The Monopolistic Competition Revolution in Retrospect

In 1977 a seminal paper was published by Avinash Dixit and Joseph Stiglitz that revolutionised the modelling of imperfectly competitive markets. It launched what might be called the second monopolistic competition revolution which has been far more successful than the first one, initiated by Edward Hastings Chamberlin and Joan Robinson in the 1930s. In this collection of original essays experts in the fields of macroeconomics, international trade theory, economic geography and international growth theory address the question of why the second revolution was so successful. They also highlight what is missing, and look forward to the next step in the modelling of imperfectly competitive markets. The text includes a comprehensive survey of both monopolistic competition revolutions, and previously unpublished working papers by Dixit and Stiglitz that led to their famous 1977 paper. Other contributors include Wilfred Ethier, Joe Francois, Richard Baldwin, Vernon Henderson, Russell Looker and Peter Neary.

STEVEN BRAKMAN is Professor of International Economics at the University of Groningen, the Netherlands. He is co-author of *The Economics of International Transfers* (with C. van Marrewijk, 1998) and *An Introduction to Geographical Economics* (with C. van Marrewijk and H. Garretsen, 2001).

BEN HEIJDRA is Professor of Macroeconomics at the University of Groningen, the Netherlands. He is co-author (with Frederick van der Ploeg) of *Foundations of Modern Macroeconomics* (2002).

The Monopolistic Competition Revolution in Retrospect

Steven Brakman and Ben J. Heijdra, Editors

CAMBRIDGE
UNIVERSITY PRESS

PUBLISHED BY THE PRESS SYNDICATE OF THE UNIVERSITY OF CAMBRIDGE
The Pitt Building, Trumpington Street, Cambridge CB2 1RP, United Kingdom

CAMBRIDGE UNIVERSITY PRESS
The Edinburgh Building, Cambridge, CB2 2RU, UK
40 West 20th Street, New York, NY 10011–4211, USA
477 Williamstown Road, Port Melbourne, VIC 3207, Australia
Ruiz de Alarcón 13, 28014 Madrid, Spain
Dock House, The Waterfront, Cape Town 8001, South Africa

http://www.cambridge.org

First published 2004

Printed in the United Kingdom at the University Press, Cambridge

Typeface Plantin 10/12 pt.   *System* LATEX 2$_\varepsilon$ [TB]

A catalogue record for this book is available from the British Library

Library of Congress Cataloguing in Publication data

The monopolistic competition revolution in retrospect/Steven Brakman
    and Ben J. Heijdra, editors.
      p.   cm.
    Includes bibliographical references and index.
    ISBN 0-521-81991-1
    1. Competition, Imperfect.   2. Competition.   3. Monopolies.
    I. Brakman, Steven.   II. Heijdra, Ben J.

    HB238.M66   2003
    338.6′048–dc21   2003048569

ISBN 0 521 81991 1 hardback

Contents

Contributors

RICHARD E. BALDWIN, Department of Economics, Graduate Institute of International Studies, Geneva

LEON BETTENDORF, OCFEB, Erasmus University, Rotterdam

JAN BOONE, Department of Economics, Tilburg University, Tilburg

STEVEN BRAKMAN, Department of Economics, University of Groningen, Groningen

RUSSELL W. COOPER, Department of Economics, Boston University, Boston, MA

AVINASH K. DIXIT, Department of Economics, Princeton University, Princeton, MA

WILFRED J. ETHIER, Department of Economics, University of Pennsylvania, Philadelphia, PA

RIKARD FORSLID, Department of Economics, University of Stockholm, Stockholm

JOSEPH FRANCOIS, Tinbergen Institute, Erasmus University, Rotterdam

HARRY GARRETSEN, Utrecht School of Economics, University of Utrecht, Utrecht

HENRI L. F. DE GROOT, Department of Spatial Economics, Vrije Universiteit, Amsterdam

BEN J. HEIJDRA, Department of Economics, University of Groningen, Groningen

J. VERNON HENDERSON, Department of Economics, Brown University, Providence, RI

MARJAN W. HOFKES, Institute for Environmental Studies, Vrije Universiteit, Amsterdam

CHRISTIAN KEUSCHNIGG, Institut für Finanzwirtschaft und Finanzrecht, St Gallen, Switzerland

THEO VAN DE KLUNDERT, Department of Economics, Tilburg University, Tilburg

CHARLES VAN MARREWIJK, Department of Economics, Erasmus University, Rotterdam

PHILIPPE MARTIN, Research Department, Federal Reserve Bank of New York, New York, NY

PETER MULDER, Institute for Environmental Studies, Vrije Universiteit, Amsterdam

J. PETER NEARY, Department of Economics, University College Dublin, Dublin

DOUGLAS NELSON, Department of Economics, Tulane University, New Orleans, LA

GIANMARCO OTTAVIANO, Department of Economics, University of Bologna, Bologna

JOLANDA J. W. PEETERS, DNB (Netherlands Central Bank), Amsterdam

FREDERIC ROBERT-NICOUD, Centre for Economic Performance, London School of Economics, London

MARC SCHRAMM, Center for German Studies, University of Nijmegen, Nijmegen

SJAK SMULDERS, Department of Economics, Tilburg University, Tilburg

JOSEPH E. STIGLITZ, Department of Economics, Columbia University, New York, NY

Preface

This collection of papers is the result of the conference 'The Monopolistic Competition Revolution After 25 Years' which was held at the University of Groningen on 30–31 October 2000. The main reason for organising a conference on this topic was that we realised that the second monopolistic competition revolution, initiated by Avinash Dixit and Joe Stiglitz in the 1970s, has been far more successful than the first monopolistic competition revolution that started in the 1930s. In sharp contrast to the first revolution, the second fundamentally influenced fields such as macroeconomics, international trade theory, growth theory and economic geography. It therefore seemed a good idea to ask the founding fathers of the second revolution why they thought that their reformulation has been so successful. Furthermore, we invited well-known international researchers in each of the above-mentioned fields to shed their light on the question. In addition we invited researchers that are currently active in these fields to provide an application of the Dixit–Stiglitz model and to show how it was useful in their current research. Hopefully this set-up has resulted in a interesting collection of papers. We have also included the previously unpublished working papers of Dixit and Stiglitz. These papers give a more comprehensive version of the basic model and also include extensions of the model that later had to be, independently, rediscovered by others.

This workshop is the fourth in a series of international conferences organised by the Economics Department of the University of Groningen.[1] The conference was made possible by the financial support of the research school of the economics department of the University of Groningen (SOM), the Dutch Central Bank (DNB), the Ministry of Economic

---

[1] The results of the first three of these conferences were published in E. Sterken and S. K. Kuipers (eds.), *Methods and Applications of Economic Dynamics, Contributions to Economic Analysis*, 228, Amsterdam, North-Holland (1995); S. Brakman, H. van Ees, and S. K. Kuipers (eds.), *Market Behaviour and Macroeconomic Modelling*, London and New York, Macmillan/St Martin's Press (1998); A. van Ark, S. K. Kuipers and G. H. Kuper (eds.), *Productivity, Technology, and Growth*, Amsterdam and Boston, Kluwer Academic (2000).

Affairs of the Netherlands, the University Trust Fund (GUF) and the Faculty of Economics at the University of Groningen. We should like to thank SOM for their organisational backing during the conference, especially Annet Huisman and Rina Koning; Simon Kuipers (chairman of the board of the University of Groningen) for his support during the organisation of the conference, and finally Chris Harrison of Cambridge University Press for his encouragement and patience.

1   Introduction

Steven Brakman and Ben J. Heijdra

1.1   Introduction

> In speaking of theories of monopolistic or imperfect competition as 'revolutions,' I know in advance that I shall provoke dissent. There are minds that by temperament will define away every proposed revolution. For them it is enough to point out that Keynes in 1936 had some partial anticipator in 1836. Newton is just a guy getting too much credit for the accretion of knowledge that covered centuries. A mountain is just a high hill; a hill merely a bulging plain. Such people remind me of the grammar-school teacher we all had, who would never give 100 to a paper on the ground that 'No one is perfect.' (Samuelson, 1967, p. 138)

> Edward Hastings Chamberlin is the author of one of the most influential works of all time in economic theory – *The Theory of Monopolistic Competition*, which entered its eighth edition in 1962. Along with Lord Keynes's *General Theory*, it wrought one of the two veritable revolutions in economic theory in this century. (Dust cover text of Kuenne, 1967)

Although we stress the importance of the contribution by Avinash Dixit and Joseph Stiglitz (1977) throughout this book, the history of monopolistic competition is much longer than the past twenty-five years or so and goes back at least seventy years. The success of the Dixit–Stiglitz model of monopolistic competition might have come as a surprise to students of the history of economic thought, as it was by no means the first attempt to deal with imperfect markets or monopolistic competition. However, where the earlier attempts failed the Dixit–Stiglitz approach turned out to be very successful and has the potential 'for classic status' (see Neary,[1] chapter 8 in this volume).

In this introduction we will briefly review the two waves of literature on monopolistic competition theory, namely the one that started in 1933 and the one that commenced in 1977. The claim of this book is that the second attempt to model monopolistic competition was far more successful than the first, essentially because the second attempt introduced

We thank Avinash Dixit for comments on an earlier draft.

[1] According to Peter Neary, 'the first step on the road to classic status [is]: to be widely cited but never read. (The second step, to be widely quoted but never cited.)'

a formalisation that had all the relevant characteristics of monopolistic competition but was still relatively easy to handle.

This collection of papers will show that the re-formulation by Dixit and Stiglitz has contributed significantly to many areas of research; the main ones being international trade theory, macroeconomics, growth theory and economic geography. But even today the concept of monopolistic competition is not always appreciated. As David Kreps puts it in his influential micro textbook 'were it not for the presence of this theory in most lower level texts we would ignore it here altogether' (1990, p. 344). Kreps dismisses monopolistic competition as being too unrealistic, and challenges his readers to come up with at least one sector that could convincingly be described by monopolistic competition. This collection of essays, however, takes for granted that the Dixit–Stiglitz reformulation of monopolistic competition has become very successful, and asks why that is the case. This does not mean that the authors of the essays are uncritical about the model. The aim of this collection is to show why the model has become mainstream in such a short period of time and what we can expect from future developments regarding the modelling of imperfect markets.

This introductory chapter is organised as follows. In section 1.2 we briefly discuss the literature predating the first monopolistic competition revolution. This literature strongly hinted at the importance of increasing returns to scale and imperfect market forms but was unable to come up with a satisfactory model in which both phenomena could play a meaningful role.

In section 1.3 we briefly discuss (what we call) the first monopolistic competition revolution, namely the one that was started by Edward Hastings Chamberlin and Joan Robinson in the 1930s. We show that by the mid-1960s most (but not all) leading economists had come to the conclusion that the Chamberlin–Robinson revolution had essentially failed. In our view, there are two reasons for this lack of acceptance of the theory. First, the *timing* of the first revolution was unfortunate in that it coincided with the Great Depression and the emergence of the Keynesian revolution in macroeconomics. Second, and perhaps more importantly, Chamberlin and co-workers failed to come up with a canonical model embodying the key elements of the theory. It was not so much Chamberlin's ideas that were rejected but rather his *modelling approach* that was deemed to be unworkable.

In section 1.4 we turn to the second monopolistic competition revolution, namely the successful one that was started in the mid-1970s by Dixit, Stiglitz and Michael Spence. The timing of this second revolution was much better. The events in the world – the petroleum cartel, high inflation, productivity slowdown, etc. – made the profession painfully aware of the limitations of the paradigm of perfect competition, and made it more receptive to theories that departed from that paradigm in all its dimensions, i.e. returns to scale, uncertainty and information, strategic behaviour, etc. In addition, the second revolution caught on because Dixit and Stiglitz managed to come up with a canonical model of monopolistic competition. We present a very simple version of the Dixit–Stiglitz model and show how it manages to capture the key Chamberlinian insights.

Finally, in section 1.5 we present a broad overview of the chapters in this book.

1.2   Precursory thoughts on imperfect competition[2]

By the end of the nineteenth century two market forms dominated the discussion of economic analysis, namely monopoly and perfect competition. The former assumes a single firm with exclusive control over its output and the market, resulting in profits that are larger than in any other market form. In contrast, the latter assumes a large number of sellers of a homogeneous product, where each individual firm has no control over its price. Free entry and exit of firms ensures that long-run profits are zero. Perfect competition was introduced to show that in some sense it is optimal and in fact represents an end-state, meaning that competition between buyers or sellers has come to an end and neither party can increase utility or profits by changing its behaviour. Changes occur only if exogenous variables change, but the question then becomes how fast and under what circumstances the new equilibrium will be reached. Competition might not actually lead to the blissful state but market forces are always pointing the economy in the right direction.[3] Monopoly by contrast maximises profits of the firm but from a social point of view is sub-optimal.

This state of affairs is reflected in Alfred Marshall's *Principles of Economics*, that presented these two market forms as the basic analytical tools to analyse markets. Other market forms are hybrids in between these two

---

[2] Our historical overview is rather succinct owing to space considerations. Interested readers are referred to Triffin (1940), Eaton and Lipsey (1989, pp. 761–6) and Archibald (1987, pp. 531–4) for more extensive surveys.

[3] As Arrow and Debreu showed, in general the conditions for a unique and stable (Walrasian) equilibrium are that (1) production is subject to constant or diminishing returns to scale, (2) commodities are substitutes (meaning that a price increase raises the demand for other products), (3) external effects are absent and (4) there is a complete forward market for all goods. Assumptions (1) and (3) in particular are dropped in monopolistic competition.

polar cases.[4] Mainstream economics did not bother too much to analyse imperfect market forms, because 'the large majority of cases that occur in practice are nothing but mixtures and hybrids of these two' (Schumpeter, 1954, p. 975).

However, Marshall was aware that other market forms were not simple combinations of perfect competition and monopoly. The special nature of imperfect markets were conveyed to him in the form of the duopoly models developed by Cournot, Bertrand and Edgeworth in the second half of the nineteenth century. The analysis of Cournot (1838) was particularly important for him, as it handed him the apparatus to analyse market forms in the first place. The problem with these models was that the results depended very much on special assumptions. Although Marshall did not develop his own theory of imperfect competition, his awareness of the so-called 'Special Markets' paved the way for later theories of imperfect competition developed by Chamberlin and Robinson.

Notwithstanding some lip-service to the theory of imperfect competition, perfect competition dominated the analysis during this time and other market forms were considered to be 'imperfect'. However, in perfect competition, where each seller or buyer has no influence on market prices, there is no longer room for individual competition, and forces leading to *industry* growth are absent. The difficulty was then to reconcile the theory of the market and that of the individual firm. Simple observation of reality often contradicted the conclusions of (partial) supply and demand analysis: diminishing returns for the individual firm is not an obstacle to expand production. And average costs are diminishing at the point were firms stop expanding output. This state of affairs troubled Marshall, as decreasing (average) cost curves are incompatible with perfect competition. Marshall tried to solve this by introducing diminishing returns for the individual firm (for individual firms, production factors are in fixed supply), and external economies for the whole industry. The introduction of external economies of scale at the industry level ensured that the competitive equilibrium could be rescued. The central idea is that external economies of scale create an interdependence between supply curves; the combined supply of all firms reduces industry costs and ensures that the combination of lower prices and increased supply can be an equilibrium. External economies of scale are compatible with an industry equilibrium, because an increase in demand will still increase the price for *individual*

---

[4] However, according to Schumpeter, Marshall 'had no theory of monopolistic competition. But he pointed toward it by considering a firm's Special Market' (Schumpeter, 1954, p. 840).

firms, as the marginal cost curve of each firm is upward sloping and each firm is operating at the minimum of its average cost curve. The price increase could stimulate new firms to enter the market, reducing (average) costs and raising combined supply. With internal economies of scale a market equilibrium is not possible as each individual firm can always undercut its rivals.

According to Marshall whether or not external economies could be encountered in practice depended on the general characteristics of an industry and the environment of the industry, like the localisation of an industry. In Marshall's words:

subsidiary trades grow up in the neighbourhood, supplying it with implements and materials, organizing its traffic, and in many ways conducing to the economy of its material ... the economic use of expensive machinery can sometimes be attained in a very high degree in a district in which there is a large aggregate production of the same kind, ... subsidiary industries devoting themselves each to one small branch of the process of production, and working it for a great many of their neighbours, are able to keep in constant use machinery of the most highly specialized character, and to make it pay its expenses. (Marshall, 1920, p. 225)

In modern jargon the linkages described in this quotation are so-called backward and forward linkages; the backward linkage is that firms use other firms' output as intermediate production factors, the forward linkage is that its own product is also used as an intermediate production factor by others.[5]

Furthermore, according to Marshall a thick labour market also benefits firms:

Employers are apt to resort to any place where they are likely to find a good choice of workers with the special skill which they require; while men seeking employment naturally go to places where there are many employers who need such skill as theirs and where therefore it is likely to find a good market. (Marshall, 1920, pp. 225–6)

These factors combined explain industry growth and show why:

the mysteries of the trade become no mysteries; but are as it were in the air ... if one man starts a new idea, it is taken up by others and combined with suggestions of their own; and thus it becomes the source of further new ideas. (Marshall, 1920, p. 225)

---

[5] The quote from Marshall merely seems to shift the problem to a different level, in the sense that external economies of scale in one industry must be explained by internal economies of scale in an upstream or downstream industry linked to it, and that raises doubts about sustainability of perfect competition in that other industry.

For Marshall, however, his analysis of external economies created an additional problem, because he thought that internal economies of scale were at least as important as external economies (Blaug, 1997). In the presence of internal economies of scale the growth of an industry would benefit the largest firms (and create monopolies) and thus change the competitive forces within such an industry. Marshall had to introduce the concept of the representative firm to deal with this incompatibility. By introducing the representative firm, perfect competition and (external) economies of scale could be made consistent. But again in this case, as with perfect competition, strategic interaction between firms has been assumed away because firms are by assumption 'representative' for the whole industry.

But the consistency problems in Marshall's analysis of the market were not solved even by the representative firm. Marshall's famous period analysis assumed that in the long run the supply curve was a straight line. And this means that *in the long run* the volume of production of an individual firm is indeterminate: there is no unique intersection of the supply curve and a given price. So, Marshall's theory of perfect competition has no way of dealing with situations where the (long-run) marginal costs are constant (or declining in the presence of economies of scale). This state of affairs was most poignantly put forward by Sraffa (1926). According to Sraffa market imperfections due to returns to scale are not simple frictions, 'but are themselves active forces which produce permanent and even cumulative effects'. And he added yet another problem. Declining marginal costs would imply that the market is served by a single firm. But, according to Sraffa, in practice firms operate under declining marginal costs without monopolising the whole market. According to him, the combination of a declining supply curve and a negatively sloped demand curve limits the size of production. The idea behind a declining demand curve is that buyers are not indifferent between different suppliers. Each firm has his own *special market*; products are usually imperfect substitutes and have their own *special* characteristics.

In a sense Sraffa added to the confusion rather than solving the problem of combining increasing returns and the theory of market competition. The error Sraffa made was that he did not distinguish between price and marginal revenue, which was remarkable because the concept of marginal revenue had already been developed in a mathematical appendix in Marshall's *Principles*, in which he restates the monopoly theory developed by Cournot.[6] This was pointed out (again) by Harrod in

---

[6] Marshall casts his analysis in terms of net revenue, and only implicitly discusses marginal revenue. The concept of marginal revenue had to be re-invented (Robinson, 1933). This

1930.[7] For Marshall it was a minor issue and he did not make use of this instrument any further, because he did not need it in his analysis of perfect competition.

This was broadly speaking the state of affairs in the 1920s and 1930s. It was realised that the existence of economies of scale (of one sort or another) implied imperfect market forms, but it remained difficult to construct a satisfactory equilibrium concept for such imperfect market forms. On the one hand there was perfect competition, and on the other hand there was monopoly. Other market forms were considered to be some kind of hybrid of these two extreme forms of competition. So, one could suffice to analyse the two extreme cases in treating all other forms as an implicit mix of the two fundamental forms of competition. But no satisfactory theory of the market existed in which constant or declining marginal and average costs could be made consistent with market equilibrium. This led in the 1930s to a new theory of price determination. One can agree with Schumpeter (1954, p. 1150) that the confusion caused by Marshall was a very fertile one.[8] Marshall's analysis of the firm and economies of scale led him to develop the concept of the representative firm which invited a lively discussion on market equilibrium and returns to scale and this set the stage for the analysis of monopolistic competition.

1.3   Monopolistic competition in the 1930s

In 1933 two books appeared that changed the way economists dealt with imperfect competition, namely Joan Robinson's *The Economics of Imperfect Competition* and Edward Hastings Chamberlin's *The Theory of Monopolistic Competition*. Although Robinson revived the marginal revolution, in general Chamberlin is considered to be 'the true revolutionary' (Blaug,

---

is even more surprising considering that Cournot already used the concept of marginal revenue in 1838, and derived the familiar first-order condition for profit maximisation: marginal revenue equals marginal cost (Cournot, 1838).

[7] See Harrod (1967) for a review of his thoughts on this matter.

[8] Chamberlin, for example, attributed the origins and inspiration of his theory to the famous Taussig–Pigou controversy on railway rates which took place around 1900. This controversy was about the explanation of different railway rates. Taussig tried to fit different railway rates into the Marshallian theory of (competitive) joint supply by assuming that a unit rail supply is not homogeneous and that different demand elasticities for different stretches of railway result in different prices. In contrast, Pigou stated that it was not an issue of heterogeneity, but of monopoly coupled with the conditions necessary for price discrimination which could explain price differences. In general it is thought that Pigou won the debate.

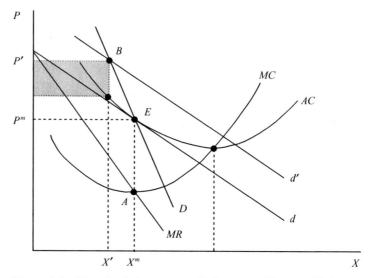

Figure 1.1   Chamberlinian monopolistic competition equilibrium

1997, p. 376).[9] This radical new analysis was a first answer to the question that was raised in 1926 by Sraffa: is it possible in a market characterised by monopolistic competition and declining average and marginal costs to reach an equilibrium? Figure 1.1 illustrates the equilibrium in the monopolistic equilibrium. Chamberlin makes four basic assumptions (Bishop, 1967, p. 252):

- The number of sellers in a group of firms is sufficiently large so that each firm takes the behaviour of other firms in the group as given (Cournot–Nash assumption)
- The group is well defined and small relative to the economy
- Products are physically similar but economically differentiated: buyers have preferences for all types of products
- There is free entry and exit.

The monopolistic elements are all those elements that distinguish a product from another product and give the firm some market power; 'each "product" is rendered unique by the individuality of the establishment in which it is sold, including its location (as well as by trade marks, qualitative differences, etc); this is its monopolistic aspect' (Chamberlin, 1933, p. 63). The large number of firms in the market and the possibility of

---

[9] Moreover, the history of Chamberlin's seminal work dates back to 1921 – see the remarks by Schumpeter (1954, p. 1150).

entry and exit of many firms provides the competitive elements; 'Each [product] is subject to the competition of other "products" sold under different circumstances and at other locations; this is its competitive aspect' (1933, p. 63).

We illustrate the Chamberlinian model with the aid of figure 1.1.[10] We assume that all actual and potential suppliers in the group face the same demand and cost conditions and depict the situation for one particular firm in isolation. There are two demand curves in the diagram. The individual firm under consideration faces demand curve d. This curve represents the firm's price–sales combinations under the assumption that all other firms in the group keep their prices unchanged. Archibald calls this the 'perceived' demand curve (1987, p. 532). The steeper curve labelled D is the demand facing each firm if all firms in the group set their prices identically. Archibald (1987, p. 532) refers to this curve as the 'share-of-the-market' demand curve. As usual MR is marginal revenue (associated with the perceived demand curve d), AC is the firm's average cost, MC is marginal cost, P is the price of the differentiated commodity, and X is the volume of sales.

The Chamberlinian equilibrium under free entry/exit of firms is at point E, where the price is P^m and output is X^m. Point E is the equilibrium because (a) the individual firm attains an optimum in that point, and (b) there are no unexploited profit opportunities, excess profits are exactly zero and no entry/exit of firms takes place. The validity of these requirements can be demonstrated as follows. The individual firm maximises its profit, taking as given the demand curve d. It finds the optimum point by equating marginal revenue and marginal cost (see point A directly below point E). In point E the demand curve d is tangent to the average cost curve, AC, so the firm makes zero profits. This is the famous Chamberlinian tangency condition. Since all firms are identical, no firm makes profits or losses and there is no entry or exit of firms.

Chamberlin (1933, p. 91) also sketched the adjustment process towards the equilibrium point. Assume that all firms in the group are initially operating along the demand curve d' at point B, set a price of P', and produce a quantity X'. At this price–output combination, each firm would make a positive profit equal to the shaded area in figure 1.1. But point B cannot be an equilibrium. Indeed, in that point the individual firm will have an incentive to lower its price (and increase its profits) by moving to the right along the d' curve (recall that each firm operates under the assumption that its competitors will continue to charge P'). But each firm has exactly the same incentives, so they will all follow suit and cut their

---

[10] This diagram is adjusted from Bishop (1967, p. 252).

prices. As a result the d' curve will shift down along the D curve towards the Chamberlinian equilibrium at point E.[11]

Obviously, owing to the downward sloping individual demand curve, there is a difference between equilibrium average cost and minimum average cost in the Chamberlinian equilibrium. This implies that there are unexploited economies of scale and the question arises whether this represents a waste of resources. The answer to this question is both 'yes' and 'no'. 'Yes', in the sense that indeed there is excess capacity and 'no', in the sense that product differentiation introduces variety and this expands the extent of consumer choices and thereby welfare. As Eaton and Lipsey put it, 'in a society that values diversity, there is a trade-off between economizing on resources, by reducing the costs of producing existing products, and satisfying the desire for diversity, by increasing the number of products' (1989, p. 763). We will return to this topic in more detail when discussing the second monopolistic competition revolution.

Given the elegance of the monopolistic competition model it is surprising to see how little influence it had on economic theory. The first attacks on the early monopolistic competition revolution came from Hicks (1939, pp. 83–5) and somewhat later from Stigler (1949) and Friedman (1953). Hicks rejected the theory because he was unable to translate it into a workable model. Stigler (1949) rejected the theory for methodological reasons. He claimed that the predictions derived from the theory of monopolistic competition are not very different from those of perfect competition. Occam's razor then suggests that perfect competition should be favoured over monopolistic competition, a line of reasoning to which Friedman also adheres. It was put forward even more strongly by Archibald (1961, p. 14): 'The theory is not totally empty, but very nearly so' (see also Samuelson, 1967, for a further discussion of this debate). In addition Stigler raised an important point by noting that:

Professor Chamberlin's failure to construct an analytical system capable of dealing informatively with his picture of reality is not hard to explain. The fundamental fact is that, although Chamberlin could throw off the shackles of Marshall's view of economic life, he could not throw off the shackles of Marshall's view of economic analysis. Marshall's technique was appropriate to the problem set to it: it deals informatively and with tolerable logic with the world of competitive industries and monopolies. But it is lost in the sea of diversity and unsystematism, and Chamberlin is lost with it. (Stigler, 1949, p. 22)

---

[11] Note that the position of the D curve depends on the number of firms in the group. In figure 1.1, D is consistent with the Chamberlinian equilibrium at E. As a result, the thought experiment conducted above does not prompt entry of firms. It just shows that E is the only conceivable Chamberlinian (Cournot–Nash) equilibrium.

Archibald (1987, p. 532) mentions two further criticisms that were raised against the Chamberlinian model. First, the notion of the 'group' (of products) was ill-defined. In the common definition, goods belong to a group if (1) the cross-elasticity of demand between these goods is 'high' and (2) the cross-elasticity between goods in the group and all other goods is 'low'. The problem with this definition is that there is no logical way to determine what is a high elasticity and what is a low one. Second, Kaldor (1934, 1935) suggested very early on that reality may be better approximated by a market structure with chains of overlapping oligopolies (localised competition) than by Chamberlin's monopolistically competitive structure. Of course, in such an oligopolistic setting the Cournot–Nash assumption is clearly untenable.

Not surprisingly, in well-known textbooks that appeared in the 1960s and 1970s, monopolistic competition is only briefly mentioned, if at all – see, for example, Henderson and Quandt (1971) and Malinvaud (1972). Akerlof (2002, p. 413) recollects about this period that, 'monopolistic competition and Joan Robinson's equivalent were taught in graduate and even undergraduate courses. However, such "specific" models ... were presented not as central sights, but instead as excursions into the countryside, for the adventurous or those with an extra day to spare'.

The *Festschrift* that was published in honour of Chamberlin also paints a rather bleak picture. Harry Johnson, for example, not only observes that the theory had by 1967 no discernible impact on the theory of international trade, but continues that 'some beginnings have been made towards the analytical and empirical application of monopolistic competition concepts; but the work has been very much ad hoc, and much synthesizing remains to be done' (1967, p. 218). What is needed is an 'operationally relevant analytical tool capable of facilitating the quantification of those aspects of real-life competition' (1967, p. 218).

But not only Johnson is rather sceptical on the contribution of monopolistic competition; other contributors seem to have the same opinion. Fellner, for instance, concludes that these models are convenient tools of exposition 'on specific symmetry assumptions ... In situations lacking these traits of symmetry ... [they] lose much of their usefulness' (1967, p. 29) and Tinbergen (1967) observes that the influence on econometrics and macroeconomics is limited.

Only Paul Samuelson is more positive, though still on the defensive, as the following rather lengthy quotation shows:

If the real world displays the variety of behaviour that the Chamberlin–Robinson models permit – and I believe the Chicago writers are simply wrong in denying that these important empirical deviations exist – then reality will falsify *many* of the important qualitative and quantitative *predictions* of the competitive model.

Hence, by the pragmatic test of prediction adequacy, the perfect-competition model fails to be an adequate approximation ... The fact that the Chamberlin–Robinson model is 'empty' in the sense of ruling out few empirical configurations and being capable of providing only formalistic descriptions, is not the slightest reason for abandoning it in favor of a 'full' model of the competitive type *if reality is similarly* 'empty' and 'non-full'. (1967, p. 108n, emphasis in the original)

Samuelson concludes that 'Chamberlin, Sraffa, Robinson, and their contemporaries have led economists into a new land from which their critics will never evict us' (1967, p. 138).

It might have come as a surprise, even to a relative optimist like Paul Samuelson, that the theory of monopolistic competition was given a new lease on life so quickly. Indeed, less than a decade after the 1967 Chamberlin festivities, Dixit and Stiglitz (1977) managed to again place monopolistic competition theory on the centre stage.

1.4   The second monopolistic revolution

As we pointed out in section 1.3, the monopolistic competition revolution by no means started with the seminal article by Dixit and Stiglitz (1977), but had already had a long (and somewhat troublesome) history. However, one of the reasons why we have gathered the collection of studies in the present volume is that we claim that the second monopolistic competition revolution has been much more successful than the first. The reason for this success is that Dixit and Stiglitz managed to formulate a canonical model of Chamberlinian monopolistic competition which is both easy to use and captures the key aspects of Chamberlin's model. Though it is by now widely recognised that the Dixit–Stiglitz approach is somewhat unrealistic, it has nevertheless become the 'workhorse model' incorporating monopolistic competition, increasing returns to scale and endogenous product variety. As is stressed by Peter Neary in chapter 8 in this volume, the main contributions of the Dixit–Stiglitz model are:[12]

- The definition of an industry (or large group of firms) is simplified: all product varieties are symmetric and are combined in a constant-elasticity-of-substitution (CES) aggregation function (see below).
- Overall utility is separable and homothetic[13] in its arguments, implying that we can use a two-stage budgeting procedure. In the first stage

[12] There are actually two models in the original Dixit–Stiglitz (1977) paper, which they label, respectively, the Constant Elasticity Case and the Variable Elasticity Case. The first model has become known as *the* Dixit–Stiglitz model. Note that both models have been used in international trade theory, notably Krugman (1979, 1980).

[13] This is the main distinction from the model developed by Spence (1976), who uses a quasi-linear utility specification.

usually a Cobb–Douglas specification is used, and in the second stage a CES utility function is applied.

- On the production side, technology features increasing returns to scale at firm level. The typical formulation models the average cost curve as a rectangular hyperbola. All firms are symmetrical.

In the remainder of this section we present a very simple version of the Dixit–Stiglitz model and characterise its key properties. Readers who are familiar with the model may skip this section and proceed directly to section 1.5 below.

1.4.1   The model

Preferences

There are two sectors in the economy. The first sector produces a homogeneous good under constant returns to scale and features perfect competition. The second sector consists of a large group of monopolistically competitive firms who produce under increasing returns to scale at firm level. The utility function of the representative household[14] is Cobb–Douglas:

$$U = Z^\delta Y^{1-\delta}, \qquad 0 < \delta < 1, \tag{1.1}$$

where U is utility, Z is consumption of the homogeneous good and Y is the consumption of a *composite* differentiated good. This composite good consists of a bundle of closely related product 'varieties' which are close but imperfect substitutes for each other. Following the crucial insights of Spence (1976) and Dixit and Stiglitz (1977), a convenient formulation is as follows:

$$Y \equiv \left[\sum_{i=1}^{N} X_i^{(\sigma-1)/\sigma} \right]^{\sigma/(\sigma-1)}, \qquad 1 < \sigma \ll \infty, \tag{1.2}$$

where N is the existing number of different varieties, X_i is consumption of variety i and σ is the Allen–Uzawa cross-partial elasticity of substitution. Intuitively, the higher is σ, the better substitutes the varieties are for each other.[15] In this formulation, $1/(\sigma-1)$ captures the notion of 'preference for diversity (PFD)' (or 'love of variety') according to which households prefer to spread a certain amount of production over N differentiated

---

[14] There is a large number of identical households. To avoid cluttering the notation, however, we normalise the number of households to unity.

[15] In the limiting case, as σ approaches infinity, the varieties are *perfect* substitutes, i.e. they are identical goods from the perspective of the representative household.

goods rather than concentrating it on a single variety (see Bénassy, 1996, for this definition).[16]

The household faces the following budget constraint:

$$\sum_{i=1}^{N} P_i X_i + P_Z Z = I,$$ (1.3)

where P_i is the price of variety i, P_Z is the price of the homogeneous good and I is household income (see below).

The household chooses Z and X_i (for $i = 1, \ldots, N$) in order to maximise utility (1.1), subject to the definition of composite consumption (1.2) and the budget constraint (1.3), and taking as given the goods prices and its income. By using the convenient trick of two-stage budgeting we obtain the following solutions:[17]

$$P_Z Z = \delta I,$$ (1.4)

$$P_Y Y = (1 - \delta) I,$$ (1.5)

$$X_i = (1 - \delta) \left(\frac{P_i}{P_Y} \right)^{-\sigma} \left(\frac{I}{P_Y} \right), \qquad (i = 1, \ldots, N),$$ (1.6)

where P_Y is the *true price index* of the composite consumption good Y:

$$P_Y \equiv \left[\sum_{i=1}^{N} P_i^{1-\sigma} \right]^{1/(1-\sigma)}.$$ (1.7)

Intuitively, P_Y represents the price of one unit of Y given that the quantities of all varieties are chosen in an optimal (utility-maximising) fashion

---

[16] In formal terms *average* PFD can be computed by comparing the value of composite consumption (Y) obtained if N varieties and X/N units per variety are chosen with the value of Y if X units of a single variety are chosen ($N = 1$):

$$\text{Average PFD} \equiv \frac{Y(X/N, X/N, \ldots, X/N)}{Y(X, 0, \ldots, 0)} = N^{1/(\sigma-1)}.$$ (a)

The elasticity of this function with respect to the number of varieties represents the *marginal* taste for additional variety which plays an important role in the monopolistic competition model. By using (a) we obtain the expression for the marginal preference for diversity (MPFD):

$$\text{MPFD} = \frac{1}{\sigma - 1}.$$ (b)

[17] For a pedestrian derivation of such expressions, see for example Brakman, Garretsen and van Marrewijk (2001, ch. 3).

by the household.[18] Equations (1.4)–(1.5) feature the usual result that income spending shares on Z and Y are constant for the Cobb–Douglas utility function. Equation (1.6) is the demand curve facing the producer of variety i. It features a constant price elasticity, i.e.[19]

$$-\frac{\partial X_i}{\partial P_i}\frac{P_i}{X_i} = \sigma.$$

Note that (1.6) provides a formal definition for the individual firm's perceived demand curve (i.e. the d curve in figure 1.1). To derive the industry demand curve (the D curve) we postulate symmetry (see below), set $P_i = P$ and $X_i = X$ (for all $i = 1, \ldots, N$), and obtain from (1.6):

$$X = \frac{1}{N}(1 - \delta)\frac{I}{P}. \tag{1.8}$$

Whereas the d curve features a price elasticity of σ (which exceeds unity by assumption), the Cobb–Douglas specification ensures that the D curve is unit elastic, i.e. the *industry* demand curve is less elastic than the demand curve facing individual firms, as was asserted by Chamberlin (1933), and illustrated in figure 1.1, where the D curve intersects the d curve from above.

Technology and pricing

The supply side of the economy is as follows. There is one factor of production, labour, which is perfectly mobile across sectors and across firms in the monopolistic sector. As a result, there is a single wage rate which we denote by W. Production in the homogeneous goods sector features constant returns to scale and technology is given by:

$$Z = \frac{L_Z}{k_Z}, \tag{1.9}$$

where L_Z is the amount of labour used in the Z-sector and k_Z is the (exogenous) technology index in that sector. The Z-sector operates under perfect competition and marginal cost pricing ensures that there are zero

---

[18] Formally, P_Y is defined as follows:

$$P_Y \equiv \left\{ \min \sum_{i=1}^{N} P_i X_i \text{ subject to } \left[\sum_{i=1}^{N} X_i^{(\sigma-1)/\sigma} \right]^{\sigma/(\sigma-1)} = 1 \right\}.$$

[19] In deriving this elasticity, we follow Dixit and Stiglitz (1977) by ignoring the effect of P_i on the price index P_Y. See Yang and Heijdra (1993), Dixit and Stiglitz (1993) and d'Aspremont, Dos Santos Ferreira and Gérard-Varet (1996) for a further discussion of this point.

profits and the price is set according to:

$$P_Z = k_Z W. \tag{1.10}$$

Production in the monopolistically competitive Y-sector is characterised by internal economies of scale. Each individual firm i uses labour to produce its product variety and faces the following technology:

$$X_i = \begin{cases} 0 & \text{if } L_i \leq F \\ (1/k_Y)[L_i - F] & \text{if } L_i \geq F \end{cases}, \tag{1.11}$$

where X_i is the marketable output of firm i, L_i is labour used by the firm, F is fixed cost in terms of units of labour and k_Y is the (constant) marginal labour requirement. The formulation captures the notion that the firm must expend a minimum amount of labour ('overhead labour') before it can produce any output at all (see Mankiw, 1988, p. 9). As a result, there are increasing returns to scale at firm level as average cost declines with output.[20]

The profit of firm i is denoted by Π_i and equals revenue minus total (labour) costs:

$$\Pi_i \equiv P_i X_i - W[k_Y X_i + F]. \tag{1.12}$$

The firm chooses its output in order to maximise profit (1.12) subject to its price-elastic demand curve (1.6), ignoring the effects its decisions may have on P_Y and/or I (see n. 19). The first-order condition for this optimisation problem yields the familiar markup pricing rule:

$$P_i = \mu W k_Y, \qquad \mu \equiv \frac{\sigma}{\sigma - 1}, \tag{1.13}$$

where μ (>1) is the gross markup of price over marginal cost.

Chamberlinian equilibrium

The key thing to note is that the model is completely symmetric. According to (1.13), all active firms face the same price elasticity (and thus adopt the same markup), pay the same wage rate, and face the same technology. Hence, all firms set the same price, i.e. $P_i = P$ for all i. But this means, by (1.6) and (1.11)–(1.12), that output, labour demand and

---

[20] Note that (1.11) implies that the average cost curve of active firms is a hyperbola. This is standard in the Dixit–Stiglitz model. Most graphical presentations of the Chamberlinian model use U-shaped average cost curves. Dixon and Lawler (1996, p. 223) propose the following technology which features a U-shaped average cost curve:

$$X_i = \begin{cases} 0 & \text{if } L_i \leq F \\ (1/k_Y)[L_i - F]^\gamma & \text{if } L_i \geq F \end{cases}$$

with $0 < \gamma < 1$.

the level of profit are also the same for all firms in the differentiated sector, i.e. $X_i = X$, $L_i = L$, and $\pi_i = \pi$ for all $i = 1, \ldots, N$. The symmetry property allows us to suppress the i-index from here on.

Before characterising the model developed in this section, we must tie up some loose ends. First, the representative household inelastically supplies H units of labour and is the owner of all firms and thus receives all profits (if there are any). Household income is thus given by:

$$I = HW + N\Pi. \tag{1.14}$$

The second loose end concerns the labour market clearing condition, according to which the demand for labour by the two sectors must equal the exogenously given supply:

$$NL + L_Z = H. \tag{1.15}$$

Owing to its simple structure, the model can be solved in closed form. We start by noting that (1.12) and (1.13) can be combined to obtain a simple expression for profit per active firm in the monopolistic sector:

$$\Pi = W[(\mu - 1)k_Y X - F]. \tag{1.16}$$

With free entry/exit of firms, profits are driven down to zero and the unique output level per active firm follows directly from (1.16):

$$X = \frac{F}{(\mu - 1)k_Y}. \tag{1.17}$$

Output per firm is constant and depends only on features of the technology (F and k_Y) and on the gross markup ($\mu \equiv \sigma/(\sigma - 1)$). The lower is σ, the higher is μ and the smaller is each firm's output. In terms of figure 1.1, the Chamberlinian equilibrium is represented by point E: P^m is given by (1.13) and X^m corresponds to (1.17).

Since profits are zero in the Chamberlinian equilibrium, it follows from (1.14) that $I = HW$ and from (1.4) that $Z = \delta HW/P_Z$. By using this result in (1.9) and (1.10) we find the equilibrium levels of output and employment in the homogeneous goods sector:

$$Z = \frac{L_Z}{k_Z} = \frac{\delta H}{k_Z}. \tag{1.18}$$

A constant share of the labour force is employed in the homogeneous goods sector.

From (1.11) and (1.17) we find that in the symmetric equilibrium $L = k_Y X + F = \mu k_Y X$ or in aggregate terms $NL = \mu k_Y NX$. By using (1.15) and (1.18) we find that $NL = (1 - \delta)H$. Since output per firm is known, we can combine these two expressions for NL and solve for the equilibrium number of firms:

$$N = \frac{(1 - \delta) H}{\sigma F},$$
(1.19)

where we have used the fact that $\mu \equiv \sigma/(\sigma - 1)$ to simplify the expression somewhat. The equilibrium number of firms depends positively on the amount of labour attracted into the monopolistically competitive sector and negatively on the demand elasticity and the level of fixed cost that each firm must incur. All these effects are intuitive.

Aggregate output of the monopolistically competitive sector can be computed as follows. Equation (1.2) implies that in the symmetric equilibrium $Y = N^{\mu} X$. By using this result and noting (1.17) and (1.19) we find:

$$Y = \Omega_0 L_Y^{\mu},$$
(1.20)

where $\Omega_0 \equiv (\sigma - 1)\sigma^{-\mu} F^{1-\mu}/k_Y$ is a positive constant and $L_Y \equiv (1 - \delta) H$ is the total labour force employed in the monopolistically competitive sector. The key thing to note about (1.20) is that, since $\mu > 1$, labour features increasing returns to scale in the Chamberlinian model. Inspection of (1.17) and (1.19) reveals that a larger market (prompted, say, by an increase in the labour force H) leaves the equilibrium firm size unchanged but expands the number of product varieties. Note that by using (1.7) in the symmetric equilibrium, (1.10), and (1.13) we find that the relative price of the composite differentiated good can be written as follows:

$$\frac{P_Y}{P_Z} = \left(\frac{\mu k_Y}{k_Z}\right) N^{1-\mu}.$$
(1.21)

This expression provides yet another demonstration of the scale economies that exist in the Chamberlinian model. These scale economies originate from the love-of-variety effect (see also n. 18). Provided μ exceeds unity, the relative price of the differentiated good falls as the number of product varieties rises.

An attractive feature of the Dixit–Stiglitz model is that it contains the perfectly competitive case as a special case. Indeed, by letting σ approach infinity and, at the same time, letting F go to zero, both sectors in the economy are perfectly competitive. Since $\mu = 1$ in that case, it follows from (1.16)–(1.21) that profits are identically equal to zero ($\Pi = 0$), output per firm and the number of firms are undetermined, aggregate output features constant returns to scale and the relative price only depends on relative productivity (k_Y/k_Z).

Welfare properties

Does the Chamberlinian market equilibrium provide too much or too little variety? This is one of the classic questions that has been studied extensively in the monopolistic competition literature. The problem is illustrated by figure 1.1. At point E there are unexploited economies of scale owing to markup pricing. Salop (1979, p. 152) uses a spatial model of monopolistic competition and concludes that the market produces too much variety. He is careful to note, however, that this result is not robust. In contrast, in the standard Dixit–Stiglitz model the first-best ('unconstrained') social optimum calls for more product varieties than are provided by the market (1977, p. 302) – see also below.[21] Spence reaches the same conclusion in a special case of his model but argues that the problem is inherently difficult to study because:

there are conflicting forces at work in respect to the number or variety of products. Because of setup costs, revenues may fail to cover the costs of a socially desirable product. As a result, some products may be produced at a loss at an optimum. This is a force tending towards too few products. On the other hand, there are forces tending toward too many products. First, because firms hold back output and keep price above marginal cost, they leave more room for entry than would marginal cost pricing. Second, when a firm enters with a new product, it adds its own consumer and producer surplus to the total surplus, but it also cuts into the profits of the existing firms. If the cross elasticities of demand are high, the dominant effect may be the second one. In this case entry does not increase the size of the pie much; it just divides it into more pieces. Thus, in the presence of high cross elasticities of demand, there is a tendency toward too many products. (1976, pp. 230–1)

In the remainder of this sub-section we study what (our version of) the Dixit–Stiglitz model has to say about this issue.[22]

First-best social optimum   In the first-best social optimum the social planner chooses the combination of Z, Y and N such that the representative household's utility (1.1) is maximised given the technology (1.9) and (1.11) and the resource constraint (1.15). In the aggregate this problem can be written as:

$$\max_{\{Z,Y,N\}} U = Z^{\delta} Y^{1-\delta} \text{ subject to:}$$
$$H = k_Y N^{1/(1-\sigma)} Y + FN + k_Z Z, \tag{1.22}$$
$$N \geq N^{MIN},$$

---

[21] In the 'unconstrained' social optimum, only the resource constraint is taken into account. In the 'constrained' social optimum the additional requirement of non-negative profit per active firm is added.

[22] The welfare analysis follows the approach of Broer and Heijdra (2001).

where N^{MIN} is the (exogenous) lower bound on the number of product varieties that can be produced. This lower bound is typically ignored in the literature but is nevertheless important because there are internal scale economies in the differentiated sector. Using the subscript 'u' to denote the first-best optimum values we find the following first-order conditions:

$$\frac{(1 - \delta) / Y_u}{\delta / Z_u} = \frac{k_Y N_u^{1/(1-\sigma)}}{k_Z}, \tag{1.23}$$

$$(N_u - N^{MIN}) \left[\zeta_u - \frac{\sigma}{\sigma - 1} \right] = 0, \tag{1.24}$$

where ζ_u is a measure for the scale economies at firm level:

$$\zeta_u \equiv \frac{k_Y X_u + F}{k_Y X_u}, \tag{1.25}$$

and where X_u is production per active firm in the first-best optimum. Equation (1.23) says that the marginal rate of substitution between the homogeneous and the composite good must be equated to their relative social price. Equation (1.24) has two important implications. First, if the scale economies at firm level are very strong, and ζ_u exceeds $\sigma/(\sigma - 1)$, then the term in square brackets on the left-hand side of (1.24) is positive and it is socially optimal to produce as few as possible product varieties. In that case the 'business-stealing effect'[23] is stronger than the preference-for-diversity effect.

The second implication that can be derived from (1.24) is that the existence of an internal solution to the optimal number of firms ($N_u > N^{MIN}$) implies that the diversity preference must be sufficiently strong compared to the internal scale economies. Indeed, if the optimal number of varieties is strictly greater than the lower bound, then the term in square brackets on the left-hand side of (1.24) is zero (so that $\zeta_u = \sigma/(\sigma - 1)$) and (1.25) determines the optimal size of each active firm:

$$X_u = \frac{F}{k_Y (\mu - 1)}, \tag{1.26}$$

where we have used the definition of μ, given in (1.13) above, to facilitate the comparison with the corresponding market solution (1.17). By using the resource constraint and (1.23) and noting that $Y_u = N_u^\mu X_u$ we can solve for the optimal number of firms and the production and

---

[23] See Mankiw and Whinston (1986, p. 49) for this terminology. The 'business-stealing effect' is operative if output per firm falls when the number of firms increases.

employment levels in the homogeneous sector:[24]

$$N_u = \frac{(1-\delta)(\mu-1)}{\delta+\mu(1-\delta)} \frac{H}{F},$$ (1.27)

$$Z_u = \frac{L_{Yu}}{k_Z} = \frac{\delta}{\delta+\mu(1-\delta)} \frac{H}{k_Z}.$$ (1.28)

Market equilibrium We are now in a position to examine the welfare properties of the model by comparing the first-best socially optimal values of the different variables to their market-produced counterparts (for which we use the subscript 'e'). A comparison of (1.18) and (1.28) reveals that $L_{Ze} > L_{Zu}$ and $Z_e > Z_u$, i.e. employment and output in the homogeneous goods sector are too large in the market equilibrium. But this means, of course, that aggregate employment in the differentiated sector is too small, i.e. $N_e L_e < N_u L_u$.

Comparing (1.17) and (1.26) shows that $X_e = X_u$, i.e. the market yields the optimal firm size. Finally, by comparing (1.19) and (1.27) we find that $N_e < N_u$, i.e. the market provides *too few varieties*! Since output per active firm is the same in the two cases, it follows that $Y_e < Y_u$.[25]

Decentralisation It is not difficult to show that the first-best social optimum can be decentralised by means of a product subsidy on differentiated goods, provided it can be financed in a non-distorting fashion (e.g. with a lump-sum tax levied on the representative household). Assume that each active firm receives an ad valorem product subsidy so that (1.12) becomes $\Pi_i \equiv (1+s_P)P_i X_i - W[k_Y X_i + F]$ where s_P is the product subsidy. Each firm will now set its price according to the augmented markup rule $P_i = \mu W k_Y / (1 + s_P)$. Since the first-best equilibrium calls for marginal cost pricing ($P_i = W k_Y$) it follows that the optimal product subsidy which decentralises the first-best social optimum is:

$$s_{Pu} = \mu - 1.$$ (1.29)

Provided the product subsidy is set according to (1.29), no lump-sum payments to active firms are needed to ensure the optimal amount of variety.

Extensions It is not surprising, in view of Spence's remarks quoted above, that the deficient-diversity result can be easily reversed in a suitably

---

[24] The resource constraint simplifies to $H = k_Z Z_u + \mu k_Y N_u X_u$ and (1.23) can be simplified to $(1-\delta)k_Z Z_u = \delta k_Y N_u X_u$. Since X_u is known, these two expressions can be solved for N_u and Z_u.

[25] Dixit and Stiglitz are careful to note that this conclusion is specific to the symmetric CES case considered here.

modified version of the Dixit–Stiglitz model. In recent years a number of authors have argued that household preference-for-diversity and market power of individual firms are conceptually distinct phenomena.[26] One way to bring this distinction into focus is by generalizing (1.2) to:

$$Y = N^{\eta-\mu} \left[\sum_{i=1}^{N} X_i^{1/\mu} \right]^{\mu}, \tag{1.30}$$

where η and $\mu \equiv \sigma/(\sigma - 1)$ are allowed to be distinct.[27] In this formulation, μ (>1) parameterises the market power of differentiated goods producers whereas η (≥ 1) captures the preference-for-diversity effect.[28] If $\eta = 1$ then households do not value variety *per se* but firms nevertheless possess market power as μ exceeds unity. In the standard Dixit–Stiglitz model, $\eta = \mu$, and it is impossible to switch off the preference-for-diversity effect without at the same time eliminating the basis for monopolistic competition.

Following the same steps as before, it is easy to show that the market-equilibrium values for X, Z, and N are still as given in, respectively, (1.17), (1.18) and (1.19). The relative price of the composite differentiated good is given by:

$$\frac{P_Y}{P_Z} = \left(\frac{\mu k_Y}{k_Z} \right) N^{1-\eta}, \tag{1.31}$$

and aggregate output in the differentiated sector is:

$$Y = \Omega_0' L_Y^{\eta}, \tag{1.32}$$

where $\Omega_0' \equiv \eta^{-\eta} (\eta - 1)^{\eta-1} F^{1-\eta}/k_Y$ and $L_Y = (1 - \delta) H$. Comparing (1.20) and (1.32) we find that it is the preference-for-diversity parameter, η, which regulates whether or not there are increasing returns to labour. Indeed, if $\eta = 1$, then returns to scale are constant despite the fact that there is monopolistic competition in the differentiated sector.

---

[26] See Bénassy (1996) and Broer and Heijdra (2001).

[27] The true price index associated with (1.30) is:

$$P_Y \equiv N^{\mu-\eta} \left[\sum_{i=1}^{N} P_i^{1-\sigma} \right]^{1/(1-\sigma)}.$$

The demand for variety i is now given by:

$$\frac{X_i}{Y} = N^{(\eta-\mu)/(\mu-1)} \left(\frac{P_i}{P_Y} \right)^{-\sigma}.$$

[28] Interestingly, preferences such as (1.30) actually appear and are analysed in the May 1974 and February 1975 versions of the Dixit–Stiglitz paper which are reprinted here as chapters 3 and 4, respectively. Unfortunately, they apparently did not survive the refereeing process and were eliminated from the published paper. They do, however, feature in Ethier (1982) though in a slightly different context.

The welfare analysis is also affected by the alternative definition of Y given in (1.30). Indeed, it is not difficult to show that the first-best interior social optimum calls for:[29]

$$Z_u = \frac{\delta}{\delta + \eta (1 - \delta)} \frac{H}{k_Z}, \tag{1.33}$$

$$X_u = \frac{F}{(\eta - 1) k_Y}, \tag{1.34}$$

$$N_u = \frac{(1 - \delta)(\eta - 1)}{\delta + \eta (1 - \delta)} \frac{H}{F}, \tag{1.35}$$

$$Y_u = N_u^\eta X_u. \tag{1.36}$$

We can once again compare the socially optimal solutions to their market counterparts. Provided η is strictly greater than unity, it follows from (1.18) and (1.33) that the homogeneous sector is too large in the market equilibrium, i.e. too little labour enters the differentiated sector. All the other welfare comparisons depend in a critical manner on the magnitude of the preference-for-diversity parameter, η, relative to the markup μ. Indeed, the comparison of (1.17) and (1.34) reveals that $X_e \gtreqless X_u$ for $\eta \lesseqgtr \mu$. In the first-best social optimum, preference for diversity determines firm size in the differentiated sector, whereas in the Chamberlinian model the markup performs this role. If individual firms possess a lot of market power (σ close to unity so that μ is large), then output per variety is kept small and the market mechanism produces firms that are too small from a social point of view.

The comparison of (1.19) and (1.35) yields the following conclusion regarding the number of product varieties:

$$N_e \lesseqgtr N_u \quad \Longleftrightarrow \quad [\sigma - (1 - \delta)](\eta - 1) \gtreqless 1. \tag{1.37}$$

Dixit and Stiglitz (1977, p. 302) study the special case for which $\eta = \mu$. In that case, $\sigma = \eta/(\eta - 1)$ and the market must yield too few varieties (see also p. 23 above). If, however, we allow η and μ to be different, then the conclusion is less clear-cut. If the diversity effect is strong, and $\eta > \mu$, then the market still produces too few varieties. In contrast, if the diversity effect is weak ($\eta \approx 1$), market power is strong ($\sigma \approx 1$), and the differentiated sector is relatively large ($\delta \approx 0$), then it may well be the case that the N_e exceeds N_u and there is excessive product differentiation. In that case active firms in the market are very small (because they possess a lot of market power) and a large part of the labour force is employed in the differentiated sector.

---

[29] We limit attention to the interior solution for which the preference for diversity effect is strong enough to dominate the internal scale economies. It is not difficult to show that condition (1.24) for the augmented model is $(N_u - N^{MIN})[\zeta_u - \eta] = 0$.

Decentralisation of the first-best equilibrium is more complex in the augmented model. In addition to a product subsidy, the policy maker must now be able to directly affect the zero-profit condition by means of a firm-based lump-sum tax or transfer. In particular, if we denote this instrument by T_u and index it with P_Y, then the profit definition (1.12) is augmented to $\Pi_i = (1 + s_P) P_i X_i - W[k_Y X_i + F] - P_Y T_u$. The first-best equilibrium can be decentralised if the product subsidy is set equal to $s_{Pu} = \mu - 1$ (see (1.29)) *and* if the lump-sum tax is set according to:

$$T_u = (\mu - \eta) N_u^{\eta-1} X_u. \tag{1.38}$$

The product subsidy restores marginal cost pricing and the lump-sum instrument is needed to ensure that active firms have the socially optimal size and the optimal number of product varieties is produced. The expression in (1.38) is intuitive. For example, if $\eta > \mu$ then lump-sum transfers are needed. It is optimal to have many small firms but, in the absence of a lump-sum transfer, such firms are unable to cover their fixed costs despite the fact that they receive a product subsidy. The opposite holds if $\mu > \eta$.

If the policy maker does not possess the lump-sum instrument for firms, the first-best cannot be decentralised and a more restricted welfare criterion must be employed. As Dixit and Stiglitz themselves put it, 'it would therefore appear that a more appropriate notion of optimality is a constrained one, where each firm must have nonnegative profits' (1977, p. 300). Clearly, in view of our previous discussion, the non-availability of the lump-sum instrument is irrelevant in case $\eta = \mu$ – see (1.38). In the general case, however, the second-best (or 'constrained') social optimum is indeed different from the first-best ('unconstrained') social optimum.

In the constrained social optimum the planner must find an optimal trade-off between two tasks, namely removing the monopoly distortion (as parameterised by $\mu - 1$) and producing the optimal number of product varieties. For our version of the Dixit–Stiglitz model, the constrained social optimum can be determined as follows. First we note that for a given value of the product subsidy, s_P, the Chamberlinian market equilibrium yields the following solutions:

$$X_e = \frac{F}{(\mu - 1) k_Y}, \tag{1.39}$$

$$Z_e = \frac{L_{Ze}}{k_Z} = \frac{\delta}{1 + (1 - \delta) s_P} \frac{H}{k_Z}, \tag{1.40}$$

$$N_e = \frac{(1 - \delta) H}{\sigma F} \left(\frac{1 + s_P}{1 + (1 - \delta) s_P} \right), \tag{1.41}$$

$$Y_e = N_e^{\eta} X_e. \tag{1.42}$$

In the constrained social optimum, the social planner maximises household utility, $U \equiv Z_e^\delta X_e^{1-\delta} N_e^{\eta(1-\delta)}$, taking into account the relations (1.39)–(1.42). It is already clear, from the inspection of (1.17) and (1.39), that the planner is unable to affect firm size in the constrained equilibrium, i.e. $X_c = X_e$, where the subscript 'c' is used to denote the constrained social optimum. The planner can, however, affect both the number of product varieties and the size of the homogeneous goods sector. By using, respectively, (1.40) and (1.41) we find:

$$\frac{1}{Z_e}\frac{\partial Z_e}{\partial s_P} = -\frac{1-\delta}{1+(1-\delta)\,s_P} < 0, \tag{1.43}$$

$$\frac{1}{N_e}\frac{\partial N_e}{\partial s_P} = \frac{\delta}{(1+s_P)\,[1+(1-\delta)\,s_P]} > 0. \tag{1.44}$$

Increasing the product subsidy leads to a shrinkage of the homogeneous goods sector and an expansion of the number of firms in the differentiated sector. By differentiating the utility function with respect to s_P we find after some manipulation:

$$\begin{aligned}
\frac{dU}{ds_P} &= U\left[\frac{\delta}{Z_e}\frac{\partial Z_e}{\partial s_P} + \frac{\eta\,(1-\delta)}{N_e}\frac{\partial N_e}{\partial s_P}\right] \\
&= \frac{\delta\,(1-\delta)\,U}{1+(1-\delta)\,s_P}\left[-1+\frac{\eta}{1+s_P}\right].
\end{aligned} \tag{1.45}$$

This expression clearly shows that in the constrained social optimum, the preference-for-diversity effect provides the rationale for a product subsidy. This stands in stark contrast with the unconstrained social optimum, in which the product subsidy aims to restore marginal cost pricing and thus depends on the index for market power, $\mu - 1$ – see (1.29). In the constrained social optimum, the policy maker sets the product subsidy such that $dU/ds_P = 0$, or:

$$s_{Pc} = \eta - 1. \tag{1.46}$$

By using (1.46) in (1.40) and (1.41) and rearranging somewhat, we find the expressions for Z_c and N_c:

$$Z_c = \frac{L_{Zc}}{k_Z} = \frac{\delta}{\delta+\eta\,(1-\delta)}\frac{H}{k_Z}, \tag{1.47}$$

$$N_c = \left(\frac{(1-\delta)\,(\mu-1)}{\delta+\eta\,(1-\delta)}\right)\frac{\eta}{\mu}\frac{H}{F}. \tag{1.48}$$

By using (1.33), (1.40) (with $s_P = 0$ imposed), and (1.47) we find that $Z_u = Z_c < Z_e$, i.e. the homogeneous sector has the same size in the unconstrained and the constrained social optimum but is too large in the Chamberlinian equilibrium. The comparison for the number of product varieties proceeds as follows. First, we note from (1.44) that N_e is increasing in s_P. If $\eta > 1$ then it follows from (1.46) that $s_P > 0$. As a result, we find that $N_c > N_e$, i.e. the constrained social optimum also calls for a larger number of product varieties. Second, the comparison of (1.35) and (1.48) reveals:

$$\frac{N_c}{N_u} = \frac{\eta (\mu - 1)}{\mu (\eta - 1)}. \tag{1.49}$$

In the standard Dixit–Stiglitz case, $\eta = \mu$ and it follows from (1.49) that $N_c = N_u$. In the generalised model, we find that $N_c \gtreqless N_u$ for $\eta \lesseqgtr \mu$.

1.4.2   Evaluation

We have shown above that the Dixit–Stiglitz model, though rather specific in its assumptions, offers a neat way of dealing with increasing returns to scale at firm level while maintaining a well-defined industry equilibrium. In addition we have shown how the model captures the key insights of Chamberlin and is rather flexible.

This is not to say that the Dixit–Stiglitz model has not been criticised in the literature. Though the model was originally intended as a contribution to the product differentiation literature, it has come under serious attack in that literature. Eaton and Lipsey, for example, suggest a number of so-called 'awkward facts' about product differentiation which the model fails to accommodate (1989, pp. 725–6, 731). First, in reality each consumer buys only a *small sub-set* of the available commodities. Second, in reality tastes are revealed to differ among individuals in that 'different consumers purchase different bundles of differentiated commodities and these differences cannot be fully accounted for by differences in their incomes' (Eaton and Lipsey, 1989, p. 726). In the Dixit–Stiglitz model there is a *representative* consumer who buys *all* existing varieties. In the product differentiation literature the aim is therefore to go beyond the representative-agent world of Dixit and Stiglitz and to search for microeconomic foundations of the Chamberlin model.[30]

Though the Dixit–Stiglitz model has failed to impress most students of product differentiation, it has nevertheless attained 'workhorse' status in

---

[30] Eaton and Lipsey (1989, pp. 731–4) present a brief (and now somewhat dated) survey of some of this micro-foundations literature. Weitzman (1994) has more recently demonstrated that a generalised aggregator function like (1.30) can be interpreted as the reduced form of a spatial model of monopolistic competition on the circle, provided the firm can choose its level of specialisation.

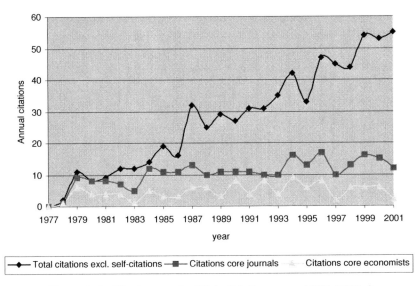

Figure 1.2   Citations to the Dixit–Stiglitz paper, 1977–2001

a large number of different fields of economics. The analytical flexibility of the model in particular has proved to be very convenient in the last quarter-century or so. In figure 1.2 we plot the number of citations of the published version of the Dixit–Stiglitz paper.[31] There has been a steady increase in the total number of citations and even in core journals the paper holds its ground. This book shows where these citations are coming from. The specific formalisation of the model, and the fact that it can deal with imperfect markets without getting lost in details of strategic interaction, has led to innovations in various fields of economics, as this volume aims to show.

1.5   Structure of the book

The structure of this book is as follows. The book consists of six parts, of which two are general and four are more specific and each covers a separate discipline. We selected those disciplines where the Dixit–Stiglitz model has contributed the most, namely international trade theory, geographical economics, macroeconomics and growth theory.

Each discipline part consists of a survey paper that is followed by a critical appraisal of the Dixit–Stiglitz model in that particular field, and one

---

[31] We thank Harry van Dalen of Erasmus University for providing us with this figure.

or two original applications of the Dixit–Stiglitz model. We hope that this volume shows that, although the model has unrealistic features, it nevertheless gives interesting answers to many diverse problems. Furthermore, we hope to show that the second monopolistic competition revolution has indeed been more successful than the first.

Part I: underground classics

In part I we include some 'underground classics', i.e. one previously unpublished paper by Stiglitz on the capital market (chapter 2) and two preliminary versions of the Dixit–Stiglitz paper dated, respectively, May 1974 and February 1975 (chapters 3 and 4). These working papers not only develop the basic model in more detail than the published version does, but also contain some interesting material that later had to be, independently, re-discovered by others. For example, the May 1974 version of the model includes the following features: (a) preference for diversity and market power are clearly distinguished (see also the discussion surrounding (1.30), p. 22), and (b) preferences are modelled in terms of a continuum of product varieties. Similarly, the February 1975 version of the paper contains an interesting discussion of the public good aspect of product variety. We wholeheartedly concur with Bénassy who argues that especially the February 1975 version of the Dixit–Stiglitz paper 'should become required reading for all serious students of the field' (1996, p. 46 n. 3). By incorporating it (and its May 1974 precursor) in this book we hope to have significantly lowered the barrier to such students.

Part II: current perspectives

In part II of the book, the intellectual founding fathers of the Dixit–Stiglitz model reflect on their contribution to the monopolistic competition literature. In addition, one of the earliest adopters of the Dixit–Stiglitz model, Wilfred Ethier, reflects on the usefulness of this model to international trade theory.

In chapter 5, Avinash Dixit is rather critical of the Dixit–Stiglitz approach, and wants to go beyond the simplifying assumptions of the benchmark model, such as new perspectives from game theory. He argues that one of the reasons the first monopolistic competition revolution failed was because of the absence of any strategic interaction between firms. In essence this criticism mirrors the ones voiced against Marshall's representative firm almost a century ago. Also in Marshall's analysis strategic interaction is basically absent. Dixit states that this is also true for the second monopolistic competition revolution, where all firms are in essence 'price-index' takers, and the determination of this price index is left to higher levels of aggregation. Dixit is in favour of a more eclectic view in which no single model should dominate economic analysis – more than one model is needed to describe a complex reality. What is needed is a taxonomy of different models that can be applied to different situations. And in this sense Dixit welcomes the – sometimes criticised – trend towards numerical simulations of theoretical models that 'make the theoretical models come alive in a way that complex algebraic comparative static expressions do not'.

In chapter 6, Joseph Stiglitz recalls that four decades after Chamberlin had written his book, the theory of monopolistic competition called out for formalisation. The only formal model of monopolistic competition available at that time was one in which product differentiation showed up as a series of stores located on a circle: each store having only two neighbours with whom to compete. But this particular formalisation seems at odds with the central idea of the monopolistic competition model: it was not realistic to assume the absence of (complex) strategic interactions between these stores. Stiglitz remembers that 'we wanted to formulate a benchmark model' (see p. 136). He continues that with hindsight it seems that the benchmark model was taken 'too seriously', and shows that other modelling perspectives are potentially more promising, such as dealing with the consequences of imperfect information.[32]

In chapter 7, Wilfred Ethier calls the Dixit–Stiglitz paper 'a truly great tool-paper'. Ethier (1982) was a rather early application of the Dixit–Stiglitz framework to international trade, though he himself considers his own paper as yet 'another tool-paper' – it has never been among his favourites. But obviously this sentiment is not shared by people working in growth theory where the Ethier-formalisation of the Dixit–Stiglitz framework has become very popular. Furthermore (as an aside) Ethier, in his contribution to this volume, gives a funny insight into the refereeing process and his perceptive response to one of Krugman's first papers on New Trade Theory.

Part III: international trade

Background

Until 1975 international trade theory was dominated by the competitive paradigm embodied in the Heckscher–Ohlin–Samuelson (H–O–S)

---

[32] Similar critical remarks on the benchmark model can be found elsewhere. Fujita, Krugman and Venables (1999, p. 6), for example, mention that the popularity of the Dixit–Stiglitz model is 'baffling', given the unrealistic nature of this model (they also mention that their book might have been called 'Games You Can Play With CES Functions', indicating, inter alia, the benefits of the Dixit–Stiglitz formalisation of monopolistic competition).

framework. Things changed quite dramatically following the empirical study of Grubel and Lloyd (1975). They showed the importance of intra-industry trade between countries with similar factor endowments. The H–O–S model, with its explicit reliance on differences in relative factor endowments and homogeneous goods, could not explain this empirical regularity. Initially, this led to many mutually unrelated approaches to deal with intra-industry trade – see the *Handbook of International Economics* chapter by Helpman (1984) for a survey. In the words of Paul Krugman, 'inevitably, given the state of the field at that time, the general impression conveyed in that chapter was of a collection of highly disparate and messy approaches, standing both in contrast and in opposition to the impressive unity and clarity of the constant-returns, perfect competition trade theory' (1995, p. 1244).

During the late 1970s and early 1980s it became clear that the Dixit–Stiglitz approach provided a simple and elegant way of modelling imperfect competition and increasing returns to scale. Using this approach one could avoid being 'messy', and for this reason the Dixit–Stiglitz model quickly became the dominant benchmark model in international trade theory. The first applications were by Krugman (1979, 1980) himself and by Dixit and Norman (1980).[33]

Using the Dixit–Stiglitz framework it is quite easy to explain intra-industry trade. The basic idea of Krugman (1980) can be explained with the aid of our simple version of the Dixit–Stiglitz model (see subsection 1.4.1 above). Assume that there are two countries that are identical in all respects except (possibly) for their labour endowments. In the absence of trade, Chamberlinian monopolistic competition ensures that there are $N = (1 - \delta)H/(\sigma F)$ domestic product varieties and $N^* = (1 - \delta)H^*/(\sigma F)$ foreign varieties, where H^* is labour supply in the foreign country. The opening up of trade between the two countries ensures that both domestic and foreign consumers can now choose $N + N^*$ product varieties.[34] Provided domestic and foreign consumers exhibit preference for diversity, the greater choice of variety improves welfare to both. The key thing to note is that this welfare effect does not hinge on differences between factor endowments, i.e. it still holds if $H = H^*$ in

---

[33] See Krugman (1995) for a survey. Section 9.3 of Dixit and Norman (1980) is attributed to unpublished material by Norman. During the preparation of this book we received the handwritten version of this earlier work by Norman. His paper is incomplete and the policy consequences of the basic model are absent. The model developed in section 9.3 of Dixit and Norman (1980) is very similar to this version. A PDF file of Norman's unpublished paper can be downloaded from: http://www.eco.rug.nl/˜heijdra/norman76.pdf. Apparently Norman did not attempt to publish his paper as a separate article once it was included in this well-known textbook.

[34] As Krugman (1980, p. 951) points out, costless product differentiation ensures that no (domestic or foreign) firm will want to produce a variety that already exists.

our example. This framework is now a standard part of economics curriculum. Although real wages might differ between countries of different sizes in autarky, after trade they become the same as each consumer now has the same choice among varieties – see (1.7). In this sense trade completely substitutes for international factor mobility (as in the H–O–S model).

Ethier (1982) argued that most international trade is not in final products (as in the Krugman, 1980, model) but rather in intermediate goods. In terms of our model, Ethier interprets Y in (1.1) as a homogeneous commodity which is produced according to the production function (1.2), where X_i now represents an intermediate input variety. This formulation implies that, in addition to *internal* economies of scale in the production of each intermediate input variety, there are *external* economies at the final goods stage. The intuition behind this so-called *Ethier-effect* is as follows. An increase in the number of input varieties ensures that Y-producers can use a more 'roundabout' production process and thus lower product costs.[35] In Ethier's model, opening up of trade is beneficial because it causes external effects in the production of final goods in both countries. Interestingly, Ethier's formulation has become quite popular in the macroeconomic and growth applications of the Dixit–Stiglitz model – see below.

The book

In chapter 8, Peter Neary presents a critical survey of monopolistic competition and international trade theory. He discusses trade theory but also gives a clear account of why the Dixit–Stiglitz (1977) model has become so popular: it is its *formalisation* that has contributed to its success. Although the model has become standard in trade theory, it has rather mixed success with respect to empirical testing. But not only the limited empirical success of the model makes Neary critical of the whole approach. Like Kaldor before him, Neary argues that 'in its assumptions about entry and strategies, monopolistic competition resembles perfect competition much more than it resembles the market structure of many industrial sectors in the real world'. What is needed according to Neary is a GOLE: a theory of General Oligopolistic Equilibrium.[36]

In chapter 9, Joe Francois and Douglas Nelson present a state-of-the-art overview of all classes of trade models; classical models, the new trade models, and models based on the Ethier framework. They show the differences and similarities between these models and provide a generic representation of the new trade models and Ethier type of models,

---

[35] In fact, Ethier uses a production function like (1.30) in which η captures the Ethier-effect and μ represents the market power by input variety producers.

[36] Recently, Neary (2002) has proposed such a model.

combining them with neoclassical elements. Their geometric representation of five classes of models shows why some models give identical results and why some do not. This is a complex issue because the Ethier-type models are usually characterised by multiple-equilibria, and instability. Although various authors express the need for additions, extensions, and better empirical work in this area, the Francois–Nelson taxonomy of models and their geometric representation, show that still not all applications of the basic Dixit–Stiglitz framework have been exploited in international trade theory.

Part IV: Economic geography

Background

As we already argued above, for otherwise identical countries, a difference between labour force sizes $(H \neq H^*)$ implies that the larger country will have a higher real wage in autarky due to the larger number of available varieties (see also (1.7) and n. 18). In the presence of impediments to trade (such as transport cost or tariffs), however, it is no longer the case that trade substitutes for factor mobility – see Krugman (1979, 1980). The larger region now offers a higher real wage because of a larger *local* market (which does not face transport costs or tariffs). The effect of this seemingly small addition to the model is surprisingly large and leads to a so-called *home-market effect*: the country with the largest economy tends to be a net exporter of products of the monopolistically competitive industry. Helpman and Krugman (1985) show that if one country is large enough compared to its trading partner, all Y (see (1.1)) might be concentrated in that country. In standard trade models location does not matter, because when transport cost are absent there is nothing to gain from being in a specific location. The home-market effect is interesting by itself, but takes the distribution of labour (or income) as given. If workers would be mobile all workers would end up in the largest market in order to forgo transport cost, and the multi-country model would simply collapse into a single country/region model.

A decade ago, Krugman (1991a, 1991b) realised that his trade model, appended with transport costs, could explain centre–periphery patterns in the world economy once factor mobility between countries is allowed. According to Krugman:

it is obvious – in retrospect – that something special happens when factor mobility interacts with increasing returns . . . This observation is, as I suggested, obvious in retrospect; but it certainly took me a while to see it. Why exactly I spent a decade between showing how the interaction of transport costs and increasing returns at the level of the plant could lead to the 'home market effect' (Krugman, 1980) and realising that the techniques developed there led naturally to simple models of regional divergence (Krugman, 1991) remains a mystery to me. The only good news was that nobody else picked up that $100 bill lying on the sidewalk in the interim. (Krugman, 1999)

In order to prevent the model from collapsing into a single-country/ region model, Krugman (1991a, 1991b) makes some additional assumptions regarding the labour market. First, he divides (exogenously) the labour market into two parts: a share is allocated to the homogeneous good sector Z (agriculture in his terminology), and a share is allocated to Y (which he calls manufactures). To simplify notation Krugman assumes that a share δ goes to Z, and $1 - \delta$ to the Y sector (compare with (1.18)). Furthermore, workers in the manufacturing industry are assumed to be mobile between countries, whereas farmers are immobile; and farmers cannot become workers or vice versa.

This implies that we can no longer assume a single wage rate for the homogeneous sector and the manufacturing sector (compare with sub-section 1.4.1). Assuming costless trade in agriculture (homogeneous sector), prices and wages in agriculture can be used as a numéraire (by convenient choice of units). In principle the nominal wage rate in the Y-sector can easily be calculated by asking at what price the optimal amount per firm (as indicated by (1.17)) is exactly met by total demand. Total demand comes from two sources: domestic sales and foreign sales. For consumers the price difference between these two sources consists of transport costs (and we have to adapt (1.6) and (1.7) accordingly). This line of reasoning gives us the equilibrium price at which demand equals optimal supply. From this equilibrium price one can derive the corresponding nominal wage rate in the manufacturing sector by using (1.13). The real wage follows from dividing the nominal wage by the exact price index (raised to the power $1 - \delta$).

If the real wage between countries differs this will lead to labour migration until real wages in the manufacturing sector are equalised. Depending on the model parameters, all workers might concentrate in a single region, or might be divided over different regions. By assumption complete agglomeration is not possible, because of the immobile farmers.

Once the $100 bill had been picked up by Krugman, geographical economics turned into one of the most active fields in international trade theory, although not everyone is convinced of the 'revolutionary' character of this new field.[37]

---

[37] See Neary (2001) for a critique. Brakman, Garretsen and van Marrewijk (2001) present an extensive description of the intellectual history of this approach.

The book

In chapter 10, Richard Baldwin, Rikard Forslid, Philippe Martin, Gianmarco Ottaviano and Frédéric Robert-Nicoud develop and explain the key features of the core–periphery model (as the Krugman model is now called). They show that the core–periphery model is much more complex than the standard Dixit–Stiglitz trade model. They furthermore explain some of the more difficult issues in these types of models, such as normalisations, characteristics of equilibria (e.g. their (in)stability), and how the model deals with expectations. The chapter shows how two seemingly innocuous changes to the standard Dixit–Stiglitz trade model – the introduction of transport cost and international factor mobility – can give rise to complicated and interesting models.

The debate of the effects of globalisation on labour markets often takes place in the H–O–S framework. In chapter 11, Jolanda Peeters and Harry Garretsen show that the neoclassical framework might not be the most appropriate one to study the consequences of globalisation on labour markets in the OECD countries. By allowing for wage rigidities in a geographical economics model, they are able to show that the effects of globalisation can be very different in different countries. It is by no means certain that low-skilled workers are always worse off following increased globalisation. If globalisation can be represented by a reduction in transportation costs, then agglomerating and spreading forces both determine long-run outcomes of the model. This makes the conclusions less clear-cut than those obtained from neoclassical models. Potentially, however, the Peeters–Garretsen model can accommodate the rather different institutional circumstances existing in apparently similar countries. Obviously more empirical research is needed to find out whether their model is indeed better equipped to deal with all kinds of different circumstances.

In his critical survey of the geographical economics approach, Peter Neary (2001) notes that empirical work in the field is largely absent. Indeed, with a few exceptions, it is almost totally lacking. This might come as a surprise as the great interest in the Dixit–Stiglitz trade model was caused by the existence of a recalcitrant empirical irregularity, namely the phenomenon of intra-industry trade. This phenomenon made researchers look for theoretical models that could explain these facts. In chapter 12, Steven Brakman, Harry Garretsen, Charles van Marrewijk and Marc Schramm explain why it is difficult to test geographical economics models. Basically, the problem is that many observations are consistent with many competing models. In general, testing is restricted to some of the implications of the geographical economics models, but often these characteristics are consistent with more than one model. It is however, possible to estimate the structural equations of a variant of the standard model, as has been done by Hanson (1998) for the USA. Brakman *et al.* test an extended version of the Hanson model for Germany. They show that it is possible to find some empirical support for this model. It is, however, not always clear how to interpret the results owing to the possibility of multiple equilibria. Also more empirical work needs to be done here before one can conclude that the geographical economics approach is better able to explain some of the geographical stylised facts than alternative models are.

To conclude part IV of the book, in chapter 13 Vernon Henderson gives a critical appraisal of the geographical economics approach. As a researcher of a neighbouring discipline, urban economics, he discusses the merits of the model with respect to the insights it offers in its urban applications. Henderson welcomes the tendency of mainstream economists to put more geography into their models, but notes that all elements of the Krugman model are familiar to those working in regional economics.[38] Furthermore, modern models in urban economics have incorporated some of the more relevant stylised facts of cities and city formation, whereas the Krugman model deals only with a simplified model of a city – see Fujita and Thisse (2002). The Krugman model, for example, in its basic formulation predicts that the cost of living in a city falls with city size, a prediction that is at odds with the congested reality of cities. Furthermore, the absence of a land development market is also troublesome for urban economists. Also, from a theoretical perspective the geographical economics models, when applied to the analysis of cities, quickly become complex and predict many possible equilibria. And because we have no idea about the size of relevant parameter values, it is not possible to choose between the different equilibria. As a consequence Henderson is very critical of the application of the Dixit–Stiglitz type of geography models to the analysis of cities and highlights some of the, in his eyes, more promising theoretical developments in urban economics.

Part V: Economic growth

Background

Following a period of relative neglect, the theory of economic growth was given a new impetus in the mid-1980s and early 1990s by authors such as Paul Romer (1987, 1990), Robert Lucas (1988), and Gene Grossman and Elhanan Helpman (1991). The body of literature that has emerged

---

[38] This point is acknowledged by Krugman himself, who argues that 'in fairness it should be reported that many geographers feel that the new literature is only telling them what they already knew, with a few technical gimmicks' (1995, p. 1265).

subsequent to – and as a result of – their pioneering efforts is often referred to as the 'endogenous growth' literature. Whereas the long-run growth rate is essentially exogenous in the older growth literature in the Solow–Swan tradition, the distinguishing feature of the new literature is that long-run growth is endogenously determined within the model. Whereas the accumulation of human capital is the central feature in the Lucas (1988) model, the Romer–Grossman–Helpman type models all make explicit use of the Dixit–Stiglitz approach in one way or another.

We can use our version of the Dixit–Stiglitz model to illustrate the way in which endogenous growth emerges in (a simplified version of) the model by Grossman and Helpman (1991, ch. 3).[39] In this model research and development (R&D) activities form the basis of economic growth. There is a single homogeneous good, Y, which is produced with the production function (1.2), where X_i is a differentiated input variety (as in the Ethier approach). The number of existing input varieties, N, is predetermined at any moment in time but can be increased by means of labour-consuming R&D activities. Labour is the only production factor and ownership titles on patents present the only financial asset for savings purposes. Intermediate input producers each hold a blueprint telling them how to produce their own, slightly unique, variety X_i and act as Dixit–Stiglitz monopolistic competitors using the technology $X_i = L_i / k_X$, where L_i is labour use and k_X is a technology index.[40] Technology in the perfectly competitive R&D sector is given by:

$$\dot{N} = \frac{NL_R}{k_R},\tag{1.50}$$

where $\dot{N} \equiv dN/dt$ is the number of *new* blueprints (patents), k_R is a productivity index and L_R is the amount of labour used in the R&D sector. Equation (1.50) constitutes the 'engine of growth' in the model. It incorporates the assumption, due to Romer (1990), that the stock of existing blueprints positively affects the productivity of researchers. As Romer puts it, '[t]he engineer working today is more productive because he or she can take advantage of all the additional knowledge accumulated as design problems were solved during the last 100 years' (1990, pp. S83–84).

The infinitely lived representative household chooses its optimal time profile for consumption in order to maximise the lifetime utility function, $\Lambda \equiv \int_0^\infty \log C(\tau) e^{-\rho\tau} d\tau$, subject to the budget identity $C + P_N \dot{N} = WH + N\Pi$, where C is consumption of the homogeneous good

---

[39] This example is taken from Bénassy (1998). See also Heijdra and van der Ploeg (2002, pp. 461–6) for details of the solution method.
[40] There are no fixed costs.

(equalling Y in equilibrium), ρ is the rate of time preference, P_N is the market value of a patent, W is the real wage rate and Π is profit per intermediate input firm. The budget identity shows that income (right-hand side) is spent on the consumption of final goods and on the accumulation of patents (i.e. on saving). The optimal savings plans of the household in effect determines the fraction of labour allocated to the R&D sector and thus, via (1.50), the rate of innovation in the economy. It can be shown that the endogenous growth rates for the number of input varieties and for aggregate output are:[41]

$$\frac{\dot{N}}{N} = \frac{(\mu - 1)\,H}{\mu k_R} - \frac{\rho}{\mu}, \qquad \frac{\dot{Y}}{Y} = (\mu - 1)\,\frac{\dot{N}}{N}. \tag{1.51}$$

The innovation rate increases with the monopoly markup and the side of the labour force but decreases with the rate of time preference. Intuitively, the markup-effect operates as follows. If the markup is high then input producers keep their output small so that, for a given number of varieties, the amount of labour absorbed by the input-producing sector is small.[42] As a result, the R&D sector is relatively large so that the economy innovates at a high rate.

The example presented here, of course, represents no more than the tip of the iceberg. It nevertheless serves to illustrate yet another area where the Dixit–Stiglitz approach has proven to be very useful. Indeed, the mere analytical flexibility of the Dixit–Stiglitz model has enabled growth theorists to incorporate the notion of monopolistic competition within a fully specified dynamic general equilibrium model with optimising households and firms.

The book

In chapter 14, Sjak Smulders and Theo van de Klundert confirm that the Dixit–Stiglitz model of monopolistic competition has been an important building block for a number of theories of economic growth. Their chapter examines the role played by monopolistic competition in several theories of economic growth. They discuss these theories in a general equilibrium framework with two types of R&D. First, new product lines can be introduced by incurring a sunk cost. Second, incumbent firms can raise productivity by in-house investment in tacit knowledge. Special

---

[41] It is assumed that not all labour is absorbed by the monopolistically competitive sector, i.e. some labour is employed in the R&D sector.

[42] It can be shown that there is no transitional dynamics in $L_X \equiv k_X N X$ and that $L_X = (H + \rho k_R)/\mu$. The results mentioned in the text follow from this expression. Note also that output per intermediate firm declines according to $\dot{X}/X = -\dot{N}/N$, i.e. it gets smaller and smaller as time goes on.

cases of the model include a dynamic version of the Dixit–Stiglitz model, the semi-endogenous growth model, the semi-endogenous growth model based on variety expansion, the endogenous growth model based on in-house R&D, and a combination of the latter two. It is shown that the intensity of competition play quite a different role in the various cases distinguished.

In chapter 15, Sjak Smulders studies the effects of capital mobility on welfare and the speed of adjustment in a two-country growth model. R&D allows monopolistic firms to improve their productivity level while national and international knowledge spillovers affect the returns to R&D. The two countries considered differ only with respect to the initial pro-ductivity level. The country with the lowest productivity level gradually catches up with the leading country. There is complete convergence in the long run if there is no capital mobility. Under perfect capital mobility, countries end up with equal long-run productivity levels, but permanent differences in consumption. The speed of convergence is larger with per-fect capital mobility than with balanced trade. The difference increases with substitution between product varieties and the rate of intertemporal substitution. Capital mobility harms (benefits) the leader (lagging) coun-try if domestic spillovers are more important than international spillovers.

In chapter 16, Henri de Groot, Marjan Hofkes and Peter Mulder ap-ply the Dixit–Stiglitz approach in yet another area. Their chapter studies the adoption and diffusion of energy-efficient technologies in a vintage model. An important characteristic is that vintages are complementary; there are returns to diversity of using different vintages. De Groot, Hofkes and Mulder argue that this is a potentially relevant part of the explana-tion of the energy-efficiency paradox. They also analyse how diffusion patterns and adoption behaviour are affected by learning-by-doing and tax policies. It is shown that the stronger the complementarity between different vintages and the stronger the learning by doing, the longer it takes before firms scrap (seemingly) inferior technologies.

Part VI: macroeconomics

Background

Perhaps the two main dividing issues among macroeconomists are (1) the assumed coordination power of markets and (2) the degree of flexibility of prices and wages. Economists who derive their inspiration from the clas-sicals tend to exhibit a great belief in frictionless markets and emphasise price and wage flexibility. At the other end of the spectrum, economists working in the Keynesian tradition tend to display a higher tolerance for imperfect markets and emphasise that prices and wages may be sticky.

During the latter half of the 1980s, economists from the Keynesian group applied the Dixit–Stiglitz model to study some classic macroeconomic questions. For example, Akerlof and Yellen (1985a, 1985b) and Blanchard and Kiyotaki (1987) develop models with monopolistically competitive price and/or wage setters. They show that price and/or wage stickiness may (a) be optimal to individual price/wage setters and (b) be a general equilibrium phenomenon if there exist small (non-convex) costs associated with price/wage changes, so-called *menu costs*. Intuitively, since under monopolistic competition objective functions are flat at the top, such menu costs ensure that quantity adjustment replaces price adjustment following an exogenous shock. Since the economy is not in a first-best equilibrium to start with, there are first-order welfare effects associated with second-order small menu costs.

The monopolistic competition model has also been used in a setting of flexible prices/wages. Kiyotaki (1988), for example, studies the 'vintage-Keynesian' notion of animal spirits and multiple, Pareto-rankable, equilibria. He builds a two-period model incorporating monopolistic competition in the goods market and real investment decisions by entrepreneurs and shows that there exist two rational expectations equilibria, namely a 'pessimistic' one and an 'optimistic' one. He thus shows that the state of entrepreneurs' expectations regarding the future can have important implications for allocation and welfare in a monopolistically competitive world.

The monopolistic competition model has also been used to provide foundations for the 'Keynesian' multiplier – see Mankiw (1988) and Startz (1989).[43] In all macroeconomic applications of the Dixit–Stiglitz approach, the endogenous labour supply response plays a vital role. For the multiplier model this can be illustrated quite easily with the aid of the simple model presented in sub-section 1.4.1.[44] Instead of choosing two types of goods (as in (1.1)), the representative household now chooses the composite differentiated good, Y, and leisure, $1 - H$ (where 1 is the time endowment and H is labour supply). The household has a Cobb–Douglas utility function, $U = (1 - H)^{\delta} Y^{1-\delta}$. The household budget constraint (1.3) is augmented to $P_Y Y + W(1 - H) = I$, where $I \equiv W + N\Pi - T$ is full income, W is the wage rate, $N\Pi$ is aggregate profit income and T is the lump-sum tax. Equations (1.5)–(1.6) are still relevant but (1.4) is replaced by $W(1 - H) = \delta I$. The government consumes a composite good G (defined analogously to (1.2)) and its budget constraint will be

---

[43] Dixon (1987) remarks that this multiplier is more Walrasian than Keynesian because perfect flexibility of prices and wages is assumed.

[44] The model is loosely based on Mankiw (1988). Details of the solution approach can be found in Heijdra and van der Ploeg (2002, pp. 359–77).

$T = P_Y G$, where P_Y is defined in (1.7). Individual firms face a demand from both the government and the representative household but since these demand curves feature the same elasticity the price is the same for both customers, i.e. $P_i = \mu W k_Y$ (see (1.13)). In the symmetric equilibrium, the goods market equilibrium condition is $NPX = P_Y [Y + G]$ and aggregate profit income can be written as $N\Pi = \frac{1}{\sigma} NPX - WNF$.

We follow Mankiw (1988) by assuming that the number of firms is constant in the (very) short run. In that case, the model can be condensed to two simultaneous equations determining composite household consumption, Y, and real aggregate output, NPX/P_Y, as a function of the exogenous variables:

$$\frac{NPX}{P_Y} = Y + G, \tag{1.52}$$

$$Y = \Omega_0 + \left(\frac{1-\delta}{\sigma}\right) \frac{NPX}{P_Y} - (1 - \delta)G, \tag{1.53}$$

where $\Omega_0 \equiv (1 - \delta) W (1 - NF) / P_Y$ is a constant. The system is reminiscent of the Samuelsonian Keynesian Cross diagram – (1.52) says that aggregate output equals demand by the household and the government while (1.53) shows that household demand itself depends positively, via its effect on aggregate profit income, on real aggregate output. It is therefore not surprising that the model features a short-run multiplier effect. Indeed, it follows from (1.52)–(1.53) that the short-run output multiplier is given by:

$$0 < \frac{d\left(\frac{NPX}{P_Y}\right)}{dG} = \frac{\delta}{1 - \frac{1-\delta}{\sigma}} < 1. \tag{1.54}$$

The intuition behind the multiplier is as follows. The increase in government consumption necessitates an increase in the lump-sum tax which renders households poorer. Since Y and $1 - H$ are both normal goods, the consumption of both is reduced. The reduction in leisure consumption is effectuated by an increase in labour supply. This enables the expansion of aggregate output. Note that under perfect competition (with $\sigma \to \infty$) fiscal policy would also increase aggregate output though by less. The key mechanism under both perfect and monopolistic competition is the labour supply response by households.

The book

In chapter 17, Russell Cooper reviews the contribution of monopolistic competition to macroeconomics. He begins by assessing the various types of theoretical structures that admit monopolistic competition in either product or factor markets. He then studies the quantitative implications of this form of market power as well as implications for the conduct of fiscal and monetary policy. Cooper concludes that macro models based on monopolistic competition are useful because they provide a source of inefficiency (that is not present under perfect competition) and can be used to study price setting behaviour by firms. From a quantitative perspective, however, the fact that markets are monopolistically competitive – rather than perfectly competitive – does not seem to matter very much.

In chapter 18, Jan Boone gives a formalisation of defensive and enterprising strategies for firms. He asks the question whether a rise in competition tends to make firms more enterprising or more defensive. Distinguishing three ways in which competition can be intensified, Boone finds the following results. First, a rise in the number of opponents and a reduction in opponents' costs both make a firm more defensive. Second, an increase in the aggressiveness of interaction between firms makes the top firms in an industry more enterprising while the laggards become more defensive. These results are evaluated in light of the discussion on green production and downsizing.

In chapter 19, Christian Keuschnigg presents an intertemporal equilibrium model of monopolistic competition and start-up investment with variable capacity. Reflecting a trade-off between the number and capacity of new machines, aggregate investment may be extensive or intensive and may therefore advance the degree of either specialisation or rationalisation of industrial production. Investment externalities are identified that result in under-accumulation of capital. The chapter compares the effectiveness of a proportional investment tax credit with a fixed start-up subsidy that shifts the direction of investment towards a more extensive form with a larger number of smaller machines.

Finally, in chapter 20 Leon Bettendorf and Ben Heijdra construct a dynamic overlapping-generations model of a semi-small open economy with monopolistic competition in the goods market. Using the Dixit–Stiglitz framework, they show that there are two distortions that must be addressed by the policy maker, namely the one due to increasing returns to scale (resulting from monopolistic competition) and the one due to national market power (resulting from a downward sloping export demand function). It is natural in this setting to consider two policy instruments, namely the product subsidy and the import tariff. While in the first-best situation the instrument targeting principle is relevant, it turns out that in the second-best case the two policy instruments are complementary.

The Dixit–Stiglitz framework thus yields precise and intuitively understandable prescriptions about the interaction between the optimum tariff and pre-existing uncorrected domestic distortions and vice versa.

REFERENCES

Akerlof, G. A. (2002). Behavioral macroeconomics and macroeconomic behavior. *American Economic Review*, 92: 411–433

Akerlof, G. A. and Yellen, J. (1985a). Can small deviations from rationality make significant differences to economic equilibria? *American Economic Review*, 75: 708–721

(1985b). A near-rational model of the business cycle, with wage and price inertia. *Quarterly Journal of Economics, Supplement*, 100: 823–838

Archibald, G. C. (1961). Chamberlin versus Chicago. *Review of Economic Studies*, 24: 2–28

(1987). Monopolistic competition, in Eatwell, J., Milgate, M. and Newman, P. (eds.), *The New Palgrave: A Dictionary of Economics*. London, Macmillan

d'Aspremont, C., Dos Santos Ferreira, R., and Gérard-Varet, L.-A. (1996). On the Dixit–Stiglitz model of monopolistic competition. *American Economic Review*, 86: 623–629

Bénassy, J.-P. (1996). Taste for variety and optimum production patterns in monopolistic competition. *Economics Letters*, 52: 41–47

(1998). Is there always too little research in endogenous growth with expanding product variety? *European Economic Review*, 42: 61–69

Bishop, R. L. (1967). Monopolistic competition and welfare economics, in Kuenne, R. E. (ed.), *Monopolistic Competition Theory: Studies in Impact: Essays in Honor of Edward H. Chamberlin*. New York, John Wiley

Blanchard, O. and Niyotaki, N. (1987). Monopolistic competition and the effects of aggregate demand. *American Economic Review*, 77: 647–666

Blaug, M. (1997). *Economic Theory in Retrospect*, 5th edn. Cambridge, Cambridge University Press

Brakman, S., Garretsen, H. and van Marrewijk, C. (2001). *An Introduction to Geographical Economics*. Cambridge, Cambridge University Press

Broer, D. P. and Heijdra, B. J. (2001). The investment tax credit under monopolistic competition. *Oxford Economic Papers*, 53: 318–351

Chamberlin, E. H. (1933). *The Theory of Monopolistic Competition: A Re-orientation of the Theory of Value*, 8th edn. (1962). Cambridge, MA, Harvard University Press

Cournot, A. (1838). *Recherches sur les Principles Máthematique de la Théorie des Richesses*. Paris; translated as *Researches into the Mathematical. Principles of the Theory of Wealth*, N. T. Bacon (trans.). New York: A. M. Kelley (1960)

Dixit, A. and Norman, V. (1980). *The Theory of International Trade*. Cambridge, Cambridge University Press

Dixit, A. K. and Stiglitz, J. E. (1977). Monopolistic competition and optimum product diversity. *American Economic Review*, 67: 297–308

(1993). Monopolistic competition and optimum product diversity: reply. *American Economic Review*, 83: 302–304

Dixon, H. D. (1987). A simple model of imperfect competition with Walrasian features. *Oxford Economic Papers*, 39: 134–160

Dixon, H. D. and Lawler, P. (1996). Imperfect competition and the fiscal multiplier. *Scandinavian Journal of Economics*, 98: 219–231

Eaton, B. C. and Lipsey, R. G. (1989). Product differentiation, in Schmalensee, R. and Willig, R. D. (eds.), *Handbook of Industrial Organization*, vol. 1. Amsterdam, North-Holland

Ethier, W. (1982). National and international returns to scale in the theory of international trade. *American Economic Review*, 72: 389–405

Fellner, W. (1967). The adaptability and lasting significance of the Chamberlin contribution, in Kuenne, R. E. (ed.), *Monopolistic Competition Theory: Studies in Impact: Essays in Honor of Edward H. Chamberlin*. New York, John Wiley

Friedman, M. (1953). The methodology of positive economics, in Friedman, M., *Essays in Positive Economics*. Chicago University Press, Chicago

Fujita, M., Krugman, P. and Venables, A. J. (1999). *The Spatial Economy*. Boston, MIT Press

Fujita, M. and Thisse, J.-F. (2002). *Economics of Agglomeration: Cities, Industrial Location, and Regional Growth*. Cambridge, Cambridge University Press

Grossman, G. M. and Helpman, E. (1991). *Innovation and Growth in the Global Economy*. Cambridge, MA, MIT Press

Grubel, H. and Lloyd, P. (1975). *Intra-Industry Trade: The Theory and Measurement of International Trade in Differentiated Products*. London, Macmillan

Hanson, G. H. (1998). Market potential, increasing returns, and geographic concentration. NBER Working Paper 6429, February (rev. 1999)

Harrod, R. F. (1967). Increasing returns, in Kuenne, R. E. (ed.), *Monopolistic Competition Theory: Studies in Impact: Essays in Honor of Edward H. Chamberlin*. New York, John Wiley

Heijdra, B. J. and van der Ploeg, F. (2002). *Foundations of Modern Macroeconomics*. Oxford, Oxford University Press

Helpman, E. (1984). Increasing returns, imperfect markets, and trade theory, in Jones, R. and Kenen, P. (eds.), *Handbook of International Economics*, vol. 1. Amsterdam, North-Holland

Helpman, E. and Krugman, P. (1985). *Market Structure and Foreign Trade*. Cambridge, MA, MIT Press

Henderson, J. M. and Quandt, R. E. (1971). *Microeconomic Theory*, 2nd edn. New York, McGraw-Hill

Hicks, J. R. (1939). *Value and Capital*. Oxford, Oxford University Press

Johnson, H. G. (1967). International trade theory and monopolistic competition theory, in Kuenne, R. E. (ed.), *Monopolistic Competition Theory: Studies in Impact: Essays in Honor of Edward H. Chamberlin*. New York, John Wiley

Kaldor, N. (1934). Mrs. Robinson's 'Economics of Imperfect Competition'. *Economica*, 1: 335–341

(1935). Market imperfections and excess capacity. *Economica*, 2: 33–50

Kiyotaki, N. (1988). Multiple expectational equilibria under monopolistic competition. *Quarterly Journal of Economics*, 103: 695–714

Kreps, D. M. (1990). *A Course in Microeconomic Theory*. Princeton, Princeton University Press

Krugman, P. (1979). Increasing returns, monopolistic competition, and international trade. *Journal of International Economics*, 9: 469–480

(1980). Scale economies, product differentiation, and the pattern of trade. *American Economic Review*, 70: 950–959

(1991a). *Geography and Trade.* Cambridge, MA, MIT Press

(1991b). Increasing returns and economic geography. *Journal of Political Economy*, 99: 483–499

(1995). Increasing returns, imperfect competition and the positive theory, in Grossman, G. M. and Rogoff, K. (eds.), *Handbook of International Economics*, vol. 3. Amsterdam, North-Holland

(1999). Was it all in Ohlin?, Cambridge, MA, MIT, mimeo; downloadable from: http://www.wws.princeton.edu/~pkrugman/ohlin.html

Kuenne, R. E. (ed.) (1967). *Monopolistic Competition Theory: Studies in Impact: Essays in Honor of Edward H. Chamberlin.* New York, John Wiley

Lucas, R. E. (1988). On the mechanics of economic development. *Journal of Monetary Economics*, 22: 3–42

Malinvaud, E. (1972). *Lectures on Microeconomic Theory.* Amsterdam, North-Holland

Mankiw, N. G. (1988). Imperfect competition and the Keynesian cross. *Economics Letters*, 26: 7–13

Mankiw, N. G. and Whinston, M. D. (1986). Free entry and social inefficiency. *Rand Journal of Economics*, 17: 48–58

Marshall, A. (1920). *Principles of Economics*, 8th edn. (reprinted edn. 1994). London, Macmillan

Neary, J. P. (2001). Of hypes and hyperbolas: introducing the new economic geography. *Journal of Economic Literature*, 39: 536–561

(2002). The road less travelled: oligopoly and competition policy in general equilibrium, in Arnott, R., Greenwald, B., Kanbur, R. and Nalebuff, B. (eds.), *Imperfect Economics: Essays in Honour of Joseph Stiglitz.* Cambridge, MA, MIT Press

Robinson, J. (1933). *The Economics of Imperfect Competition.* London, Macmillan

Romer, P. M. (1987). Growth based on increasing returns due to specialization. *American Economic Review, Papers and Proceedings*, 77: 56–62

(1990). Endogenous technological change. *Journal of Political Economy*, 98: S71–S101

Salop, S. C. (1979). Monopolistic competition with outside goods. *Bell Journal of Economics*, 10: 141–156

Samuelson, P. A. (1967). The monopolistic competition revolution, in Kuenne, R. E. (ed.), *Monopolistic Competition Theory: Studies in Impact: Essays in Honor of Edward H. Chamberlin.* New York, John Wiley

Schumpeter, J. A. (1954). *History of Economic Analysis.* Oxford, Oxford University Press

Spence, A. M. (1976). Product selection, fixed costs, and monopolistic competition. *Review of Economic Studies*, 43: 217–235

Sraffa, P. (1926). The law of returns under competitive conditions. *Economic Journal*, 36: 535–550

Startz, R. (1989). Monopolistic competition as a foundation for Keynesian macroeconomics. *Quarterly Journal of Economics*, 104: 737–752

Stigler, G. J. (1949). *Five Lectures on Economic Problems*. London, Longmans, Green

Tinbergen, J. (1967). Quantitative economics, macroeconomics, and monopolistic competition, in Kuenne, R. E. (ed.), *Monopolistic Competition Theory: Studies in Impact: Essays in Honor of Edward H. Chamberlin*. New York, John Wiley

Triffin, R. (1940). *Monopolistic Competition and General Equilibrium Theory*. Cambridge, MA, Harvard University Press

Weitzman, M. L. (1994). Monopolistic competition with endogenous specialization. *Review of Economic Studies*, 61: 57–80

Yang, X. and Heijdra, B. J. (1993). Monopolistic competition and optimum product diversity: comment. *American Economic Review*, 83: 295–301

Part I

Underground classics

2   Monopolistic competition and the capital market

Joseph E. Stiglitz

2.1   Introduction

It is often suggested that the market for shares in firms is one of the more competitive markets. There are a large number of buyers and sellers, and for most widely held firms – most of the largest firms in the USA – no single individual owns more than a few per cent of the shares. Moreover, shares in one firm are closely competitive with shares in other firms.

On the other hand, it is often alleged that if a firm were to increase its issue of shares, it would face a downward sloping demand schedule for its shares.

If the former view were correct, then a security which was uncorrelated with the business cycle,[1] should be treated as essentially a safe security, and a firm, in evaluating a project, should ignore the variance of the project, and be concerned only with its correlation with the business cycle. There is a widespread view that this is in fact not the case.

These contrasting views would be resolved if the capital market were monopolistically competitive rather than perfectly competitive: different securities are close but not perfect substitutes for one another.

If different risky securities are not perfectly correlated, then they are imperfect substitutes for one another (in the absence of a full set of Arrow–Debreu securities). If there are many such securities, they will be *close* substitutes for one another, i.e. there are gains from dividing one's assets among $n + 1$ risky securities rather than n risky securities, but the marginal gain from the additional diversification allowed by the $n + 1$st security may be relatively small. A risk averse individual will want to hold some of all the available securities, no matter how large the number

This work was supported by National Science Foundation Grant SOC74-22182 at the Institute for Mathematical Studies in the Social Sciences, Stanford University. This chapter is part of a paper originally presented at the Far Eastern Meetings of the Econometric Society, Tokyo, 27–29 June 1970. Research support from the Guggenheim Foundation, National Science Foundation, and Ford Foundation is gratefully acknowledged. I am indebted to A. Dixit and M. Spence for extremely helpful discussions.

[1] Assuming for simplicity that the business cycle constitutes the major undiversifiable risk.

of firms. As a result, all risky firms will perceive themselves as facing a negatively sloped demand schedule for their securities.

Consider, for instance the situation where all risky firms are identical but not perfectly correlated; in equilibrium an individual will hold exactly the same amount of all the risky securities. If one of the firms were to contemplate raising its level of investment, it could induce individuals to hold more of its securities only by lowering the price of a unit of its securities. (The amount by which it will be lowered will not necessarily decrease as the number of firms increase; see Stiglitz, 1972a.) Alternatively, assume the firm contemplated raising the price of its shares. This would result in a slight change in the demand for them; in contrast a slight change in the price of one of two commodities that were perfect substitutes (one of two securities that were perfectly correlated) would result in the demand shifting entirely to one or the other of the commodities (securities).

One must then ask, why do individuals hold sufficiently few securities in their portfolios that they are not, effectively, perfect substitutes. Several reasons can be put forth: (a) Transactions costs prevent individuals from holding more than a few securities in their portfolios. This is an unconvincing explanation, since with mutual funds, these transactions costs can be made negligible. (b) Information costs make it desirable for individuals to concentrate their portfolios. A quite forceful argument can be made on these grounds and is pursued elsewhere.[2] (c) There are only a finite number of firms and the number of states of nature are infinite. The income patterns of any two arbitrarily chosen firms differ in at least some states of nature. Obviously, if there were no costs associated with setting up new firms (creating new assets), then, so long as there is a return from further diversification of risk, additional firms would be created. To explain a limitation on the number of firms there must be some non-convexity in the production process, e.g. some fixed cost associated with setting up a new firm.

It is this view which we wish to pursue in this chapter. In particular, we wish to investigate whether there will be too few or too many risky firms, whether the risky firms will be too small or too large, whether there will be 'errors' in the choice of technique, etc. Interest in these questions is motivated by three considerations.

---

[2] There are in fact two separate aspects to the argument. If individuals are well informed about a few stocks and uninformed about others, it can be shown that they may own sufficient amounts of the stock about which they are well informed that they will be risk averse with respect to the actions of those firms (see Stiglitz, 1974). Secondly, because of the fundamental non-convexity associated with information, it is optimal only to obtain information about a limited number of securities (see Radner and Stiglitz, 1974).

In our earlier work analysing the optimality of the stock market (Stiglitz 1972a), in the context of a mean variance model, we established that if firms maximised their stock market value, taking the rate of interest and the risk discount factor as given, the equilibrium would not be Pareto optimal. This result has been the subject of some discussion. One objection raised to our analysis was that under our assumptions there would be a strong motivation for entry. With sufficient entry, as we argued above, different securities with the same correlation with the business cycle will become essentially perfect substitutes. But fixed costs associated with creating firms act as a deterrent to entry. It is therefore important to determine exactly the nature of the equilibrium when the number of firms is endogenous. In particular there remains the question of how to interpret our earlier result. One interpretation we offered at the time was that in the absence of a complete set of securities, the market ought to be viewed as monopolistically competitive. This chapter investigates in detail that interpretation.[3]

Even if firms fail to recognise the effect of their scale of operation on their value (per unit scale) there remains the question of which firms should operate. Earlier analyses with a fixed number of firms, and no firm having any choice of technique, showed that if firms believed that doubling their scale doubled their market value then the equilibrium would be a constrained Pareto optimal (Diamond, 1971). But if we allow for entry will this still be the case? An example presented in our earlier paper (Stiglitz, 1972a) suggested that this would not in fact be the case, but the generality of this result remained in question. In this chapter, we wish to show that *when the number of firms producing is not fixed, the market solution will err both with respect to the number and choice of firms*

---

[3] It should be emphasised that this is not the only appropriate interpretation. In particular, we argued in our earlier paper that what is 'price taking behaviour' is not unambitious; in a mean variance model, firms could act as price takers relative to what they consider to be the relevant variables, i.e. they take the rate of interest and the risk discount factor as given. Such an interpretation would have them acting not as monopolistic competitors but as essentially perfect competitors. It should also be observed that there are other sources of potential inefficiency in the stock market allocation of investment, discussed at greater length in Stiglitz (1972a).

There are other objections which have been raised concerning our analysis, particularly associated with the choice of the objective function of the firm. As we mentioned briefly in our earlier study and elaborated at greater length in the original version of the paper (presented at the Far Eastern Meetings of the Econometric Society in 1970) the policy which the individual stockholder wishes the firm to pursue depends on whether the individual plans to sell shares (so that he is concerned with market value maximisation) or simply to retain his shares. If the ratio of retained shares to shares sold is zero, maximisation is desired, and our earlier analysis is applicable. In the extreme case where no one wishes to change his portfolio, then the policy voted for will be Pareto optimal. These issues are discussed in more detail in Stiglitz (1970).

to produce, even when all firms take their value per unit scale as given. More generally the analysis of equilibrium in the capital market with entry under competitive conditions provides the second motivation for this chapter.

Finally, a better understanding of monopolistic competitive equilibrium provides the third motivation for undertaking this study.

It is often asserted that monopolistic competition leads to too much product differentiation and to each firm, as a consequence, producing too little output. It has long been recognised, however, that the usual argument for this, which makes note of the 'excess capacity' in monopolistic competition (i.e. production at levels below the point of minimum average costs) is incorrect, for it fails to take into account the gains from product differentiation:[4] after all, the reason that one commodity is not a perfect substitute for another (that is, the reason that we do not have *perfect* competition) is that at least some individuals perceive there to be a difference in these commodities for which they are willing to pay a price.[5] Thus, what must be compared are the gains from product differentiation with the 'losses' from the inefficiency of producing below minimum average cost. Without some appropriate parameterisation of the problem it is difficult to determine whether there will normally be under- or over-diversification, or even to determine conditions under which one would expect one or the other. So far, unfortunately, only one such parameterisation has appeared in the literature – the Hotelling (1929) formulation of the problem of spatial location, which has been substantially generalised in the ... work of Lovell (1970) and Stern (1972). The latter study raises some important questions concerning the general validity of the conventional wisdom that in monopolistic competition there are too many firms producing too little output. Although the model of spatial location has an interpretation in the case when products are differentiated by some physical characteristic (say, colour), that model has a number of features which limits its applicability as a description of the general problem of optimal product differentiation. The most important of these is the assumption that individuals purchase from only one store (buy one kind of

---

[4] Chamberlin himself was careful to avoid this error. See Chamberlin (1950, pp. 85–92). Unfortunately, he never developed a theory of optimal product differentiation. See also Bishop (1967).

[5] Some economists have suggested that these are not 'real' differences, only perceived differences – and in fact it is only advertising which makes individuals think that there is a difference. Why the difference between commodities which are close substitutes should be any less 'real' than differences between other commodities is never made clear in these arguments. The fact that the commodities differ less means that individuals are willing to pay less to have one commodity rather than another, but does not vitiate the fact that these are real differences.

commodity, e.g. only red balloons not red balloons, white balloons and pink balloons). Although this assumption makes sense in the context of the transportation problem, in most other contexts it is not so persuasive. Conventional economics has long embodied the principle of 'Variety is the Spice of Life' in the assumption of quasi-concave indifference curves; the assumption that individuals buy either red or white balloons, but not both, denies the validity of this hypothesis.[6] A second important limitation is that the analysis is never embedded in a general equilibrium model. For example, consider a simple two-sector model, one sector of which is perfectly competitive, the other of which is described by our monopolistic competition model. Surely, one of the important questions which we wish to answer is, is the effect of monopolistic competition to divert resources from or to the perfectly competitive sector, or are its only consequences felt within the monopolistic competitive sector itself? The conventional location models fail even to address themselves to these questions.

A third difficulty arises in making welfare comparisons. By making firms closer together, individuals who happen to live on the fringes of a market area are made better off, others are made worse off. Hence, stronger welfare criteria than Pareto optimality are required; conventionally, arguments making use of consumer and producer surplus are employed; compensation could be paid to those who are worse off, but such compensation is never in fact made, for if it were, it would presumably affect the demand curves, and in the analysis, the demand curves are assumed to remain unchanged.[7]

The analysis of monopolistic competition in the capital market provides us with an opportunity to calculate precisely the social benefits and costs of creating a new firm and to compare the optimal allocation with the market allocation.

In the analysis of this chapter, we shall consider a highly simplified version of the capital market model. All risky firms will be assumed to be identical but not perfectly correlated, and all safe firms (i.e. firms whose returns are perfectly certain) are identical. Since one safe security is a perfect substitute for another safe security, the safe firms will constitute a perfectly competitive industry, the risky firms the monopolistically competitive industry. In sections 2.2–2.5 the returns to the risky firms will be assumed to be independently (but identically) distributed, while in section 2.6 they will all be correlated with a general market factor. All individuals will be assumed to be identical and risk averse.

[6] This may not be an unreasonable assumption for certain large consumer durables, e.g. houses or automobiles. For many everyday commodities, it is clearly inappropriate.

[7] This point is, of course, closely related to the previous point that all the analyses are completely partial equilibrium in character.

This formulation allows us to avoid the pitfalls of the previous studies of monopolistic competition: individuals purchase not one but all the produced 'commodities'; there is a perfectly competitive sector, so we can enquire into the diversion of resources from the perfectly competitive to the monopolistically competitive sector; and since all individuals are identical and purchase the same portfolio (market basket of goods) they are all worse off in the 'competitive' situation than in the optimal.

Hence, we would argue that the results are of interest not only for what they suggest about the workings of the capital market, but for the light they shed on the more general question of resource allocation in economies with a monopolistically competitive sector.

In subsequent studies, using considerably different parameterisations of the problem, Dixit and Stiglitz and Spence (1975a, 1975b) have been able to show that the basic results of this study do appear to have more general applicability. In the concluding section of this chapter, we shall comment further on these more general results.

2.2   The model[8]

The representative individual evaluates alternative portfolios in terms of their means and variances, i.e.

$$U = U(\mu_Y, \sigma_Y), \tag{2.1}$$

where μ_Y is his mean income and σ_Y is the standard deviation of his income.

There is a fixed cost, a of setting up a risky firm.

In this and the immediately following sections we shall assume that the returns to all firms are independently distributed, and that the fixed costs of establishing a risky firm are independent of the number of firms.

The mean and standard deviation of the firm's returns are a function of the 'variable' capital alone. If X_i are the profits available for distribution to shareholders of the ith firm[9] then

$$\bar{X}_i = EX_i = h_i(I_i)$$

$$\sigma_i = \sqrt{E(X_i - \bar{X}_i)^2} = g_i(I_i), \tag{2.2}$$

where I_i is the capital, in excess of the fixed cost of setting up the firm, invested in the ith firm (we shall refer to I_i as 'variable' capital as opposed

---

[8] For a more extensive discussion of the basic model, the reader is referred to Stiglitz (1972a).

[9] We assume without loss of generality that the firm is entirely financed by equity; under the assumptions of this model, the financial structure of the firm has no consequences.

to, a, the 'fixed' capital). We assume that increasing investment increases both mean and standard deviation of income

$$h'_i > 0, \qquad g'_i > 0, \tag{2.3a}$$
$$h''_i \leq 0. \tag{2.3b}$$

We shall first investigate the case where all risky firms (and potential firms) are identical, i.e. $g_i = g_j$, $h_i = h_j$ all i, j. Accordingly, in this and the immediately following sections we shall drop the subscripts on h and g. The safe firm is assumed to have constant returns to scale with the return given by r.

The total amount available for investment is assumed to be fixed: let I_R be the total invested in the risky industry, I_S in the safe industry and n the number of firms in the risky industry,[10]

$$I = I_R + I_S = an + nI_i + I_S. \tag{2.4}$$

Our problem is the choice of n, I_i, and I_S subject to the resource constraint (2.4) to maximise utility (2.1).

One of the main advantages of the mean variance model is that it allows us to separate out questions of productive efficiency from those of 'portfolio choice based on consumer preferences', that is, we can first describe the efficiency frontier, the allocation of resources (the determination of the number and the size of risky firms) which minimises risk for given mean and then ask what point on the efficiency frontier is optimal given the preferences of the representative individual. The market solution may differ from the optimal solution in either or both of these: it may or may not be productively efficient, and even if it is productively efficient, it may not choose the optimal point on the efficiency frontier. Indeed, in our earlier analysis (Stiglitz, 1972a) with a fixed number of firms we showed that, if there were no choice of technique – only a choice of scale – then the economy would be productively efficient, but the market solution resulted in too little allocation of resources to risky investments compared to the optimal allocation. On the other hand, if there were a choice of technique, the economy was not likely to be productively efficient.

Let us first describe then the efficiency frontier. We wish to minimise the standard deviation for a given mean. It is easy to show that, given our symmetry assumptions concerning the risky firms, it is optimal to have all firms which produce, produce at the same scale. Thus, we can formulate

---

[10] Throughout the discussion, we shall treat n as a continuous variable; the modifications required to take account of the fact that n can take on only integer values are straightforward.

our problem as

$$\min \sigma_Y = \sqrt{n}\, g(I_i) \tag{2.5a}$$

subject to

$$\mu_Y = nh(I_i) + r(I - nI_i - an). \tag{2.5b}$$

Letting θ be the Lagrangian multiplier associated with constraint (2.5b), we obtain the following first-order conditions

$$\frac{\partial \sigma_Y}{\partial n} = \frac{g}{2\sqrt{n}} = \theta\,[h - r(I_i + a)] = \theta\,\frac{\partial \mu_Y}{\partial n} \tag{2.6a}$$

$$\frac{\partial \sigma_Y}{\partial I_i} = \sqrt{n}\, g' = \theta n[h' - r] = \theta\frac{\partial \mu_Y}{\partial I_i}. \tag{2.6b}$$

(2.6a) gives the effects of changing the number of firms, keeping the size of each firm constant, while (2.6b) gives the effects of changing the investment in the risky industry, keeping the total number of firms constant. Dividing (2.6b) and (2.6a), we have the result that the mean–standard deviation trade-off, keeping n constant, must be the same as that keeping I_i constant; this implies that letting I_i^o be the optimal size of the firm,

$$\frac{g}{2g'} = \frac{h - r\left(I_i^o + a\right)}{h' - r}. \tag{2.7}$$

(2.7) has one very strong implication. The optimal size of the risky firm is independent of preferences.

In the special case when there is constant returns to scale to variable capital, i.e. $h'' = g'' = 0$ we can solve explicitly for I_i^o:

$$I_i^o = \frac{2ra}{h' - r}, \tag{2.7'}$$

which depends only on the relation between the marginal returns in the risky and safe industries and the fixed cost of setting up a new firm.

We may draw the opportunity locus in mean variance space. In figure 2.1, we have marked the perfectly safe point by S. If I_R is invested in the risky industry, the mean and variance are given by

$$\sigma_Y = \left(\frac{I_R}{a + I_i^o}\right)^{1/2} g(I_i^o) \tag{2.8a}$$

$$\mu_Y = \frac{I_R}{a + I_i^o}\, h(I_i^o) + r(I - I_R) \tag{2.8b}$$

$$\frac{d\mu_Y}{d\sigma_Y} = \frac{2(\mu_Y - rI)}{\sigma_Y} \tag{2.8c}$$

$$\frac{d^2\mu_Y}{d\sigma_Y^2} = \frac{2(\mu_Y - rI)}{\sigma_Y^2} > 0. \tag{2.8d}$$

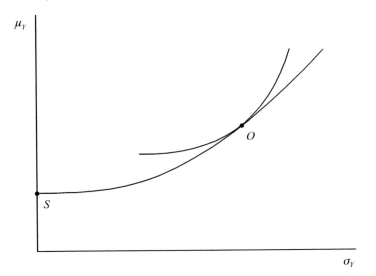

Figure 2.1 The efficiency frontier

Because of diversification, the risk increases more slowly than the mean; the opportunity locus is convex. This is true even if there is constant returns to scale to variable capital in the risky industry.

The choice of the optimal point on the opportunity locus is straightforward: it is simply the tangency between the indifference curve and the opportunity locus, as in figure 2.1. Analytically we, require that

$$\frac{\partial U/\partial \mu_Y}{\partial U/\partial \sigma_Y} = \theta = \frac{\partial \sigma_Y/\partial n}{\partial \mu_Y/\partial n} = \frac{\partial \sigma_Y/\partial I_R}{\partial \mu_Y/\partial I_R} = \frac{2(\mu_Y - rI)}{\sigma_Y}. \tag{2.9}$$

2.3   The market solution

In our mean variance model, it is well known that the value of a firm in equilibrium is given by[11]

$$V_i = \frac{h(I_i) - kg^2(I_i)}{r}, \tag{2.10}$$

where k is the risk discount factor, i.e. we first calculate the certainty equivalent of the risky return by taking the mean and subtracting off a 'risk premium'; the risk premium is simply equal to the risk discount factor times the variance of the security (if the securities are uncorrelated, as we have assumed here). Market equilibrium is characterised by the following two conditions:

[11] See, e.g., Stiglitz (1972a) or Lintner (1965).

(a) Each firm takes k and r as given and maximises the value of the equity of the original shareholders, i.e.

$$\max \ V_i - I_i \tag{2.11}$$

so that

$$h' - r = 2\,kgg'. \tag{2.12}$$

(b) Firms enter until there are zero profits for the marginal entrant, i.e.

$$V_i - I_i = a \tag{2.13}$$

Substituting (2.10) into (2.13) and the result into (2.12) we obtain upon simplification:

$$\frac{g}{2g'} = \frac{h - r\left(I_i^c + a\right)}{h' - r}, \tag{2.14}$$

where I_i^c is the competitive equilibrium size of a risky firm. Equation (2.14) should be contrasted with (2.7). The two expressions are identical. The *market solution is efficient*. For any given number of firms, the size is optimal, for any given total investment in the risky industries, the number of firms is optimal.

2.4   Competitive versus optimal size of risky industry

In order to compare the competitive versus the optimal size of the risky industry, we must relate the risk discount factor to properties of the utility function. It is easy to show that

$$k = -\frac{U_2}{U_1 \sigma_Y}. \tag{2.15}$$

Substituting this into (2.12) we obtain (upon simplification)

$$-\frac{U_2}{U_1} = \frac{h' - r}{2gg'}\sigma_Y = \sqrt{n}\left(\frac{h' - r}{2g'}\right) = \frac{1}{2\theta}\left(= \frac{1}{2}\frac{\partial \mu_Y/\partial I_i}{\partial \sigma_Y/\partial I_i}\right). \tag{2.16}$$

This should be contrasted with the optimal allocation where, using (2.10), we have

$$-\frac{U_2}{U_1} = \sqrt{n}\left(\frac{h' - r}{g'}\right) = \frac{1}{\theta}. \tag{2.17}$$

The market solution results in the slope of the indifference curve being half the slope of the opportunity locus, i.e. there is an under-allocation of resources to the risky industry (see figure 2.2). This entails that there are too few risky firms, not too many.

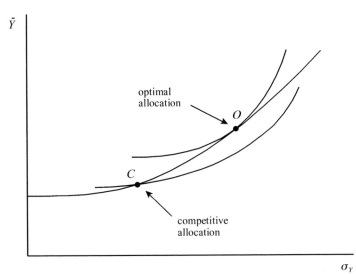

Figure 2.2   Competitive versus optimal allocation of resources

Not surprisingly, to operate the risky industry at an optimal level would require some subsidy for the marginal entrant. This follows from substituting (2.15) into (2.10), to obtain

$$V_i = \frac{h - \frac{1}{\theta}\frac{g}{\sqrt{n}}}{r} \tag{2.18}$$

then using (2.6a) to show:[12]

$$V_i < a + I_i^o. \tag{2.19}$$

Indeed, this will in general be true for all points to the right of C in figure 2.2: *the monopolistic competition equilibrium is a constrained optimum*, where the government is not allowed to subsidise the fixed costs of establishing private firms.[13]

---

[12] I.e.

$$h - \frac{g}{\theta\sqrt{n}} < r(a + I_i)$$

$$\theta[h - r(a + I_i)] = \frac{g}{2\sqrt{n}} < \frac{g}{\sqrt{n}}.$$

[13] When I is elasticity supplied, unless a lump-sum tax is feasible, the taxes required to obtain the revenue for paying the fixed costs of setting up firms creates distortions. Elsewhere, we have shown that if the utility function is additive, then when all individuals are identical, optimal taxation requires that the riskier industry be taxed at a higher (lower) ad valorem rate if the wealth elasticity of the demand for the risky assets is less

We would argue that this is not an unreasonable constraint; though production subsidies and taxes are feasible, as are franchise taxes, a subsidy for a firm simply to exist is not. (How, for instance, is the government to stop an individual from declaring himself a 'firm' with high fixed costs? To differentiate such phony firms from real firms would require either detailed and costly information and administration, or the reliance on easily obtained data, like output, in which case we no longer have a lump-sum subsidy.)

But, as we shall now see, this result as well as the more general result on the productive efficiency (in mean variance terms) of the monopolistically competitive capital market, do not extend to the case with correlated returns.

2.5   Correlated returns: the competitive analysis

One widely employed model of the stock market suggests that the returns to a firm, X_i, may be written[14]

$$X_i(I_i, \theta) = h_i(I_i)\left[1 + \beta_i M(\theta) + \epsilon_i(\theta)\right],\qquad(2.20)$$

where $M(\theta)$ is the state of the business cycle and

$$E\epsilon_i\epsilon_j = E\epsilon_i = EM(\theta) = E\epsilon_i M = 0.$$

For simplicity, let us again assume all firms are identical. Then 'efficiency' requires

$$\max\ nh(I_i) + r\left[I - n(I_i + a)\right] \equiv \mu_Y$$

s.t.

$$\sigma_Y = h(I_i)b(n) \le \bar{\sigma}_Y,$$

where

$$b(n) = \sqrt{[E\epsilon^2 + (2n-1)\beta^2 EM^2]n},$$

i.e.

$$\frac{h' - r}{h - r(a + I)} = \frac{h'}{h}\frac{b}{b'n}.$$

(greater) than unity. The economy will accordingly operate to the left (right) of the point of tangency of the indifference curve and the efficiency curve (although if I is reduced the whole frontier shrinks down) (see Stiglitz, 1972b).

[14] Note that (2.20) is consistent with 'multiplicative uncertainty', i.e. increasing investment increases returns in all states of nature proportionately.

Let $\frac{b}{b'n} = 1 - \gamma$

$$\frac{h'}{h} = \frac{r - \gamma h'}{r(1 - \gamma)(a + I_i)} \tag{2.21}$$

or letting

$$\frac{h'I}{h} = v < 1$$

$$I_i = \frac{av(1 - \gamma)r}{r - \gamma h' - r(1 - \gamma)v}. \tag{2.21'}$$

It has been suggested that in this context, it would be 'reasonable' for firms to assume that their value was proportionate to h_i; if they did, then, with a fixed number of firms, the economy would be efficient. But if the number of firms is variable, the economy will not be efficient: In equilibrium, we have

$$V_i = \frac{h_i(1 - k[((n-1)h(I_i^*) + h_i)\beta^2 EM^2 + h_i E\epsilon^2])}{r} \equiv h_i\rho. \tag{2.22}$$

I_i is chosen to maximise $V_i - I_i$

$$\frac{\partial V_i}{\partial I_i} = h_i'\rho = 1. \tag{2.23}$$

Firms will enter until

$$V_i - I_i = h_i\rho - I_i = a. \tag{2.24}$$

Hence, instead of (2.21) we have (using (2.23) and (2.24))[15]

$$\frac{h'}{h} = \frac{1}{I_i + a} \tag{2.25}$$

or

$$I_i = \frac{a}{\frac{1}{v} - 1}. \tag{2.26}$$

Note that if $\gamma = 0$, (2.26) and (2.21') are identical. But

$$\gamma = 1 - \frac{b}{b'n} = 1 - \frac{1}{\frac{1}{2} + \frac{n\beta^2 EM^2}{E\epsilon^2 + (2n-1)\beta^2 EM^2}}$$

$$= \frac{\beta^2 EM^2 - E\epsilon^2}{E\epsilon^2 + (4n-1)\beta^2 EM^2} \gtrless 0 \qquad \text{as } \beta^2 \gtrless \frac{E\epsilon^2}{EM^2},$$

---

[15] Note that if r is not constant, this may not be a unique solution to (2.25).

i.e. depending on the relative importance of the independent variation and the variations relating to the business cycle.

Since

$$\frac{r - \gamma h'}{r(1 - \gamma)(a + I_i)} - \frac{1}{a + I_i} = -\frac{\gamma(h' - r)}{r(a + I_i)(1 - \gamma)}.$$

$$I_i^o \lessgtr I_i^c \text{ as } \gamma \lessgtr 0$$

To compare the optimal number of firms with the market solution, we observe that the former requires

$$-\frac{U_2}{U_1} = \frac{(h' - r)}{h'}\frac{n}{b} \tag{2.27}$$

while in the latter

$$-\frac{U_2}{U_1} = \frac{h' - r}{h'}\frac{b}{n\beta^2 EM^2 + E\epsilon^2}. \tag{2.28}$$

For any given value of I_i, the right-hand side of (2.28) exceeds that of (2.27) since

$$n^2\beta^2 EM^2 + nE\epsilon^2 \leq nE\epsilon^2 + n(2n - 1)\beta^2 EM^2$$

for $n \geq 1$.

Consider first the case of $\gamma = 0$, so $I_i^o = I_i^c$. Then at n^c, the left-hand side of (2.27) exceeds the right-hand side. $\gamma = 0$ implies b is proportional to n, so the right-hand side of (2.27) is independent of n. An increase in n increases mean and variance; it can be shown that this increases $-U_2/U_1$. Thus, *in this central case, there are more risky firms in the market equilibrium than in the optimal allocation.* If $\gamma > 0$, $I_i^o > I_i^c$, and since $[d(h' - r)/h']/dI_i = rh''/(h')^2 < 0$, again the right-hand side of (2.28) would exceed that of (2.27) if n were the same.

But at the same time, since $I_i^o > I_i^c$, the left-hand side of (2.27) normally would exceed that of (2.28), i.e. at a higher mean and variance $-U_2/U_1$ is larger. A decrease in n decreases both the left- and right-hand side of (2.27), but, provided γ is not too large, the former effect dominates. Thus again there will be too many risky firms in equilibrium. More generally, since both right-hand sides depend simply on the properties of technology, while the left-hand sides on tastes as well, it is apparent that either effect may dominate; there may be more or fewer risky firms in the market equilibrium than in the optimal allocation.

Notice that in the preceding section, we showed that the market solution was not optimal when returns were uncorrelated, i.e. $\beta = 0$. The difference between the results arises from the difference in behavioural hypotheses; in the former, we assumed that firms took the risk discount factor and the rate of interest as given, in the latter we simply assumed that firms took the ratio of market value to scale as given.[16]

The above analysis did not explicitly take into account the constraint on the viability of the firm. If we require that each firm have at least a value equal to its expenditure on investment, i.e.

$$V_i \geq I_i + a$$

or

$$h_i(I_i)\rho - I_i \geq a, \tag{2.29}$$

we can show that the market solution is not a constrained optimum.

The behavioural hypothesis employed in the previous section is, however, not totally convincing. At least equally plausible is the hypothesis employed in our earlier analysis that firms are aware that as they change their scale, their value per unit scale changes. In the mean variance formulation employed here, we assume that firms take the risk discount factor and the rate of interest as given. Then in equilibrium instead of (2.23) we obtain

$$h' \left[\rho - \frac{kh_i(\beta^2 EM^2 + E\epsilon^2)}{r} \right] = 1 \tag{2.23'}$$

or

$$h' \left[\frac{1 - hk(n+1)\beta^2 EM^2 + 2E\epsilon^2}{r} \right] = 1$$

so, using (2.24)

$$\frac{h'}{h} = \frac{1}{(a + I_i)} \frac{1}{(1 - z)}, \tag{2.30}$$

where

$$z = \frac{kh(\beta^2 EM^2 + E\epsilon^2)}{1 - kh[n\beta^2 EM^2 + E\epsilon^2]}$$

If h is of constant elasticity, it is clear that since $z > 0$, $I_i^c < I_i^o$, the market solution entails too small firms.

2.6   Increasing marginal entrance costs

Thus far in the analysis, we have assumed that all firms face the same fixed costs of entry. We now consider what happened when the fixed

[16] Which is a more 'realistic' hypothesis seems a question of some debate. For a more extended discussion of this issue, see Stiglitz (1972a, pp. 55–5).

costs of entry is an increasing function of the number of firms already in the risky industry, i.e. the firms best suited for the risky industry enter first, and then those less suited enter. For simplicity, we only consider the case of independently distributed firms. We let $f'(n)$ be the fixed cost of establishing the marginal firm; $f'' > 0$.

Then, instead of (2.7), we obtain for the optimal size of the firm

$$\frac{g}{2g'} = \frac{h - r\left(I_i^o + f'\right)}{h' - r}$$

which, in the case where this is constant returns to scale to variable capital reduces to

$$I_i^o = \frac{2rf'}{h' - r}.$$

Thus, the optimal scale of the firm increases as the number of firms in the risky industry increases.

We still obtain, however, the result that the market solution is efficient when the marginal entrant must pay his (own) fixed cost.

On the other hand, in a number of industries which might be described by a monopolistically competitive model, the cost of entering to the marginal firms is simply the average cost (as in the familiar fisheries or oil well problems). Then, the larger the number of entrants, the larger the fixed cost each must pay. In that case the condition for no entry becomes

$$V_i - I_i = \frac{f(n)}{n}.$$

In that case, as one might expect, the economy does not operate on its mean variance efficiency frontier. Examples may be constructed where there are too many as well as too few risky firms.

2.7   Reinterpretation in partial equilibrium terms[17]

The nature of the competitive equilibrium solution can be depicted in terms of the familiar partial equilibrium diagrams. Let $\bar{X}_i$ be our measure of the output for the firm. If $h_i'' < 0$, the total average cost curve is u-shaped. The 'perceived demand function' giving price per unit of output $V_i/h(I_i)$ is[18]

$$\frac{V_i}{h(I_i)} = \frac{1}{r} - \frac{kg^2(h^{-1}(\bar{X}_i))}{r\bar{X}_i}.$$

---

[17] This discussion is meant to be heuristic, to relate our results to the older literature on monopolistic competition. Thus we shall use consumer surplus analysis without rigorously justifying it.

[18] This demand schedule assumes that k and r are given.

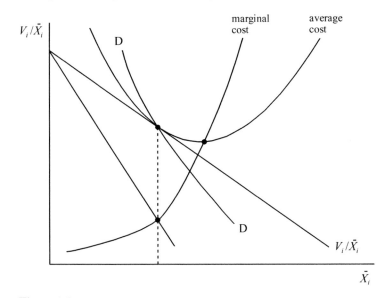

Figure 2.3

With free entry the equilibrium is given at the tangency of the demand schedule and the average cost schedule. We have also drawn the demand schedule corresponding to the situation where all the risky firms increase their *output* simultaneously. This demand schedule will in general be steeper than that given when only one firm's investment varies, since, at fixed n, as I_i increases for all firms, k will increase (if there is decreasing absolute risk aversion) (see figure 2.3).

The gain from the additional diversity resulting from a new firm can be measured by the area under the demand curve. The magnitude of that consumer surplus needs to be compared with the magnitude of the fixed cost. The central result of section 2.4 could thus be interpreted as saying that in the market solution, the magnitude of the consumer surplus exceeds the fixed cost, but that additional entry is not possible without providing lump-sum subsidies to pay for the fixed cost.

Let us now consider the model of section 2.5, with correlated returns. Then the perceived demand schedule becomes

$$\frac{V_i}{h_i} = \frac{1}{r} - \frac{k\beta_i \sum \beta_j h_j(I_j)}{r} - \frac{kh_i(I_i)\left[E\epsilon_i^2 + \beta_i^2 EM^2\right]}{r}.$$

The major biases of monopolistic competition, discussed at greater length by Spence and Dixit–Stiglitz, become evident. The elasticity of the perceived demand schedule is a function of the magnitude of own

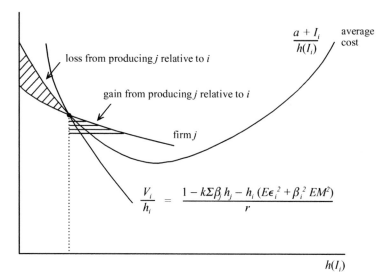

Figure 2.4

variance

$$\left[E\epsilon_i^2 + \beta_i^2 EM^2 \right] h^2$$

relative to covariance with the market

$$h_i \beta_i \sum \beta_j h_j (I_j).$$

As figure 2.4 illustrates, we can find two industries with the same fixed costs, but different ratios of own variance to covariance, such that the firm with the lower own variance is infra-marginal, and the one with the higher own variance is just below the margin, but because of the larger consumer surplus associated with the latter, it would be preferable to produce the latter. (And indeed, if the former were not produced, the latter might even be feasible.) This argues that the market systematically is biased against firms with high own variance and high correlation with the market factor, and biased in favour of those with a low correlation with the rest of the market.

There are additional biases when we take into account the restriction on viability of firms. Since we argued that in the market equilibrium, additional entry is desirable at the margin, there is a social return to lowering k, the risk discount factor. (This shifts the demand curve upwards, making some marginal entry feasible.) The precise determination of the risk discount factor is a complex matter, except for the constant

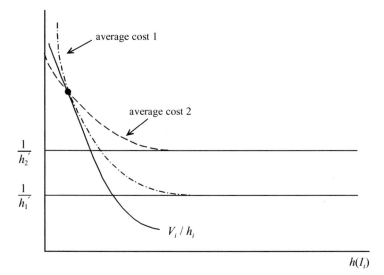

Figure 2.5

absolute risk aversion utility functions (in which case it is a constant) and the quadratic utility function. In the latter case, substitution of a low mean firm for a high mean firm reduces k, and thus makes further risk diversification possible. But the quadratic utility function has the property of increasing absolute risk aversion, and so one might expect that this result is rather special. Since at higher levels of wealth individuals are likely to be less risk averse, securities with a high mean but high own variance may reduce the risk discount factor k, and if this is correct, it strengthens our earlier presumption that the market is biased against risky firms.

Finally, figure 2.5 illustrates the bias of the market solution against firms with high fixed costs relative to variable costs. In figure 2.5 we have depicted the cost and demand curves for two firms with identical risk properties, with stochastic constant returns to scale, but with one having higher fixed costs ($a_1 > a_2$) but lower marginal costs ($h_1' > h_2'$). Firm 2 is initially viable, firm 1 is not. But if firm 2 is eliminated, firm 1 would be viable, and the switch is clearly desirable.

2.8   Concluding comments

We have examined a model in which different commodities are close – but not perfect – substitutes for each other. Under normal assumptions of quasi-concave indifference curves, individuals would consume some of all the different varieties of goods produced; if there were no fixed costs to producing a different variety, all the varieties that could be produced would be produced. There are, however, in general some fixed costs with producing a different commodity, and even if they are small, they will put a limit on the number of different commodities which it is optimal to produce. The question is, how does this optimal allocation compare with that of a monopolistically competitive economy? We have examined this question in the context of a capital market where the different commodities are different securities. We have assumed that individuals evaluate incomes in terms of means and variances, which allows us to derive simple expressions for the valuation (demand) functions for the different securities. We have shown that

(a) If the returns to different securities are independent,

    (i) for any given level of investment in the monopolistically competitive sector (the risky industry), the number of firms and size of each firm is optimal, but

    (ii) there is under-investment in the monopolistically competitive industry; however

    (iii) the monopolistically competitive allocation is the optimal allocation in the absence of government subsidies for the fixed cost of establishing a new firm.

(b) If the returns to different securities are correlated, the economy will not be operating on its mean variance efficiency frontier, even if all firms believe that their market value is proportional to their scale. If they recognise the dependence of market value on scale, the distortion is increased. There is some presumption that the market solution does entail too small firms, consistent with the conventional wisdom, but contrary to it, there may be too few risky firms. Moreover, the market solution is biased in favour of firms with low own variances relative to covariances with respect to the rest of the market, and to low fixed costs – high marginal cost firms.

These results suggest that the misallocations associated with monopolistically competitive industries are far more complicated – and perhaps more important – than much of the conventional wisdom would imply.

REFERENCES

Bishop, R. L. (1967). Monopolistic competition and welfare economics, in Kuenne, R. (ed.), *Monopolistic Competition Theory*. New York: John Wiley

Chamberlin, E. H. (1950). Product heterogeneity and public policy. *American Economic Review, Papers and Proceedings*, 40: 85–92

Diamond, P. (1971). A model of price adjustment. *Journal of Economic Theory*, 3: 156–168

Hotelling, H. (1929). Stability in competition. *Economic Journal*, 39: 41–57 (reprinted in Stigler and Boulding, 1952)

Lintner, J. (1965). The valuation of risk assets and the selection of risky investments in stock portfolios and capital budgets. *Review of Economics and Statistics*, 47: 13–37

Lovell, M. C. (1970). Product differentiation and market structure. *Western Economic Journal*, 8: 120–143

Radner, R. and Stiglitz, J. E. (1974). A fundamental non-convexity in the value of information, Stanford, mimeo

Spence, M. (1975a). Product selection, fixed costs, and monopolistic competition. Technical Report, 157, Institute for Mathematical Studies in the Social Sciences. Stanford University, January

(1975b). Nonlinear prices and welfare. Technical Report, 158, Institute for Mathematical Studies in the Social Sciences. Stanford University, January

Stern, N. H. (1972). The optimal size of market areas. *Journal of Economic Theory*, 4:159–173

Stigler, G. and Boulding, K. (eds.) (1952). *Readings in Price Theory*. Irwin, Homewood, IL

Stiglitz, J. E. (1970). On the optimality of the stock market allocation of investment. Paper presented to the Far Eastern–Meetings of the Econometric Society, Tokyo, 27–29 June, mimeo

(1972a). On the optimality of the stock market allocation of investment. *Quarterly Journal of Economics*, 86: 25–60 (originally, paper presented to the Far Eastern Meetings of the Econometric Society, Tokyo, June 1970)

(1972b). Taxation, risk taking, and the allocation of investment in a competitive economy, in Jensen, M.C. (ed.), *Studies in the Theory of Capital Markets*. New York, Praeger

(1974). Information and the capital market. Oxford, mimeo

3   Monopolistic competition and optimum product diversity (May 1974)

Avinash K. Dixit and Joseph E. Stiglitz

3.1   Introduction

This chapter is an attempt to formalise a simple general equilibrium version of the Chamberlinian monopolistic competition model, in order to test whether there is any validity in the oft-quoted assertion that monopolistic competition leads to too much product diversification. Chamberlin (1950) himself was careful not to make any such assertion; as a matter of fact he saw the central issue very clearly, and expressed it succinctly as follows: 'It is true that the same total resources ... may be made to yield more units of product by being concentrated on fewer firms. The issue might be put as efficiency versus diversity.' Kaldor (1935), too, saw that excess capacity did not mean excessive diversification. He said that if economies of scale were exploited to a greater extent, 'the public would be offered finally larger amounts of a smaller number of commodities; and it is impossible to tell how far people prefer quantity to diversity and vice versa.' What this really means is that a model must be specified in greater detail to determine conditions under which the one or the other might be expected. The one example which has been worked out in some detail, the Hotelling spatial location model, has led many economists to the presumption that there is in fact excessive diversity associated with monopolistic competition.[1] The results of our analysis throw considerable doubt on this presumption. Indeed, in one central case, we establish that the monopolistically competitive equilibrium is a *constrained* Pareto optimum, where the constraint is that the government is unable to subsidise firms. Relative to the unconstrained Pareto optimum, this equilibrium has too *few* firms.

As will soon become clear, proper analysis of this problem requires a model with a 'large number' of firms. It is then natural to formulate the model with a continuum of firms. This model has several features which are of interest in their own right. First, conventional partial equilibrium

---

[1] Hotelling (1929). But see also Stern (1972) which casts doubt on that presumption even in the context of location.

analysis, which ignores income effects and repercussions in other sectors of the economy, finds a rigorous justification in such a model. Second, it is commonly supposed that if there are a large number of firms in a given industry, then the industry will be close to being purely competitive. But if there are matching large numbers of commodities that can be produced, as is clearly the case in the dimensions of sizes, shapes and qualities, then additional firms can produce different commodities, and as we establish, even with a continuum of firms, the monopoly power of each can be greater than zero.

The model which we formulate differs from the spatial location model in one important respect. There, each consumer purchases only one of the products in the industry. Increasing product differentiation leads to the consumer being able to purchase a commodity closer to his liking, i.e. to go to a store closer to his residence. The model we formulate entails each consumer enjoying product diversity directly. There are numerous examples where this formulation is clearly more appropriate than one modelled on location. The ability to diversify a portfolio by spreading one's wealth over a large number of assets was one of the instances that provided the original motivation for formulating this kind of model, and is discussed elsewhere in more detail (Stiglitz, 1973). Clothes suited to different climatic conditions, or flavours of ice-cream, are other examples of this type.

We will assume that the consumers' preferences are exogenous, and that the social welfare function respects them. Thus considerations of advertising and of its welfare implications are excluded. We feel that prevailing thinking on the problem has over-stressed these aspects at the expense of some of the basic allocative issues, and that effects of incorporating then into a model like the one we discuss should be fairly evident.

3.2   The basic model

As we noted in the introduction, the model formulated is the simplest one in which we can appropriately analyse the questions of interest. Thus, we neglect differences of tastes and incomes among consumers, and assume that there are only two sectors, the monopolistically competitive sector and a purely competitive one which aggregates the rest of the economy. The latter is chosen as numéraire, and the amount of the economy's endowment of that commodity is normalised at unity; it can be thought of as the time at the disposal of the consumers.

Preferences are characterised by an expenditure function

$$E = uG(1, q), \tag{3.1}$$

where G is concave and homogeneous of degree one in its arguments, u is the utility level (the multiplicative separability implies unitary income elasticities of demand), 1 is the price of the numéraire, included in the arguments as a reminder, and q is an *index* of the market prices of the commodities produced in the monopolistically competitive sector:

$$q = \left[\int_0^n p(i)^{-\alpha} dF(i) \right]^{-1/\alpha} n^{-\beta + 1/\alpha}, \qquad 1 + \alpha > 0. \tag{3.2}$$

Here $p(i)$ is the price of the commodity labelled i in the monopolistically competitive sector, $F(i)$ is the cumulative function of the 'number' of firms in this sector, each producing one commodity. The integral is a Stieltjes integral, and the case of a discrete number of commodities can be thought of as a special case where $dF(i) = 1$ for integer i and zero elsewhere. The continuum case will have $dF(i) = di$ for the whole interval $[0, n]$. We shall concentrate on the continuum case, and mention special results for the discrete case in footnotes.

Once the number of commodities produced has been fixed, $(1 + \alpha)$ has the conventional interpretation of the elasticity of substitution between pairs of commodities in the monopolistically competitive sector. Since one of the main questions on which we focus is the number of commodities, the model must be formulated in such a way that no commodity is essential but that there is a return from diversity. Thus we must have $\alpha > 0$, i.e. the elasticity of substitution between any pair of commodities within the monopolistically competitive sector should be greater than unity. We can then view our model as follows. Every niche between zero and infinity can be occupied, in principle, by a firm, each producing a different commodity. We rearrange these intervals so that actual firms are packed together between 0 and n, and the range beyond n is either disregarded or has all its $p(i)$ set at infinity. If necessary, we can shuffle firms in the interval $[0, n]$ to give the function $p(i)$ some regularity properties. Thus n is the farthest location occupied on the possible spectrum of commodities, and therefore provides a measure of the degree of product diversity achieved.

The crucial measure of the value of product diversity is provided by β. Assume, for instance, that all firms charge the same price, with $p(i) = p$ for all i. Then (3.2) becomes

$$q = pn^{-\beta}. \tag{3.3}$$

For fixed p, this is a decreasing function of n, provided $\beta > 0$. The greater β, the greater is the value of product diversity relative to the price reductions for each variety. Since the effects on utility are channelled through the index q, we see that a 1 per cent increase in the number of commodities

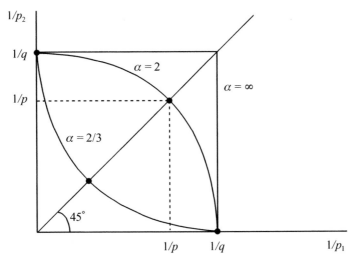

Figure 3.1

in the bundle is equivalent to a β per cent reduction in the price of each unit in the bundle.

In the subsequent analysis, a special case of (3.2) will play a central role. This is where

$$\alpha\beta = 1 \tag{3.4}$$

and therefore

$$q = \left[\int_0^n p(i)^{-\alpha} dF(i) \right]^{-1/\alpha}. \tag{3.2*}$$

This is the natural case where the value of diversity is simply that embodied in the degree of quasi-concavity of the utility function, and n does not appear directly. Figure 3.1 illustrates this with two commodities, showing contours of (3.2*), and thus of the indirect utility function, in the space $1/p_1$ and $1/p_2$. The curves have the same value of q but different values of α. If the two commodities are perfect substitutes, i.e. if $\alpha = \infty$, then the consumer is not willing to pay any higher price for each commodity for the sake of having both of them available, and thus the contour is rectangular. If the two are imperfect substitutes, α is finite, and the common price p for each of the two, such that the consumer is indifferent between this situation and paying q for one of them with the other one unavailable, exceeds q. In the example of figure 3.1, it is easy to verify that $1/q = (1/p)\sqrt{2}$, i.e. $q = p.2^{-1/2}$, which is just (3.3) with $n = 2$, and $\beta = 1/\alpha = 1/2$. It is also clear from figure 3.1 that the premium on variety increases as α decreases. If α is zero or negative, all commodities are essential. As explained earlier, such cases are not of interest in the present context.

A somewhat unattractive feature of this model is the complete symmetry: the elasticity of substitution between each pair of commodities within the monopolistically competitive sector is the same, and further it is independent of the number of these commodities. In many actual problems there is some concept of distance between commodities, whether geographical, physical or psychological, and two commodities that are thus closer together have a higher elasticity of substitution than a pair farther apart. Also, if the total range of variation in this dimension is fixed, then commodities have to crowd closer together as their total number increases, and thus the elasticities of substitution increase. As regards the first point, we are following the tradition of earlier analysis on the subject, including that of Chamberlin, and can offer only the defence of analytic simplicity. We do not think that the main points we make would be upset by a more general model, although specific results would be harder to obtain and could differ. As for the second point, this is a matter of degree. It may be more reasonable to allow the elasticity of substitution to go to infinity with the number of commodities. But in the real world we have a finite number of firms, and in many industries the elasticity of substitution between commodities produced by different firms is finite. As the number of firms becomes large, certain 'income' and 'repercussion' effects *do* become small, and the elasticity of substitution *may* become large. The present model can be thought of as assuming that the 'income' and 'repercussion' effects become small faster than the elasticities of substitution become large. This model with a large number of firms and finite elasticities of substitution can at worst be thought of as a polar case. More than that, at least in certain markets, it may provide a better approximation to the real world with a finite number of firms and finite elasticities of substitution than does the alternative polar case of a large number of firms with infinite elasticities of substitution.

The analysis of consumer behaviour is now straightforward. The budget constraint can be written

$$X_0 + \int_0^n p(i)x(i)dF(i) = E = 1 + \pi, \qquad (3.5)$$

where X_0 is the quantity of the numéraire, $x(i)$ is the density of quantity of commodity i (i.e. $x(i)dF(i)$ is the quantity of commodities between i and $i + di$) and π is the amount of profits, distributed to the consumers in a lump-sum manner. From standard results in demand theory (with some care in handling the continuum formulation), we can derive the demand functions

$$X_0 = uG_1(1, q) = \frac{EG_1(1, q)}{G(1, q)} \tag{3.6}$$

$$x(i) = uG_2(1, q)\left[\frac{p(i)}{q}\right]^{-(1+\alpha)}$$

$$= E \frac{q G_2(1, q)}{G(1, q)} \frac{p(i)^{-(1+\alpha)}}{I}, \tag{3.7}$$

where I is the integral in (3.2). The total expenditure on the goods of the monopolistically competitive sector is given by

$$\int_0^n p(i)x(i)dF(i) = E \frac{q G_2(1, q)}{G(1, q)}$$

and the budget share of the sector is

$$s(q) = \frac{q G_2(1, q)}{G(1, q)}. \tag{3.8}$$

In the continuum case, the interesting property of these demand functions for the commodities in the monopolistically competitive sector is that the response of demand to a change in the price of the commodity is just the compensated price derivative. Since a negligible amount of expenditure is accounted for by each of these commodities, the income effects vanish. Thus

$$-\frac{p(i)}{x(i)}\frac{\partial x(i)}{\partial p(i)} = 1 + \alpha. \tag{3.9}$$

Similarly, for the responses to changes in prices of other commodities in the sector, we find repercussion effects negligible:

$$\frac{p(j)}{x(i)}\frac{\partial x(i)}{\partial p(j)} = 0 \qquad \text{for } i \neq j. \tag{3.10}$$

We can therefore neglect game-theoretic considerations in our analysis.[2]

We assume that firms in the monopolistically competitive sector set their prices to maximise profits, taking the prices of other firms in the sector as given. We assume that there is a fixed cost a of setting up each firm in this sector, and that the marginal cost of production is constant and equal to c for each commodity. The non-convexity resulting from the fixed cost is an essential feature of the problem: without it, all conceivable commodities could be produced in infinitesimal amounts without

---

[2] In the discrete case the right-hand sides of (3.9) and (3.10) become $1 + \alpha - O(1/n)$ and $O(1/n)$, respectively.

any need to incur higher average costs, and there would then be no trade-off between efficiency and variety. The fixed cost and constant marginal cost formulation is the simplest that permits such non-convexity; some comments on possible generalisations will be made later. The assumptions also preserve symmetry between all firms in the group.

3.3   Monopolistically competitive equilibrium

The profit-maximisation condition for each firm is the familiar equality between marginal revenue and marginal cost. Since the elasticity of demand and the marginal cost are both constant, this takes the simple form

$$p(i) \left[1 - \frac{1}{1+\alpha} \right] = c, \qquad \text{for all } i \in [0, n], \text{ or}$$

$$p(i) = \left[\frac{1+\alpha}{\alpha} \right] c, \qquad \text{for all } i \in [0, n]. \tag{3.11}$$

Thus the equilibrium profit margin depends simply on the elasticity of substitution between commodities within the sector. Write p_e for the equilibrium price of each commodity being produced in this sector.

The second condition of equilibrium is that firms enter until the marginal entrant makes exactly zero profit, i.e.

$$[p(n) - c]x(n) = a. \tag{3.12}$$

Using (3.7) and observing that symmetry implies zero profit for all other firms in the sector as well, and therefore $E = 1$, this becomes

$$\frac{1}{1+\alpha} \frac{1}{n} \frac{q\,G_2}{G} = a, \qquad \text{or}$$

$$\frac{s(p_e n^{-\beta})}{n} = a(1 + \alpha). \tag{3.13}$$

This defines the number of active firms in equilibrium, n_e. We have a unique equilibrium provided the left-hand side of (3.13) is a monotonic function of n. Since $s(q)$ is bounded between 0 and 1, the left-hand side goes to zero as n goes to infinity, and thus could not be an increasing function of n. We shall see the economic significance of it being a decreasing function in a moment. An overly strong sufficient condition is that $s(q)$ be a non-decreasing function. Standard manipulations with expenditure functions show that

$$\theta(q) \equiv \frac{q\,s'(q)}{q} = [1 - s(q)]\,[1 - \sigma(q)], \tag{3.14}$$

where $\sigma(q)$ is the elasticity of substitution between the two sectors, i.e.
$\sigma(q) = GG_{12}/(G_1 G_2)$. This elasticity of substitution being less than or
equal to one is thus sufficient for the uniqueness of equilibrium.

A more interesting and instructive formulation is in terms of the familiar dd and DD curves. Define

$$X_1 = \int_0^n x(i)dF(i) \tag{3.15}$$

and call it the total output of the monopolistically competitive sector. This
is a simple arithmetic sum and not an index dual to q. It is introduced in
order to relate our analysis to the traditional one. Now the DD curve is

$$D(p; n) = \frac{X_1}{n} = \frac{s(pn^{-\beta})}{pn}. \tag{3.16}$$

Thus $s(pn^{-\beta})/n$ decreases as n increases for each fixed p provided the
DD curve shrinks to the left as the number of firms increases. i.e. if such
entry does not shift demand towards this sector so much as to increase
the demand facing each firm when they all vary prices together. Using
the chain rule, we can write this condition as

$$\beta\theta(q) + 1 > 0. \tag{3.17}$$

As $s(q)$ and $\sigma(q)$ must both be non-negative, we see from (3.14) that

$$\theta(q) < 1 \tag{3.18}$$

and this ensures that the DD curve slopes downward. Finally, the conventional assumption that the DD curve is less elastic than the dd curve
amounts to

$$1 + \alpha > 1 - \theta(q) \qquad \text{or} \qquad \alpha + \theta(q) > 0. \tag{3.19}$$

We will assume that all three of these conditions hold, and they will prove
useful later.

Chamberlin's analysis in fact implicitly assumes that an increase in the
number of firms leaves the total demand for the sector output unchanged.
Now X_1 will be independent of n if either $\beta = 0$ or $s'(q) = 0$. The former is equivalent to assuming that individuals do not value diversity at
all, and so is contrary to the intent of the analysis. Thus, implicitly, conventional Chamberlinian analysis assumes $s'(q) = 0$, i.e. $\theta(q) = 0$. This
gives a constant budget share for the monopolistically competitive sector,
and from (3.14) a unitary elasticity of substitution with the competitive
sector. Note that this ensures (3.17) and thus uniqueness of equilibrium,
and also (3.18) and (3.19).

Finally, using the DD curve, we can easily calculate the output x_e produced by each firm in equilibrium. From (3.16), (3.11) and (3.13), we have

$$x_e = \frac{a\alpha}{c}. \tag{3.20}$$

We can also write down an expression for the budget share of the monopolistically competitive sector in equilibrium:

$$s_e = s(q_e) \qquad \text{where } q_e = p_e n_e^{-\beta}. \tag{3.21}$$

These will be useful for subsequent comparisons.

3.4   Constrained optimality

The notion of optimality naturally depends on the constraints that must be imposed on welfare maximisation. This is particularly problematic in the present context. Since there are economies of scale in the relevant range of production, a first-best allocation, i.e. one subject to constraints of resource availability and technology alone, can be decentralised only if the government can give lump-sum subsidies to firms. The theoretical and practical difficulties of doing so, and of raising the necessary revenue without causing new distortions, are clearly formidable. It would therefore appear that a perhaps more appropriate notion of optimality in this context is a constrained Pareto optimality where each firm must operate without making a loss. The government can control the number of firms and the prices they charge through conventional regulatory policies.

There now arises the question of whether the basic symmetry of our model is preserved. There is some unavoidable asymmetry, as some firms are active and others are not. Fortunately, in the case of large numbers, it is optimal for all active firms to charge the same price. Figure 3.2 shows the argument for a cross-section of two of these firms. Their respective profits π_1 and π_2 depend to a negligible extent on the price charged by the other firm, and the functional forms $\pi_1(p_1)$ and $\pi_2(p_2)$ are the same. The feasible region is therefore a square as shown. Also, total profit π is a symmetric function of (p_1, p_2), and then so is the utility $u = (1 + \pi)/G(1, q)$. Finally, we can examine the dependence of utility on prices to say more about the contours of u. First, when marginal costs of production are constant, any radial move of the vector of prices away from the vector of marginal costs reduces utility. Second, if all commodities are Hicksian substitutes, then moving the price which is proportionately farthest away

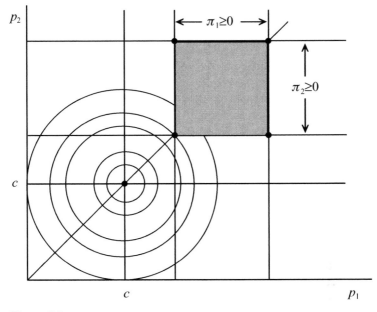

Figure 3.2

from the corresponding marginal cost towards the latter increases utility.[3]
These conditions are satisfied in our model. The condition for all commodities to be substitutes can be shown to be $\alpha + \theta(q) + s(q) > 0$, and
(3.19) is sufficient for this. Thus contours of u must slope downward in
the region to the north-east of (c, c), and those farther away from this
point correspond to a lower value of utility. The constrained optimum
must then have $p_1 = p_2$, and each firm must make exactly zero profit
there, as shown.

When the number of firms is smaller, and each firm's profit depends
to a significant extent on the prices charged by other firms, iso-profit
lines will have the U-shapes conventional in duopoly theory. Downward
sloping contours of u will no longer suffice to prove symmetry, for a
symmetric tangency solution may prove to be only a local optimum. This
possibility gives another reason, besides usual oligopoly considerations,
for restricting the validity of the conventional monopolistic competition
analysis to the large group case.

When all firms just break even, we have $E = 1$, and $u = 1/G(1, q)$.
Thus maximising u is equivalent to minimising q. The constraint is that
each active firm just breaks even. The constrained optimum problem can

---

[3] These results are proved in e.g. Dixit (1974).

then be written as

$$\min_{p,n} \ pn^{-\beta} \qquad \text{subject to:} \qquad \frac{p-c}{p} \frac{s(pn^{-\beta})}{n} = a. \tag{3.22}$$

Now consider the curve defined by (3.22) in the (p, n) space. We have assumed that the left-hand side is a decreasing function of n for fixed p. Thus (3.22) defines n as a single-valued function of p, for all values of p above d defined by

$$\frac{d-c}{d} \lim_{n \to 0} \frac{s(dn^{-\beta})}{n} = a. \tag{3.23}$$

In particular, if this limit is infinite, we have $d = c$.

Differentiating along the constraint logarithmically, we evaluate the elasticity

$$\frac{p}{n} \frac{dn}{dp} = \frac{\frac{c}{p-c} + \theta(q)}{1 + \beta\theta(q)}. \tag{3.24}$$

The denominator has been assumed positive. The numerator is positive if $\theta(q)$ is positive. Else the numerator is positive when

$$p < c \left[1 - \frac{1}{\theta(q)} \right]. \tag{3.25}$$

This is true for p near enough to c. If $\theta(q)$ fluctuates, there may be alternate intervals where (3.25) holds and fails, and thus the constraint curve may have alternately rising and falling portions. Only the initial rising portion will matter in all that follows. Figure 3.3 shows the case where $\theta(q)$ is negative; the other case is even simpler.

The contours of the objective function have equations

$$n = \text{constant} \times p^{1/\beta} \tag{3.26}$$

and the first-order condition for optimality is the equality between the slopes or elasticities of (3.22) and (3.26). Equating the right-hand side of (3.24) to $(1/\beta)$ yields the price at the constrained optimum

$$p_{co} = c(1 + \beta). \tag{3.27}$$

We show that this unique solution to the first-order condition satisfies the second-order condition. The contour of the objective function has a constant elasticity, $(1/\beta)$. First suppose $\theta(q)$ is constant. Then the right-hand side of (3.24) is a decreasing function of p, i.e. the constraint curve has an elasticity greater than $(1/\beta)$ to the left of p_{co} and

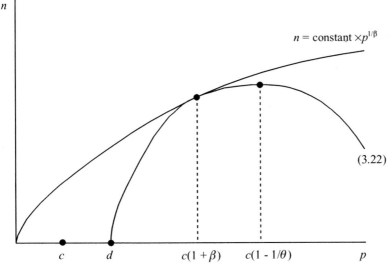

Figure 3.3

less than $(1/\beta)$ to its right. Since $q = pn^{-\beta}$ is stationary at the point, variations in $\theta(q)$ do not matter. The second-order condition is thus established.

Comparing (3.11) and (3.27), we see that in the case $\beta\alpha = 1$, the two prices are equal. Since the same break-even constraint is satisfied in the two cases, they have the same number of firms as well, and the values of all other variables can be calculated from these two. This proves our assertion in the introduction: in the central case where the desirability of diversity is simply that embodied in the quasi-concavity of the utility function, the monopolistically competitive equilibrium is the Pareto optimum constrained by the lack of lump-sum subsidies. Chamberlin (1933, p. 94) once called this equilibrium 'a sort of ideal'; our analysis gives some precision to that concept, and establishes when it is valid.

Outside of this central case, comparisons between the constrained optimum equilibrium are quite easy to make. The basic point is that the two satisfy the same break-even constraint. If $\theta(q)$ is positive, this constraint defines a positive association between p and n. Even if $\theta(q)$ is negative, (3.17) and (3.19) ensure that $1/\alpha$ and β are each less than $-1/\theta(q)$ for all q, and therefore both p_e and p_{co} lie in the first rising portion of the constraint curve. Thus the situation with the higher price also has the larger number of firms. From (3.16) and (3.22), we see that each firm in the constrained optimum produces

$$x_{co} = \frac{a}{c\beta}. \tag{3.28}$$

We can then put together all the comparisons possible so far:

$$\beta\alpha \gtrless 1 \text{ as } p_{c\hat{o}} \gtrless p_e \text{ as } n_{co} \gtrless n_e \text{ as } x_{co} \lessgtr x_e. \tag{3.29}$$

Finally, the budget share of the monopolistic sector in the constrained optimum is

$$s_{co} = s(q_{co}) \qquad \text{where } q_{co} = p_{co} n_{co}^{-\beta}. \tag{3.30}$$

Since the constrained optimum and the market equilibrium face the same constraint, while the former minimises q, except in the case where the two coincide we have

$$q_{co} < q_e \tag{3.31}$$

and therefore the budget shares satisfy

$$s_{co} \gtrless s_e \text{ as } \theta(q) \lessgtr 0, \qquad \text{i.e. as } \sigma(q) \gtrless 1 \tag{3.32}$$

over the relevant range of q. If $\theta(q)$ fluctuates in sign over this range, an unambiguous comparison is not possible.

3.5   Unconstrained optimum

These solutions may in turn be compared to the unconstrained (first-best) optimum. The argument accompanying figure 3.2 has already established the first-best optimality of marginal cost pricing. Denoting unconstrained optimum values by the subscript *uo*, we write

$$p_{uo} = c. \tag{3.33}$$

This is less than the price both in the constrained optimum and in the market equilibrium.

Now each firm will only just cover its variable costs, and with n firms, the total losses financed by lump-sum transfers will be (an). Then $E = 1 - an$, and the optimisation problem becomes

$$\max_{n} \frac{1 - an}{G(1, cn^{-\beta})}.$$

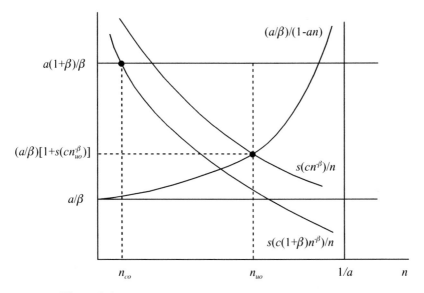

Figure 3.4

The first-order condition can be written in two alternative ways

$$\frac{s\left(cn^{-\beta}\right)}{n} = \frac{a/\beta}{1 - an} \tag{3.34}$$

$$= \frac{a}{\beta}[1 + \beta s\left(cn^{-\beta}\right)]. \tag{3.35}$$

As n increases, the left-hand side of (3.34) decreases and the right-hand side increases. Their intersection to determine n_{uo} is shown in figure 3.4. From (3.35) and the fact that values of s must lie in the interval $(0, 1)$, we conclude that the ordinate at the point of intersection must be less than $a(1 + \beta)/\beta$. Figure 3.4 then helps us compare n_{uo} and n_{co}. The latter is defined by

$$\frac{s\left(c(1 + \beta)n^{-\beta}\right)}{n} = \frac{a(1 + \beta)}{\beta}, \tag{3.36}$$

where we have used (3.22) and (3.27). If $\theta(q)$ is negative or zero, the left-hand side of (3.36) will lie below that of (3.34), as shown in figure 3.4, and we will have

$$n_{uo} > n_{co}. \tag{3.37}$$

If $\theta(q)$ is positive, the opposite conclusion is possible. Consider the case where θ is constant. The second curve then lies above the first, the ratio of their ordinates being $(1 + \beta)^\theta$. If the inequality of (3.37) is to be reversed, this must exceed $(1 + \beta)/[1 + \beta s(c n_{uo}^{-\beta})]$. This is clearly possible. But if s is reasonably small and θ is not too close to 1, i.e. the monopolistically competitive sector is a relatively small part of the economy and the DD curve is not too inelastic, then the presumption is that (3.37) will continue to hold.

The comparison of the size of firms is unambiguous. Equations (3.16), (3.33) and (3.35) can be put together to give

$$x_{uo} = \frac{a}{c\beta} \left[1 + \beta s \left(c n_{uo}^{-\beta} \right) \right] \tag{3.38}$$

and therefore, comparing (3.28), we find

$$x_{uo} > x_{co}. \tag{3.39}$$

Thus the unconstrained optimum always exploits economies of scale further than the constrained one, and often has more firms as well.

Turning to the budget shares, we note that the unconstrained optimum has a lower value of E than the constrained one, but of course a higher level of utility. Therefore we must have

$$q_{uo} < q_{co} \tag{3.40}$$

and can conclude that

$$s_{uo} \gtrless s_{co} \text{ as } \theta(q) \lessgtr 0, \text{ i.e. as } \sigma(q) \gtrless 1 \tag{3.41}$$

provided these hold over the entire relevant range of q.

In our central case $\beta\alpha = 1$, the constrained optimum and the market equilibrium coincide. All the above statements therefore incorporate the comparisons between the unconstrained optimum and the market equilibrium for this case. Firms in the unconstrained optimum are always larger, and there are usually more of them. Thus we have proved that, in an important case, at least one of the usual presumptions is valid: the unconstrained optimum makes fuller use of the economies of scale than the market. However, closer scrutiny shows that the essential reason for this 'excess capacity' result is not the one conventionally given. We have also shown that the constrained optimum does not push economies of scale beyond the extent achieved by the market. Thus it is not the positive degree of monopoly power, but the underlying non-convexity and the unavailability of lump-sum subsidies that constitute the real reason for our result. We shall have more to say about the distinct reasons for possible non-optimality of the market in our concluding remarks.

Outside the central case, we have two ways of comparing the full optimum with the market equilibrium. We could work via the constrained optimum, and see where transitive chains of corresponding inequalities can be found. Alternatively, we could look for direct comparisons. Once again, we have a simple result for comparative size of firms:

$$x_{uo} \gtrless x_e \text{ as } 1 + \beta s\left(cn_{uo}^{-\beta}\right) \gtrless \beta\alpha. \tag{3.42}$$

Comparison of the number of firms is more difficult. In the Chamberlinian case where $\theta(q) = 0$, i.e. $s(q) = \bar{s}$, a constant, it is easy to show that

$$n_{uo} \gtrless n_e \text{ as } 1 + \beta\bar{s} \lessgtr \beta(1 + \alpha). \tag{3.43}$$

If $\theta(q)$ is non-zero, the results are less complete. An argument similar to that accompanying figure 3.4 shows that

$$\text{If } \theta(q) < 0 \text{ and } 1 + \alpha > \frac{1}{\beta} + s\left(cn_{uo}^{-\beta}\right), \quad \text{then } n_{uo} > n_e \tag{3.44}$$

$$\text{If } \theta(q) > 0 \text{ and } 1 + \alpha < \frac{1}{\beta} + s\left(cn_{uo}^{-\beta}\right), \quad \text{then } n_{uo} < n_e. \tag{3.45}$$

In the Chamberlinian case, (3.42) and (3.43) show that it is not possible for the unconstrained optimum to have both fewer and smaller firms than the equilibrium, but the other three combinations are all possible. For example, if $\beta\alpha > 1$ and $\bar{s}$ is sufficiently small, then the optimum has more and smaller firms.

To conclude the discussion of the first best, consider Chamberlin's (1950) statement on the effect of product diversity: 'Marginal cost pricing no longer holds as a principle of welfare economics, nor is the minimum point on the cost curve for the firm to be associated with the ideal.' We have shown that the first part of this applies only to a constrained optimum. The second part is more generally valid.[4] It is only when

$$\lim_{n \to 0} s(cn^{-\beta}) < \frac{a}{\beta} \tag{3.46}$$

that the two curves in figure 3.4 will have a degenerate intersection at $n = 0$, corresponding to the case where economies of scale for only one product type are pushed as far as possible, and no other product types are produced at all.

---

[4] Bishop (1967) discusses the unconstrained optimum in a partial equilibrium context in Chamberlin's model. A very general analysis of the problem in the location context can be found in Starrett (1973).

3.6   Possible generalisations

We indicate some lines along which our model might be generalised. On the demand side, the expenditure function can be written

$$E = uG(1, p_1, p_2, \ldots ; n) \tag{3.47}$$

where the prices cover all conceivable commodities, and n is the number actually being produced. An unproduced commodity is understood to have an infinite price and zero budget share. This still keeps unitary income elasticities, but an extension in that direction does not seem particularly urgent in this context. We still have the demand functions,

$$x_i = EG_i / G. \tag{3.48}$$

If all actual firms charge the same price p, we can write (3.47) as $E = uG(p, n)$ and the budget share of the monopolistically competitive sector as $s(p, n)$. The break-even constraint is

$$\frac{p - c}{p} \frac{s(p, n)}{n} = a. \tag{3.49}$$

The constrained optimum can be depicted by a tangency between this and a level contour of G, exactly as in figure 3.3. The condition is

$$\frac{nG_n}{pG_p} = \frac{1 - ns_n/s}{c/(p - c) + ps_p/s}. \tag{3.50}$$

The market solution is given by combining (3.49) with the condition for profit maximisation neglecting income and repercussion effects:

$$\frac{G_i}{G} + (p - c)\left[\frac{G_{ii}}{G} - \left(\frac{G_i}{G}\right)^2 \right] = 0. \tag{3.51}$$

Unfortunately, no immediate relationship between the two solutions can be seen.

On the side of production, we can relax the assumptions of constant marginal cost and of constant set-up cost per firm. The former poses only technical problems. The latter brings some conceptual difficulties. If the cost $A(n)$ of setting up n firms is not proportional to n, we must specify the manner in which this is allocated among firms. If each firm is charged the average set-up cost $A(n)/n$, this introduces an externality between firms: setting up a new firm affects the cost charged to existing firms. If marginal set-up cost is charged to each firm (the ith firm paying $A'(i)$, with $A''(i)$ positive), this introduces an asymmetry between firms, and uniform pricing need not have any optimality features. In either case, the problem becomes much more difficult.[5]

3.7   Concluding remarks

We should like to draw a distinction between two related reasons why the market may fail to achieve optimality in this model, and to conclude with some reflections based on this. The first aspect of the problem is the economies of scale in production. The conventional implications of this need no elaboration. The particular aspect of interest here is the fact that it is costly to bring into existence a new product type. This is what gives force to the second aspect of the problem, which has to do with the possible failure of the market even to achieve constrained Pareto optimality in the sense used here. We have shown that the market equilibrium is a constrained Pareto optimum if the desirability of product diversity is reflected solely in the quasi-concavity of utility. The existence of a product type is a feature of the economy that is available in common to all consumers. Since there is a cost associated with the introduction of an additional product type, while the marginal cost of an additional individual availing himself of the existence of the new product type is zero (i.e. nothing in excess of the conventional marginal cost of producing an extra unit of the good, which in our model is the same for all goods), the set of commodities actually produced takes on very much the aspect of a pure public good. The analogy is closer with the older Dupuit–Hotelling analysis than with the newer Samuelson tradition. There are two related but distinct questions involved. The first is whether to undertake a particular project, which entails an infra-marginal calculation, and the second is the level at which to carry on the activity of a project that is chosen, which entails a marginal calculation. In the same way and for the same reason, the choice of the output of a commodity that is being produced involves a marginal calculation, while the choice of whether to produce it at all involves the infra-marginal gains from its provision.

Unlike many public goods, exclusion is feasible here, in the form of fixed charges for the right to purchase certain commodities. If all the individuals are identical, this is easy to implement by means of a two-part tariff provided we have enough information to calculate the rates. If there is diversity of tastes, the full optimum will require the fixed charges to be different for different individuals, which is much harder to arrange. Moreover, projections of demand for a new variety will fail to capture that part of the gain which is associated with the common good of making it

---

[5] Some aspects of this generalisation are discussed by Stiglitz (1973).

available, including the infra-marginal gains to individuals who purchase it.

If, as we have suggested, the set of private goods actually produced can itself be a public good, then the distinction conventionally made between the activities that 'ought' to be in the public sector and those that 'ought' to be in the private sector becomes somewhat blurred. But these are questions which will have to be pursued on another occasion.

REFERENCES

Bishop, R. L. (1967). Monopolistic competition and welfare economics, in Kuenne, R. (ed.), *Monopolistic Competition Theory: Studies in Impact: Essays in Honor of Edward H. Chamberlin*. New York, John Wiley

Chamberlin, E. H. (1933). *The Theory of Monopolistic Competition*. Cambridge, MA, Harvard University Press
  (1950). Product heterogeneity and public policy. *American Economic Review, Papers and Proceedings*, 40: 85–92

Dixit, A. K. (1974). Welfare effects of tax and price changes. April, manuscript; subsequently published in *Journal of Public Economics*, 4: 103–123

Hotelling, H. (1929). Stability in competition. *Economic Journal*, 39: 41–57 (reprinted in Stigler and Boulding, 1952)

Kaldor, N. (1935). Market imperfection and excess capacity. *Economica*, 2: 33–50 (reprinted in Stigler and Boulding, 1952)

Starrett, D. A. (1973). Principles of optimal location is a large homogeneous area. Technical Report, 90, Institute for Mathematical Studies in the Social Sciences. Stanford University, February; subsequently published in *Journal of Economic Theory*, 9: 418–448

Stern, N. H. (1972). The optimal size of market areas. *Journal of Economic Theory*, 4: 159–173

Stigler, G. and Boulding, K. (eds.) (1952). *Readings in Price Theory*. Homewood, IL, Irwin

Stiglitz, J. E. (1973). Monopolistic competition and optimal product differentiation: an example. March manuscript; chapter 2 in this volume

4   Monopolistic competition and optimum product diversity (February 1975)

Avinash K. Dixit and Joseph E. Stiglitz

4.1   Introduction

This chapter began as an attempt to formalise a simple general equilibrium version of the Chamberlinian monopolistic competition model, in order to see whether there is any validity in the common assertion that monopolistic competition leads to too much product diversification. Chamberlin (1950, p. 89) himself was careful not to make any such assertion; as a matter of fact, he saw the central issue very clearly, and expressed it succinctly as follows: 'It is true that the same total resources . . . may be made to yield more units of product by being concentrated on fewer firms. The issue might be put as efficiency versus diversity'. Kaldor (1933, p. 50), too, saw that excess capacity was not the same as excessive diversity. He said that if economies of scale were exploited to a greater extent, 'the public would be offered finally larger amounts of number of commodities; and it is impossible to tell how far people prefer quantity to diversity and vice versa'. What this really means is that a model must be specified in greater detail to determine conditions under which the one or the other might be expected. The one example which has been worked out in detail, the Hotelling spatial location model, has led many economists to the presumption that there is in fact excessive diversity associated with monopolistic competition.[1] The results of our analysis throw considerable doubt on this presumption.

Further, it soon becomes apparent that the issue of diversity is only part of the more general question of a comparison between the market equilibrium and the optimum allocation: not only may the numbers produced be incorrect, but the choice of which commodities to produce,

The research for this chapter was initiated while Dixit was at Balliol College, Oxford, and Stiglitz was Visiting Fellow at St Catherine's College, Oxford. Stiglitz's research was supported in part by National Science Foundation Grant SOC74-22182 at the Institute for Mathematical Studies in the Social Sciences, Stanford University. The authors are indebted to Michael Spence for comments and suggestions on an earlier draft.

[1] Hotelling (1929). However the article by Stern (1972) casts doubt on that presumption even in the context of location.

and how much of each to produce, may differ. There are a number of effects at work. Whether a commodity is produced depends on revenues relative to total costs. Social profitability depends, on the other hand, on a number of factors. In deciding whether to produce a commodity, the government would look not only at the profitability of the project, but also at the consumer surplus (the profitability it could attain if it were acting as a completely discriminating monopolist), and the effect on other industries and sectors (on the consumer surplus, profitability and viability). The effects on other sectors result both from substitution and income effects.

The whole problem hinges crucially on the existence of economies of scale. In their absence, it would be possible to produce infinitesimal amounts of every conceivable product that might be desired, without any additional resource cost. Private and social profitability would co-incide given the other conventional assumptions, and the repercussions on other sectors would become purely pecuniary externalities. With non-convexities, however, we shall see that all these considerations are altered.

Moreover, given economies of scale in the relevant range of output, market realisation of the 'unconstrained' or first-best optimum, i.e. one subject to constraints of resource availability and technology alone, re-quires pricing below average cost, with lump-sum transfers to firms to cover losses. The conceptual and practical difficulties of doing so are clearly formidable. It would therefore appear that perhaps a more appro-priate notion of optimality is a constrained one, where each firm must operate without making a loss. The government may pursue conventional regulatory policies, or combinations of excise and franchise taxes and sub-sidies, but the important restriction is that lump-sum subsidies are not possible.

The permissible output and price configurations in such an optimum reflect the same constraints as the ones in the Chamberlinian equilibrium. The two solutions can still differ because of differences implicit in the objective functions.

Consider first the manner in which the desirability of variety can enter into the model. Some such notion is already implicit in the convexity of indifference surfaces of a conventional utility function defined over quan-tities of all the varieties that might exist. Thus, a person who might be indifferent between the combinations of quantities $(1, 0)$ and $(0, 1)$ of two product types would prefer the combination $(\frac{1}{2}, \frac{1}{2})$ to either extreme. If this is the only relevant consideration, we shall show that in one central case the Chamberlinian equilibrium and the constrained optimum coin-cide. In the same case, we shall also show that the first-best optimum has firms of the same size as in the other two solutions, and a greater number of such firms. These results undermine much of the conventional wisdom concerning excess capacity as well as excessive diversity.

However, it is conceivable that the range of products available is by itself an argument of the utility function, over and above what is taken into account through the amounts actually consumed. This may reflect the desirability of accommodating a sudden future change of tastes, or of retaining one's identity by consuming products different from those consumed by one's neighbours, or some such consideration. Variety then takes on some aspects of a public good, and this raises the usual problems for the optimal provision of such goods in a market system.

Even if variety is not a public good, its private and social desirability can still differ on account of the failure to appropriate consumers' surplus as noted above. In the large group case, it so happens that if the elasticity of demand is constant and the same for all products, the consumers' surplus is proportional to the revenue, with the same factor of proportionality for all goods. The difference in the objectives of firms and of welfare maximisation then does not matter. Otherwise, we expect the equilibrium outcome to be biased against those varieties for which the ratio of consumers' surplus to revenue is large. However, this simple principle does not yield much direct insight. A change in the output of a commodity, or the introduction of a new commodity, affect the demands for all other goods. With possible changes in the levels as well as the elasticities of all demands, the consumers' surpluses and revenues can change in complicated ways. Therefore the answers to the questions of the equilibrium and the optimum levels of output, including possibly considerations of the viability of these commodities, involve a very large range of possibilities. We need an explicit model with a detailed formulation of demand, in order to isolate and analyse the various questions. The rest of the chapter attempts to provide such analyses. In section 4.2 we discuss the problems of modelling the demand for variety, and set up the model of the special case mentioned above. In section 4.3, this case is analysed in detail. Sections 4.4–4.6 consider the various generalisations mentioned above. In each case, we compare various features of the Chamberlinian equilibrium with those of the two types of optima, with particular regard to (1) the number and mix of products, (2) their prices and quantities and (3) the total resource allocation for this group of products.

We focus on the allocation problems that are of interest here, and neglect two other issues. The first is that of income distribution. We assume utility to be a function of market aggregate quantities. This is justified if the consumers have identical tastes, and either identical incomes or linear Engel curves; alternatively we can assume that lump-sum redistributions take place to maximise an individualistic social welfare function, thus yielding Samuelsonian social indifference curves. Also, we assume that the consumers' preferences are exogenous, thus excluding considerations of advertising and its welfare implications. We feel that prevailing thinking has overstressed this aspect at the expense of some basic allocative issues, and that the qualitative effects of adding these considerations to our model should in any case be fairly evident.

Our model differs from the spatial location model in one important respect. There, each consumer purchases only one of the products in the industry. Increasing product differentiation leads to the consumer being able to purchase a commodity closer to his liking, i.e. to go to a store closer to his residence. Our model includes such considerations in its interpretation with heterogeneous consumers and social indifference curves. But in addition, it can allow each consumer to enjoy product diversity directly. There are numerous examples where this formulation is clearly more appropriate than one modelled on location. The ability to diversify a portfolio by spreading one's wealth over a large number of assets was one of the instances that provided the original motivation for formulating this kind of model, and is discussed in more detail elsewhere (Stiglitz, 1973). Clothes suited to different climatic conditions, or flavours of ice-cream, are other examples of this type.

4.2   The demand for variety

Consider a potentially infinite range of related products,[2] numbered $1, 2, \ldots n, \ldots$ A competitive sector labelled 0 aggregates the rest of the economy. Good 0 is chosen as the numéraire and the amount of the economy's endowment of it is normalised at unity; this can be thought of as the time at the disposal of the consumers.

If the amounts of the commodities consumed are x_0 and $\underline{x} = (x_1, x_2, \ldots x_n, \ldots)$ we define a utility function

$$u = U(x_0, x_1, x_2, \ldots, x_n, \ldots). \tag{4.1}$$

This function, assumed to have convex indifference surfaces, considers variety as a private good in the sense defined before. If a sub-set S of commodities is actually being produced, i.e. $x_i > 0$ for $i \in S$ and $x_i = 0$ for $i \notin S$, then the public good case can be modelled by allowing u to

---

[2] An earlier version of this chapter considered the aesthetically more pleasing case of a continuum of products. However, it was discovered that [the] technical difficulties of that case led to unnecessary confusion.

depend explicitly on S, i.e.

$$u = U(x_0, x_1, x_2, \ldots, x_n, \ldots; S). \tag{4.2}$$

We shall take up this case in section 4.4.

It is clear that at this level of generality, nothing specific or interesting could be said. We proceed to impose some structure on U in order to isolate issues for sharper focus. First, we assume that the group of products in question is separable from the aggregated sector, i.e.

$$u = U(x_0, V(x_1, x_2, \ldots, x_n, \ldots)). \tag{4.3}$$

For most of this chapter, we assume that V is a symmetric function. This, combined with an assumption about the symmetry of costs, removes the issue of the product mix. The number of products is still a relevant consideration, but given this number n, it does not matter what labels they bear. Then we may as well label them $1, 2, \ldots n$, and potential products $(n + 1), (n + 2), \ldots$ are not being produced. This is a restrictive assumption, for in such problems we often have a natural sense of order along a spectrum, and two products closer together on this spectrum are better substitutes than two products farther apart. This makes V asymmetric, and the actual labels of products available become important. This is naturally recognised in the spatial context, but the Chamberlin tradition where the nature of the products in the group is left unspecified has implicitly assumed symmetry. We shall follow this tradition, but in section 4.6 we shall return to the question of the product mix.[3]

The next simplification is to consider an additively separable form for the function $V(\underline{x})$, i.e.

$$u = U\left(x_0, \sum_i v(x_i)\right). \tag{4.4}$$

We take up this case in section 4.5. In section 4.4, we consider an even more special form where $V(\underline{x})$ has a constant elasticity of substitution, i.e.

$$u = U\left(x_0, \left[\sum_i x_i^\rho\right]^{1/\rho}\right). \tag{4.5}$$

For concavity, we need $\rho < 1$. Further, since we wish to allow a situation where several of the x_i are zero, we need $\rho > 0$.

---

[3] Spence (1974) focuses on this issue in greater detail.

Finally, we assume that U is homogeneous of degree one in x_0 and $V(\underline{x})$. Then, with unit income elasticities, we can study substitution between the sectors without the added complication of unequal income effects.

In the remainder of this section we shall derive the demand functions for the special case (4.5), and comment on their properties. Suppose products $1, 2, \ldots n$ are being produced, and write the budget constraint as

$$x_0 + \sum_{i=1}^{n} p_i x_i = I, \tag{4.6}$$

where I is income in terms of the numéraire, i.e. the endowment which has been normalised at 1, plus the profits of firms distributed to consumers, or minus the lump-sum transfers to firms, as the case may be.

We omit the details of utility maximisation. The interesting feature is that a two-stage budgeting procedure is applicable.[4] Thus we can define a quantity index $y = V(\underline{x})$, and a price index $q = Q(\underline{p})$ such that (x_0, y) maximise $U(x_0, y)$ subject to $x_0 + qy = I$, and then $\underline{x}$ maximises $V(\underline{x})$ subject to $\sum_i p_i x_i = qy$. Moreover, with the quantity index of a constant elasticity form, so is the price index. Thus, when

$$y = \left[\sum_{i=1}^{n} x_i^\rho \right]^{1/\rho} \tag{4.7}$$

we have

$$q = \left[\sum_{i=1}^{n} p_i^{-1/\beta} \right]^{-\beta}, \tag{4.8}$$

where $\beta = (1 - \rho)/\rho$. From the conditions imposed on ρ, we know that β is positive.

Now consider the first stage of budgeting. Since U is homogeneous of degree one, x_0 and y are each proportional to I, and the budget shares are functions of q alone. Let $s(q)$ be the budget share of y, i.e.

$$y = \frac{I s(q)}{q}. \tag{4.9}$$

The ratio x_0/y is a function of q alone, and its elasticity is defined as the intersectoral elasticity of substitution, which we shall write as $\sigma(q)$. The behaviour of budget shares depends on the relation between $\sigma(q)$ and 1

---

[4] See, e.g., Green (1964, p. 21).

in the standard manner; thus we have the elasticity

$$\theta(q) = \frac{qs'(q)}{s(q)} = [1 - \sigma(q)] [1 - s(q)].$$ (4.10)

We see at once that

$$\theta(q) < 1.$$ (4.11)

Turning to the second stage of the problem, it is easy to show that for each i,

$$x_i = y \left(\frac{q}{p_i} \right)^{1/(1-\rho)},$$ (4.12)

where y is defined by (4.9). Consider the effect of a change in p_i alone. This affects x_i directly, and also through q and thence through y as well. Now from (4.8) we have the elasticity

$$\frac{\partial \log q}{\partial \log p_i} = \left(\frac{q}{p_i} \right)^{1/\beta}.$$ (4.13)

So long as the prices of the producers in the group are not of different orders of magnitude, this is of the order $(1/n)$. We shall assume that n is reasonably large, and accordingly neglect the effect of each p_i on q and thus the indirect effects on x_i. This leaves us with the elasticity

$$\frac{\partial \log x_i}{\partial \log p_i} = - \left(\frac{1}{1 - \rho} \right) = \frac{1 + \beta}{\beta}.$$ (4.14)

In the Chamberlinian terminology, this is the elasticity of the *dd* curve, i.e. the curve relating the demand for each product type to its own price with all other prices held constant.

In our large group case, we also see that for $i \neq j$, the cross-elasticity $\partial \log x_i / \partial \log p_j$ is negligible.

However, if all prices in the group move together, the individually small effects add to a significant amount. This corresponds to the Chamberlinian *DD* curve. Consider a symmetric situation where $x_i = x$ and $p_i = p$ for all i from 1 to n. We have

$$y = xn^{1/\rho} = xn^{1+\beta}$$ (4.15)
$$q = pn^{-\beta} = xn^{-(1-\rho)/\rho}$$ (4.16)

and then, from (4.8) and (4.12)

$$x = \frac{Is(q)}{pn}.$$ (4.17)

The elasticity of this is easy to calculate; we find

$$\frac{\partial \log x}{\partial \log p} = -[1 - \theta(q)].$$ (4.18)

Then (4.11) shows that the DD curve slopes downward. The conventional condition that the dd-curve be more elastic is seen from (4.14) and (4.18) to be

$$\frac{1}{\beta} + \theta(q) > 0.$$ (4.19)

Finally we observe that; for $i \neq j$,

$$\frac{x_i}{x_j} = \left(\frac{p_j}{p_i}\right)^{1/(1-\rho)}.$$ (4.20)

Thus $1/(1 - \rho)$ is the elasticity of substitution between any two products within the group. This calls for some comment. A constant intra-sectoral elasticity of substitution has some undesirable features in a model of product diversity. Some problems of assuming symmetry were pointed out earlier. For a spectrum of characteristics, we would expect the elasticity to depend on the distance between i and j. In addition, the total number of products being produced may be thought to influence the elasticities. If the total conceivable range of variation is finite, then products have to crowd closer together as their number increases, and thus the elasticity of substitution should on the whole increase and tend to infinity in the limit. However, it is often the case that the total range is very large, and most practicable product ranges can only hope to cover a negligible fraction of it. This is particularly true if there are several relevant characteristics, and therefore several dimensions to the spectrum. Since this is a very likely situation, we think it interesting to have a model where there is an infinity of conceivable products but only a finite number are ever produced, and the elasticities of substitution are all bounded above, thus always leaving some monopoly power in existence. With fresh apologies for symmetry, the assumption of constancy then offers some simplicity and an interesting result. In section 4.5, we shall relax constancy to some extent.

As regards production, we assume for most of the chapter that each firm has the same fixed cost, a, and a constant marginal cost, c, also equal for all firms. All our results remain valid if the variable cost of production is allowed to depend on output, but the algebra is considerably more complicated. In section 4.6 we consider a case where different firms have different values of a and c, and in the concluding remarks we mention some other problems.

4.3   The constant elasticity case

4.3.1   Market equilibrium

In this section we study the consequences of the utility function (4.5) and the associated demand functions derived in section 4.2. Let us begin with the Chamberlinian group equilibrium. The profit-maximisation condition for each firm is the familiar equality of marginal revenue and marginal cost. With a constant elasticity of demand and constant marginal cost for each firm, this becomes

$$p_i \left[1 - \frac{1}{1/(1 - \rho)} \right] = c, \text{ for } i = 1, 2, \ldots, n.$$

Write p_e for the common equilibrium price for each variety being produced. Then we have

$$p_e = \frac{c}{\rho} = c(1 + \beta). \tag{4.21}$$

The second condition of equilibrium is that firms enter until the next potential entrant would make a loss, i.e. n is defined by

$$\left. \begin{array}{c} (p_n - c)x_n \geq a \\ (p_{n+1} - c)x_{n+1} < a \end{array} \right\}.$$

We shall assume that n is large enough that 1 can be regarded as a small increment. Then we can treat n as if it were a continuous variable, and write the condition approximately as an equality,

$$(p_n - c)x_n = a. \tag{4.22}$$

With symmetry, this implies zero profit for all other firms as well. Then we have $I = 1$, and using (4.12) and (4.21) we can write the condition in a way that defines the number of firms in the equilibrium, n_e:

$$\frac{s\left(p_e n_e^{-\beta}\right)}{p_e n_e} = \frac{a}{\beta c}. \tag{4.23}$$

Equilibrium is unique provided $s(p_e n^{-\beta})/(p_e n)$ is a monotonic function of n. This relates to our earlier discussion about the two demand curves. From (4.17) we see that the behaviour of $s(pn^{-\beta})/(pn)$ as n increases tells us how the demand curve DD for each firm shifts as the number of firms increases. It is natural to assume that it shifts to the left, i.e. the function above decreases as n increases for each fixed p. The condition for this in elasticity form is easily seen to be

$$1 + \beta \theta(q) > 0. \tag{4.24}$$

This is exactly the same as (4.19), the condition for the *dd* curve to be more elastic than the *DD* curve, and we shall assume that it holds.

The condition can be violated if $\sigma(q)$ is sufficiently higher than one. In this case, an increase in n lowers q, and shifts demand towards the monopolistic sector to such an extent that the demand curve for each firm shifts to the right. However, this is rather implausible.

Conventional Chamberlinian analysis assumes a fixed demand curve for the group as a whole. This amounts to assuming that nx is independent of n, i.e. that $s(pn^{-\beta})$ is independent of n. This will be so if $\beta = 0$, or if $\sigma(q) = 1$ for all q. The former is equivalent to assuming that $\rho = 1$, when all products in the group are perfect substitutes, i.e. diversity is not valued at all. That would be contrary to the intent of the whole analysis. Thus, implicitly, conventional analysis assumes $\sigma(q) = 1$. This gives a constant budget share for the monopolistically competitive sector. Note that in our parametric formulation, this implies a unit elastic *DD* curve, (4.24) holds and so equilibrium is unique.

Finally, using (4.12) and (4.23), we can calculate the equilibrium output for each active firm:

$$x_e = \frac{a}{\beta c}. \tag{4.25}$$

We can also write down an expression for the budget share of the group as a whole:

$$s_e = s(q_e) \text{ where } q_e = p_e n_e^{-\beta}. \tag{4.26}$$

These will be useful for subsequent comparisons.

4.3.2   Constrained optimum

Turning to the constrained optimum, we wish to find an n and the corresponding p_i and x_i for the active firms so as to maximise utility subject to the constraint that no firm makes a loss. There now arises the question of whether the basic symmetry of our model is preserved. There is some unavoidable asymmetry, as some firms are active and the others are not. It would still simplify the problem greatly if we could know in advance that all active firms would have the same price and output.

Fortunately, this is so in the large group case. Suppose two firms are producing unequal but positive outputs x_1 and x_2, each without making a loss. By (4.12), we see that each firm's revenue $p_i x_i$ is proportional to x_i^ρ, where the factor of proportionality is the same for both, and depends on q, thus being independent of each firm's decisions to order $(1/n)$. Since $\rho < 1$, revenue is a concave function of output. With constant marginal cost, therefore, any output between x_1 and x_2 would also yield non-negative profit. Thus it would be feasible to have each firm produce $(x_1 + x_2)/2$ instead, and by the convexity of the indifference surfaces it would be preferable to do so.

Complications arise with few firms, and also if marginal cost can vary with output, and declines fast enough to offset the concavity of revenue. Note also why the argument cannot be applied with one active firm and one inactive firm: the fixed cost presents a basic non-convexity at zero.

Finally, it is easy to show that moving all prices proportionately towards the corresponding marginal costs will increase utility, provided marginal costs are non-decreasing functions of the respective outputs.[5] In the present situation, this implies that the optimum price should lie on the boundary of the feasible set, i.e. each active firm should make exactly zero profit.

Thus we have $I = 1$, and indirect utility is a (decreasing) function of q alone. The constrained optimum problem can then be written as

$$\min_{p,n} \quad pn^{-\beta}$$

subject to

$$\frac{(p - c)s(pn^{-\beta})}{pn} = a. \tag{4.27}$$

Consider the curve defined by (4.27) in the (p, n) space. We have assumed that the left-hand side is a decreasing function of n for each fixed p. Thus (4.27) defines n as a single-valued function of p, for all values of p above $p_{\min}$ defined by

$$(p_{\min} - c) \lim_{n \to \infty} \frac{s(p_{\min}n^{-\beta})}{p_{\min}n} = a. \tag{4.28}$$

In particular, if this limit is infinite, $p_{\min} = c$.

Differentiating along the constraint logarithmically, we evaluate the elasticity

$$\frac{d \log n}{d \log p} = \frac{\frac{c}{p-c} + \theta(q)}{1 + \beta\theta(q)}. \tag{4.29}$$

The denominator has been assumed positive. The numerator will always be positive if $\theta(q)$ is positive. Even if $\theta(q)$ is negative, conditions (4.19) ensures that the numerator will be positive for $p \leq c(1 + \beta)$. It may become negative for higher values of p, and may even fluctuate in sign if $\theta(q)$ fluctuates. Thus the constraint curve may have alternatively rising

---

[5] See, e.g., Dixit (1975, Theorem 1).

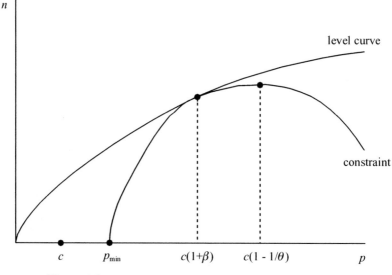

Figure 4.1

and falling portions. However, we will show that only the initial rising portion matters. Figure 4.1 shows the case where $\theta(q)$ is negative; the other case is even simpler.

The contours of the objective function have equations

$$n = \text{constant} \times p^{1/\beta} \tag{4.30}$$

and the first-order condition for optimality is the equality between the slopes or elasticities of (4.27) and (4.30). Equating the right-hand side of (4.29) to $(1/\beta)$ yields a unique solution p_c:

$$p_c = c(1 + \beta). \tag{4.31}$$

We show that this unique solution satisfies the second-order condition for a maximum, and therefore that p_c is the constrained optimum price. Note that the level curves of the objective function have the constant elasticity $(1/\beta)$. First suppose $\theta(q)$ is constant. Then the right-hand side of (4.29) is a decreasing function of p, i.e. the constraint curve has an elasticity greater than $(1/\beta)$ to the left of p_c and less than that to its right. Since $q = pn^{-\beta}$ is stationary at that point, variations in $\theta(q)$ have only a second-order effect, and thus neglecting them does not matter. Since utility increases as p decreases and as n increases, the proof is complete.

Comparing (4.21) and (4.31), we see that the two solutions have the same price. Since they face the same break-even constraint, they have the same number of firms as well, and the values of all other variables can be calculated from these two. Thus in this case the monopolistically competitive equilibrium is the optimum constrained by the lack of lump-sum subsidies. Chamberlin (1933, p. 94) once called this equilibrium 'a sort of ideal'; our analysis gives some precision to that concept, and establishes when it is valid.

4.3.3   Unconstrained optimum

These solutions may in turn be compared to the unconstrained (first-best) optimum. Considerations of convexity once again establish that all active firms should produce the same output. Thus we want to choose n firms each producing output x in order to maximise

$$u = U[1 - n(a + cx), xn^{1+\beta}] \tag{4.32}$$

where we have used (4.15) and the economy's resource balance constraint. The first-order conditions are

$$-ncU_0 + n^{1+\beta}U_y = 0 \tag{4.33}$$

$$-(a + cx)U_0 + (1 + \beta)xn^{\beta}U_y = 0. \tag{4.34}$$

From the first stage of the budgeting problem, we know that $q = U_y/U_0$. Using (4.33) and (4.16), we find the price charged by each active firm in the unconstrained optimum, p_u, to equal marginal cost

$$p_u = c. \tag{4.35}$$

This, of course, is no surprise. Next, from the first-order conditions, we have $(a + cx)/(nc) = (1 + \beta)x/n$, which gives the output of each active firm, x_u. We have

$$x_u = \frac{a}{c\beta}. \tag{4.36}$$

Finally, with (4.35), each active firm covers its variable cost exactly. The lump-sum transfers to firms then equal an, and therefore $I = 1 - an$, and

$$x = (1 - an)\frac{s(pn^{-\beta})}{pn}.$$

The number of firms n_u is then defined by

$$\frac{s\left(cn_u^{-\beta}\right)}{n_u} = \frac{a/\beta}{1 - an_u}. \tag{4.37}$$

We can now compare these magnitudes with the corresponding ones in the equilibrium or the constrained optimum. The most remarkable result is that the output of each active firm is the same in the two situations. The fact that in a Chamberlinian equilibrium each firm operates to the left of the point of minimum average cost has been conventionally described by saying that there is excess capacity. However, when variety is desirable, i.e. when the different products are not perfect substitutes, it is not in general optimum to push the output of each firm to the point where all economies of scale are exhausted.[6] We have shown, in one case that is not an extreme one, that the first-best optimum does not exploit economies of scale beyond the extent achieved in the equilibrium. We can then easily conceive of cases where the equilibrium exploits economies of scale too far from the point of view of social optimality. Thus our results undermine the validity of the folklore of excess capacity, from the point of view of the unconstrained optimum as well as the constrained one.

A direct comparison of the numbers of firms from (4.23) and (4.37) would be difficult, but an indirect argument turns out to be easy. The one clear thing about the unconstrained optimum is that it has higher utility than the constrained optimum. Also, the level of lump-sum income in it is less than that in the latter. It must therefore be the case that

$$q_u < q_c = q_e. \tag{4.38}$$

Further, the difference must be large enough that the budget constraint for x_0 and the quantity index y in the unconstrained case must lie outside that in the constrained case in the relevant region, as shown in figure 4.2. Let C be the constrained optimum, A the unconstrained one, and let B be the point where the line joining the origin to C meets the budget constraint in the unconstrained case. By homotheticity, the indifference curve at B is parallel to that at C, so each of the moves from C to B and from B to A increase the value of y. Since the value of x is the same in the two optima, we must have

$$n_u > n_c = n_e. \tag{4.39}$$

Thus the unconstrained optimum actually allows more variety than the constrained optimum and the equilibrium; this is another point contradicting the folklore on excessive diversity.

Using (4.38) we can easily compare the budget shares. In the notation we have been using, we find

$$s_u \gtrless s_c \text{ as } \theta(q) \lessgtr 0, \text{ i.e. as } \sigma(q) \gtrless 1 \tag{4.40}$$

provided these hold over the entire relevant range of q.

[6] Chamberlin appears to have confused the issue by saying that 'monopoly is necessarily a part of the welfare ideal', see his article (1950, p. 86). As far as the first best is concerned, that is not so. See also Bishop (1967) and Starrett (1974) for analyses of the first best.

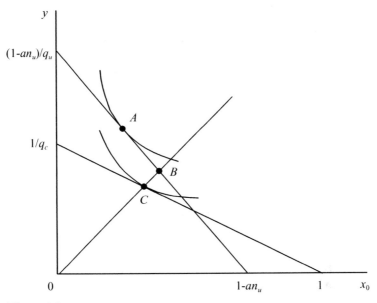

Figure 4.2

It is not possible to have a general result concerning the relative magnitudes of x_0 in the two situations; an inspection of figure 4.2 shows this. However, we have a sufficient condition:

$$x_{0u} = (1 - an_u)(1 - s_u)$$
$$< 1 - s_u$$
$$\leq 1 - s_c = x_{0c} \text{ if } \sigma(q) \geq 1.$$

In this case the equilibrium or the constrained optimum use more of the numéraire resource than the unconstrained optimum. On the other hand, if $\sigma(q) = 0$, we have L-shaped isoquants and in figure 4.2, points A and B coincide giving the opposite conclusion.

4.4   Diversity as a public good

In this section we consider the consequences of having the range of products actually produced as a direct argument of utility, over and above the effect through the amounts consumed. The general formulation of this public good problem was given in (4.2). Once again, it is too general to be useful, and we specialise it in several ways. In particular, we retain symmetry, so that the only feature of the set S of goods produced that is relevant is the number of elements in it, i.e. the number n of goods being produced. Next, we assume the separable constant elasticity of substitution form for utility as a function of the amounts consumed. Finally, we assume that the direct argument n is separated with the products in the group, and at this stage much is gained in analytic convenience without changing the qualitative features further if we assume a multiplicative power form. Thus the utility function is

$$u = U\left(x_0, \left[\sum_i x_i^\rho\right]^{1/\rho} n^\delta\right). \tag{4.41}$$

While we shall normally speak of the public good case, the formal analysis allows δ to be positive or negative, i.e. variety to be a public good or a public bad. However, we will need $(\beta + \delta)$ positive, where β is as before.

The analysis of demand is almost unchanged from section 4.2. The two-stage budgeting property still holds, and we define the quantity index

$$y = \left[\sum_{i=1}^n x_i^\rho\right]^{1/\rho} n^\delta \tag{4.42}$$

and the associated price index

$$q = \left[\sum_{i=1}^n p_i^{-1/\beta}\right]^{-\beta} n^{-\delta}. \tag{4.43}$$

In the symmetric situation, with $x_i = x$ and $p_i = p$ for all i, we have

$$y = xn^{\delta+1/\rho} \tag{4.44}$$
$$q = pn^{-(\beta+\delta)}. \tag{4.45}$$

These can be contrasted with (4.7), (4.8), (4.15) and (4.16).

The first-stage demand function $y(I, q)$ is exactly as before, i.e. (4.9) continues to hold, while, at the second stage, we have

$$x_i = I \frac{s(q)}{q} \left(\frac{qn^{\delta\rho}}{p_i}\right)^{1/(1-\rho)}. \tag{4.46}$$

In the symmetric situation, this simplifies to

$$x = I \frac{s\left(pn^{-(\beta+\delta)}\right)}{pn}. \tag{4.47}$$

These define the *dd* curve and the *DD* curve, respectively. The break-even constraint is

$$(p - c) \frac{s \left(pn^{-(\beta+\delta)} \right)}{pn} = a. \tag{4.48}$$

The solutions for the equilibrium and the two types of optima can be found by the same methods as before, and we shall only state the results. Once source of difference should be evident: the elasticity of the dd curve and therefore the equilibrium price–cost margin is unaffected by δ, but q and therefore the objective in the constrained optimum, depends on δ.

In the equilibrium, as before,

$$p_e = c(1 + \beta) \tag{4.49}$$

$$x_e = \frac{a}{c\beta} \tag{4.50}$$

while in the constrained optimum

$$p_c = c(1 + \beta + \delta) \tag{4.51}$$

$$x_e = \frac{a}{c(\beta + \delta)}. \tag{4.52}$$

In each case, the number of firms is defined by (4.48) with the appropriate value of p.

The conditions for the dd curve to be more elastic than the DD curve, and for the latter to shift to the left as n increases, ensure that both the equilibrium and the optimum lie on the initial rising portion of the constraint curve like that in figure 4.1. Thus we have

$$n_c \gtrless n_e \text{ as } p_c \gtrless p_e \text{ as } x_c \lessgtr x_e \text{ as } \delta \gtrless 0. \tag{4.53}$$

The government can achieve the constrained optimum by imposing a specific tax of $c\delta/(1 + \beta)$ on each product in the group, and using the proceeds to finance a franchise subsidy.

Comparisons between the constrained and the unconstrained optima are even easier. The former minimises q given by (4.45) subject to (4.48), while the latter maximises $u = U(1 - n(a + cx), xn^{(1+\beta+\delta)})$. This problem is the same as that of the previous section with β replaced by $(\beta + \delta)$ everywhere. Thus we have

$$p_u = c \ < \ p_c \tag{4.54}$$

$$x_u = \frac{a}{c(\beta + \delta)} = x_c \tag{4.55}$$

and n_u is defined by

$$\frac{s \left(cn_u^{-(\beta+\delta)} \right)}{n_u} = \frac{a/(\beta + \delta)}{1 - an_u} \tag{4.56}$$

with

$$n_u > n_c. \tag{4.57}$$

It is easy to compare the unconstrained optimum with the equilibrium as far as the output and price of each active firm are concerned. The number of firms is somewhat harder. If δ is positive, we know $n_u > n_c > n_e$. If δ is negative, the situation is not clear. An argument similar to that accompanying figure 4.2 will show that the quantity index y is higher in the unconstrained optimum, but so is the output of each firm, and thus a higher y could be consistent with a lower n. In the special case where $\theta(q)$ is always zero, i.e. $s(q)$ is constant and equal to $\bar{s}$, say, we can make an explicit calculation which shows that

$$n_u \gtrless n_e \text{ as } \bar{s} + \frac{1}{\beta + \delta} \lessgtr 1 + \frac{1}{\beta}. \tag{4.58}$$

Then, provided the monopolistic sector is a small part of the economy, and δ is not too large in absolute value, we can expect the unconstrained optimum to have more firms.

We conclude this section with some reflections on the public good problem. This, too is related to the existence of a fixed cost. The existence of a product type is a feature of the economy that is available in common to all consumers. While there is a cost associated with the introduction of an additional product type, the marginal cost of an additional individual availing himself of this feature is zero. This way of thinking about a pure public good is in the Dupuit–Hotelling tradition, and somewhat different from the newer Samuelson approach. There are two distinct but related questions involved. The first is whether to undertake a particular project, which entails an infra-marginal calculation, and the second is the level at which to carry on the activity of a chosen project, which is a marginal calculation. In the same way and for the same reason, the choice of the output of a commodity that is being produced involves a marginal calculation, but the choice of whether to produce it at all involves an infra-marginal one, of gains from its provision.

Unlike many public goods, exclusion is feasible here, in the form of fixed charges for the right to purchase certain commodities. If all the individuals are identical, this is easy to implement by means of a two-part tariff. If there is diversity of tastes, the full optimum will require the fixed charge to be different for different individuals, which is much harder to arrange. Moreover, projections of demand for a new variety based on the offer-price of it will fail to capture that part of the gain which is associated with the common good of making it available.

If, in the manner treated in this section, the *set* of private goods actually produced can itself be a public good, the distinction that is conventionally made between the activities that 'ought' to be in the public sector and those that 'ought' to be in the private sector becomes somewhat blurred. But these are questions that will have to be pursued on another occasion.

4.5   Variable elasticity utility functions

In this section we revert to considering variety as a private good, but remove the assumption of a constant elasticity of substitution within the monopolistic sector.[7] We retain separability as in (4.4); in fact we consider a somewhat more restrictive form

$$u = x_0^{1-\gamma} \left[\sum_{i=1}^{n} v(x_i) \right]^{\gamma} \tag{4.59}$$

This is somewhat like assuming a unit inter-sectoral elasticity of substitution. However, since the group utility $V(\underline{x}) = \sum v(x_i)$ is not in general homothetic, two-stage budgeting is inapplicable and such an elasticity does not have any rigorous meaning.

Considering demand functions in this case, we have the first-order conditions

$$\frac{1 - \gamma}{x_0} = \lambda, \qquad \frac{\gamma v'(x_i)}{V(\underline{x})} = \lambda p_i \tag{4.60}$$

where λ gives the marginal effect of income on $\log u$. As before, if the number of products is sufficiently large, we can take each of them to be a negligible fraction of expenditure, and then the second set of equations in (4.60) will define the dd curves with $V(\underline{x})$ and λ held constant. The demand elasticities are

$$-\frac{\partial \log x_i}{\partial \log p_i} = -\frac{v'(x_i)}{x_i v''(x_i)}. \tag{4.61}$$

Clearly we will need v to be a concave function.

The analysis will be similar to that in section 4.3, but some magnitudes that were constant there will now be functions of the x_i. For recognition and comparison, we will denote these functions by the same symbols as

---

[7] We are indebted to Michael Spence for pointing out to us the strong implications of assuming constant elasticity functions.

were used for the parameters in section 4.3. Thus we define $\beta(x)$ by

$$1 + \frac{1}{\beta(x)} = -\frac{v'(x)}{xv''(x)}. \tag{4.62}$$

Finally, solving for λ using the budget constraint and reducing to the symmetric situation, i.e. one with $x_i = x$ and $p_i = p$ for all i, we have the DD curve defined implicitly by

$$x = \frac{I}{np} \frac{\gamma\rho(x)}{\gamma\rho(x) + (1-\gamma)}, \tag{4.63}$$

where

$$\rho(x) = \frac{xv'(x)}{v(x)}. \tag{4.64}$$

As was the case when ρ was constant, we shall assume that $\rho(x)$ lies between 0 and 1. It can be verified that if $\rho(x)$ is constant, we have $\beta(x)$ also constant and the two are related as in section 4.3. Otherwise, the relationship between the two is different; it is easy to verify that

$$\frac{x\rho'(x)}{\rho(x)} = \frac{1}{1+\beta(x)} - \rho(x) \tag{4.65}$$

Also, we have the demand for the numéraire

$$x_0 = I \frac{1-\gamma}{\gamma\rho(x) + (1-\gamma)}. \tag{4.66}$$

Now consider the Chamberlinian equilibrium. The profit-maximisation condition yields, for each active firm,

$$p = c\left[1 + \beta(x)\right]. \tag{4.67}$$

Substituting this in the zero-pure-profit condition, we have x_e defined by

$$x\beta(x) = \frac{a}{c}. \tag{4.68}$$

Finally, the number of firms can be calculated using the DD curve and the break-even condition, yielding

$$n = \frac{1}{a+cx} \frac{\gamma\rho(x)}{\gamma\rho(x) + (1-\gamma)}. \tag{4.69}$$

Evaluating this for $x = x_e$ yields n_e.

For uniqueness of equilibrium once again we need conditions relating to the shift of the DD curve, relative elasticities etc. However, these conditions are now rather involved and not transparent. We shall omit them to save space, and indicate where they are used in the subsequent discussion.

Let us now turn to the constrained optimum. We wish to choose n and x to maximise u, with x_0 defined by (4.66), and subject to the constraint that each firm make zero profit while choosing a point on its DD curve. This condition is precisely (4.69), and we can make explicit substitutions to obtain a maximand in terms of x alone. This finally becomes

$$u = \frac{\gamma^\gamma (1-\gamma)^{1-\gamma}}{\gamma\rho(x) + (1-\gamma)} \left[\frac{\rho(x)v(x)}{a + cx} \right]^\gamma.$$

Choosing x to maximise this, we find the condition

$$\frac{cx}{a + cx} = \frac{1}{1 + \beta(x)} - \frac{\rho(x)}{\gamma\rho(x) + (1-\gamma)} \frac{x\rho'(x)}{\rho(x)}. \qquad (4.70)$$

The corresponding condition for equilibrium could be written

$$\frac{cx}{a + cx} = \frac{1}{1 + \beta(x)}. \qquad (4.67')$$

Now the left-hand side as a function of x increases from 0 to 1 as x increases from 0 to ∞. If we draw the right-hand sides in each case as functions of x, and use the second-order conditions and conditions for the uniqueness of equilibrium, we find that, provided ρ' is one-signed,

$$x_c \gtrless x_e \text{ as } \rho'(x) \lessgtr 0. \qquad (4.71)$$

Comparison of the numbers of firms uses (4.69), but the algebra is in this instance more easily understood from a diagram. This is figure 4.3. Both the equilibrium and the constrained optimum have each firm's price and output combination on the average cost curve, and also on the appropriate DD curve. The actual point is determined by some other consideration; the tangency of the average cost curve and the dd curve for the equilibrium, and something not geometrically obvious for the optimum. However, if in the equilibrium each firm that is active produces more output, the price–output point must be further down the average cost curve than it is for the optimum, i.e. it must lie on a DD curve further to the right. Given our assumption, this can only result with fewer firms, thus yielding the result

$$n_c \gtrless n_e \text{ as } \rho'(x) \gtrless 0. \qquad (4.72)$$

Finally, (4.71) shows that $\rho(x_c) < \rho(x_e)$, and then from (4.66)

$$x_{0c} > x_{0e}. \qquad (4.73)$$

A different degree of inter-sectoral substitution could yield the opposite. This is an opposition of income and substitution effects as in figure 4.2.

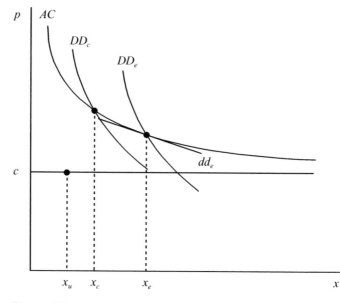

Figure 4.3

An intuitive reason for these results can be given as follows. With our large group assumptions, the revenue of each active firm is proportional to $xv'(x)$. However, the contribution of its output to group utility is $v(x)$. The ratio of the two is $\rho(x)$. Therefore, if $\rho'(x) > 0$, at the margin the firms in equilibrium find it more profitable to expand than what would be desirable in the optimum. Given the break-even constraint, this has to happen at the infra-marginal cost of having fewer firms.

Note that if $\rho(x)$ is constant over an interval, the right-hand side of (4.65) is zero, and on differentiating it, $\beta(x)$ is also constant. However, if $\rho(x)$ is non-constant, we cannot infer a relationship between the signs of $\rho'(x)$ and $\beta'(x)$. Thus the relevant consideration here is not how the elasticity of demand varies with output, but how the elasticity of utility varies.

Normally, we would expect that as the number of commodities produced increases, the elasticity of substitution between any pair of them should increase. In the symmetric equilibrium, this is just the inverse of the elasticity of marginal utility. Further, we can expect $-xv''/v'$ and xv'/v to be positively related (e.g. for the family $(k + mx)^j$ with $m > 0$, $0 < j < 1$). Then a higher x would correspond to a lower n, and so lower substitution, higher $-xv''/v'$, and higher xv'/v, i.e. $\rho'(x) > 0$. Then the equilibrium would have fewer and bigger firms than the constrained optimum. Once again the common views concerning excess capacity and excessive diversity are called into question.

The unconstrained optimum problem is to choose n and x to maximise

$$u = [nv(x)]^\gamma [1 - n(a + cx)]^{1-\gamma}.$$

This yields the conditions

$$\gamma [1 - n(a + cx)] = (1 - \gamma)n(a + cx) \tag{4.74}$$

$$\gamma \rho(x) [1 - n(a + cx)] = (1 - \gamma)ncx. \tag{4.75}$$

Using these and (4.63) and recalling that $I = 1 - an$ in the unconstrained optimum, we find

$$p_u = c \tag{4.76}$$

and x_u is defined by

$$\frac{cx}{a + cx} = \rho(x). \tag{4.77}$$

Subtracting the right-hand side of this from the right-hand side of (4.70) yields the expression

$$\frac{1}{1 + \beta(x)} - \rho(x) - \frac{\rho(x)}{\gamma\rho(x) + (1 - \gamma)} \frac{x\rho'(x)}{\rho(x)}$$

$$= \left[1 - \frac{\rho(x)}{\gamma\rho(x) + (1 - \gamma)}\right] \frac{x\rho'(x)}{\rho(x)}$$

$$= \frac{(1 - \gamma)[1 - \rho(x)]}{\gamma\rho(x) + (1 - \gamma)} \frac{x\rho'(x)}{\rho(x)}.$$

This has the same sign as $\rho'(x)$. Then, using second-order conditions, we find

$$x_u \gtreqless x_c \text{ as } \rho'(x) \lesseqgtr 0. \tag{4.78}$$

This is in each case transitive with (4.71) to yield output comparisons between the equilibrium and the unconstrained optimum.

Even though the unconstrained and the constrained optima have the same objective, roughly speaking, the break-even constraint forces the latter to pay more attention to revenue. Therefore, the consideration of the ratio of revenue to utility helps us to understand the output comparisons in (4.78).

The DD curve on which the price–output combination in the unconstrained optimum lies differs from that in the other two situations, because of differences in the lump-sum incomes as well as the numbers of firms.

The latter cannot therefore be compared using an argument like that of figure 4.3. However, we have from (4.74) that

$$n_u = \frac{\gamma}{a + cx_u} \tag{4.79}$$

and

$$n_c = \frac{\gamma}{a + cx_c} \frac{\rho(x)}{\gamma\rho(x) + (1 - \gamma)} < \frac{\gamma}{a + cx_c}.$$

This yields a one-way comparison:

$$\text{If } x_u < x_c, \text{ then } n_u > n_c. \tag{4.80}$$

We also have a similar result comparing the unconstrained optimum with the equilibrium. These leave open the possibility that the unconstrained optimum has both bigger and more firms. That is not unreasonable; after all the unconstrained optimum uses resources more efficiently.

4.6   Asymmetric cases

The next important modification is to remove the assumption of symmetry. We can then ask the broader question: will the right set of commodities be produced in monopolistically competitive equilibrium? And if not, can we say anything about the nature of the biases?[8] Not surprisingly, the answer to the first is that a wrong commodity bundle may result. The determination of the set of commodities produced depends on a number of factors: the fixed cost of establishing each firm, the marginal cost of producing the commodity, the elasticity of the demand schedule, the level of the demand schedule and the cross-elasticities of demand. The following simple example illustrates the fact that there may be multiple equilibria, in one of which everyone is better off than in the other. Assume we have four commodities, coffee, tea, sugar and lemons. Coffee and sugar are strong complements, as are tea and lemons. But coffee–sugar and tea–lemon are strong substitutes. Then there might exist an equilibrium in which coffee and sugar are produced, but tea and lemons are not, and conversely. Given that no tea is produced, the demand for lemons is so low that it cannot meet fixed costs, and conversely, given that no lemons are produced, the demand for tea is equally low. But everyone might prefer a tea–lemon equilibrium to a coffee–sugar one.

This anecdote illustrates the kinds of interactions that are relevant, but does not provide insight into the determinants of the bias possible.

---

[8] For a more exhaustive treatment of these questions, see Spence (1974).

Further, it is open to the objection that with complementary commodities, the availability of one increases the demand for the other, so that there is an incentive for one entrant to produce both. In the above example, an entrepreneur who believes that consumers prefer tea–lemon to coffee–sugar will expect a profit from joint production of tea and lemons. However, the problem remains even when there is no complementarity. We illustrate this by means of an example.

Suppose there are two sets of commodities beside the numéraire, the two being perfect substitutes for each other and each having a constant elasticity sub-utility function. Further, we assume a constant budget share for the numéraire. Thus the utility function is

$$u = x_0^{1-s} \left\{ \left[\sum_{i_1=1}^{n_1} x_{1i_1}^{\rho_1} \right]^{1/\rho_1} + \left[\sum_{i_2=1}^{n_2} x_{2i_2}^{\rho_2} \right]^{1/\rho_2} \right\}^s . \tag{4.81}$$

We assume that each firm in group i has a fixed cost a_i and a constant marginal cost c_i.

Consider two types of equilibria, in each of which only one commodity group is being produced. These are given by

I	II	
$\bar{x}_1 = \dfrac{a_1}{c_1\beta_1}$	$\bar{x}_1 = 0$	
$\bar{x}_2 = 0$	$\bar{x}_2 = \dfrac{a_2}{c_2\beta_2}$	
$\bar{p}_1 = c_1(1+\beta_1)$	$\bar{p}_2 = c_2(1+\beta_2)$	(4.82)
$\bar{n}_1 = \dfrac{s\beta_1}{a_1(1+\beta_1)}$	$\bar{n}_2 = \dfrac{s\beta_2}{a_2(1+\beta_2)}$	
$\bar{q}_1 = \bar{p}_1\bar{n}_1^{-\beta_1}$	$\bar{q}_2 = \bar{p}_2\bar{n}_2^{-\beta_2}$	
$\bar{u}_1 = s^s(1-s)^{1-s}\bar{q}_1^{-s}$	$\bar{u}_2 = s^s(1-s)^{1-s}\bar{q}_2^{-s}$	

The first is a Nash equilibrium iff it does not pay a firm to produce a commodity of the second group. The demand for such a commodity is

$$x_2 = \begin{cases} 0 & \text{for } p_2 \geq \bar{q}_1 \\ s/p_2 & \text{for } p_2 < \bar{q}_1 . \end{cases}$$

Hence we require

$$\max_{p_2} (p_2 - c_2)x_2 = s(1 - c_2/\bar{q}_1) < a_2$$

or

$$\bar{q}_1 < \frac{sc_2}{s - a_2}. \tag{4.83}$$

Similarly, the second is a Nash equilibrium iff

$$\bar{q}_2 < \frac{sc_1}{s - a_1}. \tag{4.84}$$

Now consider the optimum. Both the objective and the constraint are such as to lead the optimum to the production of commodities from only one group. Thus, suppose n_i commodities from group i are being produced at levels x_i each, and offered at prices p_i. The utility level is given by

$$u = x_0^{1-s} \left\{ x_1 n_1^{1+\beta_1} + x_2 n_2^{1+\beta_2} \right\}^s \tag{4.85}$$

and the resource availability constraint is

$$x_0 + n_1(a_1 + c_1 x_1) + n_2(a_2 + c_2 x_2) = 1. \tag{4.86}$$

Given the values of the other variables, the level curves of u in (n_1, n_2) space are concave to the origin, while the constraint is linear. We must therefore have a corner optimum. As for the break-even constraint, unless the two $q_i = p_i n_i^{-\beta_i}$ are equal, the demand for commodities in one group is zero, and there is no possibility of avoiding a loss there.

Note that we have structured our example so that if the correct group is chosen, the equilibrium will not introduce any further biases in relation to the constrained optimum. Therefore, to find the constrained optimum, we have only to look at the values of $\bar{u}_i$ in (4.82) and see which is the greater. In other words, we have to see which $\bar{q}_i$ is the smaller, and choose the situation (which may or may not be a Nash equilibrium) defined in (4.82) corresponding to it.

Figure 4.4 is drawn to depict the possible equilibria and optima. Given all the relevant parameters, we calculate $(\bar{q}_1, \bar{q}_2)$ from (4.82). Then (4.83) and (4.84) tell us whether either or both of the situations are possible equilibria, while a simple comparison of the magnitudes of $\bar{q}_1$ and $\bar{q}_2$ tells us which is the constrained optimum. In the figure, the non-negative quadrant is split into regions in each of which we have one combination of equilibria and optima. We have only to locate the point $(\bar{q}_1, \bar{q}_2)$ in this space to know the result for the given parameter values. Moreover, we can compare the location of the points corresponding to different parameter values and thus do some comparative statics.

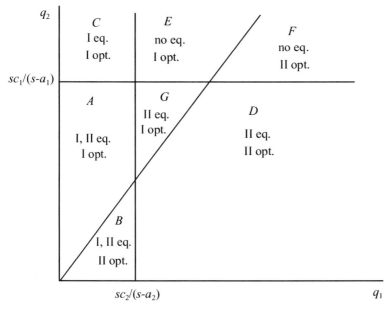

Figure 4.4

To understand the results, we must examine how much $\bar{q}_i$ depends on the relevant parameters. It is easy to see that each is an increasing function of a_i and c_i. We also find

$$\frac{\partial \log \bar{q}_i}{\partial \beta_i} = - \log \bar{n}_i \qquad (4.87)$$

and we expect this to be large and negative. Further, we see from (4.14) that a higher β_i corresponds to a lower own price elasticity of demand for each commodity in that group. Thus $\bar{q}_i$ is an increasing function of this elasticity.

Consider initially a symmetric situation, with $sc_1/(s - a_1) = sc_2/(s - a_2)$, $\beta_1 = \beta_2$, so that the region G vanishes, and suppose the point $(\bar{q}_1, \bar{q}_2)$ is on the boundary between regions A and B. Now consider a change in one parameter, e.g. a higher own elasticity for commodities in group 2. This raises $\bar{q}_2$, moving the point into region A, and it becomes optimal to produce commodities from group 1 alone. However, both I and II are possible Nash equilibria, and it is therefore possible that the high-elasticity group is produced in equilibrium when the low-elasticity one should have been. If the difference in elasticities is large enough, the point moves into region C, where II is no longer a Nash equilibrium.

But, owing to the existence of a fixed cost, a significant difference in elasticities is necessary before entry from group 1 commodities threatens to destroy the 'wrong' equilibrium. Similar remarks apply to regions B and D.

Next, begin with symmetry once again, and consider a higher c_1 or a_1. This increases $\bar{q}_1$ and moves the point into region B, making it optimal to produce the low-cost group alone while leaving both I and II as possible equilibria, until the difference in costs is large enough to take the point to region D. The change also moves the boundary between A and C upward, opening up a larger region G, but that is not of significance here.

If both $\bar{q}_1$ and $\bar{q}_2$ are large, each group is threatened by profitable entry from the other, and no Nash equilibrium exists, as in regions E and F. However, the criterion of constrained optimality remains as before. Thus we have a case where it may be necessary to prohibit entry in order to sustain the constrained optimum.

If we combine a case where $c_1 > c_2$ (or $a_1 > a_2$) and $\beta_1 > \beta_2$, i.e. where commodities in group 2 are more elastic and have lower costs, we face a still worse possibility. For the point $(\bar{q}_1, \bar{q}_2)$ may then lie in region G, where only II is a possible equilibrium and only I is constrained optimum, i.e. the market can produce only a low-cost, high-demand elasticity group of commodities when a high-cost, low-demand elasticity group should have been.

The basic principle underlying the analysis of biases in the choice of commodities is that while the viability of a firm in monopolistically competitive equilibrium depends on the ability to earn sufficient revenues in excess of variable costs to pay for the fixed costs, the desirability of having a firm operate from a social viewpoint depends on the magnitude of revenue *plus* consumer surplus relative to total costs. Thus, although low own elasticity commodities would appear to have the potential of earning large revenues in excess of variable costs, they may not be able to do so if there is a high cross-elasticity with a commodity with a high own elasticity, and low own price elasticity commodities also tend to have large consumer surpluses associated with their production. In the above example, the inefficient equilibrium is the one in which the high-demand elasticity commodity group is produced, when the other commodity group 'ought' to have produced.

In the interpretation of the model with heterogeneous consumers and social indifference curves, inelastically demanded commodities will be the ones which are intensively desired by a few consumers. Thus we have an 'economic' reason why the market will lead to a bias against opera relative to football matches, and a justification for subsidisation of the former and a tax on the latter, provided the distribution of income is optimum.

Even when cross-elasticities are zero, there may be an incorrect choice of commodities to be produced (relative either to an unconstrained or constrained optimum) as figures 4.5–4.6 illustrate. Figure 4.5 illustrates a case where commodity A has a more elastic demand curve than commodity B; A is produced in monopolistically competitive equilibrium, while B is not. But clearly, it is socially desirable to produce B, since ignoring consumer surplus, it is just marginal. Thus, the commodities that are not produced but ought to be are those with inelastic demands. Indeed, if, as in the usual analysis of monopolistic competition, eliminating one firm shifts the demand curve for the other firms to the right (i.e. increases the demand for other firms), if the consumer surplus from A (at its equilibrium level of output) is less than that from B (i.e. the cross-hatched area exceeds the striped area), then constrained Pareto optimality entails restricting the production of the commodity with the more elastic demand.

A similar analysis applies to commodities with the same demand curve but different cost structures. Commodity A is assumed to have the lower fixed cost but the higher marginal cost. Thus, the average cost curves cross but once, as in figure 4.6. Commodity A is produced in monopolistically competitive equilibrium; commodity B is not (although it is just at the margin of being produced). But again, observe that B should be produced, since there is a large consumer surplus; indeed, since were it to be produced, B would produce at a much higher level than A, there is a much larger consumer surplus; thus if the government were to forbid the production of A, B would be viable, and social welfare would increase.

In the comparison between constrained Pareto optimality and the monopolistically competitive equilibrium, we have observed that in the former, we replace some low-fixed cost–high-marginal cost commodities with high-fixed cost–low-marginal cost commodities, and we replace some commodities with elastic demands with commodities with inelastic demands.

On the side of production, there is one related problem that we should mention.[9] We have assumed that the fixed cost for any firm is independent of the number of firms in existence. However, it is often thought that economies of scale in a primary production or servicing industry, or results of standardisation, will mean that the cost $A(n)$ of setting up n firms is not proportional to n. If this is so, we must specify the manner in which this is allocated between firms. If each firm is charged the average set-up cost $A(n)/n$, this introduces an externality among firms: setting up a new firm affects the cost charged to existing firms.

---

[9] Some aspects of this generalisation are discussed by Stiglitz (1973).

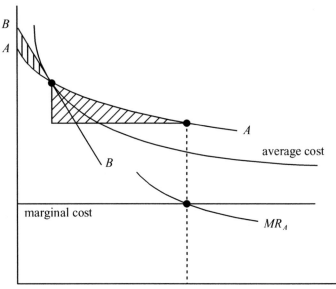

Figure 4.5

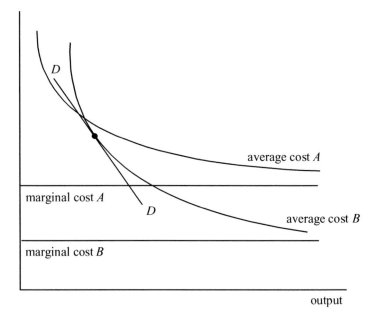

Figure 4.6

Competitive equilibrium can exist even if $A(n)/n$ is declining, in the standard manner of Marshallian parametric external economies, but there is now one more reason for it to be inefficient. On the other hand, if each firm is charged the marginal set-up cost, i.e. the ith firm pays $A(i) - A(i - 1)$, then economies of scale will mean non-existence of competitive equilibrium, since the infra-marginal firms will be paying higher fixed costs and thus making losses when the marginal one is just breaking even. Also, the optimum will involve a complicated asymmetry that is not easy to handle.

4.7   Concluding remarks

We have constructed in this chapter a series of models to study various aspects of the relationship between market and optimal resource allocation in the presence of some non-convexities. The following general conclusions seem worth pointing out.

Monopoly power, which is a necessary ingredient of markets with non-convexities, is usually considered to distort resources away from the sector concerned. However, in our analysis monopoly power enables firms to pay fixed costs, and entry cannot be prevented, so the relationship between monopoly power and the direction of market distortion is no longer obvious.

In the central case of a constant elasticity utility function, the market solution was constrained Pareto optimal, regardless of the value of that elasticity (and thus the implied elasticity of the demand functions). With variable elasticities, the bias could go either way, and the direction of the bias depended not on how the elasticity of demand changed, but on how the elasticity of utility changed. We suggested that there was some presumption that the market solution would be characterised by too few firms in the monopolistically competitive sector.

When demand curves were independent, we also observed a bias against products with low price elasticities or high fixed costs. With interdependent demands, the failure of each firm to take account of the effects on other firms would presumably lead to the possibility of further biases. The polar case examined here confirmed that hypothesis and indicated some particular outcomes of wrong product choice.

A more general theory would attempt to incorporate these various effects into a single model. The problem is one of suitable parameterisation to yield interesting results. Michael Spence has considered one such model in a partial equilibrium context. The Lancaster approach of relating interdependence in demand to product attributes is another possibility. Such general models are a subject for further research.

REFERENCES

Bishop, R. L. (1967). Monopolistic competition and welfare economics, in Kuenne, R. (ed.), *Monopolistic Competition Theory: Studies in Impact: Essays in Honor of Edward H. Chamberlin*. New York, John Wiley

Chamberlin, E. H. (1933). *The Theory of Monopolistic Competition*. Cambridge, MA, Harvard University Press

(1950). Product heterogeneity and public policy. *American Economic Review, Papers and Proceedings*, 40: 85–92

Dixit, A. K. (1975). Welfare effects of tax and price changes. *Journal of Public Economics*, 4: 103–123

Green, H. A. J. (1964). *Aggregation in Economic Analysis*. Princeton, Princeton University Press

Hotelling, H. (1929). Stability in competition. *Economic Journal*, 39: 41–57 (reprinted in Stigler and Boulding, 1952)

Kaldor, N. (1934). Market imperfection and excess capacity. *Economica, N.S.*, 2: 33–50 (reprinted in Stigler and Boulding, 1952)

Spence, A. M. (1974). Product selection, fixed costs and monopolistic competition. manuscript; subsequently published in *Review of Economic Studies*, 43: 217–235, 1976

Starrett, D. A. (1974). Principles of optimal location in a large homogeneous area. *Journal of Economic Theory*, 9: 418–448

Stern, N. H. (1972). The optimal size of market areas. *Journal of Economic Theory*, 4: 159–173

Stigler, G. and Boulding, K. (eds.) (1952). *Readings in Price Theory*. Homewood, IL, Irwin

Stiglitz, J. E. (1973). Monopolistic competition and optimal product differentiation: an example. March, manuscript; chapter 2 in this volume

Part II

Current perspectives

5 Some reflections on theories and applications of monopolistic competition

Avinash K. Dixit

5.1   Introduction

Models of monopolistic competition are now well established as standard tools for the analysis of many economic issues. This is a relatively recent development. If we count the number of times the phrase 'monopolistic competition' appears in the entries (consisting of titles, and abstracts since 1989) for articles in the database Econ-Lit for the entire timespan it covers, we find the situation in table 5.1.

The rapid and continued increase in the numbers is impressive. Another fact is also noteworthy. During the 1990s, when abstracts have been available, the total number of appearances increased even while the number of appearances in titles fell. This suggests that this approach is becoming well established; users of the framework feel increasingly more assured about using it as a normal part of their toolkit without having to make a big deal about it.

This is noteworthy because the starting date of 1969 for this data was immediately after George Stigler published his important book, *The Organization of Industry*, which included a chapter on monopolistic competition. Reviewing the work of Robinson and Chamberlin through the lens of Triffin's general equilibrium formulation, Stigler reached a basically negative conclusion about the theory.[1] Triffin had argued that in principle all products in a general equilibrium system formed a continuum with degrees of greater or smaller substitution. Abstract principles did not tell us where to break this chain in order to define a group or an industry. But in concrete economic applications one could use the

This is a slightly revised version of the paper presented at the conference. I thank Steven Brakman and Ben Heijdra for organising the conference and thereby giving me the opportunity to develop these thoughts. I also thank the participants in the conference, especially Russell Cooper and Peter Neary, for their comments and suggestions, and the National Science Foundation for research support.

[1] Keppler (1994) gives an interesting account of the history of thought on monopolistic competition. However, I disagree with many of his judgements about the current state of the theory and its uses.

Table 5.1 *Appearances of the phrase 'monopolistic competition'*

Year	In title	Anywhere
1995–99	69	211
1990–94	100	176
1985–89	98	NA
1980–84	26	NA
1975–79	16	NA
1969–74	19	NA

concept to reduce the scope of the investigation to manageable proportions. Stigler dismissed this as *ad hoc* empiricism. He accepted the logic of Chamberlin's tangency solution, but argued that in practice the cross-elasticities would be so large as to make the solution indistinguishable from the Marshallian model of perfect competition. Stigler's final verdict was that economists should keep in their toolbox only the two extreme models of perfect competition and pure monopoly, and use whichever is appropriate for studying the question being posed. Sometimes one aspect of the same industry might be better understood in the light of one theory and another aspect using the other theory. Thus, when studying the New York housing market, '[i]f we are interested in the effects of rent ceilings and inflation, the theory of competition provides informative predictions. If we are interested in why one location rents for more than another, the theory of monopoly may be an informative guide' (Stigler, 1968, p. 320).

Most interesting for us is the reason Stigler offers for the alleged failure of the theory of monopolistic competition: 'although Chamberlin could throw off the shackles of Marshall's view of economic life, he could not throw off the shackles of Marshall's view of economic analysis' (Stigler 1968, pp. 318–19). Ironically, the same can be said of Stigler. His preferred extreme models of perfect competition and pure monopoly have one feature in common – neither is game-theoretic. Neither has any strategic interaction. In perfect competition each firm takes the price as given; the determination of the price is an equilibration or fixed-point problem solved at a different level. In pure monopoly each firm takes the demand curve as given; that comes from separate analysis at an economy-wide level with no feedback from the monopoly, which is only a small part of the economy.

I think what has enabled our generations to go beyond Chamberlin and Stigler, and make progress in the theories of market structures that are neither perfectly competitive nor pure monopolies, is our new perspective coming from game theory and its more general concept of Nash equilibrium. True, in monopolistic competition the game-theoretic aspects are minimal. We can regard each firm as a price-*index* taker instead of a price taker, and leave the determination of the price index to a higher level of equilibration. But we would not feel comfortable with even this small departure from the Marshallian apparatus unless we were able to visualise it as a part of a general set of models of imperfect competition, and think of it alternatively as the case of a large group oligopoly, usually with free entry.

5.2   Alternative models of monopolistic competition

There are many different models of monopolistic competition, and some heated arguments as to which is the correct model. I take an eclectic viewpoint on this issue. Models are merely devices to simplify a complex reality to the point where one can understand and analyse some aspect of it that is of immediate interest. I can put this approach in the clearest way by contrasting it with Pearce (1970, p. 17, cited by Jones and Neary, 1984, n. 1): 'There is but one world and only one model is needed to describe it.' If that were true, such a description would be called 'the world', not 'a model'. Different contexts require one to focus on different aspects of reality. Therefore there need not be one correct or uniformly best model.

From this viewpoint, what we need is not a contest for superiority, but a taxonomy of the different models and their merits or defects in particular applications. I hope to make a start on such an enterprise here, by looking at a few prominent models in this way.

At the broadest level, we can divide the set of models into two categories, *structural* and *reduced form*. Structural models give an explicit model of a consumer's choice where diversity plays a role; discrete choice from a collection of products differentiated by location in a characteristic space is the most common framework. Aggregation of individual demands to obtain aggregate demands for all available varieties is carried out explicitly. Reduced form models regard aggregate demands as if they result from the maximisation of a utility function defined directly over the quantities of goods, and the form of the utility function is intended to capture the desire for variety.

Economists are trained to regard structural models as *ipso facto* superior to reduced form models. There are indeed strong arguments favouring the former, the most important being the Lucas critique. The parameters that enter the reduced form equations are really functions of underlying deep parameters of the consumers' preferences and of other variables pertaining to the economic 'environment' of the industry we focus on, including the policy variables that bear on it. When these environmental variables change, the reduced form parameters should change with them. But pure reduced form analysis ignores such changes, and can therefore give seriously misleading answers to questions of comparative statics with respect to changes in the environment or policy.

However, structural models have their own limitations. Most importantly, one must immediately choose one particular structure. In the locational model, for example, one must specify whether the product characteristic space is a finite or infinite straight line or a circle, or some region in a higher-dimensional space. Each consumer is usually restricted to buying just one variety; this is often an unrealistic restriction even for large durables like cars and houses. And different specifications of the structure can yield dramatically different results. Here a good reduced form model can have the advantage of flexibility – it can capture some pertinent features of several different structures. Of course the qualifier 'good' is important but elusive, and involves much trial and error. But the risk of such errors is a normal part of theoretical research, and learning from such errors is a normal part of the process by which theorists acquire the skill or the art of modelling.

An analogy from the literature, to set against the Lucas critique analogy, is Nash's bargaining model. It sets up an abstract cooperative game and offers a solution based on axioms that have at best a normative appeal. A structural model would specify the actual strategies – offers, counteroffers, acceptances, refusals, delay, and so on – that actual bargainers deploy in a non-cooperative game, and look for an appropriate equilibrium concept, hemi-demi-strictly neo-Bayesian diabolical equilibrium or whatever. But, as Binmore (1996, p. xv) expressed it, 'How could one possibly construct a noncooperative game that is sufficiently general to capture each twist and turn that a negotiation might conceivably take? Nash recognised that a frontal attack on the bargaining problem is not practical ... The reason for using a cooperative solution concept for predictive purposes, rather than analysing a noncooperative model of the actual bargaining procedure, is that the latter will necessarily incorporate all kinds of fine detail about which the modeller is unlikely to be fully informed, and which are probably irrelevant to the final outcome.' But 'there are certain issues to which bargaining outcomes are highly sensitive'. So 'how are we to know in what circumstances a given cooperative solution concept may legitimately be applied? One cannot expect a simple and unambiguous answer to such a broad question.' What one should do is to pursue both types of analysis, and 'narrow down the class of possible answers'. That is exactly what the 'Nash program' was all about. I think that the theory of monopolistic competition should pursue a similar parallel development of reduced form and structural models, to refine our understanding of when the flexibility of the former is useful and when the details of the latter make a significant difference.

5.2.1   Reduced-form models

These begin with a utility function of the form

$$U(x_0, F(x_1, x_2, \ldots)), \tag{5.1}$$

where x_1, x_2, ... are the quantities of the differentiated goods on which the analysis focuses, and x_0 is the quantity of an aggregate representing the rest of the economy. The rest of the economy is usually assumed to be perfectly competitive with constant returns to scale, and x_0 is chosen as the numéraire. This is a standard part of the simplification that goes with the focus on one sector, and is common to almost all models of monopolistic competition. Differences emerge in the specification of the sectoral subutility function F, and the form of the top-level function $U(x_0, F)$.

The two obvious and common choices in the specification of U are the quasi-linear (Spence) and the homothetic (Dixit–Stiglitz). Each has its advantages and costs. The quasi-linear form eliminates feedbacks of income effects on the sector in question; this is most useful in the context of industrial organisation. The homothetic form enables the sector to expand in proportion with the rest of the economy as the size of the economy changes. This is useful in international trade, where one wishes to separate out comparative advantage effects from size effects, and thus to separate out inter-industry trade from intra-industry trade. It is also useful in growth theory, where the steady state in which all quantities grow equiproportionately is a useful benchmark. In macroeconomics, a clear choice is not dictated by analytical convenience. Cooper (2003, n. 12) argues that the quasi-linear form provides a better match to long-run observations.

Both the Spence and the Dixit–Stiglitz models use a CES form for F. This has some immediate consequences that simultaneously explain the attraction of these models and the objections to them. Together with the large group approximation, which becomes exact if the set of products is modelled as a continuum, the CES form implies a constant elasticity of demand for any one product, and therefore each firm's pricing decision yields a constant markup on marginal cost. If the cost function consists of a fixed cost and a constant marginal cost, then we have an immediate and simple solution for the price in terms of the cost and utility parameters. The sectoral price index also takes a very simple form, and gets only a little more complex in applications to international trade and economic geography, where the sector is split into two by country or location, and transport costs are recognised.

However, the advantage turns into a handicap – the model cannot let price converge to marginal cost even if fixed costs go to zero, or the demand density goes to infinity which has the same effect of making fixed costs relatively negligible. Then entry should drive the number of firms to infinity; one expects that the products should become close to perfect substitutes, the price elasticity of demand for each product should increase and go to infinity, and the markup should fall to zero.[2]

Some people regard this as a fatal flaw; for them, a model that does not have the competitive limit is no good at all. I regard it as a limitation on the use of the model. If one is not interested in the range of fixed costs so small that the industry is close to being perfectly competitive, then a falling markup may be a dispensable complication. So long as one is aware of the issue, one can intelligently use the model in situations where the industry is not close to the competitive limit. As an example, consider the question of gains from monopolistically competitive trade. There are several sources of such gains: (1) availability of greater variety, (2) better exploitation of economies of scale and (3) greater degree of competition, driving prices closer to marginal costs. The last is absent in the CES model; therefore it will under-estimate gains from trade. But once we understand this, we can get useful results from the CES model. If we can identify sufficient conditions for gains from trade in the CES model, we can be confident that the same conditions will also suffice in more general models that let markups decrease as trade expands.

The CES demand specification, in conjunction with a constant marginal cost specification, immediately yields a solution for the quantity of each variety in terms of the cost and demand conditions. In a closed economy (or for international trade without transport costs), expansion occurs solely through an increase in the number of varieties produced, without any increase in the quantity of each. In reality one expects an

---

[2] The elasticity and markup can be made a function of the number of firms by allowing each firm to recognise the effect of its price on the price index; for example Yang and Heijdra (1993). However, this change is not enough to yield a competitive limit.

increase in both. Again this is a matter one should be aware of; it may be important for some applications but not for others.

Some other forms of F can be found in the literature; a more general additively separable form appears in the Spence and Dixit–Stiglitz papers. A quadratic F has been used as a reduced form, and also comes from a structural model of portfolio choice; more on this below.

5.2.2   Structural models

The most popular location models follow the work of Hotelling and Lancaster. Salop, Eaton and Lipsey, and several others built complete equilibrium models of monopolistic competition based on this structure. It was soon applied to international trade by Helpman in a characteristically thorough and elegant model. These are too well known to need citations, and subsequent applications are too numerous to list here.

This structure has a lot of intuitive appeal, and has the desirable limiting property – as fixed costs decrease or demand density increases, products crowd closer together in characteristic space, their cross-price elasticities of demand increase and in the limit we get perfect competition. On the negative side, for tractability one must generally restrict the characteristic space to one dimension.[3] Then each product has zero substitution elasticities with all others except its two immediate neighbours. This seems quite unrealistic.

An advantage of the location model in normative analysis is that it can reveal conflicts of interest with regard to the effects of growth, trade, or policy changes in a way that the aggregate models (especially reduced form ones) cannot. An increase in the variety that is available in the aggregate can hurt some people if a variety they especially liked ceases to be available. For example, if shirts were previously available in collar sizes of whole and half inches, and growth of trade led to an increase in variety so that now we had collar sizes of whole, one-third, and two-third inches, then people with an ideal size close to half-inches would be losers. The importance of having this possibility in one's model depends on the questions one wants to ask.

Models of vertical product differentiation are close cousins, and are appropriate where quality, rather than fit closest to one's tastes, is the issue. Everyone agrees that one product is better than another, but people differ in their willingness to pay for the higher quality. This model too found an early use; the work of Gabszewicz, Shaked, Sutton and Thisse on

[3] See Stiglitz (1986) for interesting analysis in higher dimensions and comments on how the choice of models makes a difference.

industrial organisation and international trade is noteworthy here. This model can yield dramatically different results than the one with horizontal differentiation. Depending on how fast costs of producing high quality rise relative to the willingness to pay for it, we can get an equilibrium with a large Chamberlinian group or one with a few firms that form a natural oligopoly. Again, the choice of model can depend on the context of the application.

In the usual location model, each consumer buys only one of the available spectrum of varieties; there is diversity in the aggregate because different consumers buy different varieties. Many people regard this as a desirable property, but I disagree. Individuals do buy two or more even of such large durable items as houses or cars. They definitely buy diverse collections of clothes, patronise many restaurants of diverse types, and diversify their portfolios. While this can provide a justification for a reduced form model using a representative consumer approach, there are also structural models where individuals can purchase some of several related goods. The combinable characteristics model of Gorman and Lancaster is the best known. Its underlying structure is the same as the general equilibrium model of state-contingent commodities and their linear combinations called securities. Therefore portfolio theory is a natural place for monopolistic competition. In standard finance theory, contingent claims and securities can be repackaged costlessly, and the focus is on pricing complex combinations (derivatives) in terms of a basic spanning set. But suppose each repackaging requires a fixed cost. Then it is too costly for most individuals to tailor a portfolio that fits their tastes precisely. Instead we will see a finite number of pre-packaged combinations or mutual funds that are imperfect substitutes for each other. Each will sell at a price above marginal cost. If the technology changes in such a way that the fixed cost goes down, then we will see more and more specialised or boutique funds appear, and each will have a smaller excess of price over marginal cost. This seems to be consistent with casual observation of this market, but I have not seen a theoretical model or an empirical study of the phenomenon. Stiglitz (1973) had an early example but it was not developed very far; more recent studies of costly creation of financial securities, for example Pesendorfer (1995), have a different focus.

Kyle (1989) develops a model of financial markets where the demands for assets are linear, as if derived from a quadratic utility function. This comes from an underlying structure with a von Neumann–Morgenstern utility function with constant absolute risk aversion and normal distributions of returns. Kyle's focus is quite different, however, namely the strategic transmission of information in financial markets when some traders have private information and all have rational expectations.

Random-utility models of discrete choice are most useful in econometrics, but they have also been used as a basis for the theory of demand for differentiated products by Anderson, de Palma and Thisse (1992). Most interestingly, they provide some microfoundations for the representative-consumer reduced form models. Indeed, the special case where the random terms in the linear random utility model have double negative exponential distributions generates the same demands as the reduced form CES model. Of course the underlying structure enables Anderson, de Palma and Thisse to pose several other questions including those requiring rigorous normative criteria for policy evaluation.

Finally, a simple and direct microfoundation for the specification (5.1) of diversity goes back to Ethier (1982). He modelled diversity in production. The consumer consumes two homogeneous goods x_0 and x to get utility $U(x_0, x)$. The final good x is produced under constant returns to scale using several intermediate inputs x_i, and

$$x = F(x_1, x_2 \ldots)$$

becomes the production function, and it is taken to be CES in many applications. Each intermediate good is in turn produced under increasing returns to scale, and the intermediate goods form the monopolistically competitive industry. This has the great merit of preserving the simplicity and tractability of the Dixit–Stiglitz model while removing the stigma of the lack of deep parameters in a reduced form.

5.3   Some themes from the conference papers

The dominant impression a reader of these papers will retain is that they are indeed an impressive collection. Specifically, progress in modelling using monopolistic competition has been nothing short of amazing. I can say that without any boasting, because I have not taken any part in these subsequent developments. Two particularly noteworthy technical contributions are the extension to include transport costs and tariffs that came from the work of Krugman, Venables and others, and the dynamics that came from the work of Grossman and Helpman, Obstfeld and Rogoff and others.

The subject and its applications have expanded and matured to the point that differences and skirmishes are emerging as they do in any large family; I was amused to see the economic geographers taking a few pot-shots at one another. More seriously, I share Peter Neary's concern about interpreting the demand-side parameter σ as a measure of economies of scale. True, it is *tied to* such a measure, namely the ratio of average to marginal costs, in equilibrium, but that is not the same thing as *being* that measure. Unless care is exercised, regarding exogenous increases in σ as increases in the degree of economies of scale can lead to errors. While I am on the subject of the interpretation of parameters, I should say that I liked Boone's use of various parameters as measures of different aspects of the severity of competition.

A feature common to many of these papers, and increasingly common in the research literature in economics more generally, is the use of numerical solutions to theoretical models for wide ranges of parameter values. Such solutions make the theoretical models come alive in a way that complex algebraic comparative static expressions do not, and give us a much clearer idea of whether the theory is of significant importance or merely a logical curiosum. Simulations also help improve one's conceptual understanding and intuition, and can suggest analytical solutions. Thus they are a useful complement to theory even when analytical solutions are available, and a useful tool of research when they are not. Therefore I applaud the use of numerical solutions. Most of the authors do not tell us what algorithms or programs they used; I suspect in most cases the solution methods were developed *ad hoc* for the particular application. I applaud the efforts and the results, and think that future progress down the road of numerical solution will be much faster because of the general methods developed and expounded by Judd (1998).

5.4   Concluding remarks

I am often asked if Joe Stiglitz and I realised just how useful our model would turn out to be when we were working on it. Of course the answer is – not by a long way. We were interested in a specific substantive issue, namely whether the market provides optimal varieties and quantities when there are scale economies, product diversity and imperfect competition; we developed the tools as we needed them. Of course we are happy that the tools have found so many uses. If we had recognised all the possible uses, we would have written many of these papers ourselves!

This is true of many papers that have played important roles as 'tool papers'. Perhaps the all-time classic of this genre is Mirrlees (1971), which launched the whole field of mechanism design. Mirrlees developed the tools for his specific application, namely optimal non-linear income taxation; in the hands of Spence, Wilson and others, the tool was found to have a thousand other uses.

And that brings me to my final point. A tool becomes successful only through its use. Each user demonstrates its useability, and gives confidence to other users to take the tool to farther uses in the same area or to new applications. Therefore the users of a tool deserve as much credit for its success as the original developers. This conference honours and celebrates all the participants and several others in the profession, not just Dixit and Stiglitz.

REFERENCES

Anderson, S. P., de Palma, A. and Thisse, J.-F. (1992). *Discrete Choice Theory and Product Differentiation*. Cambridge, MA and London, MIT Press

Binmore, K. (1996). Introduction, in J. F. Nash, Jr., *Essays on Game Theory*. Cheltenham, Edward Elgar

Cooper, R. W. (2002). Monopolistic competition and macroeconomics: theory and quantitative implications, chapter 17 in this volume.

Ethier, W. J. (1982). National and international returns to scale in the modern theory of international trade. *American Economic Review*, 72: 389–405

Jones, R. W. and Neary, J. P. (1984). The positive theory of international trade, in Jones, R. W. and Kenen, P. B. (eds.), *Handbook of International Economics, I*. Amsterdam, North-Holland

Judd, K. L. (1998). *Numerical Methods in Economics*. Cambridge, MA, MIT Press

Keppler, J. (1994). *Monopolistic Competition Theory*. Baltimore and London, Johns Hopkins University Press

Kyle, A. S. (1989). Informed speculation with imperfect competition. *Review of Economic Studies*, 56: 317–355

Mirrlees, J. A. (1971). An exploration in the theory of optimum income taxation. *Review of Economic Studies*, 38: 175–208

Pearce, I. F. (1970). *International Trade*. New York, Norton

Pesendorfer, W. (1995). Financial innovation in a general equilibrium model. *Journal of Economic Theory*, 65: 79–116

Stigler, G. (1968). *The Organization of Industry*. Chicago and London: University of Chicago Press

Stiglitz, J. E. (1973). Monopolistic competition and optimal product differentiation: an example. Unpublished manuscript; chapter 2 in this volume

   (1986). Toward a more general theory of monopolistic competition, in Peston, M. H. and Quandt, R. E. (eds.), *Prices, Competition, and Equilibrium*. Oxford, Philip Allan

Yang, X. and Heijdra, B. J. (1993). Monopolistic competition and optimum product diversity: comment. *American Economic Review*, 83: 295–301

6   Reflections on the state of the theory of monopolistic competition

Joseph E. Stiglitz

6.1   Introduction

I welcome this opportunity, almost twenty-five years after the publication of our paper on monopolistic competition,[1] to reflect on some of the broader issues which underlie our analysis, and some of the issues which arose in the subsequent literature. It seemed abundantly clear at the time – and even more so now – that many, if not most firms in the economy face downward sloping demand curves. Indeed, in the absence of some forms of imperfections of competition, it would be hard to explain the macroeconomic problems which have beleaguered capitalism, even in small open economies; all they would need to do is to lower their exchange rate, and they would face an infinite demand for their products. How, then, could there be a Keynesian problem of insufficiency of aggregate demand?[2] It also seemed abundantly clear that much competition took the form not of price competition, but of product differentiation. The market itself, in fact, created the imperfections of competition.

The widespread application of our model in trade theory, growth theory, and other areas of economics bears testimony to the fact that there are numerous important economic phenomena that seem inconsistent with, or at least cannot be convincingly explained by, a model with perfect competition (in which all products are produced, or at least are priced). Product differentiation and limited competition are central to understanding modern economies – perhaps not the markets for wheat and corn and other agricultural commodities which were the centre of attention in the nineteenth century–, but certainly for the industrial commodities of the twentieth century, and the intellectual products that are likely to play such an important role in the twenty-first.

There had been at least three strands in the early development of the theory of imperfect competition – Chamberlin's theory of monopolistic competition, Schumpeter's theory of innovative competition, and the

---

[1] See Dixit and Stiglitz (1977).

[2] For a more extensive discussion of the point, see Greenwald (1999).

134

theory of strategic competition, which can be traced back to Cournot and Bertrand. The Dixit–Stiglitz model follows the monopolistic competition framework of Chamberlin; accordingly, this is the topic on which I want to focus here.

6.2   Chamberlin's theory of monopolistic competition

Chamberlin's theory seemed to us to have considerable merit. In many industries there were enough firms that each could ignore its strategic impact on others, yet few enough firms (or firms with products which were sufficiently differentiated) that each faced a downward sloping demand curve. Besides, in the theory of monopolistic competition, one side-stepped the unsettled areas of strategic interaction; results in that arena seemed to depend so strongly on behavioural assumptions, e.g. whether firms were price or quantity setters, and no consensus seemed to be emerging about the circumstances under which one behavioural assumption seemed more plausible than another. Unfortunately, in the four decades since Chamberlin wrote his book, it did not receive the attention due, at least in terms of further development of the theory. This was particularly surprising, given that the economics profession itself had become increasingly mathematically model-oriented, and Chamberlin's theory called out for formalisation. Yet, the major formalisation of the model (one which was partially motivated by Chamberlin himself) actually was inconsistent with the theory. The simplest way to model product differentiation was based on geography, and the simplest way of modelling that was a series of stores located around a circle (e.g. Salop, 1979). While that model provided a tight parameterisation, which generated strong, concrete results, each store had two, and only two, neighbours with whom it competed. It was not *plausible* that there be no strategic interaction! Having a large number of firms might be necessary for the absence of strategic interaction, but surely it was not sufficient. One needed a plausible model in which each firm competed directly with a large number of other firms.

There were several other motivations for developing a more adequate model. The standard wisdom concerning monopolistic competition was that firms produced too little. This could be seen in two different ways: they produced at a lower output than that at which average costs were minimised; and price exceeded marginal cost. In standard formulations, economic efficiency required price to equal marginal cost. Thus, monopolistic competition was associated with under-production. If there were fixed costs of production, however, both of these arguments seemed to have shortcomings. The first one did not take into account the trade-off between variety and costs: one could produce more goods, i.e. have greater product variety, at higher average costs. The issue was, whether markets made the correct decision concerning product diversity. This was not effectively addressed within the standard competitive paradigm, where convexity assumptions ruled out the problem. The second argument was out of tune with second-best concerns which, in the years preceding our work, had increasingly received attention. If price were to equal marginal cost, if there were fixed costs, the government would have to provide a subsidy. The revenues to finance the subsidy would have to be raised somehow, almost surely from distortionary taxation. Though the general theories of imperfect information, which underlie the theory of distortionary taxation, were only in the process of being formulated, it was plainly clear that, at least at the margin, additional revenues were associated with additional tax distortions.[3] Thus, if the fixed costs associated with an additional firm were to be paid for through a government subsidy, there would be a distortion, just as there was a distortion under monopolistic competition. The relevant question was thus not whether there were distortions, but whether the allocation of resources generated by the market could be improved upon by government intervention and, if so, whether the optimal resource allocation would involve more or fewer firms, more or less diversity.[4]

What had made other models of monopolistic competition simple and tractable was symmetry. The constant elasticity utility function allowed us to formulate a symmetric model with which all of the questions in which we were interested could be effectively addressed. The results were striking: the market generated the optimal amount of diversity. Unfortunately, many took our model too seriously. We had wanted to formulate a benchmark model that would allow one to ascertain what kinds of products might be under-produced or over-produced in the market economy (relative to a well-defined norm). We certainly did not

---

[3] With perfect information, governments could levy equitable lump-sum taxes, differentiating the levies by, say, the individual's ability to pay. With imperfect information, the government either had to tax everyone the same, which would be viewed as inequitable, or differentiate among individuals through taxes which depended on endogenous variables, like income or consumption; such taxes inevitably were distortionary. The path-breaking work in this area was due to Mirrlees (1971). See also Stiglitz (1987a). Note that much of the theory of differential taxation, such as Ramsey (1927) and Diamond and Mirrlees (1971) did not have a coherent theory of the underlying restrictions on the set of admissible taxes.

[4] As I comment below, our analysis side-stepped a key issue by assuming everyone was identical. Everyone benefited the same from a gain in diversity, and they all bore the same costs. In practice, individuals differ; some may gain more from additional product diversity, and from the production of particular products. The implicit taxes associated with monopolistic competition (as those associated with innovative competition supported through the patent system) can be thought of as benefit taxes. Those who consume the product pay the fixed costs.

believe that the economy was, in any sense, constrained Pareto efficient (where the constraint here refers to the inability to raise revenues costlessly).[5]

Before illustrating what is at issue, I want to discuss other approaches to modelling.

6.3   Alternative modelling approaches

The approach we took to analysing monopolistic competition is not the only one which is consistent with the objective of incorporating *limited* but *non-strategic* competition. In the subsequent years, several others were explored.

The first represented an extension of the geographic models. The problem with the circle model was that each firm had only two neighbours. In three dimensions, each firm is surrounded by many more firms. If distances are measured in the 'taxi-cab metric' (the sum of vertical and horizontal distances), then in three dimensions, each firm has six neighbours – a far larger number than two. It was far more plausible that firms ignore strategic interactions when there are six neighbours than when there are two. In the Festschrift in honour of Baumol,[6] I asked the question: in n-dimensional space, would markets provide too little or too much product diversity? As n increased, each firm had more and more neighbours, and therefore the assumption of non-strategic interaction became more and more plausible. The analysis, unfortunately, was highly complicated,[7] but the answer was relatively simple – it depended just on whether n was greater or less than 5.

The way to think about these higher dimensional spaces is that they represent preferences over characteristics, not individuals distributed over space. Most commodities have large numbers of characteristics, which can be combined together in a multitude of ways, suggesting that a high-dimension characteristics model would be appropriate.[8] The characteristics model has one distinct advantage: it reflects the fact that in the process

---

[5] Indeed, my later work with Bruce Greenwald (1986, 1988) and others made it abundantly clear that with incomplete markets and imperfect information, markets were essentially never constrained Pareto efficient, where the 'constraint' refers to the costs of creating or transacting in markets or obtaining information. Similar analyses would apply to situations, as here, where there are fixed costs of production.

[6] See Stiglitz (1986).

[7] Few readers found it comfortable thinking in four or more dimensional space.

[8] However, the assumption that individuals are spread evenly over space, as implausible as it may be in the geographical context, is even more stretched here. Since many of the properties of the monopolistic competitive equilibrium depend critically on the impact, *at the margin*, of lowering prices, assumptions about the density function (over space or characteristics) are critical. (The same observation holds, with equal force, for the search models, illustrated by the contrasting results of Diamond, 1971 and Stiglitz, 1984.)

of product differentiation, products that match better the preferences of different individuals are created. Individual heterogeneity is critical. By contrast, in the Dixit–Stiglitz model, all individuals are identical. Heterogeneity of individuals poses serious problems for welfare analyses, as we comment below.

The recognition of the existence of sub-markets within markets in which there are large numbers of firms is absolutely essential for many purposes of applied analysis, including anti-trust. To be sure, there are many banks within the USA, but the number of banks serving small businesses in rural Washington may be very limited, and a merger even among two of these banks could have anti-competitive effects.

A second advantage of this modelling approach is the way it deals with the consequences of imperfect information, e.g. associated with search. Earlier studies (e.g. Diamond, 1971) had shown that even with arbitrarily small search costs, the market equilibrium would be that characterised by *monopoly pricing*, even though there were many firms in the market.[9] A slight change in assumption, from that where all consumers faced a fixed but strictly positive search cost, to that where there was a probability distribution of search costs, with a positive density at an interval around zero, leads to a model which is more appropriately thought of as one with *monopolistic competition*. In this model, behaviour is markedly different either from traditional models of competition or monopoly. In particular, equilibrium may be characterised either by price distributions or by price rigidities.[10] But the basic property of monopolistic competition persists; that there is a large number of firms. However, each firm still believes that the amount it sells depends on the price it charges but it believes, and plausibly so, that the action it undertakes has no affect on the behaviour of its rivals. In practice, I believe that the imperfections of competition, which arise from imperfections in information, do play an important role in the economy.

The implications of competition imperfections that arise from costly information are markedly different from those that arise from other sources; in general, improvements in information such as associated with new technologies that allow lower search costs (at least with respect to price), lead to less monopoly power and an increase in the efficiency

---

[9] For a more complete survey, see Stiglitz (1989a).

[10] The demand curve facing a firm may have a kink. If the demand curve is 'concave', then the marginal revenue from increasing output is markedly lower than from decreasing output, so that output remains unchanged, even in face of marked charges in marginal costs of production. See Stiglitz (1987c). In other circumstances, the only equilibrium consists of price distributions; if all firms charged the same price, it would pay some firms to deviate, and offer a lower price. See Salop and Stiglitz (1977, 1982) and Varian (1980).

of the market. Welfare analyses in the other models are far more complicated.[11]

There is a broader set of issues which needs to be explored once one recognises that competition is limited: firms do not have to limit themselves to charging a single price in the market.[12] The price charged can depend on the quantity purchased; there can be complicated tie-in (bundling) arrangements.[13] A variety of mechanisms can be used to attempt to extract more 'rents' out of consumers, some of which can be quite costly to consumers. Firms may randomise prices (over time or across space), which allows discrimination between those with high and low search costs.[14] These devices for 'rent' (or surplus) extraction mean that, in equilibrium, there might be greater product diversity than there would be if such devices did not exist.[15] While standard economic theory condemns such price discrimination (it interferes with one of the key characteristics of Pareto efficiency, exchange efficiency, which requires all individuals face the same (marginal) price), in the theory of the second best, in which we are immersed, the losses from this inefficiency may be less than the gains from greater product diversity. This is but one example of the complexities of normative analysis, to which we turn shortly.

First, however, I want to note that as the basic *idea* behind monopolistic competition became applied to other areas, other natural parameterisations arose. For instance, in the capital market, all securities may be imperfect substitutes for each other, when there are an infinite set of states of nature and only a limited number of securities. Mean variance analysis provides a natural way for analysing such markets, generating clear results showing the non-optimality of monopolistically competitive market allocations (Stiglitz, 1989b).

[11] For instance, in Dixit–Stiglitz, a change in the magnitude of fixed costs (which, in a sense, gives rise to the limitations in competition) will result in more firms in the market, but the markup will remain the same. One of the peculiar features of the Diamond (1971) model is that the price remains the monopoly price, so long as search costs are not reduced to zero. This is not true, for instance, of more general search models, as in Stiglitz (1987c).

[12] By now, the general theory of non-linear monopoly pricing is a well-developed branch of the theory of asymmetric information. For an early analysis, see Stiglitz (1977). Under certain circumstances, if there exist good 'resale' markets, they may still be restricted (e.g. Katz, 1981, 1983).

[13] See, for instance, Adams and Yellen (1976).

[14] See, e.g., Salop (1977).

[15] In general, if the quantities of each of the goods which a firm sells to a particular customer are observable (there is no resale), he can confront the customer with a non-linear interdependent set of charges: $R = R(q_1, q_2, \cdots)$. The standard pricing function is of the form $R = p_1 q_1 + p_2 q_2 + \cdots$, while standard non-linear pricing (e.g. with quantity discounts) are of the form $R = f_1(q_1) + f_2(q_2) + \cdots$

6.4   Normative analysis

One way of thinking about monopoly power under monopolistic competition is that the gap between price and marginal cost is a tax that is used to finance the fixed costs. The symmetry assumption (with all firms having the same elasticity of demand) implies that the optimal tax rate should be the same for all firms. (In Dixit–Stiglitz, all individuals are identical; but in a more general model, there is a further advantage of having the fixed costs in the industry being borne by a tax on the industry – the tax is like a benefit tax, with those who benefit from the availability of the product paying the costs.)

But in more general models, with interdependent demand curves, Ramsey optimal taxes do not depend just on the elasticity of demand within the industry; tax rates have to be adjusted so that the percentage reduction in the demand (along the compensated demand curve) for all commodities is the same. Thus, there is no presumption that the optimal tax rates would correspond to the implicit taxes generated by monopoly power. Matters become more complicated if we impose the additional constraint that taxes imposed on an industry or firm cannot be redistributed from one to another.

All of this reinforces the presumption that the monopolistic competition equilibrium (with its implicit taxes financing the fixed costs) is *not* constrained Pareto efficient. (For a similar critique of the interpretation of monopoly prices as Ramsey prices, see Sappington and Stiglitz, 1987.)

But designing the welfare enhancing interventions may be far from easy. But when there are large sectors of the economy which, on average, differ significantly in some of their key attributes (e.g. manufacturing and retailing), there may be a stronger case for some forms of systematic interventions.[16]

Key to all normative analyses is an appropriate identification of the relevant constraints. I have argued that an important determinant of these constraints are the information sets available, for example, to the government.[17] One of the constraints about designing optimal interventions in general, and in monopolistic competition situations in particular, is that the government has to know a great deal about properties of demand curves and technology. Firms might claim that they face larger fixed

---

[16] As the British government tried in the 1960s.

[17] Many analyses have also focused on *political* constraints, but these are often hard to formulate analytically. I have been surprised how frequently, in practice, what seemed to be a political constraint appears not to be. Whether the original assertion was incorrect, or some change has occurred in the world which led to the removal of the constraint, is not always obvious. The important lesson for modelling, however, is that one should be wary about simply asserting that there is some political constraint. (See Stiglitz, 1998.)

costs than they really do, and that is one of the reasons that firm-specific subsidies aimed at the fixed costs (so that firms could charge a price equal to marginal cost and still break even) are not likely to be feasible.

Ramsey's analysis of the optimal tax problem has been criticised on the grounds that underlying his model was an implausible set of constraints on the set of taxes that could be levied, *given* the assumptions that went into the analysis: if all individuals were in fact identical, there would be no plausible reason not to impose a lump-sum tax. It is only because individuals differ, and the government wishes to differentiate tax burdens among individuals in different circumstances, that other taxes need to be resorted to. But in *developed* countries, it is hard to make a persuasive case for limiting taxes to commodity taxes, and indeed, once income or progressive consumption taxes are imposed, the case for distortionary commodity taxation becomes questionable.[18] I raise these issues because many of the same concerns arise in the context of monopolistic competition. If the problem is financing the fixed costs (which, after all, give rise to the limitations in competition), then there may be no compelling reason to limit oneself to what amounts to a uniform tax; given the limitations in competition, firms can, and often do, resort to a variety of forms of price discrimination. The welfare economics of these price discrimination regimes too are rather complicated; while there is again no presumption that the market equilibrium that emerges is constrained Pareto efficient, again it may be hard to design restrictions/regimes which are unambiguously welfare enhancing. It is even hard to assess the desirability of restrictions on price discrimination (such as those embodied in American competition laws).[19] The higher prices paid by some groups of customers allow others to pay lower prices. Price discrimination means that firms are able to capture more of the consumer surplus, so that the general standard criterion for the establishment of a new firm – that there be positive consumer surplus – is more likely to be satisfied. Without perfect price discrimination, it may be possible that there exist products which would be socially profitable to produce, if only firms could capture

---

[18] See Atkinson and Stiglitz (1976), Mirrlees (1976). The question is: can government's objectives (raising revenue in ways which minimise distortions with particular distributive considerations) be enhanced further through differential commodity taxation? In some central cases (e.g. where there is separability in the utility function between leisure and consumption of different goods), the answer is unambiguously, 'no'. In other cases, differential commodity taxation may be desirable, but the rates and structure are markedly different in the presence of an income tax than without, and the additional gain in social welfare (say using a utilitarian social welfare function) may be limited.

[19] While it is *difficult* to make such welfare judgements, as a matter of policy it is often necessary to do so. There is concern, for instance, about the consequences of the discriminatory practices which have become commonplace in the airline industry.

more of the benefits which accrue to consumers. Indeed, in general, there will exist such products. Thus, at first blush, price discrimination, even if not perfect, would seem to be a move in the right direction. But a problem arises from asymmetries in the ability to price discriminate when assessing the general equilibrium repercussions. Products which allow more perfect price discrimination, might drive out products which generate high consumer welfare but where the scope for price discrimination is more limited.

Price discrimination raises another set of issues: typically, some individuals are forced to pay higher prices than they would without price discrimination, while others pay lower prices (particularly in a monopolistically competitive equilibrium where profits are driven down to zero). Eliminating price discrimination will, accordingly, not be a Pareto improvement *unless* compensation is paid; and such compensation seldom occurs. This implies that the criteria of Pareto efficiency may prove to be an insufficient guide to policy; one would need to resort to stronger criteria, such as evaluating outcomes through a utilitarian or other social welfare function.[20]

Overall, I find it remarkable how little these issues have been explored over the past quarter-century (see Salop and Stiglitz, 1987).

6.5   Contestability doctrines

Since the publication of our [original] paper, a major strand [has arisen] in the literature on industrial organisation called the theory of contestability (see, e.g., Baumol, 1982), based on the notion that even if there are large fixed costs, so that there are a limited number of firms, market equilibria are characterised by zero profits and are *constrained Pareto efficient* (though much of the literature has not actually attempted to establish this result, or to explicate the assumptions under which it might hold, but rather has contented itself to arguing the point within a partial equilibrium context). There are, indeed, some superficial similarities between the theory of monopolistic competition and contestability; in both, competition drives profits to zero, though in one case, there is a tangency between the average cost curve and the perceived market demand curve, while in the other, the price charged is the lowest price at which the firm breaks even. The fact that profits are zero suggests a form of constrained Pareto optimality, that is, welfare could not be increased without some government subsidy.

---

[20] Similar issues arise even without price discrimination in technologies involving joint products, where different individuals consume the different commodities (in different proportions). See the discussion below of the airline industry.

But there is a key difference: the plausibility of non-strategic behaviour. The usual articulation of contestability doctrines is that if the firm charged a higher price, some other firm would enter, undercut, and become the dominant firm. Potential competition, not actual competition, is what matters. But entry is affected not by the level of profits before entry, but anticipations about profit levels afterwards, and strategic behaviour can affect (rational) expectations about those. Indeed, so long as *any* of the fixed costs are sunk (that is, not recoverable after entry), potential entry does not act as an effective discipline device; high profits can be sustained (Farrell, 1986; Stiglitz, 1987b). The large literature on the airline industry, once thought to be the paragon of contestability, has demonstrated forcefully in the post-regulation world that potential competition does not suffice to keep prices at competitive levels even when sunk costs are relatively small.[21]

More generally, the airline industry presents an interesting application of some of the issues of monopolistic and strategic competition. There is a high level of product differentiation and fixed costs are relatively low. Think of airlines as producing two commodities, business and leisure travel, by means of a joint production function. Under the contestability doctrine, or in a monopolistically competitive equilibrium, prices are driven down to the point where there are zero profits, i.e.

$$R(p_1^*, p_2^*) = C(p_1^*, p_2^*),$$

where we assume that the prices charged affect the composition of demand, and thus the cost of providing the services. There may, in fact, be many values of $\{p_1, p_2\}$ satisfying the above equation. Assume that an entrant believes that the existing firm will continue to offer the services at the quoted prices, regardless of what he does. By assumption, he cannot capture the entire market and still make a profit, but he may be able to wrest away a sub-market, say the leisure travellers, by offering them a lower price. But given the economies of scale, even if he were successful in doing so, there might be no price that he could charge (lower than p_1^*, the price charged by the incumbent) at which he would break even. And this would be true for many or any of the pairs of $\{p_1, p_2\}$ satisfying the zero profit condition. Thus, there are multiple Nash equilibria which may or may not be Pareto rankable.[22]

---

[21] See, for instance, Borenstein (1989).

[22] If all individuals were identical, then while the price-game described above could yield Pareto inefficient equilibria, if firms offered tied bundles, presumably only a Pareto-efficient equilibrium would emerge. But if individuals were to differ, with some individuals consuming commodity 1 and others commodity 2, then the different equilibria would, in general, not be Pareto rankable.

On the other hand, there might be strategic equilibria where the airline firm makes a pure profit on at least some subset of its markets, charging prices considerably in excess of marginal costs. (In other markets, there might be a standard, monopolistically competitive equilibrium with profits driven to zero.) Other carriers with the same technology do not enter because they know for instance that entry will result in a Bertrand equilibrium, with price equalling marginal cost, so that the fixed sunk costs, no matter how small, cannot be recovered. At the same time, there might exist a stand-alone technology that provides leisure travellers with transportation at a competitive price of say p_1^{**}, lower than p_1^{*} charged by the incumbent, and below the Latter firm's marginal cost of production. It may be profitable for the incumbent to engage in predation to drive the entrant out of business because the profits that the incumbent can make if he limits himself to supplying the business travellers are far lower than his current profits. Yet, because his profits from providing the services to the business traveller are so high, his overall profits are positive, even as he engages in predation in the leisure market.

Pushing the analysis one step back, it is possible that at the time a market opened up (in this case, at the time of deregulation), there was a 'race' to be the firm that came to dominate the market, in order to earn the monopoly rents. Competition *for* the market might, in these instances, be associated with dissipative activities, like intense advertising or heavy scheduling. Competition *for* the market might yield zero long-term profits, even though once the firm is established, and the costs of attaining its dominant position are put aside, the firm earns strictly positive profits. There is, however, a strong presumption that the resulting equilibrium is not Pareto efficient; much of the money expended to establish the dominant position in the market may have been wasteful, and there exist further distortions associated with exercising market power.

6.6   Schumpeterian competition

This brings me to the final form of competition, Schumpeterian competition. There are some close affinities between Schumpeterian competition and monopolistic competition. Both are concerned with creating new commodities, the latter from a well-defined opportunity set, and the former by an expansion of the opportunity set. It was never clear whether under Schumpeterian competition profits (after taking into account R&D expenditures) were driven down to zero. What was clear was that the threat of new entry (potential competition) forced firms to innovate, and greatly limited their ability to exercise monopoly power (similar, in that sense, to contestability doctrines). The issue of whether one should model the process as entailing strategic behaviour or not, is not clear. The model that Schumpeter seems to have had in mind, a dominant firm producing a particular commodity with no close substitutes, seems to be one in which it is hard to ignore strategic considerations, even if there be large numbers of potential competitors. That is, at least the incumbent firm has to think about how potential competitors might respond to actions, which it takes. And the criticism of the contestability doctrine given above applies with equal force here: given the sunk cost nature of research, profits of the incumbent need not be driven down to zero. He could expend enough on research simply to convince a potential entrant that were he to enter the race, he would lose. In short, potential competition might have only a limited effect in spurring innovation.[23] On the other hand, in the case of markets with many firms producing a range of products that are relatively close substitutes and research strategies that are aimed at improving those products and lowering costs of production, strategic considerations may be less important. Analyses closer to those of the standard monopolistic competitive paradigm may be applicable here.[24]

6.7   Conclusion

The theory of monopolistic competition has one, overarching lesson: competition in many markets is imperfect, even though there might be many firms; products are highly differentiated, and firms face downward sloping demand curves. Models that assume perfect competition provide an inadequate description of how markets behave, how they respond to different perturbations, and thus are an uncertain guide to welfare, either in assessing the impact of alternative proposed policies[25] or the desirability of alternative interventions. In *some* cases, there are enough firms interacting with each other that one can credibly assume that they do not act strategically, and these situations fall in the domain of theories of monopolistic competition.

The model that Avinash Dixit and I formulated a quarter of a century ago provided an important tool that was a simple formulation for analysing a variety of problems, from growth to trade. Indeed, I would argue that there is a need for still further application, for example, into every area of public finance, where the perfect competition paradigm has

---

[23] See Dasgupta and Stiglitz (1988) or Fudenberg *et al.* (1983).

[24] See, for instance, Dasgupta and Stiglitz (1980).

[25] See, for instance, Hoff and Stiglitz (1997) for an analysis of how monopolistic competition theory in less developed capital markets in the rural sector alters standard policy recommendations concerning government interventions to lower the cost of capital.

remained dominant. At the very least, it needs to be shown that the results obtained with the perfect competition model are robust; we need to know what might be altered if, as is so often the case, there are limitations on competition.

The perfect competition paradigm is a powerful one, partly because it provides a benchmark. With perfect competition markets are Pareto efficient: the invisible hand ensures the efficient workings of the market, and no government, no matter how efficient, can improve upon the *efficiency* of the market's resource allocation. The Dixit–Stiglitz model can also be thought of as a benchmark, within the theory of monopolistic competition. But we have to understand the limitations of any theory, and what drives the results. The assumption that all individuals are identical is perhaps the most crucial assumption within the Dixit–Stiglitz model; it simplifies the analysis, and allows for clear welfare analyses. But the results might give us a false sense of how well markets work. When the simplifying assumptions are dropped, it becomes apparent that the invisible hand is partly invisible because it is simply not there: resource allocations will not, in general, be constrained Pareto efficient. Yet there are demanding requirements on the information that the government must have to implement Pareto improvements. Nor can 'political economy' considerations be ignored. And the imperfections of information provide wide scope for interest groups to attempt to 'persuade' politicians (sometimes with material inducements) that the world is such that their sector is one that requires special assistance in the form of protection or subsidies. Thus, while a half century ago, some may have marvelled at the wonders of the market, believing that some how we had the best of all possible worlds, today we are cognisant of the limitations of our world – but are unsure how, or in fact whether, it can be improved upon. Making matters more complicated is the fact that individuals do differ in their preferences, and that a major source of product differentiation is the response to these differences; but accordingly, policies which affect the extent of diversity of product differentiation, can have markedly different effects on different individuals. While this greatly complicates welfare analysis, in practice, applied welfare analysis has seldom limited itself to identifying Pareto improvement, and effectively always has had to rely on stronger criteria, for example based on social welfare functions.

Hopefully, twenty-five years from now, we will gather again, to see how much further progress we have made in understanding market economies, not using the idealised models of perfect competition, but the far more relevant ones based on the limitations of competition.

REFERENCES

Adams, W. J. and Yellen, J. L. (1976). Commodity bundling and the burden of monopoly. *Quarterly Journal of Economics*, 90: 475–498

Atkinson, A. B. and Stiglitz, J. E. (1976). The design of tax structure: direct versus indirect taxation. *Journal of Public Economics*, 6: 55–75

Baumol, W. J. (1982). Contestable markets: an uprising theory of industry structures. *American Economic Review*, 72: 1–15

Borenstein, S. (1989). Hubs and high fares: dominance and market power in the US airline industry. *RAND Journal of Economics*, 20: 344–365

Dasgupta, P. and Stiglitz, J. E. (1980). Uncertainty, industrial structure, and the speed of R&D. *Bell Journal of Economics*, 11: 1–28

(1982). Market structure and resource depletion: a contribution of the theory of intertemporal monopolistic competition. *Journal of Economic Theory*, 28: 128–164

(1988). Potential competition, actual competition and economic welfare. *European Economic Review*, 32: 569–577

Diamond, P. (1971). A model of price adjustment. *Journal of Economic Theory*, 3: 156–168

Diamond, P. A. and Mirrlees, J. A. (1971). Optimal taxation and public production I: production efficiency. *American Economic Review*, 61: 8–27; Optimal taxation and public production II: tax rules. *American Economic Review*, 61: 261–278

Dixit A. K. and Stiglitz, J. E. (1977). Monopolistic competition and optimum product diversity. *American Economic Review*, 67: 297–308

Farrell, J. (1986). How effective is potential competition?. *Economic Letters*, 20: 67–70

Fudenberg, D., Gilbert, R., Stiglitz, J. E. and Tirole, J. (1983). Preemption, leapfrogging and competition in patent races. *European Economic Review*, 22: 3–32

Greenwald, B. (1999). International adjustment in the face of imperfect financial markets, in *Proceedings of the World Bank Annual Conference on Development Economics 1998*, Washington DC, World Bank

Greenwald, B. C. and Stiglitz, J. E. (1986). Externalities in economies with imperfect information and incomplete markets. *Quarterly Journal of Economics*, 101: 229–264

(1988). Pareto inefficiency of market economies: search and efficiency wage models (in search behaviour in labor and product markets). *American Economic Review, Papers and Proceedings*, 78: 351–55

Hoff, K. and Stiglitz, J. E. (1997). Moneylenders and bankers: price-increasing subsidies in a monopolistically competitive market. *Journal of Development Economics*, 52: 429–462

Katz, M. (1981). Imperfect competition and heterogeneous consumers: the theory of screening in product markets. PhD dissertation, Oxford University, unpublished

(1983). Non-uniform pricing, output, and welfare under monopoly. *Review of Economic Studies*, 50: 37–56

Mirrlees, J. A. (1971). An exploration in the theory of optimum income taxation. *Review of Economic Studies*, 38: 135–208

(1976). Optimal tax theory: a synthesis. *Journal of Public Economics*, 6: 327–58

Ramsey, F. (1927). A contribution to the theory of taxation. *Economic Journal*, 37: 47–61

Salop, S. (1977). The noisy monopolist: imperfect information, price dispersion, and price discrimination. *Review of Economic Studies*, 44: 393–406

(1979). Monopolistic competition with outside goods. *Bell Journal of Economics*, 10: 141–156

Salop, S. and Stiglitz, J. E. (1977). Bargains and ripoffs: a model of monopolistically competitive price dispersions. *Review of Economic Studies*, 44: 493–510 (reprinted in S. A. Lippman and D. K. Levine, eds., *The Economics of Information*, Cheltenham, Edward Elgar, 1995, pp. 198–215)

(1982). The theory of sales: a simple model of equilibrium price dispersion with identical agents. *American Economic Review*, 72: 1121–1130

(1987). Information, welfare and product diversity, in Feiwel, G. (ed.), *Arrow and the Foundations of the Theory of Economic Policy*. London, Macmillan, pp. 328–340

Sappington, D. and Stiglitz, J. E. (1987). Information and regulation, in Bailey, E. (ed.), *Public Regulation*. London, MIT Press, pp. 3–43

Stiglitz, J. E. (1977). Monopoly, non-linear pricing and imperfect information: the insurance market. *Review of Economic Studies*, 44: 407–430

(1984). Price rigidities and market structure. *American Economic Review, Papers and Proceedings*, 74: 350–355

(1986). Towards a more general theory of monopolistic competition, in Peston, M. and Quandt, R. (eds.), *Prices, Competition, & Equilibrium: Festschrift in Honor of Baumol*. Oxford, Philip Allan/Barnes & Noble Books, pp. 22–69

(1987a). Pareto efficient and optimal taxation and the new new welfare economics, in Auerbach, A. and Feldstein, M. (eds.), *Handbook on Public Economics*. Amsterdam, North Holland/Elsevier Science Publishers, pp. 991–1042 (also NBER Working Paper 2189)

(1987b). Technological change, sunk costs, and competition. *Brookings Papers on Economic Activity* 3 (special issue of *Microeconomics*, M. N. Baily and C. Winston, eds., 1988, pp. 883–947)

(1987c). Competition and the number of firms in a market: are duopolies more competitive than atomistic markets? *Journal of Political Economy*, 95: 1041–1061

(1989a). Imperfect information in the product market, in Schmalensee, R. and Willig, R. D. (eds.), *Handbook of Industrial Organization, I*. Amsterdam, Elsevier Science Publishers, pp. 769–847

(1989b). Monopolistic competition and the capital market, in Feiwel, G. (ed.), *The Economics of Imperfect Competition and Employment – Joan Robinson and Beyond*. New York, New York University Press, pp. 485–507

(1998). The private uses of public interests: incentives and institutions. *Journal of Economic Perspectives*, 12: 3–22

Varian, H. R. (1980). A model of sales. *American Economic Review*, 70: 651–659

7   Dixit–Stiglitz, trade and growth

Wilfred J. Ethier

7.1   Introduction

Great papers come in two flavours. Some are *idea-papers*, providing new and fruitful ways to look at the world. Others are *tool-papers*, giving us new and useful techniques or models with which to exploit the ideas. Dixit–Stiglitz (1977) is a truly great tool-paper.

The basic idea of monopolistic competition had been around for decades. Everyone (almost) knew that it was very important, so important that it had become standard fare in undergraduate microeconomics courses at even the most introductory level. So important that it was usually not mentioned at all in graduate theory courses. No one had been able to express the idea in a formal model that could both endow the theory with professional respectability and also apply it to significant problems in a professional way. As a result it was widely regarded as an idea – inherently important though it might be – that had simply not proven to be useful. Any professor iconoclastic enough to discuss monopolistic competition in his or her graduate course would be ignored by students preoccupied with mastering the formal models crucial to passing qualifying examinations and to gaining future employment. Graduate students typically learned about monopolistic competition only when they became teaching assistants for the first undergraduate course and so were forced to learn about it; those graduate students fortunate enough to get by on fellowships often never encountered the concept at all.

Dixit–Stiglitz (1977) changed all that forever. It is now commonplace to employ models of monopolistic competition, and, since this is one of the basic market structures, these models are employed throughout economics. This is reflected in the schizophrenic way in which our gathering is truly an unusual professional conference: unusually narrow by being concerned with just one single paper; unusually broad in touching on many diverse areas of economics!

Fundamental as its contribution has been, Dixit–Stiglitz, at least as regards its impact on the theory of international trade (my own field), has not been well served by the surveys so important to students. Perhaps it is just the luck of timing. The first two volumes of North-Holland's *Handbook of International Economics* (Jones and Kenen, 1984) appeared a bit too early to give Dixit–Stiglitz-and-trade full justice – the key contributions had not yet been fully digested by the profession – and the third volume (Grossman and Rogoff, 1995) appeared too late – the research frontier had moved on. The *New Palgrave* (Eatwell, Milgate and Newman, 1988) appeared at just the right time, but, curiously, its chosen contributors did not have a lot of interest.

My remarks will largely concern how the Dixit–Stiglitz paper has influenced and has been related to my own work ('Dixit–Stiglitz and Me', I must confess). This is not because I have lost my distaste for comments of such a self-centred sort – I just can't think of anything else to say that could not be said much better by others.

7.2   Trade

Dixit–Stiglitz made its way into the international trade literature as a way to address intra-industry trade. During the 1970s economists became aware that the largest, and the fastest-growing, part of world trade was the exchange of similar goods (intra-industry trade) between similar (advanced) economies. By contrast, the dominant international trade theory, that of comparative advantage, viewed trade as a way to exploit *differences* between countries. There is no logical contradiction here, but that was not universally appreciated at the time, so the contrast did cause economists to long for an alternative to comparative advantage. An 'underground' literature did develop ('underground' only in the sense that it did not employ formal models to the degree necessary for respectability by the standards of contemporary trade theory, and was therefore largely ignored by respectable trade theorists, such as myself).

A two-country version of the Dixit–Stiglitz model provided an attractive way to model intra-industry trade between similar economies as the exchange of differentiated final products in international monopolistically competitive markets. This was accomplished in the late 1970s in an unpublished paper by Victor Norman (1976), and, in published work, by Paul Krugman (1979) and by Dixit and Norman (1980) independently and simultaneously, I believe.

At this time I was also concerned with intra-industry trade between similar economies, but from a quite different point of view. My starting point was the theory of trade based on external economies of scale; notable examples include R. C. O. Matthews (1949–50), Murray Kemp (1969), and James Markusen and James Melvin (1984). This theory provided an (old) alternative to comparative advantage, but, as it tended to imply extreme specialisation, it was not an obvious candidate to explain intra-industry trade.

My approach (1979) was to formulate the external economies of scale as originating in an increased division of labour permitted by a more extensive market, *à la* Adam Smith, and to insist upon the crucial role of trade in intermediate goods for this division of labour. International trade increases the extent of the market. Dissimilar countries, by specialising in production and engaging in inter-industry trade, can both increase the division of labour and exploit those dissimilarities. However, if intermediate goods can be traded, *similar* countries can also increase the division of labour, but by engaging in *intra-industry* trade they can concentrate on different parts of the production process and exchange intermediate goods. Thus this reformulation of external economies of scale as international economies rather than national economies allowed it to explain intra-industry trade (in producer goods) between similar (advanced) economies. In all this I was not at all concerned with monopolistic competition – I had gone through graduate school on fellowships.

I did believe that indivisibilities had to come in at a micro level for the division of labour to be limited by the extent of the market, but I was content to follow traditional 2 × 2 international trade theory (including that on economies of scale) by implicitly burying such considerations under aggregation. I had not yet needed Dixit–Stiglitz.

7.2.1   A digression

My paper was published in the *Journal of International Economics* (*JIE*) at the start of 1979. Dixit and Norman's contribution was of course part of their book (1980), but other central contributions to intra-industry trade, those of Paul Krugman (1979), Kelvin Lancaster (1980) and Elhanan Helpman (1981), were also submitted in due course to the *Journal of International Economics*. (At that time the *JIE* was attracting much of the best work in trade theory.) As my paper had been the first to arrive, the editor, Jagdish Bhagwati, sent me each of the other papers to referee as it was submitted (an outcome not unusual in the world of journal editing).

In each case I submitted a report with suggestions for improvements (or, at least, for changes) and enthusiastically recommended acceptance. For example, my letter of 21 November 1978 to Jagdish Bhagwati concerning Krugman's paper (1979) stated that the paper, 'is skillfully and elegantly executed, and yields interesting and original insights about trade . . . [my] suggestions do not address the substance of the paper, and, even if Krugman should be completely recalcitrant, you should not hesitate to publish the paper.'

As a result, for years I thought of myself as, in addition to one of the contributors to the theory of intra-industry trade, also a midwife to many of the other central contributions. (I use the term 'midwife' deliberately: I had no reason to think any of my suggestions had been heeded, so I saw myself as assisting only at the delivery, not in the determination of what was to be delivered.)

Years later the *Journal of Economic Perspectives* published an article, by Joshua S. Gans and George B. Shepherd (1994), about famous papers that had originally been rejected for publication. Krugman's paper was one of those featured – it had been rejected by the *Quarterly Journal of Economics* before its submission to the *JIE*. Imagine my dismay when I saw Jagdish Bhagwati quoted (p. 170) as saying: 'I published it myself *despite* two adverse referee reports by very distinguished experts on the theory of increasing returns! It did take some courage and also a strong sense of the importance of the paper for me to do so.'

Though having thought of myself for years as a successful midwife, I was apparently just another frustrated abortionist.

7.2.2   Back to Dixit–Stiglitz

I finally utilised Dixit–Stiglitz when it occurred to me that it would be natural to combine my earlier paper (1979) with Dixit–Stiglitz (and its international trade applications). I regarded this as a straightforward technical exercise, making the underlying indivisibilities explicit, that might furnish a useful model (another tool-paper!) and would at least highlight for the theory of international trade the role played by trade in producer goods, which is predominant in actual trade. But I have never regarded the resulting paper (1982) as intellectually significant: The ideas that I find interesting had already all been clearly presented in my earlier paper (1979), and the micro modelling was little beyond simply reinterpreting and reformulating Dixit–Stiglitz (and its international trade applications). This article has never been one of my own favourites among the papers that I have written.

Fortunately for me, this disdain has not been widely shared.

7.3   Growth

If the division of labour is limited by the extent of the market, anything that widens that extent has the potential to produce the externalities that can be generated by that division. Opening the economy to international trade is one way to widen that extent; economic growth is another. Indeed, the central role of economic growth was quite clear – indeed, it was absolutely fundamental – to Adam Smith and to the classical economists, centrally concerned with economic growth, as well as to later major contributors to the subject, such as Allyn Young (1928).

So it is quite understandable that the 'new' growth theory, emerging in the mid-1980s (Paul Romer, 1986, is a key contribution), should also draw on these ideas. My (1982) paper served at least as a conduit for the new growth theory to utilise the Dixit–Stiglitz formulation.

This new growth theory is often distinguished from the 'old' by the claim that the former allows the rate of growth to be endogenously determined by acknowledging that it is sensitive to the (endogenous) rate of technical progress, in addition to the rate of accumulation of physical factors. Of course, the earlier theory had never described itself as 'old'. 'Neoclassical' was the adjective of choice, indicating that its practitioners were returning, with neoclassical techniques, to the growth concerns that had preoccupied the classical economists before the subsequent decades of largely static analysis (itself brought on by the development of neoclassical economics). Neoclassical growth dominated economic theory in the 1960s, only to disappear almost without a trace in the 1970s.

Although an emphasis on endogenous growth working through technical change is indeed a distinguishing characteristic of the new growth theory, neoclassical growth theory actually had had quite a bit to say about technical change, including technical change that results from the deliberate actions of economic agents and thus is not just a statistical 'residual'. But primary emphasis was put on physical factor accumulation. Nevertheless, perhaps a more important distinguishing feature of the new growth theory – or at least of a large part of it – is its consideration of pervasive externalities and spillovers as central to the way in which (endogenous) technical change interacts with growth. And these externalities are just what international trade theory had been wrestling with in the late 1970s and early 1980s, a process ably described and analysed by Elhanan Helpman (1984).

But this interaction across fields has gone both ways. Externalities associated with an increased division of labour are also associated with the introduction of new (intermediate) goods, and concern with the growth process acclimatises one to think explicitly about the process of introducing new goods. The development of the new growth theory utilising externality concepts – concepts worked out in part by international trade theory – soon fed back from growth theory and stimulated the elaboration by trade theorists of further growth theories oriented toward an international economy (Grossman and Helpman, 1991).

So what should come next? One school of thought, embraced by some trade theorists and no doubt influenced by the success of the new growth theory, emphasises the need to focus on the dynamics of decision making and to sort out how the intertemporal decisions of firms and other agents determine how technical change and market development actually come about over time: more dynamics.

There is something to this. But I fear it could be a recipe for the type of sterility that led neoclassical growth theory to an early death. More importantly, though, I think it detracts from what I regard as the big issue. This is what determines the nature of the firm.

In (the simpler) discussions of monopolistic competition, each differentiated product is associated with a separate firm. This remains true in growth models treating the introduction of new products. All this despite an obvious potential for gains from cooperation or agglomeration among such firms. The basic logic of monopolistic competition ought to force theoretical attention directly upon the determinants of the extent of the firm, or, more generally, upon the nature of the relationships (contractual or otherwise) between the individual units producing distinct differentiated goods. I regard this as the central problem for future research, much more important than more dynamics (though, of course, this problem, too, should have a dynamic component).

Economists working in industrial organisation (IO) have, of course, hardly been blind to such concerns: they are in fact central to that field. So a possible strategy for trade theorists and for growth theorists is simply to wait and see what further answers to this question our colleagues in IO come up with. But I don't recommend this attitude. As my account of the relation between trade and growth illustrates, a two-way relation between fields can be invaluable.

The question of the determinants of the firm very naturally intrudes itself into that part of international trade theory devoted to the multinational firm, where the extent of the firm is the central issue. So there has been action here. But the question obviously ought to be equally central to all those fields of economics utilising the concept of monopolistic competition. And, much more often than not, even the literature on the multinational firm has declined to address this basic question, which it refers to as the 'internalisation' issue. This reflects, I think, how difficult it is to obtain useful answers. If this were not so, industrial organisation theorists would presumably have already given us all those answers we need.

My response to this is to look at what our young economists are actually doing. Amy Glass and Kamal Saggi wrestle with the endogenous determination of the multinational firm; Allesandra Casella, Giovanni Maggi and John McLaren investigate contractual and institutional issues. This is just as it should be; I am encouraged.

7.4   Concluding remarks

With hindsight, it is clear that Dixit–Stiglitz appeared at just the right moment to maximise its impact on both the literature on international trade and also that on economic growth. Trade theorists had become aware of the importance of intra-industry trade and were looking for ways to model it when Dixit–Stiglitz was handed to them. They in turn used it to explore externalities and to model the division of labour, just in time to serve the needs of the new growth theory. The timing could not have been better. In closing, let me say that what most impresses me about Dixit–Stiglitz – and its impact on economics – is that it demonstrates how a truly great tool-paper, even if not claiming to address deep issues, can, if it is in fact great enough, have a much deeper influence on how those issues are addressed than those idea-papers claiming actually to do so.

REFERENCES

Dixit, A. K. and Norman, V. (1980). *Theory of International Trade.* Cambridge, Cambridge University Press
Dixit, A. K. and Stiglitz, J. E. (1977). Monopolistic competition and optimum product diversity. *American Economic Review* 67: 297–308
Eatwell, J., Milgate, M. and Newman, P. (eds.), *The New Palgrave: A Dictionary of Economics.* London, Macmillan
Ethier, W. J. (1979). Internationally decreasing costs and world trade. *Journal of International Economics* 9: 1–24
    (1982). National and international returns to scale in the modern theory of international trade. *American Economic Review* 72: 389–405
Gans, J. S. and Shepherd, G. B. (1994). How are the mighty fallen: rejected classic articles by leading economists. *Journal of Economic Perspectives* 8: 165–179
Grossman, G. M. and Helpman, E. (1991). *Innovation and Growth in the Global Economy.* Cambridge, MA, MIT Press
Grossman, G. M. and Rogoff, K. (1995). *Handbook of International Economics,* 3. Amsterdam, North-Holland
Helpman, E. (1981). International trade in the presence of product differentiation, economies of scale, and imperfect competition: a Chamberlin–Heckscher–Ohlin approach. *Journal of International Economics* 11: 305–340
    (1984). Increasing returns, imperfect markets, and trade theory, in Jones, R. W. and Kenen, P. B. (eds.), *Handbook of International Economics,* 1. Amsterdam, North-Holland
Jones, R. W. and Kenen, P. B. (eds.) (1984), *Handbook of International Economics,* 1, 2. Amsterdam, North-Holland

Kemp, M. C. (1969). *The Pure Theory of International Trade and Investment.* Englewood Cliffs, NJ, Prentice-Hall

Krugman, P. (1979). Increasing returns, monopolistic competition, and international trade. *Journal of International Economics* 9: 469–479

Lancaster, K. (1980). Intra-industry trade under perfect monopolistic competition. *Journal of International Economics* 10: 151–176

Markusen, J. and Melvin, J. (1984). The gains-from-trade theorem with increasing returns to scale, in Kierzkowski, H. (ed.), *Monopolistic Competition and International Trade.* Oxford, Oxford University Press

Matthews, R. C. O. (1949–50). Reciprocal demand and increasing returns. *Review of Economic Studies*, 37: 149–158

Norman, V. (1976). Product differentiation and trade. Unpublished manuscript, UK Economic Study Group, University of Warwick, UK, downloadable from http://www.eco.rug.nl/˜heijdra/norman76.pdf

Romer, P. (1986). Increasing returns and long-run growth. *Journal of Political Economy* 94: 1002–1037

Young, A. A. (1928). Increasing returns and economic progress. *Economic Journal* 38: 527–542

Part III

International trade

8 Monopolistic competition and international trade theory

J. Peter Neary

8.1 Introduction

[T]he theory of monopolistic competition has had virtually no impact on the theory of international trade. (Harry G. Johnson, 1967, p. 203)

My opening quotation, taken from a *Festschrift* for E. H. Chamberlin, is almost as close in time to us as it is to Chamberlin's pioneering *Theory of Monopolistic Competition* (1933). Yet it belongs to a bygone era. The theory of monopolistic competition has had a huge impact on modern trade theory, and no serious student of the subject can afford to neglect its many applications. Nor is any student likely to be allowed to neglect them. It is even rumoured that there are universities where the graduate trade curriculum covers nothing but monopolistic competition!

One development above all others is responsible for this shift: the publication in 1977 of Avinash Dixit and Joe Stiglitz's paper which introduced an elegant, parsimonious and tractable formalisation of the Chamberlinian model. Dixit and Stiglitz themselves (hereafter, 'DS') applied their innovation only to the classic issue in industrial organisation of whether monopolistically competitive industries would yield an optimal level of product diversity. But within a few years, a sizeable literature had already developed applying their approach to international trade. The DS approach provided a framework for modelling some distinctive features of contemporary international trade, especially trade in manufactured goods between developed countries, which traditional competitive models failed to capture. Above all, it allowed consideration of the implications of increasing returns to scale and product differentiation in general equilibrium. It is not that there is any inherent virtue in general rather than partial equilibrium. It is simply that many of the principal questions which arise in trade theory are fundamentally general equilibrium: the

I am grateful to participants at the SOM conference on the Dixit–Stiglitz model, especially Avinash Dixit, Bill Ethier, Charles van Marrewijk and Jean-Marie Viaene, for helpful comments. This research is part of the Globalisation Programme of the Centre for Economic Performance at LSE, funded by the UK ESRC.

determinants of trade patterns, the impact of trade policy on income distribution and the effects of international factor mobility, to name only a few. Some way of linking goods and factor markets is essential if these issues are to be addressed at all, and until 1977 the only framework within which this could be done was that of competitive general equilibrium.

The DS approach was not the only formal model of monopolistic competition which was proposed around this time. Spence (1976) developed his own variant, very similar to that of DS, and the form is sometimes referred to as 'SDS' or 'Spence–Dixit–Stiglitz' preferences. (I discuss this further below.) Lancaster (1979) developed a different specification based on the idea (due originally to Gorman) that consumers have preferences over characteristics rather than over goods themselves. Each individual has an 'ideal' variety and ranks all available varieties by their distance from this ideal. Provided individual consumers have tastes which differ in a symmetric manner over varieties, aggregate demand exhibits the same preference for diversity as the one-consumer model of DS. This was in many ways a more satisfactory way of modelling demand for differentiated products, and it was successfully applied to international trade by Lancaster (1979, 1980) himself and by Helpman (1981). Ultimately though, these alternative approaches proved less tractable and hence less fruitful than the DS specification.

In this chapter I try to take stock of the progress which has been made in applying monopolistic competition to trade theory since the appearance of the DS paper. I do not attempt a comprehensive survey, partly for reasons of space and partly because there are already many other surveys available.[1] Instead I give a personal view of both the achievements and the limitations of the approach. Section 8.2 reviews the DS model and discusses very briefly some of its principal applications to trade theory. Section 8.3 tries to give the flavour of some of these applications by presenting a new one: a model which shows how multinational corporations can emerge even between countries with similar factor endowments. Section 8.4 turns to address some issues which have been neglected in the literature and section 8.5 attempts an overall assessment.

8.2   The Dixit–Stiglitz model and trade theory

'A universal adoption of the assumption of monopoly must have very destructive consequences for economic theory'. (John Hicks, 1939, p. 83)

---

[1] See in particular Helpman and Krugman (1985), Ethier (1987), Krugman (1989) and Helpman (1990). More recent applications to economic geography are surveyed in Fujita, Krugman and Venables (1999), Fujita and Thisse (2000) and Neary (2001).

Hicks could not have been more wrong. The widespread adoption of the DS approach to monopolistic competition has had hugely positive consequences for many branches of economic theory and especially for international trade theory. I begin with a brief review of the DS specification and then discuss some applications.

8.2.1 *Preferences and demand*

DS were concerned not with trade, macro or growth, but with the social optimality of a Chamberlinian industry. In particular, they revisited the once passionate but now largely forgotten debates about whether such an industry would produce too many varieties, and whether it would operate with 'excess capacity' (meaning at above minimum average cost). For the record, they overturned conventional wisdom by showing that, in a plausible central case, the outcome is of the Goldilocks kind: not too many, not too few, but just right! Specifically, with symmetric CES preferences for the differentiated products, the market equilibrium coincides with the constrained social optimum, constrained in the sense that lump-sum taxes or transfers to firms are not feasible. However, it was the technical tools they introduced rather than their substantive conclusions which were to have most effect on later work.

DS were able to address the issues clearly because they adopted a particular specification of the aggregate utility function:

$$u = U\left[x_0, V(x_1 \ldots, x_n)\right], \tag{8.1}$$

where utility depends on consumption of the numéraire good x_0 and on a sub-utility function V, which in turn is defined over a large, and potentially variable, number of differentiated products, indexed from 1 to n.

DS made two key assumptions about the structure of preferences. First, obvious from (8.1), is that utility is separable in the numéraire good x_0 and the differentiated goods. This was a simple importation into industrial organisation of a concept already well established in demand theory, and now seems natural to us. But it is worth emphasising how much it contributed to analytic clarity. Previous writers had debated the appropriate definition of an 'industry', or, in Chamberlin's preferred term, a 'group'. Typically, definitions were given in terms of cross-elasticities of demand, sometimes of *both* direct and inverse demand functions (see Bain, 1967, pp. 151 ff.). DS cut through all this fog: instead of restricting the demand functions by imposing arbitrary limits on inter- and intra-industry substitutability, they made a single restriction on the utility function, which implies that (in symmetric equilibria) all products within an industry should have the *same* degree of substitutability with other goods.

The second assumption made by DS is that u is homothetic in both its arguments. This combined with separability allows the consumer's decision to be characterised as one of two-stage budgeting, which simplifies the derivations a lot. It also leads naturally to general equilibrium applications, especially in trade theory, where the assumption of homotheticity, though patently unrealistic, is routinely made to allow a focus on supply-side determinants of trade patterns. DS themselves noted that their specification differed from that of Spence (1976), published in the preceding year, who assumed that preferences were quasi-linear: $u = x_0 + V(x_1, \ldots, x_n)$. This difference in assumptions had relatively minor implications for the Chamberlinian issues with which both papers were concerned; but it ensured that the DS specification was better suited to general equilibrium applications.

Just as important as the assumptions of separability and homotheticity was what was not in the utility function: no Hotelling beaches, Gorman–Lancaster characteristics or other indirect ways of modelling tastes for differentiated products. Instead, DS invoked the elementary property of convexity of indifference curves, with the utility function defined over consumption of all possible (not just actual) varieties. This made it a much simpler and more tractable way of modelling a preference for diversity.

Even with all this, DS might have had few emulators if they had not considered three further technical restrictions on the utility function U: symmetry of V in the x_i; a CES form for V; and a Cobb–Douglas form for U itself. DS themselves explored the implications of these three assumptions two at a time. However, most applications to trade, with only a few exceptions which I will mention below, have adopted all three. Indeed, it is now standard to refer to this very special case as 'Dixit–Stiglitz preferences', confirming that the paper has taken the first step on the road to classic status: to be widely cited but never read. (The second step, to be widely quoted but never cited, is probably imminent.) Since DS themselves did not use this special case, perhaps 'Dixit–Stiglitz lite' would be a better label.

Incorporating these restrictions, the utility function (8.1) becomes:

$$u = x_0^{1-\mu} V^\mu, \qquad V^\rho = \sum_{i=1}^{n} x_i^\rho. \tag{8.2}$$

Here μ is the share of nominal income Y spent on manufactures, while ρ measures the substitutability between varieties: ρ must be positive (since some of the x_i may be zero) and less than one (to ensure concavity).

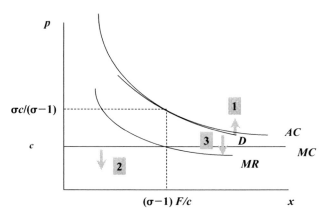

Figure 8.1   Chamberlin–Dixit–Stiglitz equilibrium

The elasticity of substitution between varieties, σ, is in turn related to ρ: $\sigma \equiv 1/(1 - \rho)$; so σ must exceed one. Utility maximisation leads to demand functions for individual varieties, which are log-linear in own price p_i and in total spending on manufactures μY, both deflated by a manufacturing price index P:

$$x_i = \mu \left(\frac{p_i}{P}\right)^{-\sigma} \frac{Y}{P} \qquad \text{where} \qquad P^{1-\sigma} = \sum_{j=1}^{n} p_j^{1-\sigma}. \qquad (8.3)$$

8.2.2   Production and equilibrium

Turning to producers, DS made two key simplifications. First, they modelled increasing returns in an ingeniously parsimonious way: 'It is easy and probably not too unrealistic to model scale economies by supposing that each potential commodity involves some fixed set-up cost and has a constant marginal cost' (DS, p. 297). Denoting the latter by F and c, respectively, the marginal cost curve is horizontal at the level c, and the average cost curve, equal to $c + F/x$, is a rectangular hyperbola with respect to the vertical axis and the marginal cost curve. See figure 8.1, where the curves are labelled MC and AC, respectively. Since all firms are identical, subscripts can be dropped from here on.

Second, DS implemented the Chamberlinian tradition of atomistic firms with no perceived interdependence by assuming that each firm takes income Y and the industry price index P as fixed when choosing its own price (more on this in section 8.4). Equation (8.3) is then a simple constant-elasticity demand function, with the elasticity of demand equal to σ, and marginal revenue in turn is a constant fraction of price:

$$MR = \frac{\sigma - 1}{\sigma} \, p. \tag{8.4}$$

The implied demand and marginal revenue curves are also illustrated in figure 8.1, labelled D and MR, respectively.

Equilibrium now exhibits the familiar Chamberlinian properties. Profit maximisation sets marginal revenue equal to marginal cost, while free entry sets price equal to average cost. For both conditions to hold, the famous tangency condition between the demand and average cost curves must be met, as figure 8.1 illustrates. Moreover, the special functional forms yield very simple solutions for equilibrium price and output. The price–marginal cost markup depends only on the elasticity of substitution σ:

$$\frac{\sigma - 1}{\sigma} \, p = c. \tag{8.5}$$

While the level of output depends only on the cost parameters F and c and on σ:

$$x = (\sigma - 1)\frac{F}{c}. \tag{8.6}$$

Changes in any other parameters or variables lead to adjustments in industry output via changes in the number of firms only.

8.2.3   Empirical anomalies

This completes the basic DS apparatus. To explain why it came to be applied to trade issues, I must digress to recall the empirical background.

Two strands of empirical work in the 1960s and 1970s had led to increasing questioning of the then-dominant competitive paradigm and especially of the Heckscher–Ohlin model. First was the finding that a great deal of international trade consisted of two-way trade in apparently similar goods. Ever since Ricardo's example of England and Portugal exchanging cloth for wine, trade theory had sought to explain the pattern of *inter*-industry trade. But it became increasingly clear that much trade did not fit that pattern. Rather it seemed to be better described as *intra*-industry. Careful empirical work by Grubel and Lloyd (1975) showed that this was not just an artefact of aggregation. Even when trade data were finely disaggregated, intra-industry trade continued to account for a large fraction of total trade. This seemed particularly true of trade between advanced countries, which in turn raised a further paradox. Trade based on comparative advantage arises from *differences* between countries (differences in technology for Ricardo, in factor endowments for Heckscher–Ohlin). But the evidence suggested that trade volumes were highest between countries that were *similar* in terms of incomes, technology and stage of development.

The second set of empirical findings concerned the degree of disruption induced by trade liberalisation. Studies by Balassa (1967) and others of the effects of the European Economic Community (EEC) in the 1950s and 1960s showed that adjustment to tariff reductions required surprisingly little change in the scale of industrial sectors. Rather it seemed to take the form of specialisation *within* sectors, as increased competition forced consolidation of product lines. As a result, the reduction of trade barriers between countries at similar stages of development did not impose large costs of adjustment.

Both of these findings were in conflict with the trade theory of the day and generated much talk of the need for a new paradigm. Was the work of Balassa, Grubel and Lloyd by itself sufficient to stimulate a new approach? I believe that it was not. The Leontief Paradox had not led to the abandonment of Heckscher–Ohlin trade theory in the 1950s, for the good reason that no other satisfactory general equilibrium theory of trade was available. Moreover, criticism of international trade theory (and indeed of neoclassical economic theory as a whole) for its neglect of imperfect competition had been widespread for many decades. What was new in the late 1970s was simultaneous progress in the theory of industrial organisation, and especially the development of the DS approach, which provided a framework in which the empirical anomalies could be explained and, ultimately, integrated with traditional theory.

8.2.4   *Product differentiation as a cause of trade*

Applications of DS to trade issues were not slow in coming. The first to be written appears to have been a 1976 paper by Victor Norman (which also showed how to integrate the new approach with Heckscher–Ohlin theory, the subject of the next sub-section).[2] However, the first to be published and the neatest example was Krugman (1979).

To see Krugman's results, consider the special case of (8.2) with no numéraire good (or, equivalently, with $\mu = 1$).[3] Let labour be the only

---

[2] Dixit and Norman (1980), p. 281, introduce their section 9.3 with the words 'The model is based on Norman (1976), but has several similarities with Krugman (1978a, 1978b)'. The Krugman papers are cited here as Krugman (1979) and (1980) respectively. Neither cites Norman or Dixit and Norman.

[3] In other respects Krugman (1979) used a somewhat more general version of the DS model than (8.2), which I discuss in section 8.4.

factor of production and take it as numéraire. The aggregate resource constraint is then $L = n(F + cx)$. Using (8.6) to eliminate x, the equilibrium number of varieties produced equals $L/(\sigma F)$. This is unaffected by opening the economy up to trade with a foreign country: the equilibrium illustrated in figure 8.1 is unchanged. The only effect is that consumers have a wider choice. Since they prefer diversity, they consume foreign as well as home varieties: more varieties in total, with less consumption of each.

Note that the two countries may be *ex ante* identical in this case. Hence the DS model implies that trade will take place between countries with identical technology and factor endowments. Moreover, the pattern of trade, with countries exchanging relatively similar differentiated products, is consistent with the empirical evidence on the importance of intra-industry trade. *All* trade is intra-industry, consumers unambiguously gain from greater variety, and trade liberalisation need not imply any changes in relative sector sizes, consistent with the evidence of Balassa (1967) cited in sub-section 8.2.3.

8.2.5   *The return of factor endowments*

Showing that monopolistic competition could be an independent source of trade, and that the outcome resembled real-world intra-industry trade, was a useful contribution. However, it is unlikely that it would have come to dominate the literature if it had not been integrated with the standard Heckscher–Ohlin approach. In fact, this integration was carried out almost immediately. Here the main original contributions were Dixit and Norman (1980, section 9.3), Helpman (1981) and Ethier (1982).[4] (All three of these were circulated at least as early as 1979. Ethier, 1979, may have been the first to explain intra-industry trade between similar economies, though as discussed in the next sub-section, his model lacked satisfactory microfoundations.)

Return to the two-sector specification in (8.2). Think of the numéraire good as labour-intensive 'agriculture', produced under constant returns to scale by a competitive sector. Similarly, think of the differentiated products as capital-intensive 'manufactures'. Finally, in the tradition of the Heckscher–Ohlin–Samuelson model, assume two countries and confine attention to free-trade equilibria in which both sectors remain active

---

[4] Krugman (1981) also looked at the interaction of factor endowments and monopolistic competition, but only for a special case of symmetric international endowment differences.

in both countries and in which factor prices are equalised internationally. Once again, figure 8.1 (with factor prices suitably normalised) illustrates any such trading equilibrium.

The key idea is that Heckscher–Ohlin trade is driven by *differences* between countries, whereas DS trade is driven by *similarities*. Heckscher–Ohlin, like any comparative advantage-based theory, postulates international differences (specifically, in factor endowments) which generate differences in equilibrium autarky prices and hence an incentive to trade. The greater the differences, the greater the volume of trade is likely to be. (With factor-price equalisation, two countries, and fixed world factor endowments, this result is strengthened: the volume of inter-industry trade is a linear function of the differences in factor endowments.) By contrast, under DS assumptions, each variety is unique, and consumers want to consume as many varieties as possible. Hence the volume of trade between two countries will be greatest when they are identical in size. Combining the two sources of trade leaves the results basically unchanged, except of course that the Heckscher–Ohlin prediction applies to inter-industry trade and the DS one to intra-industry trade. This synthesis was consistent with the empirical evidence on intra-industry trade discussed in sub-section 8.2.3; it has proved empirically fruitful (see sub-section 8.2.8); and it constitutes one of the major 'bottom-line' messages of the new trade theory.

8.2.6   Intermediate goods

All the papers discussed so far considered trade in final goods only. By contrast, intermediate goods constitute a much higher fraction of world trade, one of the considerations which motivated Ethier (1982) to extend the DS approach to trade in differentiated intermediate goods. He used the same functional form as the right-hand side of (8.2), but reinterpreted 'V' as a production function rather than a sub-utility function. Hence the driving force in the model is not that more varieties raise consumers' utility but rather that they increase total factor productivity. He showed that the implications which held in models with differentiated consumer goods, for intra- and inter-industry trade, and for the distributional consequences of trade policy, continued to hold.[5] More importantly, he showed that increased specialisation leads to productivity gains which depend on the world rather than the national scale of the industry.

---

[5] Whence the assertion by Krugman (1989, p. 1186) that the extension to differentiated intermediate goods makes little difference.

Extending Adam Smith's vision, the division of labour is limited by the extent of the *global* rather than the local market: production of inputs need not be geographically concentrated. This specification provided a microeconomic rationale for a model of *international* returns to trade (in contrast with traditional national returns to scale) which Ethier (1979) had earlier explored. It has also proved very influential in growth theory. Romer (1987, 1990) adopted Ethier's specification explicitly in his work on endogenous growth, where increasing returns arise from specialisation in the production of intermediate inputs. Subsequent work on growth in both closed and open economies, covered in other contributions to this conference, has made extensive use of the DS specification to model horizontal product differentiation.

8.2.7   New trade theory goes global: multinationals and economic geography

So far, I have described the applications of new trade theory to important old questions: the pattern of trade and the consequences of trade liberalisation. However, it was not long before the new approach was also applied to questions which had not been previously addressed. The first of these was the rationale for multinational corporations, which could not be explained in a competitive framework. Helpman (1984) extended the DS approach to explain why a firm might choose to vertically disintegrate. He postulated the existence of different activities within the firm: in the simplest case, production of a final good required both 'headquarter services' (finance, marketing, R&D, etc.) and manufacturing. Crucially, these two activities had different factor intensities, so it would be profitable to locate different activities in countries with factor endowments appropriate to them. For example, if manufacturing is more unskilled-labour-intensive, it would be located in the more unskilled-labour-abundant country. (In Helpman's model, the fact that all firms behaved in this way would by itself equalise factor prices, but nevertheless the initial incentive for vertical disintegration came from an incipient divergence of factor prices.)

The second novel issue to which new trade theory came to be applied was the possibility of industrial agglomeration. Krugman (1980) had allowed for transport costs on monopolistically competitive goods and had shown that they generate a 'home-market effect'. A rise in the number of home firms is associated with a fall in the local price index for manufactures (since home-produced varieties do not incur transport costs, whereas imported ones do). Since (at initial wages) an increase in home demand can be accommodated only by a fall in the local price index, it leads to a magnified increase in the number of home firms. Hence larger countries produce disproportionately more manufacturing varieties and so tend to export them.

The home-market effect is of some interest in itself, but since it takes incomes as exogenous its implications were unclear. Hence the lead was not followed for some time, not least by Krugman himself, who in his book with Helpman (Helpman and Krugman, 1985) concentrated on the case discussed in section 8.2.4 where all trade barriers are absent so factor prices are equalised internationally. In Krugman (1991) he returned to his 1980 model and made incomes endogenous by adding the possibility of international factor mobility. Now the home-market effect generates a 'demand linkage': an extra firm in one country raises demand for labour there which encourages in-migration; the resulting increase in local demand raises profits which encourages more firms to enter, and so on, in a process reminiscent of the Keynesian multiplier or the 'cumulative processes' of 1950s development economics. (With the difference that, as in many other contexts surveyed by Matsuyama, 1995, they now have a simple but rigorous theoretical foundation.) This effect shifts the demand and marginal revenue curves upwards in figure 8.1, as indicated by the arrow numbered '1'. The fact that larger countries have lower price levels also generates a 'cost linkage' since this too encourages further in-migration (workers are attracted by the lower cost of living in a large location). The resulting fall in local wages shifts the average and marginal cost curves downwards, as indicated by the arrow numbered '2'. Both these linkages therefore tend to encourage agglomeration. However, this outcome is not inevitable, since there is always an orthodox competition effect which tends to lower profits and so work against agglomeration: the fall in the local price index shifts the demand and marginal revenue curves downwards, as indicated by the arrow numbered '3'. Whether agglomeration results or not depends on the balance between these competing forces, which in turn depends on the underlying parameters of the model: transport costs work against agglomeration, while high demand (i.e. a higher value of μ) and a high preference for diversity (i.e. a *lower* value for σ) work in favour of it.

While international labour mobility on the scale needed may seem implausible, Venables (1996) showed that the same outcomes could arise in a model with no migration but with intermediate goods. These two mechanisms form the basis for what Krugman has termed the 'new economic geography'. Though it has not met with universal enthusiasm (for reasons I discuss in Neary, 2001), it undoubtedly represents an interesting development.

8.2.8   The proof of the pudding?: testing the new trade theory

As I have noted, the starting point of the new trade theory was a dissatisfaction with the alleged inability of traditional competitive theories to explain the observed patterns of international trade. Hence one might expect that the widespread acceptance of the new approach arose from its empirical success. But in fact this was not the case. Though the early theoretical papers made much of the *plausibility* of their stories and their consistency with stylised facts, they did not attempt to test the new theories formally.[6] When such testing did eventually come, the results were mixed. Even for Krugman (1994, p. 20): 'It must be admitted that the state of empirical work on the new trade theory is a bit disappointing.'

The first attempt to test the predictions of the models based on DS was that of Helpman (1987). He specified an empirical model consistent with the theory and showed that it gave a plausible account of the level and pattern of intra-industry trade. In particular, bilateral intra-industry trade was closely related to relative country sizes. However, subsequent work questioned whether this was indeed a test of the monopolistically competitive theory. As reviewed by Deardorff (1998), the central issue is that Helpman's specification, often called a 'gravity equation' since it resembles Newton's law of gravity, is consistent with any theory in which countries specialise in different goods. Helpman (1998) in response has questioned whether alternative theories can account for the observed trade patterns. But the fact that there is no clear discriminating test between perfectly and monopolistically competitive trade theories is a drawback. Leamer and Levinsohn (1995), in their influential survey paper, have responded with the nihilistic advice 'Estimate, do not test', but taken literally this would preclude the application of scientific method to this field.

When transport costs are admitted to the model, however, it is possible to devise a test which can in principle discriminate between perfectly and monopolistically competitive models. A series of papers by Davis and Weinstein (e.g. 1998) have implemented this idea. (Their research is mostly unpublished, so a summary may be premature. I discuss it in more detail in Neary, 2001, section 6.) They draw on Krugman's 'home-market effect' (discussed in section 8.2.7) which predicts that, in monopolistically competitive models, a larger home market should encourage exports. By contrast, competitive models predict that it should encourage imports. The results of their tests are close to a tie, with monopolistic competition

---

[6] Note I am not suggesting that the *same* people who make theoretical contributions should be expected to check their empirical validity. Taken literally, this would forgo all the benefits of division of labour within the economics profession.

apparently accounting for just over 50 per cent of OECD trade in manufactures.

Clearly this line of research is important and may yet coalesce into a coherent picture of the empirical value of the new approach. For the present, the results are sufficiently mixed that both proponents and opponents of the new approach can derive some satisfaction from them.

8.3   An extension

[M]odeling the role of economies of scale as a cause of trade . . . requires that the impact of increasing returns on market structure be somehow taken into account, but in this literature the main concern is usually to get the issue of market structure out of the way as simply as possible. (Krugman, 1989, p. 1179)

The main response to decreasing costs on the part of mainstream 'new' trade theory has been to muffle the impact of scale economies by 'convexifying' assumptions, e.g. the Dixit–Stiglitz (1977) model of monopolistic competition in which firms' profitability gains from returns to scale are strictly limited by consumers' desires for product diversity. (Ocampo and Taylor, 1998, p. 1524)

A striking feature of general equilibrium models with monopolistic competition à la DS, especially when they assume international factor-price equalisation, is that they end up looking very like competitive equilibrium models, except with more interesting interpretations. This can be seen as either a positive or negative feature, as my two quotations above, respectively, show. To illustrate how this happens, let me work through a simple model which has the additional virtue of being new.

My starting point is Helpman's theory of multinational corporations, discussed in section 8.2. Recall that Helpman assumed that multinational corporations were vertically integrated firms engaged in monopolistic competition. Different activities within the firm had different factor intensities, and so each firm had an incentive to vertically disintegrate, locating in different countries in a way which matched the factor demands of each activity with local factor supplies. This gave a plausible description of multinational activity, which has proved influential in subsequent work. However, it made one key counter-factual prediction: multinationals could emerge only between countries with very different relative factor endowments. Even moderate similarity between countries in their relative factor endowments implied that factor prices were equalised when firms were solely national, and so there was no incentive to go multinational.

A number of authors have addressed this deficiency of the Helpman model. Ethier (1986) models firms' behaviour in a context where the outcome of R&D (headquarter services in Helpman's terminology) is uncertain, but it is not possible to write a state-contingent contract with an outside firm. The greater the costs of a poor R&D outcome, therefore, the greater the incentives firms have to internalise their downstream activities. The resulting model predicts when firms will choose to become multinational and operate their own plants in foreign countries (in Dunning's terminology, to 'internalise' their production activities) rather than to license their technology to foreign firms: a choice which is taken for granted in Helpman's model and in mine. In the process it provides an explanation of intra-industry foreign direct investment. An alternative approach adopted by Markusen and Venables (1998) is to assume that there are international transport costs, so that firms locate production facilities abroad if the fixed costs of operating an extra plant are outweighed by the advantages of better market access. Both these approaches are of interest, and both allow for multinationals to emerge between similar economies. However, these models are more complicated than mine, and by way of compensation, they assume that goods are homogeneous. Here I sketch an alternative model which stays closer to Helpman but abandons the Heckscher–Ohlin assumptions about factor markets.

The approach I adopt generalises the specific-factors model to allow for multinational corporations.[7] Assume a two-country world with two sectors, agriculture and industry, and three factors, land, unskilled labour and skilled labour. All three factors are internationally immobile and only unskilled labour is intersectorally mobile. Agriculture requires land as well as unskilled labour. Industry consists of two activities, headquarter services and manufacturing. Both require skilled as well as unskilled labour, with headquarter services more skill-intensive.

The equilibrium of the model is now easily illustrated, using a diagrammatic technique introduced by Dixit and Norman.[8] Assume first that all factors can move freely across international boundaries. In the resulting 'integrated equilibrium', goods prices, factor prices and factor intensities are determined. In figure 8.2, *OB* represents the land and unskilled labour used in the production of agriculture, while *OA* represents the unskilled labour used to produce industrial goods (at both stages of production) along with skilled labour. Assume for concreteness that, when we diverge from the integrated equilibrium, the endowment of skilled labour is equally divided between the two countries. Then, the line

---

[7] See Neary (1978) for references on the specific-factors model and Caves (1971) for an early discussion of multinational corporations in that context.

[8] The trick is to combine the Edgeworth–Bowley boxes for two countries in a world box, and to consider the effects of changes in relative endowments as movements of the endowment point within the box. With three factors, the world Edgeworth–Bowley box is three-dimensional. Dixit and Norman (1980, p. 124) consider a cross-section parallel to the axis of one of the specific factors, whereas figure 8.2 illustrates the external face of the world box, perpendicular to the skilled labour axis.

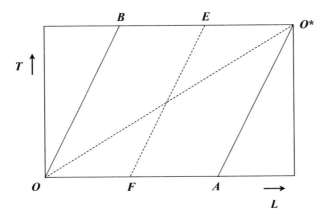

Figure 8.2   World factor endowments

EF denotes the factor-price equalisation set: only if land and unskilled labour endowments lie along this line will it be possible, in the absence of multinational corporations, to produce the same vector of goods as in the integrated equilibrium.

The role of multinational corporations now becomes clear. If the endowments of land and unskilled labour do not lie along the line *EF*, there is an incentive to relocate the more unskilled-labour-intensive manufacturing activities to the country with the lower unskilled wages. The process of relocating such activities will itself tend to equalise unskilled wages internationally. Provided endowments lie in the set *OBO*A*, and provided techniques in headquarter services and manufacturing are sufficiently different, it will be possible to find an allocation of activities between countries which replicates the integrated equilibrium. Intra-industry trade will occur for all distributions of factor endowments. Inter-industry trade will occur (given homothetic tastes) provided the equilibrium does not lie at the point of intersection of the diagonal *OO** and the line *EF*. Finally, multinational activity will occur provided the endowment point does not lie along *EF*. Clearly it is possible to have either high or low levels of multinational activity coexisting with either high or low levels of inter-industry trade: trade and multinational activity may be either substitutes or complements. Moreover, the model shows how multinational corporations can emerge even between countries with similar (though not identical) factor endowments.

Finally, note that the model is isomorphic to a competitive model with the same assumptions about factor markets except that skilled labour is internationally mobile. (The dynamics of that model are worked out in

Neary, 1995.) As my quotations on p. 171 suggest, the DS approach can be seen either as a brilliantly parsimonious approach to incorporating product differentiation and returns to scale into general equilibrium, or as a sleight of hand which forces these features into a largely neoclassical mould. In the next section I turn to consider the objections in more detail.

8.4   Lacunae

[O]ligopolistic markets seem empirically more important than those that combine atomism with product differentiation. (Bain, 1967, p. 175)

We have seen that the DS specification is extremely tractable and, because it embodies homotheticity, it lends itself easily to general equilibrium applications. But there is a price to be paid for this. The relatively clean functional forms for demand and supply impose a variety of special assumptions. And, like all versions of monopolistic competition, it neglects many issues which the modern theory of industrial organisation highlights.

8.4.1   Variety

Taste for variety was DS' starting point, so it is appropriate to begin by considering their treatment of it. In symmetric equilibria, utility rises steeply with the number of varieties for a given total outlay, all the more so the lower is σ. Figure 8.3 conveys the same information from a different perspective, showing how rapidly the true cost of living falls with the number of varieties.[9] Those familiar with the debates prompted by the Boskin Commission's report (which concluded that, because of substitution and other biases, the US consumer price index over-estimates the growth in the true cost of living by up to $1\frac{1}{2}$ percentage points per annum) may be surprised to see product diversity alone causing the true index to lie so far below the market prices of all goods. In a trade context, an implication is that greater product diversity can be a major source of gains from trade. Dixit himself has an elegant paper showing how this suggests a more benign view than usual of the

---

[9] The price of each individual variety, p, is normalised to unity in figure 8.3. From section 8.2.1, $\ln V = \ln x + [\sigma/(\sigma - 1)]\ln n$. Letting $I = npx$ denote total expenditure on the differentiated goods, and eliminating x, we can solve for the indirect utility function: $\ln V = \ln(I/p) + [1/(\sigma - 1)]\ln n$. Hence utility is increasing in n and convex for σ less than 2. Inverting (or, alternatively, solving from (8.3)), the true cost-of-living index in symmetric equilibria is: $\ln P = \ln p - [1/(\sigma - 1)]\ln n$. This is decreasing and convex in n.

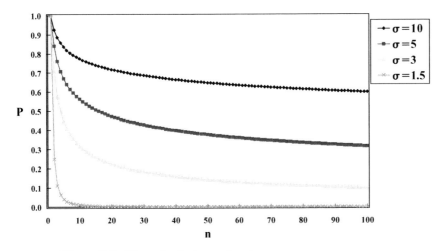

Figure 8.3 The price index and variety

implications for developing countries of long-term trends in the terms of trade (Dixit, 1984). But does this optimistic perspective not follow directly from the assumptions? Variety may be the spice of life, but is it really so tasty?

One way out of this difficulty is suggested by Ethier (1982). The standard DS specification conflates two distinct aspects of consumer behaviour, responsiveness to price and taste for diversity. Ethier's generalisation disentangles the two:[10]

$$V = n^\gamma \left[\sum_{i=1}^{n} \frac{x_i^\rho}{n} \right]^{1/\rho}. \tag{8.7}$$

The specification is unwieldy, but it has a nice implication. The parameter σ (equal as before to $1/(1-\rho)$) continues to measure the elasticity of demand and hence the market power of a typical firm. By contrast, the parameter γ measures the preference for diversity (or, in a production context, the gains from specialisation).[11] These two parameters can be varied independently, whereas the usual specification, which implicitly sets γ equal to $1/\rho$ or $\sigma/(\sigma-1)$, does not permit this. In particular, it

[10] This specification has had a shadowy history. It first appeared in a working paper version of the original DS paper (Dixit and Stiglitz, 1975, section 4), with the rationalisation that diversity as measured by n was a public good. However, this discussion was omitted in the published version. It was independently rediscovered in a consumption context by Bénassy (1996) and Broer and Heijdra (2001).

[11] As in n. 9, V equals xn^γ in symmetric equilibria. Constant total outlay then implies that $\ln V = \ln(I/p) + (\gamma - 1)\ln n$. So $\gamma - 1$ measures the preference for diversity.

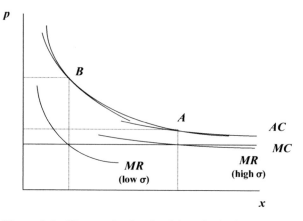

Figure 8.4   Changes in the elasticity of substitution

is possible to assume a very low preference for diversity (γ close to one) while still allowing demand elasticities to be relatively low.

Yet the worry remains that, even when extended in this way, the DS specification imposes too benign a view of product diversity. It clearly fails to capture one of the concerns of anti-globalisation protesters: that liberalising trade may reduce rather than increase variety. Explaining this possibility would require taking account of both consumer heterogeneity and asymmetries between goods in the degree to which they benefit from economies of scale, especially in distribution.[12]

8.4.2   Returns to scale

As we have just seen, σ serves two roles in describing preferences. It is often pressed into service for a third, as an inverse measure of 'equilibrium returns to scale'. Figure 8.4 (from Neary, 2001a) illustrates how the equilibrium of the firm is affected by a reduction in the elasticity of substitution. This implies that demand becomes less elastic, products become more differentiated, and there is a greater preference for diversity. As a result, the equilibrium moves from A to B: other things equal, average firm output falls and more varieties are produced. It is also true that the average cost curve is more steeply sloped and that many conventional measures would suggest that returns to scale are greater. (Note that $\sigma/(\sigma - 1)$, which has risen, equals the equilibrium ratio of the composite factor's marginal product to its average product, or one over the output

[12] Francois and van Ypersele (2000) present an interesting model which goes in this direction.

elasticity of total costs.) But it is clear that technology is unchanged: saying that returns to scale are greater at B does not correspond to what we usually mean when we discuss differences between industries.

If σ is given, and if the cost parameters are unchanged, then (8.6) shows that the output of each firm is given. In particular, it cannot be affected by trade policy. This is an unsatisfactory and counter-factual property. It can be overcome by working with a more general version of the basic model, drawn from section II of DS. Instead of a CES utility function for manufactures, this assumes a general additively separable form:

$$V = \sum_{i=1}^{n} v(x_i). \tag{8.8}$$

As DS showed, the elasticity of demand is inversely related to the curvature of the function v: $\varepsilon_i = -v'/(v''x_i)$; and, as Krugman (1979) showed, the derivative of this elasticity with respect to output, $d\varepsilon_i/dx_i$, determines the response of firm output to an expansion in market demand. In particular, average firm size rises provided this derivative is negative. The latter assumption is plausible, and so the extended DS model rationalises the empirical observations of Balassa mentioned in sub-section 8.2.3.[13] However, the specification in (8.8) has not proved tractable, and from Dixit and Norman (1980) and Krugman (1980) onwards, most writers have used the CES specification in (8.2), with its unsatisfactory implications that firm size is fixed by tastes and technology, and all adjustments in industry size (due to changes in trade policy, for example) come about through changes in the number of firms.[14]

8.4.3 Entry

Where entering firms come from, and where exiting ones go to, is never explained in models of monopolistic competition, any more than it is in models of perfect competition. New firms, exact replicas of existing firms, are assumed ready to spring up like dragon's teeth whenever a

[13] Krugman justified this assumption 'without apology' since it 'seems plausible' and 'seems to be necessary if the model is to yield reasonable results'. It can be shown that, as with many results in imperfectly competitive models, it must hold provided demand is not 'too' convex. The elasticity of ε_i with respect to x_i equals $1 + 1/\varepsilon_i + \rho_i$, where ρ_i equals $-x_i v'''/v''$ and is a measure of the concavity of the demand function.

[14] There is, however, a mechanism whereby firm size can be influenced by extra-industry influences even in the simple DS model. Lawrence and Spiller (1983) and Flam and Helpman (1987) allow for differences in factor proportions between fixed costs and variable costs. Hence general equilibrium effects on relative factor prices lead to changes in equilibrium size. This effect is absent from most applications of the DS approach, which assume that the production function is homothetic, so that fixed and variable costs have identical factor proportions.

tiny profit opportunity presents itself; and existing firms exit without a murmur following any downturn in industry fortunes. This is justified as a long-run or equilibrium assumption. But, except over secular time horizons, it seems particularly inappropriate in applications to countries at different stages of economic development. Even in a developed-country context, it is unsatisfactory from many points of view. It implies that there is no value to incumbency, no learning by doing and no binding limit on the supply of entrepreneurial skills. Of course I am not saying that models with 'unlimited supplies of firms' are useless. But even a cursory consideration of modern industry suggests that they provide a plausible description of very few sectors.

8.4.4   Strategies

My final worry about the DS approach is reflected in the contributions to this volume. DS has been extensively applied in many fields, but it has had relatively little influence on the field of industrial organisation itself. This is an IO model for export only! It is far removed from the concerns of IO practitioners (theorists of course, but also a growing body of empirical scholars) with all aspects of 'perceived interdependence' between firms.

The DS model ignores perceived interdependence to the extent of assuming myopic behaviour by firms. It explicitly assumed that each firm ignores the effects of its price–output decision on the industry price index. Yang and Heijdra (1993) suggested that this neglect was unnecessary, while d'Aspremont, Dos Santos Ferreira and Gérard-Varet (1996) pointed out that DS firms also ignore the 'Ford effect': the impact of their own pricing behaviour on income. Omitting these effects can be justified as an approximation, satisfactory for large n, and exact in the case of a continuum of firms.[15]

More serious in my view is that DS firms do not engage in any form of strategic behaviour. They cannot make commitments since they do not engage in any intertemporal behaviour. (Expenditures on fixed and variable costs are incurred simultaneously.) So investments in capacity, R&D or advertising ('selling costs' in Chamberlin's terminology) do not arise. For many purposes these omissions do not matter. But they restrict the usefulness of the model for discussing many aspects of industrial policy, technological progress or structural change.

---

[15] Ironically, the first version of DS, Dixit and Stiglitz (1974), assumed a continuum of firms. In the second version they switched to the discrete case, because (as they laconically explained in a footnote which was in turn omitted from the published version) [the] 'technical difficulties of that case led to unnecessary confusion' (Dixit and Stiglitz, 1975, p. 53 – see p. 92 in this volume).

My own conclusion is that, in its assumptions about entry and strategies, monopolistic competition resembles perfect competition much more than it resembles most models of oligopoly – and, arguably, more than it resembles the market structure of many industrial sectors in the real world (especially in relatively mature industries). This seems to have been the view of most pre-DS industrial economists (as in my quotation on p. 174 from Bain), and even of Chamberlin himself, who suggested that monopolistic competition was appropriate to the study of retail outlets, filling stations and other markets where the twin assumptions of atomistic firms and differentiated products fit the facts well. The relevance of the model to international trade in particular, where exporting firms are typically above-average in size and have significant market power, is more questionable.

What is needed is a GOLE: a theory of General Oligopolistic Equilibrium! There are formidable obstacles to developing such a theory. Even in partial equilibrium the predictions of oligopoly models suffer from indeterminateness and sensitivity to changes in solution concepts. Extending them to general equilibrium introduces further problems of non-existence and sensitivity to choice of numéraire which have been extensively discussed by theorists such as Gabszewicz and Vial (1972), Roberts and Sonnenschein (1977), Bohm (1994) and Dierker and Grodal (1999). Yet the pay-off to even modest progress in this direction would be enormous. Perhaps the way to go is to adopt some of the same technical tricks, such as symmetry and aggregation over many agents, which have made the DS approach to monopolistic competition so useful.[16]

8.5   Conclusion

I began with a quote from Harry Johnson's 1967 survey of monopolistic competition and international trade theory. Let me end with a second quote from the same source: 'what is required at this stage is to convert the theory from an analysis of the static equilibrium conditions of a monopolistically competitive industry ... into *an operationally relevant analytical tool* capable of facilitating the quantification of those aspects of real-life competition so elegantly comprehended and analyzed by Chamberlin but excluded by assumption from the mainstream of contemporary trade theory' (Johnson, 1967, p. 218, italics added).

In retrospect, Johnson articulated clearly what was missing from the literature on monopolistic competition in the decades between Chamberlin and Dixit–Stiglitz. The model's partial equilibrium implications had been

---

[16] For a sketch of a model along these lines, see Neary (2002).

worked out in geometric detail; and some of its insights had been incorporated into the general Arrow–Debreu model.[17] But it had little impact on the middle ground of applied theoretical fields which try to address real-world issues without neglecting economy-wide links between goods and factor markets. What was missing was 'an operationally relevant analytical tool' which would allow Chamberlinian insights to be incorporated into applications-oriented general equilibrium models. This was exactly what DS provided.

The pay-off to trade theory in particular has been immense. I have tried to show that the DS approach has thrown a great deal of light on many central issues in the field: the interaction between inter- and intra-industry trade, the nature of adjustment to trade liberalisation, the role of trade in intermediate goods, the basis for multinational corporations and the conditions favouring agglomeration. Nor are its potential applications exhausted. In section 8.3 I sketched a model which combines DS preferences with the specific-factors model, and provides a parsimonious explanation of why multinational corporations may emerge even between countries with similar factor endowments.

However, I have also argued that, contrary to the claims of Krugman (1994), DS-based trade theory tells many of the same 'big lies' as traditional competitive theory.[18] While it allows for differentiated products and increasing returns to scale, it retains the assumptions of identical, atomistic firms, free entry and no perceived interdependence. And of course, the price of tractability is a reliance on very special functional forms. These deficiencies do not matter for many purposes: the model makes distinctive predictions, and explains many phenomena which cannot even be discussed in a competitive framework. However, they make the model less relevant to many important issues than it may seem. And they call into question the extent to which it represents an advance in descriptive realism over traditional competitive models.

---

[17] Negishi, Nikaido and others had constructed models of general equilibrium with Chamberlinian monopolistic competition. However, they were primarily interested in issues of existence and stability under very general specifications, rather than in comparative statics implications, which as we now know require much more structure.

[18] The passage is worth quoting at length: 'All economic theory involves untrue simplifying assumptions. Traditional trade theory, however, makes its big untrue assumptions – constant returns, perfect competition – at the beginning of the game, and plays by strict rules thereafter. The result is that traditional models, especially the 2-by-2 Heckscher–Ohlin–Samuelson model, tend to have a spurious air of generality and necessity: once you have become accustomed to the big untruths, you lose sight of the essential unrealism of the set-up. By contrast new trade theory models *avoid these big lies* but make many small ones along the way in order to keep matters tractable; the theorist can never forget the degree of falsification involved' (Krugman, 1994, p. 15, italics added). As I hope I make clear in the text, it just ain't so.

Of course, a twenty-fifth birthday conference should be an occasion for celebration rather than complaint. So it may seem churlish to criticise the model, especially when one of the authors is present. I hope not: better to see my comments in section 8.4 as an agenda – or a wish-list – for future research than as criticisms of what has been achieved so far. And if the achievements of the monopolistic competition revolution in trade theory have sometimes been exaggerated, Dixit and Stiglitz cannot be held responsible for the more extreme claims of their followers. Indeed, their original paper contained no hint of the many applications which their approach would make possible. Maybe DS were lucky, in developing a persuasive but tractable model of monopolistic competition which had implications far beyond the IO topic which was their direct concern, and at just the moment when the empirical failures of competitive trade theory were being highlighted. But it would be more correct to say that it is the rest of us who have been lucky. Without the DS specification, trade theory, like many other fields, would have been much less exciting, and would have made much less progress, in the past quarter-century.

REFERENCES

Bain, J. S. (1967). Chamberlin's impact on microeconomic theory, in Kuenne, R. E. (ed.), *Monopolistic Competition Theory: Studies in Impact: Essays in Honor of Edward H. Chamberlin*. New York, Wiley

Balassa, B. (1967). *Trade Liberalization among Industrial Countries*. New York, McGraw-Hill

Bénassy, J.-P. (1996). Taste for variety and optimum production patterns in monopolistic competition. *Economics Letters*, 52: 41–47

Bohm, V. (1994). The foundation of the theory of monopolistic competition revisited. *Journal of Economic Theory*, 63: 208–218

Broer, D. P. and B. J. Heijdra (2001). The investment tax credit under monopolistic competition. *Oxford Economic Papers*, 53: 318–351, originally circulated as Research Memorandum 9603, OCFEB, Erasmus University, 1996

Caves, R. E. (1971). International corporations: the industrial economics of foreign investment. *Economica*, 38: 1–27.

Chamberlin, E. H. (1933). *The Theory of Monopolistic Competition*. Cambridge, MA, Harvard University Press

d'Aspremont, C., Dos Santos Ferreira, R. and Gérard-Varet, L.-A. (1996). On the Dixit–Stiglitz model of monopolistic competition. *American Economic Review*, 86: 623–629

Davis, D. R. and Weinstein, D. E. (1998). Market access, economic geography and comparative advantage: an empirical assessment. NBER Working Paper 6787

Deardorff, A. V. (1998). Determinants of bilateral trade: does gravity work in a neoclassical world?, in Frankel, J. A. (ed.), *The Regionalization of the World Economy*. Chicago, Chicago University Press

Dierker, E. and Grodal, B. (1999). The price normalization problem in imperfect competition and the objective of the firm. *Economic Theory*, 14: 257–284

Dixit, A. K. (1984). Growth and terms of trade under imperfect competition, in Kierzkowski, H. (ed.), *Monopolistic Competition and International Trade*. Oxford, Clarendon Press

Dixit, A. K. and Norman, V. (1980). *Theory of International Trade: A Dual, General Equilibrium Approach*. London, Cambridge University Press

Dixit, A. K. and Stiglitz, J. E. (1974). Monopolistic competition and optimum product diversity. Balliol College, Oxford and Cowles Foundation, Yale, mimeo; see chapter 3 in this volume

(1975). Monopolistic competition and optimum product diversity. Warwick and Stanford, mimeo; see chapter 4 in this volume

(1977). Monopolistic competition and optimum product diversity. *American Economic Review*, 67: 297–308

Ethier, W. J. (1979). Internationally decreasing costs and world trade. *Journal of International Economics*, 9: 1–24

(1982). National and international returns to scale in the theory of international trade. *American Economic Review*, 72: 389–405

(1986). The multinational firm. *Quarterly Journal of Economics*, 100: 805–833

(1987). The theory of international trade, in Officer, L. H. (ed.), *International Economics*. Dordrecht, Kluwer Academic Publishers

Flam, H. and Helpman, E. (1987). Industrial policy under monopolistic competition. *Journal of International Economics*, 22: 79–102

Francois, P. and van Ypersele, T. (2000). On the protection of cultural goods. Department of Economics, Tilburg University, mimeo

Fujita, M., Krugman, P. and Venables, A. J. (1999). *The Spatial Economy: Cities, Regions and International Trade*. Cambridge, MA, MIT Press

Fujita, M. and Thisse, J.-F. (2000). Agglomeration and market interaction. Presented to the World Congress of the Econometric Society, Seattle

Gabszewicz, J. and Vial, J. P. (1972). Oligopoly à la Cournot in a general equilibrium analysis. *Journal of Economic Theory*, 4: 381–400

Grubel, H. G. and Lloyd, P. J. (1975). *Intra-Industry Trade: The Theory and Measurement of International Trade in Differentiated Products*. London, Macmillan

Helpman, E. (1981). International trade in the presence of product differentiation, economies of scale, and monopolistic competition: a Chamberlin–Heckscher–Ohlin model. *Journal of International Economics*, 11: 305–340

(1984). A simple theory of international trade with multinational corporations. *Journal of Political Economy*, 92: 451–471

(1987). Imperfect competition and international trade: evidence from fourteen industrial countries. *Journal of the Japanese and International Economies*, 1: 62–81

(1990). *Monopolistic Competition in Trade Theory*, Special Papers in International Finance, 16. International Finance Section, Department of Economics, Princeton

(1998). The structure of foreign trade. CEPR Discussion Paper, 2020

Helpman, E. and Krugman, P. R. (1985). *Market Structure and Foreign Trade*. Cambridge, MA, MIT Press

Hicks, J. (1939). *Value and Capital.* Oxford, Clarendon Press

Johnson, H. G. (1967). International trade theory and monopolistic competition theory, in Kuenne, R. E. (ed.), *Monopolistic Competition Theory: Studies in Impact: Essays in Honor of Edward H. Chamberlin.* New York, John Wiley

Krugman, P. R. (1979). Increasing returns, monopolistic competition and international trade. *Journal of International Economics*, 9: 469–479

(1980). Scale economies, product differentiation and the pattern of trade. *American Economic Review*, 70: 950–959

(1981). Intraindustry specialization and the gains from trade. *Journal of Political Economy*, 89: 959–973

(1989). Industrial organization and international trade, in Schmalensee, R. and Willig, R. (eds.), *Handbook of Industrial Organisation*, 2. Amsterdam, North-Holland

(1991). Increasing returns and economic geography. *Journal of Political Economy*, 99: 483–499

(1994). Empirical evidence on the new trade theories: the current state of play, in *New Trade Theories: A Look at the Empirical Evidence*. London, CEPR

Lancaster, K. J. (1979). *Variety, Equity and Efficiency.* New York, Columbia University Press

(1980). Intraindustry trade under perfect monopolistic competition. *Journal of International Economics*, 10: 151–175

Lawrence, C. and Spiller, P. T. (1983). Product diversity, economies of scale, and international trade. *Quarterly Journal of Economics*, 98: 63–83

Leamer, E. E. and Levinsohn, J. (1995). International trade theory: the evidence, in Grossman, G. M. and Rogoff, K. (eds.), *Handbook of International Economics*, 3. Amsterdam, North-Holland

Markusen, J. R. and Venables, A. J. (1998). Multinational corporations and the new trade theory. *Journal of International Economics*, 46: 183–203

Matsuyama, K. (1995). Complementarities and cumulative process in models of monopolistic competition. *Journal of Economic Literature*, 33: 701–729

Neary, J. P. (1978). Short-run capital specificity and the pure theory of international trade. *Economic Journal*, 88: 488–510

(1995). Factor mobility and international trade. *Canadian Journal of Economics*, 28: S4–S23

(2001). Of hype and hyperbolas: introducing the new economic geography. *Journal of Economic Literature*, 39: 536–561

(2002). Competition, trade and wages, in Greenaway, D., Upward, R. and Wakelin, K. (eds.), *Trade, Investment, Migration and Labour Market Adjustment*, Basingstoke, Palgrave Macmillan

Norman, V. (1976). Product differentiation and trade. UK Economic Theory Study Group, University of Warwick, manuscript, downloadable from http://www.eco.rug.nl/~heijdra/norman76.pdf

Ocampo, J. A. and Taylor, L. (1998). Trade liberalisation in developing countries: modest benefits but problems with productivity growth, macro prices, and income distribution. *Economic Journal*, 108: 1523–1546

Roberts, D. J. and Sonnenschein, H. F. (1977). On the foundations of the theory of monopolistic competition. *Econometrica*, 45: 101–113

Romer, P. M. (1987). Growth based on increasing returns due to specialization. *American Economic Review, Papers and Proceedings*, 77: 56–72

(1990). Endogenous technological change. *Journal of Political Economy*, 98: 71–102

Spence, A. M. (1976). Product selection, fixed costs and monopolistic competition. *Review of Economic Studies*, 43: 217–236

Venables, A. J. (1996). Equilibrium locations of vertically linked industries. *International Economic Review*, 37: 341–359

Yang, X. and B. J. Heijdra (1993). Monopolistic competition and optimum product diversity: comment. *American Economic Review*, 83: 295–301

9 Monopolistically competitive provision of inputs: a geometric approach to the general equilibrium

Joseph Francois and Douglas Nelson

9.1   Introduction

As many have noted, following Chamberlin's (1933) classic work on the subject, monopolistic competition had a peculiar relationship to economic theory and research: widely recognised as important and featured in undergraduate treatments of industrial organisation (along with monopoly, oligopoly and perfect competition), but never quite becoming a central part of the discourse of mainline economic theory.[1] The fundamental contributions of A. Michael Spence (1976) and Avinash Dixit and Joseph Stiglitz (1977) changed this situation completely. With a tractable model capturing the essential elements of Chamberlin's analysis, monopolistic competition moved right to the centre of research on a wide range of economic topics.[2] Most of this volume celebrates this essential contribution. In this chapter we focus on an additional contribution of a very similar sort. A good bit further back than Chamberlin, Adam Smith analysed the way in which the division of labour is limited by the extent of the market. As with monopolistic competition, this notion was widely referred to and recognised as somehow important, but was never integrated into economic theory or research in a serious way.[3] Wilfred Ethier (1982a) recognised that if Dixit and Stiglitz's formal

---

[1] For early examples of the widespread recognition of the importance of monopolistic competition to economic theory in these early years, see the papers collected in Kuenne (1967). Much of the early work on the subject was concerned with differentiating between Chamberlin's work and that of Joan Robinson (1933). Interestingly, one might conclude from the ease with which Robinson's work entered into the foundations of research on imperfect competition that, until the contributions of Spence (1976) and Dixit and Stiglitz (1977), with the possible exception of Lancaster's (1966, 1971) important work, Robinson had had the best of this early clash.

[2] The particular centrality of the Dixit–Stiglitz paper lies in the clarity of presentation.

[3] Buchanan and Yoon (1994) is an exceptionally well selected volume of classic and contemporary papers on this subject. In looking at this volume, one is forcefully struck by the fact that, following Smith's identification of the phenomenon, Allyn Young's (1928) brilliant essay is the only substantial contribution until Ethier (1982a). The other papers essentially illustrate the fact that the idea continued to attract attention, without calling forth any way of going beyond what was already in Smith and Young.

structure was interpreted as a formal representation of the supply side of the economy, a tractable representation of division of labour, limited by the extent of the market, was readily at hand. While Ethier's model has now become an essential part of microeconomic, trade, growth, business cycle, urban–regional and public finance theory, it lacks a tractable, geometric representation useful for intuition generation and pedagogic purposes. Drawing on our recent work (Francois and Nelson, 2002a, hereafter FN), we present such a framework in this chapter and illustrate its application.

The central role of division of labour models in modern economic analysis is undeniable. Following Ethier's (1979, 1982a) original presentation of the model as a framework for studying the interaction between national and international returns to scale, the framework diffused rapidly throughout economic analysis. In international trade theory the model has been used to study trade patterns (Ethier, 1979, 1982a; Markusen, 1988, 1989; van Marrewijk *et al.*, 1997), trade policy (Markusen, 1990a; Francois, 1992, 1994; Lovely, 1997) and factor-market adjustment to trade (Burda and Dluhosch, 1999; Francois and Nelson, 2000; Lovely and Nelson, 2000). One of the most interesting recent applications uses the multiple equilibrium property of these models to derive north–south trade structures endogenously (Markusen, 1991; Krugman, 1995; Krugman and Venables, 1995; Matsuyama 1996; Puga and Venables, 1996; Venables, 1996a). Following the important work of Romer (1987, 1990), the Ethier model has also become a standard framework in endogenous growth theory (Barro and Sala-i-Martin, 1995, ch. 6) and has been used extensively in development theory (Rodríguez-Clare, 1996; Rodrik, 1996) and regional economics (Holtz-Eakin and Lovely, 1996a, 1996b; Fujita, Krugman and Venables, 1999).

In this chapter we proceed as follows. To provide some structure to the exercise, we have divided the general family of specialisation models into four types, which are specified in table 9.1. We begin with two versions of national production externality (NPE) models. In the first, a closed-economy version of the model (unimaginatively called model Type I in table 9.1), we develop our basic geometric framework in the simplest environment. Even in this simple context, we are able to illustrate basic mechanisms that have been highlighted in the literature on endogenous growth and development. From there we develop a NPE model of trade in final goods only (called model Type II), and demonstrate that this model is operationally identical to standard models of trade with national external economies of scale. The greatest conceptual and analytical difficulties emerge with international production externalities (IPE), which surface once trade in intermediate goods is permitted (model Types III and IV).

Table 9.1 *A classification of specialisation models*

		Trade structure	Description
National Production Externality Models	I	Closed economy	The properties of this type of model are those of an external scale economy model (Markusen, 1990a).
	II	Open economy (trade in final goods only)	*Markusen model*: Final goods production in each region will exhibit increasing returns due to specialisation (Markusen, 1989). However, without direct trade in intermediates, trade has no effect on the production structure of the economy. Model behaves like standard model of trade under external economies of scale.
International Production Externality Models	III	Trade in intermediates only (or intermediates and the standard good)	*Ethier model*: International economies of scale. Trade affects production conditions, so transformation functions are no longer technological facts (Ethier, 1982a). Without trading costs, this is identical to Type III, and this is where the scale of one regional sector will directly effect the efficiency of other sectors. Types III and IV diverge in interpretation with trading costs.
	IV	Trade in intermediates and final goods	

The graphical analysis makes the locus of this difficulty clear. The general treatment of IPE models is followed by an examination of imperfect factor mobility (section 9.4) and the link between globalisation and wages (section 9.5).

9.2 National production externalities in autarky: model I

9.2.1 The basic model

We assume that there are: two factors of production, labour (L) and capital (K); and two final consumption goods, wheat (W) and manufactures (M). Wheat is taken to be produced from K and L under a standard neoclassical technology represented by a production function $f(K_w, L_w)$ which is twice differentiable, linear homogeneous and strictly concave. Both factors are costlessly mobile between sectors and the markets for

K, L, W and M are perfectly competitive. Where demand is needed, it will be taken to be generated by a representative agent whose preferences can be represented by a twice differentiable, strictly quasi-concave, homothetic utility function defined over consumption of W and M. Division of labour models diverge from standard trade models in the technology of M production. M is produced by costless assembly of components (x). Components are produced from 'bundles' of K and L denoted m. The market for components is monopolistically competitive, and bundles production is perfectly competitive.

Ethier's key insight was that the Spence (1976)–Dixit–Stiglitz (1977) model of preference for variety, applied to international trade by Krugman (1979, 1980), when applied to production constitutes the basis of a model of division of labour. The model contains two main elements: (1) A technology reflecting increasing returns to 'division of labour'; and (2) something limiting the division of labour (i.e. 'the extent of the market').[4] The first element is given by a CES function that costlessly aggregates components (x_i) into finished manufactures:

$$M = \left[\sum_{i \in n} x_i^\phi \right]^{1/\phi}. \tag{9.1}$$

Here n types of components are costlessly assembled into final manufactures and ϕ is an indicator of the degree of substitutability between varieties of inputs (x_i).[5] In particular, note that if $x_i = x \; \forall \; I \in n$, (9.1) reduces to $M = n^{1/\phi} x$. Then, for n constant, output of manufactures is linearly related to output of components and if $0 < \phi < 1$ (as we assume it to be) there are increasing returns to the variety of inputs, i.e. $\partial M / \partial n = (1/\phi) n^{1/\phi - 1} x > 1$.[6] The smaller is ϕ, the stronger are the returns to the division of labour. As in the SDS formulation, fixed costs in the production of intermediates and finite resources limits the number of types of components produced and thus, since aggregate output of M is increasing in varieties of component types, economies of scale are limited by the extent of the market.

The transformation of the SDS model of preferences into a model of the division of labour, along with the trick of using 'bundles' of inputs in the production of intermediates, not only makes the model exceptionally tractable from an analytical point of view, but also lends itself to

---

[4] Appendix 1 of FN contains a full development of the Ethier model.

[5] Note the harmless abuse of good mathematical notation: n is being used as both the label of an index set and the number of elements in that set.

[6] Since, as we show in the appendix, x is constant in equilibrium, it is easy to see that the production of M is homogeneous of degree $1/\phi > 1$.

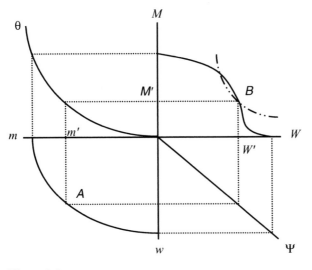

Figure 9.1

straightforward graphical representation. The first element of this representation is the *bundles transformation function*: $w = B(m)$. In each industry, 'bundles' of capital and labour are produced according to standard neoclassical production functions of K and L: $m = g(K_m, L_m)$ and $w = f(K_w, L_w)$. Since capital and labour exist in finite quantities, $\{\bar{K}, \bar{L}\}$, and if we assume, say, manufacturing is K-intensive relative to wheat at all relative factor prices, the bundles transformation function will have the usual concave shape. This is plotted in figure 9.1 in the SW quadrant. The NW and SE quadrants contain functions mapping bundles into final good outputs: $W = \psi(w)$ and $M = \theta(m)$. In the HOS case, $\psi(\cdot)$ is just a 45° line.[7]

The real core of the graphical analysis is the $\theta(\cdot)$ function. In mapping bundles into final manufactures, this function embodies the market structure assumptions in both production of intermediates (internal increasing returns due to fixed cost and monopolistic competition) and final assembly (external increasing returns due to division of labour). It is straightforward to show that:

$$M = \theta(m) = Am^{1/\phi}, \tag{9.2}$$

where A is a constant and, as shown in (9.1), ϕ is an indicator of the degree of substitutability between varieties of inputs. It will be useful in

---

[7] That is, the 'bundles', w, used in wheat production just are the inputs from standard analysis.

the later analysis to have expressions for the first and second derivatives of θ:

$$\theta'(m) = \frac{1}{\phi} A m^{1/\phi - 1} > 0, \qquad \theta''(m) = \frac{1}{\phi}\left(\frac{1}{\phi} - 1\right) A m^{1/\phi - 2} > 0.$$
(9.3)

Following Mayer's (1972, figure 1) analysis of production and trade under increasing returns to scale, we can use the information contained in the bundles transformation function and the two mapping relations to derive the transformation relation between final manufactures and wheat, $W = T(M)$, presented in the NE quadrant in figure 9.1. That is, every point on the bundles transformation curve, $B(\cdot)$, is mapped to a point on the final goods transformation curve, $T(\cdot)$.

Herberg and Kemp (1969) and Mayer (1972) have intensively studied precisely the system we have just described for the case of variable returns to scale in both sectors (in our notation, θ and ψ are both permitted to be non-linear). From Mayer (1972, p. 103) we have expressions for $T'(\cdot)$ and $T''(\cdot)$ in terms of θ, ψ, and $B(m)$. Note that in these expressions we are working with the inverses of B and T. That is, $\beta = B^{-1}$ and $\tau = T^{-1}$[8]

$$\tau' = \frac{dM}{dW} = \left(\frac{\theta'}{\psi'}\right)\beta', \quad \text{and} \quad \tau'' = \frac{d^2 M}{dW^2} = \frac{\theta'}{(\psi')^2}$$
$$\times \left[\left(\frac{\theta''}{\theta'}\right)(\beta')^2 \left(\frac{\psi''}{\psi'}\right)\beta' + \beta''\right].$$
(9.4)

In the baseline case of HOS structure for bundles production, $\psi' = 1$ and $\psi'' = 0$, so the expressions in (9.4) are considerably simplified to:

$$\tau' = \frac{dM}{dW} = \theta'\beta', \quad \text{and} \quad \tau'' = \frac{d^2 M}{dW^2} = \theta'\left[\left(\frac{\theta''}{\theta'}\right)(\beta')^2 + \beta''\right].$$
(9.5)

The expressions for τ' show the interaction between $B(\cdot)$, θ, and ψ that are illustrated at any point on $T(\cdot)$ frontier in the right panel of figure 9.1. As with Herberg–Kemp and Mayer, we are particularly interested in $T''(\cdot)$ if we want to know about the curvature of $T(\cdot)$.

We can show that if $\theta''/\theta' \to \infty$ as $m \to 0$, then the transformation function must be convex in the neighbourhood of zero manufacturing

---

[8] Since $B(m)$ is the standard HOS production frontier, we know that it possesses a unique inverse. We adopt this both for expositional convenience and because, as graphically portrayed, the slope in (W, M) space is naturally seen as dM/dW.

output.[9] Given the derived expressions in (9.3), it is easy to see that

$$\frac{\theta''}{\theta'} = \frac{1}{m}\left(\frac{1}{\phi} - 1\right) > 0 \tag{9.6}$$

which (since $0 < \phi < 1$) clearly approaches infinity as m approaches zero. This equation is just a measure of local curvature (like the Arrow–Pratt measure of absolute risk aversion). Thus, because the function taking m into M is extremely (i.e. almost infinitely) tightly curved in the neighbourhood of zero manufacturing output, the transformation function is pulled in toward the origin. As the β'' term in the expression for τ'' suggests, the concavity of $B(m)$ works against the convexity of θ and can produce a concave portion of $T(M)$ in the neighbourhood of zero W output. In particular, it is easy to see that (9.6) and β' both get smaller as the output of M increases, implying that the first term in the square brackets in (9.5) gets smaller. Unfortunately, while the first term should decline monotonically, unless we are willing to make some strong assumptions about the magnitude of T'', *we are unable to say anything definite about curvature away from the neighbourhood of zero M output*. This is an important point. The frontier may, in general, be characterised by multiple convexities and alternative stable and unstable regions.

9.2.2   *Ricardian variations*

Given the structure that we have developed to this point, it is easy to illustrate two standard variants of the basic model: the Ricardian and Ricardo–Viner technologies for bundle production. In the Ricardian case (Chipman 1970; Ethier 1982b; Gomory 1994) labour is the only productive factor, as a result the resource constraint takes the simple form of a straight line with a slope of negative unity in the SW quadrant (figure 9.2). Wheat is produced with a constant returns to scale production function, components are produced with a fixed and variable component (now paid entirely in labour) and manufactures are produced from components according to (9.1). We now have that the 'bundles' transformation function (i.e. the labour constraint) is characterised by $B' = -1$ and $B'' = 0$. Since ψ is still a linear map with a slope of 1, we derive $T' = -\theta'$ and $T'' = \theta''$. That is, the shape of the transformation function between finished manufactures and wheat is defined entirely by θ, and T is concave throughout its length. The explanation of this is quite clear in

[9] This is a result of Mayer's (1972, pp. 106–9) which refines a result originally presented in Herberg and Kemp (1968).

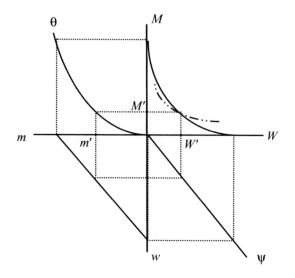

Figure 9.2   Ricardian technology for bundles production

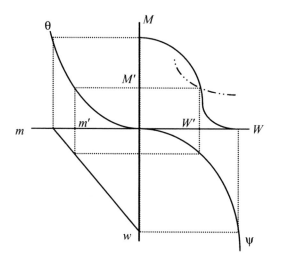

Figure 9.3   Ricardo–Viner technology for bundles production

figure 9.2 since the θ function is the only source of curvature, while both B and ψ have unit slopes.

The Ricardo–Viner structure (figure 9.3) has been extensively used in an important series of papers by Markusen (1988, 1989, 1990a, 1990b,

1991). Consider the simplest version of this model: wheat is produced with mobile labour and specific capital; components are produced with labour only (again there is a fixed and a variable part needed in production of components); and manufactures are produced by costless assembly of components. As with the Ricardian model, the resource constraint for the Ricardo–Viner model is given by the labour constraint, which will again be a straight line with a slope of negative one. The θ function, determined by monopolistic competition among component producers and the CES aggregator, has the same qualitative properties and graphical appearance as in the HOS and Ricardian cases. Unlike the two previous cases, however, the ψ function is no longer linear but, reflecting the presence of the specific capital, shows diminishing returns to mobile labour (i.e. $\psi' > 0$ and $\psi'' < 0$). As a result, we cannot use the expressions for τ' and τ'' in (9.4) but must use those in (9.5). On the other hand, the Ricardian resource constraint still permits us to take $B' = \beta' = -1$ and $B'' = \beta'' = 0$, so we can write:

$$\tau' = \frac{dM}{dW} = -\left(\frac{\theta'}{\psi'}\right), \text{ and } \tau'' = \frac{d^2M}{dW^2} = \frac{\theta'}{(\psi')^2}\left[\left(\frac{\theta''}{\theta'}\right) + \left(\frac{\psi''}{\psi'}\right)\right].$$

(9.7)

As with the HOS case, in the Ricardo–Viner case the term in square brackets contains a strictly positive term and a strictly negative term. The first term in the square brackets, still given by (9.6), goes to positive infinity in the neighbourhood of zero output of final manufactures. The second (negative) term is strictly finite at that point, so T will be convex at that point. We also know that the first term will decline smoothly as output of finished manufactures increases. Unfortunately, other than sign, we have very little information about the properties of the negative term, so *we cannot be certain about the structure of T away from the neighbourhood of zero manufacturing output.*[10] This is an important source of multiple equilibria in the literature.

---

[10] Following Markusen (1989) we can get some additional leverage by considering specific functional forms. For example, in the Cobb–Douglas case we have $\psi''/\psi' = (\alpha - 1)/L_W < 0$. This expression goes to negative infinity as output of wheat goes to zero. Mayer (1972), again expositing a result due to Herberg and Kemp (1969), shows that in this case T must be strictly concave in the relevant neighbourhood. Since both ψ''/ψ' and θ''/θ' decline smoothly with increases in L applied to W and M, respectively, we can say for this case that T will have a single inflection (at the unique point where $\psi''/\psi' = \theta''/\theta'$).

For additional discussion of the curvature of $T(\cdot)$ in the Ricardo–Viner case, see Markusen and Melvin (1984), Herberg and Kemp (1991) and Wong (1996).

9.2.3   The closed economy equilibrium and non-tangencies

We turn next to the equilibrium structure of the closed economy. This involves consumption along the MW frontier in figure 9.1. While under S-D-S type monopolistic competition the closed economy produces the optimal number of varieties for a given allocation of resources to m production, average cost pricing and returns to specialisation mean that, even so, the relative size of the manufacturing sector will be sub-optimal.[11] As a result of average cost pricing, while autarky consumption will be at some point like B in figure 9.1, domestic prices will not be tangent to the $T(\cdot)$ frontier at this point (Markusen, 1990a). This leaves scope for policy interventions that target expansion of the manufacturing sector.

With the addition of Cobb–Douglas preferences, it can be shown that the production side of the economy exhibits the standard features of more classical models. In particular, the combination of Cobb–Douglas preferences (with fixed expenditure shares) and homotheticity of wheat and bundles production yields a sub-system of equations that is purely Heckscher–Ohlin. As a result, as shown in Ethier (1982), the standard Rybczynski and Stolper–Samuelson results hold (in terms of wheat and bundles). However, the welfare calculus is complicated by aggregate scale effects in the transformation of bundles in final manufactures which is what matters for welfare.

9.2.4   Economic growth

In addition to the implications of returns to specialisation for the shape of the static production frontier $T(\cdot)$, such returns also carry important dynamic implications. The critical difference is captured in the θ function, which is strictly linear in the neoclassical model. With capital accumulation in the classical model, there will be an expansion of the production possibility frontier (the $T(\cdot)$ frontier), with a bias toward the capital-intensive sector. With labour in fixed supply (and assuming a standard final demand system), the new equilibrium return to capital will fall. Identically, the incremental gain from an additional unit of capital will also decline. Because of these declining returns, the classical model will exhibit the dynamic property, under classical savings or Ramsey specifications, of a fixed long-run capital/labour ratio and zero growth. This process can be fundamentally altered, however, by the simple addition of returns to specialisation. Because the θ function is no longer linear, the decline in the return to capital is moderated by returns to specialisation

---

[11] See Bhagwati, Panagariya and Srinivasan (1998) for a concise discussion of the optimal variety issue.

(Grossman and Helpman, 1991, ch. 4). If returns to specialisation are sufficiently large that they effectively bound the return to capital from below, the model will produce sustained economic growth. This depends on the relative curvature of the θ function. Even if the model exhibits local long-run Solow properties (with a unique steady-state level of capital and income in the long run), the curvature of the θ function still implies a longer period of transitional growth, and a magnification effect related to efficiency shocks (as may follow from policy intervention). In conjunction with average cost pricing, the externalities related to resource accumulation mean that the laissez-faire equilibrium in the model exhibits not only a sub-optimal static allocation of resource, but also a sub-optimal dynamic one.

The curvature of the θ function also carries dynamic implications for the effects of learning by doing. For example, we can represent the accumulation of production knowledge in the manufacturing sector by temporal shifts in the $B(\cdot)$ frontier – simply reinterpret K as knowledge capital. Even in the neoclassical model, this may lead to sustained economic growth. This depends, critically, on whether there are diminishing returns to knowledge accumulation. Externalities following from knowledge accumulation – variations on AK-type growth – can lead to sustained growth. Specialisation economies can deliver the required externalities. It is the curvature of the θ function that proves critical to determining whether specialisation economies are sufficient to generate sustained economic growth, or whether instead they simply provide a magnification of static effects (and boost the Solow residual in the process).

9.3 National production externalities with trade: model II

We turn next to the open economy version of the NPE model. If we are willing to permit trade in final goods only (i.e. in W and M, but neither in components nor in factors), $B(\cdot)$, $\theta(m)$ and $\psi(w)$ continue to be technological properties of a country's economy. (By a 'technological property' we refer to a property of an economy that is not changed by opening international trade.) Since factors are taken to be immobile (except when factor mobility is the subject of analysis), it should be clear that trade will not have any effect on the bundles transformation function. Similarly, $\psi(w)$ is defined purely in terms of a national technology. Finally, examination of (9.1) reveals that, as long as only nationally produced intermediates are available to producers of final manufactures, $\theta(m)$ is also determined solely in terms of national magnitudes. Thus, figures 9.1– 9.3 continue to characterise production conditions whether or not there is trade in final goods only. This is exceptionally convenient because it permits us to appropriate the substantial body of work on international trade under increasing returns to scale virtually unchanged (Helpman, 1984).

The Type II model is an extreme version of a model with local agglomeration effects. We say 'extreme' because there are no moderating effects related to cross-border spillover of production externalities. Because the reduced form structure of the model is identical to the older external scale economy literature, we are free to stand on the shoulders of this literature when drawing policy implications about trade policy and the location of industry. One important feature of the Type II model is that, Dr Pangloss to the contrary notwithstanding, there will generally be multiple, Pareto rankable equilibria. For small countries, in particular, there is the strong likelihood that they will specialise in wheat production, and may suffer a welfare loss relative to autarky. This fact underlies the modern versions of Frank Graham's argument for protection (Ethier, 1982b; Panagariya, 1981).[12]

Many of the insights of the recent literature on forward linkages, development, and specialisation (Rivera–Batiz and Rivera-Batiz, 1991; Rodrik, 1996; Rodríguez-Clare, 1996; Venables, 1996b) follow directly from this property of local agglomeration models. Basically, because specialised primary/wheat production involves a stable equilibrium, and because more developed economies, by definition, have cost advantages related to larger and more specialised upstream industries, there is a tendency for underdeveloped countries to stay that way.

9.4   International production externalities : models III and IV

9.4.1   *Introducing international production economies in the basic model*

While, as we have seen, Ethier's model of the division of labour has provided extremely useful microfoundations for the analysis of strictly

---

[12] Where Panagariya and Ethier adopt a Ricardian model, Markusen and Melvin (1981, proposition 1) and Ide and Takayama (1993, proposition 4) present an equivalent result for the HOS case. In deriving these results, fundamental use is made of the stability properties of these models under a Marshallian adjustment process in the final goods sector. The only peculiarity, for stability analysis of our models relative to the standard external economy models is the monopolistic competition in the intermediate sector. However, Chao and Takayama (1990) have shown that, as long as production functions are homothetic, monopolistic competition of this sort is stable under the obvious firm entry process. Since homothetic production functions characterise all of our models in this chapter, for models I/II we can fully appropriate the stability results developed by: Eaton and Panagariya (1979) and Ethier (1982b) for the Ricardian Case; Panagariya (1986) for the Ricardo–Viner case, and Ide and Takayama (1991, 1993) for the HOS case.

national returns to scale, in its maiden application it was actually used to examine internationally increasing returns to scale. The notion that access to international markets permits beneficial specialisation has been an essential element of trade theoretic analysis at least since Adam Smith and David Ricardo. What is new in Ethier's formulation is the formalisation of a direct link between international trade and the technology of production: access to a wider variety of component inputs permits an increased division of labour in the production of manufactures. As we shall see, however, it is precisely the link between trade and technology that makes the analysis difficult to visualise in simple graphical form: production conditions (especially as represented by the transformation function between final goods) are no longer a 'technological fact', determined only by nationally fixed production functions and endowments, but will now be dependent on the international equilibrium.[13]

We now assume that all R countries share identical: tastes; technologies for producing factor bundles ($w = f(K_w, L_w)$ and $m = g(K_m, L_m)$); technologies for producing components from factor bundles; and the technology for transforming w into wheat (i.e. $\psi(w)$). In all countries, all markets are taken to be perfectly competitive, except the market for components which is monopolistically competitive. A given country, $j \in R$, assembles components into final manufactures according to the following aggregator function:

$$M^j = \left[\sum_{r \in R} \sum_{i \in n_r} \left(x_i^r \right)^\phi \right]^{1/\phi}. \tag{9.8}$$

Roman subscripts and superscripts are country identifiers, Greek superscripts are numbers (i.e. powers). In the two-country case the Home country will have no superscript and Foreign magnitudes will be starred – i.e. when $n = 2$, $n = \{ , *\}$. With traded intermediate goods, it will no longer be the case that, at the level of a given national economy, the amount produced by a given component producer (which we now denote by y_r) will be equal to the amount of that component consumed in the country (x_r). In fact, since some strictly positive share of every component producing firm's output is exported, $x_r < y_r$. As a result, we can no longer simply substitute the expression for y into (9.8) unless we are working with global output. We can, however, exploit the fact that under

---

[13] A variation of the basic model type developed here incorporates value-added at the final assembly stage of intermediates into final goods. This leads to explicit interaction between division of labour effects and intermediate linkages. See, for example, Brown's (1994) discussion in the context of large applied general equilibrium models, and Puga and Venables' (1998) similar application in the context of smaller numerical models.

the assumption of a constant elasticity of substitution among varieties of components and zero transportation costs, if price per unit of every component is the same, every final manufacturing firm will purchase the same quantity of the intermediate from every intermediate producer in the world. Thus, we can set $x_i^r = x^r \; \forall I$ and r.[14] As a result, since $\sum_{i \in n_r} (x_i^r)^\phi = n_r x_r^\phi$, and letting $n^G = \sum_{r \in R} n^r$, we can write (9.8) as:

$$M^j = \left[\sum_{r \in R} n^r (x^r)^\phi \right]^{1/\phi} = \left(n^G \right)^{1/\phi} x. \tag{9.9}$$

Furthermore, since all component producers produce the same quantity and all manufacturing firms consume the same quantities of each component, it will be the case that $x^j = \delta_j y_r$. Since country j consumes δ_j of every variety, it is implicitly consuming δ_j of the total allocation of factors to bundle production, and denoting implicit consumption of bundles in country j by m^j, we have:

$$\delta_j = \frac{m^j}{m^G}. \tag{9.10}$$

What we are really interested in is an expression for $\theta(m)$ incorporating the possibility of imported intermediate components. The aggregator in (9.9) is essentially the same as that in (9.1), so for national component producers the underlying competitive conditions are essentially unchanged from those underlying the analysis presented above. Thus, we can now write $M^j = \theta(m_j, m^{-j})$:[15]

$$M^j = \theta^j (m^j, m^{-j}) = A \left(\sum_{r \in R} m_r \right)^{1/\phi - 1} m^j, \tag{9.11}$$

where θ is now functions of the *global* level of component production.

Before considering the two-country case (as an approach to the R-country case), we briefly note the analytical simplification purchased by assuming either that the country in question is either the only economically large country or is economically small. In the first case, the analysis is identical to that in the closed economy case (the Type I model). In the small-country case, rest-of-world (or large-country) production completely determines the magnitude of the term in parentheses on the

---

[14] That is, every final assembly firm will buy the same quantity of every type of component and, since M production is produced by competitive firms under identical technologies, we can treat the economy's output as being produced by a single firm with that technology.

[15] Appendix 2 of FN presents the analytics underlying this claim.

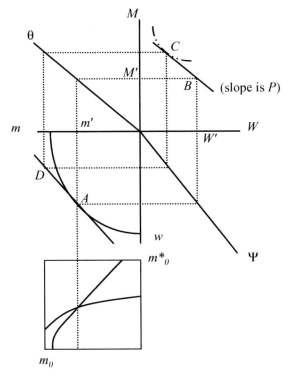

Figure 9.4

right-hand side making $M^j = A^+ m_j$ (where A^+ is a constant that includes everything but m_j). This is, of course, a linear function, so the small country behaves like a small country under constant returns to scale.

9.4.2   Large economies: the realised product transformation frontier

Now suppose that there are two countries (Home and Foreign), both large. Ethier's allocation curves, graphed below the SW quadrant in figure 9.4, are used to identify the equilibrium quantities m and m^*.[16] At this equilibrium, m and m^* are determined and so θ is a linear function. That is, θ is a linear function (shown in the NW quadrant of figure 9.4). The

---

[16] Recall that the allocation curves give, for either country, the (m, m^*) combinations that are consistent with domestic equilibrium for that country – i.e. where the domestic supply price is equal to the world demand price. The intersection of these curves identifies an (m, m^*) combination consistent with simultaneous equilibrium in both national markets and, thus, the world market.

allocation curve diagram picks out the equilibrium point on the bundles transformation function (point A in figure 9.4) which, via ψ and the linear θ, is mapped to equilibrium outputs of final goods (point B). If point A is an interior point on $B(\cdot)$, competitive conditions and technology ensure that the slope of the tangent at that point gives the equilibrium price (in units of wheat) per unit of m (which we denote p). If there is trade in intermediate goods only (i.e. all trade is intra-industry trade), consumption occurs at point B as well: $m_P^j = m_C^j$.

The same logic will also work for the case of trade in components and wheat (the Type III model), with local assembly of components into final manufactures for local consumption (the case considered in Ethier). However, if intermediate goods can be exchanged for wheat (as well as other intermediate goods), it will no longer be generally true that $m_P^j = m_C^j$. We have already seen how to find the production point on the bundles frontier (A) and the implicit final goods production point (B). The equilibrium at the intersection of the allocation curves reflects an equilibrium price of manufactures (P, taking wheat as the numéraire). As a result of zero profits, full employment of the factor endowment, and balanced trade, we know that consumption will occur on the national income line through point B (with a slope of $-P$). As illustrated at point C in figure 9.4, this will be a tangency between an indifference curve and the national income line. Using the equilibrium (linear) θ and ψ again, this time from point C, we can find the pair of factor bundles (m_C^j, w_C^j) needed to produce the consumption bundle of final goods. We know that the national income line tangent to the bundles frontier (at A) reflects the same national income as that given by the line through B, with an adjustment for scale.[17] Thus, D will lie on the national income line through A, the slope of which is $-p$ (i.e. the price per unit m). This is a full characterisation of equilibrium in the Ethier model with trade in intermediate goods and wheat (model III).

It is essential to note that we have not yet drawn a production set in the NE quadrant. This is because of the fundamental difference between models I/II and models III/IV highlighted by the general equilibrium nature of θ in the latter case. Since θ is not a technological fact, we cannot draw a purely technological production frontier. There are only equilibrium points. In fact, at the equilibrium defined by the allocation curve intersection, we have taken the equilibrium θ as linear to draw figure 9.4. As a result, there cannot be offer curves or excess supply curves of the usual sort. This, of course, is why Ethier developed the allocation curve technique.

---

[17] That is, we must make adjustment for the fact that $kP = p$.

As an aid to visualising the role of economic policy, we now construct an *experiment dependent set of production and consumption schedules*.[18] Recall that $B(\cdot)$ is a technological fact (it depends only on a fixed technology and a fixed factor endowment). Appropriate economic policy can pick out any point on the $B(\cdot)$ frontier. Consider, for example, a subsidy for home intermediate manufactures production. Such a subsidy will have a direct effect related to home output, and a second effect that captures the interaction between home production and rest-of-world production in the manufacturing sector. The net effect, involving changes in m and m^*, reflects the shifts in the home and foreign allocation curves that will be realised in the fifth quadrant in figure 9.4. (see Ethier, 1979, on this point). From (9.11), these in turn imply a shift in the efficiency of the economy in transforming m into M. As discussed more formally in the appendix, every level of home m output is associated with a new policy-dependent equilibrium characterised by a new production point in final goods space, a new relative price for manufactured goods P and a new consumption point related back to implicit trade in bundles.

Moving to our graphic apparatus, we define Θ as the locus of all equilibrium points on the linear θ functions in mM space. This embodies the interaction between changes in the subsidy and changes in $[m + m^*]$. The Θ function can now be used to trace out the experiment dependent production frontier $T(\cdot)$ in figure 9.5, which we will refer to this as the realised product transformation (RPT) frontier, defined in terms of final consumption goods.[19] This is effectively the production side of the economy. The next step involves finding the locus of all points identified by consumption of final goods at the experiment equilibria along the RPT. This follows from the imposition of final preferences and an income identity for consumption. If we impose identical homothetic preferences, we can then map the consumption locus as follows. First, along the RPT curve in figure 9.5, we have a price P associated with each point on the surface. One such price line is P_0 – associated with production point e_0. At the same time, from our imposition of homothetic preferences, this price P_0 also has associated with it an income expansion path E_0. The intersection of the price line, projected from the production point e_0, and the income expansion path E_0 projected from the origin gives us the associated consumption point C_0. We can map such consumption points for each production point on the RPT curve, yielding the consumption locus FN.

---

[18] Appendix 3 of FN contains the algebra underlying the analysis of this section.

[19] In this section we are speaking in terms of trade in intermediates (an Ethier model). Identically, the same discussion can be viewed in terms of specialised consumer goods, with M denoting the sub-utility index for differentiated consumer manufactures.

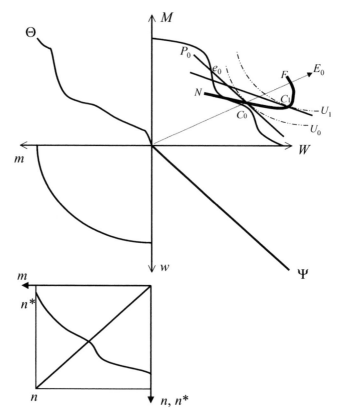

Figure 9.5

We can actually go a step further, and discuss welfare rankings along the policy-dependent consumption locus in figure 9.5. The bottom line is that we are able to represent welfare ranking through shifts along social indifference curves in figure 9.5. Hence, in figure 9.5, social welfare U_1 is greater than U_0.

9.5   Factor market flexibility and industrialisation patterns

In this section, we consider the implications of factor market structures for the location of industry. We are interested in the importance of factor mobility within countries for the manifestation of agglomeration and location effects emphasised in the new economic geography literature, and the older literature on trade with scale economies.[20] In essence, this involves a fusion of issues covered in the older literature on factor mobility (see, for example, Hill and Mendez, 1983; Casas, 1984) with the more recent literature on agglomeration.

Maintaining the structure developed above, we now want to explore the properties of the bundled transformation function. If we start, for example, with a pure Ricardian transformation surface, then we have implicitly assumed full mobility of our single factor. The result is a transformation frontier like that in figure 9.2. Alternatively, suppose that labour is not fully mobile, but rather that effective units of labour can be shifted between sectors m and w according to the transformation function $L_m = h(L_w)$ where $h' < 0$ and $h'' < 0$.

As we move away from full labour mobility, our economy moves from one as in figure 9.2 toward one instead as represented by figure 9.1. Though note that, as in Mayer's (1974) discussion of the relationship between short- and long-run production frontiers, this increasingly concave production frontier lies increasingly inside the full-mobility frontier. The implication is that, as factor mobility between sectors falls, the concavity of the bundles transformation function will become increasingly important relative to the curvature of the θ function. The stable, concave region will be a relatively larger share of the product transformation surface in the upper-right quadrant. In addition, the probability of catastrophic collapse or agglomeration would appear to be reduced.

9.6   Globalisation and wages

Now consider the linkages between relative wages and specialisation models along the lines of Ethier (1982a) and Lovely and Nelson (2000). Building on the basic analysis of Type III/IV models sketched above, we proceed as follows. To keep the analysis simple, consider the completely symmetric case. That is, countries have identical endowments, technologies, and preferences. We have a Heckscher–Ohlin technology in bundles space, giving us the relative wage mapping Ω in figure 9.6. Given symmetry, Samuelson's angel simply divides the integrated equilibrium by allocating factors in equal quantities between the two economies. With costly trade, both economies will look qualitatively like that in figure 9.6, but since the transformation surface in the upper left quadrant is determined by conditions in both countries, as we reduce trading costs, there will be an outward shift in the surface as, along the lines of Krugman's

---

[20] This section builds on Francois (2001).

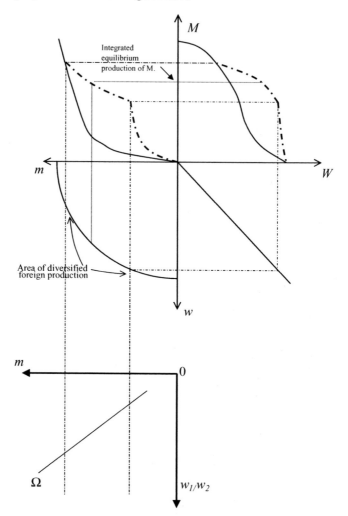

Figure 9.6 Relative wages in a large Heckscher–Ohlin–Chamberlin country with trade and trade costs

(1980) initial discussion of home-market effects, we observe a substitution from home to foreign varieties.

What are the implications of this shift for relative wages? As with most honest answers in economics, 'it depends'. Consider, in figure 9.7, that with the shift in the RPT surface, equilibrium might shift from point e_0 to $e_{0,A}$ or to $e_{0,B}$. In both cases, we have an expansion in manufacturing output, linked to global productivity gains that ultimately relate

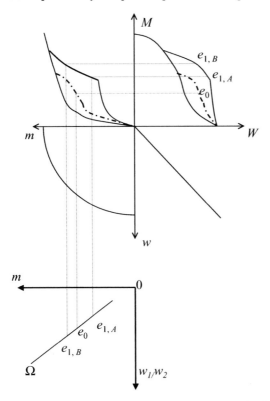

Figure 9.7 The impact of globalisation: reducing trade costs in the Heckscher–Ohlin–Chamberlin country

to an increased scale of global production. However, there is an under-lying ambiguity as to whose wages go up, and whose go down. This is reflected in the lower, fifth quadrant. This ambiguity also follows from related efficiency gains related to the global volume of FDI within this class of models (Francois and Nelson, 2000; Markusen and Venables, 1997). To complicate the situation further, the possibility of instabil-ity along the global transformation surface means that globalisation may imply dramatic shifts in production and trade volumes, with underly-ing productivity gains from international specialisation, but again with an underlying ambiguity as well. The class of global specialisation (i.e. monopolistic competition) models does point to a link between global integration through rising trade and investment levels on the one hand, and wages on the other. However, the direction of this link is ultimately an empirical question.

What does this type of analysis tell us about trade and wage linkages? In a related paper (Francois and Nelson, 2002b), we have argued that, in the literature on trade and labour markets, more attention needs to be given to North–North trade, which is considerably larger in magnitude than the North–South trade that implicitly motivates much of the existing research. In this context, an expanding body of scholarship in research on directions of trade suggests that, if North–North trade is relevant, frameworks alternative to the HOS model and its extensions are potentially useful.

9.7   Summary

Division of labour models have become a standard analytical tool, along with competitive general equilibrium models (like the Ricardian, Heckscher–Ohlin–Samuelson, and Ricardo–Viner models), in public finance, trade, growth, development and macroeconomics. Yet unlike these earlier general equilibrium models, specialisation models so far lack a canonical representation. This is because they are both new and also highly complex. Typically, they are characterised by multiple equilibria, instability and emergent structural properties under parameter transformation.

Given the prominence of specialisation models in modern economics, the value of a generic representation seems considerable. In this chapter we have developed such a framework. In the process, we demonstrate that important results in the recent literature depend critically on the stability and transformation properties that characterise the generic model. We have also highlighted why one sub-class of these models is particularly difficult to illustrate easily.

REFERENCES

Barro, R. and Sala-i-Martin, X. (1995). *Economic Growth*. New York, McGraw Hill
Bhagwati, J., Panagariya, A. and Srinivasan, T. N. (1998). *Lectures in International Trade*. Cambridge, MA, MIT Press
Brown, D. (1994). Properties of applied general equilibrium trade models with monopolistic competition and foreign direct investment, in Francois, J. and Shiells, C. (eds.), *Modeling Trade Policy: Applied General Equilibrium Assessments of North American Free Trade*. Cambridge, Cambridge University Press
Buchanan, J. and Yoon, Y. (eds.) (1994). *The Return to Increasing Returns*. Ann Arbor, University of Michigan Press
Burda, M. and Dluhosch, B. (2000). Globalization and European labour markets, in Siebert, H. (ed.), *Globalization and Labour*. Tübingen, Mohr Siebeck

Casas, F. R. (1984). Imperfect factor mobility: a generalization and synthesis of two-sector models of international trade. *Canadian Journal of Economics*, 17: 747–761

Chamberlin, E. H. (1933). *The Theory of Monopolistic Competition*. Cambridge, MA, Harvard University Press

Chao, C. C. and Takayama, A. (1990). Monopolistic competition, non-homotheticity, and the stability of the Chamberlinian tangency solution. *International Economic Review*, 31: 73–86

Chipman, J. (1970). External economies of scale and competitive equilibrium. *Quarterly Journal of Economics*, 84: 347–385

Dixit, A. and Norman, V. (1979). *Theory of International Trade*. Cambridge, Cambridge University Press

Dixit, A. K. and Stiglitz, J. E. (1977). Monopolistic competition and optimum product diversity. *American Economic Review*, 67: 297–308

Eaton, J. and Panagariya, A. (1979). Gains from trade under variable returns to scale, commodity taxation, tariffs and factor market distortions. *Journal of International Economics*, 9: 481–501

Ethier, W. (1979). Internationally decreasing costs and world trade. *Journal of International Economics*, 9: 1–24

(1982a). National and international returns to scale in the modern theory of international trade. *American Economic Review*, 72: 388–405

(1982b). Decreasing costs in international trade and Frank Graham's argument for protection. *Econometrica*, 50: 1243–1268

Francois, J. (1992). Optimal commercial policy with international returns to scale. *Canadian Journal of Economics*, 25: 184–195

(1994). Global production and trade: factor migration and commercial policy with international scale economies. *International Economic Review*, 35: 565–581

(2001). Factor mobility, economic integration, and the location of industry. CIES Discussion Paper

Francois, J. and Nelson, D. (2000). Victims of progress: globalization, specialization, and wages for unskilled labour. CEPR Discussion Paper, 2527

(2002a). A geometry of specialization. *Economic Journal*, 112: 649–678

(2002b). Globalization and relative wages: some theory and evidence. CEPR Discussion Paper

Fujita, M., Krugman, P. and Venables, A. (1999). *The Spatial Economy: Cities, Regions, and International Trade*. Cambridge, MA, MIT Press

Gomory, R. (1994). A Ricardo model with economies of scale. *Journal of Economic Theory*, 62: 394–419

Grossman, G. and Helpman, E. (1991). *Innovation and Growth in the Global Economy*. Cambridge, MA, MIT Press

Helpman, E. (1984). Increasing returns, imperfect markets and trade theory, in Jones, R. and Kenen, P. (eds.), *Handbook of International Economics*, I. Amsterdam, North-Holland

Helpman, E. and Krugman, P. (1985). *Market Structure and Foreign Trade*. Cambridge, MA, MIT Press

Herberg, H. and Kemp, M. (1969). Some implications of variable returns to scale. *Canadian Journal of Economics*, 2: 403–415

(1991). Some implications of variable returns to scale: the case of industry specific factors. *Canadian Journal of Economics*, 24: 703–704

Hill, J. and Mendez, J. (1983). Factor mobility in the general equilibrium model of production. *Journal of International Economics*, 15: 19–25

Holtz-Eakin, D. and Lovely, M. (1996a). Scale economies, returns to variety, and the productivity of public infrastructure. *Regional Science and Urban Economics*, 26: 105–23

(1996b). Technological linkages, market structure, and production policies. *Journal of Public Economics*, 61: 73–86

Ide, T. and Takayama, A. (1991). Variable returns to scale, paradoxes and global correspondences in the theory of international trade, in Takayama, A., Ohyama, M. and Ohta, H. (eds.), *Trade, Policy, and International Adjustments*. San Diego, Academic Press

(1993). Variable returns to scale, comparative statics paradoxes, and the theory of comparative advantage, in Herberg, H. and Long, N.V. (eds.), *Trade, Welfare and Economic Policies*. Ann Arbor, University of Michigan Press

Kemp, M. C. (1964). *The Pure Theory of International Trade*. Englewood Cliffs, NJ, Prentice-Hall

Kemp, M. C. and Negishi, T. (1970). Variable returns to scale, commodity taxes, factor market distortions and their implications for trade gains. *Swedish Journal of Economics*, 72: 1–11

Krugman, P. (1979). Increasing returns, monopolistic competition, and international trade. *Journal of International Economics*, 9: 469–479

(1980). Scale economies, product differentiation, and the pattern of trade. *American Economic Review*, 70: 950–959

(1995). Complexity and emergent structure in the international economy, in Levinsohn, J., Deardorff, A. and Stern, R. (eds.), *New Directions in Trade Theory*. Ann Arbor, University of Michigan Press

Krugman, P. and Venables, A. (1995). Globalization and the inequality of nations. *Quarterly Journal of Economics*, 110: 857–880

Kuenne, R. (ed.) (1967). *Monopolistic Competition Theory: Studies in Impact. Essays in Honor of Edward H. Chamberlin*. New York, John Wiley

Lancaster, K. (1966). A new approach to consumer theory. *Journal of Political Economy*, 74: 132–157

(1971). *Consumer Demand: A New Approach*. New York, Columbia University Press

Lovely, M. (1997). Playing by the new subsidy rules: capital subsidies as substitutes for sectoral subsidies. *Journal of International Economics*, 43: 463–482

Lovely, M. and Nelson, D. (2000). Marginal intraindustry trade and labour adjustment. *Review of International Economics*, 8: 436–447

Markusen, J. (1988). Production, trade, and migration with differentiated, skilled workers. *Canadian Journal of Economics*, 21: 492–506

(1989). Trade in producer services and in other specialised inputs. *American Economic Review*, 79: 85–95

(1990a). Micro-foundations of external economies. *Canadian Journal of Economics*, 23: 495–508

(1990b). Derationalizing tariffs with specialized intermediate inputs and differentiated final goods. *Journal of International Economics*, 28: 375–383

(1991). First mover advantages, blockaded entry, and the economics of uneven development, in Helpman, E. and Razin, A. (eds.), *International Trade and Trade Policy*. Cambridge, MA, MIT Press

Markusen, J. R. and Melvin, J. R. (1981). Trade, factor prices, and gains from trade with increasing returns to scale. *Canadian Journal of Economics*, 14: 450–469

(1984). The gains from trade theorem with increasing returns to scale, in Kierzkowski, H. (ed.), *Monopolistic Competition and International Trade*. New York, Oxford University Press

Markusen, J. and Venables, A. (1997). The role of multinational firms in the wage-gap debate. *Review of International Economics*, 5: 435–451

Marrewijk, C. van, Stibora, J., de Vaal, A. and Viaene, J. M. (1997). Producer services, comparative advantage, and international trade patterns. *Journal of International Economics*, 42: 195–220

Matsuyama, K. (1996). Why are there rich and poor countries? Symmetry-breaking in the world economy. *Journal of the Japanese and International Economies*, 10: 419–439

Mayer, W. (1972). Homothetic production functions and the shape of the production possibility locus. *Journal of Economic Theory*, 8: 101–110

(1974). Short-run and long-run equilibrium for a small open economy. *Journal of Political Economy*, 82: 955–967.

Panagariya, A. (1981). Variable returns to scale in production and patterns of specialization. *American Economic Review*, 71: 221–230

(1986). Increasing returns, dynamic stability, and international trade. *Journal of International Economics*, 20: 43–63

Puga, D. and Venables, A. (1996). The spread of industry: spatial agglomeration in economic development. *Journal of the Japanese and International Economies*, 10: 440–464

(1998). Trading arrangements and industrial development. *World Bank Economic Review*, 12: 221–249

Rivera-Batiz, F. and Rivera-Batiz, L. (1991). The effects of direct foreign investment in the presence of increasing returns due to specialization. *Journal of Development Economics*, 34: 287–307

Robinson, J. (1993). *The Economics of Imperfect Competition*. London, Macmillan

Rodríguez-Clare, A. (1996). The division of labour and economic development. *Journal of Development Economics*, 49: 3–32

Rodrik, D. (1996). Coordination failures and government policy: a model with applications to East Asia and Eastern Europe. *Journal of International Economics*, 40: 1–22

Romer, P. (1987). Growth based on increasing returns due to specialization. *American Economic Review*, 77: 56–62

(1990). Endogenous technical change. *Journal of Political Economy*, 98: S71–S102

Spence, A. M. (1976). Product selection, fixed cost and monopolistic competition. *Review of Economic Studies*, 43: 217–235

(1996a). Trade policy, cumulative causation, and industrial development. *Journal of Development Economics*, 49: 179–197

(1996b). Equilibrium location of vertically linked industries. *International Economic Review*, 37: 341–358

Wong, K. Y. (1996). A comment on 'Some implications of variable returns to scale: The case of industry-specific factors'. *Canadian Journal of Economics*, 29: 240–244

Young, A. (1928). Increasing returns and economic progress. *Economic Journal*, 38: 527–540

Part IV

Economic geography

10   The core–periphery model: key features and effects

Richard E. Baldwin, Rikard Forslid, Philippe Martin, Gianmarco I. P. Ottaviano and Frédéric Robert-Nicoud

10.1   Introduction

More than twenty-five years ago, Avinash Dixit and Joe Stiglitz developed a simple model for addressing imperfect competition and increasing returns (ICIR) in a general equilibrium setting. Its first application, in Dixit and Stiglitz (1977), was to an issue that now seems rather banal – whether the free markets produce too many or too few varieties of differentiated products. But ICIR considerations are so crucial to so many economic phenomena, and yet so difficult to model formally, that the Dixit–Stiglitz framework has become the workhorse of many branches of economics. In this chapter, we present one of its most recent, and most startling applications – namely, to issues of economic geography. While there are many models in this new literature, almost all of them rely on Dixit–Stiglitz monopolistic competition, and among these, the most famous is the so-called core–periphery (CP) model introduced by Paul Krugman, (1991a).

The basic structure of the CP model is astoundingly familiar to trade economists. Take the classroom Dixit–Stiglitz monopolistic competition trade model with trade costs, add in migration driven by real wage differences, impose a handful of normalisation, and *voilà*, the CP model! The fascination of the CP model stems in no small part from the fact that these seemingly innocuous changes so unexpectedly and so radically transform the behaviour of a model that trade theorists have been exercising for more than twenty-five years.

This chapter presents the CP model – or, more precisely, the version in chapter 5 of Fujita, Krugman and Venables (1999) (hereafter, FKV).[1] We survey or describe all the main properties of the model including catastrophe, hysteresis and global stability.

---

[1] The original model appears in Krugman (1991a, 1991b). Venables (1996) is its vertical-linkages version.

10.2   The standard core–periphery model

The basic structure of the CP model assumes two initially symmetric regions (north and south), fixed endowments of two sector-specific factors (industrial workers H and agricultural labourers L), and two sectors (manufactures M and agriculture A). Agricultural labourers are not geographically mobile, but industrial workers do migrate in response to the North–South real wage differences. Trade in industrial goods is costless, so both firms and consumers care about location.

The technology is simple. The M-sector is a standard Dixit–Stiglitz monopolistic competition sector, where manufacturing firms (M-firms for short) employ H to produce output subject to increasing returns. Production of each M-variety requires a fixed cost of F units of H in addition to a_m units of H per unit of output, so the cost function is $w(F + a_m x)$, where x is a firm's output of a specific variety and w is the reward to H. The A-sector produces a homogeneous good under perfect competition and constant returns using only L.

Both M and A are traded, with M trade is inhibited by iceberg trade costs. Specifically, it is costless to ship M-goods to local consumers but to sell one unit in the other region, an M-firm must ship $\tau \geq 1$ units. The idea is that $\tau - 1$ units of the good 'melt' in transit. As usual, τ captures all the costs of selling to distant markets, not just transport costs, and $\tau - 1$ is the tariff-equivalent of these costs. Importantly, trade in A is costless.[2]

Preferences of the representative consumer in each region consists of CES preferences over M-varieties nested in a Cobb–Douglas upper-tier function that also includes consumption of the homogeneous good, A. Specifically:

$$U = C_M^\mu C_A^{1-\mu}; \qquad C_M \equiv \int_0^{n+n^*} \left[c_i^{(\sigma-1)/\sigma} \, di \right]^{\sigma/(\sigma-1)},$$
$$0 < \mu < 1 < \sigma, \tag{10.1}$$

where C_M and C_A are, respectively, consumption of the M composite and consumption of A; n and n^* are the measure of north and south varieties (often we loosely refer to these as the number of varieties), μ is the expenditure share on M-varieties, and σ is the constant elasticity of substitution between M-varieties.

---

[2] Chapter 7 of FKV shows that this is an assumption of convenience in that qualitatively identical results can be obtained in a more complex model that allows for A-sector trade costs.

Migration is governed (as in FKV) by the ad hoc migration equation:

$$\frac{\dot{s}_H}{s_H} = (\omega - \omega^*)(1 - s_H), \qquad \omega \equiv \frac{w}{P},$$

$$P \equiv P_A^{1-\mu}\left[\int_0^{n+n^*} p_i^{1-\sigma}\, di\right]^{\mu/(1-\sigma)}, \qquad (10.2)$$

where $s_H \equiv H/H^w$ is the share of world H in the north, H is the northern labour supply, H^w is the world labour supply, ω and ω^* are the northern and southern real wages, w is the northern nominal wage for H, and P is the north's region-specific perfect price index implied by (10.1); p_A is the price of A and p_i is the price of M-variety i (the variety subscript is dropped were clarity permits). Analogous definitions hold for southern variables, which are denoted with an asterisk.

10.2.1   Equilibrium expressions

As is well known,[3] utility optimisation yields a constant division of expenditure between M and A, and CES demand functions for M varieties, namely:

$$c_j \equiv \frac{p_j^{-\sigma}\mu E}{\int_0^{n+n^*} p_i^{1-\sigma}\, di}, \qquad E = wH + w_L L, \qquad (10.3)$$

where E is region-specific expenditure and w_L is the wage rate of L. As usual in the Dixit–Stiglitz monopolistic competition setting, free and instantaneous entry drives pure profits to zero, so E involves only factor payments. Demand for A is $C_A = (1 - \mu)E/p_A$.

On the supply side, perfect competition in the A-sector forces marginal cost pricing, i.e. $p_A = a_A w_L$ and $p_A^* = a_A w_L^*$, where a_A is the unit input coefficient. Costless trade in A equalises northern and southern prices and thus indirectly equalises L wage rates internationally, viz. $w_L = w_L^*$. In the M-sector, 'milling pricing' is optimal, so the ratio of the price of a northern variety in its local and export markets is just τ. Summarising these equilibrium-pricing results:

$$p = \frac{w a_M}{1 - 1/\sigma}, \qquad p^* = \frac{\tau w a_M}{1 - 1/\sigma}, \qquad p_A = p_A^* = w_L = w_L^*,$$

$$(10.4)$$

where p and p^* are the local and export prices of a home-based M-firm. Analogous pricing rules hold for southern M-firms.

---

[3] Details of all calculations can be found in 'All you wanted to know about Dixit–Stiglitz but were afraid to ask', available on http://heiwww.unige.ch/~baldwin/.

A well-known result for the Dixit–Stiglitz monopolistic competition model is that operating profit (call this π) is the value of sales divided by σ, where the value of sales is either shipments at producer prices, or retail sales at consumer prices.[4] Using milling pricing from (10.4) and the shipments-based expression for operating profit in the free entry condition, namely $px/\sigma = wF$, yields the equilibrium firm size. This and the full employment of H – i.e. $n(F + a_M x) = H$ – yields the equilibrium number of firms, n. Specifically:

$$n = \frac{H}{\sigma F}, \qquad \bar{x} = \frac{F(\sigma - 1)}{a_M}, \tag{10.5}$$

where $\bar{x}$ is the equilibrium size of a typical M-firm. Similar expressions define the analogous southern variables. Two features of (10.5) are worth highlighting. First, the number of varieties produced in a region is proportional to the regional labour force. H migration is therefore tantamount to industrial relocation and vice versa. Second, the scale of firms is invariant to everything except the elasticity of substitution and the size of fixed costs. Note also that one measure of scale, namely the ratio of average cost to marginal cost, depends only on σ.

The market for northern M-varieties must clear at all moments and from (10.5) firm output is fixed, so using (10.3), the market clearing condition for a typical Northern variety is[5]:

$$p\bar{x} = R, \qquad R \equiv \frac{w^{1-\sigma}\mu E}{nw^{1-\sigma} + \phi n^*(w^*)^{1-\sigma}} + \frac{\phi w^{1-\sigma}\mu E^*}{\phi nw^{1-\sigma} + n^*(w^*)^{1-\sigma}}, \tag{10.6}$$

where R is a mnemonic for 'retail sales'. Due to markup price and iceberg trade costs, the value of a typical firm's retail sales at consumer prices always equals its revenue at producer prices; R is thus also a mnemonic for revenue. Also, $\phi = \tau^{1-\sigma}$ measures the 'free-ness' (phi-ness) of trade and note that the free-ness of trade rises from $\phi = 0$ (with infinite trade costs) to $\phi = 1$ with zero trade costs. Equilibrium additionally requires that the equivalent of (10.6) for a typical southern variety, and the market

---

[4] A typical first-order condition for local sales is $p_i(1 - 1/\sigma) = wa_M$. Rearranging this, operating profit on local sales is $(p - wa_M)c_i = pc/\sigma$. A similar rearrangement of the first-order condition for export sales and summation yields the result for consumer prices. Noting that $p^*c^* = w\tau c^* = w\tau x_h^h/\tau$, where x_h^h is export shipments, yields the result for producer prices.

[5] Local sales of a northern variety are $w^{1-\sigma}/[nw^{1-\sigma} + n^*(\tau w^*)^{1-\sigma}] \times \mu E$ since the price of imports is τw^*. The expression for export sales is $(\tau w)^{1-\sigma}/[n(\tau w)^{1-\sigma} + n^*(w^*)^{1-\sigma}] \times \mu E^*$.

clearing condition for A hold. The latter requires:

$$(1 - \mu)(E + E^*) = \frac{2L}{p_A}. \tag{10.7}$$

Equation (10.6) and its southern equivalent are often called the wage equations since they can be written in terms of w, w^*, H and H^*. One can make some progress by plugging (10.7) instead of the southern wage equation into (10.6), but unfortunately there is no way to solve for the equilibrium w analytically since $1 - \sigma$ is a non-integer power. Numerical solutions for particular values of m, σ and ϕ are easily obtained.[6]

10.2.2   Choice of numéraire and units

Both intuition and tidiness are served by appropriate normalisation and choice of numéraire. In particular, we take A as numéraire and choose units of A such $a_A = 1$. This simplifies both the expressions for the price index and expenditure since it implies $p_A = w_L = w_L^* = 1$. In the M-sector, we measure M in units such that $a_M = (1 - 1/\sigma)$, so that the equilibrium prices become $p = w$ and $p^* = \tau w$, and the equilibrium firm size becomes $\bar{x} = F\sigma$.

The next normalisation, which concerns F, has engendered some confusion. Since we are working with the continuum-of-varieties version of the Dixit–Stiglitz model, we can normalise F to $1/\sigma$.[7] With this, $\bar{x} = 1$, $n = H$ and $n^* = H^*$. These results simplify the M-sector market-clearing condition, (10.6). The results that $n = H$ and $n^* = H^*$ also boost intuition by making the connection between migration and industrial relocation crystal clear.

We have not yet specified units for L or H. Choosing the world endowment of H, namely H^w, such that $H^w = 1$ is useful since it implies that the total number of varieties is fixed at unity (i.e. $n^w = 1$) even though the production location of varieties is endogenous. The fact that $n + n^* = 1$ is useful in manipulating expressions. For instance, instead of writing s_H for the northern share of H^w, we could write s_n or simply n. Finally, it proves convenient to have $w = w^* = 1$ in the symmetric outcome (i.e.

---

[6] A MAPLE spreadsheet that shows how to solve this model numerically can be found on http://heiwww.unige.ch/~baldwin/.

[7] Since units of the sector-specific factor are also normalised elsewhere, it may seem that there is one too many normalisations. As it turns out, the normalisation is OK in the continuum of varieties version of Dixit–Stiglitz, but not OK in the discrete-varieties version. With a continuum of varieties, n is not the number of varieties produced in the north (if n is not zero, an uncountable infinity of varieties are produced in the north), it is a measure and we are free to choose the unit of this measure. In the discrete-varieties version, n and n^* are pure numbers, so this degree of freedom is absent.

where $n = H = 1/2$) and core periphery outcomes (i.e. where $n = H = 1$ or 0). This can be accomplished by choosing units of L such that the world endowment of the immobile factor, i.e. L^w, equals $(1 - \mu)/2\mu$.[8]

In summary, the equilibrium values with these normalisation are:

$$p = w, \qquad p^* = w\tau, \qquad \bar{x} = 1,$$
$$p_A = p_A^* = w_L = w_L^* = 1, \qquad nw + n^*w^* = 1, \qquad n + n^* = H + H^* = 1,$$
$$n = H = s_H = s_n, \qquad n^* = H^*, \qquad E^w = 1/\mu,$$

$$(10.8)$$

where s_H and s_n, are the north's shares of H^w and n^w respectively, and, by construction, $w = w^* = 1$ in the symmetric outcome.

Note that with these normalisations the nominal wage in the core equals unity in the core–periphery outcomes. The nominal wage in the periphery in such outcomes varies with trade costs. Specifically, the periphery's wage is $(\phi\mu(1 + L) + \mu L/\phi)^{1/\sigma}$. Of course, this is a sort of 'virtual' nominal wage, viz. the wage that a small group of workers would earn if they did work in the periphery.

10.3   The long-run equilibria and local stability

In solving for long-run equilibria, the key variable – the state variable – is the division of the mobile factor H between north and south.[9] Inspection of the migration equation (10.2) reveals two types of long run equilibria. The first type – CP outcomes – is where $s_H = 1$ or 0. The second type – interior outcomes – is where $w = w^*$ but $0 < s_H < 1$. Given symmetry, it is plain that ω does equal ω^* when $s_H = 1/2$, so $s_H = 1/2$ is also always a long-run equilibrium.[10] It is equally clear from the migration equation that when $s_H = 1$ or 0, the economy is also in equilibrium since no migration occurs.

10.3.1   A caveat on full agglomeration

Only one dispersion force operates in the CP model and this (local competition) becomes very weak as trade gets very free. As a result, the model predicts that sufficiently high levels of trade free-ness are inevitably associated with full agglomeration. The world, however, is full of

---

[8] FKV takes L^w as μ and A^w as $1 - \mu$, but wages are unity as long as L^w/A^w equals $\mu/(1 - \mu)$.

[9] With our normalisation, we can write the state variable as n, H, s_n or s_H.

[10] Are there other interior steady states? Robert-Nicoud (2001) actually confirms analytically that there can also be at most two other interior steady states. More on this below.

dispersion forces – comparative advantage, congestion externalities, natural resources, 'real' geography such as rivers, natural ports, etc. – and these can change everything.

The point is that the model's agglomeration forces also decrease with trade costs. This implies that for low enough trade costs other dispersion forces that are not eroded by trade free-ness, such as comparative advantages, will dominate the location decisions of firms when trade becomes sufficiently free. In the literature this is called the 'U-shaped result'. Dispersion is the likely outcome both when trade costs are very high and when they are very low. This appealing feature is not, unfortunately, present in the simple CP model.[11]

What all this means is that the CP model should not be construed as predicting that the world must end up in an agglomerated equilibrium as trade costs are lowered. Rather the model predicts that dramatic changes in location may happen for some levels of trade costs.

Identification of these long-run equilibria, however, is only part of the analysis. Complete analysis requires us to evaluate the local stability of these three equilibria.

10.3.2   Local stability analysis

The literature relies on informal tests to find the level of trade costs where the symmetric equilibrium becomes unstable and where the full agglomeration outcome becomes stable. In particular, for the symmetric equilibrium, one sees how a small northward migration *changes* the real wage gap $\omega - \omega^*$; if it is negative, the equilibrium is stable, otherwise it is unstable. For the core–periphery outcomes, (CP outcomes), the test is whether the *level* of the periphery real wage exceeds that of the core; if so, the CP equilibrium is unstable, otherwise, it is stable. Symbolically the stability tests are:

$$\left.\frac{d(\omega - \omega^*)}{ds_H}\right|_{sym} < 0, \qquad \omega_{CP} > \omega_{CP}^*, \qquad (10.9)$$

where '*sym*' and '*CP*' indicate evaluation at $s_H = 1/2$ and $s_H = 1$, respectively. The ϕ where the first expression in (10.9) holds with equality is called the 'break' point, ϕ^B. The ϕ where the second expression holds with equality is called the 'sustain' point, ϕ^S. The validity of these informal tests in (10.9) can easily be proved. The dynamic aspects of the CP model can be expressed a single non-linear differential equation. Formally, local stability is evaluated by linearising this equation around

---

[11] See FKV for various modifications that lead to the 'U-shaped result'.

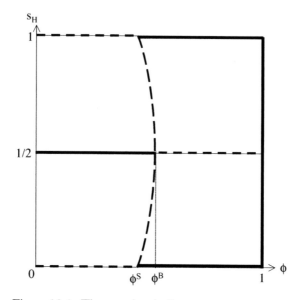

Figure 10.1 The tomahawk diagram

an equilibrium point. Doing so exactly lines up with the informal stability tests in (10.9) above (Baldwin, 2001).

Using (10.9), FKV establish that the symmetric equilibrium is stable only for sufficiently low levels of trade free-ness, specifically for $\phi < \phi^B$, and that CP outcomes are stable only for sufficiently high levels of trade free-ness, specifically for $\phi > \phi^S$. Using numerical simulation, FKV also establish that there is a range of ϕ for which both the symmetric and CP outcomes are stable, i.e. that $\phi^S < \phi^B$.

These three facts and the long-run equilibria can be conveniently illustrated with the so-called 'tomahawk' diagram, figure 10.1 (the 'tomahawk' moniker comes from viewing the stable-part of the symmetric equilibrium as the handle of a double-edged axe). The diagram plots s_H against the free-ness of trade, ϕ and shows locally stable long-run equilibria with heavy solid lines and locally unstable long-run equilibria with heavy dashed lines. Thus the three horizontal lines $s_H = 1$, $s_H = 1/2$ and $s_H = 0$ are steady states for any permissible level of ϕ. Note that for most levels of ϕ, there are three long-run equilibria, while for the levels of ϕ corresponding to the bowed curve, there are five equilibria – two CP outcomes, the symmetric outcome and two interior, asymmetric equilibria.[12]

---

[12] Of course when there is no trade cost, i.e. $\phi = 1$, distance has no meaning and the location of production is not determined; any division of H^w is a steady state.

10.4 Catastrophic agglomeration and locational hysteresis

Catastrophe is the most celebrated hallmark of the CP model – probably because it is so unexpected. Specifically, starting from a symmetric outcome and very high trade costs, marginal increases in the level of trade free-ness ϕ has no impact on the location of industry until a critical level of ϕ is reached. Even a tiny increase in ϕ beyond this point causes a catastrophic agglomeration of industry in the sense that the only stable outcome is that of full agglomeration.[13]

The key requirement for catastrophe is that the stable interior outcome becomes locally unstable beyond a critical ϕ – the so-called break point – and that at the same level of trade costs, the full agglomeration outcomes are the only stable equilibrium.

The literature traditionally uses the tomahawk diagram (figure 10.1) to illustrate the catastrophe feature. The idea is that trade costs have, roughly speaking, fallen over time. Thus starting in the distant past – say the pre-industrial era – trade costs were very high and economic activity was very dispersed. As time passed, ϕ rose, eventually to a level beyond ϕ^B, at which point industry rapidly became agglomerated in cities and in certain nations. Perhaps the most striking feature of the CP model is the result that a symmetric reduction in trade costs between initially symmetric nations eventually produces catastrophic agglomeration. That is, rising ϕ has no impact on the location of industry until a critical level of openness is reached. However, even a tiny increase in ϕ beyond this point results in a very large location effect as the even division of industry becomes unstable. That non-marginal effects come from marginal changes is certainly one of the hallmarks of the economic geography models.

The second famous feature of the CP model is hysteresis. That is, suppose we start out with an even division of industry between the two regions and a ϕ between the break and sustain points (i.e. in the so-called 'overlap'). Given that the symmetric outcome and both full agglomeration outcomes (core-in-the-north and core-in-the-south) are all locally stable, some location shock, or maybe even an expectations shock, could shift industry from the symmetry outcome to one of the core outcomes. Importantly, the locational impact would not be reversed when the cause of the shock were removed. In other words, this model features sunk-cost hysteresis of the type modelled by Baldwin (1993), Baldwin and Krugman (1989) and Dixit (1989).[14] The key requirement for locational hysteresis is the existence of a range of ϕs where there are multiple, locally stable equilibria.

[13] In the jargon, the catastrophe property is called 'super-critical bifurcation'.
[14] The feature is also sometimes called 'path dependency', or 'history matters'.

10.5   The three forces: intuition for the break and sustain points

The complex equilibrium structure and extremely non-neoclassical behaviour of this model is curious, to say the least, given the fairly standard assumptions behind the model. This section provides intuition for the complexity.

10.5.1   *The three forces and the impact of trade costs*

There are three distinct forces governing stability in this model. Two of them – demand-linked and cost-linked circular causality (also called backward and forward linkages) – favour agglomeration, i.e. they are destabilising. The third – the local competition effect (also known as the market crowding effect) – favours dispersion, i.e. it is stabilising.

The expressions $E = wL + w_A A$ and $E^* = w^*(L^w - L) + w_A A$ help illustrate the first agglomeration force, namely demand-linked circular causality. Starting from symmetry, a small migration from south to north would increase E and decrease E^*, thus making the northern market larger and the southern market smaller since mobile workers spend their income locally. In the presence of trade costs, and all else being equal, firms will prefer the big market, so this migration induced 'expenditure shifting' encourages 'production shifting'. Of course, firms and industrial workers are the same thing in this model, so we see that a small migration perturbation tends to encourage more migration via a demand-linked circular causality.

The definition of the perfect price index in (10.2) helps illustrate the second agglomeration force in this model, namely cost-linked circular causality, or forward linkages. Starting from symmetry, a small migration from south to north would increase H and thus n while decreasing in H^* and n^*. Since locally produced varieties attract no trade cost, the shift in ns would, other things equal, lower the cost of living in the north and raise living costs in the south, thus raising the north's relative real wage. This in turn tends to attract more migrants.[15]

The lone stabilising force in the model, the so-called local competition, or market crowding, effect, can be seen from the definition of retail sales, R, in (10.6). Perturbing the symmetric equilibrium by moving a small mass of H northward, raises n and lowers n^*. From (10.6), we see that this tends to increase the degree of local competition in the north and thus lower R (as long as $\phi < 1$).[16] To break even, northern firms would have to

---

[15] FKV call it the 'price index effect'.

[16] In Dixit–Stiglitz competition, the price–cost mark up never changes, so this local competition effect is not a pro-competitive effect. This is why some authors prefer the term 'market crowding'.

pay lower nominal wages. All else equal, this drop in w and corresponding rise in w^* makes north less attractive and thus tends to undo the initial perturbation. In other words, this is a force for dispersion of industry activity.

The catastrophic behaviour of the model stems from two facts, which we explore more below. The first is that the dispersion force is stronger than the agglomeration forces at high trade costs. The second is that raising the level of trade free-ness reduces the magnitude of each of the three forces, but it erodes the strength of the dispersion force faster. As a result, at some level of trade costs – the break point – the agglomeration forces become stronger than the dispersion force and industry collapses into just one region. For readers who wish to understand these forces in more depth, we turn now to a series of thought experiments that more precisely illustrate the forces and their dependence on trade costs.

10.5.2   A series of thought experiments

Focusing on each of the three forces separately boosts intuition and we accomplish this via a series of thought experiments. These focus on the symmetric equilibrium for a very pragmatic reason. In general, the CP model is astoundingly difficult to manipulate since the nominal wages are determined by equations that cannot be solved analytically. At the symmetric equilibrium, however, this difficulty is much attenuated. Due to the symmetry, all effects are equal and opposite. For instance, if a migration shock raises the northern wage, then it lowers the southern wage by the same amount. Moreover, at the symmetric outcome, $w = w^* = 1$, so much of the intractability – which stems largely from terms involving a nominal wage raised to a non-integer power – disappears.

The local competition effect
To separate the production shifting and expenditure shifting aspects of migration, the first thought experiment supposes that H migration is driven by *nominal* wages differences and that all H earnings are remitted to the country of origin.[17] Thus, migration changes n and n^* but not E and E^*.

---

[17] This may be thought of as corresponding to the case where H is physical capital whose owners are immobile. Note also that under these suppositions, the model closely resembles the pre-economic geography models with monopolistic competition and trade costs (e.g. Venables, 1987 and chapter 10 of Helpman and Krugman, 1985).

Log differentiating (10.6) yields (using ''^' to indicate proportional change):

$$\sigma \hat{w} = s_R(\hat{s}_E - \hat{\Delta}) + (1 - s_R)(\hat{s}_E^* - \hat{\Delta}^*), \quad \sigma \hat{w}|_{s_n=1/2} = 2(s_R - 1/2)(\hat{s}_E - \hat{\Delta}),$$
$$(10.10)$$

where $\Delta = nw^{1-\sigma} + \phi n^* (w^*)^{1-\sigma}$, $\Delta^* = \phi nw^{1-s} + n^* (w^*)^{1-\sigma}$, $s_R \equiv nw^{1-\sigma}/\Delta$ is share of a typical north firm's total sales, R, that are made in the north and the second expression follows due to the equal and opposite nature of all changes around symmetry; all share variables such as s_R, s_E and s_n lie in the zero–one range. Observe that at the symmetric outcome (i.e. $s_n = s_H = 1/2$), s_R exceeds $1/2$ when trade is not perfectly free, i.e. $\phi < 1$. Moreover, s_R falls toward $1/2$ as ϕ approaches unity; specifically, $s_R = 1/(1 + \phi)$ at $s_H = 1/2$.

By supposition, expenditure is repatriated so $\hat{s}_E = 0$, and given the definition of Δ:

$$\hat{\Delta}|_{s_n=1/2} = 2(s_M - 1/2)(\hat{n} - (\sigma - 1)\hat{w}), \quad\quad (10.11)$$

where s_M is the share of northern expenditure that falls on northern M-varieties. With positive trade costs, s_M exceeds $1/2$ with the difference shrinking as ϕ increases; in fact using the demand functions and symmetry we can show that $2(s_M - 1/2) = (1 - \phi)/(1 + \phi)$. Using (10.11) in (10.10) with $ds_E = 0$ yields:

$$\hat{w} = \left(\frac{-4(s_R - 1/2)(s_M - 1/2)}{\sigma - 4(s_R - 1/2)(s_M - 1/2)(\sigma - 1)} \right) \hat{n}. \quad\quad (10.12)$$

This is the 'local competition' effect in isolation. Note that s_R and s_M lie in the zero–one range.

There are four salient points. First, since the denominator must be positive (since $4(s_R - 1/2)(s_M - 1/2)$ is always less than unity and $\sigma > 1$) and the numerator must be negative, northward migration always lowers the northern nominal wage and, by symmetry, raises the southern wage. Second, this shows directly that migration is not, *per se*, destabilising. When the demand or cost linkages are cut, as in this thought experiment, the symmetric equilibrium is always stable despite migration. Third, the magnitude of this 'competition for consumers' effect diminishes roughly with the square of trade costs since as trade free-ness rises, $(s_R - 1/2)$ and $(s_M - 1/2)$ fall. Specifically, $4(s_R - 1/2)(s_M - 1/2) = [(1 - \phi)/(1 + \phi)]^2$. Note that in FKV terminology $(s_R - 1/2)$ and $(s_M - 1/2)$ are denoted as 'Z' since at the symmetric equilibrium both equal $(1 - \phi)/(1 + \phi)$.

The final point is that in this thought experiment the break and sustain points are identical; this can be seen by noting that s_n doesn't enter

(10.12). Both points equal $\phi = 1$ since the symmetric outcome is stable, and the CP outcome is unstable for any positive level of trade costs. When there are no trade costs, any locational outcome is an equilibrium.

Demand linkages

In the next thought experiment, suppose that, for some reason, H bases its migration decision on nominal wages but spends all of its income in the region it is employed. While this would not make much sense to a rational H-worker, the assumption serves intuition by allowing us to restore the connection between production shifting $(dH = dn)$ and expenditure shifting dE without at the same time adding in the cost-linkage (i.e. cost-of-living) effect. Since E equals $L + wH$ and this equals $L + wn$ with our normalisations, the restored term from (10.10) is:

$$\hat{s}_E = \left(\frac{wn}{E}\right)(\hat{w} + \hat{n}) = \mu(\hat{w} + \hat{n}). \tag{10.13}$$

The second expression follows since, from (10.8), $w = 1$, $n = 1/2$ and $E = 1/2\mu$ at the symmetric outcome. Using (10.13) and (10.11) in (10.10), we find:

$$\hat{w}|_{s_n=1/2} = \frac{2\mu(s_R - 1/2)\hat{n} - 4(s_R - 1/2)(s_M - 1/2)\hat{n}}{\sigma - 4(s_R - 1/2)(s_M - 1/2)(\sigma - 1) - \mu}. \tag{10.14}$$

Note that the denominator is always positive, since $0 \leq 4(s_R - 1/2)(s_M - 1/2) \leq 1$.

Six aspects of (10.14) are worth highlighting. First, the destabilising aspects of demand-linked circular causality can be seen by the fact that the first term in the numerator is positive. Second, the size of the destabilising demand linkage increases with the M-sector expenditure share, μ. This makes sense since as μ rises, a given amount of expenditure shifting has a bigger impact on the profitability of locating in the north. Third, the size of this destabilising effect falls as trade gets freer since s_R approaches $1/2$ as ϕ approaches unity. Fourth, the magnitude of the stabilising local* competition effect erodes faster than the destabilising force since both s_R and s_M approach $1/2$ as ϕ approaches unity. Fifth, the symmetric outcome is stable with very high trade costs. To see this observe that $4(s_R - 1/2)(s_M - 1/2) = 2(s_R - 1/2) = 1$ at $\phi = 0$ and $\mu < 1$. Finally, at some level of trade free-ness, namely $\phi^{b'} = (1 - \mu)/(1 + \mu)$, dw/dn is zero. This critical value is useful in characterising the strength of agglomeration forces since it defines the range of trade costs where agglomeration forces outweigh the dispersion force. Thus an expansion of this range (i.e. a fall in the critical value) indicates that agglomeration dominates over a wider range of trade costs.

Cost-of-living linkages

The above thought experiments isolate the importance of the local competition effect and demand-linked circular causality. The final force operating in the model works through the cost-of-living effect. Since the price of imported varieties bears the trade costs, consumers gain – other things equal – from local production of a variety. This effect, which we dub the 'location effect', is a destabilising force. A northward migration shock leads to production shifting that lowers the cost-of-living in the north and thus tends to makes northward migration more attractive. To see this more directly, we return to the full model with H basing its migration decisions on real wages and spending its income locally. Log differentiating the northern real wage, we have $\hat{\omega} = \hat{w} - \hat{\Delta}\mu/(1 - \sigma)$. Using (10.11):

$$\hat{\omega}|_{s_n=1/2} = [1 - 2\mu(s_R - 1/2)]\,\hat{w} + \left(\frac{2\mu}{\sigma - 1}\right)(s_R - 1/2)\hat{n}.$$

$$(10.15)$$

The second term is the cost-of-living effect, also known as cost-linked circular causality, cost linkages, or backward linkages. Since this is positive, the cost-of-living linkage is destabilising in the sense that it tends to make the real wage change stemming from a given migration shock more positive. Moreover, consumers care more about local production as $\mu/(\sigma - 1)$ increases, so the magnitude of the cost-of-living effect increases as μ rises and σ falls. Higher trade costs also amplify the size of the effect since s_R rises towards 1 as ϕ approaches zero.

Two observations are in order. First, note that the cost-linkage can be separated entirely from the demand and local competition effects. The first term in (10.15) captures the demand-linkage and the local competition effect, while the second term captures the cost-linkage. Second, note that the coefficient on $\hat{w}$ is positive – since $2(s_R - 1/2) \leq 1$ – so the net impact of the demand-linkage and local competition effects on ω depends only on the sign of (10.14).

The no-black-hole condition

To explore stability at very high trade costs, we use (10.14) and set $\phi = 0$ to get that $\hat{\omega}$ at $s_n = 1/2$ equals $-(1 - \mu)\hat{n} + \mu\hat{n}/(1 - \sigma)$. Stability requires this to be negative and solving we see that this holds only when $\mu < (1 - 1/\sigma)$. If this, which FKV call the 'no black hole' condition, holds, then the dispersed equilibrium is stable with very high trade costs. Otherwise, the symmetric equilibrium is never stable.

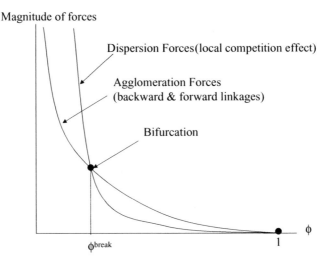

Figure 10.2   Agglomeration and dispersion forces erode with ϕ

10.5.3   The break point

We have seen that the magnitude of both the agglomeration and dispersion forces diminishes as trade cost falls, but the dispersion force diminishes faster than the agglomeration forces. We also saw that when the 'no black hole' condition holds, the symmetric equilibrium is stable – i.e. the dispersion force is stronger than the agglomeration forces – for very high trade costs.

Figure 10.2 illustrates both of these facts. The bifurcation point (i.e. the level of trade costs where the nature of the model's stability changes) is where the agglomeration and dispersion forces are equally strong.

Finally, noting that $2(s_R - 1/2) = 2(s_M - 1/2) = (1 - \phi)/(1 + \phi)$, we can find the level of ϕ where the bifurcation occurs by plugging (10.14) into (10.15), setting the result equal to zero and solving for ϕ. The solution is:

$$\phi^B = \frac{\sigma(1 - \mu) - 1}{\sigma(1 + \mu) - 1} \left(\frac{1 - \mu}{1 + \mu} \right). \qquad (10.16)$$

The break point can be used as a metric for the relative strength of agglomeration forces. For example, if a particular parameter change reduces ϕ^B, it must be that the change leads the agglomeration forces to overpower the dispersion force at a higher level of trade costs. This, in turn, implies that the change has strengthened the agglomeration forces relative to the dispersion forces.

Note that from (10.16), the break point falls when μ rises and when σ falls. This should make sense since μ magnifies both the demand-linked and the cost-linked agglomeration forces, while a fall in the substitutability of varieties, i.e. a rise in $1/(\sigma - 1)$, magnifies the cost-of-living linked agglomeration (by strengthening the utility benefit of local production). Of course, with free entry, $1/\sigma$ is also a measure of scale, so, loosely speaking, we can also say that an increase in equilibrium scale economies magnifies the cost-of-living agglomeration force.

10.5.4   The sustain point

The sustain point is much easier to characterise since it involves the comparison of levels rather than the signing of a derivative. Specifically, we evaluate w/P and w^*/P^* at the CP outcome (we take $s_n = s_H = 1$, although $s_n = s_H = 0$ would do just as well) and look for the level of ϕ where the two real wages are equal. Given our normalisation, w and P equal unity at the CP outcome (to see this plug $n = 1$ and $n^* = 0$ into (10.6) to find $w = 1$ and then use this and $n = 1$ and $n^* = 0$ in the definition of P). Using the southern equivalent of (10.6), we have $(w^*)^\sigma = \phi\mu(1 + L) + \mu L/\phi$ at the CP outcome, where L is each region's endowment of the immobile factor and $L = (1 - \mu)/2\mu$ with our normalisations. Plainly, this w^* is a sort of 'virtual' nominal wage since no labour is actually employed in the south when $s_H = 1$. Finally, in the south all M-varieties are imported when $s_H = 1$, so $P^* = \phi^{\mu/(1-s)}$. Putting these points together, the sustain point is implicitly defined by:

$$1 = \frac{w}{P} = \frac{w^*}{P^*} = \frac{[\phi^S\mu(1 + L) + \mu L/\phi^S]^{1/\sigma}}{(\phi^S)^{\mu/(1-\sigma)}}, \qquad L = \frac{1 - \mu}{2\mu}. \tag{10.17}$$

With some manipulation, this can be shown to be equivalent to the following implicit definition for the sustain point:

$$1 = (\phi^S)^{\mu/(1-1/\sigma)-1}\left(\frac{1 + \mu}{2}(\phi^S)^2 + \frac{1 - \mu}{2}\right). \tag{10.18}$$

10.5.5   Tomahawk bifurcation

The bifurcation diagram has the shape a tomahawk, as Figure 10.1 shows. This means that the sustain point occurs at a lower level of trade free-ness than the break point and that there are at most three interior steady-states at all levels of trade free-ness short of full integration, namely for all ϕ in [0, 1). We now turn to these issues.

Comparing the break and sustain points

The fact that the sustain point occurs at a lower level of trade free-ness than the break point is well known and has been demonstrated in thousands of numerical simulations by dozens of authors. Yet a valid proof of this critical feature of the model was never undertaken until recently.[18]

The most satisfying approach to proving that $\phi^S < \phi^B$ would be direct algebraic manipulation of expressions for the two critical points. This is not possible since ϕ^S can be defined implicitly only as in (10.17). Instead, we pursue a two-step proof. First we characterise how the function,

$$f(\phi) \equiv \phi^{\mu/(1-1/\sigma)-1}\left[(1+\mu)\phi^2 + \left(\frac{1-\mu}{2}\right)\right] - 1,$$

(this is just a transformation of the second expression in (10.17)) changes with ϕ. This function is of interest since ϕ^S is its root. With some work we can show three facts: that $f(1) = 0$ and $f'(1)$ is positive, that $f(0)$ is positive and $f'(0)$ is negative, and that $f(.)$ has a unique minimum. Taken together, this means f has a unique root between zero and unity. In short, it looks like the f drawn in figure 10.3. Next, we show that $f(\phi^B) < 0$, which is possible only if $\phi^S < \phi^B$, given the shape of $f(\phi)$. To this end, observe that $f(\phi^B)$ is a function of μ and σ. Call this new function $g(\mu, \sigma)$ and note that the partial of g with respect to μ is negative and $g(0, \sigma)$ is zero regardless of σ. The point of all this is that the upper bound of g, and thus the upper bound of $f(\phi^B)$, is zero. We know, therefore, that for permissible values of μ and σ, $\phi^S > \phi^B$.

On the number of interior steady states

Until recently, no analytical study supported the tomahawk configuration of the bifurcation diagram (figure 10.1): thousands of simulations showed that when there were asymmetric interior steady states they featured the following characteristics. First, they always come in symmetric pairs (this is hardly surprising given the symmetry of the model), namely, if some s_H different to $1/2$ is a solution to $\Omega[s_H] = 0$, then $1 - s_H$ is a solution, too. Second, these asymmetric steady states are always unstable: $d\Omega/ds_H$ is positive for all $s_H > 1/2$ such that $\Omega[s_H] = 0$. Finally, there are at most two of them.

To show this result, it is sufficient to invoke the result in sub-section 10.5.5 and that $\Omega[.] = 0$ admits at most three solutions. See figure 10.1

---

[18] The first draft of the excellent paper by Peter Neary (2001), was seen by us before we wrote this chapter. That draft contained a brief proof in a footnote that turned out to be incorrect. One of the authors showed the proof's error and provided a correct proof, which Peter Neary incorporated (with accreditation) in subsequent drafts of his paper. See also Robert-Nicoud (2001).

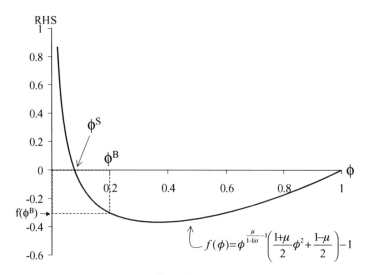

Figure 10.3   Proving the $\phi^B > \phi^S$

to get convinced. The proof for this result involves essentially two steps. The first step is to rewrite the model in its 'natural' state space, namely the mobile nominal expenditure $s_H w$ rather than the mass of mobile workers s_H. To this end, it is useful to note that the Cobb–Douglas specification for tastes in (10.1) implies $s_H w + (1 - s_H)w^* = 1$, hence $s_H w$ is the share of mobile expenditure spent in the North. The second step is to show that the alternative CP model developed by Forslid and Ottaviano (2001) is *identical* to the original version surveyed here when expressed in the same, natural, state space. Since this model is known to admit at most three interior steady states, the same must be true for the original CP model analysed here. This methodology extends to geography models in which agglomeration is driven by input–output linkages (FKV, chapter 14). See Robert-Nicoud (2001) for details.

10.6   Caveats

10.6.1   *When does symmetry break? Pareto dominance and migration shocks*

The analysis to this point has focused only on local stability, as is true of the vast majority of the literature. This is not enough. For instance, when does symmetry break as trade costs fell gradually from prohibitive to negligible? The standard answer is that it breaks at the break point. This is not necessarily true. For levels of trade free-ness between ϕ^S and ϕ^B, there are three locally stable equilibrium: $s_n = 1/2$, $s_n = 1$ and $s_n = 0$. In game theory, where multiple equilibria is viewed as a problem, it is common to apply the 'Pareto refinement'. That is, if a particular equilibrium is Pareto dominated by another, there is some presumption that agents would be able to coordinate sufficiently to avoid the inferior outcome. The technical name of the equilibria that survive this refinement are 'coalition proof equilibria' (Bernheim, Peleg and Whinston, 1987). As it turns out, $s_n = 1/2$ is not coalition proof when $\phi^S < \phi < \phi^B$.

With ϕ between ϕ^S and ϕ^B, all workers are better off at either CP outcome than they are at the symmetric outcome – due to the cost-of-living effect. One might therefore presume that a sufficiently large coalition of workers would agree to migration once trade costs got low enough to make the CP outcome locally stable. This would be rational since if they all did move their instantaneous real wage would rise. All this goes to challenge the standard analysis that claims that starting with very high trade costs, the economy remains at the symmetric outcome until the break point is reached. If coalitions of workers can migrate, it is possible – and indeed would be very rational – for symmetry to collapse when trade costs fall to the sustain point. More formally this just says that while symmetry is locally stable when $\phi^S < \phi < \phi^B$, it is not globally stable.

This brings us to issues of global stability. This, together with other issues, will however not be tackled in detailed here so as to be parsimonious.

10.7   Global stability and forward-looking expectations

Baldwin (2001) provides a rigorous analysis on the dynamic properties of the model. In particular, he shows how to study the global stability properties of the model as well as how to extend it to allow for forward-looking agents. We survey the results of this analysis in turn.

10.7.1   Global stability and myopic expectations

Local stability analysis (as carried out in sub-section 10.3.2) is fine for most uses, but it is not sufficient for fully characterising the model's behaviour when s_H is away from a long-run equilibrium (e.g. when the process of agglomeration is 'en route'). The economic geography literature typically avoids discussing what happens between long-run equilibria, but where it does it relies on a heuristic approach. Namely, it is asserted that the system approaches the nearest stable equilibrium that does not require crossing an unstable equilibrium. Baldwin (2001) uses

Liaponov's direct method to show that this heuristic approach can be justified formally.

10.7.2   Local stability and forward-looking expectations

Perhaps the least attractive of the CP model assumptions concerns migrant behaviour. Migrants are assumed to ignore the future, basing their migration choices on *current* real wage differences alone. This is awkward since migration is the key to agglomeration, workers are infinitely lived, and migration alters wages in a predictable manner. While the shortcomings of myopia were abundantly clear to the model's progenitors, the assumption was thought necessary for tractability. This turns out not to be true. The first thing to note is that myopic behaviour is tantamount to static expectations. Also, an important and somewhat unexpected result is that the break and sustain points are exactly the same with static and with forward-looking expectations. In this sense, the law of motion in (10.2) is merely an assumption of convenience.

10.7.3   Global stability and forward-looking expectations

When trade costs are such that the CP model has a unique stable equilibrium, local stability analysis is sufficient. After any shock, the asset value of migration (a co-state variable) jumps to put the system on the saddle path leading to the unique stable equilibrium (if it did not, the system would diverge and thereby violate a necessary condition for intertemporal optimisation). For ϕs where the model has multiple stable steady states things are more complex. With multiple stable equilibria, there will be multiple saddle paths. In principle, multiple saddle paths may correspond to a given initial condition, thus creating what Matsuyama (1991) calls an indeterminacy of the equilibrium path. In other words, it is not clear to which path the system will jump, so the interesting possibility of self-fulfilling prophecies and sudden takeoffs may arise.

Assume $\phi^S < \phi < \phi^B$ throughout so that the system is marked by three stable steady states. Three qualitatively different cases are considered for the migration cost parameter γ. The first case is when γ, the migration cost parameter, is very large, so horizontal movement is very slow. Numerical simulations show there is no overlap of saddle paths in this case, so the global stability analysis with static expectations is exactly right. That is, the basins of attraction for the various equilibria are the same with static and forward-looking expectations. This is an important result. It says that if migration costs are sufficiently high, the global as well as the local stability properties of the CP model with forward-looking expectations are qualitatively identical to those of the model with myopic migrants.

The second case is for an intermediate value of migration costs. Here the saddle paths overlap somewhat. The existence of overlapping saddle paths changes things dramatically, as Krugman (1991c) showed. If the economy finds itself with a level of s_n in the area of overlap, then a fundamental indeterminacy exists. Both saddle paths provide perfectly rational adjustment tracks. Workers individually choose a migration strategy taking as given their beliefs about the aggregate path. Consistency requires that beliefs are rational on any equilibrium path. That is, the aggregate path that results from each worker's choice is the one that each of them believes to be the equilibrium path. Putting it more colloquially, workers chose the path that they think other workers will take. In other words, expectations, rather than history, can matter.

Because expectations can change suddenly, even with no change in environmental parameters, the system is subject to sudden and seemingly unpredictable takeoffs and/or reversals. Moreover, the government may influence the state of the economy by announcing a policy, say a tax, that deletes an equilibrium even when the current state of the economy is distant to the deleted equilibrium.

The final case is the most spectacular. Here migration costs are very low, so horizontal movement is quite fast. Interestingly, the overlap of saddle paths includes the symmetric equilibrium. This raises the possibility that the economy could jump from the symmetric equilibrium onto a path that leads it to a CP outcome merely because all the workers expected that everyone else was going to migrate. Plainly, this raises the possibility of a big-push drive by a government having some very dramatic effects.

We conclude with two remarks. First, note that the region of overlapping saddle paths will never include a CP outcome. Thus, although one may 'talk the economy' out of a symmetric equilibrium, one can never do the same for an economy that is already agglomerated. Finally, Karp (2000) assumes that agents have 'almost common knowledge' in the sense of Rubinstein (1989) about history (economic fundamentals) rather than common knowledge. In a setting akin to Matsuyama (1991) and Krugman (1991c), Karp shows that the equilibrium indeterminacy brought about by the possibility that expectations might prevail above history washes away. Common knowledge and rational expectations together give rise to the possibility that expectations might prevail over history in the first place, so it is not surprising that altering the information structure alters the equilibrium set considerably. We conjecture that the same holds true in the present CP model with forward-looking expectations. As Karp (2000) points out, the restoration of the determinacy implies that 'the unique competitive equilibrium can be influenced by government policy, just as in the standard models'.

10.8   Concluding remarks

In ending, we can do no better than to quote an early draft of Peter Neary's (2001) *Journal of Economic Literature* article on the new economic geography literature:

'New economic geography' has come of age. Launched by Paul Krugman in a 1991 *Journal of Political Economy* paper; extended in a series of articles by Krugman, Masahisa Fujita, Tony Venables and a growing band of associates; soon to be institutionalised with the appearance of a new journal; it has now been consolidated and comprehensively synthesised in a recent book from MIT Press.

Such rapid progress would make anyone dizzy, and at times the authors risk getting carried away by their heady prose style. Thus, the structure of equilibria predicted by one model suggests a story which they call (following Krugman and Venables (1995)) 'History of the World, Part I' (page 253); the pattern of world industrialisation suggested by another is described as 'a story of breathtaking scope' (page 277); and on his website Krugman expresses the hope that economic geography will one day become as important a field as international trade. This sort of hype, even if tongue-in-cheek, is not to everyone's taste, especially when the results rely on special functional forms and all too often can only be derived by numerical methods. What next, the unconvinced reader may be tempted to ask? The tee-shirt? The movie?

This reaction is even more remarkable when one notes that the basic elements of the model have been in circulation since Dixit and Stiglitz (1977) and Krugman (1980). In this chapter, we propose an exhaustive presentation of the CP model, decomposing the effects at work so as to boost intuition. We have described all the main properties of the model (using analytical analysis rather than simulations whenever it was possible), including catastrophe, hysteresis, the number of steady states and global stability. For lack of space, we were content with merely mentioning some of them, especially the most technical ones. Baldwin *et al.* (2003) cover these properties in depth and also consider the case of intrinsically asymmetric regions.

REFERENCES

Baldwin, R. E. (1988). Hysteresis in import prices: the beachhead effect. *American Economic Review*, 78: 773–785
    (2001). The core–periphery model with forward-looking expectations. *Regional Science and Urban Economics*, 31: 21–49

Baldwin, R. E., Forslid, R., Martin, P., Ottaviano, G. I. P. and Robert-Nicoud, F. (2003). *Economic Geography and Public Policies*, Princeton, Princeton University Press

Baldwin, R. E. and Krugman, P. (1989). Persistent trade effects of large exchange rate shocks. *Quarterly Journal of Economics*, 104: 635–654

Bernheim, B. D., Peleg, B. and Whinston, M. D. (1987). Coalition-proof Nash equilibria I: concepts. *Journal of Economic Theory*, 42: 1–12

Dixit, A. K. (1989). Hysteresis, import penetration, and exchange rate pass-through. *Quarterly Journal of Economics*, 104: 205–28

Dixit, A. K. and Stiglitz, J. E. (1977). Monopolistic competition and optimum product diversity. *American Economic Review*, 67: 297–308

Forslid, R. and Ottaviano, G. (2001). Trade and agglomeration: two analytically solvable cases. Lund University, mimeo

Fujita M., Krugman P. and Venables, A. (1999). *The Spatial Economy: Cities, Regions and International Trade*. Cambridge, MA, MIT Press

Helpman, E. and Krugman, P. R. (1985). *Market Structure and Foreign Trade*. Cambridge, MA, MIT Press

Karp, L. (2000). Fundamentals versus beliefs under almost common knowledge. UC Berkeley, mimeo

Krugman, P. (1980). Scale economies, Pronet differentiation, and the pattern of trade. *American Economic Review*, 70: 950–959

    (1991a). Increasing returns and economic geography. *Journal of Political Economy*, 99: 483–499

    (1991b). *Geography and Trade*. Cambridge, MA, MIT Press

    (1991c). History versus expectations. *Quarterly Journal of Economics*, 106: 651–667

Krugman, P. R. and Venables, A. J. (1995). Globalization and the inequality of nations. *Quarterly Journal of Economics*, 110: 857–880

Matsuyama, K. (1991). Increasing returns, industrialization and indeterminacy of equilibrium. *Quarterly Journal of Economics*, 106: 617–650

Neary, J. P. (2001). Of hype and hyperbolas: introducing the new economic geography. *Journal of Economic Literature*, 39: 536–561

Robert-Nicoud, F. (2001). The structure of standard models of the New Economic Geography. London School of Economics, mimeo

Rubinstein, A. (1989). The electronic email game: strategic behavior under almost common knowledge. *American Economic Review*, 79: 385–391

Venables, A. (1987). Trade and trade policy with differentiated products: a Chamberlinian–Ricardian model. *Economic Journal*, 97: 700–717

    (1996). Equilibrium locations of vertically linked industries. *International Economic Review*, 37: 341–359

11   Globalisation, wages and unemployment: a new economic geography perspective

Jolanda J. W. Peeters and Harry Garretsen

11.1   Introduction

There is considerable cross-country variance in unemployment and employment performance as well as in the evolution of industrial and occupational structure. Differences are in particular striking between the US and Europe, but there are also substantial differences among European countries. (Burda and Dluhosch, 1998, p. 5)

This quotation is from an interesting study that tries to analyse the relevance of globalisation for the observed changes in wages and unemployment of low-skilled labour in Western industrialised countries. The empirical evidence suggests that this relevance varies significantly across these countries (OECD, 1997). In some countries globalisation, either through increased trade or increased factor mobility, is thought to have had an adverse impact on particularly the relative wages of low-skilled workers, whereas in other countries relative low-skilled wages are hardly affected or have even increased. Moreover, in some cases the impact of globalisation does not seem to show up in relative wage changes but (also) in an increase in the relative unemployment of low-skilled labour (Dewatripont, Sapir and Sekkat, 1999). One possibility to explain these differences is that there may be considerable cross-country variation in the degree of globalisation as well as in the workings of national labour markets. With respect to the latter the well-known differences in wage flexibility between notably the USA and the UK and the continental European countries come to mind (Layard, Nickell and Jackman, 1991). So, one would expect that the theoretical model which has been most widely used to analyse the possible impact of globalisation on labour markets to take these differences into account. This is, however, clearly not the case.

At the time of the writing of this chapter both authors were affiliated with the Department of Applied Economics, University of Nijmegen, the Netherlands. We would like to thank Steven Brakman, Charles van Marrewijk, Albert de Vaal and participants at the conference (notably Peter Neary, Russell Cooper and our discussant Theo van de Klundert) for their comments. Of course, the usual disclaimer applies. This chapter is a revised version of our CESifo Working Paper, 256, Center for Economic Studies, Munich, February 2000.

The model we refer to is, of course, the Heckscher–Ohlin model and in many discussions on globalisation the simple $2 \times 2 \times 2$ textbook version of this model is used (see for instance the contributions to Collins, 1998). This model makes unambiguous predictions about the impact of globalisation. The empirical validity of these predictions is not our concern here (but see Peeters, 2001). What matters for our present purposes is that these predictions are based on a 'one size fits all' analysis of globalisation. Countries are homogeneous with respect to the degree and contents of globalisation that they experience and also with respect to the workings of the labour market (typically wages are fully flexible).[1] Given the afore-mentioned cross-country variation, this is a rather unsatisfactory state of affairs.

One solution is to use an alternative trade model that enables a richer menu of possibilities as far as the impact of globalisation on labour markets is concerned. In our view and following Dluhosch (2000) the new economic geography approach may offer such an alternative. Krugman and Venables (1995) develop a two-country new economic geography model to analyse the effects of globalisation on the relative wage *between* these two countries. In their model there is, however, only one type of transportation costs, one type of labour and the labour market always clears. This seriously limits the relevance of the model for the issue of globalisation and its impact on labour markets. In this chapter we build a highly stylised new economic geography model in which two types of labour (low- and high-skilled) are distinguished and in which, owing to wage rigidities, unemployment may arise. Moreover, we also introduce two types of transportation costs (for goods and services, respectively) to allow for a more intricate analysis of the ways in which globalisation can influence the economy.

In sum, the purpose of this chapter is to analyse the impact of globalisation, which we mainly define as the fall in the transportation costs of goods and/or services, on the labour market position of low-skilled workers. By making use of a new economic geography model that allows for wage rigidities, we expect to find part of the theoretical explanation for the diverging labour market experiences across the advanced countries in the globalisation era. The paper will proceed along the following lines. Section 11.2 briefly discusses the model and focuses on its two most relevant and novel features, the production structure and the workings of the labour market. Section 11.3 investigates the short-run equilibrium of the model, in which labour cannot move between regions. As a first

---

[1] For exceptions in terms of a Heckscher–Ohlin framework see Krugman (1995) and Davis (1998).

approximation this is a reasonable assumption because the international mobility of labour is still relatively unimportant as a determinant of globalisation compared to the role of international trade and capital mobility (IMF, 1997). In the end, however, we must also deal with the implications of the mobility of labour (if only because the mobility of labour (and firms) distinguishes the new trade theory from the new economic geography). Section 11.4 is therefore concerned with the long-run implications of globalisation by allowing for the mobility of high-skilled labour. Section 11.5 concludes.

11.2   The model

11.2.1   The main ingredients of the model

Our model is based on the new economic geography model developed by de Vaal and van den Berg (1999) but there are some notable differences between their and our approach. The main similarity is to be found in the modelling of the production structure (see below). The main differences are that we include two instead of only one factor(s) of production (high- and low-skilled labour) and allow not only for flexible wages but also for rigid wages.[2] Apart from the handling of the production structure and the labour market, our model resembles the standard two-region new economic geography model as laid out in, for example, Fujita, Krugman and Venables (1999, chapters 4 and 5) or Brakman, Garretsen and van Marrewijk (2001, chapters 3 and 4).

Demand
The world is divided in two regions, Home and Foreign. Both regions are capable of producing a homogeneous agricultural good A and varieties of the heterogeneous manufactured good M. The agricultural good, which serves as the numéraire, is produced with a constant returns to scale (CES) technology, whereas the manufactured good is produced under economies of scale. All individuals are assumed to have a Cobb–Douglas utility function of the form $U = C_M^\mu C_A^{1-\mu}$, where C_M is consumption of the manufactures aggregate and C_A is consumption of the agricultural good. The manufactures aggregate is given by

$$C_M = \left[\sum_{N_h} c_{hh}^\theta + \sum_{N_f} c_{fh}^\theta \right]^{1/\theta},$$

---

[2] In a twin paper, Peeters and de Vaal (2000), the same model is used but labour market rigidities are not part of the analysis.

where N_h is the number of varieties that originate in Home and N_f is the number of varieties that originate in Foreign. As the manufacturing varieties are imperfect substitutes for each other $(0 < \theta < 1)$, the Home consumer consumes both Home (c_{hh}) and Foreign (c_{fh}) varieties.[3] This merely restates the crucial role of the Dixit–Stiglitz model in new economic geography. The relative demand is a function of relative prices only:

$$\frac{c_{hh}}{c_{fh}} = \left(\frac{p_{hh}}{p_{fh}}\right)^{1/(\theta-1)}, \tag{11.1}$$

where p_{hh} denotes the price of a Home good consumed by a Home consumer, whereas p_{fh} is the price of a Foreign good consumed by a Home consumer. Utility-maximisation gives us in addition the true price index of consumers in Home which, as we will see below, is necessary to derive real wages:

$$\tilde{P}_h = \left[N_h p_{hh}^{\theta/(\theta-1)} + N_f p_{fh}^{\theta/(\theta-1)}\right]^{(\theta-1)/\theta}. \tag{11.2}$$

Supply

The demand side of our model is standard within the new economic geography approach but this is not the case for the production structure. The production of manufactures in Home consists of two activities: the production of unfinished goods, $\bar{x}_h$, and the adding of producer services from Home and Foreign, S_h and S_f. While the production of unfinished goods is performed by the manufacturing firms, the production of producer services is performed by services firms.[4] It is assumed that the unfinished goods are produced by *low-skilled labour* only and that the production of unfinished goods entails scale economies: $L_{\bar{x}_h}^m = F + B\bar{x}_h$, where $L_{\bar{x}_h}^m$ is the low-skilled labour used to produce the output $\bar{x}_h$ and $F(B)$ are the fixed (marginal) cost in terms of low-skilled labour. Part of the unfinished output of the Home manufacturing firm is intended for the Home region (x_{hh}), whereas the other part is exported to Foreign (x_{hf}); thus: $\bar{x}_h = x_{hh} + x_{hf}$. Producer services are produced by *high-skilled labour* only and its production also entails scale economies: $H_{S_h} = f + bS_h$, where H_{S_h} is the high-skilled labour used to produce services output S_h. As producer services typically require close interaction between the consumer and the producer, we assume that producer services have to be added locally. An example helps to clarify the production structure. Suppose a Home firm

---

[3] We describe the Home region, simply noting that analogous conditions hold in Foreign.
[4] Thus, a manufacturing firm 'buys' the producer services from the services firms. In this respect, producer services can be regarded as an intermediate input to the manufacturing firms.

produces a variety of a particular manufactured good, let's say a car. The car itself is the unfinished good (x_h) and it requires the addition of producers services produced in Home and Foreign before it can be sold as a final consumption good to the consumers in both regions. In the case of the car, the producer services that are required are for instance all kinds of dealer, sales and financing services without which the consumption good cannot be sold to the consumer.[5]

Finally, for the *location* of production to matter, it must the case that both the trade of unfinished goods and producer services involves transportation costs. We assume the familiar 'iceberg' transportation costs for unfinished goods (τ) and producer services (ρ), so that a part of the transported item 'melts' away. The production functions of a Home manufacturing firm can then be given by:

$$m_{hh} = x_{hh}^{\alpha} \left[\sum_{n_h} S_{hhh}^{\gamma} + \sum_{n_f} (\rho S_{fhh})^{\gamma} \right]^{(1-\alpha)/\gamma} \tag{11.3}$$

$$m_{hf} = (\tau x_{hf})^{\alpha} \left[\sum_{n_h} (\rho S_{hhf})^{\gamma} + \sum_{n_f} S_{fhf}^{\gamma} \right]^{(1-\alpha)/\gamma}, \tag{11.4}$$

where m_{hh} and m_{hf} denote the amount of the final consumption good a Home manufacturing producer makes for consumers in Home and Foreign; n_h and n_f are the number of producer services varieties from Home and Foreign; S_{ijk} refers to the use of a region i service by a region j manufacturing producer to finish its good in region k; γ is the elasticity of substitution of producer services and α is the unfinished good intensity in final production.

Equilibrium prices and production

Given this particular production structure which will play an important part in our analysis, the determination of equilibrium prices and production is more or less straightforward so we will be brief here. Manufacturing producers maximise their profits. This yields the following price equations:[6]

$$p_{hh} = \frac{C}{\theta} w_h^{\alpha} \tilde{V}_h^{1-\alpha} \tag{11.5}$$

$$p_{hf} = \frac{C}{\theta} \tau^{-\alpha} w_h^{\alpha} \tilde{V}_f^{1-\alpha}, \tag{11.6}$$

---

[5] In a way we could also denote our two production factors as labour type A and type B instead of as low-skilled and high-skilled labour. The skill level as such is not important in what follows.

[6] For a derivation, see Peeters (2001, appendix C).

with $C = B^\alpha \alpha^{-\alpha}(1-\alpha)^{-(1-\alpha)} > 0$ and where w_h denotes the nominal wage of low-skilled workers in Home (the equilibrium level). $\tilde{V}_i$ denotes the price index of producer services in region $i = h, f$ and is for Home given by:

$$\tilde{V}_h = \left[\sum_{n_h} v_h^{\gamma/(\gamma-1)} + \sum_{n_f} \left(\frac{v_f}{\rho}\right)^{\gamma/(\gamma-1)} \right]^{(\gamma-1)/\gamma}. \qquad (11.7)$$

If there is free entry and exit of firms into manufacturing, profits must be zero. Substitution of earlier results then leads to the result that the total production of unfinished goods and its use of low-skilled labour is alike for all manufactures throughout the economy and is equal to (per firm):

$$\bar{x}_h = \frac{\alpha\theta}{1-\theta}\frac{F}{B} \qquad L_{\bar{x}_h}^M = \frac{1-\theta(1-\alpha)}{1-\theta}F. \qquad (11.8)$$

Equilibrium on the market for unfinished manufactured goods requires that total sales of one firm equals total demand (per firm). Hence:

$$\bar{x}_h = \frac{\alpha\theta}{B}\frac{p_{hh}m_{hh} + p_{hf}m_{hf}}{w_h}. \qquad (11.9)$$

Let us now turn to the prices and production of producer services. Producer services firms also maximise their profits; this yields:

$$v_h = \frac{b}{\gamma}r_h, \qquad (11.10)$$

where r_h is the nominal wage of high-skilled labour in Home. Here also, free entry and exit of firms into the services market drives profits to zero and leads to the result that the output and the labour use of producer services firms is alike for all services firms and is equal to (per firm):

$$S_h = \frac{\gamma}{1-\gamma}\frac{f}{b} \qquad H_{S_h} = \frac{f}{1-\gamma}. \qquad (11.11)$$

Equilibrium on the services market requires total sales per firm $(v_h S_h)$ to equal total demand, so the services market equilibrium is represented by:[7]

$$v_h S_h = (1 - \alpha)\theta v_h^{\gamma/(\gamma-1)} \big[(N_h p_{hh} m_{hh} + N_f p_{fh} m_{fh}) \tilde{V}_h^{\gamma/(1-\gamma)}$$

$$+ (N_f p_{ff} m_{ff} + N_h p_{hf} m_{hf})(\rho \tilde{V}_f)^{\gamma/(1-\gamma)} \big]. \qquad (11.12)$$

The model can be closed by specifying the equilibrium conditions for the labour market and the market for final consumption goods. Our specification of the labour market deviates, however, from the standard new economic geography models in two important ways. First, our model includes two types of labour and, second, our labour market should somehow allow for wage rigidities. The next sub-section therefore takes a closer look at the workings of the labour market in our model.

11.2.2   *The labour market and wage rigidity*

Recall that there are two factors of production in each economy: low-skilled labour ($\bar{L}$) and high-skilled labour ($\bar{H}$). In Home as well as Foreign low-skilled labour is employed in both the agricultural and the manufacturing sector and is assumed to be immobile between sectors or regions: $\bar{L} = L^A + L^M$. The low-skilled workers employed in the agricultural sector (L^A) are equally divided between the two regions: $L_i^A = l\bar{L}/2$ ($i = h, f$). The low-skilled workers employed in the manufacturing sector (L^M) are not necessary divided equally between Home and Foreign: λ_l is the share of low-skilled manufacturing workers in Home. Due to wage rigidities, to which we turn below, the labour market for low-skilled manufacturing workers in Home does not have to clear and unemployment can arise. If this is the case, U_h refers to the number of unemployed in Home, while $L_h^{M,e}$ refers to the number of *employed* low-skilled manufacturing workers in Home. Note that in Foreign the labour market for low-skilled manufacturing workers always clears. The high-skilled workers in both regions are always fully employed and they are assumed to be mobile between Home and Foreign in the long run: λ_h is the share

---

[7] To derive total demand, note that each services firm delivers to Home and Foreign manufacturing firms:

$$S_h = \sum_{N_h}(S_{hhh} + S_{hhf}) + \sum_{N_f}(S_{hfh} + S_{hff}).$$

From the first-order condition of profit-maximisation of manufacturing firms, it follows that the demand for the output of a region i services firm by a region j manufacturing producer for consumers in region k is equal to:

$$S_{ijk} = \begin{cases} \theta(1-\alpha) p_{jk} m_{jk} v_i^{-1/(1-\gamma)} \tilde{V}_k^{\gamma/(1-\gamma)} & \text{for } i = k \\ \theta(1-\alpha)\rho^{\gamma/(1-\gamma)} p_{jk} m_{jk} v_i^{-1/(1-\gamma)} \tilde{V}_k^{\gamma/(1-\gamma)} & \text{for } i \neq k. \end{cases}$$

of high-skilled workers in Home. Substitution between low-skilled and high-skilled workers is not possible. The set-up of the labour market is given by equations (11.13) and (11.14):

$$N_h L_{\tilde{x}_h}^M = \begin{cases} (1-l)\lambda_l \bar{L} & \text{if flexible} \\ (1-l)\lambda_l \bar{L} - U_h & \text{if rigid} \end{cases} \qquad N_f L_{\tilde{x}_f}^M = (1-l)(1-\lambda_l)\bar{L}$$

$$(11.13)$$

$$n_h H_{S_h} = \lambda_h \bar{H} \qquad n_f H_{S_f} = (1-\lambda_h)\bar{H}. \qquad (11.14)$$

Equations (11.13) and (11.14) give labour demand (left-hand sides) and labour supply (right-hand sides). As can be seen, with the notable exception of the low-skilled labour market with rigid wages, the various labour markets clear. In case the labour market clears it is also immediately clear that the equilibrium number of varieties is determined. Note, however, that this is not true for N_h if $U_h > 0$.

The specification of the equilibrium conditions for the market of manufactured goods closes the model. Note that the unemployed have nothing to spend in this model which inter alia means that total income is always smaller with unemployment. Given the Cobb–Douglas representation of the demand side, so that consumers spend a fixed share of their income on both goods, namely, μ on manufactured goods and $(1 - \mu)$ on agricultural goods, the equilibrium conditions for the market for manufactures in Home and Foreign are, respectively:

$$N_h p_{hh} c_{hh} + N_f p_{fh} c_{fh} = \begin{cases} \mu \left(w_h L_h^M + L_h^A + r_h H_h \right) & \text{if flexible} \\ \mu \left(w_h^{rig} L_h^{M,e} + L_h^A + r_h H_h \right) & \text{if rigid} \end{cases}$$

$$(11.15)$$

$$N_f p_{ff} c_{ff} + N_h p_{hf} c_{hf} = \mu \left(w_f L_f^M + L_f^A + r_f H_h \right), \qquad (11.16)$$

where w_h^{rig} is the absolute wage of low-skilled workers in Home if the labour market does not clear. Given the importance attached to wage rigidity in our analysis of the effects of globalisation, it is useful to elaborate upon the implications of wage rigidity. *We distinguish two labour market regimes in Home.* The first is the *flexible (FLEX) regime*, in which the labour market for low-skilled manufacturing workers always clears (i.e. U_h equals zero). In fact, in this regime our labour market is equivalent to the specification of the labour market in the core new economic geography model (see Fujita, Krugman and Venables, 1999, p. 52). The number of varieties N_i and n_i (with $i = h, f$) are then determined on the labour market (see (11.13) and (11.14)), whereas the wages of low-skilled and high-skilled workers are determined on the goods market (11.15) and (11.16). As long as the distribution of high- and low-skilled workers between Home and Foreign is fixed, labour supplies are also fixed and this gives the equilibrium number of varieties of unfinished goods and producer services.

Our second labour market regime is the *relative wage rigidity (RWR) regime*, in which it is assumed that the low-skilled wages are set so as to equal the high-skilled wages, hence $w_h^{rig} = w_h^{RWR} = r_h$. In fact, this is a very stringent wage norm because it implies that there is no wage differential whatsoever. For our analysis it does, however, not make much difference whether low-skilled wages are 50 per cent, 75 per cent or, as in our case, 100 per cent of high-skilled wages. This rigidity reflects a wage norm which is thought to be very relevant for, e.g., the countries in continental Europe. This wage rigidity always binds (because $w_h^{FLEX} < r_h^{FLEX}$), meaning that part of the low-skilled manufacturing labour force in Home will be unemployed. To see how unemployment arises, in case of relative wage rigidity (*RWR*) and in contrast with the *FLEX* regime, note that N_h can no longer be looked upon as being determined on the labour market. Instead, N_h is then determined on the goods market. With w_h fixed at the level of the high-skilled wage in Home and, also important, assuming that N_f, n_h and n_f are still determined on their respective labour markets, N_h has to adjust in order for the goods market (11.15) and (11.16) to continue to clear. This means that the labour market for low-skilled in Home will not clear. This shows up in the rigid wage version of (11.13) where U_h represents the disequilibrium on this labour market. In fact, it turns out that with relative wage rigidity, N_h has to decrease thereby reducing the number of varieties produced.[8]

11.3   Short-run implications of globalisation

To see how globalisation affects the relative labour market position of the low-skilled in Home, we focus in this section on the short-run equilibrium and take therefore the distribution of low-skilled and high-skilled labour between regions as given. We think that the short-run equilibrium is interesting from a globalisation perspective because, as was stated in the introduction, the international mobility of labour is still relatively low. This means that globalisation in terms of our model occurs through the

---

[8] Of course, other types of wage rigidity are also possible. In Peeters and Garretsen (2000) we also analyse the implications of a minimum wage for the low-skilled in Home. The main conclusions are, however, in that case not different from the ones derived in sections 11.3 and 11.4 for the *FLEX* and *RWR* regimes.

effects of a fall in transportation costs of goods and services between our two regions. The short-run equilibrium is contained in (11.1), (11.5), (11.6), (11.9), (11.12), their Foreign equivalents and equations (11.13)–(11.16). As with most new economic geography models the complexity of our model precludes an analytical solution, so we will conduct our analysis through simulations. The numerical values for the benchmark case are:

$$\bar{L} = 800, \quad F = 1, \quad \alpha = 0.6, \ \theta = \gamma = 0.6, \ B = 0.05, \ l = 0.5$$
$$\bar{H} = 100, \quad f = 0.5, \ \mu = 0.6, \ \tau = \rho = 0.5, \ b = 0.1, \quad \lambda_l = \lambda_h = 0.4.$$

11.3.1   *Relative wages between regions*

This section investigates the impact of globalisation (a reduction in transportation costs of unfinished goods and/or producer services) on the relative wages of low-skilled and high-skilled workers *between* regions (w_h/w_f and r_h/r_f). Since most new economic geography models have only one factor of production they can address the impact of globalisation only on the relative wage *between* regions (e.g. Krugman and Venables, 1995). Focusing first on relative wages between regions allows us, albeit in the context of a short-run equilibrium, to compare our results with the results of these one-factor models. In short, the standard conclusions (essentially based on Krugman, 1991, p. 491) can be stated as follows: (1) if both regions are equally well endowed with labour, the relative wage will equal one; (2) if labour is then shifted from one region to another, the relative wage can move either way depending on the trade-off between the Home Market and Extent of Competition effect; (3) the level of transportation costs is very important in settling the balance between both these effects.[9]

In order to investigate whether these effects are present in our model, consider figure 11.1 which shows the effect of a reduction in the transportation costs of unfinished goods (*increase* in τ) on the relative wage of low-skilled workers *between* regions (w_h/w_f) in the regime with flexible wages. Three distributions of labour are shown: the first one is simply the benchmark case, in which Home is smaller in terms of low-skilled and high-skilled labour ($\lambda_h = \lambda_l = 0.4$), the second one is the symmetrical case ($\lambda_h = \lambda_l = 0.5$), and the third one is for Home being the larger region ($\lambda_h = \lambda_l = 0.6$). In the symmetrical case, w_h/w_f indeed equals one

---

[9] In a nutshell, the home market effect gives firms in the larger region a competitive advantage by allowing them to better exploit economies of scale, which enables them to offer higher wages, whereas the extent of competition effect gives firms in the smaller region an advantage as they face less competition for the local demand, which enables them to offer higher wages (see Krugman, 1991).

at all levels of τ; as there are no differences between the two regions all endogenous variables will have the same values in Home compared to Foreign. In the case Home is the smaller region ($\lambda_h = \lambda_l = 0.4$), however, the relative wage does not equal one and a fall in the transportation costs of unfinished goods implies that w_h/w_f decreases for low levels of τ. After a critical level of transportation costs ($\tau > 0.46$), w_h/w_f starts to increase again. Figure 11.1 shows that if Home is instead the larger region ($\lambda_h = \lambda_l = 0.6$) exactly the opposite happens with the relative wage w_h/w_f. The relation between transportation costs and the relative wage is thus non-linear; a fall in the transportation costs of unfinished goods can either increase or decrease the relative wage depending upon the *level* of transportation costs.

Figure 11.1 thus allows us to reproduce the two other aforementioned standard results. To see this, note that a shift of labour from one region to another, what in figure 11.1 boils down to comparing, for a *given* level of τ, the relative wage in the symmetrical case with the two other λ-distributions implies that w_h/w_f can move either way depending upon the level of τ. At low levels of τ, a shift of labour from Home to Foreign implies that the relative wage of low-skilled workers in Home increases, as the extent of competition effect dominates over the home market effect. At higher values of τ, the balance between both effects is reversed though, and a shift of labour from Home to Foreign implies a fall in the relative wage of low-skilled workers in Home. With Home being the larger region, the opposite happens.

Of course, this kind of analysis can be repeated for the relative wage of high-skilled workers *between* regions (r_h/r_f) or for a reduction in the transportation costs of producer services (increase in ρ). This leads to similar conclusions. If one looks at absolute wages it is noteworthy that wages in the same region always move in the same direction. So if for instance w_h increases, so will r_h. This is to be expected because the 'tug of war' between the home market effect and the extent of competition effect has a similar qualitative impact on intra-regional wages.[10]

By and large similar conclusions with respect to relative wages between regions hold in the *RWR* regime (not shown here). There is one notable difference with the case of flexible wages, namely, the relative wage need to be equal to one in the symmetrical case. Thus, although both kinds of labour are equally divided between Home and Foreign, the absolute wages of the same type of labour differ between Home and Foreign. This can be explained by the fact that unemployment exists in the case of

---

[10] This raises the question as to how globalisation can lead to changes in relative regional wages, this question will be addressed in sub-section 11.3.2.

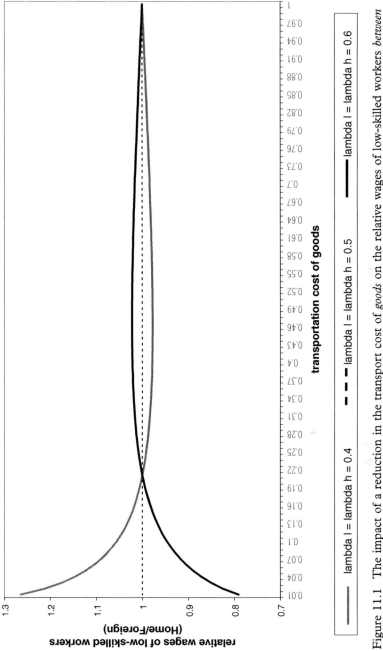

Figure 11.1 The impact of a reduction in the transport cost of *goods* on the relative wages of low-skilled workers *between* regions.

relative wage rigidity and unemployment reduces the number of *employed* workers and therefore decreases the size of the Home region (because the unemployed have, by assumption, nothing to spend). This implies that, although we assumed an equal distribution of labour, an asymmetry between the two regions exists so that the relative wage does not have to equal one.

Finally, and again in accordance with the core model of new economic geography, we know what happens to the absolute wages in Foreign. They move in precisely the opposite direction from absolute wages in Home. When w_h and r_h increase, it is always the case that w_f and r_f decrease by the same amount. The upshot of figure 11.1 is that changes in transportation costs lead to changes in relative wages between regions and to changes in absolute wages as well that can be understood in terms of the by now standard battle in new economic geography models between the home market and extent of competition effect. How this battle is decided depends crucially on the λ-distribution between Home and Foreign and on the level of transportation costs. In what follows is important to keep in mind that these two standard effects remain relevant when transportation costs fall.

11.3.2   *Relative intra-regional wages and unemployment*

Although sub-section 11.3.1 gives rise to interesting (but well-known) results, the main interest of this chapter is the impact of globalisation on the relative wage of the low-skilled (w_h/r_h) or the unemployment rate (U_h) *within* a region, here the Home region. This sub-section investigates the distributional effects of globalisation *within* the two regions in the short run and here we can compare our results with the results found by more traditional models like the Heckscher–Ohlin model. In the streamlined $2 \times 2 \times 2$ version of this last model, which has dominated the globalisation debate (see Collins, 1998 or Wood, 1998), the effect of a reduction of transportation costs on the relative wages in the country which is relatively well-endowed with high-skilled labour is clear-cut. Such a reduction leads to a decrease of relative low-skilled wages. In the Heckscher–Ohlin approach, the supply side (i.e. the distribution of endowments) drives this result. In our model, the action is very much on the demand side of the economy.

We first investigate the decline in the transportation costs of unfinished goods (i.e. increase in τ) and then turn to the decline in the transportation costs of producer services (i.e. increase in ρ). Before doing so, it is important to make clear that in addition to the familiar home market and extent of competition effect, there are with respect to intra-regional labour market developments two effects to take into account. Both of these two additional effects relate to the specifics of our model:

1. Although w_i and r_i always move in the same direction after a fall in the transportation costs (see sub-section 11.3.1), our production structure implies that the absolute wages react *quantitatively* different to a change in either τ or ρ. In particular, a change in the transportation costs of unfinished goods (τ) always has a relatively larger impact on low-skilled wages, while a change in the transportation costs of producer services (ρ) is more important for high-skilled wages.[11] This result is due to the fact that an increase in τ (ρ) is of direct relevance to the low-skilled (high-skilled) as they are the only factor of production used in the unfinished goods (producer services) production. This is of course relevant for the determination of the relative wage since any change in w_h/r_h is simply a result of the changes in w_h and changes in r_h. Given that an increase in τ implies a larger change in w_h than in r_h (and also that the opposite holds with respect to an increase in ρ), it is possible to understand the developments in w_h/r_h, even though the absolute wages are affected (qualitatively) in the same way. Of course, this is a partial line of reasoning and there are other intricate ways in which changes in transportation costs influence wages in our model but this line of reasoning is supported by the simulations.

2. If wages are no longer flexible (in our case: a fixed relative wage in Home), this obviously also creates a channel thorough which intra-regional labour markets are affected. This is in particular true in Home where, as we will see below, the wage rigidity gives rise to unemployment.

We now turn to the simulation results which are thus the summation of the standard new economic geography effects of sub-section 11.3.1 and the two above-mentioned effects. Given the complexity of the model we thus have to rely on simulation results and it will (unfortunately) often be impossible to fully disentangle these effects for specific simulation results. This is a problem with the new economic geography approach in general (Neary, 2001).

Fall in the transportation costs of unfinished goods (increase in τ)
Figure 11.2 depicts for Home the relative wage of low-skilled workers and the unemployment rate, respectively, for the benchmark case where $\lambda_h = \lambda_l = 0.4$ (Home is thus the smaller region). The left-axis displays

---

[11] To see this, note from (11.6) and (11.9) that an increase in τ has a direct impact on w_h. Also, from (11.10) and (11.12) it can be discerned that an increase in ρ has a direct impact on r_h. The finding that w_i (r_i) is affected quantitatively more by a change in τ (ρ) is supported by the simulations.

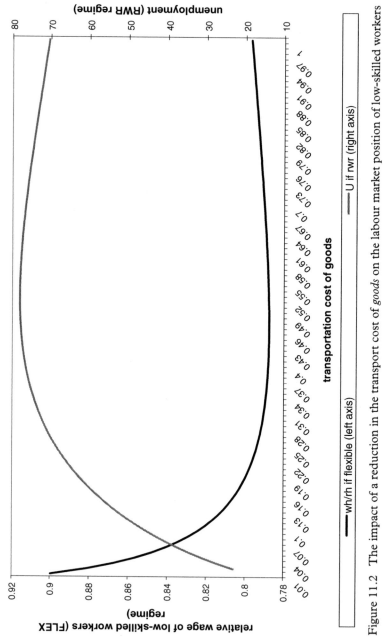

Figure 11.2 The impact of a reduction in the transport cost of *goods* on the labour market position of low-skilled workers

the relative wage w_h/r_h and is relevant for the *FLEX* regime. The right-axis displays the unemployment U_h and this variable is of interest in the *RWR* regime. The figure immediately reveals one important conclusion: the relationship between the transportation costs of unfinished goods and the relative wages of low-skilled workers and unemployment is non-linear and it does depend very much on the *level* of τ what the impact of globalisation on labour market in Home will be. This result sets our analysis apart from the traditional Heckscher–Ohlin conclusion that a fall in transportation costs leads to a clear-cut change in relative wages. That is to say, in the latter the change in w_h/r_h does not depend on the degree of globalisation (i.e. the level of transportation costs). Hence, the stylised fact that industrialised countries differ considerably in terms of the changes in relative wages or unemployment in the globalisation era may thus have something to do with differences in the level of transportation costs across countries.

Consider for instance w_h/r_h and hence the *FLEX* regime in figure 11.2: at low levels of τ (i.e. high transportation costs), an increase in τ is bad news for low-skilled workers as they face a decline in the relative wage; however, after a certain level of τ (to be precise,) $\tau > 0.47$, a further decline in the transportation costs of unfinished goods ceases to have much impact (in % change). In fact, for low levels of transportation costs (high τ) the relative wage increases slightly. The same applies in the *RWR* regime, where the labour market deterioration of the low-skilled at low levels of τ is now reflected in rising unemployment. The main point to notice for both regimes is that the simulation results in figure 11.2 show that the impact of globalisation on the labour market position of low-skilled workers depends crucially on the *level* of transportation costs.[12] A similar conclusion was reached in case of relative wages *between* regions.

As we argued in section 11.2, the disequilibrium in the labour market for low-skilled workers in Home is caused by the fall in the number of unfinished goods varieties in Home (N_h) as the latter are now determined on the goods market. This implies that the number of unfinished goods varieties is larger in the *FLEX* regime as compared to the *RWR* regime. Our simulation results show that this is indeed the case: $N_h^{FLEX} > N_h^{RWR}$. As an aside to the existence of unemployment it can

[12] In order to test the robustness of this result, we performed an extensive sensitivity analysis. In most cases, the non-linear relationship between τ and w_h/r_h is found. In addition we found that the distribution of labour between regions is also crucial to determine the impact of globalisation on the labour market position of low-skilled workers in Home. So if we assumed that Home was the larger region in terms of low-skilled and high-skilled labour, globalisation turned out to be good news for the low-skilled at low levels of τ and bad news at higher levels of τ. We return to the distribution of labour between regions in section 11.4.

be added that globalisation invariably leads to *deindustrialisation* in Home if the fall in transportation costs implies unemployment. Unemployment of low-skilled manufacturing labour in Home decreases the share of the manufacturing goods sector (*vis-à-vis* the agricultural sector) in employment and production.

Finally, note that the fall in the transportation costs of unfinished goods has also implications for Foreign workers (not shown here). It turns out that invariably: $w_f^{FLEX} < w_f^{RWR}$ and $r_f^{FLEX} < r_f^{RWR}$.[13] How can this be explained? Note that the wage rigidity in Home increases the absolute wages of low-skilled workers in Home. The zero profit condition then implies that the prices of Home varieties will increase (see (11.5) and (11.6)), which, by (11.1), decreases total demand for Home varieties and increases total demand for Foreign varieties. The latter then translates into higher absolute wages for low-skilled workers in Foreign. This conclusion for wages in Foreign supports the affirmative answer given by Davis (1998) to the question 'Does European unemployment prop up American wages?' and it underscores his plea for a general equilibrium analysis of the impact of wage rigidities. Interestingly enough, Davis (1998) reached this conclusion with a Heckscher–Ohlin model but it thus carries over to our new economic geography model. Unemployment in Home is good news for all workers in Foreign.

Fall in the transportation costs of producer services (increase in ρ)

Figure 11.3 depicts the relative wage of low-skilled workers and the unemployment rate, respectively, for Home in the two labour market regimes when ρ increases (again the left-axis (right-axis) displays the relative real wage (low-skilled unemployment) which is our focus in the *FLEX* (*RWR*) regime). From figure 11.3 it can be seen that there is also a non-linear relationship between the transportation costs of producer services and the relative wage of low-skilled workers. The main message is that if globalisation occurs through a fall in the transportation costs of producer services, the relative wages of the low-skilled labour show a downward trend for very low transportation costs (to be more precise, for $\rho > 0.63$), but for higher transportation cost, a fall in the transportation costs of services is good news for the low-skilled in Home. This result can be compared with the corresponding simulation result as shown by figure 11.2. It then turns out that for the *FLEX* regime it may matter a great deal for the relative wage in Home whether τ or ρ changes. This leads us to conclude that for the impact of globalisation one must also look at the *type*

---

[13] Recall that the labour market always clears in Foreign. The superscript in the notation of foreign wages relates to the labour market regime in Home.

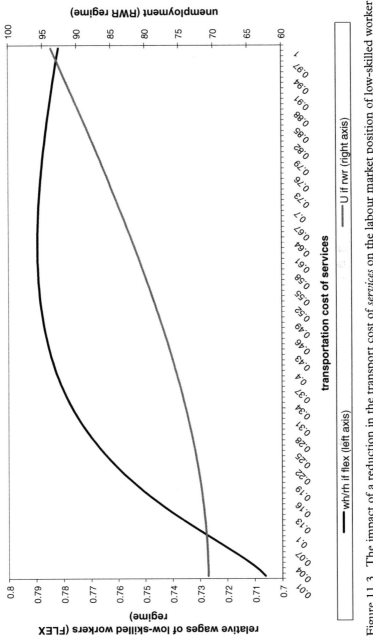

Figure 11.3 The impact of a reduction in the transport cost of *services* on the labour market position of low-skilled workers

of transportation costs that is being reduced. Our way to account for this conclusion is given by point 1 at the end of the introduction to subsection 11.3.2. There we argued that a change in τ has a larger impact on low-skilled labour and the same for ρ and high-skilled labour. Given that an increase in τ implies a larger change in w_h than in r_h (and also that the opposite holds with respect to an increase in ρ), it is possible to understand the deviating developments in w_h/r_h for the case of flexible wages when comparing the relative wages in figures 11.2 and 11.3.

The simulation result in figure 11.3 for the relationship between unemployment and the fall in the transportation costs of producer services tell a similar story. For the *RWR* regime it also turns out that for unemployment the consequences of globalisation depend on the type of transportation costs which is being reduced. The differences in the outcome for unemployment in case τ or ρ changes can be traced back to the efficiency or productivity effect related to a fall in the transportation costs of producer services (see (11.3) and (11.4)). An increase in ρ implies that fewer services are being lost in international trade; implicitly, this increases the number of producer services available per low-skilled worker and thus the productivity of low-skilled workers rises. An increase in τ does not have this effect, it merely reduces the transportation costs of unfinished goods between Home and Foreign without affecting the productivity of the factors of production.

11.4   Long-run implications of globalisation

We finally turn to the impact of globalisation in the long run and introduce a second aspect of globalisation: factor mobility. In the new economic geography models, the inter-regional mobility of labour differentiates the long run from the short run.[14] So far, neither low-skilled nor high-skilled workers were mobile. This assumption is partly relaxed in this section because it is now assumed that high-skilled workers can move between Home and Foreign and that low-skilled workers remain immobile. This is a reasonable assumption given that high-skilled workers are typically more mobile than low-skilled workers (e.g. Siebert, 1999) and the still very limited mobility of low-skilled labour in Europe (OECD 1997). As is common in the new economic geography literature, it is assumed that high-skilled workers move until either real high-skilled wages are equalised or until all high-skilled workers have moved to one region.

---

[14] It also differentiates the new economic geography from the new trade theory (see Neary 2001). In this sense the discussion so far (with λ fixed) has even more in common with, for instance, Krugman and Venables (1990) than with Krugman (1991) and the literature that builds on the latter.

In order to investigate the long-run equilibrium, we first derive the relative real wage of high-skilled workers (Home/Foreign). Real wages of high-skilled workers in region $i = h, f$ are a function of nominal wages and prices as follows: $\upsilon_i = r_i / \tilde{P}_i^\mu$, where $\tilde{P}_i$ is the price index as given in (11.2). Now substitute the price equations in the price indices and define the relative real wage of high-skilled workers as υ_h/υ_f which is then given by:

$$\frac{\upsilon_h}{\upsilon_f} = \frac{r_h}{r_f}\left(\frac{\tilde{V}_f}{\tilde{V}_h}\right)^{(1-\alpha)\mu}\left(\frac{\left[N_f w_f^{\alpha\theta/(\theta-1)} + N_h(w_h/\tau)^{\alpha\theta/(\theta-1)}\right]^{(\theta-1)/\theta}}{\left[N_h w_h^{\alpha\theta/(\theta-1)} + N_f(w_f/\tau)^{\alpha\theta/(\theta-1)}\right]^{(\theta-1)/\theta}}\right)^\mu.$$

$$(11.17)$$

Given the relative real wage of high-skilled workers, we are interested in the following questions. What are the characteristics of the long-run equilibria and, related to this, how are these equilibria affected by globalisation?[15]

Figure 11.4 shows the computed values of υ_h/υ_f as a function of λ_h for two different levels of transportation costs and with $\lambda_l = 0.4$ in the regime with flexible wages. Figure 11.5 does the same but now for $\lambda_l = 0.6$. It is clear that the long-run outcome for υ_h/υ_f and hence for the equilibrium distribution of high-skilled labour depends on the level of transportation costs and the fixed distribution of low-skilled labour. For high transportation costs ($\tau = \rho = 0.2$), there is a stable intermediate equilibrium for λ_h. However, this intermediate equilibrium ceases to exist if transportation costs fall. With $\tau = \rho = 0.5$, the mobile labour force ends in either Home (figure 11.5) or Foreign (figure 11.4) depending on the value of λ_l. The relevance of λ_l is clear when comparing figures 11.4 and 11.5, if a region has more low-skilled labour it *ceteris paribus* ends up with more high-skilled labour. Simulations like those shown in figure 11.4 for the relative wage rigidity regime yield by and large similar conclusions.[16]

---

[15] Another question is, of course, how in the long run relative (real) wages within a region change as λ_h, ρ or τ change. Since the simulations (not shown here) show that the conclusions as to the behaviour of relative (real) wages in the long run are comparable as for the relative intra-regional wages in the short run, in the sense that the labour market outcomes depend crucially on the level and type of transportation costs being reduced, the distribution of labour across regions and the labour market regime, we do not address this question here.

[16] There is one big difference between the *FLEX* and the *RWR* regime. In the *RWR* regime, the stable intermediate equilibrium is reached only if Home is assumed to be the larger region ($\lambda_l = 0.6$) and transportation costs are sufficiently high ($\tau = \rho = 0.2$); if Home is the smaller region ($\lambda_l = 0.4$), the stable intermediate equilibrium ceases to exist even for $\tau = \rho = 0.2$. For an explanation, see Peeters (2001, pp. 142–9).

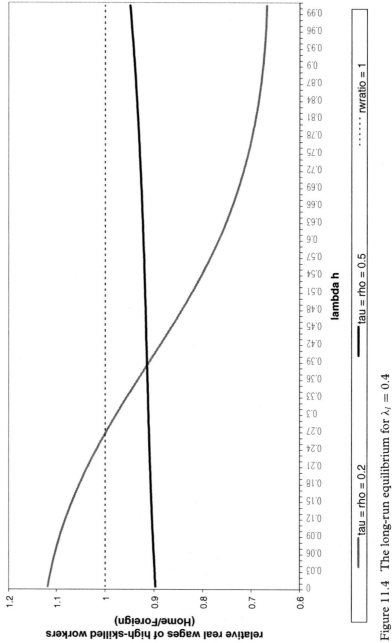

Figure 11.4 The long-run equilibrium for $\lambda_l = 0.4$

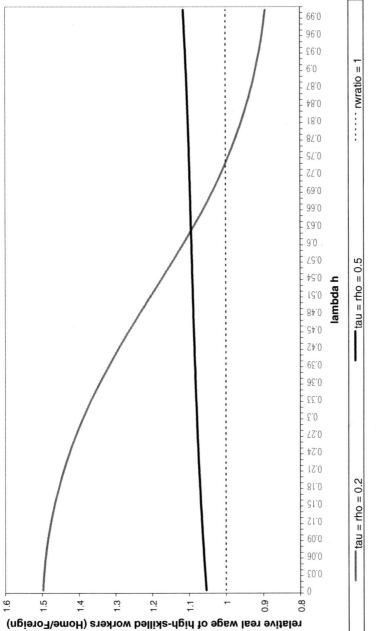

relative real wage of high-skilled workers (Home/Foreign)

lambda h

tau = rho = 0.2   tau = rho = 0.5   rwratio = 1

Figure 11.5   The long-run equilibrium for $\lambda_l = 0.6$

The shift from a stable intermediate equilibrium to a stable monocentric equilibrium ($\lambda_h = 0$ for $\lambda_l = 0.4$ and $\lambda_h = 1$ for $\lambda_l = 0.6$) is in line with the standard new economic geography result based on Krugman (1991). The reason behind this result is that below some level of transportation costs, the home market and, now also, the price index effect dominate the extent of competition effect.[17] High-skilled workers will therefore all move to the larger region and complete agglomeration of high-skilled workers will be the outcome. For high transportation costs, this order is reversed, and, in our model, the relative strength of the extent of competition effect ensures a stable spreading equilibrium for high-skilled workers.

11.5   Conclusions

In this chapter, we have developed an alternative for the Heckscher–Ohlin model to analyse the effects of globalisation. In our model, essentially a two-factor new economic geography model with the possibility of relative wage rigidity, the impact of globalisation (proxied by a fall in transportation costs and labour mobility) on the labour market varies considerably. A first conclusion is that the impact of globalisation on relative wages and unemployment turns out to depend critically on the level and type of the transportation costs that is being reduced, the flexibility of wages and the distribution of low- and high-skilled labour across countries. Globalisation is by no means always bad news for the low-skilled. On the contrary, in some of the simulations we performed, the low-skilled are better off in terms of the relative wage and/or the unemployment outcome as globalisation proceeds. Because the OECD countries differ in all these factors, our model can give a theoretical account for the diverging labour market outcomes across the OECD countries. A second conclusion relates to the difference between the short run and the long run in this type of model. In the short run, thus for a given distribution of labour, globalisation typically has a larger (positive or negative) impact in its initial stages. In the long run, though, in which globalisation proceeds by the mobility of labour too, it is difficult to say when globalisation implies a change in the agglomeration pattern. A final conclusion is that our analysis illustrates that it can be very misleading to analyse the effects of globalisation based on a model with fully flexible wages for countries in which wage rigidity

---

[17] The price index effect implies that the price index which consumers face will be lower in the larger region. Consumers/workers in the larger region have the advantage that they pay a relatively lower price for the final manufacturing good they consume and this advantage shows up as a relatively higher real wage thus enhancing the attractiveness for mobile workers to move/stay in the larger region.

prevails. It matters a great deal for the effects of globalisation whether or not wages are rigid. Our analysis points to two promising avenues for further research. The first is to try to substantiate the theoretical conclusions with empirical evidence. The second is to extend the theoretical model by analysing the consequences of productivity differences between sectors and regions in order to deal with this other alleged villain in the globalisation debate (skill biased) technological change.

REFERENCES

Brakman, S., Garretsen, H. and van Marrewijk, C. (2001). *An Introduction to Geographical Economics: Trade, Location and Growth*. Cambridge, Cambridge University Press

Burda, M. C. and Dluhosch, B. (1998). Globalization and European labour markets. CEPR Discussion Paper, 1992

Collins, S. M. (1998). *Imports, Exports and the American Worker*. Washington, DC, Brookings Institution Press

Davis, D. R. (1998). Does European unemployment prop up American wages? National labor markets and global trade. *American Economic Review*, 88: 478–494

Dewatripont, M., Sapir, A. and Sekkat, K. (1999). *Trade and Jobs in Europe: Much Ado about Nothing?* Oxford, Oxford University Press

Dluhosch, B. (2000). *Industrial Location and Economic Integration, Centrifugal and Centripetal Forces in the New Europe*. Cheltenham, Edward Elgar

Fujita, M. Krugman, P. R. and Venables, A. J. (1999). *The Spatial Economy: Cities, Regions and International Trade*. Cambridge, MA, MIT Press

International Monetary Fund (IMF) (1997). *World Economic Outlook*. Washington, DC, May

Krugman, P. R. (1991). Increasing returns and economic geography. *Journal of Political Economy*, 99: 483–499.

   (1995). Growing world trade: causes and consequences. *Brookings Papers on Economic Activity*, 1: 327–362

Krugman, P. R. and Venables, A. J. (1990). Integration and the competitiveness of peripheral industry, in Bliss, C. and de Macedo, J. B. (eds.), *Unity with Diversity in the European Community*. Cambridge, Cambridge University Press

   (1995). Globalization and the inequality of nations. *Quarterly Journal of Economics*, 110: 857–880

Layard, R., Nickell, S. and Jackman, R. (1991). *Unemployment: Macroeconomic Performance and the Labour Market*. Oxford, Oxford University Press

Neary, J. P. (2001). Of hype and hyperbolas: introducing the new economic geography. *Journal of Economic Literature*, 39: 536–561

Organisation for Economic Co-operation and Development (OECD) (1997). Trade, earnings and employment: assessing the impact of trade with emerging economies on OECD labour markets. *Employment Outlook* (chapter 4). Paris, OECD

Peeters, J. (2001). Globalisation, location and labour markets. PhD thesis, University of Nijmegen

Peeters, J. and Garretsen, H. (2000). Globalisation, wages and unemployment: a new economic geography perspective. CESifo Working Paper, 256, Munich

Peeters, J. and de Vaal, A. (2000). Explaining the wage gap: Heckscher–Ohlin, economic geography and services availability. SOM Research Report, 00C21, University of Groningen

Siebert, H. (1999). *The World Economy*. London and New York, Routledge

Vaal, A. de and van den Berg, M. (1999). Producer services, economic geography, and services tradability. *Journal of Regional Science*, 39: 539–572

Wood, A. (1998). Globalisation and the rise in labour market inequalities. *Economic Journal*, 108: 1463–1482

12 Empirical research in geographical economics

Steven Brakman, Harry Garretsen, Charles van Marrewijk and Marc Schramm

12.1 Introduction

Since the 1980s, the monopolistic competition model has become very popular. It has been applied to a large number of aggregate phenomena in industrial organisation, international trade theory, economic growth and economic geography, with great success. The benchmark model has been developed by Avinash Dixit and Joseph Stiglitz (1977). Their model develops a specific form of imperfect competition, that explains the model's attractiveness, ease of use, and popularity. In particular the following characteristics are important:
- Increasing returns at the firm level
- Firms are symmetric
- Each firm produces one differentiated product
- The firm is able to set its own price
- The number of firms is large, such that individual firms do not have to deal with strategic interactions with other firms
- Free entry and exit drive profits in the industry down to zero.

These features of the model are attractive because ad hoc assumptions on conjectural variations are absent, and the combination of price-setting behaviour, free entry and exit in the presence of increasing returns leads to well-defined equilibria. These characteristics make the model well suited for applications in various fields.

One of the first uses of this monopolistic competition model was in international trade theory (Krugman, 1979, 1980; Dixit and Norman, 1980). A central question in trade theory is: what happens if two economies integrate if these economies are identical in preferences and technologies, but differ in size (labour supply)? The answer depends on what is assumed with respect to the mobility of labour and whether or not international trade is costly. If, as is standard in trade theory, labour is immobile across borders, but mobile within countries, while simultaneously

We thank our discussant Arjen van Witteloostuijn for useful comments.

products are freely tradable, free trade implies that each country can consume the same consumption basket and each firm is of equal size and pays the same wage. The only difference is that the larger country produces more varieties (in proportion to the relative size measured in terms of labour). Which varieties each country produces, however, is undetermined (Helpman and Krugman, 1985).

This story changes fundamentally if trade is no longer free and manufacturing labour becomes mobile (workers in the numéraire or agricultural sector are immobile). In fact this is the core model of the new economic geography, or, the term we prefer and use, *geographical economics* approach.[1] The existence of transport costs makes it worthwhile for consumers to migrate to the larger region where they can avoid such costs, which increases (potentially) their real wage. This implies that the large economy grows while the small economy shrinks. Economies of scale (pecuniary externalities) are realised through clustering or agglomeration. In this model one group definitely is worse off; the immobile workers in the smaller region, who now have to import manufactures and pay for the transport costs. This story does not only hold on a country level but also applies to smaller geographical units, like regions, cities or locations within cities. It is not surprising that these models are used to explain core–periphery patterns within countries, or under-development traps on a global level.

The attractiveness of the geographical economics model is that it incorporates more realism than the standard new trade model and that it produces testable hypotheses of its own. One such testable hypothesis is that manufacturing wages fall the further one moves away from industrial centres. This hypothesis will be at the heart of the empirical part of our chapter.

At present, empirical evidence on geographical economics models is in short supply. Not only do different models predict different outcomes, but the various equilibria in a geographical economics model also depend on specific values of the relevant parameters. Both agglomeration and spreading can be consistent in the same geographical economics model, depending on the specific values of those parameters. This becomes especially awkward if parameter values change over time, or differ across space.

This paper is structured as follows. In section 12.2, we will briefly assess the current state of empirical research in geographical economics.

---

[1] We prefer the term 'geographical economics' because we think that this approach is above all an attempt to put more geography into economics than the other way around as the phrase 'new economic geography' suggests; see also Fujita and Thisse (2000) or Brakman, Garretsen and van Marrewijk (2001).

This section will make clear that empirical research on the relevance of the geographical economics is sketchy at best, and mostly indirect. Next we will show what difficulties one encounters in empirical research, and at the same time show how some of the empirical difficulties can be circumvented. Our test case is Germany. As such the German reunification forms an excellent 'laboratory' experiment to test a geographical economics model. It must be emphasised beforehand that for various reasons (like the lack of time-series data) we do not provide any new insights as to the relevance of the geographical economics approach for German reunification. We are, however, able to use the German case to estimate the main structural parameters of the model and establish whether or not a so-called 'spatial wage structure' can, as predicted by the theoretical model, indeed be observed for Germany. Data on the German county level are available and it is possible to test some (but certainly not all) of the implications of geographical economics model for Germany. First we review the empirical literature on economic geography. In sub-section 12.3.1 we briefly sketch the situation in Germany. In subsection 12.3.2 a geographical economics model developed by Hanson (1998) will be applied to Germany. Sub-section 12.3.3 discusses the results. Section 12.4 produces some conclusions and suggestions for future research.

12.2   Empirical research in economic geography[2]

12.2.1   The problem defined

Empirical surveys like Brülhart (1998) show clearly that agglomeration can be observed at various levels of aggregation (country, region, city). Two questions then arise. First, can these facts be reconciled with economic theory at large? Second, if the answer to the first question is affirmative, how can we discriminate between different theories in general, and with respect to geographical economics in particular?

First of all, agglomeration can be observed on a supranational or regional level. The relevance of agglomeration at this level is linked to studies of economic growth pointing to persistent differences in GDP *per capita* between (groups of) countries. Both neoclassical and new growth theory can account for this state of affairs. If the speed of convergence is very slow, and/or if one looks at conditional convergence instead

---

[2] This section is largely taken from chapter 5 of Brakman, Garretsen and van Marrewijk (2001).

of absolute convergence, the existence of agglomeration need not be at odds with neoclassical growth theory. Similarly, the relevance of new trade theory as well as geographical economics in accounting for the observed relevance of intra-industry trade is obvious, but the existence of intra-industry trade can also be explained in modern versions of the neoclassical trade model, where technology differs between countries (see, for example, Davis, 1998).[3] Trade theory can thus not only be called upon to give a foundation for specialisation patterns across space, but also for agglomeration. This is not only true for the geographical economics model, but also for neoclassical trade theory in which endowments are geographically concentrated. The basic new trade model has not much to offer here because it has nothing to say on the issue *where* production will take place.

The conclusion must be that the same empirical facts about specialisation or agglomeration can be explained using different theoretical approaches. On the one hand this is good news, because it means that these are not facts in search of a theory. On the other hand, this conclusion is not satisfactory for our present purposes, because it leaves unanswered the question as to the (relative) empirical relevance of individual theories like geographical economics. This point has, of course, not gone unnoticed in the literature. Several studies try to test for the relevance of one or more theories of location by investigating how much of the observed specialisation or agglomeration can be ascribed to each theory. A good example is the study of the US city-size distribution by Black and Henderson (1998, 1999), testing for the importance of actual geography and characteristics of city neighbours as determinants of city size. Both forces turn out to be relevant. Following up on the development of the Ellison–Glaeser index, Dumais, Ellison and Glaeser (1997) try to show how much of the observed concentration is due to each of the three well-known Marshallian externalities. They find evidence lending support to one of these externalities, labour market pooling, and thus also indirectly find evidence for theories that rely on pecuniary external economics like geographical economics. This does not mean that a neoclassical foundation of the observed geographic concentration in the USA is irrelevant. On the contrary, Ellison and Glaeser (1999, p. 315) estimate that approximately 20 per cent of this concentration can be explained by geographical advantages (endowments).

In many studies, the variables underlying the neoclassical approach as well as those that serve as proxies for the modern trade or growth theories are all empirically relevant. Haaland *et al.* (1999), for example, regress

---

[3] The same is true for the gravity model (see Deardorff, 1995).

for a group of thirteen European countries and thirty-five industries the concentration of each industry upon variables capturing up to four trade theoretical approaches. Two variables, namely labour intensity and human capital intensity of industry production, are used as proxies for the factor abundance model, whereas technological differences between industries represent the Ricardian technology model. The new trade model and geographical economics are represented using the relative concentration of expenditures (market size), and a variable measuring economies of scale. Both *neoclassical* variables, such as human capital intensity, and *new* variables, such as market size, are important determinants of industry concentration in Europe.[4] These conclusions are important if one wants to explain industry concentration in Europe, thinking that various determinants (and hence theories) might be relevant. It is only if one wants to discriminate between theories that the usefulness of such an approach is limited

The problem is aptly summarised by Brülhart (1998, p. 792) who argues that such a 'regression analysis of industry concentration suggests that all major theoretical approaches are relevant. However they have not been used so far to assess relative merits of competing models across industries or countries.' For geographical economics there are two other important problems. First, that allegedly independent variables in some studies, notably proxies for market size, are *not* independent variables, but endogenous variables determined by the location of industries, workers and firms in the geographical economics approach.[5] Second, the geographical economics model is characterised by multiple equilibria. Which equilibrium gets established depends on the initial conditions. Without knowledge of the initial conditions it is difficult to test the model. The geographical economics approach allows for both full agglomeration as well as spreading of economic activity to be long-run equilibria. One solution is to study whether or not some of the specific implications of the model can be tested. The so-called spatial wage structure is an obvious candidate.[6]

---

[4] Other examples include Kim (1995) and van den Berg and Sturm (1997)

[5] See also Haaland *et al.* (1999, p. 9) and Midelfart-Knarvik *et al.* (2000).

[6] In his survey of geographical economics Paul Krugman (1998, p. 172) concludes that empirical work has 'failed to offer much direct testing of the specifics of the models'. According to Krugman recent empirical work by Donald Davis and David Weinstein on the home market effect is an exception. In a series of papers, Davis and Weinstein (1996, 1997, 1998a, 1998b, 1999) have developed an empirical methodology that enables them 'to distinguish a world in which trade arises due to increasing returns as opposed to comparative advantage' (Davis and Weinstein, 1998a, p. 8). Although their work to test for the home market effect is interesting in its own right, we do not think that it provides a test for the empirical relevance of geographical economics (see Brakman, Garretsen and van Marrewijk, 2001, pp. 141–5; for a similar view see Neary, 2001).

12.2.2   A spatial wage structure

Given the (reasonable) assumption that labour supply is not perfectly elastic, the core geographical economics model due to Krugman (1991) predicts that regions which face a relatively high demand for manufactures also pay relatively higher wages. That is to say, wages fall the further one moves away from industrial centres. This testable implication of the core model sets geographical economics apart from the two alternative trade theories. In neoclassical trade theory, there is no foundation for such a spatial wage structure. The existence of economic centres can be rationalised by location-specific endowments but this does not imply a spatial wage structure. Even with (endowment-driven) agglomeration, the main prediction of the neoclassical trade theory is that trade will lead to factor price equalisation. In the new trade models it is true that in autarky wages are higher for the country with the larger labour force, but when trade opens up wages are equalised. This follows from the specialisation in production of varieties of the manufactured good, such that some varieties are produced in one country and the other varieties in the other country. This rules out a spatial wage structure in new trade models because there is no endogenous agglomeration of manufacturing production across space, and thus no possibility of a centre of manufacturing production.[7]

This is what is new in the Hanson (1997, 1998, 1999) approach. Hanson's starting point is 'that the level of economic activity in a location is conditioned by that location's access to markets for its goods. While this view may seem narrow – it ignores climate, natural resource supplies, and other factors which surely influence city location – I attempt to show that market access provides a useful way to characterize the forces that contribute to the *geographic concentration of economic activity*' (Hanson, 1998, p. 1, emphasis added).

The implied reference to the market potential function is not coincidental, Krugman (1995, p. 99) already observed that the equilibrium condition for the nominal wage equation in the new economic geography model, in a qualitative sense, closely resembles a market potential function as introduced by Harris (1954). In the core new economic geography model, the nominal wage equation can be looked upon as a spatial labour demand function to the extent that wages (and hence labour demand) in a region are higher, the nearer this region is to areas with a high demand for this region's products. Hanson (1998), therefore, considers the market-potential function as a 'reduced form' of the nominal wage

---

[7] This point also holds for the Davis and Weinstein studies of the home market effect, essentially dealing with the concentration of industries across regions/countries.

equation from the core new economic geography model. So he uses the market-potential function as the empirical specification to estimate the spatial wage structure for the USA (see also section 12.3).

We briefly discuss the theoretical approach in Hanson (1998).[8] Following Helpman (1998) and Thomas (1996), the agricultural sector of the core model of geographical economics is replaced by a housing sector. The reason is that the standard Krugman model displays a bias towards monocentric equilibria: all manufactures end up being produced at a single location. This is clearly not in accordance with the facts about the spatial distribution of manufacturing activity for the USA, or any other industrialised country. The perfectly competitive housing sector serves as the spreading force, because housing is relatively more expensive in the centres of production where demand for housing is high. This extension of the geographical economics model typically results in a more even distribution of manufacturing activity than the standard Krugman model. The equilibrium conditions are very similar to this model, in particular the wage equation, which is central to the empirical analysis, is identical to the normalised equation:[9]

$$
W_j = \left[\sum_k Y_k I_k^{\varepsilon-1} T^{D_{jk}(1-\varepsilon)} \right]^{1/\varepsilon},
\tag{12.1}
$$

in which W is the wage rate, Y is income, I is the price index, ε is the elasticity of substitution, T is the transport cost parameter and $T_{jk} = T^{D_{jk}}$, where D_{jk} is the distance between locations j and k. Transport costs T is defined as the number of goods that have to be shipped in order to ensure that one unit arrives over one unit of distance. Given the elasticity of substitution ε, it can directly be seen from (12.1) that for every region wages are higher when demand in surrounding markets (Y_k) is higher, when access to those markets is better (lower transport costs T), and when there is less competition for the varieties the region wants to sell in those markets (competition effect, measured by the price index I_k).

Two empirical specifications of (12.1) are actually estimated. In the first version, (12.1) is simplified by assuming that wages in region j depend only on a constant and income Y_k.[10] This specification is in fact

---

[8] We also deal extensively with Hanson (1998) to build upon his approach below, when investigating the spatial wage structure in Germany.

[9] In the housing model of geographical economics, Hanson assumes that real wages are equal between regions, which means that the economy is by definition in its long-run equilibrium (see below). The condition that housing payments in each region equal the share of expenditures allocated to housing is added as an equilibrium condition (Hanson, 1998, p.12).

[10] Distance is measured relative to the economic centre of a state (see Hanson, 1998, p. 32

an example of a market potential function, but with wages as the dependent variable. The advantage is that it is easy to estimate and indicates if there is a spatial wage structure or not. The disadvantage is that there is no clear-cut connection with the theoretical model and its structural parameters. In this sense the first specification still suffers from the same drawbacks as the empirical specification of the wage equation in Hanson (1997). The second specification of (12.1) therefore bases the estimation results upon the theoretical model. To do this, Hanson rewrites (12.1) by assuming that the equilibrium real wages are equal between regions and by imposing the equilibrium condition for the housing market:[11]

$$\log W_j = k_0 + \frac{1}{\varepsilon} \log \left[\sum_k Y_k^{\varepsilon + (1-\varepsilon)/\delta} H_k^{(1-\delta)(\varepsilon-1)/\delta} W_k^{(\varepsilon-1)/\delta} T^{(1-\varepsilon)D_{jk}} \right] + err_j.$$

$$(12.2)$$

Where k_0 is a parameter, H_k is the housing stock in region k, and δ is the share of income spent on manufactures. Note that (12.2) includes the three structural parameters of the core model, namely share of income spend on manufactures, δ, the substitution elasticity, ε and the transport costs, T. Given the availability of data on wages, income, the housing stock, and a proxy for distance, (12.2) can be estimated. In both empirical specifications of the theoretical wage equation (12.1), the dependent variable is the wage rate measured at the county level. For both specifications Hanson finds strong confirmation for a spatial wage structure and thus for the relevance of geographical economics.

12.2.3   Some critical remarks

The approach developed by Hanson constitutes one of the most elaborate attempts to date to arrive at an empirical validation of the geographical economics approach. Still, there are a number of objections that can be

---

for details). Actually, the first specification is:

$$\log W_j = \kappa_0 + \kappa_1 \log \left(\sum_k Y_k e^{-\kappa_2 D_{jk}} \right) + err_j,$$

where κ_0, κ_1, and κ_2 are parameters to be estimated. We use this also as a first specification in the case study for Germany.

[11] Lack of reliable data on the regional price index of manufactures I_k and on the regional price of housing P_k makes this rewriting necessary. To get from wage equation (12.1) to (12.2) use (i) the equilibrium for the housing market: $P_j H_j = (1 - \delta) Y_j$ (the value of the fixed stock of housing equals the part of income spent on housing), and (ii) real wage equalisation between regions: $W_j / (P_j^{1-\delta} I_j^\delta) = W_k / (P_k^{1-\delta} I_k^\delta)$.

raised against his methodology, some of which are also mentioned by Hanson (1998, p. 31) and (partly) remedied in Hanson (1999).

First, there is no role for fixed region-specific endowments determined by actual geography and so there is no role for neoclassical trade theory in Hanson (1998). Access to the sea, the location of mountain ranges and other physical features of the USA are also relevant in explaining regional wages and the concentration of economic activity across space.[12]

Second, Hanson (1998) assumes that the USA is a closed economy. Only national demand matters for regional wages. This is not an unreasonable assumption as a first approximation for the USA, but even there it is clear that the concentration of economic activity (and hence of regional wages) is also determined by the degree of openness of the US economy. For more open economies, the 'closed economy assumption' is obviously more problematic.

Third, the theoretical model used by Hanson is taken from Thomas (1996), who builds on Helpman (1998). A central issue in Thomas (1996) is the non-linear relationship between transport costs on the one hand and industrial agglomeration and relative wages on the other. It implies that as transport costs decrease from very high to intermediate levels, the agglomeration of economic activity is strengthened and the relative wage of large regions increases. If transport costs fall even further from intermediate to low levels, however, firms and workers relocate to the smaller regions, the share of large regions in manufacturing production decreases and the wage differential between large and small regions narrows. For an intermediate range of transport costs, the advantages of market proximity outweigh the disadvantages for firms and workers of the relatively large region. The advantages of market proximity arise from the backward and forward linkages that enable firms in the centres of production to pay relatively higher wages. The disadvantages of agglomeration arise from the higher wage costs for firms and from congestion costs for workers. The latter are incorporated in Thomas (1996), and thus also in Hanson (1998), by a relatively high housing price in the centre of production. At a certain point transport costs get so low that the advantages of market proximity fall short of the disadvantages, and a relocation process starts. This is illustrated in figure 12.1.

Why is the theoretical possibility of a non-linear relationship, or U-curve, between transport costs and relative wages important from an empirical point of view? Because it implies that models of geographical

---

[12] To deal with this point Hanson (1999, p. 5) adjusts for exogenous amenities, such as average heating and cooling days, average humidity, whether the county borders the sea coast, etc. The results hardly change when wages are adjusted for these amenities.

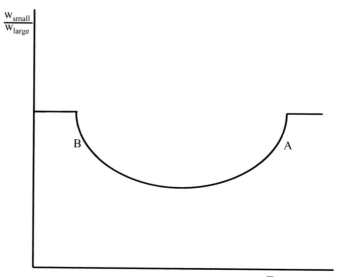

Figure 12.1   Relative wage and transport costs

economics can be in accordance with the results found by Hanson (1998), as well as with a tendency towards regional wage equalisation, depending on the position of the economy on the U-curve. Without an hypothesis about the initial level of transport costs it is not clear whether increasing regional wage differentials, as in the Hanson study, is evidence in favour of geographical economics or not. Hanson (1998) concludes that the significance of transport costs for regional wages has increased in the period 1970–90, and that the benefits of spatial agglomeration have also increased over time. Figure 12.1 illustrates this point with transport costs *rising* as one moves from left to right along the horizontal axis. This means that either the US economy is on the part of the U-curve where a fall in transport costs stimulates agglomeration and regional wage differentials (point *A* in figure 12.1), or the US economy is on the downward sloping part (point *B* in figure 12.1) with *in*creasing transport costs.[13]

Hanson (1998) does not deal with the issues raised in figure 12.1. This may be due to his assumption of real wage equalisation across

---

[13] An increase of transport costs is in line with the results found by Hanson. Thomas (1996), however, concludes that regional wage differentials have narrowed in the USA, which he attributes to the fact that the USA is on the downward sloping part of the U-curve where a fall in transport costs favours the relatively smaller region.

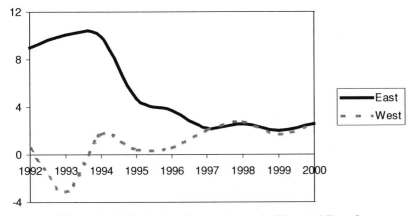

Figure 12.2 Evolution of growth rates in West and East Germany

regions, implying that the US economy is always in a long-run equilibrium. If real wage equalisation is not imposed, priors for the initial spatial distribution of economic activity, and for the initial values for the structural parameters are needed. In other words, because geographical economics is characterised by multiple equilibria, it remains difficult to test for the empirical relevance as long as the test does not include a prediction of the equilibrium distribution of economic activity and wages.

12.3   Germany

12.3.1   The German unification

The objective of this section is to establish whether or not a spatial wage structure exists for Germany. The German case is interesting against the background of the fall of the Berlin Wall in October 1989, and the formal reunification of West and East Germany in October 1990. After the initial optimism following the German reunification, it was quickly pointed out that the reasons for this optimism were far from obvious from the perspective of new trade theory and new growth theory and geographical economics. Although some convergence in GDP *per capita* took place in the period 1991–5, the clear *lack* of convergence since then indicates that geographical economics, with its emphasis on core–periphery outcomes, might be of some relevance for post-unification Germany (see figure 12.2).[14] In fact, the core model of geographical economics was

[14] Data source: Statistisches Bundesamt.

called upon to show that a so-called *Mezzogiorno* scenario (with West Germany as the core and East Germany as the periphery) could not be ruled out for the German case.[15]

Brakman and Garretsen (1993) use the core geographical economics model due to Krugman (1991) (extended with productivity differences between the two countries) to investigate the prospects for East Germany of becoming a centre of production assuming that initially the centre of manufacturing production is located in West Germany. One of the advantages of the case of German reunification is that we know the initial conditions; in 1990 virtually all (profitable) manufacturing German production was located in the western part. Given the assumption about the initial distribution of manufacturing production and the parameter values δ, ε and T, the question is whether or not this initial distribution is a stable equilibrium in the long run. To answer this question Brakman and Garretsen (1993) also assume that labour costs in East Germany are initially higher than in West Germany, which is equivalent to assuming that labour productivity in East Germany is relatively lower.[16] The simulations based on this model lead to the conclusion that it is very difficult for East Germany to become the centre of production. Two simulation results tell the story. First, given a moderate value for transport costs T, the initial core–periphery pattern is not sustainable if, and only if, East German labour productivity somehow became *higher* than West German labour productivity. Second, without such a productivity spurt, East Germany can become the centre of production only with very high transport costs. In reality, labour productivity is East Germany is not higher, and the fall of the Berlin Wall and subsequent massive investments in infrastructure, have lowered transport costs between east and west considerably. Hence, applying the core model to the case of the German reunification yields a rather pessimistic conclusion for the prospects of East Germany in the near future.

The last conclusion is subject to two important caveats. First, the core model is a static model: for a fixed level of overall income it deals with the allocation of economic activity between the two regions. This forecloses the analysis of how economic growth may induce firms to locate and produce in East Germany. As pointed out by Brakman and Garretsen (1993) the introduction of economic growth does not necessarily alter the pessimistic view, since the new growth theory also allows for the

---

[15] The term '*Mezzogiorno*' refers to the core–periphery pattern in Italy.

[16] In the production function underlying the core model $l_i = \alpha + \beta x_i$ (where l_i is the amount of labour necessary to produce x_i, and αW and βW are, respectively, fixed and marginal costs), it is assumed that parameter β is higher in East Germany.

initial conditions to determine long-run equilibrium in terms of growth of GDP *per capita*. In fact, some versions of new growth theory are analytically similar to the core model of geographical economics (see, for example, Grossman and Helpman, 1991, chapter 3). The second caveat concerns the empirical relevance of geographical economics for the German case. It is one thing to argue that simulations with the core model show that East Germany may very well remain the periphery. It is quite something else, however, to actually test for the relevance of the underlying model for post-reunification Germany. We now turn to the empirical evidence.

12.3.2   Empirical results: part I

Our purpose is to test for a spatial wage structure in Germany. Compared to for instance the USA, the German case creates several challenges. First of all, unlike the USA, Germany is typically considered to be an open economy. To test for a spatial wage structure, one has to take economic activity from abroad into account. Second, the labour market in Germany is considered to be rigid. If one detects a spatial wage structure, despite this institutional set-up, that would mean a clear case in favour of the agglomeration dynamics, which are described by the models of the geographical economics. Third, also typical of the German case are, of course, the differences between the western and eastern economy. Nominal wages are lower in the east than in the west, due to a lower labour productivity (see Sinn, 2000, p. 19).

Before we turn to the estimation results a few words on the construction of our data set are in order. Germany is administratively divided into about 440 districts (*Kreise*). Of these districts a total of 118 districts are so called city-districts (*kreisfreie Stadt*), in which the district corresponds with a city. We use district statistics provided by the regional statistical offices in Germany. The data set contains local variables, like the value-added of all sectors (GDP), the wage bill and the number of hours of labour in firms with twenty or more employees in the mining and manufacturing sector. In the empirical analysis we include 114 city-districts in our sample, of which twenty-six are East German. This group of city districts represents 47 per cent of total German GDP and about 40 per cent of total German urban population. Since we also want to analyse the cities' *Hinterland* we also included thirty-seven country districts, constructed using 326 country districts. The total number of districts in our sample is thus 151, namely 114 city districts and thirty-seven country districts. Transport costs are, of course, a crucial variable. We do not use the geodesic distance between districts, because this measure does not distinguish between highways and secondary roads. Instead, distance is measured by the average number of minutes of travel by car it takes to get from A to B. The data are obtained from the *Route Planner 2000* (Europe, AND Publishers, Rotterdam). For the data on the housing stock, required to estimate (12.2), we use the number of rooms in residential dwellings per district. Since we have one observation per district for the average hourly wage and for GDP (1994–5) we have to estimate the wage equations in levels. The latter is a difference with Hanson. Another difference is, recall wage equation (12.2), then we measure the wage W_j and GDP Y_k both at the county level whereas Hanson measures GDP at the level of the US states in order to deal with the fact that Y_k is an endogenous variable and to prevent wages having an impact on GDP. Our 'solution' to this issue is to include 1995 data on wages and 1994 data on GDP in our estimations.

Estimating the market potential function[17]

The first specification, following Hanson, is an approximation of the equilibrium wage equation (12.1):

$$\log W_j = \kappa_1 \log \left[\sum_k Y_k e^{-\kappa_2 D_{jk}} \right] + \kappa_3 D_{east} + \kappa_4 D_{country} + \text{constant},$$

(12.1′)

where W_j is the nominal hourly wage in city-district j, Y_j is the value-added of all sectors in city-district j, D_{jk} is the distance between city-districts j and k, with distance measured in minutes of travel by car. D_{east} is a dummy variable which takes into account that in East Germany (dummy is 1) wages are relatively low (in 1995 East German wages were about 35 per cent lower than West German wages) because of productivity differences. $D_{country}$ is a dummy variable which takes into account that country districts are geographically defined differently than city-districts. The estimation results hardly change if both dummies are excluded.

The main conclusion is that for Germany as a whole (here, 151 districts) we find strong confirmation of the relevance of a spatial wage structure. The coefficients κ_1 and κ_2 are both significantly different from zero. Distance clearly matters. Wages in district j depend positively on the economic activity and the resulting demand from other districts (κ_1 is positive), but the impact of this demand on wages in city-district j is localised (κ_2 is positive). In other words, the results confirm the idea that

[17] See Brakman, Garretsen and Schramm (2000) for further details.

Table 12.1 *Estimation of the spatial wage structure of Germany*[a]

	Coefficient	Standard error	t-statistic
κ_1	0.167	0.018	8.846
κ_2	0.199	0.045	4.389
κ_3	−0.257	0.045	−5.686
κ_4	−0.500	0.051	−9.992
Constant	2.657	0.175	15.173

Note: [a] $\bar{R}^2 = 0.61$; number of observations = 151; estimation method: non-linear least squares.

wages will be higher when a district is close to, or part of, an economic centre, that is a clustering of districts with relatively high Y. Both dummies are also significant and have the expected sign, indicating that wages are relatively low for East German and/or country districts. Another feature worth mentioning is that equation (12.1′) assumes that Germany is a closed economy. Germany's main trading partners are the other member states of the European Union (EU). Adding the market access to these fourteen EU countries has, however, no additional impact whatsoever on wages and the estimation results reported in table 12.1. The spatial wage structure in Germany does not seem to be affected by economic activity abroad.

Estimating the structural parameters by the means of the reduced form wage equation (12.2)

In our search for a spatial wage structure in Germany that supports geographical economics we now turn to the attempt to estimate the structural parameters using the reduced form wage equation (12.2) for Germany. In doing so, we will be able to verify the so-called 'no-black hole' condition, giving an indication for the convergence prospects in Germany.[18] The data and sample are the same as before. Given that we have already established that the openness of the German economy does not have a bearing on our results, we estimate for the case of a closed economy.

---

[18] In Fujita, Krugman and Venables (1999, p. 58) the so-called 'no-black-hole' condition is introduced. It says that if this condition is not fulfilled 'the forces working toward agglomeration would always prevail, and the economy would tend to collapse into a point'. Stated differently, if the 'no-black-hole' condition is not met full agglomeration occurs irrespective of the level of transport costs.

Table 12.2 *Estimating the structural parameters for Germany*[a]

	Coefficient	Standard error	*t*-statistic
δ	1.869	0.887	2.105
ε	3.914	0.618	6.327
$\log T$	0.008	0.001	7.257

Note: [a] $\bar{R}^2 = 0.481$; number of observations = 151; estimation method: non-linear least squares. The implied estimate for $\varepsilon/(\varepsilon - 1)$ is 1.343. The implied estimate for $\varepsilon(1 - \delta)$ is -3.401, with a standard error of 2.773.

Table 12.2 gives the estimation results. We also included a dummy variable for East German districts and a dummy variable for country districts. As these results are immaterial for the conclusions with respect to the structural parameters they are not reported here.

The results are somewhat mixed. The substitution elasticity ε is significant and the coefficient implies a profit margin of 34 per cent (given that $\varepsilon/(\varepsilon - 1)$ is the markup) (see table 12.2), which is fairly reasonable,[19] although higher than found for the USA by Hanson (1998, 1999). Note that the value $\varepsilon(1 - \delta)$ is used to determine whether a reduction of transport costs affects spatial agglomeration of economic activity: is $\varepsilon(1 - \delta) < 1$? The share of income spent on manufactures δ is (implausibly) large because it does not differ significantly from one, which would mean that Germans do not spend any D-Marks on housing, the non-tradable good in the model underlying equation (12.2). Even though Hanson also finds this share to be quite large for the USA (above 0.9 and in some cases also not significantly different from 1), this is a somewhat puzzling result. The transport cost parameter has the correct sign and is highly significant. In discussing the Hanson results we criticised his assumption of real wage equalisation (imposing a long-run equilibrium). Specifically for the German case this *a priori* is too strong an assumption. We know that real wages in the two parts of Germany were not equal in 1995. So we re-estimated (12.2) allowing for a real wage differential between (but not within) East and West Germany. The coefficient (not shown here) measuring the real wage differential indeed indicated that real wages are

---

[19] Estimates of profit margins in industry range from 14 per cent in the USA (Norrbin, 1993), 100 per cent in the UK (Haskel, Martin and Small, 1995) to over 100 per cent in the US (Hall, 1988).

Table 12.3 *Structural parameters for Germany, restricting δ Panel (a)*[a]
$\delta = 0.67998 = 1-($income share spent on non-tradable services$)$

	Coefficient	Standard error	*t*-statistic
ε	2.876	0.276	10.409
$\log T$	0.009	0.001	7.278

Note: [a] $\bar{R}^2 = 0.455$; number of observations $= 151$; log likelihood $= 1.22$; estimation method: non-linear least squares. The implied estimate for $\varepsilon/(\varepsilon - 1)$ is 1.533. When the restriction $\delta = 0.67998$ is imposed, the implied estimate for $\varepsilon(1 - \delta)$ equals 0.920, with a standard error of 0.088.

not equal, but (surprisingly) did not differ significantly from zero. The results shown in table 12.2 are therefore a good first approximation for Germany.

A final estimation of (12.2) addresses the problem that the share of income spent on manufactures δ was found to be too high in table 12.3 (namely above 1). To remedy this we consulted statistical information on German expenditure shares, which is relatively easy to obtain. The appropriate δ can be chosen either as $1 - 0.32002$, with 0.32002 being the share of income spent on non-tradable services (see panel (a) of table 12.3), or as $1 - 0.17153$, with 0.17153 being the share of income spent on non-tradable housing services (see panel (b) of table 12.3).[20] We thus estimated (12.2) again, restricting the parameter δ to either of the two values above.

As table 12.3 shows, restricting the share of income spent on manufactures to 0.68 or 0.82 reduces the estimated elasticity of substitution between manufacturing varieties from almost 4 to roughly 3, and thus increases the estimated markup over marginal costs from 1/3 to 1/2. The estimated size and significance of the transport costs T are, however, not affected by imposing the restrictions. (Though it should be noted that the restrictions are statistically not valid, as a likelihood ratio test shows.)[21]

[20] Based on the weights in the German CPI, February 1999, Statistisches Bundesamt.
[21] The log likelihood of the unrestricted specification (12.2) is 5.39. The likelihood ratio test is 8.34 ($\delta = 0.68$) and 5.52 ($\delta = 0.82$), which implies rejection of the restriction.

*Panel (b)[a] $\delta = 0.82847 = 1 - (income\ share$
spent on housing services)

	Coefficient	Standard error	t-statistic
ε	3.100	0.318	9.734
$\log T$	0.009	0.001	7.568

Note: [a] $\bar{R}^2 = 0.465$; number of observations $= 151$; log likelihood $= 2.63$; estimation method: non-linear least squares. The implied estimate for $\varepsilon/(\varepsilon - 1)$ is 1.476. When the restriction $\delta = 0.82847$ is imposed, the implied estimate for $\varepsilon(1 - \delta)$ equals 0.532, with a standard error of 0.055.

We started our discussion about Germany in this section by mentioning the lack of convergence prospects. The estimation results in tables 12.2 and 12.3 show that $\varepsilon(1 - \delta) < 1$, although not significantly, except for the case in which δ is fixed at 0.82847. This implies in the geographical economics model with a housing sector based on Helpman (1998) that transport costs might have an impact on the degree of agglomeration, that is agglomeration is not inevitable if transport costs can be sufficiently reduced. For Germany this seems to indicate that a lowering of transport costs might lead to more even spreading of economic activity, which is good news for the peripheral districts, the bulk of which are located in East Germany. It also means that the pessimistic view about the German convergence process based on simulations with the core model of geographical economics may be too pessimistic.

12.3.3   Empirical results: part II

Ideally one would like to estimate both equilibrium equations of the economic geography model, that is the wage equation and the price index equation. This is to be preferred to the estimation of either an approximate method like (12.1$'$) or the reduced form equation (12.2) which uses the *a priori* untested assumption of real wage equalisation between German regions.

If there are R regions, the equilibrium wage equation (12.3) and the price index equation (12.4) are:

$$W_s = \left[\sum_{r=1}^{R} Y_r (T^{D_{rs}})^{1-\varepsilon} I_r^{\varepsilon-1} \right]^{1/\varepsilon} \tag{12.3}$$

$$I_r = \left[\sum_{s=1}^{R} \lambda_s (T^{D_{rs}})^{1-\varepsilon} W_s^{1-\varepsilon} \right]^{1/\varepsilon}, \tag{12.4}$$

where I_r is region r's exact price index of manufactures, Y_r is its income level, W_r is its manufacturing wage rate λ_r is its share of manufacturing workers, D_{rs} is its distance to region s and ε is the elasticity of substitution between manufactures. Empirical application of this set of equations is difficult because of the non-linearities and the summations involved. For a large number of regions this becomes highly impracticable. One can, however, circumvent some of the difficulties in estimating this set of equations and thereby estimate the structural parameters without invoking real wage equalisation.

Trick 1. We can simplify price equation (12.4). The price index of manufactures in region r exists of prices of each manufacturing good produced in all regions s. Wages are multiplied by a distance factor $T^{D_{rs}}$ and weighted by the region's share in the number of varieties λ_s. Equation (12.4) can be simplified by not considering all prices in all regions, but using the *average* price outside region r instead. The relevant distance would be the distance between the region analysed and this average region. However, the distance to the most important region is *a priori* the most relevant. The *average* region is therefore substituted by the *most important* or *centre* region. This centre is obtained by weighing the distances with the measure of relative Y.[22] The economic centre of Germany turns out to be *Landkreis Giessen* (near Frankfurt), which is in West Germany. Equation (12.4) then becomes:

$$I_r = \left[\lambda_r W_r^{1-\varepsilon} + (1 - \lambda_r)(\bar{W} T^{D_{r-centre}})^{1-\varepsilon} \right]^{1/(1-\varepsilon)}, \tag{12.4'}$$

where $\bar{W}$ is the average wage and $D_{r-centre}$ is the distance from region r to the economic centre. Data on the weights λ_r, region r's share of employment in manufacturing, which is proportional to the number of varieties, is available.

Trick 2. The marginal productivity of labour (MPL) differs between East Germany and West Germany (see the discussion of Brakman and Garretsen, 1993, above). It is assumed that there is a uniform level of MPL in the West, θ_{west}. There is also a uniform level of MPL in the East, θ_{east}, which is lower than in the West. Incorporating this difference means

---

[22] For each region r the weighted average distance to the other regions $\sum_s weight_s D_{rs}$ is calculated, using $weight_s = Y_s / \sum_j Y_j$. The region with the smallest average distance is the economic centre.

that the basic equations of the model change to.[23]

$$W_s = \text{constant} \times \left(\frac{\theta_{west}}{\theta_r}\right)^{(1-\varepsilon)/\varepsilon} \left[\sum_{r=1}^{R} Y_r (T^{D_{rs}})^{1-\varepsilon} I_r^{\varepsilon-1}\right]^{1/\varepsilon} \qquad (12.3'')$$

$$I_r = \left[\lambda_r \left(W_r \frac{\theta_{west}}{\theta_r}\right)^{1-\varepsilon}\right.$$

$$\left. + (1 - \lambda_r)(\bar{W} T^{D_{r-center}})^{1-\varepsilon}\right]^{1/(1-\varepsilon)}. \qquad (12.4'')$$

Results of the tricks

Equation (12.4″) is substituted into (12.3″), which provides us with the reduced form of the short-run equilibrium. The equation to be estimated is:

$$\log W_s = \kappa_0 + \frac{1}{\varepsilon} \log \left[\sum_{r=1}^{R} Y_r \left(T^{D_{rs}}\right)^{1-\varepsilon} I_r^{\varepsilon-1}\right]$$

$$+ \kappa_2 D_{east} + \kappa_3 D_{country} + err_s \qquad (12.5)$$

where

$$I_r^{1-\varepsilon} = \lambda_r [W_r(1 + \kappa_1 D_{east})]^{1-\varepsilon} + (1 - \lambda_r)(\bar{W} T^{D_{r-center}})^{1-\varepsilon}.$$

Table 12.4 shows the regression results of the reduced form of the short-run equilibrium. The parameter κ_1 is set equal to zero, as it (perhaps surprisingly, because κ_2 is significantly different from zero) turned out to be not significantly different from zero.

The results in table 12.4 show that a spatial wage structure is present. Again, the estimated distance parameter is significantly positive, and virtually identical to previous estimates, indicating the robustness of the estimated transport costs with respect to the estimated specification. This time, however, the elasticity of substitution between different types of manufactures increases substantially. The markup over marginal costs therefore reduces to about 10 per cent. This arises from the significance

---

[23] Employment in a typical Western firm is $\alpha + \beta x_i$. Employment in a typical Eastern firm is $\alpha + \beta x_i(\theta_{west}/\theta_{east})$. Sales of a firm located in region r equals total demand for its product. Dropping subscript i for the individual firm:

$$\frac{(\varepsilon - 1)\alpha}{\beta(\theta_{west}/\theta_r)} = \sum_{k=1}^{R} \left[\left(\frac{\varepsilon}{\varepsilon - 1} \frac{\beta W_r T^{D_{rk}}(\theta_{west}/\theta_r)}{I_k}\right)^{-\varepsilon} T^{D_{rk}} \delta \frac{Y_k}{I_k}\right],$$

which gives (12.3″) above, where $\theta_{west}/\theta_r = 1$ if r is in West, and $\theta_{west}/\theta_r > 1$, if r is in East.

Table 12.4 *Estimating the reduced form of the short-run equilibrium for Germany*[a]

	Coefficient	Standard error	t-statistic
ε	10.564	2.599	4.064
$\log T$	0.007	0.002	4.172
κ_2	−0.358	0.053	−6.777

Note: [a] $\bar{R}^2 = 0.455$; number of observations = 151; estimation method: non-linear least squares. The implied estimate for $\varepsilon/(\varepsilon - 1)$ is 1.105. When the restriction $\delta = 0.82847$ is imposed, the implied estimate for $\varepsilon(1 - \delta)$ equals 1.812, with a standard error of 0.055.

of the estimated dummy variable for East Germany, which increases the predictive power of the estimated equation to about 52 per cent.

12.4 Conclusions

In this chapter we have discussed the empirical relevance of geographical economics, and our analysis leads to two main conclusions. First, a large number of empirical studies are not only consistent with geographical economics models, but also with other theories of trade and location. This is not surprising since these studies are mostly not aimed at testing specific theories, such as geographical economics. Second, those attempts that try to test directly for the relevance of geographical economics do confirm some of its main predictions, in particular the existence of a spatial wage structure. Despite this empirical validation, the nature of the geographical economics approach, and specifically the existence of multiple equilibria, make it difficult to test in a conclusive manner for the relevance of this theory. However, applications of the geographical economics model to a real-world case, here Germany after the unification, shows that the model does indeed confirm the existence of a spatial wage structure. In order to be able to say more on German reunification we first of all need (remember figure 12.1) multiple years of observation. Also, for this model to be perhaps better suited for the German case, one likes to take specific German features into account such as the degree of labour market flexibility or transfers between western and eastern Germany (see Brakman, Garretsen and Schramm, 2001 for a first attempt)

The analysis also raises a number of questions. It remains unclear what geographical economics adds empirically to our understanding of the relationships between location and economic activity. Is it that we are now able to discover new facts, or does geographical economics 'merely' provide a better theoretical foundation for stylised facts that were already established long ago? The empirical evidence is clearly in favour of a spatial wage structure. However, the implications of the estimated structural parameters for convergence or divergence in Germany are not clear-cut. Some parameters, notably the estimated elasticity of substitution, depend substantially on the estimation procedure. Others, such as the estimated transport costs parameter, are more robust in this respect, but these are, as figure 12.1 clearly shows, difficult to interpret, particularly since we can only perform cross-section estimations. Moreover, interpreting some of the implications of the estimated parameters, such as the extent to which transport costs matter as indicated by the 'no-black-hole' condition, depend on the structural specification of the model. Now that we have some reasonable estimates of the most important structural parameters one can, in principle, start to perform some counterfactual experiments in order to determine the outcome of specific policy changes. Obviously, the outcome will at least partially depend on the structural model used for these policy simulations.

REFERENCES

Berg, M. van den and Sturm, J. E. (1997). The empirical relevance of location factors modelled by Krugman. SOM Research Report 97C01, University of Groningen

Black, D. and Henderson, V. (1998). Urban evolution in the USA. Brown University Working Paper, 98-21, Brown University

(1999). Spatial evolution of population and industry in the United States. *American Economic Review, Papers and Proceedings*, 89: 321–327

Brakman, S. and Garretsen, H. (1993). The relevance of initial conditions for the German unification. *Kyklos*, 46: 163–181

Brakman, S., Garretsen, H. and van Marrewijk, C. (2001). *An Introduction to Geographical Economics: Trade, Location and Growth*. Cambridge, Cambridge University Press

Brakman, S., Garretsen, H. and Schramm, M. (2000). The empirical relevance of the new economic geography: testing for a spatial wage structure in Germany. CESifo Working Paper, 395, Munich

(2001). New economic geography in Germany: estimating the Helpman–Hanson model. University of Nijmegen, mimeo

Brülhart, M. (1998). Economic geography, industry location and trade: the evidence. *World Economy*, 21: 775–801

Davis, D. R. (1998). The home market, trade and industrial structure. *American Economic Review*, 88: 1264–1276

Davis, D. R. and Weinstein, D. E. (1996). Does economic geography matter for international specialization? Harvard University, mimeo

(1997). Increasing returns and international trade: an empirical confirmation. Harvard University, mimeo

(1998a). Market access, economic geography and comparative advantage: an empirical assessment. Harvard Institute of Economic Research Discussion Paper, 1850, Harvard University

(1998b). An account of global factor trade. NBER Working Paper, 6758

(1999). Economic geography and regional production structure: an empirical investigation. *European Economic Review*, 43: 379–407

Deardorff, A. (1995). Determinants of bilateral trade: does gravity work in a neoclassical world? NBER Working Paper, 5377

Dixit, A. K. and Norman, V. (1980). *Theory of International Trade*. Cambridge, University Press

Dixit, A. K. and Stiglitz, J. E. (1977). Monopolistic competition and optimal product diversity. *American Economic Review*, 67: 297–308

Dumais, G., Ellison, G. and Glaeser, E. L. (1997). Geographic concentration as a dynamic process. NBER Working Paper, 6270

Ellison, G. and Glaeser, E. L. (1999). The geographic concentration of industry: does natural advantage explain agglomeration? *American Economic Review, Papers and Proceedings*, 89: 311–316

Fujita, M., Krugman, P. R. and Venables, A. J. (1999). *The Spatial Economy*. Cambridge, MA, MIT Press

Fujita, M. and Thisse, J.-F. (2000). Economics of agglomeration, in Huriot, J.-M. and Thisse, J.-F. (eds.), *The Economics of Cities*. Cambridge, Cambridge University Press

Grossman, G. M. and Helpman, E. (1991). *Innovation and Growth in the Global Economy*. Cambridge, MA, MIT Press

Haaland, J. I., Kind, H. J., Midelfart-Knarvik, K. H. and Torstensson, J. (1999). What determines the economic geography of Europe? CEPR Discussion Paper, 2072

Hall, R. E. (1988). The relation between price and marginal cost in US industry. *Journal of Political Economy*, 96: 921–947

Hanson, G. H. (1997). Increasing returns, trade and the regional structure of wages. *Economic Journal*, 107: 113–133

(1998). Market potential, increasing returns, and geographic concentration. NBER Working Paper, 6429

(1999). Market potential, increasing returns, and geographic concentration. University of Michigan, mimeo (revised version of Hanson, 1998)

Harris, C. D. (1954). The market as a factor in the localization of industry in the United States. *Annals of the Association of American Geographers*, 44: 315–348

Haskel, J., Martin, C. and Small, I. (1995). Price, marginal cost and the business cycle. *Oxford Bulletin of Economics and Statistics*, 57: 25–41

Helpman, E. (1998). The size of regions, in Pines, D., Sadka, E. and Zilcha, I. (eds.), *Topics in Public Economics*. Cambridge, Cambridge University Press

Helpman, E. and Krugman, P. R. (1985). *Market Structure and Foreign Trade.* Cambridge, MA, MIT Press

Kim, S. (1995). Expansion of markets and the geographic distribution of economic activities: the trends in US regional manufacturing structure, 1860–1987. *Quarterly Journal of Economics*, 110: 881–908

Krugman, P. R. (1979). Increasing returns, monopolistic competition and international trade. *Journal of International Economics*, 9: 469–479

(1980). Scale economies, product differentiation, and the pattern of trade. *American Economic Review*, 70: 950–959

(1991). Increasing returns and economic geography. *Journal of Political Economy*, 99: 483–499

(1995). *Development, Geography and Economic Theory*. Cambridge, MA, MIT Press

(1998). Space: the final frontier. *Journal of Economic Perspectives*, 12: 161–174

Midelfart-Knarvik, K. H., Overman, H. G., Redding, S. J. and Venables, A. J. (2000). The location of European industry. *Economic Papers*, 142, European Commission, Brussels

Neary, J. P. (2001). Of hype and hyperbolas: introducing the new economic geography. *Journal of Economic Literature*, 29: 536–561

Norrbin, S. C. (1993). The relation between price and marginal cost in US industry: a contradiction. *Journal of Political Economy*, 101: 1149–1164

Sinn, H.-W. (2000). Germany's economic unification: an assessment after ten years. CESifo Working Paper, 247, Munich

Thomas, A. (1996). Increasing returns, congestion costs and the geographic concentration of firms. International Monetary Fund, Washington, mimeo

13   The monopolistic competition model in urban economic geography

J. Vernon Henderson

13.1   Introduction

The development of the modern monopolistic competition model by Dixit and Stiglitz (1977), as well as by Spence (1976), started as a key innovation in industrial organisation. It provides a rigorous version of the Chamberlin–Robinson model of imperfect competition and clarifies long-standing issues such as whether, in fact, markets will generate too many varieties of differentiated products. But it quickly became apparent that the neat technical form to the model has other, perhaps even more important uses. The framework provides a convenient forum to model both scale economies in trade and growth models and the role of transport costs in trade models. These considerations led later to the formulation of the 'new' economic geography and to innovations in more traditional urban economics. While Dixit or Stiglitz cannot be praised nor held accountable for these developments *per se*, they would not have occurred in a timely fashion, without the Dixit–Stiglitz model. In this review, I focus on applications of Dixit–Stiglitz in urban modelling, so much of the discussion evaluates work by researchers such as Fujita, Krugman, Venables and their students.

There are two main types of applications in urban economic analysis. First are Krugman's (1991) core–periphery model and its urban variants by Krugman (1993) and Fujita, Krugman and Mori (1999). The core–periphery model is used extensively to model regional interactions, but also is interpreted widely as modelling urban phenomena. The more specific urban variants of the model try to better capture interactions across cities, as opposed to regions. The second type of application of Dixit–Stiglitz is to model the micro-foundations of agglomeration within a city (Hobson, 1987 and Fujita, 1988) and the integration of these

I thank Duncan Black, Diego Puga and Will Strange for their perceptive and helpful comments on a preliminary version of the paper, as well as Jim Davis. They saved me from some embarrassing omissions and helped me better orient the paper and better represent the literature. But they couldn't save me entirely from my own biases.

micro-foundations into traditional systems of cities models (Abdel-Rahman and Fujita, 1990).

In section 13.2, I start by reviewing the core–periphery model and its fundamental insights. With this review, in section 13.3, I then focus on key concerns with the core–periphery model and its more urban variants. These concerns involve the depiction of geography, empirical validation and theoretical limitations, such as the inability to date to conduct welfare and key policy analysis, to accommodate economic growth and to analyse situations with complete land development markets. Since some of these criticisms are in the context of an implicit or explicit comparison with the traditional systems of cities model, I start section 13.3 with a review of that model. In section 13.4, I turn to the second type of application of the Dixit–Stiglitz model – its use in modelling the micro-foundations of agglomeration within a city and then the integration of that modelling into the general equilibrium context of a system of cities. Finally, in section 13.5, I turn to recent developments. There is a new generation of systems of cities models that incorporates key aspects of core–periphery models, as well as Dixit–Stiglitz or other models of local imperfect competition, into the urban systems framework. They focus on modelling the diverse processes of large metro areas today – headquarters activity, R&D activity and producer service production.

This chapter will argue that, while the core–periphery model itself may be a useful addition to models of regional interactions and inter-regional trade and factor movements, it is not a very useful model of cities, or urban economic geography. Even its specifically urban variants have limited usefulness. However the integration of Dixit–Stiglitz and aspects of the core–periphery model into traditional systems of cities models has helped spur a new generation of systems of cities models. These account in a reasonable fashion for spatial frictions – transport and transactions costs – between cities. And the Dixit–Stiglitz model, along with other imperfect competition models, is used to represent key aspects of the service, R&D and headquarters functions of large metro areas. This has been a missing ingredient of most urban modelling.

13.2   Krugman's application of Dixit–Stiglitz

The natural extension of the Dixit–Stiglitz model into the 'new' economic geography took off with Krugman's (1991) *Journal of Political Economy* paper. This paper spawned a whole literature, much of it focused on the core–periphery model and represented in the book by Fujita, Krugman and Venables (1999), *The Spatial Economy*. It is important to appreciate Krugman's key innovations, in terms of traditional location theory. To do so, I start by outlining the model.

Krugman analyses a two-region economy. Agricultural labourers are fixed in number and immobile: they neither migrate between economic sectors nor regions. There is also a population of manufacturing worker/consumers, who are perfectly mobile between the regions, but not sectors. The key issue is when will regions specialise with all manufacturing worker/consumers migrating to one region, yielding a core manufacturing centre and a periphery region with only agricultural production. Krugman focuses on 'tipping points', when having two manufacturing regions will be unstable because any perturbation of a situation where both regions do manufacturing will result in manufacturing workers in one region all flowing into the other, induced by evolving real wage gains. As in all urban and location models, agglomeration into the core region is driven by scale economies. The Dixit–Stiglitz model has plant fixed costs of production and national economies of scale through the scale benefits of a larger country being able to support more varieties, in a model where there is an unlimited demand for varieties. But there is a new ingredient in Krugman's agglomeration recipe.

In the analysis, the key innovation relative to traditional location theory is that manufacturing sectors provide their own internal force for local agglomeration: they are focal points of consumer demands for products. In Losch (1954), Berry (1967), Beckman (1968) and other traditional hierarchy and location models, manufacturing plants serve an agriculture population but their workers have no residential location and themselves generate no demand for their own product. In Krugman, the Dixit–Stiglitz model, combined with Samuelson iceberg-type transport costs, provides a story of enhanced agglomeration through backward and forward linkages. The more consumers there are in a region the more firms need employ workers to supply the consumers, the more varieties that then get produced, the higher real incomes are, then the more worker/consumers are attracted to the region, and so on. This potentially unlimited benefit of agglomeration is the centripetal force to create a specialised core region. The centrifugal force working against all manufacturing being agglomerated in the core is the fixed agriculture population in the periphery. That population is its own source of demand for manufactured products. If transport costs are low, that doesn't stop the formation of the core. However if transport costs are high, then producers can be induced to move from the core to the periphery to serve the agricultural population, resulting in symmetrically populated regions.

Of course core–periphery models are not new in mainstream economies. While not called core–periphery, there are a various models of differential regional size and economic compositions such as traditional regional models with a mobile versus immobile factor across regions (e.g.

see Borts and Stein, 1964) or the regional public goods literature. And tipping, the analysis of what population allocations are stable, is central to urban systems models (Henderson, 1974; Fujita, 1989); and it is part of modern regional models that experience population growth (Henderson, 1986; Anas, 1992). However Krugman's analysis highlights the role of transport costs and backward and forward linkages in determining regional specialisation, an almost forgotten aspect of these other models. In most traditional urban models, transport costs are of a (0,1) nature: either there are no transport costs for a good or transport costs are so large as to render the good non-tradable across regions. That is, no transport costs are ever incurred. A world with incurred transport costs introduces interesting and compelling considerations.

Since Krugman's paper, there have been on-going extensions to the basic core–periphery model, as presented in Fujita, Krugman and Venables (1999). There is a nice review in Fujita and Thisse (2000) and this is not the place to attempt another review of such an enormous literature. The extensions include Venables' (1996) introduction of intermediate products that I will discuss separately below, the analysis of growth in a two-region context, the analysis of transport hubs (Fujita and Mori, 1996), and other considerations of forces for dispersion such as internal commuting costs (Tabuchi, 1998). These particular extensions are still focused on a core–periphery paradigm.

In critically examining the model below, I will argue that the core–periphery model is inadequate for understanding the key aspects of a modern urbanised economy and a number of its predictive outcomes contradict empirical evidence. Despite this, many extensions of the core–periphery model still treat the model as though it is a model for analysing cities.

Krugman is well aware of the problem and has been involved in two different attempts to create an urban version of the model, where there are an endogenous number of region/cities. First he devised a clock-dial, or race-track model, where agricultural space is circular and there are a number of potential urban sites (Krugman, 1993). Specifying a naive adjustment mechanism for manufacturing labour flows across sites, using computer simulations, he computes when one versus two versus more sites will end up being occupied, from an initial allocation where there are, say, twelve sites with an arbitrary initial endowment of manufacturing workers. Most of his computations again involve two symmetrical sites being occupied in equilibrium – same size and opposite each other on the circle. In a more sophisticated version of this, Fujita and Mori working with Krugman were able to solve the 'holy grail' of location theory – a general equilibrium model of an urban hierarchy. After years of work (Fujita and Krugman, 2000), using simulation, Fujita, Krugman and Mori (1999) were able to simulate an urban hierarchy equilibrium, with a hierarchy of cities stretched along a line of agricultural land and production. The central city produces the largest range of differentiated products, and smaller peripheral cities more limited ranges.

The Fujita, Krugman and Mori work is an important achievement. But most of the problems with the core–periphery model carry over to this more specific urban version as well, in terms of the modelling, policy analysis and empirical support.

13.3   Issues with the core–periphery model and its derivatives

To examine issues with the core–periphery model, it is helpful to review the traditional systems of cities model and have that as one of several perspectives on the core–periphery model. That review will also facilitate the discussion in sections 13.4 and 13.5, on the use of the Dixit–Stiglitz model to represent micro-foundations of agglomeration and to incorporate these into a system of cities model. I start with a review of the systems of cities model, and then examine three sets of issues concerning the core–periphery model.

13.3.1   Systems of cities models

In the basic general equilibrium model of urban systems as devised by Henderson (1974) and in the major extensions (e.g. Hochman, 1977; Kanemoto, 1980), capital and labour are perfectly mobile within a country. Cities form on urban sites that are in unlimited supply on the national landscape. Agriculture is not explicitly modelled (although it could be considered as the smallest type of city in the system). The USA is the prototype for this model where at most 2 per cent of the labour force is in agriculture and roughly 2/3 of the national land area is 'vacant' – not used in urban areas, roads, rural settlements and farmhouses and cultivation. There are hundreds of cities and their numbers change continuously. Technological developments and infrastructure investments in transport and telecommunications have diminished the role of spatial frictions for trade across cities. Rather than modelling inter-city transport costs, the focus is on internal city transport costs in the form of commuting costs (Fujita and Thisse, 2000).[1] Cities have explicit or implicit spatial

---

[1] One can argue that commuting costs are a far more important cost of friction than transport costs of goods. From section 21 of the *Statistical Abstract of the USA 1997*, in 1995 in the USA, $441 billion was spent on freight transport. Out-of-pocket costs of consumer transport was $774 billion. These numbers represent the total expenditures

structures with a business district and commuting from residential areas. Commuting costs are the key force for dispersion; the limit on increasing individual city sizes is rising congestion and commuting costs.

The initial version of the model focused on two issues. First there is the idea that cities are specialised in production, exploiting local own industry external scale economies and producing different goods entirely – textiles versus steel versus automobiles versus gambling and entertainment versus health services, and so on. For each product type, there are an endogenous number of cities with different sizes for each type. The second issue concerns the formation of cities. What is the number of cities overall and of each type that will occur in equilibrium? Henderson (1974) considered two alternative city formation mechanisms. First involves tipping, or what is now called 'self-organisation'. As population grows in an economy, a new city (or cities) forms only when a single worker (or tiny firm) would gain by leaving any existing city and living in a settlement size of one person. Self-organisation is a depressing outcome – the urban economists' version of a Malthusian world – where new cities arise only when old ones get so overgrown and congested that individuals are driven out 'into the wilderness'.

The alternative city formation mechanism is that there exists a land development market for new cities, so land development markets are complete. There are 'large agents' who facilitate *en masse* movement of workers and firms. Such agents recognise when a new city can be sustained. They then set contract terms (zoning for size and composition of settlements, financial inducements and guarantees) that induce *en masse* movements of workers and firms into their new cities, at the limit achieving efficient city sizes. Rauch (1993) and Mitra (1994) have a nice game theoretic analysis of this phenomenon of developers inducing *en masse* movements of workers. Helsley and Strange (1997) focus on the role of land developers when land assembly is costly or faces uncertain prospects and Henderson and Mitra (1996) analyse the phenomenon of edge-city formation (Garreau, 1991). Henderson and Becker (2000) formulate a modern version of city formation with local governments and politics, where efficient city sizes can be achieved in a market context through a combination of local growth controls imposed by vote-seeking local

in those years on new capital, labour, gas, insurance, maintenance, etc. In addition, the tables suggest that time costs of urban consumers equal out-of-pocket costs – these are the total number of urban miles in non-interstate automobile transport in a year times $12 per hour times the average time to travel a mile. This could be an under-estimate of commuting costs: traditional transport analysis stresses that time costs are much higher than out-of-pocket commuting costs. Of course the frictional costs of trading services across cities are omitted in calculating costs of trade.

governments on existing cities and the formation of new cities through either self-organisation or actions of land developers.

There have been a variety of extensions to this basic model. Some consider important aspects of urban systems, such as the role of diversified cities (e.g. Abdel-Rahman, 1996), the skill composition of cities (e.g. Black, 1998), and the micro-foundations of scale economies that are discussed in section 13.4 below. Others point to fundamental extensions that are essential to application of urban analysis to the real world – dynamics, welfare analysis and policy. Exogenous growth is analysed in Kanemoto (1980) and Henderson and Ioannides (1981) and endogenous growth in Eaton and Eckstein (1997) and Black and Henderson (1999). These growth models examine the technological forces driving on-going population and economic growth of individual cities, as well as differences in human capital and knowledge accumulation across different types of cities. Extensive welfare analysis comparing equilibrium with efficient outcomes started in a static context with Henderson (1977) and Arnott (1979). The impact on urban systems of various policy distortions such as national minimum wages, tariffs and national government favouritism of key cities such as the national capital is first modelled in Henderson (1982a, 1982b).

I now turn to issues with the core–periphery model and its urban variants. These include depiction of geography, empirical support and the 'usability' of the model as a model that examines urban policy issues.

13.3.2   Geography

A basic *raison d'être* of the core–periphery model and its extensions is to have an explicit geography in economic models. 'Space' in the core–periphery model does not involve explicit spatial dimensions; there is just 'geography' – two regions with shipping costs between them. But I will argue below that having geography may be more important than having explicit spatial dimensions between cities. Apart from this issue, from a US perspective, Krugman's world is a nineteenth-century world, where farmers still provide a key demand for urban products and the geography of agriculture land and production determines the geography of cities. Different types of workers are immobile across either regions or economic sectors. Moreover within this framework, agricultural products have zero transport costs while urban products are transport cost-intensive. Reality suggests the relative transport costs go the other way. But these criticisms are really too strict. The model from the perspective of countries in the European Union or from the perspective of a single developing country could well represent portions of regional labour forces that are immobile across regions even in the relatively long term, and possibly immobile across economic sectors in the shorter run. The products of immobile workers do not need to be literally agricultural and hence they may not be more transport intensive than those of the mobile workers.

More critically, as urban models, the core–periphery world has a fixed number of regions and Krugman's clock-dial world is talking of a world of two versus three cities. As in much of economics, a world of twos is very different from a world of many. With ten–fifteen cities, catastrophic changes in city populations do not occur (i.e. changes are not catastrophic) and the tipping story with catastrophic changes found in Krugman seems of limited interest. Even medium size countries have fifty–sixty major urban areas whose numbers increase over time with population growth and their sizes with technological development. However the Fujita, Krugman and Mori work has explicit spatial dimensions – agriculture and cities on a line – and many cities. Admittedly it is in an agricultural hierarchy framework, where there is a sense of one metro area dominating a group of dependent towns and then villages within a limited agricultural region (see later). However it is the most convincing completed general equilibrium model of an economy with explicit spatial dimensions.

One might argue that we can have a richer model with more geography, without the complexity of explicit space between cities (see section 13.5). In terms of geography, there are other considerations than shipping costs of final products among regions. There is the fact that manufacturing requires raw material inputs that are found in discrete geographic locations often in the hinterlands of countries, while final products are shipped internationally from natural harbours, typically in coastal areas. And on a larger international scale, there is Jeff Sach's story of climate, disease, economic growth and location.

13.3.3   Empirical support

A basic tenet of economic science is that a model doesn't need to look like the real world. Here, in some sense, it doesn't matter if core–periphery models have any similarity to real geography or if urban systems models capture only the internal and not the external space of cities. Rather, what matters is how well models predict. Do they work so as to predict the key economic phenomena of the real urban world?

Unfortunately, there has been almost no empirical work on urban aspects of the core–periphery model and its urban versions. An exception is Hanson (1996, 1998a, 1998b), who combines concepts from the core–periphery and urban systems models to look at spatial patterns of wages in Mexico and to look at the effect of market potential on wage patterns across US counties. The lack of empirical work central to the core–periphery model could be just that too little time has passed to find supporting evidence for the core–periphery. But this means that we have not directly quantified the upstream and downstream circular causality forces of agglomeration in Krugman. They are surely there; we just haven't developed and implemented a strong empirical test to determine the extent to which they matter, although Holmes (1999b, 2000) has some work that bears on the issue. In contrast, dating back to, for example, Hoover (1939) and Chinitz (1961), economists have examined the nature and extent of technological external economies of scale in systems of cities models with more recent work by Ciccone and Hall (1996) for example. Econometric work by Sveikauskas (1975), Nakamura (1985) and Henderson (1988) documents that such economies of scale for standardised manufacturing tend to be own industry ones, where efficiency of a factory depends just on the scale of closely related activities nearby, rather than overall urban scale *per se*. The magnitude of such externalities seems to justify the sizes of observed cities in simple simulation work.

Some of the basic predictions of the core–periphery model are at odds with the data. In particular, the core–periphery and Krugman urban models suggest that costs-of-living in a city fall with city size. We have known for years that the opposite is the case. For example Thomas (1978) indicates that costs of living in the biggest cities are twofold those in the smallest, as suggested by worldwide comparisons today made possible by the UNCHS data set from Habitat. A variety of researchers before and after Roback (1982) have shown the close positive relationships between urban housing costs, land costs, commuting times and city sizes.

In terms of the relations among cities, there is older work on urban hierarchies (Berry, 1967), focused on agricultural areas which support networks of small towns. The analysis concerns the distribution of urban services to farmers in a confined agricultural area – which order of town will offer dry cleaning services versus haircuts versus repair services and how many of these personal and repair services will be offered in towns of different sizes and ranks. The work is very interesting, particularly in its application to analysing systems of rural villages and towns, in relation perhaps to a local small–medium-size metro area in an agricultural county, or province of a country. But it doesn't tell us much about a more modern system of cities – how many steel versus textile cities there are nationally and how that is influenced by growth, factor endowments and tariff policy. The urban systems empirical work examines urban specialisation in industrial and exportable service products among different size metro areas, as documented in Alexandersson (1959), Bergsman, Greenston and Healy (1972) and Henderson (1988).

There is no modern empirical work on growth in a hierarchy *per se*, while there is an on-going literature on growth based on urban systems models (Eaton and Eckstein, 1997; Beeson, Dejong and Troesken, 1999; Black and Henderson, 2000; Dobkins and Ioannides, 2000). However it could be that some of this work could be interpreted in an urban hierarchy model. The work examines increases in city sizes and numbers and the relation to knowledge accumulation and population growth, as well as tracking the evolution of the relative size distribution of cities. One observation is the remarkable stability of the relative size distribution over decades, where city types seem to grow in size in parallel. The Beeson, Dejong and Troesken work is of particular interest in terms of geography because it demonstrates that the mid-nineteenth-century population allocations across cities are well explained by first nature geography – proximity to natural resources and amenities such as ports. However subsequent population growth and patterns are little explained by first nature. Rather they are more explained by history (and luck) – second nature considerations such as the location of historical investments in transport infrastructure and historical internal city conditions such as the education of the local population and the provision of local public services.

13.3.4   Theory

The Fujita, Krugman and Mori (1999) model of an urban hierarchy spread along a line of farmland represents a remarkable achievement, providing the economic foundations in a general equilibrium context for the historical work on urban hierarchy models. But the work also reveals that a basic problem with trying to do urban versions of the core–periphery model is that it becomes immensely complex. As a result, researchers quickly turn to simulating a variety of examples, with no general analysis of what types of equilibria may exist under different sets of parameter values. With the onset of simulation, everything goes into a black box and outcomes are examples of things that can happen that researchers choose to explore or report. But that may a matter of style, as well as a reasonable compromise, given the complexity of the problem.

Depending on the researchers' tastes, the real issue may not be the simulation *per se*. The issue is that because the model becomes so complex, key topics are omitted entirely. There is no welfare analysis of efficient allocations compared to market ones. There is no analysis of endogenous or exogenous economic growth in urban hierarchies where capital or knowledge can grow through investment decisions and the numbers and sizes of cities can change with economic growth. There is no analysis of the impact of government policies on the urban hierarchy. These are distressing absences, which limit the usability of the model, in terms of standard types of economic investigations.

From the perspective of urban modelling there is a further problem. In the urban hierarchy models there is no land development market (i.e. an assumption of incomplete land markets), where developers can facilitate city formation and assemblage of land. In these models space does not really involve land as a commodity; it is just there to create distance between cities. Having land development markets facilitates the formation of cities in a timely fashion, moving us away from the potentially Malthusian outcomes of self-organisation. It correspondingly allows for the internalisation of various externalities in the migration and city formation process. An absence of land development markets is a denial of reality – an imposition of incomplete markets in a situation where markets are generally complete. The existence of large-scale developers, whether it be late twentieth-century edge-city developers in the USA (Garreau, 1991) and enormous land development companies worldwide, or it be large rail and manufacturing firms, regional and national governments, or the church setting up cities over the centuries is well known. Again the problem in the urban hierarchy model is one of complexity; no one has yet to conceive of a way to model city formation with urban land development markets in the core–periphery model and its urban variants.

Finally there is an issue that concerns location theorists in the modelling of the transport costs in the core–periphery and hierarchy models. Iceberg transport costs are not the form that transport costs take in 'reality' and the implications are not innocent. Most products have a fixed and variable-with-distance transport cost component, dependent on mode, so they are better approximated as a linear function for each mode. Iceberg transport costs support a Dixit–Stiglitz world where any new manufacturing producer anywhere in the world always chooses to produce a new variety. All products are consumed at every location no matter where they are produced, since products never completely melt away. In reality, with linear transport costs, at some point the cost of transport of a good exceeds the worth of the good. Then geographic points cease to ship to each other, and Dixit–Stiglitz scale economies are exhausted. New producers in one location could choose to duplicate the products of a non-competing location. This in itself would be the basis for industrialisation of distant peripheral regions. And non-interactive regions could simply duplicate what each other does, limiting national returns to scale.

13.4   Dixit–Stiglitz as micro-foundations for agglomeration

The original urban systems models treated economies of scale in a model of a single city (e.g. Mills, 1967; Mirrlees, 1972), as well as in the systems of cities model as a 'black box'. There is a series of papers providing micro-foundations for the 'black box'. Fujita and Ogawa (1982) and more recently Berliant, Reed and Wing (2000) examine the spatial decay of information spillovers as the basis of agglomeration. Helsley and Strange (1990) consider a matching model with heterogeneous worker matching to technology choices of firms – larger scale results in better matches. They also develop a model of improved resale opportunities for the immobile capital of failed firms, where larger cities provide a better resale market (Helsley and Strange, 1991). In essence, scale provides better insurance. Becker and Henderson (1999) model the scale benefits of greater intra-industry specialisation by firms in a local area.

However, the urban literature recognised the value of the Dixit–Stiglitz model in analysing the provision of locally traded services, shopping and intermediate inputs, well before the development of the core–periphery model. The goods considered are non-traded across cities, so that the scale of production and the extent of diversity within a city is based on the extent of local agglomeration. Just as in the Dixit–Stiglitz model where there are national increasing returns to scale, in the urban version at the local level there are increasing returns to scale, given the diversified products are non-traded across cities. The early work utilised the Dixit–Stiglitz model in the context of a single city, where local consumers value varieties of local consumer services or retail goods, as the micro-basis for agglomeration benefits. Hobson (1987) has a Dixit–Stiglitz model at the local level without local transport costs or spatial dimensions to the local business district, and shows that the Henry George Theorem (Flatters, Henderson and Mieszkowski, 1974; Stiglitz, 1977) applies: lands rents can be used to subsidise the optimal provision of varieties. Abdel-Rahman (1988) has a similar model and has some discussion of optimal city size for a single city, as well as some discussion of an equilibrium with two cities.

Building upon his earlier work with Ogawa, Fujita (1988) models the spatial dimensions of a city providing a variety of locally produced traded consumer goods, in a context where the business district has spatial dimensions and consumers experience transport costs of shopping for each item consumed. Transport costs for a consumer for any variety are an increasing function of the distance from the consumer's house to the location of supplier of the variety. Thus each person buys different amounts of each variety and consumer product bundles vary with their location.

Fujita shows the condition under which the business district is in the city centre, and analyses the optimal provision of varieties and the nature of agglomeration benefits for a city of a fixed population.

At the same time as Fujita's paper, Rivera-Batiz (1988) used the Dixit–Stiglitz model to analyse the provision of varieties of non-traded intermediate inputs used in production of a city's standardised export good. The idea is related to out-sourcing as well as diversity. Larger cities provide a larger variety of intermediate material and service inputs to final producers; that makes their production process more efficient since they can obtain more finely tuned inputs, with diversity offering productivity gains. Implicitly this encourages out-sourcing by firms. This is the micro-foundations model based on Dixit–Stiglitz that people tend to think of being most relevant to agglomeration in cities. Although not done as an urban application, Venables (1996) takes the formulation one step further by having diversity and imperfect competition in both one final good and in an intermediate input to it. That creates a 'virtuous circle' of agglomeration benefits where, with enhanced scale, as final good producers become more efficient that feeds back into increased demand for intermediate inputs which further enhances efficiency.

Abdel-Rahman and Fujita (1990) as well as Fujita (1989) take this type of micro-foundations formulation – diversity of local non-traded intermediate inputs – and apply it to a systems of cities model. Following the standard analysis, they solve for the range of equilibrium city sizes under self-organisation and under a national government that optimises with respect to the number of cities. All the work reviewed in this section foreshadows recent developments in systems of cities models.

13.5   Recent developments

There are two very recent inter-connected avenues of exploration, some of which use the Dixit–Stiglitz model, that are very exciting. The first is that there are now systems of cities models that incorporate key features of the core–periphery model. Second is the use of the Dixit–Stiglitz model or other models of imperfect competition to try to better represent the essence of modern urban economies that are moving away from manufacturing into traded service and high-tech activities. Headquarters activities, producer services, financial services and R&D are the core activities of very large metro areas. The first question, which starts to be addressed in this new generation models of systems of cities, asks how these metro areas integrate/interact with the rest of the manufacturing and resource-oriented cities of an economy, in a context in which there are transport or transactions costs of trade across cities. The second question asks how the service sectors of large metro areas are organised. It looks at issues such as the out-sourcing decisions of firms, the spatial extent to which services (or in fact any economic activities) are exported and the range of products that individual multi-product firms may offer. Some of these models use Dixit–Stiglitz CES or related technologies, but introduce Cournot competition. Either firms produce the same variety in a context where the overall number of varieties is fixed or firms produce different ranges of varieties, rather than a single variety, and compete over the extent of their ranges.

13.5.1   New generation models

The new generation models introduce into the systems of cities models generalised transport costs of commodities (or ideas) across cities (Xiong, 2000). The number of cities is endogenous and cities may specialise in distinctly different activities, with attendant results for city size differences. Cities form on urban sites and there is an unexhausted supply of such sites. There may be both cross-region and within-region transport costs across cities. The idea of regions is to allow more geography, where there are coastal regions with ports and interior regions with raw material endowments. But within and across regions there is in an endogenous number of cities that trade with each other, with the degree of urban specialisation influenced by the transport costs of trade and communications. But this new generation is mostly not about improving the aesthetics. The papers are trying to model the basics of modern urban economies which are not addressed in the older systems of cities work. In particular, there is the role of large metro areas as centres of innovation, R&D and headquarters and producer service activities that provide key inputs for the multitude of smaller manufacturing metro areas.

Two examples stand out. In Duranton and Puga (1999), specialised manufacturing cities trade with diversified cities that innovate for them. The innovation model focuses on urban scale economies dependent on the diversity of local experimental activity. New products are developed in diversified cities, which facilitate firm sequential experimentation with an array of processes, until a firm finds its ideal process. Then the firm starts mass production, relocating to a smaller specialised city. The model is the first to provide micro-foundations of Jacobs-type (1969) scale economies. Trade is costly, so cities may not actually specialise in manufacturing versus innovation. But with reasonably low trade costs, there is specialisation, with an endogenous number of both innovative metro areas and specialised manufacturing cities.

Davis (2000) has a two-region model, a coastal exporting region and an interior natural resource-rich region. There are specialised manufacturing activities which, for production and final sale, require business service activities, summarised as headquarters functions which purchase local Dixit–Stiglitz intermediate services such as R&D, marketing, financing, exporting and so on. Headquarters activity is in port cities. The issue is whether manufacturing activities are also in these ports versus in specialised coastal hinterland cities versus in interior cities. Scale economies in manufacturing and headquarters activities are different and independent of each other, so that, based on scale considerations, these activities would be in separate specialised cities. However if the costs of interaction (shipping manufactured goods to port and transactions costs of headquarters-production facility communication) between headquarters and manufacturing functions are extremely high, then both manufacturing and headquarters activities can be found together in coastal port cities. Otherwise they will be in separate types of cities. In that case, manufacturing cities will be in coastal hinterlands if costs of headquarters–manufacturing interaction are high relative to shipping natural resources to the coast. However if natural resource shipping costs are relatively high, then manufacturing cities will be found in the interior.

13.5.2 Services

Services used by manufacturing firms and their headquarters may be produced in-house or out-sourced. If all activities are out-sourced we have the Abdel-Rahman and Fujita (1990) model, where as city scale increases that increases the range of intermediate inputs and the efficiency of final producers. But service activities are much more complicated than that, with extensive in-house activity by final producers. One set of papers with underlying Dixit–Stiglitz technology in production (Holmes, 1999a; Ono, 2000) argues that, as city scale rises, that increases the demand and scale of service activity. Then, for example, if services are heterogeneous in their in-house costs of production, vertical disintegration, or out-sourcing, will increase with urban scale as market scale lowers the cost of any out-sourced activity. That induces firms to out-source a larger range of service activities, as well as increasing the use of already out-sourced activities. Ono (2000) has a fixed range of services, where part of the scale benefits are that, for any one variety, a larger market can support more producers of that same variety. Then the benefits of increased scale are pecuniary: increased Cournot-style competition which lowers prices firms have to pay for out-sourced services.

This idea of introducing Cournot competition into a world with differentiated products is also explored in Ottaviano and Thisse (1999). In that paper, firms produce non-overlapping ranges of differentiated products (where apart from fixed costs to varieties, there is a fixed cost to firm formation). Firms compete not just over prices of varieties, but also over the range of varieties offered. People, who study service development in metro areas, think there are both Dixit–Stiglitz scale benefits of larger cities in the sense of increasing ranges of local services offered, but also Cournot benefits where there are increasing numbers of producers of the same varieties. The Ottaviano and Thisse model captures an aspect of this. While firms produce non-overlapping sets of varieties, they are oligopolistic competitors, in terms of the range of varieties offered. In countries where the number of service producers may be locally restricted (e.g. China), this model provides a starting point from which to analyse the impact of such restrictions on city productivity.

REFERENCES

Abdel-Rahman, H. (1988). Product differentiation, monopolistic competition, and city size. *Regional Science and Urban Economics*, 18: 69–76

——— (1996). When do cities specialize in production? *Regional Science and Urban Economics*, 26: 1–22

Abdel-Rahman, H. and Fujita, M. (1990). Product variety, Marshallian externalities, and city sizes. *Journal of Regional Science*, 30: 165–183

Alexandersson, G. (1959). *The Industrial Structure of American Cities*. Lincoln, University of Nebraska

Anas, A. (1992). On the birth and growth of cities: laissez-faire and planning compared. *Regional Science and Urban Economics*, 22: 243–258

Arnott, R. (1979). Optimum city size in a spatial economy. *Journal of Urban Economics*, 6: 65–89

Becker, R. and Henderson, V. (1999). Intra-industry specialization and urban development, in Huriot, J.-M. and Thisse, J.-F. (eds.), *Economics of Cities*. New York, Cambridge University Press

Beckman, M. J. (1968). *Location Theory*. New York, Random House

Beeson, P. E., Dejong, D. N. and Troesken, W. (1999). Population growth in US counties, 1840–1990. University of Pittsburgh, mimeo

Bergsman, J., Greenston, P. and Healy, R. (1972). The agglomeration process in urban growth. *Urban Studies*, 9: 263–288

Berliant, M., Reed, R. and Wing, P. (2000). Knowledge exchange matching and agglomeration. Federal Reserve Bank of Minneapolis Discussion Paper, 135

Berry, B. B. L. (1967). *Geography of Market Centers and Retail Distribution*. Englewood Cliffs, NJ, Prentice-Hall

Black, D. (1998). Essays on growth and inequality in urbanized economies. Brown University. PhD dissertation

Black, D. and Henderson, V. (1999). A theory of urban growth. *Journal of Political Economy*, 107: 252–284

(2000). Urban evolution in the USA. Brown University, Mimeo.

Borts, G. and Stein, J. (1964). *Economic Growth In a Free Market*. New York, Columbia University Press

Chinitz, B. (1961). Contrasts in agglomeration: New York and Pittsburgh. *American Economic Review*, 51: 279–289

Ciccone, A. and Hall, R. E. (1996). Productivity and the density of economic activity. *American Economic Review*, 86: 54–70

Davis, J. (2000). Headquarters-service and factory urban specialization with transport costs. Brown University, mimeo

Dixit, A. K. and Stiglitz, J. E. (1977). Monopolistic competition and optimum product diversity. *American Economic Review*, 67: 297–308

Dobkins, L. and Ioannides, Y. (2000). Dynamic evolution of the size distribution of US cities, in Huriot, J.-M. and Thisse, J.-F. (eds.), *Economics of Cities*. New York, Cambridge University Press

Duranton, G. and Puga, D. (1999). Nursery cities. London School of Economics, mimeo

Eaton, J. and Eckstein, V. (1997). Cities and growth: theory and evidence from France and Japan. *Regional Science and Urban Economics*, 27: 443–474

Flatters, F., Henderson, V. and Mieszkowski, P. (1974). Public goods, efficiency and regional fiscal equalization. *Journal of Pubic Economics*, 3: 99–112

Fujita, M. (1988). A monopolistic competition model of spatial agglomeration: differentiated product approach. *Regional Science and Urban Economics*, 18: 87–124

(1989) *Urban Economic Theory*. New York, Cambridge University Press

Fujita, M. and Krugman, P. (2000). A monopolistic competition model of urban systems and trade, in Huriot, J.-M. and Thisse, J.-F. (eds.), *Economics of Cities*. New York, Cambridge University Press

Fujita, M., Krugman, P. and Mori, T. (1999). On the evolution of hierarchical urban systems. *European Economic Review*, 43: 209–251

Fujita, M., Krugman, P. and Venables, A. (1999). *The Spatial Economy*. Cambridge, MA, MIT Press

Fujita, M. and Mori, T. (1996). The role of ports in the making of major cities: self-agglomeration and hub-effect. *Journal of Development Economics*, 49: 93–102

Fujita, M. and Ogawa, H. (1982). Multiple equilibria and structural transition of non-monocentric urban configurations. *Regional Science and Urban Economics*, 12: 161–196

Fujita, M. and Thisse, J.-F. (2000). The formation of economic agglomerations, in Huriot, J.-M. and Thisse, J.-F. (eds.), *Economics of Cities*. New York, Cambridge University Press

Garreau, J. (1991). *Edge City: Life on the New Frontier*. New York, Doubleday

Hanson, G. H. (1996). Agglomeration, dispersion and the pioneer firm. *Journal of Urban Economics*, 39: 255–281

(1998a). Market potential, increasing returns, and geographic concentration. University of Michigan, mimeo

(1998b). Market potential, increasing returns, and geographic concentration. NBER Working Paper, 6429

Helsley, R. W. and Strange, W. C. (1990). Matching and agglomeration economies in a system of cities. *Regional Science and Urban Economics*, 20: 189–212

(1991). Agglomeration economies and urban capital markets. *Journal of Urban Economics*, 29: 96–112

(1997). Limited developers. *Canadian Journal of Economics*, 30: 329–348

Henderson, J. V. (1974). The size and types of cities. *American Economic Review*, 64: 640–656

(1977). *Economic Theory and the Cities*. New York, Academic Press

(1982a). Systems of cities in closed and open economies. *Regional Science and Urban Economics*, 12: 325–350

(1982b). The impact of government policies on urban concentration. *Journal of Urban Economics*, 12: 280–303

(1986). The timing of regional development. *Journal of Development Economics*, 23: 275–292

(1988). *Urban Development: Theory: Fact and Illusion*. New York, Oxford University Press

Henderson, V. and Becker, R. (2000). Political economy of city size and formation. *Journal of Urban Economics*, 48(3): 453–84

Henderson, V. and Ioannides, Y. (1981). Aspects of growth in a system of cities. *Journal of Urban Economics*, 10: 117–139

Henderson, V. and Mitra, A. (1996). The new urban landscape, developers and edge cities. *Regional Science and Urban Economics*, 26: 613–643

Hobson, P. (1987). Optimum product variety in urban areas. *Journal of Urban Economics*, 22: 190–197

Hochman, O. (1977). A two factor three sector model of an economy with cities. Department of Economics, Ben-Gurion University of the Negev Beer, mimeo

Holmes, T. (1999a). Location of industry and vertical disintegration. *Review of Economics and Statistics*, 81: 314–325

(1999b). Scale of local production and city size. *American Economic Review, Papers and Proceedings*, 89: 317–320

(2000). Specialization of cities and local demand: evidence from the wholesale sector. University of Minnesota, mimeo

Hoover, E. M. (1939). *Location Theory and the Shoe and Leather Industries*. Cambridge, MA, Harvard University Press

Jacobs, J. (1969). *The Economy of Cities*. New York, Random House

Kanemoto, Y. (1980). *Theories of Urban Externalities*. Amsterdam, North-Holland

Krugman, P. R. (1991). Increasing returns and economic geography. *Journal of Political Economy*, 99: 483–499

(1993). On the number and location of cities. *European Economic Review*, 37: 293–298

Losch, A. (1954). *The Economics of Location*. New Haven, CT, Yale University Press

Mills, E. S. (1967). An aggregative model of resources allocation in a metropolitan area. *American Economic Review*, 57: 197–210

Mirrlees, J. A. (1972). The optimum town. *Swedish Journal of Economics*, 74: 114–136

Mitra, A. (1994). Agglomeration economies and land development games. Brown University, PhD dissertation

Nakamura, R. (1985). Agglomeration economies in urban manufacturing industries: a case study of Japanese cities. *Journal of Urban Economics*, 17: 108–124

Ono, Y. (2000). Scope of firms and city size. Brown University, mimeo

Ottaviano, G. and Thisse, J.-F. (1999). Monopolistic competition, multiproduct firms and optimum product diversity. CORE, mimeo

Rauch, J. E. (1993). Does history matter only when it matters little? The case of city-industry location. *Quarterly Journal of Economics*, 108: 843–867

Rivera-Batiz, F. L. (1988). Increasing returns, monopolistic competition, and agglomeration economies in consumption and production. *Regional Science and Urban Economics*, 18: 125–153

Roback, J. (1982). Wages, rents and quality of life. *Journal of Political Economy*, 90: 1257–1278

Spence, A. M. (1976). Product selection, fixed costs, and monopolistic competition. *Review of Economic Studies*, 43: 217–236

Stiglitz, J. E. (1977). A theory of local public goods, in Feldstein, M. S. and Inman, R. P. (eds.), *The Economics of Public Services*. New York, Macmillan

Sveikauskas, L. (1975). The productivity of cities. *Quarterly Journal of Economics*, 89: 393–413

Tabuchi, T. (1998). Urban agglomeration and dispersion: a synthesis of Alonso and Krugman. *Journal of Urban Economics*, 44: 333–351

Thomas, V. (1978). The measurement of spatial differences in poverty: the case of Peru. World Bank Staff Working Paper, 273

Venables, A. J. (1996). Equilibrium locations of vertically linked industries. *International Economic Review*, 37: 341–359

Xiong, K. (2000). Intercity trade and the industrial diversification of cities. Chase Manhattan Bank, mimeo

Part V

Economic growth

14 Monopolistic competition and economic growth

Sjak Smulders and Theo van de Klundert

14.1 Introduction

The Dixit–Stiglitz (1977) model of monopolistic competition has been the essential building block for the new generation of growth models that was developed by Romer (1990) and others. It is a well-known property of neoclassical theory that exogenous forces ultimately drive growth. By relying on perfect competition neoclassical growth theory could not model productivity growth and technical change as endogenous variables. R&D efforts lead to increases in productivity, but typically R&D expenditures are a fixed cost, which can be recouped only if firms make profits.

Monopolistic competition can generate profits in the short run if the number of competing firms is not too large. In the Dixit–Stiglitz model entry of new firms will lead to zero profits in the long run. However, the standard assumption that new firms appear out of the blue does not seem realistic. Each new firm in the model of monopolistic competition introduces a new product variant, which may require innovative effort in the first place. The development of a new product requires an up-front R&D expenditure. Entry then takes place as long as the R&D costs do not exceed the net present value of future profits that can be reaped by bringing the new product on the market.

In the Dixit–Stiglitz model the number of firms is finite in the long run. Entry of new firms reduces profits of all firms in the industry. This result is not changed if account is taken of up-front expenditure to develop new products. After the dust of entry is settled we are back in a static economy. What really changes this picture is Romer's idea of intertemporal knowledge spillovers. As the number of products increases the cost of developing new products falls, because innovating firms can build on the knowledge developed by their predecessors. Therefore, the number of products already developed can be associated with the stock of ideas on which researchers can build. It is a public good that creates an intertemporal knowledge spillover. As a result the cost of R&D decreases and a never-ending process of entry and introduction of new products drives economic growth.

Various other models build on Romer's approach and can be classified as 'variety expanding models' (cf. Grossman and Helpman, 1991, ch. 3). In alternative approaches it is not entry but quality improvement and creative destruction that induces growth (cf. Aghion and Howitt, 1992, 1998; Grossman and Helpman, 1991, ch. 4). Knowledge spillovers are also the driving force but competition is often modelled as limit pricing rather than monopolistic pricing. As there appears to be no clear connection with the Dixit–Stiglitz model we will not discuss these other growth models in the present survey.

Instead we would like to focus on a third approach in endogenous growth theory that also starts from the Dixit–Stiglitz approach, but does not rely on the somewhat unrealistic feature of never-ending entry. Thompson and Waldo (1994), Smulders and van de Klundert (1995), Peretto (1996) and Peretto and Smulders (2002) have developed a growth model in which monopolistic competing firms undertake in-house R&D that results in productivity improvements for each firm. As all existing firms expand their production growth is economywide. Economic growth is sustained since private research creates a tacit knowledge stock that reduces future R&D costs. In these models the knowledge stock is not a pure public good, as in the endogenous growth theories referred to above, but can be appropriated fully or at least to a large extent by the firms themselves. The models with in-house R&D are representative for the system of 'trustified capitalism', which Schumpeter in his later work had in mind as one of regimes of growth and competition (e.g. Soete and Ter Weel, 1999). In the regime of trustified capitalism large firms with unthreatened market positions dominate the economy and undertake their own R&D to reduce cost and improve productivity or product quality.

In the models with in-house R&D entry may be possible in the early stages of development in which the number of firms is small and profits are excessive. Newcomers have to invest in R&D in order to develop new product lines. Under certain conditions it may be profitable to engage in this type of R&D, but after a while entry stops as excessive profits vanish. In this view entry is not essential to explain economic growth. Once entry has stopped incumbents dominate the market and growth is driven by the in-house creation of knowledge. The window of opportunity for new entrants is closed and economic growth is determined by large firms with their own history and future.

This chapter aims at discussing the role monopolistic competition plays in several theories of economic growth. We develop a general equilibrium model with in-house R&D as well as R&D that results in the creation of new product lines. It will be shown that different growth models in the growth literature are special cases of our more general model. Throughout the analysis we are concerned with the determinants of equilibrium growth and product variety. Welfare properties of the equilibria are beyond the scope of the present chapter.

The chapter is organised as follows. In section 14.2 we introduce our model of economic growth allowing for two types of R&D. On the demand side account is taken of differentiated goods and a taste for variety. In accordance with the Dixit–Stiglitz model there is monopolistic competition on the markets for goods. Perfect competition prevails in the labour market and in the capital market. Variety expansion models are discussed in section 14.3. Special cases considered relate to the dynamic version of the Dixit–Stiglitz models with a finite number of firms, the semi-endogenous growth model of Jones (1995) and the model of endogenous growth of Romer (1990) and Grossman and Helpman (1991, ch. 3). The model with in-house R&D is analysed in section 14.4. To focus on the engine of growth the number of firms is fixed. The latter assumption is relaxed in section 14.5, where two types of innovation – variety expansion and productivity improvement – are introduced. It is shown that depending on the number of firms in the initial state there may be two phases of economic growth. In the first phase both types of R&D generate the same rate of return and variety expansion goes along with productivity improvement. In the second phase entry stops and growth is driven by productivity improvements within existing firms. Conclusions are presented in section 14.6.

14.2 The model

14.2.1 Households

The composite consumption good is defined over a continuum of varieties, a mass N of which is available in the market:

$$C = N^{v-1/(\varepsilon-1)} \left[\int_0^N X_i^{(\varepsilon-1)/\varepsilon} \right]^{\varepsilon/(\varepsilon-1)}. \tag{14.1}$$

Following the Dixit–Stiglitz (1977) approach, the elasticities of substitution between different varieties is constant and equal to $\varepsilon > 1$. We generalise this approach along the lines of Heijdra and van der Ploeg (1996) and Bénassy (1996, 1998) by disentangling the assumption of product differentiation (measured by ε) from the taste for variety (measured by

v; $v = 0$ implies no taste for variety, $v = 1/(\varepsilon - 1)$ brings us back to the canonical Dixit–Stiglitz model).

Intertemporal utility is discounted utility of the composite consumption good:

$$U = \frac{1}{1 - \rho} \int_0^\infty C(t)^{1-\rho} e^{-\vartheta t} dt. \tag{14.2}$$

We assume a constant discount rate ϑ. The curvature of the utility function is governed by the constant rate of relative risk aversion ρ. The main advantage is that the elasticity of intertemporal substitution equals a constant $1/\rho$, which accompanies the constant elasticity of *intra*temporal substitution (ε) familiar from the static Dixit–Stiglitz model. As we will see below, the relative size of both elasticities determines the nature of the dynamics in the model.

Utility-maximisation gives rise to a two-stage maximisation problem. First, consumers trade off current consumption against future consumption, taking as given the relative price of consumption over time, viz. the real interest rate $r - \hat{p}_C$. This gives rise to the Ramsey rule:

$$r - \hat{p}_C = \vartheta + \rho \hat{C}, \tag{14.3}$$

where hats denote growth rates, and

$$p_C = N^{-[v-1/(\varepsilon-1)]} \left[\int_0^N p_i^{1-\varepsilon} \right]^{1/(1-\varepsilon)} \tag{14.4}$$

denotes the consumer price index. Second, consumers allocate per-period consumption expenditures over the different varieties, which gives rise to the familiar iso-elastic demand function for good i:

$$X_i = \left(\frac{p_i}{P_C} \right)^{-\varepsilon} C. \tag{14.5}$$

In the sequel we assume symmetry so that X_i and p_i are the same for each variety i. Hence we may write $C = N^v(NX_i)$ for the consumption index and $p_C = N^{-v} p_i$ for the price index. Differentiating with respect to time and substituting the results into the Ramsey equation, we find:

$$r = \vartheta + \rho(\widehat{NX_i} + v\hat{N}) + (\hat{p}_i - v\hat{N}) \equiv r_c. \tag{14.6}$$

We interpret the expression on the right-hand side as the required rate of return in the capital market. The first term is the utility discount rate. The last term in parenthesis is the consumption price index inflation rate. When consumer prices increase, households require higher nominal interest rates. The second term reflects consumption smoothing: households require a premium for postponement of consumption; the smaller the elasticity of intertemporal substitution $(1/\rho)$, the larger the required premium for a given rate of change in consumption (which equals the first term in parenthesis).[1]

14.2.2   Firms

Firms produce with labour only. Firm i needs $1/A_i$ units of labour to produce one unit of its variety:

$$X_i = A_i L_{xi}. \tag{14.7}$$

Variable A_i can be interpreted as the stock of firm-specific knowledge that determines the productivity of the firm. Note that the units of measurement of X are such that X directly enters the utility function, which means that A also reflects the firm's capability to produce a certain level of product quality per unit of labour input. Hence, any increase in A reflects productivity or quality improvements, which terms we will use interchangeably.

Each firm can expand this stock and thus improve its own productivity over time by allocating research labour to research and development (R&D) activities. The productivity of research labour L_{Ai} depends on the stock of knowledge already accumulated (A_i) and on other sources of knowledge, which we will later identify as spillovers from other firms, denoted by S_A:

$$\dot{A}_i = S_A A_i^{\alpha} L_{Ai}. \tag{14.8}$$

We do not restrict the sign of α. If α is positive, firms use the knowledge they have accumulated in the past as an input in new R&D projects and benefit from experience and learning by doing. If α is negative, further improving productivity becomes harder the more productive the firm already is.

Profits equal revenue minus labour costs:

$$\pi_i = p_i(X_i, \cdot) X_i - w(L_{Xi} + L_{Ai}). \tag{14.9}$$

Firms maximise the net present value (NPV) of profits, taking into account the downward sloping demand for their product. The first-order conditions for maximisation imply the following pricing and no-arbitrage

---

[1] We will show that $\widehat{NX_i} = 0$ in the steady state. Note that then a change in variety has two opposing effects: a consumption smoothing effect (growing variety means growing consumption, so households require higher rate of return) and a price effect (growing variety means declining effective prices so a lower nominal interest rate is accepted). The first dominates if $\rho > 1$.

equation:

$$p_i = \left(\frac{\varepsilon}{\varepsilon - 1}\right)\frac{w}{A_i} \tag{14.10}$$

$$\frac{wL_{Xi}}{w/(S_A A_i^{\alpha-1})} + (\hat{w} - \hat{S}_A) \equiv r_A = r. \tag{14.11}$$

The elasticity of substitution (price elasticity ε) determines the markup over unit labour costs w/A_i.[2] The no-arbitrage equation equates costs savings per euro invested in R&D, that is the rate of return to R&D, r_A, to the cost of capital, that is the required (nominal) rate of return r. The first term on the left-hand side represents marginal labour cost savings in production from investing in knowledge divided by the marginal cost of knowledge accumulation. We see that the larger firm size L_{Xi}, or the larger marginal research productivity $S_A A_i^{\alpha-1}$, the higher the returns. The second term on the left-hand side captures the increases in research costs over time due to factors the firms cannot control (wage cost and spillovers). The larger these cost increases, the more attractive it is to undertake R&D now rather than later, that is, the higher the current return to R&D. The equation applies only in an interior solution with R&D ($L_{Ai} > 0$). In a corner solution without research, $r_A < r$ and $L_{Ai} = 0$.

Substituting the markup pricing result (14.10) into the profit function (14.11), we find:

$$\pi_i = w\left[\frac{1}{\varepsilon - 1}L_{Xi} - L_{Ai}\right]. \tag{14.12}$$

14.2.3   Market structure: entry

To model entry as a dynamic process, we assume that potential entrants have to incur a sunk cost to develop a blueprint for a new product line. The introduction of new product lines, or *variety expansion* for short, can be considered as the second type of R&D in the model, alongside in-house R&D directed to quality improvement within existing product

---

[2] In the tradition of the Dixit–Stiglitz model of monopolistic competition, firms ignore the impact of their own actions on total consumption and the price index of consumption, because there is a continuum of firms and the actions of each firm on the total are negligible. In contrast, if the number of firms is not that large and firms act strategically, oligopolistic competition prevails and the markup depends not only on the elasticity of substitution (ε) but also the number of (symmetric) firms (cf. Yang and Heijdra, 1993). Under oligopolistic competition the outcomes depend on the reaction hypothesis introduced with respect to firm behaviour. Different regimes of competition lead to different markups for a given number of firms and substitution parameter. The regime of competition affects growth as is shown in van de Klundert and Smulders (1997). In the present chapter we ignore strategic interactions and oligopoly.

lines as described above. The research technology is such that if L_N units of labour are allocated to variety expansion, a flow of $S_N L_N$ new firms is created.

$$\dot{N} = S_N L_N. \tag{14.13}$$

Free entry in R&D ensures that the price of a blueprint equals the cost of developing a blueprint w/S_N. The price of a blueprint in turn equals the value of a blueprint for an entrant, $q = w/S_N$. This value q must be such that investing money in blueprints gives a return that equals the return in the bonds market, which implies $\pi/q + \hat{q} = r$. Substituting π and q we find the following no-arbitrage equation:

$$\frac{w\left[\frac{1}{\varepsilon-1}L_{Xi} - L_{Ai}\right]}{w/S_N} + (\hat{w} - \hat{S}_N) \equiv r_N = r. \tag{14.14}$$

The left-hand side represents the return to investing in new product lines, the return to entry (r_N) for short. The first term represents the profit flow from a new product line relative to the cost to develop the new line. The second term represents the increase in development cost over time. This equation holds only in an interior equilibrium ($L_N > 0$). If no entry takes place, we must have $r_N < r$ and $L_N = 0$.

14.2.4 Labour market equilibrium

Labour supply is exogenous at level L and grows at rate g_L. Total labour demand equals demand for production, and for the two types of research. With symmetric firms, this implies the following labour market clearing condition:

$$L = (L_{Xi} + L_{Ai})N + L_N. \tag{14.15}$$

14.3   Growth through variety expansion

We first study growth driven by the expansion of product variety. We show how the seminal growth models developed by Romer (1990), Grossman and Helpman (1991, ch. 3) and Jones (1995) can be seen as a dynamic version of the Dixit–Stiglitz model extended for knowledge spillovers that govern the cost of entry.

To focus on entry, we assume that all research effort in the economy is devoted to developing new product lines ($L_{Ai} = 0$).[3] Moreover we

---

[3] This situation can arise endogenously in the full model, for example if S_A is sufficiently small. Below, we will return to the determination of which type of research is undertaken in equilibrium.

assume that the cost of entry endogenously changes over time. The idea is that research on new product lines builds on a stock of public knowledge. Individual research efforts contribute to public knowledge, that is, there are knowledge spillovers from private research to the public knowledge stock. Since research aims at expanding N, we can relate the knowledge stock to N. In particular, research productivity S_N increases with N:

$$S_N = \chi N^\phi, \qquad \phi \le 1. \tag{14.16}$$

From the labour market clearing condition, we can derive $\hat{N} = \chi(L/N^{1-\phi}) - \chi\left(N^\phi L_{Xi}\right)$, which we can rewrite as an expression for how $L/N^{1-\phi}$ evolves over time:

$$\widehat{L/N^{1-\phi}} = g_L - (1-\phi)\chi(L/N^{1-\phi}) + (1-\phi)\chi(N^\phi L_{Xi}), \tag{14.17}$$

where g_L is the exogenous growth rate of the labour supply.

The capital market is in equilibrium if the return to innovation r_N equals the rate of return required by households r_c. Combining the Ramsey equation (14.6) and the no-arbitrage equation (14.11), solving for $\widehat{L_{Xi}}$, and rewriting using the above labour market condition, we find:

$$\widehat{(N^\phi L_{Xi})} = (N^\phi L_{Xi})\chi \left[\left(\frac{1}{\varepsilon-1} - v + \phi\right)\frac{1}{\rho} + (v+1-\phi)\right]$$

$$-(L/N^{1-\phi})\chi\left[(v+1-\phi) - \frac{v-\phi}{\rho}\right] - \frac{\vartheta}{\rho}. \tag{14.18}$$

Equations (14.17)–(14.18) form a system of two differential equations in $L/N^{1-\phi}$ and $N^\phi L_{Xi}$, the first of which is predetermined, while the second can jump. We can therefore easily set up a phase diagram with these two variables on the axes, cf. figures 14.1–14.3.[4] Recall that the relevant parameters are research productivity χ, spillover parameter ϕ, intratemporal and intertemporal substitution ε and $1/\rho$, taste for variety v discount rate ϑ and population growth rate g_L. The exact nature of the phase diagram changes with the parameters, as we will discuss below. The adjustment is saddle point stable as long as the first term in square brackets in (14.18) is positive. For $\phi < 1$, the saddle path slopes up (down) if the second term in square brackets is positive (negative), that is if the elasticity of intertemporal substitution ($1/\rho$) is small (large). Points above the 45-degree line are infeasible since they imply a violation of the labour market constraint (14.15).

---

[4] These figures are drawn for the case $\rho > (v - \phi)/(v + 1 - \phi)$.

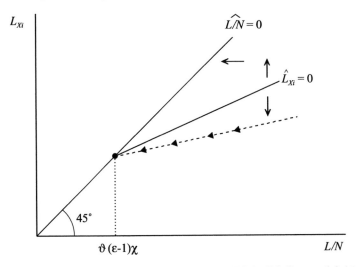

Figure 14.1 Variety expansion: dynamic Dixit–Stiglitz model ($\phi = 0$ and $g_L = 0$)

14.3.1 Special case i (Dynamic Dixit–Stiglitz model): $\phi = g_L = 0$

By assuming $\phi = g_L = 0$, we find the simplest dynamic version of the Dixit–Stiglitz model: rather than instantaneous entry, we have time-consuming entry (sunk cost rather than fixed cost). The dynamic model reduces to two differential equations in N and L_{Xi} and is represented in figure 14.1. If the number of firms happens to be large initially, such that $L/N < \vartheta(\varepsilon - 1)/\chi$, the economy is stuck in a stationary equilibrium, in which N is historically determined and $L_{Xi} = L/N$. The market has to be shared by so many firms that the rate of return to entry falls short of the minimum required rate of return ϑ and no investment takes place. In contrast, if the initial number of firms is small, such that $L/N > \vartheta(\varepsilon - 1)/\chi$, entry takes place and the economy approaches a steady state that can be characterised by:

$$L_{Xi} = (\varepsilon - 1)\frac{\vartheta}{\chi}, \qquad N = \frac{\chi L}{(\varepsilon - 1)\vartheta}. \tag{14.19}$$

This steady state can be easily related to the static Dixit–Stiglitz model. In the static version with flow fixed cost F per firm and instantaneous entry, we find $L_{Xi} = (\varepsilon - 1)F$ and $N = L/(\varepsilon F)$ (cf. Neary's chapter 8 in this volume). Hence, in the dynamic model, the term ϑ/χ takes over the role of the fixed cost in the static model. Note that this term equals the steady-state interest rate (ϑ) times the set-up cost ($1/\chi$), and therefore represents the annualised set-up cost. The preference parameters v and ρ do not affect the steady-state solution. The taste-for-variety parameter v measures how the cost of capital changes with a change in product variety (see (14.6)), the intertemporal substitution parameter ρ measures how the cost of capital changes with a change in consumption. In the steady state, both consumption and variety are constant so that the two parameters do not play a role.

The dynamics of the model enrich the picture of monopolistic competition. In the static Dixit–Stiglitz model firm size is fixed (which is criticised in Neary's chapter 8 in this volume). However, in the dynamic model outside the steady state, firm size L_{Xi} decreases or increases over time along the saddle path for two reasons. First, the number of firms cannot change instantaneously. Second, if total savings in the economy changes, total sales, which is shared among incumbents, changes. A large part of the labour force may be allocated to R&D activities in the short run, thus reducing the amount of labour for the firms that are already in the market. In particular, firm size increases (decreases) with the number of firms if the saddlepath in figure 14.1 slopes downward (upward). It slopes downward if $(1 + v)/v < 1/\rho$; it slopes upward if the latter inequality is reversed. In the canonical DS formulation (where $v = 1/(\varepsilon - 1)$) this reduces to $\varepsilon < (>)1/\rho$. So what matters is whether the intratemporal elasticity of substitution (the DS variable ε) is larger or smaller than the intertemporal elasticity of substitution. Intuitively, if the taste for variety is large (ε small) and the intertemporal elasticity is large, and if the economy starts with a small number of firms, it is attractive to postpone consumption and massively invest in more variety, which makes firms small in the short run when variety is still small, but large in the steady state when variety has expanded.

14.3.2   Special case ii (semi-endogenous growth): $0 < \phi < 1$, $g_L > 0$

By allowing for some, but limited, knowledge spillovers and population growth, we find a case in which the steady state is characterised by growth. The reason is that entry goes on forever and thus allows for gains from increasing specialisation. This case is a simplified[5] version of Jones' (1995) model of 'semi-endogenous growth' and of Eicher and Turnovsky's (1999) 'non-scale growth model'.

Figure 14.2 depicts the corresponding phase diagram. The dynamics differ from those in the previous case mainly because of population

---

[5] In Jones (1995), variety matters for production rather than for preferences, moreover physical capital is required to produce varieties, rather than just labour as in our model.

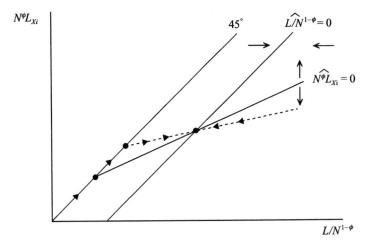

Figure 14.2 Variety expansion: semi-endogenous growth ($\phi < 1$ and $g_L > 0$)

growth, which prevents a stationary equilibrium arising. In an economy that starts with a small size relative to the number of firms such that $L/N^{1-\phi} < \vartheta(\varepsilon - 1)/\chi$, innovation is not profitable enough, as above. All labour is allocated to production ($L_{Xi} = L/N$) and population growth makes total production grow (and equilibrium moves along the 45-degree line). *Per capita* production stays constant in this first stage of economic growth (which captures some aspects of the Malthusian regime). At some moment in time, population growth has resulted in large enough markets to warrant innovation. In this second stage of growth the economy moves along the saddle path. The growth rate of *per capita* consumption now gradually increases over time, as is reflected by the vertical distance between the 45-degree line and the saddle path.

A steady state is characterised by constant $L/N^{1-\phi}$ and $N^\phi L_{Xi}$, which requires a constant rate of variety expansion $\hat{N} = g_L/(1 - \phi)$ and a constant share of production in total employment NL_{Xi}/L.[6] Hence $\hat{N} + \hat{L}_{Xi} = g_L$ and the long-run growth rate of *per capita* consumption is given by:

$$g_C - g_L = v\hat{N} = \left(\frac{v}{1 - \phi}\right)g_L. \tag{14.20}$$

The key difference with the previous case is that *per capita* growth may be

[6] Note that $NL_{Xi}/L = (N^\phi L_{Xi})/(L/N^{1-\phi})$, in which both terms in parentheses are constant.

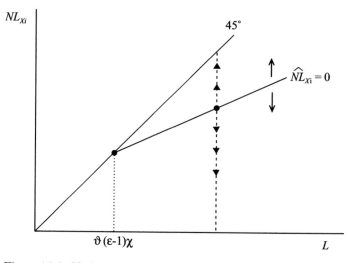

Figure 14.3   Variety expansion: endogenous growth ($\phi = 1$ and $g_L = 0$)

unbounded. This requires $v > 0$, so that growth is driven by the taste for variety. New firms enter every period, so that consumers can divide their expenditures over an increasing range of product variety, which increases real consumption to the extent that they love variety. Unbounded growth also requires population growth ($g_L > 0$). Ongoing entry is threatened by diminishing returns: more firms means smaller firms and thus lower returns to entry so that entry stops. A growing labour force offsets this.

Slightly reinterpreting the model along the lines of Ethier (1982), we may state that an ongoing process of increasing specialisation in production drives growth, so as to capture Adam Smith's view on growth. One arrives at this view by interpreting the sub-utility function for C as a production function for final goods C, in which X_i are intermediate inputs and N is the number of intermediate inputs. Parameter v then measures how much producers benefit from using a larger number of specialised inputs, that is, how much they benefit from increased specialisation.

14.3.3   Special case iii ('endogenous growth'): $\phi = 1$, $g_L = 0$

For the case of critically large spillovers, viz. $\phi = 1$, and zero population growth, the model reduces to an 'endogenous growth' model in the spirit of Grossman and Helpman (1991, ch. 3) and Romer (1990).

The phase diagram for this case – depicted in figure 14.3 – is one-dimensional since the variable on the horizontal axis $L/N^{1-\phi} = L$ is a constant. As a result $N^\phi L_{Xi} = NL_{Xi}$ immediately jumps to the value for which $\widehat{N^\phi L_{Xi}} = \widehat{NL_{Xi}} = 0$ (see 14.18). Hence, there is no transitional dynamics. From (14.1), (14.7), (14.13) and (14.15) the growth rate of consumption can be calculated as $g_C = v\hat{N} = v\chi(L - NL_{Xi})$, which implies $NL_{Xi} = L - g_C/(v\chi)$. Substituting this expression and $\widehat{N^\phi L_{Xi}} = \widehat{NL_{Xi}} = 0$ into (14.18), we find:

$$g_C = v\left(\frac{\chi L - (\varepsilon - 1)\vartheta}{\varepsilon + (\rho - 1)(\varepsilon - 1)v}\right). \tag{14.21}$$

Different from the previous case is that growth may be unbounded without population growth. More firms means lower profits per firm, but due to strong spillovers ($\phi = 1$), the cost of entry also declines strongly, so that it remains attractive to enter, no matter how large N already is.

The key difference with the previous case is that the long-run growth rate of consumption depends on intertemporal preference parameters. A higher discount rate (ϑ) or a lower rate of intertemporal substitution ($1/\rho$) implies a lower growth rate. If we introduced production taxes or research subsidies, these would affect the long-run growth rate, too. The taste-for-variety (or returns-to-specialisation) parameter affects growth positively as above.[7] Lower values of ε imply both higher profits and faster growth[8] and in this sense competition is bad for growth.

14.4   Growth through in-house R&D

A less desirable aspect of growth models based on variety expansion is that entry of new firms (or the emergence of new industries) and increased specialisation within firms (industries) cannot be disentangled. Although in reality some periods of growth may be characterised by rapid changes in market structure and extended periods of entry of new firms, in most periods growth stems from research within a limited number of established firms. Gort and Klepper (1982) show that over the life cycle of an industry, only in the initial phase is entry of new firms the dominant source of growth. Malerba and Orsenigo (1995) take a sectoral perspective and compare the dominant source of innovation in different sectors. They find that only eleven out of the thirty-three industries' patents are

---

[7] Now even the growth rate of the number of firms (see the term in parentheses) is affected. $\text{sign}(\partial\hat{N}/\partial v) = \text{sign}\,[(1 - \rho)g_C]$.

[8] Differentiating we find $\text{sign}(\partial g_C/\partial \varepsilon) = \text{sign}\,[(1 - \rho)v\chi L - (\vartheta + \chi L)]$. Positive growth requires $\chi L + \vartheta > \varepsilon\vartheta$. Bounded utility requires $\vartheta + (\rho - 1)g_C > 0$, which after substitution of g_C implies $\varepsilon\vartheta > (1 - \rho)\chi L$. Hence, if growth is positive and utility is bounded, $\vartheta + \chi L > (1 - \rho)\chi L$ and $\partial g_C/\partial \varepsilon < 0$.

predominantly granted to new innovators. This suggests the existence of two different regimes of the innovation process that drives growth, one based on entry and another based on in-house R&D. Schumpeter elaborated on both regimes, labelled 'competitive capitalism' and 'trustified capitalism', respectively. In the latter, innovation is conducted by large and established firms that engage in monopolistic competition and try to capture some of the market shares of their rivals. Established firms have an advantage over entrants because they can build on experience and tacit firm-specific knowledge. Innovation strengthens their position in the market, since it expands the stock of firm-specific knowledge.

We now model some elements of trustified capitalism by studying growth driven by quality improvement *within* product lines. We consider the case that is opposite to the one analysed in the previous section: we abstract from entry, and assume that all innovation takes the form of quality improvement within existing firms ($L_N = 0$, N is treated as a parameter). This results in a model similar to Thompson and Waldo (1994) and Smulders and van de Klundert (1995).[9]

As in the previous section, we also allow for knowledge spillovers to capture the idea that research builds on public knowledge. The public knowledge stock rises with research effort. Since research aims at increasing A, we can now relate the knowledge stock to average A in the economy, which equals A_i because of our symmetry assumption. In particular, research productivity S_A increases with A:

$$S_A = \xi A^\psi. \tag{14.22}$$

Parameter ψ captures intertemporal *between*-firm knowledge spillovers. We already introduced intertemporal *within*-firm knowledge spillovers as captured by α. We denote total intertemporal spillovers by $\psi + \alpha \equiv \phi^*$. From this specification of spillovers, the R&D function (14.8), the symmetry assumption ($A_i = A$), and the labour market clearing condition

[9] Thompson and Waldo (1994) model research as a stochastic process and ignore within-firm intertemporal spillovers (this case arises in our model if $\alpha = 0$ and $\psi = 1$). The key element of trustified capitalism is that 'creative accumulation' rather than 'creative destruction' drives growth. In this respect, the trustified capitalism model contrasts to the 'Schumpeterian' models of Grossman and Helpman (1991, ch. 4) and Aghion and Howitt (1992, 1998), which all rely on creative destruction. What our model of trustified capitalism has in common with these models is that growth is possible without an increase in variety. In these 'Schumpeterian' models with creative destruction, new firms replace old firms. There are two reasons not to deal with this class of models in this chapter. First, these models are often structurally isomorph with the variety expansion models (see Grossman and Helpman, 1991, p. 98) and yield similar insights. Second, these models rely on perfect substitutability and (Bertrand) limit pricing rather than the Dixit–Stiglitz approach of modelling competition.

(14.15), we find:

$$\hat{A} = \xi L/(NA^{1-\phi^*}) - \chi(L_{Xi}/A^{1-\phi^*}) \qquad (14.23)$$

Using this equation, we find the following expression for how $L/(NA^{1-\phi^*})$ evolves over time:

$$\widehat{L/(NA^{1-\phi^*})} = g_{L/N} - (1 - \phi^*)\chi L/(NA^{1-\phi^*})$$
$$+ (1 - \phi^*)\chi(L_{Xi}/A^{1-\phi^*}), \qquad (14.24)$$

where $g_{L/N}$ is the growth rate of the per firm labour supply, which we take as a parameter.

The capital market is in equilibrium if the return to innovation r_A equals the rate of return required by households r_c. Combining the Ramsey equation and the no-arbitrage equation, solving for $\hat{L}_{Xi}$, and rewriting using the above labour market condition, we find:

$$\widehat{L_{Xi}/A^{1-\phi^*}} = (L_{Xi}/A^{1-\phi^*})\xi \left[\frac{\phi^* - \alpha}{\rho} + (2 - \phi^*)\right] - \xi L/(NA^{1-\phi^*})$$
$$\times \left[(2 - \phi^*) - \frac{\alpha + 1 - \phi^*}{\rho}\right] - \frac{\vartheta}{\rho}. \qquad (14.25)$$

We now have a system of two differential equations in $L/(NA^{1-\phi^*})$ and $L_{Xi}/A^{1-\phi^*}$, so that we can again set up a phase diagram to analyse the dynamics. The adjustment is saddle point stable as long as the first term in square brackets of (14.25) is positive. The saddle path slopes up (down) if the second term in square brackets is positive (negative), that is if the elasticity of intertemporal substitution $(1/\rho)$ is small (large). Figures 14.4 and 14.5 depict the phase diagrams for two parameter combinations.

The phase diagrams for the variety-expansion model and the quality-improvement model are very similar, so that we need not go through all cases. Due to the similar structure, similar conclusions hold with respect to the feasibility of growth in the long run. It can be easily checked that long-run growth is unbounded, either if some exogenous growing factor compensates for the diminishing returns ($g_{L/N} > 0$, see figure 14.4), or if spillovers are sufficiently large to result in constant returns with respect to the reproducible factor ($\phi^* = 1$ and constant returns with respect to A arise, see figure 14.5).

In the latter case of endogenous growth ($\phi^* = 1$, $g_{L/N} = 0$), the dynamic system boils down to a simple single differential equation:

$$\rho\hat{L}_{Xi} = \xi [\rho + 1 - \alpha] L_{Xi} - \xi(\rho - \alpha)\frac{L}{N} - \vartheta. \qquad (14.26)$$

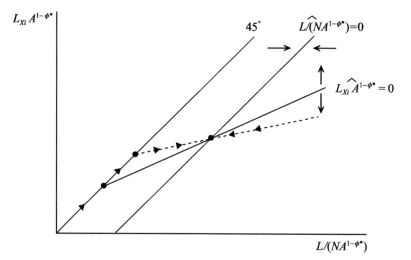

Figure 14.4 In-house R&D: semi-endogenous growth ($\phi^* < 1$ and $g_L > 0$)

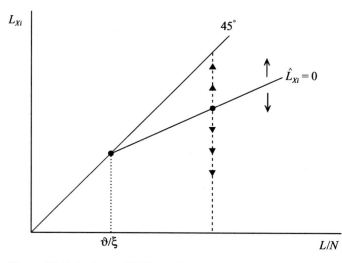

Figure 14.5 In-house R&D: endogenous growth ($\phi^* = 1$ and $g_L = 0$)

Since the differential equation is unstable, L_{Xi} immediately jumps to the steady state, which is given by:

$$L_{Xi} = \frac{1}{\rho + 1 - \alpha} \left(\frac{\vartheta}{\xi} + (\rho - \alpha)\frac{L}{N} \right). \tag{14.27}$$

The associated rate of consumption growth equals the rate of productivity growth since with symmetry $C = N^{\nu} NAL_{Xi}$ (see (14.1) and (14.7)) where N and L_{Xi} are constant:

$$g_C = \hat{A} = \frac{\xi L/N - \vartheta}{\rho + 1 - \alpha} \tag{14.28}$$

The key property of this expression is that growth depends on intertemporal preference parameters. If we introduced production taxes and research subsidies, growth would be affected by these policy variables. In short, the long-run growth rate is endogenous. Similar to the endogenous growth case of the variety-expansion model, growth increases with research productivity (ξ) and decreases with ϑ and ρ.

Intertemporal knowledge spillovers show up as a determinant of long-run growth. In particular, the degree to which intertemporal spillovers can be appropriated by firms (α) is positively related to growth. The higher α, the more the firm's own research efforts contribute to the reduction in future R&D costs (see (14.8)), and thus the higher the incentive to invest in R&D. In the variety-expansion model, no individual researcher could internalise the contribution of its own research efforts to future research cost reductions, because only the public knowledge stock affects research costs and the own contribution to the public stock is perceived as negligible.

Growth depends positively on the firm size measured by labour available per firm L/N. As in the model of endogenous growth driven by variety expansion, see (14.21), a larger firm size implies a larger market in which the results of R&D can be commercialised, so it boosts the return to innovation.

The key parameter from the Dixit–Stiglitz model (ε) does not show up in the expression for the growth rate. There are three reasons for this: symmetry among firms, no creative destruction and the assumption of a fixed number of firms.

Aghion et al. (2001) set up a growth model with a large fixed number (say, N) of industries, in each of which two firms produce goods that enter consumer preferences with a constant elasticity (say, ε) as in the Dixit–Stiglitz approach. Firms set prices as in a Cournot duopoly and choose R&D effort. Since the returns to R&D are stochastic in this model, duopolists may end up with different productivity levels even if they start at the same level. If they start at the same level, R&D is more profitable with a higher degree of substitution ε, since a given quality advantage over the rival firm produce a bigger boost in profits, the more easily consumers substitute for the rival's output.

Product market competition as measured by ε does not directly affect innovation of a fixed number of symmetric firms. However, as we have seen in the variety-expansion model, once we allow for entry, the number of firms is negatively related to the product market competition parameter ε: lower profit margins require larger firms in equilibrium. Since in the quality-improvement model growth is stimulated by larger firm size (L/N) we may expect more competition (higher ε) to result in faster growth once we relax the assumption of a fixed number of firms. This is what we turn to in the next section.

14.5   Growth with variety expansion and in-house R&D

We now combine the two models to explore the interaction between entry and in-house innovation. To simplify we assume the following:

$$g_L = \phi = 0, \qquad \phi^* = 1, \qquad \rho = 1, \qquad w = 1.$$

These assumptions imply that, first, there is neither population growth nor intertemporal spillovers in entry, second, there are strong intertemporal spillovers in productivity improvements and, third, utility is logarithmic. The fourth assumption is the numéraire choice. The third assumption only simplifies the expressions for the transitional dynamics. The first two assumptions guarantee that long-run growth is driven by productivity improvements within product lines and that the number of firms is finite. Note that with these assumptions, $\alpha = 1 - \psi$ and $S_N = \chi$ is a constant. Also note that now the phase diagrams for the variety expansion and quality improvement model can both be depicted in the $(L/N, L_{Xi})$ plane (cf. figure 14.1 and 14.5).

We first examine which type of innovation is undertaken in equilibrium. Any type of innovation can be undertaken only if its rate of return is at least the market rate r. Substituting the labour market clearing condition (14.15) into the no-arbitrage equations (14.11) and (14.14), we may write:

$$r_N \leq r \quad \Leftrightarrow \quad \chi\left(\frac{L_{Xi}}{\varepsilon - 1} - L_{Ai}\right) \leq r$$

$$\Leftrightarrow \quad \frac{1}{\varepsilon}\left(\frac{L - L_N}{N}\right) - \left(\frac{\varepsilon - 1}{\varepsilon \chi}\right) r \leq L_{Ai} \qquad (14.29)$$

$$r_A \leq r \quad \Leftrightarrow \quad \xi\left(L_{Xi} - \psi L_{Ai}\right) \leq r$$

$$\Leftrightarrow \quad \frac{1}{1 + \psi}\left(\frac{L - L_N}{N}\right) - \left(\frac{1}{\xi(1 + \psi)}\right) r \leq L_{Ai}. \qquad (14.30)$$

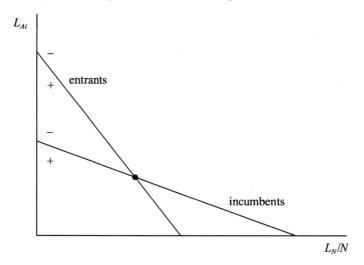

Figure 14.6   Reaction curves

Figure 14.6 depicts the two relationships as reaction curves – of entrants and incumbents, respectively – in the $(L_N/N, L_{Ai})$ plane, where r and N can be treated as parameters for firms take them as given. [10] Points above an agent's reaction curve imply that her rate of return falls short of the interest rate r as indicated by the minus sign. Both reaction curves slope negative. The point of intersection represents an equilibrium in which both types of innovation yield a return equal to the market interest rate r and in which the labour market clears.

Figure 14.6 shows that this equilibrium is stable if the entrants' reaction curve is steeper than the incumbent's reaction curve, which requires $\psi > \varepsilon - 1$. If the equality is reversed, the equilibrium is unstable: slightly increasing (decreasing) the amount of labour in entry increases the return to entry (in-house R&D). Hence, if $\psi < \varepsilon - 1$ in-house R&D and entry never occur simultaneously and equilibrium is driven by either variety expansion or in-house R&D. Since we analysed these situations in the previous sections, we can here restrict attention to the case in which both types of innovation are undertaken simultaneously because they yield the same return in a stable equilibrium. From (14.29)–(14.30) we can derive that a necessary conditions for this equilibrium to exist is

$$\psi > \varepsilon - 1 > \chi/\xi. \tag{14.31}$$

Equating the rates of return in (14.29) and (14.30), we find the rate of productivity improvement for an equilibrium with both in-house R&D

[10] Figure 14.6 is drawn for the case with $\psi > \varepsilon - 1 > \chi/\xi$ and $N < \bar{N}$.

and variety expansion:

$$\hat{A} = \xi L_{Ai} = \xi L_{Xi} \left(\frac{(\varepsilon - 1) - \chi/\xi}{(\varepsilon - 1)(\psi - \chi/\xi)} \right). \tag{14.32}$$

Substituting the second equality and the labour market equilibrium condition (14.15) into (14.13), we find the rate of variety expansion:

$$\hat{N} = \chi \frac{L}{N} - \chi \left(\frac{(\varepsilon - 1) - \chi/\xi + (\varepsilon - 1)(\psi - \chi/\xi)}{(\varepsilon - 1)(\psi - \chi/\xi)} \right) L_{Xi}. \tag{14.33}$$

Substituting this result into (14.29) and equating the resulting expression for the rate of return on investment to the required rate of return in (14.6), we find after setting $\rho = 1$:

$$\hat{L}_{Xi} = \left(\frac{\varepsilon \chi}{\varepsilon - 1} \right) L_{Xi} - \chi \frac{L}{N} - \vartheta. \tag{14.34}$$

We use (14.33)–(14.34) to set up the phase diagram in the $(L_{Xi}, L/N)$ plane, as shown in figure 14.7. Under the assumptions made in (14.31), the $\widehat{L/N} = 0$ locus has a positive slope that is smaller than 45 degrees. Points above the locus imply either $L_N < 0$ when $r_N = r_A$, which must be ruled out, or $r_N < r_A$ when $L_N = 0$, which implies a situation with constant N. The $\widehat{L/N} = 0$ locus from (14.33) cuts the $\hat{L}_{Xi} = 0$ locus derived from (14.34), which also slopes upward. If the economy starts with a small number of firms, entry takes place and the economy moves along the saddle path. Production per firm falls over time. In the long run, the number of firms approaches the following value:

$$N = \frac{\chi L}{\vartheta} \left(\frac{\psi - (\varepsilon - 1)}{(\varepsilon - 1)(\psi - \chi/\xi) + (\varepsilon - 1) - \chi/\xi} \right) \equiv \bar{N}. \tag{14.35}$$

If the economy starts with a large number of firms, $N > \bar{N}$, the rate of return to entry falls short of that of in-house R&D for any positive amount of labour allocated to variety expansion, as can be easily checked from (14.29)–(14.30). Hence, only in-house R&D can be undertaken in equilibrium. We can use the $\hat{L}_{Xi} = 0$ locus from the model with in-house R&D only, see (14.27), after setting $\rho = 1$. This line cuts the 45-degree line at $L/N = \vartheta/\xi$. Points above the 45-degree line must be ruled out since they imply $L_{Xi} > L/N$, which violates the labour market clearing condition. Hence, for $\xi L/\vartheta < N < \bar{N}$, growth is given by (14.28), and for $N < \xi L/\vartheta$, the growth rate is zero.

The most natural scenario is that the economy starts with a low number of firms $(N < \bar{N})$. Then two stages of growth emerge. In the first stage,

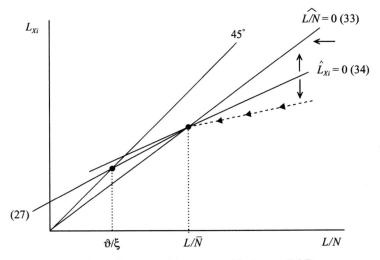

Figure 14.7   Phase diagram with entry and in-house R&D

entry and in-house R&D occur simultaneously. Once a critical number of firms has entered the market, a second stage of growth starts with in-house R&D only. Note that this growth pattern resembles the product life cycle that is empirically relevant on the industry level: in a mature economy, the number of firms is stable, and each of them devotes resources to productivity improvement. The long-run growth rate in this situation can be calculated as:

$$g_C = \hat{A} = \frac{[(\varepsilon - 1)(\xi/\chi) - 1]\,\vartheta}{\psi - (\varepsilon - 1)}. \tag{14.36}$$

Competition, as measured by a high value for ε, boosts long-run growth in this model, as is clear from (14.36). The reason is already explained above: larger price elasticities imply smaller profit margins for monopolistic firms, so that starting new firms is less attractive. Firms are larger in the mature economy, which makes in-house R&D more profitable and enhances growth. Hence, while growth did not depend on ε in the quality improvement model and did depend negatively on ε in the variety expansion model, growth depends positively on ε once we combine the two models.

Another important contrast to the results in the previous sections is that the scale of the economy, as measured by the labour force, does not affect the growth rate, but intertemporal preferences do. Hence we have endogenous growth without the so-called 'scale effect'. The scale effect implies that larger economies grow at a faster rate, basically because they can exploit knowledge in a large market. The empirics on postwar growth do not support this model prediction. In the previous sections, the scale effect showed up whenever growth was endogenous (by which we mean that it depends on intertemporal preference parameters and policy variables) (see (14.21) and (14.28)). In the semi-endogenous growth variants above, the scale effect was removed by assuming diminishing returns with respect to knowledge, but that assumption rendered growth independent of intertemporal preference parameters (or policy variables) (see (14.20)). In the model that combines quality improvement and variety expansion, an increase in the scale of the economy (larger labour force L) results – for a given number of firms – in more labour per firm, larger sales per firm and higher profits and therefore incentives to both higher levels of in-house R&D and development of new product lines. If indeed more firms enter, the process of variety expansion gradually reduces the market for individual incumbents, thus offsetting the higher incentives to in-house R&D. In the long-run equilibrium with a larger labour force, the number of firms is proportionately larger, but each firm invests at the same rate as in the economy with a smaller labour force.[11]

The rate of growth does not depend on the taste-for-variety parameter v. The number of product varieties in the steady state is constant over time so that the taste for variety does not affect the cost of capital (see our discussion of (14.19)). If we allow for population growth as well as non-unitary elasticity of intertemporal substitution $(1/\rho)$, the number of firms continuously grows as in the semi-endogenous growth model (in particular $\hat{N} = g_L$ so that L/N is constant) and v enters the expression for the long-run growth rate:

$$g_C - g_L = \hat{A} + v\hat{N} = \frac{[(\varepsilon - 1)\xi/\chi - 1]\,(\vartheta + \rho g_L) + [\psi - (\varepsilon - 1)]\,v g_L}{[\psi - (\varepsilon - 1)] - (\rho - 1)\,[(\varepsilon - 1)\xi/\chi - 1]}.$$

$$(14.37)$$

Finally it should be noted that the growth rate depends positively on the discount rate ϑ, which seems counter-intuitive. High discount rates discourage investment, but there are two types of investment now. Investment in variety is reduced (the number of firms $\bar{N}$ declines with the discount rate, see (14.35)), which in turn boosts investment in quality improvement (g).

---

[11] Young (1998), Dinopoulos and Thompson (1998) and Howitt (1999) have used this mechanism to remove scale effects; Peretto and Smulders (2002) provide the microeconomic foundation for the key assumption that the cost of in-house R&D depends on A only and not on N.

14.6   Conclusions

The Dixit–Stiglitz approach has been the main way of incorporating monopolistic competition in models of economic growth based on research and development. Monopolistic competition is an essential feature of these models since monopoly profits provide both the incentives to undertake R&D and the means to finance R&D.

The degree of monopolistic competition, as measured by (some measure inversely related to) the elasticity of substitution between product varieties (ε) affects growth in different directions in the various types of growth models. If variety expansion (entry) drives growth (and in models of creative destruction), more competition (higher ε) is bad for growth as it reduces the profits that can be reaped by the innovators that enter the market with new product lines. If in-house R&D drives growth, which is the case in the 'trustified capitalism' regime, an increase in competition is good for growth. A higher elasticity of substitution implies lower profits margins and a smaller number of firms that can survive in the market. On average firm size will be larger, which boosts innovation since the return to innovation can be captured in a larger share of the market.

The role of product variety also differs in the various models. In the variety expanding growth models, an ongoing process of entry of new firms drives long-run growth. The model captures Adam Smith's idea that increasing specialisation drives productivity gains. However, in these models there is no distinction between the number of firms and the number of specialised consumption goods or intermediary inputs. While the number of *goods* (or inputs) may indeed capture specialisation, the number of *firms* is an aspect of industrial organisation, and ideally the two should be kept separate. In the model with both entry and in-house R&D, entry stops once a critical number of firms is in the market. In-house R&D becomes the engine of growth. This model reflects the industry life cycle pattern in which entry is followed by consolidation.

This survey has shown that the Dixit–Stiglitz approach has been fruitfully used as an essential building block in growth theory and that a rich set of conclusions can be derived about the dynamic implications of monopolistic competition and product variety. It is also clear that further studying the interaction between different types of R&D in monopolistic markets is a promising avenue to study stages of growth and dynamics of market structure. Finally it should be noted that we dealt only with models that explore the elementary driving forces behind growth. Twenty-five years after the publication of the Dixit–Stiglitz model and eleven years after the publication of the first Dixit–Stiglitz-based growth models, we are still witnessing a rapid growth in the literature on how growth is related to capital market imperfections, income inequality, labour markets, social norms, environmental problems and many other issues. It is the Dixit–Stiglitz model that makes it possible to study these important topics.

REFERENCES

Aghion, Ph., Harris, Chr., Howitt, P. and Vickers, J. (2001). Competition, imitation and growth with step-by-step innovation. *Review of Economic Studies*, 68: 467–492

Aghion, Ph. and Howitt, P. (1992). A model of growth through creative destruction. *Econometrica*, 60: 323–351

(1998). *Endogenous Growth Theory*. Cambridge, MA, MIT Press

Bénassy, J.-P. (1996). Taste for variety and optimum production patterns in monopolistic competition. *Economics Letters*, 52: 41–47

(1998). Is there always too little research in endogenous growth with expanding product variety? *European Economic Review*, 42: 61–69

Dinopoulos, E. and Thompson, P. (1998). Schumpeterian growth without scale effects. *Journal of Economic Growth*, 3: 313–335

Dixit, A. K. and Stiglitz, J. E. (1977). Monopolistic competition and optimum product diversity. *American Economic Review* 67: 297–308

Eicher, T. S. and Turnovsky, S. J. (1999). Non-scale models of economic growth. *Economic Journal*, 109: 394–415

Ethier, W. J. (1982). National and international returns to scale in the modern theory of international trade. *American Economic Review*, 72: 389–405

Gort, M. and Klepper, S. (1982). Time paths in the diffusion of product innovations. *Economic Journal*, 92: 630–653

Grossman, G. and Helpman, E. (1991). *Innovation and Growth in the Global Economy*. Cambridge, MA, MIT Press

Heijdra, B. J. and van der Ploeg, F. (1996). Keynesian multipliers and the cost of public funds under monopolistic competition. *Economic Journal*, 106: 1284–1296

Howitt, P. (1999). Steady endogenous growth with population and R&D inputs growing. *Journal of Political Economy*, 107: 715–730

Jones, C. (1995). R&D based models of economic growth. *Journal of Political Economy*, 103: 759–784

Klundert, Th. van de and Smulders, S. (1997). Growth, competition and welfare. *Scandinavian Journal of Economics*, 99: 99–118

Malerba, F. and Orsenigo, L. (1995). Schumpeterian patterns of innovation. *Cambridge Journal of Economics*, 19: 47–65

Peretto, P. (1999). Cost reduction, entry, and the interdependence of market structure and economic growth. *Journal of Monetary Economics*, 43: 173–195

Peretto, P. and Smulders, S. (2002). Technological distance, growth and scale effects. *Economic Journal*, 112: 603–624

Romer, P. (1990). Endogenous technological change. *Journal of Political Economy*, 98: S71–S102

Smulders, S. and van de Klundert, Th. (1995). Imperfect competition, concentration and growth with firm-specific R&D. *European Economic Review*, 39: 139–160

Soete, L. and Ter Weel, B. (1999). Innovation, knowledge creation and technology policy: the case of the Netherlands. *De Economist*, 147: 293–310

Thompson, P. and Waldo, D. (1994). Growth and trustified capitalism. *Journal of Monetary Economics*, 34: 445–462

Yang, X. and Heijdra, B. J. (1993). Monopolistic competition and optimum product diversity: comment. *American Economic Review*, 83: 295–301

Young, A. (1998). Growth without scale effects. *Journal of Political Economy*, 106: 41–63

15   Convergence and the welfare gains of capital mobility in a dynamic Dixit–Stiglitz world

Sjak Smulders

15.1   Introduction

The Dixit–Stiglitz (1977) framework has become a powerful tool to analyse monopolistic competition and market structure in general equilibrium models, in particular in (international) macroeconomics and trade theory. While the Dixit–Stiglitz model was originally phrased in a static context, its importance is at least as large in a dynamic context. In R&D-based models of economic growth, aggregate economic growth is explained from the incentives private firms have to invest in research and development (R&D) (seminal contributions are Romer, 1990; Grossman and Helpman, 1991; Aghion and Howitt, 1992). R&D generates blueprints for new product varieties, new production processes, or improved product quality. Firms are willing to invest in R&D only if they can reap some profits. The Dixit–Stiglitz framework has proved to be a most appealing and elegant way of modelling the conditions under which firms can realise profits, which provide both the incentives to innovate as well as the means to pay for the cost of innovation. The key assumption in the Dixit–Stiglitz framework is that each firm produces a good that is differentiated from other goods in the market. The elasticity of substitution in utility between product varieties from different producers captures the degree of product differentiation. This parameter determines the firm's price elasticity and hence the degree of market power it can exert. Because of this link between market conditions and investment incentives, international differences in market conditions determine international differences in growth. A central question in growth theory is what allows countries with relatively low income to grow at a relatively high rate of growth so that they can catch up with the richer countries. Under what conditions do income levels in rich and poor countries converge? How fast is the speed of convergence?

The author's research is supported by the Royal Netherlands Academy of Arts and Sciences. He thanks Peter Broer, Theo van de Klundert, and Richard Nahuis for stimulating discussions on several aspects of this chapter. He also thanks Joerg Breitscheidel.

In this chapter I study how rates of convergence are affected by market conditions as captured by firms' market power. In particular, I examine whether it becomes easier or harder for poor countries to catch up with rich countries if the degree of product differentiation among firms, and hence market power, is high. The key ingredient of the Dixit–Stiglitz framework is thus linked to the issue of convergence. The role product differentiation plays, turns out to depend on whether international capital mobility is assumed or not. I explore the implications not only for the rate of convergence, but also for welfare. It is shown that although a higher degree of substitution (and hence lower market power) causes the rate of convergence to increase under capital mobility, it also implies a larger welfare gap between rich and poor countries.

The model in this chapter is a two-country model of endogenous growth based on in-house R&D. There is a given number of firms. By spending on R&D, each of them invests in firm-specific knowledge, which determines their productivity level. The cost of R&D depends on the firm-specific knowledge stock, as well as on national and international average knowledge stocks. The latter two determinants capture intertemporal knowledge spillovers and result in the familiar research externality which makes firms invest too little in R&D. The two countries considered differ only with respect to the initial productivity level.

The main results are as follows. There is complete convergence in the long run if there is no capital mobility. Under perfect capital mobility, countries converge to equal long-run productivity levels, but permanent differences in consumption remain. The speed of convergence is larger with perfect capital mobility than with balanced trade. The difference increases with substitution between product varieties. Capital mobility harms (benefits) the leader (lagging) country if domestic spillovers are more important than international spillovers.

The topic of convergence has received a lot of attention in the growth literature. Two strands stand out. The first focuses on growth driven by (human) capital accumulation with one final good produced only and perfect competition. A distinction should be made between closed and open economies. Closed economy models predict convergence between rich and poor countries as long as there is diminishing returns with respect to reproducible capital. Poor countries have low levels of capital and realise high rate of return to investment so that they grow relatively fast (Barro and Sala-i-Martin, 1995). If there is constant returns to capital, growth differentials are persistent and there is no convergence (the AK model, see Rebelo, 1991). In the open economy setting, capital is assumed to be mobile. In the simplest version, convergence in productivity levels is immediate since capital flows to the poor country that has accumulated less capital and realises a high (*ex ante*) rate of return. However, this is at odds with empirical research that finds a limited rate of convergence, of about 2 per cent only (Temple, 1999). The introduction of adjustment costs or borrowing constraints makes the rate of convergence limited again (see Barro, Mankiw and Sala-i-Martin, 1995; Turnovsky and Sen, 1995). While financial capital is internationally mobile, physical (and human) capital have to be accumulated in the country where they are used. Investment in the domestic capital stock takes time and is costly in terms of forgone consumption, even though borrowing from abroad is possible. In the present chapter, productive capital stocks (firm-specific knowledge) is home-grown, too, which explains why convergence takes time.

The second strand of literature focuses on growth driven by R&D with monopolistic competition and differentiated goods in the spirit of Dixit–Stiglitz. It is found that spillovers of knowledge between countries are important for convergence. If there are no such spillovers and if no inputs in production are traded, countries that start at different productivity levels diverge (Grossman and Helpman, 1991, ch. 8; Fung and Ishikawa, 1992; Feenstra, 1996). With international spillovers, most analyses find that international growth rates converge in the long run (Aghion and Howitt, 1998). In the literature both goods trade and international capital mobility are considered. However, so far how convergence is affected by export demand conditions (as captured by the export price elasticity, which is again related to the elasticity of substitution in the Dixit–Stiglitz framework) and how it is affected by the international capital mobility has not been explored. The present chapter aims to fill this gap.

This chapter is also related to the literature on international interdependency in international macroeconomics, with respect to both the type of models and the focus on how welfare levels of countries are interrelated (see the survey by Lane, 2001). While this literature focuses on monetary shocks, this chapter focuses on productivity. How initial cross-country differences in productivity affect international capital flows and welfare differences is investigated. The model can be interpreted as an analysis of how a permanent productivity shock in one country spills over to other countries, how international capital mobility affects the propagation of the shock, and how endogenous R&D and international knowledge spillovers affect the persistence of shocks over time.

The chapter is organised as follows. The model is presented in section 15.2. In section 15.3, the model is reduced to two systems of differential equations, one for the model with capital mobility, the other for the model without capital mobility. It is shown that the two countries converge in the long run. Section 15.4 studies how fast the countries converge. Section

15.5 focuses on welfare. Section 15.6 concludes. The appendix contains proofs of propositions.

15.2 A two-country endogenous growth model

15.2.1 Structure of the model

There are two countries that are characterised by identical preferences, technological opportunities and primary factor endowments. However, one country, indexed by superscript A, starts at a more Advanced productivity level than country B (also referred to as the Backward country). The central question is whether the two countries converge in terms of productivity levels, starting from this initial asymmetry, how fast they converge and how welfare in the two countries evolves over time.

Each country has one primary factor of production in fixed supply (labour), which is allocated over two activities, production and research. Produced goods are differentiated and each variety is produced by a single monopolistic firm. These firms control and accumulate firm-specific knowledge (as in Smulders and van de Klundert, 1995). Within each country, there is a continuum of symmetric firms on the unit interval. This allows us to save on notation by formulating the model for a single representative firm. All goods are traded in international markets at zero transport costs.[1]

The structural relationships are given in table 15.1. Countries are denoted by superscript $i = A, B$ (and if necessary also by superscript j for the other country). Each line in the table represents two equations, one for each country.

Labour productivity in production is denoted by h as appears from (T15.1.1), relating output X to input L. Firms have an opportunity to increase labour productivity h by performing R&D according to (T15.1.2). Knowledge can be increased by allocating labour (R) to R&D. Productivity in R&D depends on a fixed coefficient and three sources of knowledge (h^i, $\bar{h}^i$ and $\bar{h}^j$). First, firms build upon specific knowledge accumulated in the past. Second, all firms benefit from knowledge spillovers emanating from other firms in their country. Third, there are knowledge spillovers from abroad. Knowledge spillovers relate to the average level of knowledge in the different economies ($\bar{h}$). Productivity levels may differ across countries, but are identical across firms within a country. For this reason average knowledge levels are equal to the knowledge levels of firms in each country ($\bar{h}^i = h^i$).

---

[1] In van de Klundert and Smulders (2001), the implications of non-traded goods for growth and convergence are considered.

Table 15.1 *Structural relationships*[a]

Technology

$$X_i = h^i L^i \tag{T15.1.1}$$

$$\dot{h}^i = \xi (h^i)^{1-\alpha_h-\alpha_f} (\bar{h}^i)^{\alpha_h} (\bar{h}^j)^{\alpha_f} R^i \tag{T15.1.2}$$

Preferences

$$U_0^i = \frac{1}{1-\rho} \int_0^\infty (C_t^i)^{1-\rho} e^{-\vartheta t} dt \tag{T15.1.3}$$

$$C^i = \left[(D^i)^{(\varepsilon-1)/\varepsilon} + (M^i)^{(\varepsilon-1)/\varepsilon} \right]^{\varepsilon/(\varepsilon-1)}, \qquad \varepsilon > 1 \tag{T15.1.4}$$

Market clearing

$$X^i = D^i + M^j \tag{T15.1.5}$$

$$L^i + R^i = 1 \tag{T15.1.6}$$

Endogenous variables:		*Parameters:*	
X	output	α_f	foreign spillover parameter
h	labour productivity	α_h	domestic spillover parameter
L	labour in production	ξ	research productivity parameter
R	labour in research	ϑ	utility discount rate
D	consumption domestic good	$1/\rho$	intertemporal substitution elasticity
M	imports	ε	intratemporal substitution elasticity
C	aggregate consumption index		

Note: [a]All equations apply to $i, j = A, B$ and $j \neq i$.

Intertemporal preferences in the consumption index C are given in (T15.1.3). Infinitely lived households apply a constant utility discount rate ϑ. The relative rate of risk aversion is denoted by ρ so that the elasticity of intertemporal substitution equals $1/\rho$. The consumption index (C) combines consumption of domestically produced varieties (D) and imported varieties (M) by way of a CES sub-utility function, with an elasticity of substitution denoted by $\varepsilon > 1$ (see (T15.1.4)).

Goods markets clear (see (T15.1.5)). The supply of labour is normalised at one and equals total demand for labour (see (T15.1.6)).

15.2.2 Consumer and firm behaviour

The behavioural equations of our model are summarised in table 15.2. Consumers maximise intertemporal utility over an infinite horizon. The decision problem consists of two stages subject to the usual budget constraints. In the first stage, each consumer decides on the path of aggregate consumption over time. This gives rise to the familiar Ramsey rule, shown in (T15.2.1). The growth rate of consumption equals the difference

Table 15.2 *Behavioural relationships*[a]

Consumer behaviour

$$\frac{\dot{C}^i}{C^i} = \frac{1}{\rho}\left(r^i - \frac{\dot{p}_c^i}{p_c^i} - \vartheta\right) \tag{T15.2.1}$$

$$D^i = C^i\left(\frac{p^i}{p_c}\right)^{-\varepsilon} \tag{T15.2.2}$$

$$M^i = C^i\left(\frac{p^j}{p_c}\right)^{-\varepsilon} \tag{T15.2.3}$$

$$p_c = [(p^i)^{1-\varepsilon} + (p^j)^{1-\varepsilon}]^{1/(1-\varepsilon)} = 1 \tag{T15.2.4}$$

Producer behaviour

$$p^i = \frac{\varepsilon}{\varepsilon - 1}\frac{w^i}{h^i} \tag{T15.2.5}$$

$$p_h^i = \frac{w^i}{\xi K^i} \tag{T15.2.6}$$

$$r^i p_h^i = p^i\left(\frac{\varepsilon - 1}{\varepsilon}\right)L^i + \xi(1 - \alpha_h - \alpha_f)\left(\frac{K^i}{h^i}\right)p_h^i R^i + \dot{p}_h^i \tag{T15.2.7}$$

$$K^i = (h^i)^{1-\alpha_h-\alpha_f}(\bar{h}^i)^{\alpha_h}(\bar{h}^j)^{\alpha_f} \tag{T15.2.8}$$

Balance of payments

$$\dot{A}^i = r^i A^i + X^i p^i - C^i p_c \tag{T15.2.9}$$

Asset market equilibrium

$$A^A + A^B = 0 \tag{T15.2.10}$$

Symbols:

A	net foreign assets	p_c	price index consumption
r	nominal interest rate	p	output price
w	wage rate	p_h	firm's shadow price of knowledge

Note: [a]All equations apply to $i, j = A, B$ and $j \neq i$.

between the real consumption rate of interest and the pure rate of time preference, multiplied by the elasticity of intertemporal substitution. In the second stage consumers split total per period consumption spending over domestically produced varieties (T15.2.2) and foreign varieties (T15.2.3). The price elasticity of demand is equal to ε in all cases considered. Equations (T15.2.4) define the price index of aggregate consumption. Since there are neither transport costs nor international differences in preferences, this index is the same in both countries. By choosing the composite consumption good as the numéraire, we can set the aggregate consumption price equal to one.

Producers maximise the value of firm over an infinite horizon. Each firm faces a downward sloped total demand function for its products as appears from (T15.2.2) and (T15.2.3). Profit maximisation implies that firms set a markup over (marginal) cost equal to $\varepsilon/(\varepsilon - 1)$, as in (T15.2.5). Labour demand for R&D follows from setting marginal revenue ($\xi K p_h$) equal to marginal cost (w) (see (T15.2.6)). The shadow price of firm-specific knowledge p_h is introduced as a Lagrangian multiplier in the maximisation procedure.[2] Firms face a trade-off with respect to investing in specific knowledge as appears from the arbitrage conditions (T15.2.7). These conditions say that investing an amount of money equal to p_h in the capital market (the left-hand side of (T15.2.7)) should yield the same revenue as investing that same amount of money in knowledge creation. The latter raises labour productivity in the production sector and hence revenue in this sector (first term on the right-hand side of (T15.2.7)), it raises also the knowledge base in R&D (second term) and it yields a capital gain (last term).

Finally, (T15.2.9) imply that domestic net savings are invested in net foreign assets (A). Domestic savings are the sum of the trade balance (the term in square brackets) and interest receipts on foreign assets. Under perfect capital mobility the rate of interest is uniform across countries ($r^A = r^B$). At the other extreme there is the case of balanced trade or zero mobility implying $A = 0$. Both regimes with respect to the balance of payments will be analysed.

15.2.3   Semi-reduced model

Table 15.3 reduces the model to five key equations. In deriving the equations, it is taken into account that all firms within a country have the same productivity level, $h^i = \bar{h}^i$. The growth rates of h and C are denoted by g and g_C, respectively; $a = A/h$ denotes net foreign assets relative to productivity.

Equation (T15.3.1), which is derived from (T15.2.1) and (T15.2.4), restates the Ramsey rule. It represents the relationship between consumption growth and the required rate of return on households' savings. Equation (T15.3.2) combines (T15.2.6) and (T15.2.7). The equation represents the rate of return that firms can maximally pay to households. Equation (T15.3.3) represents labour market equilibrium. It states that the amount of labour not allocated to production, results in productivity

---

[2] The maximisation problem of firm k in country i can be represented by the following Hamiltonian:

$$H^k = p^k(X^k; .)X^k - w^i(X^k/h^k + R^k) + p_h^k[\xi(h^k)^{1-\alpha_h - \alpha_f}(\bar{h}^i)^{\alpha_h}(\bar{h}^j)^{\alpha_f} R^k],$$

where $p^k(\cdot)$ is the firm's demand function (see (T15.2.2)), $X/h = L$ is labour employed in production (see (T15.1.1)), the term in square brackets is firm-specific knowledge accumulation $\dot{h}^i$ (see (T15.1.2)), and p_h is the co-state variable. The firm's instruments are X^k and R^k and it controls the state variable h^k.

Table 15.3 *Key relationships*[a]

___

Ramsey rule

$$\rho g_C^i = r^i - \vartheta \tag{T15.3.1}$$

Investment decision

$$r^i = \xi \left(\frac{h^i}{h^j} \right)^{-\alpha_f} L^i + (1 - \alpha_h)\hat{h}^i - \alpha_f \hat{h}^j + \hat{p}^i \tag{T15.3.2}$$

Labour market equilibrium

$$g^i = \xi \left(\frac{h^i}{h^j} \right)^{-\alpha_f} (1 - L^i) \tag{T15.3.3}$$

Balance of payments

$$p^i L^i - \frac{C^i}{h^i} = \dot{a}^i - (r - g^i)a^i \tag{T15.3.4}$$

Goods market equilibrium

$$\frac{p^i}{p^j} = \left(\frac{h^i L^i}{h^j L^j} \right)^{-1/\varepsilon} \tag{T15.3.5}$$

___

Note: [a]Notation: $g_C \equiv \hat{C}$ consumption growth; $g \equiv \hat{h}$ productivity growth; $a \equiv A/h$ net foreign assets, scaled by knowledge stock. In all equations $i, j = A, B$ and $j \neq i$.

growth. The productivity in research depends on the knowledge gap h^i/h^j. A low stock of knowledge relative to the other country induces large spillovers and allows the country to grow faster at a given amount of labour allocated to research. Balance of payments equilibrium is represented by (T15.3.4) which combines (T15.1.1) and (T15.2.10). Goods market equilibrium is given by (T15.3.5) which combines (T15.1.1), (T15.1.5) and (T15.2.2)–(T15.2.3). Since preferences are homothetic and prices are the same in both countries, the ratio of consumption of goods produced by A relative to those produced by B is the same in both countries and equals the ratio of A's output relative to B's output.

If the two countries are completely symmetric – that is, if they have equal productivity levels ($h^A = h^B$), the same allocation of labour, and no foreign assets nor debt ($a = 0$) – a balanced growth path arises. On the balanced growth path, consumption and output grow at a common growth rate which is endogenous and given by:[3]

$$g_C^i \left(\equiv \frac{\dot{C}^i}{C^i} \right) = g^i \left(\equiv \frac{\dot{h}^i}{h^i} \right) = \frac{\xi - \vartheta}{\rho + \alpha_h + \alpha_f}, \qquad i = A, B. \tag{15.1}$$

___

[3] We restrict the analysis to interior solutions with $g > 0$, which requires sufficiently high productivity in research, $\xi > \vartheta$. If $\xi \leq \vartheta$, no growth occurs in the steady state. Outside the steady state, some convergence in productivity levels will take place if the two countries start with a large initial productivity gap, but the more ϑ exceeds ξ, the larger the long-run productivity gap remains.

Table 15.4 *Linearised model: country differences*

Ramsey rule

$$\rho\dot{\tilde{C}}^R = r\tilde{r}^R \tag{T15.4.1}$$

Investment decision

$$r\tilde{r}^R = \xi L\left[\tilde{L}^R - 2\alpha_f\tilde{h}^R\right] + (1 - \alpha_h + \alpha_f)\dot{\tilde{h}}^R + \dot{\tilde{p}}^R \tag{T15.4.2}$$

Labour market equilibrium

$$\dot{\tilde{h}}^R = -2\alpha_f\tilde{h}^R - \xi L\tilde{L}^R \tag{T15.4.3}$$

Balance of payments

$$L\left(\dot{\tilde{p}}^R + \tilde{L}^R + \tilde{h}^R - \tilde{C}^R\right) + 2(r - g)\tilde{a}^A = 2\dot{\tilde{a}}^R \tag{T15.4.4}$$

Goods market equilibrium

$$\tilde{p}^R = -\tfrac{1}{\varepsilon}\left(\tilde{h}^R + \tilde{L}^R\right) \tag{T15.4.5}$$

As usual, growth falls with discount rates, risk aversion and spillover parameters, but increases with the productivity of R&D. For future use, it is also useful to note that in the steady state we have:

$$\xi L = \vartheta + (\rho - 1 + \alpha_h + \alpha_f)g \tag{15.2}$$

$$r = \vartheta + \rho g. \tag{15.3}$$

To analyse the dynamics of the model, we log linearise around the symmetric steady state in which both countries are identical. Linearised variables are denoted by tildes, $\tilde{x} \equiv d\ln x = dx/x$. We solve for relative variables, that is, ratios of country A's to country B's variables, denoted by superscript R, $\tilde{x}^R \equiv \tilde{x}^A - \tilde{x}^B = d\ln(x^A/x^B)$. Hence tilded variables superscripted R describe how the variable in country A deviates from that in country B. The only exception is variable $\tilde{a}$ which relates to absolute difference from the steady state, $\tilde{a} \equiv da$. We make this exception because in the symmetric equilibrium $a = A/h = 0$. Table 15.4 directly follows from straightforward linearisation of the relations in table 15.3.

In a similar way, the model can be solved for country summations ($\tilde{x}^S \equiv \tilde{x}^A + \tilde{x}^B$ for any variable x), which allows us to analyse the dynamics of the 'integrated world economy'. Before doing so, the model has to be rewritten in terms of stationary variables. In particular, we first rewrite the model in table 15.3 such that C/h shows up as a single variable, instead of C and h as separate variables. The model in stationary variables for the integrated economy then has a very simple reduced form:

$$\rho\dot{\tilde{L}}^S = (\xi L)(\rho + \alpha_h + \alpha_f)\tilde{L}^S. \tag{15.4}$$

This single differential equation in $\tilde{L}^S = \tilde{L}^A + \tilde{L}^B$ applies both under perfect capital mobility and under balanced trade. The differential equation is unstable, so that $\tilde{L}^S$ jumps immediately to the steady state. The allocation of labour in the integrated world economy remains unchanged over the entire transition ($\dot{\tilde{L}}^S_t = 0$ for all t). It implies that all stationary variables in the integrated economy are time-invariant. Hence, $\tilde{g}^S = 0$, so that the knowledge stock growth rate of the integrated world economy does not change over time and the summation of knowledge levels must be equal to the summation of the initial deviations from the symmetrical steady-state level: $\tilde{h}^S_t = \tilde{h}^S_0$ for all t.[4] Also the stationary variable C/h is time-invariant in the integrated world economy, so $\tilde{C}^S_t - \tilde{h}^S_t = 0$. Hence, the results for the integrated world economy can be summarised as:

$$\tilde{L}^A_t + \tilde{L}^B_t = 0 \tag{15.5}$$

$$\tilde{C}^A_t + \tilde{C}^B_t = \tilde{h}^A_0 + \tilde{h}^B_0. \tag{15.6}$$

The integrated world economy behaves as a closed economy on a balanced growth path, irrespective of the level of the world knowledge stock and its distribution over the two countries. How the two countries behave separately depends on whether there is international capital mobility or not and is analysed in the next section.

15.3   Balanced trade versus capital mobility

From table 15.4, a two-dimensional phase diagram can be derived to find the rate of convergence in productivity. This will be done separately for the regime of perfect capital mobility and that of balanced trade.

15.3.1   Balanced trade

In the absence of international capital markets, total production equals total consumption in each country and net foreign assets positions are zero, $\tilde{a} = 0$. From (T15.4.4) and (T15.4.5), national production and consumption are directly linked according to:

$$\tilde{C}^R = \left(\frac{\varepsilon - 1}{\varepsilon}\right)\left(\tilde{L}^R + \tilde{h}^R\right). \tag{15.7}$$

The reduced form model in relative variables can be compressed to a system of two differential equations in $\tilde{h}^R$ and $\tilde{L}^R$. The result can be

---

[4] The solutions for country variables ($\tilde{x}^i$) follow from combining $\tilde{x}^R$ and $\tilde{x}^S$. For instance, $\tilde{L}^A_t = \tilde{L}^R_t/2 = -\tilde{L}^B_t$, and similarly for all other stationary variables. For the predetermined knowledge levels, the following holds: $\tilde{h}^A_t = (\tilde{h}^S_0 + \tilde{h}^R_t)/2$ and $\tilde{h}^B_t = (\tilde{h}^S_0 - \tilde{h}^R_t)/2$.

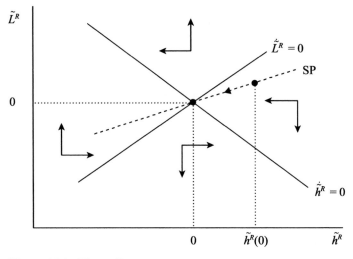

Figure 15.1 Phase diagram

presented in matrix notation as:

$$\begin{bmatrix} \dot{h}^R \\ \dot{L}^R \end{bmatrix} = \begin{bmatrix} -2\alpha_f g & -\xi L \\ -2\alpha_f \Omega_{BT} & \xi L \Phi_{BT} \end{bmatrix} \begin{bmatrix} \tilde{h}^R \\ \tilde{L}^R \end{bmatrix},$$ (15.8)

where

$$\Omega_{BT} = \frac{\varepsilon(\vartheta + 2\alpha_f g) + (\rho - 1)g}{\rho(\varepsilon - 1) + 1}$$ (15.9)

$$\Phi_{BT} = 1 + \frac{\varepsilon(\alpha_h - \alpha_f)}{\rho(\varepsilon - 1) + 1}.$$ (15.10)

The determinant of the matrix in (15.8) is negative.[5] Therefore, the system of differential equations is saddle point stable. The corresponding phase diagram is drawn in figure 15.1. As appears from (15.8) the $\tilde{h}^R = 0$ locus slopes downward. Figure 15.1 depicts a upward sloping $\dot{\tilde{L}}^R = 0$ locus, which applies under realistic parameter assumptions (e.g. $\rho > 1$ and $\alpha_h > \alpha_f$). The stable arm of the saddle path is indicated by the broken line, labelled *SP*. Its slope is unambiguously positive. Unequal productivity levels give rise to transitional dynamics. For any $\tilde{h}^R \neq 0$, the system

---

[5] The determinant equals:

$$-2\alpha_f \xi L(g\Phi_{BT} + \Omega_{BT}) = -2\alpha_f \xi L\varepsilon \left[\frac{\vartheta + (\rho + \alpha_h + \alpha_f)g}{\rho(\varepsilon - 1) + 1}\right] < 0.$$

moves along the stable arm and converges to a symmetric equilibrium in the long run. Suppose $\tilde{h}_0^R > 0$ so that country B lags behind A. During the process of convergence, the leading economy employs more labour in production than the lagging country. The lagging country allocates relatively more labour to R&D, which boosts growth.[6] In the long run there is complete catching up, $\tilde{h}_\infty^R = \tilde{L}_\infty^R = 0$, and each country's productivity expands at the same rate, given by (15.1).

By standard procedures, we can find analytical solutions for the linearised model. Let λ_{BT} be the absolute value of the negative root of the matrix in (15.8). This parameter is the adjustment speed that governs the dynamics of all variables in the case of balanced trade. We find:

$$\tilde{L}_\infty^R = \tilde{h}_\infty^R = 0, \qquad \tilde{h}_0^R \text{ given}, \tag{15.11}$$

$$\tilde{L}_t^R = \left(\frac{\lambda_{BT} - 2\alpha_f g}{\xi L} \right) \tilde{h}_t^R. \tag{15.12}$$

Consumption follows from (15.7) and (15.12):

$$\tilde{C}_t^R = \left(\frac{\varepsilon - 1}{\varepsilon} \right) \left(\frac{\lambda_{BT} + \xi L - 2\alpha_f g}{\xi L} \right) \tilde{h}_t^R. \tag{15.13}$$

15.3.2   Capital mobility

With perfect capital mobility, rates of return are equalised, $\tilde{r}^R = 0$. Equation (T15.4.1) reveals that relative consumption levels are constant over time. Formally, relative consumption follows from integration of (T15.4.1), which gives:

$$\tilde{C}^R = \tilde{v}, \tag{15.14}$$

where $\tilde{v}$ is the constant of integration, which can be solved from the initial conditions of the dynamic model. From table 15.4, with (T15.4.1) replaced by (15.14), the model can be reduced to the following system of three differential equations:

$$\dot{\tilde{a}}^A = (r - g)\tilde{a}^A + (L/2) \left(\frac{\varepsilon - 1}{\varepsilon} \right) (\tilde{h}^R + \tilde{L}^R) - (L/2)\tilde{v} \tag{15.15}$$

$$\begin{bmatrix} \dot{\tilde{h}}^R \\ \dot{\tilde{L}}^R \end{bmatrix} = \begin{bmatrix} -2\alpha_f g & -\xi L \\ -2\alpha_f \Omega_{CM} & \xi L \Phi_{CM} \end{bmatrix} \begin{bmatrix} \tilde{h}^R \\ \tilde{L}^R \end{bmatrix}, \tag{15.16}$$

---

[6] It may seem unrealistic that the poor country undertakes more R&D than the rich country. Note, however, that R&D in the model should be more broadly interpreted than merely patent development. It encompasses all activities that firms undertake to improve productivity and quality, including, for example, imitation and reverse engineering.

where

$$\Omega_{CM} = \varepsilon(\vartheta + 2\alpha_f g) + (\varepsilon\rho - 1)g \qquad (15.17)$$

$$\Phi_{CM} = 1 + \varepsilon(\alpha_h - \alpha_f). \qquad (15.18)$$

Since both assets and goods are perfectly mobile internationally, allocation of production over the two countries can be separated from the allocation of wealth and consumption. The system in (15.16) represents the allocation of production, which can be solved for independently from (15.15), which represents the allocation of consumption. Note that the structure of (15.16) is similar to the case of balanced trade, see (15.8). This gives rise to a similar phase diagram and a similar time pattern for relative productivity and labour allocation.[7] Also (15.12) and (15.13) apply after replacing λ_{BT} by λ_{CM}, where λ_{CM} is the absolute value of the negative root of the matrix in (15.16), which is the adjustment speed that governs the dynamics of all variables in the case of capital mobility.

To solve for relative consumption, we use (15.15) and the boundary values. Substituting the long run results for L and h into (15.15) we can solve for the long-run asset position:

$$\tilde{a}_\infty^A = \left(\frac{L}{2(r-g)}\right)\tilde{v} \qquad (15.19)$$

Since assets are predetermined, we have:

$$\tilde{a}_0^A = 0. \qquad (15.20)$$

Since λ_{CM} represents the adjustment speed of the economy, we may write the change of any variable as proportional to the gap between its current value and its long-run value. For assets we thus have:

$$\dot{\tilde{a}}_t^A = \lambda_{CM}\left(\tilde{a}_\infty^A - \tilde{a}_t^A\right). \qquad (15.21)$$

Substituting the last three results into (15.15) for $t = 0$, we find:

$$\tilde{v} = \left(\frac{r-g}{r-g+\lambda_{CM}}\right)\left(\frac{\varepsilon-1}{\varepsilon}\right)\left(\tilde{L}_0^R + \tilde{h}_0^R\right). \qquad (15.22)$$

Relative consumption at all $t > 0$ follows from (15.14), (15.22) and

---

[7] Saddle point stability again applies, since the determinant equals:

$$-2\alpha_f \xi L(g\Phi_{CM} + \Omega_{CM}) = -2\alpha_f \xi L\varepsilon[\vartheta + (\rho + \alpha_h + \alpha_f)g] < 0.$$

(15.11):

$$
\tilde{C}_t^R = \left(\frac{r - g}{r - g + \lambda_{CM}} \right) \left(\frac{\varepsilon - 1}{\varepsilon} \right) \left(\frac{\lambda_{CM} + \xi L - 2\alpha_f g}{\xi L} \right) \tilde{h}_0^R .
$$

$$(15.23)$$

15.3.3   Consumption and productivity over time

Figure 15.2 depicts the evolution of consumption and productivity when country A starts at a productivity level ahead that of country B ($\tilde{h}_0^R > 0$). Without capital mobility, the advanced country consumes more than the lagging one, but consumption levels converge over time. Also with capital mobility, the advanced country consumes more than the lagging one, but now this is a permanent situation. Country A maintains higher levels of consumption than country B despite the fact that productivity levels converge. The reason is that country A accumulates foreign assets. Country B uses growing export revenues to service its foreign debt. Note that capital mobility allows both countries to smooth consumption over time.

15.4   How does monopolistic competition affect convergence?

To examine how quickly productivity levels in the two countries converge, we study the properties of the stable roots of the planar systems in (15.8) and (15.16), which capture the dynamics under balanced trade and capital mobility, respectively. These roots can be written as

$$
\lambda_k = \frac{\sqrt{T_k^2 - 4D_k} - T_k}{2} > 0,
$$

$$(15.24)$$

where T_k and $D_k < 0$ are the trace and determinant, respectively, of the system in (15.8) for $k = BT$ (and of that in (15.16) for $k = CM$). From this expression we can derive the following (proofs are in the appendix):

Proposition 1 *If $\rho \geq 1$, the speed of adjustment (rate of convergence) is faster with capital mobility than with balanced trade.*

Remark 1 *In all numerical experiments I tried, I found the same result for $0 < \rho < 1$.*

Consumers prefer to smooth consumption. Capital mobility allows a country that is lagging behind to close the productivity gap at higher speed without restraining consumption a lot, by running current account deficits. The lagging country closes the gap with the leading country,

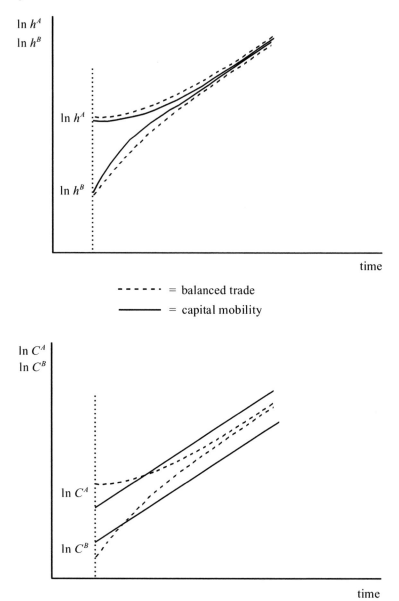

Figure 15.2 Productivity and consumption over time

since it realises (*ex ante*) a higher rate of return and invests more than the leading country. If capital is not mobile internationally, investments have to be financed fully by domestic savings, which is costly for domestic consumers who want to smooth consumption. In this case, the supply of savings is less elastic, which slows down the process of catching up relative to the case in which foreign supply of capital finances catching up.

The adjustment speed with capital mobility equals that without capital mobility only if $\rho = 0$ (since then the matrices in (15.8) and (15.16) are identical).[8] In this extreme case, utility is linear in consumption and consumption smoothing no longer plays a role. Supply of savings is perfectly elastic, independent of whether capital mobility applies or not.

The following proposition states how convergence rates change with the elasticity of substitution ε, which can be considered as the monopolistic competition parameter:

Proposition 2 *With capital mobility, the rate of convergence increases in ε. Without capital mobility, the rate of convergence decreases (increases) in ε if $\rho > 1$ ($\rho < 1$).*

The intuition behind this result is as follows. A larger price elasticity (ε) implies a smaller terms of trade loss from an increase in national output. Hence, the larger the price elasticity, the larger the future gains (in terms of export revenues) that can be reaped by the lagging country when it gradually closes its productivity gap with its trading partner. In other words, a higher price elasticity implies a higher (*ex ante*) rate of return for a given productivity gap. With capital mobility, higher rates of return attract more foreign capital and thus speed up convergence. Without capital mobility, a higher rate of return has ambiguous effects on investment since income and substitution effects work in opposite directions. In this case, domestic investment equals domestic savings so that domestic income and substitution effects determine investment. If $\rho > 1$, the intertemporal rate of substitution is low and a rise in the rate of return prompts consumers to save less, which slows down accumulation and convergence. In the opposite case of high intertemporal substitution, consumers start saving more and speed up convergence.

Table 15.5 presents a calibration exercise and sensitivity analysis. The top row presents the benchmark set of parameters. There are six degrees of freedom which I use to calibrate the model to generally accepted outcomes. I fix the growth rate g on its postwar US average. In every

---

[8] We also find $\lambda_{CM} = \lambda_{BT}$ if $\varepsilon = 1$. This is however a degenerate case since the monopoly price is no longer defined. A unitary price elasticity makes the monopolist's revenues independent of productivity levels which removes any incentive to innovation.

Table 15.5   *Calibration and sensitivity analysis*[a]

	ε (5)	ρ (5/3)	ϑ (0.025)	α_f (0.15)	α_h (0.4)	g (0.018)
λ_{CM} (3.4 per cent)	0.4	0.5	0.4	1.1	−0.4	0.6
λ_{BT} (1.0 per cent)	−0.1	−0.2	0.4	1.0	−0.1	0.6
$[\tilde{U}_0^R]_{CM}/\tilde{h}_0^R$ (0.67)	0.2	0.1	0.1	−0.1	−0.0	−0.1
$[\tilde{U}_0^A]_{CM-BT}/\tilde{h}_0^R$ (−0.01)	0.7	−0.3	−0.6	−0.3	1.1	0.6

Note: [a]Values in parentheses are benchmark parameters and results. Numbers in the table are elasticities evaluated at the benchmark parameter set.

numerical experiment, I adjust productivity parameter ξ according to (15.1) to ensure the selected growth rate. Time preference ϑ and intertemporal substitution $1/\rho$ are not far from accepted views. The price elasticity ε is chosen such that a reasonable profit margin $1/(\varepsilon - 1)$ of 25 per cent results, which is consistent with a broad range of studies (Obstfeld and Rogoff, 2000).[9] The benchmark parameters give adjustment speeds under the two alternative regimes that are close to the famous 2 per cent, found in almost all empirical studies (see Sala-i-Martin, 1996).[10] I report the results for adjustment speeds in parentheses in the first column, top rows. The other columns of the table display elasticities for the adjustment speeds evaluated at the benchmark parameter set, with respect to each of the six parameters, holding the other five parameters fixed.

It turns out that the rates of convergence under the alternative regimes differ substantially. Also, we see that the rate of convergence under capital mobility is most sensitive to the growth rate and the foreign spillover

[9] Note that ε represents both substitution among domestically produced varieties and substitution between home and foreign goods. Empirically, these elasticities differ considerably: export elasticities are considerably below 5. The current model can be easily adapted to separate aggregate export demand elasticities from firm's elasticities of demand, by adding an additional level of nesting in (T15.1.4). If we would denote the latter by η and the former still by ε, only (T15.2.5) and (T15.2.7) would change (ε has to be replaced by η in these equations) and all other equations remain the same. Hence, ε should be interpreted as the elasticity of export demand. If we choose $\varepsilon = 2$ and leave other parameters in table 15.5 unchanged, we find $\lambda_{CM} = 2.1\,percent$, $\lambda_{BT} = 1.1\,percent$, $[\tilde{U}_0^R]_{CM}/\tilde{h}_0^R = 0.43$, $[\tilde{U}_0^A]_{CM-BT}/\tilde{h}_0^R = -0.003$; the elasticities with respect to ε become significantly larger, but other elasticities remain similar to those in table 15.5.

[10] Recently, however, doubts have started to arise about the robustness of this number. In his survey on the econometrics of convergence, Temple (1999, p. 134) reports that more sophisticated studies find estimates that range between zero and 30 per cent a year.

parameter. The adjustment speed under balanced trade is fairly robust to changes in parameters.

15.5   Welfare

Rather than cross-country differences in consumption, as indicated by C^R and discussed above, cross-country differences in welfare are relevant to assess the impact of capital mobility and convergence. In this section how much welfare between a lagging and leading country differs and how capital mobility affects this difference is discussed.

15.5.1   Welfare calculus

Intertemporal welfare of the representative consumer in a country depends on the entire path of consumption, see (T15.1.3). Because of this and because in the absence of unexpected shocks consumption is continuous, a change in welfare can be decomposed in a level effect – the change in initial consumption – and a growth effect – the change in the growth rate of consumption over time. Linearising the intertemporal welfare function (T15.1.3), we find the precise expression:[11]

$$\frac{dU_0}{(1-\rho)U_0} \equiv \tilde{U}_0 = \tilde{C}_0 + \left(\frac{g}{r-g}\right)\left[\left(\frac{r-g}{r-g+\lambda}\right)\tilde{g}_{C0}\right.$$
$$\left. + \left(\frac{\lambda}{r-g+\lambda}\right)\tilde{g}_{C\infty}\right], \qquad (15.25)$$

where λ is the relevant rate of convergence. The first term on the right-hand side is the level effect, the bracketed term is the growth effect. The latter is a weighted average of the short-run change in growth ($\tilde{g}_{C0}$) and its long-run change ($\tilde{g}_{C\infty}$). The larger the adjustment speed λ, the larger is the weight on the long-run change, since long-run values are approached faster. Note that the change in welfare in (15.25) is scaled in such a way that the expression can be interpreted as the *equivalent change in permanent consumption*, that is the permanent increase in consumption on a balanced growth path that generates an equivalent change in welfare.

Taking country differences and substituting $g\tilde{g}_{Ct}^R = \dot{\tilde{C}}_t^R = \lambda(\tilde{C}_\infty^R - \tilde{C}_t^R)$, we may write for the change in country A's welfare relative to country B's welfare:

$$\tilde{U}_0^R = \left(\frac{r-g}{r-g+\lambda}\right)\tilde{C}_0^R + \left(\frac{\lambda}{r-g+\lambda}\right)\tilde{C}_\infty^R. \qquad (15.26)$$

[11] For a step-by-step derivation, see Smulders (1994, p. 294).

Substituting the solutions for C^R, from (15.13) and (15.23), and steady-state relations, (15.2) and (15.3), we find for the two regimes:

$$[\tilde{U}_0^R]_k = \left(\frac{\varepsilon - 1}{\varepsilon}\right)\left[\frac{1 + (\alpha_h - \alpha_f)\left(\frac{g}{r-g+\lambda_k}\right)}{1 + (\alpha_h + \alpha_f)\left(\frac{g}{r-g}\right)}\right]\tilde{h}_0^R, \qquad (15.27)$$

where $k = BT$, CM denotes the capital market regime.

15.5.2   Cross-country welfare differences

The expression in (15.27) gives the relative consumption differential on the balanced growth path that is equivalent to the differences in welfare stemming from the fact that country B starts at a productivity level that is $\tilde{h}_0^R$ below that of country A. With capital mobility, the expression equals the actual consumption difference, since consumption differentials are permanent and consumption grows at the balanced growth rate. Without capital mobility, the expression is a fraction of the actual short-run consumption differential, since relative consumption levels converge in the long run. Nevertheless, the equivalent consumption differential can be written both with and without capital mobility as in (15.27), which facilitates the comparison between the two regimes.

Equation (15.27) reveals some interesting properties of welfare differentials between converging countries:

Proposition 3 *Welfare of the lagging country is below that of the leading country. The welfare differential increases with ε if $(\alpha_h - \alpha_f)$ is sufficiently small.*

Proof: The first term in parentheses in (15.27) increases in ε. By Proposition 2, λ in the second term in parentheses changes with ε, but this effect never dominates if $(\alpha_h - \alpha_f)$ is sufficiently small. ∎

Remark 2 *In numerical experiments I could only identify parameter values for which the welfare differential increases with the price elasticity.*

Not surprisingly, we find that the country that lags in terms of productivity has lower intertemporal welfare than the leading country. A strong position in international markets, as measured by a low value of the price elasticity ε, mitigates the welfare differences. In other words, market power insulates a country against adverse productivity shocks. The reason is that strongly favourable terms of trade effects counterbalance the negative income effects. This effect would also apply in a static economy (with $g = 0$), in which the welfare differential would be simply $(\varepsilon - 1)/\varepsilon$ times the productivity difference. The fact that the second term in parentheses in (15.27) is smaller than unity reveals that the process of catching up associated with spillovers and growth reduces the welfare gap below the level that would apply in the static economy.

In table 15.5 some numerical results are presented. It turns out that for the benchmark parameter set a 1 per cent productivity gap causes intertemporal welfare of the lagging country to be 0.67 per cent below that of the leading country, measured in terms of permanent consumption. This number is rather insensitive to any of the parameters.

15.5.3 The gains from capital mobility

We now turn to the gains from capital mobility. A country benefits from capital mobility if its welfare is higher with capital mobility than without. We have to calculate the differences in welfare for each country under the alternative regimes. We can infer these values from the relative variables. Recall that total consumption in the world economy does not depend on the international capital market regime (see (15.5)–(15.6)). Therefore, the gains from capital mobility stem only from the change in allocation of consumption over the two countries when moving from balanced trade to capital mobility. In particular, the gain from capital mobility for country A is half of the difference between $\tilde{U}_0^R$ evaluated for capital mobility and $\tilde{U}_0^R$ evaluated for balanced trade. Country B's gain is the same number with opposite sign (see sub-section 15.3.2). From (15.27) we find:

$$
[\tilde{U}_0^A]_{CM-BT} = -[\tilde{U}_0^B]_{CM-BT} = \frac{1}{2}\left([\tilde{U}_0^R]_{CM} - [\tilde{U}_0^R]_{BT}\right)
$$

$$
= -\left(\frac{\varepsilon-1}{2\varepsilon}\right)\left(\frac{g}{1+(\alpha_h+\alpha_f)\left(\frac{g}{r-g}\right)}\right)
$$

$$
\times \left(\frac{\lambda_{CM}-\lambda_{BT}}{(r-g+\lambda_{BT})(r-g+\lambda_{CM})}\right)(\alpha_h-\alpha_f)\tilde{h}_0^R. \quad (15.28)
$$

The expression in (15.28) gives the welfare premium of capital mobility (in terms of permanent consumption) for country A. It reveals the winners and losers from international capital mobility as stated in the following proposition:

Proposition 4 *The leading country is worse off with capital mobility and the lagging country gains from capital mobility if spillovers within the country are more important than spillovers between countries ($\alpha_h > \alpha_f$).*

Proof: the sign of the expression in (15.28) depends on the sign of $-(\alpha_h-\alpha_f)\tilde{h}_0^R$. ∎

Numerical results are again presented in table 15.5. The welfare premium of capital mobility for the country that lags 1 per cent behind amounts to about 0.01 per cent of consumption. This number turns out to be relatively sensitive to the growth rate and domestic spillovers.

It might come as a surprise that the introduction of capital mobility does not improve welfare for both countries. One might expect capital mobility to be welfare-improving as it opens the possibility of consumption smoothing. However, this effect is of second order in the linear approximations around a symmetrical steady state.[12] What causes gains and losses from capital mobility is the impact of knowledge spillovers in both countries. These spillovers create externalities in research and lead to sub-optimal investment decisions, since the market for public knowledge is missing. Domestic knowledge spillovers imply under-investment from a welfare point of view. Under capital mobility, productivity in the leading country grows more slowly than under balanced trade and in the lagging country it grows faster, since capital flows to the lagging country. Therefore, capital mobility mitigates the under-investment effect in the lagging country but aggravates it in the leading country. Cross-country spillovers have an opposite effect. The returns to innovation undertaken by one country accrue partly to its trading partner, thereby deteriorating its competitive position. Hence, foreign spillovers result in over-investment from the point of national welfare. Capital mobility aggravates over-investment in country one. The proposition states that if the national externality is more severe than the international externality, there is on balance under-investment in each country. Since capital mobility speeds up investment in the lagging country, it is this country that gains from capital mobility.

15.6   Conclusions

In the two-country growth model in this chapter, initial productivity differences between countries are ultimately eliminated since the lagging country grows faster. In the long run, international growth rates fully converge. The long-run growth rate does not depend on the degree of monopolistic competition, as measured by the inverse of the elasticity

---

[12] This result also echoes some results from the static literature on capital mobility (see Wong, 1995). If the number of traded goods equals the number of factors and production functions are the same in both countries, then, starting from free goods trade, opening up to international capital markets does not affect welfare since factor prices are already equalised by goods trade. In our model, the issue is also whether capital mobility affects welfare, but in a dynamic setting with intra-sectoral (rather than inter-sectoral) trade. Without capital mobility, factor prices (wages and rates of return) are equalised only in the long run. Production functions (for goods and knowledge) are the same.

of substitution between product varieties.[13] However, since the elasticity of substitution between product varieties shapes competition between home and foreign producers, it affects the incentives to invest in home relative to foreign firms. Hence, monopolistic competition is a key determinant of the speed of convergence. With low intertemporal substitution $(1/\rho < 1)$, we have found that lower monopoly profits speed up convergence under capital mobility but reduce the convergence speed in the absence of capital mobility. For a given degree of monopolistic competition, capital mobility allows for faster convergence, but it improves welfare only in the receiving country if domestic knowledge spillovers are larger than international knowledge spillovers. Externalities in research and development make the leading country worse off as a result of international capital flows. It remains to be seen how the results change when national governments subsidise R&D to correct these externalities, and how the results change in the case of coordinated R&D policies. This is left for future research.

APPENDIX

Proof of Proposition 2

Total differentiation of (15.24) gives $d\lambda_k = -[dD_k + \lambda_k dT_k]/(2\lambda_k + T_k)$. Differentiating with respect to ε, we find:

$$\frac{d\lambda_{CM}}{d\varepsilon} = \frac{[2\alpha_f\xi - \lambda_{CM}(\alpha_h - \alpha_f)]\xi L}{2\lambda_{CM} + T_{CM}}$$

and

$$\frac{d\lambda_{BT}}{d\varepsilon} = \frac{[2\alpha_f\xi - \lambda_{BT}(\alpha_h - \alpha_f)](1 - \rho)\xi L}{[\rho(\varepsilon - 1) + 1]^2 [2\lambda_{BT} + T_{BT}]}.$$

- If $\alpha_h < \alpha_f$, it follows immediately that $d\lambda_{CM}/d\varepsilon > 0$ and sign($d\lambda_{CM}/d\varepsilon$) = sign$(1 - \rho)$.
- If $\alpha_h > \alpha_f$, $d\lambda_{CM}/d\varepsilon > 0$ if and only if $\lambda_{CM} < 2\alpha_f\xi/(\alpha_h - \alpha_f)$. This latter inequality always holds, since using the expression of λ_{CM} above, we find (i) $\lambda_{CM} = 0$ if $\varepsilon = 0$, (ii) $\lim_{\varepsilon \to \infty} \lambda_{CM} = 2\alpha_f\xi/(\alpha_h - \alpha_f)$ and (iii) λ_{CM} is a continuous function of ε.
- If $\alpha_h > \alpha_f$ and $\rho > 1$, $d\lambda_{BT}/d\varepsilon < 0$ if and only if $\lambda_{BT} < 2\alpha_f\xi/(\alpha_h - \alpha_f)$. This latter inequality holds, since (i) from (15.8) and (15.16), it follows that $\lambda_{CM} = \lambda_{BT}$ if $\varepsilon = 1$ and (ii) we have already proved that $\lambda_{CM} < 2\alpha_f\xi/(\alpha_h - \alpha_f)$. Hence, $\lambda_{BT} < \lambda_{CM}$ for all $\varepsilon > 1$ and $\rho > 1$.

---

[13] This independency allows us to focus on the role of export demand elasticities. In chapter 14 by Smulders and van de Klundert in this volume it is explained that this property arises because the number of firms is fixed.

- If $\alpha_h > \alpha_f$ and $\rho < 1$, $d\lambda_{BT}/d\varepsilon > 0$ if and only if $\lambda_{BT} < 2\alpha_f \xi/(\alpha_h - \alpha_f)$. This latter inequality holds for all $\varepsilon > 1$, since (i) $\lambda_{BT} = \lambda_{CM} < 2\alpha_f \xi/(\alpha_h - \alpha_f)$ if $\varepsilon = 1$ and (ii) λ_{BT} is a continuous function of ε.

Proof of Proposition 1

If $\varepsilon = 1$, $\lambda_{CM} = \lambda_{BT}$. From Proposition 2 we conclude that for $\rho > 1$, λ_{CM} increases with ε and λ_{BT} decreases with ε. Hence $\lambda_{CM} > \lambda_{BT}$ for all $\varepsilon > 1$ and $\rho > 1$.

REFERENCES

Aghion, Ph. and P. Howitt (1992). A model of growth through creative destruction. *Econometrica*, 60: 323–352

(1998). *Endogenous Growth Theory*. Cambridge, MA, MIT Press

Barro, R. J., Mankiw, N. G. and Sala-i-Martin, X. (1995). Capital mobility in neoclassical models of growth. *American Economic Review*, 85: 103–115

Barro, R. J. and Sala-i-Martin, X. (1995). *Economic Growth*. New York, McGraw-Hill

Dixit, A. K. and Stiglitz, J. E. (1977). Monopolistic competition and optimum product diversity. *American Economic Review*, 67: 297–308

Feenstra, R. (1996). Trade and uneven growth. *Journal of Development Economics*, 49: 229–256

Fung, K.-Y. and Ishikawa, J. (1992). Dynamic increasing returns, technology and economic growth in a small open economy. *Journal of Development Economics*, 37: 63–87

Grossman, G. M. and Helpman, E. (1991). *Innovation and Growth in the Global Economy*. Cambridge, MA, MIT Press

Klundert, Th. van de and Smulders, S. (2001). Loss of technological leadership of rentier economies: a two-country endogenous growth model. *Journal of International Economics*, 54: 211–231

Lane, Ph. (2001). The new open economy macroeconomics: a survey. *Journal of International Economics*, 54: 235–266

Obstfeld, M. and Rogoff, K. (2000). The six major puzzles in international macroeconomics: is there a common cause? NBER Working Paper, 7777

Rebelo, S. (1991). Long-run policy analysis and long-run growth. *Journal of Political Economy*, 99: 500–521

Romer, P. M. (1990). Endogenous technological change. *Journal of Political Economy*, 98: S71–S102

Sala-i-Martin, X. (1996). The classical approach to convergence analysis. *Economic Journal*, 106: 1019–1036

Smulders, S. (1994). *Growth, Market Structure and the Environment: Essays on the Theory of Endogenous Economic Growth*. PhD thesis, Tilburg University

Smulders, S. and van de Klundert, Th. (1995). Imperfect competition, concentration and growth with firm-specific R&D. *European Economic Review*, 39: 139–160

Temple, J. (1999). The new growth evidence. *Journal of Economic Literature*, 37: 112–156

Turnovsky, S. J. and Sen, P. (1995). Investment in a two-sector dependent economy. *Journal of the Japanese and International Economies*, 9: 29–55

Wong, K.-Y. (1995). *International Trade in Goods and Factor Mobility*. Cambridge, MA, MIT Press

16 A vintage model of technology diffusion: the effects of returns to diversity and learning-by-using

Henri L. F. de Groot, Marjan W. Hofkes and Peter Mulder

16.1 Introduction

A good understanding of well-documented differences in growth and productivity performance of different countries requires an understanding of the complex process of the development and diffusion of new technologies. Relatively much effort – for example, in the recent new or endogenous growth theory – has been devoted to endogenising the rate of arrival of new technologies emphasising the importance of R&D and human capital (e.g. Lucas, 1988; Grossman and Helpman, 1991). However, a good understanding of the diffusion and adoption of new technologies is in our view at least equally important (see, for example, Jovanovic, 1997). In this regard, we know that diffusion of new technologies is a lengthy process, that adoption of new technologies is costly and that many firms continue to invest in old and (seemingly) inferior technologies. The relevance of the latter phenomenon has, for example, convincingly been shown in the literature on the so-called energy-efficiency paradox; the phenomenon that firms do not (exclusively) invest in technologies that according to standard net present-value (NPV) calculations yield the highest return (see, for example, Sutherland, 1991; Howarth and Andersson, 1993; Jaffe and Stavins, 1994). The aim of this chapter is to contribute to our understanding of adoption behaviour of firms and of diffusion processes of new technologies.

The question as to why firms do not invest in seemingly superior technologies has already achieved much attention in the literature. We can categorise this literature into four groups. The first category focuses on

We acknowledge useful comments by Jan Boone, Peter Broer, Egbert Jongen, Gerard Kuper, Richard Nahuis, Bob van der Zwaan and conference participants on an earlier version of this chapter. Of course, the usual disclaimer applies. Financial support from the research programme 'Environmental Policy, Economic Reform and Endogenous Technology', funded by the Netherlands Organisation for Scientific Research (NWO) is also gratefully acknowledged.

uncertainty. It emphasises that the combination of uncertainty and some degree of irreversibility creates an option-value of waiting. Thereby, it can explain the relatively slow diffusion of new and uncertain technologies. Uncertainty can be related to the quality and performance of new technologies, the speed of arrival of new and further improved technologies, input prices of technology-specific inputs, etc. (see, for example, Balcer and Lippman, 1984; Dixit and Pindyck, 1994; Farzin, Huisman and Kort, 1998 for contributions in this area). The second line of research focuses on strategic issues in technology adoption. It elaborates on the effects of (expected) rival innovation and imitation on the timing of innovation or adoption in a world characterised by spillovers and limited appropriability (see, among others, Kamien and Schwartz, 1972; Reinganum, 1981; Spence, 1984). The third approach focuses on the role of learning and spillovers. Learning improves the performance of existing technologies and can have important spillovers to the performance of other related technologies (e.g. Davies, 1979; Jovanovic and Lach, 1989; OECD/IEA, 2000). A final category that we can distinguish focuses on the role of vested interests. It argues that switching to new technologies (temporarily) reduces expertise and destroys rents associated with relatively old technologies for particular sub-groups in the economy which may therefore engage in efforts aimed at keeping the old technologies in place (see, for example, Jovanovic and Nyarko, 1994; Krusell and Ríos-Rull, 1996; Canton, de Groot and Nahuis, 2002).

In this chapter we emphasise the role of learning as well as the relevance of complementarity between different vintages. Our model has four distinctive features. First, technology is embodied in physical capital. New vintages of capital are – when considered in isolation – more productive than old ones. Second, capital goods of different vintages are imperfect substitutes in production. Firms exhibit a 'taste for diversity' of vintages creating an incentive to simultaneously invest in new and older technologies. Third, firms gain expertise in a technology by using the technologies in the production process. In other words, we incorporate learning-by-using. Fourth, our model allows for the endogenous determination of the number of vintages used by firms, so we offer an economically motivated approach for the scrapping of vintages. We discuss these features more extensively when presenting the model in section 16.2.

There are a number of related articles in which issues of learning and technological innovation and diffusion are analysed. Without extensive discussion, we refer to, for example, Aghion and Howitt (1996); Aghion, Dewatripont and Rey (1997, 1999); Arrow (1962); Chari and Hopenhayn (1991); Jovanovic and Nyarko (1996); Parente (1994); Stokey (1988); Young (1993a, 1993b). The main differences between these studies and ours are that we (i) emphasise the importance of complementarity of vintages, (ii) emphasise diffusion instead of innovation and (iii) provide a supply-oriented explanation for the endogenous scrapping of old vintages (or, alternatively, the modernisation of the capital stock).

The chapter is organised as follows. In section 16.2 we set up the basic model. This model is solved in section 16.3. The comparative static characteristics of the model, illustrating the importance of complementarity and learning-by-using for understanding diffusion patterns of new technologies, are presented in section 16.4. Finally, section 16.5 concludes and discusses roads for future research.

16.2   The model

The model that we develop is essentially a simple two-sector vintage model that is characterised by learning-by-using and 'returns to diversity'. The two sectors that we distinguish are (i) a final goods sector in which a homogeneous consumption good is produced using labour and capital and (ii) a capital goods sector consisting of (a mass of) T monopolistically competitive firms each producing a particular vintage of capital. The only factor of production in the model is labour that is used for assemblage of final consumption goods and for the production of capital or intermediate inputs.

The model that we develop can be considered as a vintage model in the sense that capital inputs used in production are heterogeneous in their productivity or quality. For simplicity, capital is assumed to be nondurable. The model can therefore also be considered as a model with heterogeneous intermediate inputs. An advantage – at least for presentational purposes – of this assumption is that the coexistence of different vintages can, by definition, not be explained on the basis of incomplete depreciation of the existing capital stock as is common in 'traditional' vintage models. The productivity of vintages depends on its date of 'invention' and the intensity with which it has been used in the past. The latter captures the relevance of learning-by-using. Furthermore, in contrast with the more traditional vintage models, our model exhibits a 'taste for diversity' of vintages. This implies that in our model firms have incentives to invest in older technologies, even if new technologies are available that are 'better' when considered in isolation. Vintages are in other words imperfectly substitutable and thus to some degree complementary, whereas in traditional vintage models firms invest only in best practice technologies (for example, Meijers, 1994). The very reason that old and new vintages coexist in the traditional models is that once firms have incurred the (partly) sunk investment cost, it need not be optimal to replace this capital once a superior technology becomes available. By contrast, we argue that complementarity is an essential ingredient in the process of technological change and an important reason for the coexistence of different vintages. Many new technologies pass through a life cycle, in which they initially complement older technologies, and only subsequently (and often slowly) substitute for the older technologies. A number of historical examples, like for example the replacement of the waterwheel by the steam engine, illustrates the role of complementarities in this 'life cycle view' of technological change (see, for example, Rosenberg, 1976; Young, 1993b). One can argue that modern production processes consist of even more inter-related and mutually reinforcing technologies than the documented historical examples. Whereas Young (1993b) employs the idea that complementary innovation is the result of rent-seeking inventive activity on the part of innovators, we focus on the role of adopters that wish to invest in complementary technologies.

In the context of adoption of new technologies, one can think of various underpinnings – not explicitly modelled in this chapter – for these complementarities. First, firms may face uncertainty about the performance of new technologies. Older more certain technologies then complement the newer ones by providing the possibility to hedge against the uncertain performance of the new technology. Second, in large firms a range of different techniques coexists and the production process may be seen as a puzzle of a large number of technology pieces. It is then reasonable that firms continually invest in improvement of distinct pieces instead of replacing the whole puzzle at once. Third, when technological improvement takes the form of additional improvement of already adopted techniques (retrofit), there is a reason to invest in older basic techniques. The formulation that we use in our model captures these ideas in a very stylised way. It is inspired by the product-variety theory which started with the seminal work of Dixit and Stiglitz (1977) and was later extended and applied by, for example, Ethier (1982), Grossman and Helpman (1991) and Romer (1990). As first proposed by Ethier (1982), we assume returns to a diversity of capital vintages (of heterogeneous quality) instead of returns to a variety of consumer durables or intermediate goods.

16.2.1 The final goods sector

The final goods sector produces a homogeneous consumption good according to a Cobb–Douglas production function applying for a representative firm:

$$Y_t = K_t^\alpha L_{Yt}^{1-\alpha} \tag{16.1}$$

in which Y_t represents output produced in year t, and K_t and L_{Y_t} are the capital and labour input in final goods production, respectively. Capital is an aggregate of vintages of capital goods. Vintages are characterised by the first year of their availability τ. The aggregate capital stock is formulated as (building on the seminal work of Dixit and Stiglitz 1977):

$$K_t = \left[\int_{t-T}^{t} (A_{\tau,t} K_{\tau,t})^{(\varepsilon-1)/\varepsilon} d\tau \right]^{\varepsilon/(\varepsilon-1)} \qquad (16.2)$$

in which T is the (endogenous) mass of vintages in use, $K_{\tau,t}$ is the amount of capital of vintage τ used in year t (where $t - T \leq \tau \leq t$) and $A_{\tau,t}$ is a vintage-specific productivity parameter. In allowing for vintage-specific productivity and hence *asymmetric* vintages we deviate from the standard Dixit–Stiglitz framework that has been applied in many of the contributions that built on Dixit and Stiglitz (1977). Alternatively, T can be interpreted as the age of the oldest vintage in use. Technological change is embodied in new vintages. The elasticity of substitution between any pair of vintages (in efficiency units AK) is denoted by ε. Vintages are assumed to be close but imperfect substitutes ($1 < \varepsilon < \infty$).

The productivity of vintages develops according to two factors. The first is exogenous. Newer vintages – as they are introduced on the market – are more productive than older vintages when those were brought on the market. Second, vintages improve as they are used. Hence, the productivity endogenously depends on the cumulative investment in vintages. We further label this 'learning-by-using'. More specifically, we assume that the productivity of vintages ($A_{\tau,t}$) develops according to

$$A_{\tau,t} = A_0 e^{g\tau} + [1 - (1 + aC_{\tau,t})^{\lambda-1}](A_\tau^{\max} - A_0 e^{g\tau}). \qquad (16.3)$$

In this specification, A_0 is initial productivity, g is an exogenously given growth rate of the productivity of new vintages, a measures the strength of learning-by-using effects, $C_{\tau,t}$ represents past cumulative investments in vintage τ ($C_{\tau,t} \equiv \int_\tau^t K_{\tau,i} di$), λ represents the curvature of the learning-curve and $A_\tau^{\max}$ is the vintage-specific maximum productivity level (that is, the productivity level when the technology has matured). For simplicity, we assume that $A_\tau^{\max}$ is in fixed proportion $\gamma (\geq 1)$ to the productivity at the date of introduction of the vintage ($A_\tau^{\max} = \gamma A_0 e^{g\tau}$). In the special case in which $\gamma = 1$, the learning-by-using mechanism is absent and productivity of vintages depends purely on the exogenous improvements. The assumption that $0 < \lambda < 1$ implies that the productivity of a technology in the presence of learning-by-using ($\gamma > 1$) gradually converges to the mature productivity level $A_\tau^{\max}$ once the technology starts

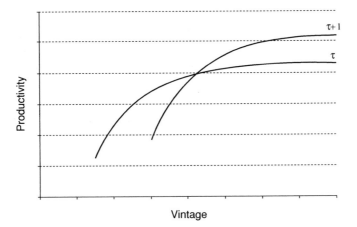

Figure 16.1 Productivity development of vintages with learning-by-using

to penetrate into the production process.[1] Figure 16.1 depicts a typical example of productivity development of two different vintages. The newer vintage (starting more to the right) is potentially more productive, but initially the old technology outperforms the new technology due to learning-by-using.

The above formulation captures the idea that the (potential) productivity level of a new vintage as it comes on the market at $t = \tau$ is higher than of an old vintage. For the purpose of this chapter, we do not further elaborate on the innovation process that underlies the improvement of new vintages, but focus on the diffusion process. We allow for effects of learning as the result of the utilisation of the technology by the final user by allowing productivity to improve with the intensity with which it has been used in the past. This learning-by-using has to be distinguished from the learning in R&D stages and learning in producing the

---

[1] From (16.3) we can also determine the learning rate. This rate indicates the percentage with which the productivity increases if installed capacity is doubled. In the specification for productivity development that we have chosen, the learning rate depends – among other things – on the capacity that has already been installed (C_0). More specifically, we can determine the learning rate as

$$\frac{\gamma - (\gamma - 1)(1 + 2aC_0)^{\lambda - 1}}{\gamma - (\gamma - 1)(1 + aC_0)^{\lambda - 1}} - 1.$$

This learning rate is declining in C_0, so the learning rate decreases as a technology penetrates further into the economy. Learning ultimately stops as the technology reaches maturity. This pattern is broadly consistent with empirical evidence on learning rates which has convincingly shown that learning rates are – at least – kinked, that is high at low levels of penetration and low at higher levels of penetration (e.g. OECD/IEA, 2000).

technology, the so-called 'learning-by-doing' (Rosenberg, 1976). As a result of the presence of learning-by-using – and in accordance with broad historical evidence (see, for example, Rosenberg, 1976; Mokyr, 1990; Young, 1993a) – new technologies can initially be inferior to more mature technologies. Learning-by-using improves the productivity and performance of the new technology over time and this learning can – at least initially – be so fast that it dominates the improvement of newly arriving vintages.

For the time being, we assume for reasons of analytical tractability of the model that learning-by-using is absent ($\gamma = 1$). We generalise and discuss the implications of allowing for learning-by-using for diffusion patterns and adoption of technologies in sub-section 16.4.2.

The behaviour of producers in the final goods sector is guided by profit-maximisation. They operate under perfect competition and a representative firm maximises profits (π):

$$\pi_t = P_{Y_t} Y_t - w_t L_{Y_t} - \int_{t-T}^{t} P_{K\tau,t} K_{\tau,t} d\tau \qquad (16.4)$$

in which P_Y, w and $P_{K\tau}$ denote the output price, the wage rate and the price of capital goods of a specific vintage, respectively (we omit time-indices if possible). Vintage capital is bought from the capital goods sector, to which we turn in the next sub-section.

16.2.2   The capital production sector

The capital production sector consists of (a mass of) T monopolistically competitive firms each producing a specific vintage according to[2]

$$K_{\tau,t} = L_{K\tau,t}. \qquad (16.5)$$

In addition, firms in this sector have to pay a fixed cost in terms of labour (L_f) before being able to produce. Firms maximise their profits ($\pi_{\tau,t}$):

$$\pi_{\tau,t} = P_{K\tau,t} K_{\tau,t} - w_t(L_{K\tau,t} + L_f). \qquad (16.6)$$

---

[2] We assume that in each period, a new vintage becomes available due to an exogenous process of technological innovation (see (16.3)) and only one firm acquires the right to produce capital of this particular vintage. It is of course possible to generalise here and to model a separate sector producing the brands and selling these to the firms producing the capital. In such a setting, firms in the capital production sector would be willing to buy the patent to produce the specific brand and acquire the monopoly right to produce, provided that the profits that can be earned over time are equal to the costs of the patent (compare, for example, Grossman and Helpman, 1991). Such a generalisation, though interesting, would not add to the basic insights we want to emphasise in this chapter.

The model is closed by imposing labour market equilibrium which – assuming a constant and exogenous labour supply L – reads as:

$$L = L_{Yt} + \int_{t-T}^{t} (L_{K\tau,t} + L_f)d\tau. \tag{16.7}$$

In section 16.3 we discuss the solution of the model, focusing on the allocation of labour and the determination of the mass of vintages used in the production process.

16.3 Solution of the model

At the heart of the solution procedure is the notion that the mass of vintages that is used is endogenous. Or, stated alternatively, the age of the oldest vintage in use is endogenous. To understand this intuitively, it is important to notice that newer vintages are more productive than older ones and the producers of vintages have to pay a fixed cost in terms of labour in order to be able to produce the vintage. As a result of the gradual increase in productivity of newer vintages, the (relative) demand for old vintages will gradually decline over time. The complementarity between vintages of different age is the reason that firms do not immediately shift to the most productive vintage. At some point in time, however, the demand for a vintage becomes so low that it can no longer profitably be supplied by the producer of that vintage. Supply will stop and the vintage is eliminated from the market. This 'scrapping' of vintages is – in contrast with the more traditional vintage literature – caused by the impossibility of profitably *supplying* the vintage, whereas the traditional vintage literature explains scrapping by the fact that at some point in time, the vintage can no longer profitably be *used* by the owner. Note that at this point the demand for this vintage is still positive but small. Our model thereby offers an alternative economically motivated approach for scrapping of vintages that differs from, for example, den Hartog and Tjan (1980) and Malcomson (1975).

Let us now turn to the solution of the model more formally. Producers in the final-goods sector solve a standard profit-maximisation problem in two stages (maximisation of (16.4)). First, they determine the optimal relative demand for (the composite of) capital and labour. This results in the standard allocation rule for a Cobb–Douglas production function implying constant cost shares of capital and labour:

$$\frac{K_t P_{Kt}}{L_{Yt} w_t} = \frac{\int_{t-T}^{t} K_{\tau,t} P_{K\tau,t} d\tau}{L_{Yt} w_t} = \frac{\alpha}{1-\alpha} \tag{16.8}$$

in which P_K is the price index of the composite capital good. In the second stage, they decide on the optimal amount of capital of each vintage by solving the following maximisation problem:

$$\max_{K_{\tau,t}} \left[\int_{t-T}^{t} (A_{\tau,t} K_{\tau,t})^{(\varepsilon-1)/\varepsilon} d\tau \right]^{\varepsilon/(\varepsilon-1)} \quad \text{subject to} \quad \int_{t-T}^{t} P_{K\tau,t} K_{\tau,t} d\tau = P_{Kt} K_t.$$

$$(16.9)$$

Optimisation yields a downward sloping demand curve for capital of a specific vintage:

$$K_{\tau,t} = K_{s,t} \left(\frac{A_{\tau,t}}{A_{s,t}} \right)^{\varepsilon-1} \left(\frac{P_{K\tau,t}}{P_{Ks,t}} \right)^{-\varepsilon}.$$

$$(16.10)$$

The relative demand for two vintages of different age thus depends on their relative productivity and their relative prices. The relative demand will be more responsive to productivity differences, the more easily vintages can be the substituted for each other.

Producers in the vintage production sector maximise their profits (16.6) subject to the downward sloping demand curve for the vintage that they produce (16.10). This results in standard markup pricing, according to which the producers of vintages put a markup over labour costs:

$$\frac{\partial \pi_{\tau,t}}{\partial L_{K\tau,t}} = 0 \quad \Leftrightarrow \quad P_{K\tau,t} = \frac{\varepsilon w_t}{\varepsilon - 1}.$$

$$(16.11)$$

The markup is larger the larger the complementarity between different vintages (i.e. the smaller ε).

This basically concludes the description of behaviour of firms in our economy. The model is subsequently solved by essentially determining the mass of vintages that can be sustained in the economy (that is, the age of the oldest vintage that can be sustained). For this, we first need to determine the allocation of labour over the production or assemblage of final goods and the production of vintages, respectively. Using the fact that cost shares of capital and intermediates are constant, we can determine the allocation of labour. Using (16.5), (16.8) and (16.11), we derive that:

$$L_{Yt} = \frac{(1-\alpha)\varepsilon}{\alpha(1-\varepsilon)} \int_{t-T}^{t} L_{K\tau,t} d\tau.$$

$$(16.12)$$

This expression reveals that more assemblage labour will be used relative to labour used for producing vintages, the smaller the share parameter in the production function of final goods and the lower the elasticity of substitution. The latter is caused by the fact that a low elasticity of substitution results in relatively high prices of vintages due to markup pricing and results in a shift from capital to labour in final goods production. Substituting this expression in the labour market equilibrium (16.7) and rewriting yields an expression for labour use in production of vintage capital:

$$\int_{t-T}^{t} L_{K\tau,t} d\tau = \frac{\alpha(\varepsilon - 1)}{\varepsilon - \alpha} \left[L - \int_{t-T}^{t} L_f d\tau \right]. \tag{16.13}$$

Firms in the capital production sector continue to produce their specific vintage as long as this is profitable. So they produce as long as

$$P_{K\tau,t} K_{\tau,t} \geq w_t (L_{K\tau,t} + L_f). \tag{16.14}$$

Using the production function for vintages and markup pricing (16.5) and (16.11), this expression can be rewritten (with equality) as

$$\frac{\varepsilon}{\varepsilon - 1} = \frac{L_{K\tau,t} + L_f}{L_{K\tau,t}}. \tag{16.15}$$

This expression basically determines the minimally required scale of operation for a producer of vintages (and hence, the minimal demand for a particular vintage that is needed for the producer of that vintage to be able to operate profitably). From (16.15), this minimal demand can be derived as

$$\bar{K} = \bar{L} = (\varepsilon - 1) L_f \tag{16.16}$$

in which $\bar{L}$ is the amount of labour used to produce the oldest vintage which is in use by the final good production sector. Clearly, the minimum scale of operation or the minimal demand for a particular vintage is larger the larger the fixed cost and the larger the elasticity of substitution (and hence the lower the markup the producers of the vintages can charge). Any firm that intends to produce an older vintage for which there would be less demand due to its lower productivity would make losses.

Having determined the production level of the oldest vintage, we can uniquely determine the production levels of more recent vintages which are in use by combining the expression for the relative demand for different vintages and the productivity difference between these vintages. Substituting the expressions for the price of capital (16.11) and the growth rate of productivity of new vintages (16.3) into (16.10) and rewriting yields (in the absence of learning-by-using, i.e. $\gamma = 1$):

$$L_{K\tau,t} = \bar{L} e^{(\varepsilon-1)g(\tau+T-t)}. \tag{16.17}$$

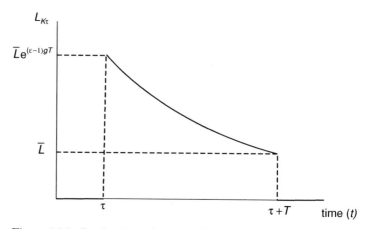

Figure 16.2   Production of one particular vintage over time

Figure 16.2 graphically illustrates this expression by displaying the production of one particular vintage (arriving on the market at $t = \tau$) over time. Expression (16.17) reveals that in the presence of exogenous improvements of the performance of newer vintages ($g > 0$), more labour is used for the production of more recent vintages (higher τ). The effect of improvement of performance on (relative) labour use is reinforced when the degree of complementarity among vintages declines. In the special case in which $g = 0$, vintages are equally productive and we end up with a symmetric solution of the model.

The total amount of labour used for the production of vintages thus equals (using (16.16) and (16.17)):

$$\int_{t-T}^{t} L_{K\tau,t}\,d\tau = \int_{0}^{T} \bar{L}e^{(\varepsilon-1)g\tau}\,d\tau = \frac{\bar{L}\left[e^{(\varepsilon-1)gT} - 1\right]}{g(\varepsilon - 1)}$$

$$= \frac{L_f\left[e^{(\varepsilon-1)gT} - 1\right]}{g}. \qquad (16.18)$$

Combining (16.13) and (16.18) we can now solve for the mass of vintages that can be sustained in the economy (or, alternatively, the age of the oldest vintages in use). This solution for T is given by the following implicit function:

$$(\varepsilon - \alpha)L_f\left[e^{(\varepsilon-1)gT} - 1\right] = \alpha g(\varepsilon - 1)[L - TL_f]. \qquad (16.19)$$

The comparative static characteristics of the model will be discussed in section 16.4.

16.4   Comparative static characteristics

The aim of this section is to illustrate the comparative static characteristics of the model. This is mainly done by relying on a graphical method that enables us to illustrate both the solution of the model as it was discussed in section 16.3 and the comparative static characteristics. In sub-section 16.4.1, we will discuss the importance of the degree of complementarity between different vintages for understanding the adoption and diffusion of new vintages. In sub-section 16.4.2, we elaborate on the importance of learning-by-using. This is done by generalising the productivity development of vintages, as introduced in section 16.2.

16.4.1   The effects of complementarity

The degree of complementarity is captured by the elasticity of substitution between the vintages. The consequences of an increase in the elasticity of substitution (that is, a lower degree of complementarity) can best be understood by dividing the total effect into three components. Note that, for the moment, we assume the learning effect to be absent. First, increased substitutability reduces the markup that producers of intermediates can charge. Consequently, the minimal demand required for these producers to operate profitably increases. Second, increased substitutability implies that the relative demand for vintages is more responsive to increases in productivity of newer vintages. Finally, the increased substitutability lowers the price of intermediates relative to wages. As a consequence, firms in the final goods sector will, *ceteris paribus*, increase their demand for intermediates. These three effects can be illustrated graphically. This is done in figure 16.3.[3]

Figure 16.3 depicts the demand for vintages of different age (on the vertical axis) as a function of the date of introduction on the market (on the horizontal axis). The most recent (current) vintage is located furthest to the right in the figure. The figure can be understood as follows. Consider first the case in which the elasticity of substitution is low (i.e. complementarity between different vintages is strong). The upward slope of the demand curve reflects the fact that newer vintages (located more to the right) are more productive and consequently have a higher demand. The demand for the oldest vintage is given as the minimal required

---

[3] Figure 16.3 is based on a discrete version of the model with the following parametrisation: $\alpha = 0.6$, $w = 1$ (numéraire), $g = 0.05$, $A_0 = 1$, $L = 300$, $L_f = 2$ and $\gamma = 1$. The elasticity of substitution is equal to $\varepsilon = 6.87$ in the low-complementarity case and $\varepsilon = 5.25$ in the high-complementarity case. This results in $T = 6$ and $T = 8$, respectively. Details on the numerical analysis are available upon request from the authors.

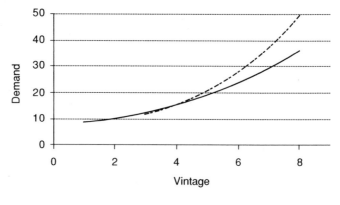

Figure 16.3 The effects of the degree of complementarity between vintages: no learning-by-using

demand as defined in (16.16) and is represented by the lowest point on the demand curve. The surface below the demand curve is equal to the amount of labour that is available for the production of vintages as given in (16.13). Combining these three elements yields a unique solution of the model that is essentially characterised by the age of the oldest vintage.

Let us now consider what happens when the elasticity of substitution increases (i.e. the degree of complementarity declines). In terms of the figure, the minimal required demand increases. This, *ceteris paribus*, implies a reduction of the equilibrium number of vintages. Second, the demand curve gets steeper as users of the vintages become more responsive to productivity differences. *Ceteris paribus*, this also implies that the equilibrium number of vintages that can be sustained in the economy declines. Third, producers of final goods shift their input towards capital as capital becomes relatively cheap. This is reflected by an upward shift of the demand curve. This effect works in an opposite way to the two previous effects and implies that more vintages can be sustained. However, the former two effects dominate for reasonable parameter values[4] and increased substitutability reduces the number of vintages that can be

---

[4] This conclusion is based on extensive simulations with the model. The details are available upon request from the authors. Applying the implicit function theorem to (16.19), we derive that the age of the oldest vintage declines with an increase in the degree of complementarity if

$$L_f\left[e^{(\varepsilon-1)gT}(1 + (\varepsilon - \alpha)gT) + \alpha gT - 1\right] > \alpha gL.$$

sustained. Complementarity thus slows down the rate of modernisation of the capital stock

16.4.2   The effects of learning-by-using

In section 16.3, we assumed the learning-by-using effect to be absent ($\gamma = 1$). We will now drop this assumption and assume that productivity of vintages initially increases at a relatively fast rate when the vintage is introduced in order to slow down at later stages and to mature ($\gamma > 1$ and $\lambda < 1$). Empirical evidence seems to suggest that the initial learning rate can indeed be quite strong (Argote, 1999; McDonald and Schrattenholzer, 2001). This would suggest that situations can arise in which productivity of vintages that have been introduced some periods ago exceeds productivity of vintages that have been introduced more recently. This possibility was already illustrated in figure 16.1. The implications of such developments of productivity should now be relatively easy to understand. The productivity development, as suggested in figure 16.1, implies that there is a vintage of intermediate age that is characterised by the highest productivity. Older vintages are less productive since their learning-by-using potential has declined (or, in other words, those vintages have matured), whereas newer vintages have not yet matured and experienced the productivity improvements due to learning-by-using. The implications of such developments for the diffusion of new technologies are illustrated in figure 16.4. This figure is comparable to

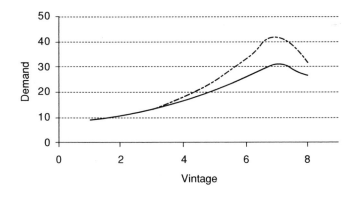

Figure 16.4   The effects of the degree of complementarity between vintages: with learning-by-using

figure 16.3, but now learning-by-using is included.[5] Clearly, new vintages are initially demanded at a relatively limited scale due to their low productivity, but as they improve due to learning-by-using they will be demanded more in order to subsequently be gradually phased out of the production process as the vintage matures and ultimately becomes obsolete. Based upon the similar logic as explained in sub-section 16.4.1, a higher elasticity of substitution will result in fewer vintages being used in the production process and at the same time lead to stronger responses to differences in productivity levels between vintages of different age.

16.5   Conclusion

The widespread adoption and diffusion of new technologies is a lengthy and costly process. In this chapter we developed a vintage model to study the diffusion of new technologies and to explain why diffusion is gradual and firms continue to invest in seemingly inferior technologies. A key characteristic of our model is that vintages are complementary; there are returns to diversity of using different vintages. We have argued that this is a potentially relevant part of the explanation for why firms continue to invest in older technologies when newer ones are available. Furthermore, we showed that this effect is intensified when we take a learning-by-using effect into account. The loss of expertise – gained by using a particular vintage and building up experience – that a firm suffers when switching to a newer vintage provides an extra argument for firms to invest in older vintages. Another important characteristic of the model is the endogenous determination of the number of vintages that is used in the production process. In our analysis we show that the stronger the complementarity between different vintages and the stronger the learning-by-using effect, the longer it takes before firms scrap (seemingly) inferior technologies. Decreased complementarity (or, alternatively, increased competition) in other words speeds up the (average) modernisation of the capital stock.

Clearly, the simple model developed in this chapter could be extended in a number of interesting directions. First, we can allow for the endogenous determination of the rate of learning-by-using and the rate of improvement of new vintages. We refer here to Aghion and Howitt (1996) for such an analysis, drawing a distinction between research (developing new vintages) and development (improving existing vintages). Second,

---

[5] Figure 16.4 is based on a discrete version of the model with the following parametrisation: $\alpha = 0.6$, $w = 1$ (numéraire), $g = 0.05$, $A_0 = 1$, $L = 300$, $L_f = 2$, $\gamma = 1.25$, $a = 0.2$ and $\lambda = 0.5$. The elasticity of substitution is equal to $\varepsilon = 5.5$ in the low-complementarity case and $\varepsilon = 5.25$ in the high-complementarity case. This results in $T = 6$ and $T = 8$, respectively. Details are available upon request from the authors.

we intend to introduce a second factor of production, energy, in order to use the model to shed light on the so-called 'energy-efficiency paradox' referred to in the introduction of this paper (e.g. Jaffe and Stavins, 1994). Finally, we intend to allow for the incomplete depreciation of capital in order to assess the importance of complementarity in understanding the development of the stock of capital of different vintages and the investment behaviour of firms.

REFERENCES

Aghion, P., Dewatripont, M. and Rey, P. (1997). Corporate governance, competition policy and industrial policy. *European Economic Review*, 41: 797–805
(1999). Competition, financial discipline and growth. *Review of Economic Studies*, 66: 825–852
Aghion, P. and Howitt, P. (1996). Research and development in the growth process. *Journal of Economic Growth*, 1: 49–73
Argote, L. (1999). *Organizational Learning: Creating, Retaining and Transferring Knowledge*. Dordrecht, Kluwer
Arrow, K. J. (1962). The economic implications of learning-by-doing. *Review of Economic Studies*, 29: 155–173
Balcer, Y. and Lippman, S. A. (1984). Technological expectations and adoption of improved technology. *Journal of Economic Theory*, 34: 292–318
Canton, E. J. F., de Groot, H. L. F. and Nahuis, R. (2002). Vested interests and resistance to technology adoption. *European Journal of Political Economy*, 18: 631–652
Chari, V. V. and Hopenhayn, H. (1991). Vintage human capital, growth, and the diffusion of new technology. *Journal of Political Economy*, 99: 1142–1165
Davies, S. (1979). *The Diffusion of Process Innovations*. Cambridge, Cambridge University Press
Dixit, A. and Pindyck, R. S. (1994). *Investment under Uncertainty*. Princeton, Princeton University Press
Dixit, A. and Stiglitz, J. E. (1977). Monopolistic competition and optimum product diversity. *American Economic Review*, 67: 297–308
Ethier, W. J. (1982). National and international returns to scale in the modern theory of international trade. *American Economic Review*, 72: 389–405
Farzin, Y. H., Huisman, K. J. M. and Kort, P. M. (1998). Optimal timing of technology adoption. *Journal of Economic Dynamics and Control*, 22: 779–799
Grossman, G. M. and Helpman, E. (1991). *Innovation and Growth in the Global Economy*. Cambridge, MA, MIT Press
Hartog, H. den and Tjan, H. S. (1980). A clay–clay vintage model approach for sectors of industry in the Netherlands. *De Economist*, 128: 129–188
Howarth, R. B. and Andersson, B. (1993). Market barriers to energy efficiency. *Energy Economics*, 15: 262–272
Jaffe, A. B. and Stavins, R. N. (1994). The energy paradox and the diffusion of conservation technology. *Resource and Energy Economics*, 16: 91–122

Jovanovic, B. (1997). Learning and growth, in Kreps, D. M. and Wallis, K. F. (eds.), *Advances in Economics and Econometrics: Theory and Applications*, II. Cambridge, Cambridge University Press

Jovanovic, B. and Lach, S. (1989). Entry, exit, and diffusion with learning by doing. *American Economic Review*, 79: 690–699

Jovanovic, B. and Nyarko, Y. (1994). The Bayesian foundations of learning by doing. NBER Working Paper, 4739

  (1996). Learning by doing and the choice of technology. *Econometrica*, 64: 1299–1310

Kamien, M. I. and Schwartz, N. L. (1972). Timing of innovations under rivalry. *Econometrica*, 40: 43–60

Krusell, P. and Ríos-Rull, J.-V. (1996). Vested interest in a positive theory of stagnation and growth. *Review of Economic Studies*, 63: 301–329

Lucas, R. E. (1988). On the mechanics of economic development. *Journal of Monetary Economics*, 22: 3–42

Malcomson, J. M. (1975). Replacement and the rental value of capital equipment subject to obsolescence. *Journal of Economic Theory*, 10: 24–41

McDonald, A. and Schrattenholzer, L. (2001). Learning rates for energy technologies. *Energy Policy*, 29: 255–261

Meijers, H. (1994). *On the diffusion of technologies in a vintage framework: theoretical considerations and empirical results*. PhD thesis, Maastricht University

Mokyr, J. (1990). *The Lever of Riches: Technological Creativity and Economic Progress*. New York, Oxford University Press

OECD/IEA (2000). *Experience Curves for Energy Technology Policy*. Paris, OECD/IEA

Parente, S. L. (1994). Technology adoption, learning-by-doing, and economic growth. *Journal of Economic Theory*, 63: 246–369

Reinganum, J. F. (1981). On the diffusion of new technology: a game theoretic approach. *Review of Economic Studies*, 48: 395–405

Romer, P. M. (1990). Endogenous technological change. *Journal of Political Economy*, 98: S71–S102

Rosenberg, N. (1976). *Perspectives on Technology*. Cambridge, Cambridge University Press

Spence, A. M. (1984). Cost reduction, competition, and industry performance. *Econometrica*, 52: 101–121

Stokey, N. L. (1988). Learning by doing and the introduction of new goods. *Journal of Political Economy*, 96: 701–717

Sutherland, R. J. (1991). Market barriers to energy-efficiency investments. *Energy Journal*, 12: 15–34

Young, A. (1993a). Invention and bounded learning by doing. *Journal of Political Economy*, 101: 443–472

  (1993b). Substitution and complementarity in endogenous innovation. *Quarterly Journal of Economics*, 108: 775–807

Part VI

Macroeconomics

17 Monopolistic competition and macroeconomics: theory and quantitative implications

Russell W. Cooper

17.1   Motivation

Models with imperfect competition have become central to macroeconomic studies of fluctuations and policy experiments. Many of these papers follow the basic framework of Dixit–Stiglitz (1977) by considering an economy with a large number of differentiated products each produced by a single firm. The success of this framework derives from its:

- simple structure that allows for rich microeconomics (product differentiation) but generates aggregate implications
- source of inefficiency in the aggregate economy and thus a basis for policy intervention
- friction and thus the potential for richer quantitative responses to shocks
- link to price setting and thus money non-neutrality.

The goal of this chapter is to discuss these various elements. The work falls naturally into three parts. We begin with the presentation of a basic theory model of monopolistic competition drawing upon the presentation in Blanchard and Kiyotaki (1987). Section 17.3 constructs a dynamic, stochastic version of this model to study business cycle properties. Section 17.4 focuses on policy implications and section 17.5 concludes.

17.2   A theory structure

Blanchard and Kiyotaki (1987) provides a convenient structure for understanding the various ways in which monopolistic competition models are used in macroeconomics.[1] The addition of imperfect competition of

This chapter was prepared for the SOM conference on the Dixit–Stiglitz model. I am grateful to the organisers for inviting the original paper and to the NSF for providing financial support. I am grateful to Ben Heijdra and conference participants for comments on the original draft of this chapter.

[1] See Blanchard and Kiyotaki (1987) for extensive citations to the existing literature. The edited volume by Dixon and Rankin (1995) illustrates the extent to which this approach has permeated macroeconomics.

this form facilitates an analysis of price-setting behaviour along with an understanding of a basic source of inefficiency through market power.

The Blanchard–Kiyotaki framework introduces monopolistic competition in both the production process and in household preferences. The model is static and thus is used here to illustrate how monopolistic competition is portrayed in macroeconomics. A refined version of the model with capital is then used for quantitative analyses in the following sections.

17.2.1   Firms

Following Blanchard and Kiyotaki, the seller of product $i = 1, 2 \ldots F$, firm i, produces output y_i from a production function given by:

$$y_i = \left(\sum_j N_{ij}^{((\sigma-1)/\sigma)} \right)^{(\sigma/(\sigma-1))}, \tag{17.1}$$

where N_{ij} is the number of units of labour of type $j = 1, 2, \ldots \mathcal{J}$ that is purchased by firm i. The important parameter here is σ which is the elasticity of substitution between the labour inputs. As $\sigma \to \infty$, labour becomes perfectly substitutable in the production process and the market power of the household as suppliers of labour will disappear.

Firms maximise profit taking as given the demand curve for their product and the wage rates for labour (ω_j). Let $R(y_i)$ denote the revenue from producing output level y_i. Of course, revenues depend on the actions of firms in other sectors of the economy but those interactions are ignored in the notation for now. The firm chooses labour inputs to

$$\max R(y_i) - \sum_j \omega_j N_{ij},$$

where output is given by (17.1). The first-order condition for labour of type j is:

$$R'(y_i) \frac{\partial y_i}{\partial N_{ij}} = \omega_j.$$

For labour of types j and k we therefore have:

$$\frac{N_{ij}}{N_{ik}} = \left(\frac{\omega_j}{\omega_k} \right)^{-\sigma}.$$

Hence σ represents the elasticity of substitution between the two types of labour (j, k) for any firm i.

17.2.2 *Households*

In the Blanchard–Kiyotaki model there are $\mathcal{J}$ households who consume goods produced in the economy and supply labour services to the firms. These households provide a unique form of labour service and thus have market power. As consumers, the households act as price takers. Letting I_j represent the total income in some unit of account, the optimisation problem of household j is specified as:

$$\max_{M_j, C_j} (F^{(1/(1-\theta))} C_j)^\gamma (M_j/P)^{(1-\gamma)} - N_j^\beta,$$

where

$$C_j = \left(\sum_i C_{ij}^{((\theta-1)/\theta)} \right)^{(\theta/(\theta-1))} \quad \text{and} \quad P = \left(\frac{1}{F} \sum_i p_i^{(1-\theta)} \right)^{1/(1-\theta)}.$$

In this problem, the household consumes a CES basket of goods, C_j, as well as a non-produced good, M_j.[2] The utility flow from the consumption basket depends on the degree of substitutability between products, indexed by θ and by the number of products, denoted by F. There is a well-defined price index P which also reflects the θ parameter. Finally, household j incurs a disutility of working N_j parameterised by β.

Given income I_j, the demand for product i by household j is simply:

$$C_{ij} = (\gamma I_j / FP) \left(\frac{p_i}{P} \right)^{-\theta}.$$

This demand function is easily explained. Household j allocates a fraction γ of its income to the consumption of the F produced goods. If product prices were all the same, then consumption of each good in real, *per capita* terms would be $(\gamma I_j/FP)$. Of course, the price of product i may not be equal to the index P and the consumption of good i by the household reflects this through the parameter θ. Let $V_j(\bar{p}, I_j)$ be the indirect utility of household j when prices are given by the vector $\bar{p}$ and household income is I_j.

The household income comes from a variety of sources: labour income, endowment of the non-produced good and profits remitted from the firms. That is,

$$I_j = \omega_j N_j + \bar{M}_j + \sum_i \alpha_{ij} \Pi_i,$$

---

[2] While this non-produced good is sometimes called money, note that this is a static economy so that generating an equilibrium with valued fiat money is difficult, particularly when one notes that putting money into the utility function is just a short cut.

where Π_i is the profit flow of firm i and α_{ij} is the shares of firm i held by household j. Note that the household *per se* does not control the firms. Instead, these firms, as noted above, simply maximise profits and these are distributed back to the households.

The households take as given the demand for their labour from the F firms. Of course, this labour demand curve depends on the wage rates set by other households as well. Let $\Xi(N_j)$ be the labour earnings from supplying N_j units of labour time. Then the household chooses the level of employment to maximise:

$$V_j(\bar{p}, \Xi(N_j) + \bar{M}_j + \sum_i \alpha_{ij}\Pi_i) - N_j^{\beta}.$$

17.2.3 Equilibrium and its properties

We consider an equilibrium in which all agents act in a similar manner. This seems quite reasonable for the economy outlined above as long as households are all identical and firms are all identical as well. Thus, we assume that households have the same endowment of the non-produced good ($\bar{M}_j = \bar{M}$ for all j) and $\alpha_{ij} = \alpha$ for all i, j.

The equilibrium is characterised by a wage (ω^*) and a price (p^*) such that:

- if other wage-setters choose ω^* and all sellers set a price of p^*, then the best response of a representative wage setter is to choose ω^* as well
- if other firms set a price of p^* and all wage-setters choose ω^*, then the best response of a representative seller is to choose p^* as well
- the markets for the non-produced good, all labour and all product markets clear.

One can think of this as a Nash equilibrium in which each seller of goods (labour) acts optimally given the prices and wages set by the other agents. This best response behaviour plus a requirement that agents meet demands forthcoming at the announced prices characterises an equilibrium.

Given the structure imposed on the problem, existence of a symmetric Nash equilibrium is not an issue. Further, Blanchard and Kiyotaki demonstrate that the equilibrium is unique. Finally, perhaps not surprisingly, the equilibrium is inefficient, reflecting the market power of sellers of goods and labour. Note, though, that here the inefficiency concerns the level of economic activity: the focus is not on the number of products *per se*.

Interestingly, the inefficiency goes beyond the usual partial equilibrium under-production due to market power. In the general equilibrium model, there are links across the decisions of agents that tend to magnify the inefficient production decisions. Blanchard and Kiyotaki call these 'aggregate demand externalities'. As discussed in Cooper and John (1988), these interactions essentially create a strategic complementarity across the decisions of these agents. In particular, the lower production by other sellers causes the demand curve to shift in for the remaining seller. This low level of demand magnifies the incentive for under-production created by the market power of this single seller.

Using this model, Blanchard and Kiyotaki analyse the effects of money in this economy as well as some of the qualitative properties of the model through comparative static exercises. There results will be discussed in the context of papers that followed their contribution.

17.3   Quantitative analysis: response to technology shocks

While certainly of theoretical interest for all the reasons given by Blanchard and Kiyotaki and the associated literature, for macroeconomists it is important to inquire about the quantitative properties of a model. In particular, the question of whether the monopolistic competition structure is quantitatively significant is not addressed by Blanchard and Kiyotaki. We explore that issue here.[3]

This section provides a number of insights. First, as in Hornstein (1993), the inefficiencies created by product differentiation and market power have very limited quantitative implications for the aggregate economy. The distortion created by imperfect competition, which is largely a level effect, will not influence the statistical properties of the basic model. Second, once we introduce entry and exit, as in Chatterjee and Cooper (1993), we do find that imperfect competition matters: shocks are both magnified and propagated over time due to product space variation.

17.3.1   Fixed product space

Our analysis builds upon Hornstein (1993) and Chatterjee and Cooper (1993) who investigate the basic model of monopolistic competition in the stochastic growth model with capital accumulation. This sub-section describes an economy in which fluctuations are driven by technology shocks where the number of producers and thus the number of products is fixed.

---

[3] This section draws very heavily on Chatterjee and Cooper (1988, 1993) and Chatterjee et al. (1993) and my paper with Andrew John (Cooper and John, 2000). I am grateful to these co-authors for endless discussions on this topic.

As in the static model of monopolistic competition, the model relies on product differentiation. As this is a dynamic economy, each produced good can either be consumed directly or used to produce an investment good which becomes capital in the future. Thus there are two CES functions which, respectively, describe the production of composite consumption and investment goods from the specific commodities. We turn to the details of the optimisation problems now.

Household optimisation

The period t utility of the representative consumer is:

$$u(c_t, l_t),$$

where l_t is leisure time and c_t is a CES aggregate defined by:

$$c_t = \left(\sum_{j=1}^{N_t} c_{jt}^{(\theta-1)/\theta} \right)^{\theta/(\theta-1)}.$$

Here c_{jt} is the consumption of product j in period t and θ parameterises the degree of substitution between products. Let N_t denote the number of products in period t so $j \in \{1, 2, \ldots, N_t\}$.[4]

To simplify the analysis of entry and exit (see below) we assume that investment is undertaken by households and the capital stock is held by them. As in Kiyotaki (1988), investment in period t is a symmetric CES aggregate as well:

$$i_t = \left(\sum_{j=1}^{N_t} i_{jt}^{(\theta-1)/\theta} \right)^{\theta/(\theta-1)}.$$

The use of these two aggregators captures the importance of diversity for consumers as well as producers without straying too far from the traditional one-sector model.[5] From the consumer's side, the CES function represents a home production function in which consumption goods purchased in period t are used to produce a consumption aggregate, c_t. Similarly, the consumer purchases a variety of investment goods which are combined to produce additional capital in the following period.

---

[4] Here there is also no independent term for the love of variety, as in Dixit–Stiglitz (1975, section 4). See the discussion of this issue in Heijdra and van der Ploeg (1996) in the context of Keynesian multipliers and Heijdra (1998). Adding a parameterised version of this effect would certaintly enrich the model.

[5] For simplicity, this specification does not allow us to capture imperfect substitutability within consumer goods as distinct from the degree of substitutability of inputs into the investment process. Adding this feature can generate richer implications, as noted in Chatterjee and Cooper (1993).

The representative household earns income from renting labour and capital to firms and also receives the profits of the firms. Resources are then spent on consumption and investment goods available in that period. Denoting the wage rate as w_t and the rental price of a unit of capital as r_t, the budget constraint within a period is given by:

$$\sum_{j=1}^{N_t} p_{jt}(c_{jt} + i_{jt}) = w_t(1 - l_t) + r_t k_t + \sum_{j=1}^{N_t} \pi_{jt},$$

where p_{jt} is the period t price of good j and prices are all quoted in the unit of account.

Given c_t and i_t, the consumption and investment demand for good j in period t is given by:

$$c_{jt} = \left(\frac{p_{jt}}{p_t}\right)^{-\theta} c_t; \qquad i_{jt} = \left(\frac{p_{jt}}{p_t}\right)^{-\theta} i_t, \tag{17.2}$$

where p_t is a price index given by:

$$p_t = \left(\sum_{j=1}^{N_t} p_{jt}^{(1-\theta)}\right)^{1/(1-\theta)}. \tag{17.3}$$

These conditions for consumer demand, given total consumption expenditures in period t (c_t), are essentially identical to those generated by the static economy. The intertemporal optimisation is, of course, reflected in the allocation of current income between consumption and investment.

These price indexes show the benefit from variety effects: if the price of all types of consumption (investment) goods is the same, then, since θ exceeds 1, the consumption (investment) price index is a decreasing function of N_t. Therefore, an increase in the number of products lowers the cost of consumption and investment relative to leisure. As discussed in detail below, this is the key avenue through which product space variations influence aggregate behaviour.

Using the price indices noted in (17.3), the budget constraint in the consumer's problem can be compactly written as:

$$p_t c_t + p_t i_t = w_t(1 - l_t) + r_t k_t + \sum_{j=1}^{N_t} \pi_{jt}.$$

Using this constraint and ignoring non-negativity constraints, the intratemporal and intertemporal efficiency conditions are:

$$u_l(c_t, l_t)/u_c(c_t, l_t) = w_t/p_t$$

and

$$u_c(c_t, l_t) = \beta u_c(c_{t+1}, l_{t+1}) \left(\frac{r_{t+1}}{p_{t+1}} + (1 - \delta) \right).$$

From the Euler equation, the consumer's loss from reducing the consumption index by a unit in period t and purchasing some of the investment index equals the gain obtained by consuming the proceeds from first renting the capital and then selling the undepreciated capital, at a price of p_{t+1} in the following period.

Firm optimisation

Each of the firms in the economy in period t produces a single, unique good. Since the capital accumulation decision is made by the consumer, firms solve static profit-maximisation problems. Each firm takes factor prices as given but recognises its market power in the commodity market. The production function $Af(n - \bar{n}, k - \bar{k})$, given more explicitly below, is characterised by overhead labour ($\bar{n}$) and overhead capital ($\bar{k}$). The overhead costs are important as they reconcile the existence of market power with no excessive profits on average. Further, they create a form of increasing returns which is dependent upon the size of the markup. Variations in the technology parameter, A, will be a source of fluctuations in the economy.

A representative firm takes as given the demand for its good and the optimisation problem is stated as:

$$\max_{n,k} p(y) Af(n - \bar{n}, k - \bar{k}) - wn - rk,$$

where $p(y)$ is the price per unit (relative to the consumption price index) if y units are produced.[6] The first-order conditions for the firm are:

$$pAf_n(n - \bar{n}, k - \bar{k}) = w\eta$$

and

$$pAf_k(n - \bar{n}, k - \bar{k}) = r\eta,$$

where

$$\eta \equiv \frac{1}{1 - (1/\theta)}$$

is the markup.

---

[6] The indicators for the sector (j) and time (t) have been suppressed to emphasise the fact that this problem pertains to a firm in any sector in any time period.

Note that the markup reflects the parameter determining the degree of substitutability between products (θ). Empirical evidence on the size of markups is then used to estimate θ.[7]

Equilibrium analysis

Since the output of each active firm appears symmetrically in the consumption and investment aggregate, the equilibrium quantity and price of each good will be the same. An equilibrium is then a sequence of consumption, output, employment, investment and prices such that individuals optimise, markets clear and firms earn zero profits (reflecting free entry). Following the analysis of Hornstein, we initially fix the number of products: $N_t = N$ for all t.[8] We return to the case of endogenous product space later.

The conditions for consumer and firm optimisation can be used to eliminate the price, wage and capital-rental terms. Therefore, the conditions of equilibrium reduce to the following equations:

$$u_l(c_t, l_t)/u_c(c_t, l_t) = A_t f_n(n_t - N\bar{n}, k_t - N\bar{k})\Lambda$$

and

$$u_c(c_t, l_t) = \beta u_c(c_{t+1}, l_{t+1})(A_{t+1}\Lambda f_k(n_t - N\bar{n}, k_t - N\bar{k}) + (1 - \delta)),$$

where $\Lambda \equiv N^{1/(\theta-1)}((\theta - 1)/\theta)$. These are the familiar intratemporal and intertemporal efficiency conditions supplemented by the Λ term which reflects the fixed product differentiation and also, through the $(\theta - 1)/\theta$ term, the markup of price over marginal cost. For this economy, the resource constraint reduces to

$$c_t + (k_{t+1} - (1 - \delta)k_t) = A_t N^{1/(\theta-1)} f(n_t - N\bar{n}, k_t - N\bar{k}).$$

Note that this system of equations nests two interesting models. One is the perfectly competitive neoclassical macroeconomic model analysed in King, Plosser and Rebelo (1988a, 1988b). This basic model corresponds to the case where all goods are perfect substitutes: $\theta \to \infty$. The second is

---

[7] This inference though is valid only if there is a single producer of each variety. Otherwise, as discussed in Cooper and John (2000), one must take into account the number of producers as well.

[8] There is a very interesting extension of the framework that comes to light here: allowing multiple producers within a given product line. This is done in theory by d'Aspremont, Dos Santos Ferreira and Gérard-Varet (1995) but the quantitative implications are quite interesting as they break the link between the markups (small) and the substitution between products (larger). See Heijdra (1998) for developments of this extension.

the model explored by Hornstein (1993) where monopolistic competition is present but there is no entry or exit. We turn to a quantitative analysis of those models below.

Quantitative results

Following the approach of King, Plosser and Rebelo (1998), Hornstein (1993) and Chatterjee and Cooper (1993), we can perform a quantitative analysis of this economy. Many aspects of the parameterisation come from the basic neoclassical growth model.

However, there are some added components due to the presence of market power. First, there is the elasticity of substitution within the consumption and investment goods aggregators. Second, there is the determination of the number of products. Third, there is the magnitude of the overhead capital and labour.

We look at three cases characterised by the size of the markup. The first, termed small markups, sets a markup of only 20 per cent, as used, for example, by Rotemberg and Woodford (1992). Here the ratio of production to non-production workers is set at 20 per cent. The second, termed medium markups, follows Hornstein (1993) and sets the markup of price over cost as 50 per cent. This is a fairly conservative estimate of markups given the estimates reported in Hall (1988). The ratio of production to non-production workers (a proxy for the overhead labour ratio) is set at 0.5, consistent with the evidence discussed in Davis and Haltiwanger (1991).[9] The final specification, termed large markups, sets a markup of 2, closer to the upper range of Hall's estimates. For these higher values of markups, the overhead labour and capital ratios are equal to 1. For all of the specification, labour's technology coefficient and labour's share remain at 0.64.

Looking at the response to temporary technology shocks is useful since this provides evidence on the response to shocks and their propagation (table 17.1).[10] The model with perfect competition has many features that we normally associate with aggregate fluctuations: consumption is less volatile than output, investment is more volatile that output and there are positive contemporaneous correlations between key macroeconomic variables and output. However, as the technology shocks which drive the economy are transitory, there is little serial correlation in output fluctuations.

---

[9] This estimate of the overhead labour ratio has the virtue of implying that our estimate of the exponent on the labour input in our production function (0.64) is the same as labour's income share. Note that we are calibrating the overhead capital and labour ratios and not the overhead capital and labour requirements directly.

[10] Details of these calculations appear in Chatterjee and Cooper (1993).

Table 17.1 *Simulated moments for IID technology shocks*

Treatment	Real sd			Corr. with Y			Serial corr.
	c	i	emp	c	i	emp	y
PC[a]	0.17	4.02	0.95	0.34	0.99	0.98	0.003
IC[a]: small markups	0.2	4.0	0.79	0.35	0.99	0.97	0.002
IC: medium markups	0.22	3.9	0.62	0.4	0.99	0.98	0.02
IC: big markups	0.27	3.84	0.46	0.43	0.98	0.96	0.04
IC: entry and exit, small markups	0.35	4.8	1.04	−0.56	0.98	0.98	0.04
IC: entry and exit, big markups	0.7	5.6	1.09	−0.54	0.94	0.97	0.13

Note: [a]PC = perfect competition; IC = imperfect competition.

The addition of monopolistic competition without allowing for variations in the number of products and/or firms over the business cycle slightly increases the volatility of consumption and its correlation with output and somewhat reduces both the volatility of investment and its correlation with output. More importantly, employment fluctuations appear to be dampened by the introduction of monopolistic competition.

Since the analysis is conducted using an approximation around the steady state, one might think initially that adding in market power through markups would have little impact on the time-series properties. In fact, looking at the conditions characterising the equilibrium, the direct effects of market power are captured by the constant terms Λ and $(\theta - 1)$. Since these enter into the total and marginal product terms multiplicatively, one would conjecture that these terms would affect the levels of variables (the usual static distortion) but not other moments.

However, this is not entirely the case. Along with markups the model includes the presence of overhead labour and capital which dampens the response of firms to variations in the state of technology. As in Rotemberg and Woodford (1992) and Hornstein (1993), these overhead inputs are necessary to avoid excessively large profits (relative to observation) at these firms. The presence of these overhead factors introduces a non-linearity into the model that depends on the markups. The economic implication is that the response of employment to technology shocks is muted.

Table 17.2 indicates similar results for the case of serially correlated technology shocks, where the autoregressive coefficient on the technology shock is 0.9. Note again that imperfect competition again dampens the employment response to shocks and increases the variability of consumption.

Table 17.2 *Simulated moments for serially correlated (0.9) technology shocks*

Treatment	Real sd			Corr. with Y			Serial corr.
	c	i	emp	c	i	emp	y
PC[a]	0.69	3.09	0.65	0.77	0.94	0.73	0.90
IC[a]: small markups	0.64	2.79	0.49	0.82	0.91	0.79	0.91
IC: medium markups	0.72	2.46	0.35	0.86	0.89	0.72	0.92
IC: big markups	0.81	2.1	0.22	0.91	0.86	0.6	0.93
IC: entry and exit, medium markups	0.7	2.86	0.58	0.75	0.86	0.88	0.93
IC: entry and exit, big markups	0.86	2.39	0.49	0.84	0.78	0.95	0.95

Note: [a]PC = perfect competition; IC = imperfect competition.

17.3.2   Product space variation

Why didn't imperfect competition matter very much in the above analysis? Intuitively, the answer is that the wedge between prices of consumption and investment goods and the associated marginal costs of production was constant. Thus, market power creates a level effect, some dampening of responses due to the overhead factors but little else. Thus it seems necessary to bring market power to life in a way that creates variations in the degree of market power.

One means of doing so is to allow for entry and exit over the business cycle. Following Chatterjee and Cooper (1993), we allow the number of products (N_t) to vary endogenously. In the absence of entry, profits of firms are highly pro-cyclical so that we would expect the product space to expand in good times and contract in bad times. As we shall see, this acts to both magnify and propagate the shocks.

Relative to these other models, there are a couple of points worth noting. First, the total factor productivity term A_t in the basic model is replaced by the composite term $A_t N_t^{1/(\theta-1)}((\theta - 1)/\theta)$. Since N_t is an endogenous variable, the effective total factor productivity in our model is endogenous and positively related to the number of products through a love of variety effect.

Intuitively, we would expect an increase in A_t to increase the equilibrium number of firms in period t. Hence a given exogenous shock to productivity would be larger in the imperfectly competitive model than in the competitive model; i.e. the imperfectly competitive model magnifies the impact of productivity disturbances.

An increase in total effective factor productivity in period t would also encourage more accumulation of capital which in turn increases the number of firms in future periods. Therefore, even if the original shock to A_t is purely temporary, effective factor productivity will be serially correlated; i.e. the imperfectly competitive model provides additional propagation of productivity disturbances.

Rows 5–6 of table 17.1 shows the results allowing for an endogenous product space. The entry treatment allows potential entrants to respond to profit opportunities in their participation decisions.

The propagation effects of the monopolistically competitive environment with entry and exit are evident from the fact that the serial correlation of output is 0.04 for the small markups case, about 20 times that produced by the competitive economy. This increased serially correlation in output comes from the sources identified in our previous discussion: a temporary technology shock induces a product space expansion which fosters more capital accumulation and, in subsequent periods, the number of products remains above its steady state value.

While not indicated in table 17.1, the standard deviation of output increases substantially in the experiment with endogenous product space variation.[11] This is evidence of the magnification of shocks created by entry and exit.

For the large markup treatment, there is substantially more endogenous propagation of the shocks. The amount of serial correlation in output from the transitory productivity shock is 0.13. There is also substantial serial correlation in consumption (0.31) though none in either investment or employment.

Rows 5–6 of table 17.2 indicate the contribution of product space variation in the case of serially correlated technology shocks. Again the endogenous propagation is apparent.

Thus we find that introducing imperfect competition along with product space variation provides for the magnification and propagation of shocks. The effects of product space variations are particularly apparent when technology shocks are transitory.

17.4   Policy implications

In addition to the quantitative responses outlined above, the monopolistic competition structures provide insights into policy interventions through both fiscal and monetary policy. The presence of market power provides a

---

[11] For perfect competition, $\text{std}(Y) = 0.0181$ and this increases to 0.0236 in the entry case with medium markups.

rationale for these interventions stemming from under-production. Further, the effects of fiscal policy are controversial and a model with market power creates a novel perspective on these policy effects. Finally, with regards to monetary policy, the presence of price-setting behaviour may, in combination with certain adjustment costs, produce a basis for monetary non-neutrality. Relative to existing literature on monetary policy, this framework provides both a reason and a channel for monetary policy.

17.4.1   Fiscal policy

The multiplier with imperfect competition

We begin this discussion with the presentation of a simple static example that builds upon Mankiw (1988). The idea here is to illustrate the ways in which government spending affects private decisions. In doing so, we stress the contribution of imperfect competition.

Suppose that the representative household has preferences over the consumption good (c) and labour time (n) represented by:

$$U(c, n) = \ln(c) + (1/\chi)(1 - n).$$

These preferences, particularly the linearity in leisure, accords with the specification used in our quantitative analysis.[12] The budget constraint of the agent is:

$$c = \omega n + \Pi - T,$$

where ω is the real wage, Π is the flow of real profits that are returned to the household by the firms and T are the taxes paid by the household. Taking these variables as given, the first-order condition for the household's labour supply is simply:

$$n = \chi + \frac{T - \Pi}{\omega} \tag{17.4}$$

and

$$c = \chi\omega.$$

So, with this specification of utility, employment depends on the income generated by the profit flow and taxes while consumption depends solely on the real wage.

There are a small number of producers who have market power as sellers but act as price takers in the factor market. One could imagine many

---

[12] In fact, the specification used in Mankiw (1988) and Startz (1995) in which utility is homogeneous in consumption and leisure does not possess the balanced growth properties needed to match long-run observations, as discussed by King, Plosser and Rebelo (1988).

firms acting as Cournot–Nash imperfect competitors within a sector or a monopolistically competitive structure.[13] Either way, assuming that the production function yields a unit of output per unit of labour input, the equilibrium real wage must satisfy:

$$1 = \eta\omega,$$

where η is the markup. Under perfect competition, $\eta = 1$ and the real wage is unity. If sellers have market power, then the real wage is less than one. Regardless of market power, given the assumption of constant returns to scale in the labour input, the real wage is constant. Thus profits can be expressed as:

$$n(1 - \omega) = n(1 - 1/\eta).$$

Using this in the agent's labour supply equation, and solving yields:

$$n = \omega\chi + T.$$

Note that this completely specifies the equilibrium level of employment and hence output in this economy. That is, the labour supply decision by the representative household implies that employment depends on the real wage and outside income (profits less taxes). Using the optimal behaviour of the firms, profits are proportional to employment and the real wage is fixed. Hence we can solve for the equilibrium level of employment as a function of the exogenously given tax.

Market clearing is satisfied if the level of private consumption (c) plus the level of government spending (G) equals the level of output (n). Using the fact that real profits are proportional to the labour input, the household's budget constraint implies that:

$$c = n - T.$$

Assuming that the government's budget is balanced, ($G = T$), this implies market clearing:

$$c + G = n.$$

Of course, labour market clearing is ensured by the fact that at the real wage given above workers are willing to supply enough labour to produce the goods that are demanded, $c + G$.

With this characterisation of the equilibrium in mind, we are ready to explore the effects of variations in government spending. Using the

---

[13] Cooper and John (2000) contains a more extended example that is closer to the model of monopolistic competition specified above. That paper also includes an extensive discussion of related work. The key, in the end, is a markup set by the seller. Heijdra (1998) provides an explicit dynamic optimising model with monopolistic competition, increasing returns and a government sector.

expression for equilibrium labour input, we find that a unit change in taxes yields a unit change in the labour input and hence in output. In equilibrium, private consumption doesn't change at all. This is independent of the market structure!

What is the channel that connects government spending to the levels of output and employment? The literature expresses these effects in two different ways. First, as in the competitive models, a change in government spending creates a wealth effect that alters labour supply. So, increases in government spending lead to higher taxes (assumed to be lump-sum) and thus increased employment and output. Second, in models of imperfect competition, there are profits which are dependent on the level of economic activity. So, economic expansions induced by government spending create higher profits and thus more spending by households. At the same time, the higher profits induce a reduction in labour supply.

These two effects can be easily seen in (17.4): labour supply is increasing in taxes and falling in profits. From the budget constraint, consumption is falling in taxes and increasing in profits. The fact that employment increases with a tax increase reflects both of these channels: holding profits fixed the change in employment would be $(1/\omega)\Delta G$ and hence larger than the change in government spending. Evidently, the increased profit flow reduces the output and employment response.

Stochastic growth model with government spending shocks and imperfect competition

We now analyse a version of the stochastic growth model with government spending shocks. A convenient starting point in the literature is the contribution of Christiano and Eichenbaum (1992) who introduced government spending shocks into the stochastic growth structure to study the implications of these shocks for the comovements of productivity and employment. The nature of the taxation process is crucial since changes in government spending generate income effects from current and anticipated taxes.

We continue to assume that government purchases are completely irrelevant for agents' optimisation decisions, that all government spending takes the form of expenditure on consumption goods, and that revenues are raised through lump-sum taxation. As emphasised in the literature on government spending shocks, the nature of taxation is critical to determining the types of correlations produced by spending shocks.[14] If, as in our case, taxes are lump-sum, then increases in government spending

---

[14] Burnside, Eichenbaum and Fisher (2000) provide a discussion of these points as well as puzzles concerning the effects of fiscal shocks.

Table 17.3 *IID Government spending shocks*

Treatment	Relative std			Corr. with Y			std(y)/std(g)
	c	i	emp	c	i	emp	y
PC[a]	1.63	36.6	2.23	−0.41	−0.98	0.75	0.021
IC[a]: small markups	1.63	31.9	1.79	−0.30	−0.99	0.7	0.022
IC: big markups	1.5	20.1	0.94	−0.04	−0.98	0.57	0.033

Note: [a]PC = perfect competition; IC = imperfect competition.

Table 17.4 *Serially correlated (0.96) government spending shocks*

Treatment	Relative std			Corr. with Y			std(y)/std(g)
	c	i	emp	c	i	emp	y
PC[a]	0.46	0.60	1.45	−0.98	0.91	0.99	0.179
IC[a]: small markups	0.45	0.51	1.21	−0.98	0.91	0.99	0.176
IC: big markups	0.44	0.33	0.72	−0.97	0.90	0.99	0.1710

Note: [a]PC = perfect competition; IC = imperfect competition.

create increases in employment due to the wealth effects associated with higher taxes. If, in contrast, the government's revenues were raised by proportional taxes, then the response of employment to a government spending shock would be the opposite. Put differently, the direction of shift of the labour supply curve in response to a government spending shock depends on whether these expenditures are financed with lump-sum or proportional taxes on labour income.

Introducing government spending into the stochastic growth model is relatively straightforward. The first-order conditions for the individual remain unchanged. The resource constraint is modified to take into account the fact that some of the resources are flowing to the government. For the quantitative analysis, we set government's steady state share of output at 20 per cent, as in Baxter and King (1993).

Tables 17.3 and 17.4 present the quantitative results for three economies: the model with perfect competition and the two cases of imperfect competition with a fixed number of products. The results in table 17.3 assume an IID process for government spending while those in table 17.4 assume that the government spending shocks are serially correlated at a level of 0.96, as estimated by Christiano and Eichenbaum (1992).

The effects of government spending shocks in the perfectly competitive economy operate through taxes. In particular, under our assumption of zero (or effectively constant) labour income taxes, an increase in government spending leads to an increase in lump-sum taxes and thus a decrease in real wealth. As in the static economy, labour supply increases in response, leading to an increase in output. For the dynamic economy, the wealth effect leads to a reduction in consumption as the agent smooths consumption. Investment falls on impact as part of this process and then recovers as part of the transitional dynamics set in place by the lower capital once the temporary government spending shock is removed.

For the economy with large markups, the same patterns as in the perfectly competitive model reappear. Note that for both of these experiments, the average product of labour (and thus the real wage) falls in response to a government spending shock.

The last column of table 17.3 is an attempt to quantify the magnification of government spending shocks on output. Here we simply compute the relative standard deviation of output to government spending. The results do indicate a slight increase in the relative standard deviation as markups increase.

As indicated in table 17.4 these patterns change once the government spending shock is highly serially correlated (as in the data). Now investment is actually positively correlated with output. Essentially, the persistent shock creates a large wealth effect and thus a larger increase in employment. Since capital and labour are complementary, the increased employment creates an incentive for the accumulation of additional capital.[15] Thus, with sufficiently correlated government spending shocks, investment increases with the shock and there is no crowding out effect. This magnification of the shock is shown by the fact that the standard deviation of output relative to government spending is now much higher.

In terms of the contribution of imperfect competition, there is relatively little differences across the rows except for the expected dampening of the effects of the shocks.[16] However, from the impulse response functions we do see that the average productivity of labour actually increases in the face of a shock: this is a consequence of the large amount of overhead factors in the production function when markups equal 100 per cent.[17]

---

[15] Baxter and King (1993) make a similar point.

[16] Devereux, Head and Lapham (1996) investigate government spending shocks in allowing for product space variation. When these effects are large enough, a government spending increase can lead to increases in consumption, investment, employment and the real wage. Further quantitative analysis of this point, combined with the love-of-variety effects described in Heijdra (1998) would be of considerable interest.

[17] By direct calculation, the average productivity of labour is increasing in the labour input for this parameterisation. However, the steady state is still saddle path stable.

17.4.2 Monetary policy

Models of imperfect competition may also admit novel insights into the desire and implications for monetary policy. Clearly, though, the model *per se* is a real model and thus something must be added to generate money non-neutralities. A common assumption is that it is costly to change prices. This assumption, along with a model of market power in which firms set prices, can generate non-neutralities and implications for the design of monetary policy.

In this section of the chapter we focus on three aspects of this lengthy literature. First, what is the evidence for menu costs in a model with monopolistic competition? Second, what are the implications for non-neutrality? Third, what are the policy implications?

Menu costs: theory and quantitative evidence

Here we consider a partial equilibrium optimisation problem of a single, monopolistically competitive firm which faces a lump-sum cost of changing its price. At the start of each period, a firm would choose to adjust its price or not, recognising the influence of this choice on its future state. One could directly embed this into a dynamic programming problem:

$$v(p, P, M, F) = max[v^N(p, P, M, F), v^A(p, P, M, F)], \text{ where}$$
$$v^N(p, P, M, F) = \pi(p, P, M,) + \beta Ev(p, P', M', F'),$$
$$v^A(p, P, M, F) = max_x \pi(x, P, M,) - F + \beta Ev(x, P', M', F').$$

Here p is the current price for a firm, P is a measure of aggregate prices, M is the stock of money and represents a shock to the firm's level of demand and F represents the cost of price adjustment. Current profits are represented by $\pi(p, P, M,)$ which are a reduced form of the profit flow of a firm in this state. These profits can be based upon a demand function coming from a CES structure, as in (17.2) above.

The first option of the dynamic programming problem entails no price change by the firm so that its price in the next period is also p. The second line allows the firm to optimally choose a new price (x) but the firm pays an adjustment cost of F. To solve this dynamic programming problem requires the firm to know the distribution of exogenous random variables (M) as well as the state-contingent evolution of the aggregate price level, P. This is a big issue since it requires the solution of an equilibrium problem along with the optimisation problem of an individual firm.

One of the interesting elements of this specification is that the firm's cost of adjustment is stochastic. While there might not be time-series variation in this cost, it is not unreasonable to allow it to vary across firms. In fact, following Willis (2000), we will discuss the estimation of the distribution of price adjustment costs.

Willis (2000) provides an empirical study of magazine pricing, building on the work of Cecchetti (1986), using a version of this dynamic optimisation problem. In his formulation, the profit function is

$$\pi = pq - \frac{d}{\gamma} q^{\gamma},$$

where

$$q = (p/P)^{-\theta} (M/P)$$

and θ again parameterises the degree of substitutability between products. Here the real money supply is intended to proxy for total industry demand as in the standard model of monopolistic competition.

Willis (2000) adopts a structural estimation approach is which the key structural parameters are chosen to minimise the distance between simulated and actual moments. The moments chosen for this exercise are regression coefficients from the estimation of a reduced form hazard model of the likelihood of price adjustment at the firm level. Willis finds that:

- the distribution of adjustment costs has a positive mean and is not degenerate
- the average adjustment cost paid is about 4 per cent of revenues
- the estimation of θ implies a markup of about 75 per cent for this industry.

One concern with this approach is that the analysis assumes that the evolution of the index of magazine prices (P) follows the empirical representation from the data. Imposing this evolution on the optimisation problem of the price setter is consistent with rational expectations. But Willis did not ensure that the resulting prices from the optimisation problem would in fact reproduce the time series of the price index. Thus there is an equilibrium link that is not explored in the already complex estimation procedures.

Monetary non-neutrality

Dotsey, King and Wolman (1999) makes progress on this problem by essentially embedding the above optimisation problem into a general equilibrium model. For their economy, Dotsey, King and Wolman argue that there is a maximal time between price changes which creates a finite state space for their analysis: they follow the distribution of firms in each of these states to characterise their equilibrium.

With this structure, they can evaluate a number of monetary policy experiments and compare the properties of their economy to the more traditional, but less convincing, time-dependent rules. Dotsey, King and Wolman find that less persistent money shocks have larger real impacts since most firms will not pay the cost of adjustment given the temporary nature of the shock. Further, their economy displays underlying cycles as part of the transitional dynamics. Finally, their economy also generates some persistence through the evolution of the cross-sectional distribution.

Monetary policy

One of the leading views of monetary policy stems from a commitment problem between a monetary authority and a set of price-setting and/or wage-setting agents. The monetary authority wishes to keep inflation low and unemployment near a target. The key elements are:

- the monetary authority lacks commitment and thus chooses its policy (inflation rate) after the agents' set prices/wages
- unemployment and inflation are determined by a Phillips curve
- there is an inefficiency in the economy so that the level of unemployment that arises if expectations are fulfilled (the so-called Natural Rate of Unemployment or NAIRU) is too high.

As is well known from the contributions of Kydland and Prescott (1977) and others, this game between the monetary authority and private agents creates an inflation bias. Essentially, the monetary authority cannot credibly convince the private sector that it will pursue a zero-inflation policy. This reflects the presence of the inefficiency: if private agents believed that the monetary authority would choose zero inflation, the monetary authority would in fact inflate in order to surprise the private agents and thus reduce unemployment below the natural rate and towards its target.

Despite its prominence in the profession, there are clearly problems with this structure and thus its conclusions. These include:

- the lack of microfoundations for any of the assumed relationships in the model
- the basis for the inefficiency of the natural rate of unemployment
- the absence of an objective function for the monetary authority that can be directly related to the objectives of the agents.

A paper by Ireland (1997) deals with these problems directly. Ireland's model has three key features:

- markets are monopolistically competitive
- sellers must set prices in advance leading to money non-neutrality
- buyers must hold cash-in-advance.

In this model, the basis of inefficiency is clear: it comes from the market power of the seller. Further, the source of money non-neutrality is made explicit by the assumption that prices must be set one period in advance. The fact that households make a portfolio decision with regard to the holding of money balances implies that any inflationary policy can distort the household's choice between goods and leisure. Thus there is a trade-off implicit in this model from inflationary policy. With this structure in mind, the monetary authority sets a policy of money transfers to maximise the lifetime utility of a representative agent. Ireland finds:

• that the optimal policy with commitment is the Friedman rule
• that this allocation may also be a 'reputational equilibrium' without commitment.

17.5   Conclusion

The point of this chapter has been to exhibit the widespread use of the basic model of monopolistic competition in macroeconomics. As described here, the use of models with some form of market power have become standard in macroeconomics. These models provide a powerful source of inefficiency and macroeconomists, looking to study price-setting behaviour, find monopolistic competition a useful structure.

Despite this widespread usage, it is, in the end, not all that clear that imperfect competition matters all that much. From a quantitative perspective, many studies that include market power at reasonable levels do not find much difference in results relative to the competitive model.

REFERENCES

Baxter, M. and King, R. (1993). Fiscal policy in general equilibrium. *American Economic Review*, 83: 315–334
Blanchard, O. and Kiyotaki, N. (1987). Monopolistic competition and the effects of aggregate demand. *American Economic Review*, 77: 647–666
Burnside, C., Eichenbaum, M. and Fisher, J. (2000). Assessing the effects of fiscal shocks. NBER Working Paper, 7459
Cecchetti, S. (1986). The frequency of price adjustment: a study of the news stand prices of magazines. *Journal of Econometrics*, 31: 255–274
   (1993). Entry and exit, product variety and the business cycle. NBER Working Paper, 4562
Christiano, L. and Eichenbaum, M. (1992). Current real business cycle theories and aggregate labor market fluctuations. *American Economic Review*, 82: 430–450
   (1994). Equilibrium selection in imperfectly competitive economies with multiple equilibria. *Economic Journal*, 104: 1106–1123

Cooper, R. and John, A. (1988). Coordinating coordination failures in Keynesian models. *Quarterly Journal of Economics*, 103: 441–463

(2000). Imperfect competition and macroeconomics: theory and quantitative implications. *Cahiers d'Economies Politique*, 37: 289–328

d'Aspremont, C., Dos Santos Ferreira, R. and Gérard-Varet, L.-A. (1995). Market power, coordination failures and endogenous fluctuations, in Dixon, H. D. and Rankin, N. (eds.) *The New Macroeconomics*. Cambridge, Cambridge University Press

Davis, S. J. and Haltiwanger, J. (1991). Wage dispersion between and within US manufacturing plants, 1963–86. *Brookings Papers on Economic Activity, Microeconomics*: 115–180

Devereux, M., Head, A. and Lapham, B. (1996). Monopolistic competition, increasing returns and the effects of government spending. *Journal of Money, Credit, and Banking*, 28: 233–254

Dixit, A. K. and Stiglitz, J. E. (1975). Monopolistic competition and optimum product diversity. Working Paper, 64, February: see chapter 4 in this volume

(1977). Monopolistic competition and optimum product diversity. *American Economic Review*, 67: 297–308

Dixon, H. and Rankin, N. (eds.) (1995). *The New Macroeconomics*. Cambridge, Cambridge University Press

Dotsey, M., King, R. and Wolman, A. L. (1999). State dependent pricing and the general equilibrium dynamics of money and output. *Quarterly Journal of Economics*, 114: 655–690

Hall, R. (1988). The relationship between price and marginal cost in US industry. *Journal of Political Economy*, 96: 921–947

Heijdra, B. (1998). Fiscal policy multipliers: the role of monopolistic competition, scale economies and intertemporal substitution in labor supply. *International Economic Review*, 39: 659–696

Heijdra, B. and F. van der Ploeg (1996). Keynesian multipliers and the cost of public funds under monopolistic competition. *Economic Journal*, 106: 1284–1296

Hornstein, A. (1993). Monopolistic competition, increasing returns to scale and the importance of productivity shocks. *Journal of Monetary Economics*, 31: 299–316

Ireland, P. (1997). Sustainable monetary policies. *Journal of Economic Dynamics and Control*, 22: 87–108

King, R. G., Plosser, C. I. and Rebelo, S. T. (1988a). Production, growth and business cycles: I. The basic neoclassical model. *Journal of Monetary Economics*, 21(2/3): 198–232

(1988b). Production, growth and business cycles: II. New directions. *Journal of Monetary Economics*, 21(2/3): 309–341

Kiyotaki, N. (1988). Multiple expectational equilibria under monopolistic competition. *Quarterly Journal of Economics*, 103: 695–714

Kydland, F. and Prescott, E. (1977). Rules rather than discretion: the inconsistency of optimal plans. *Journal of Political Economy*, 85: 473–491

Mankiw, N. G. (1988). Imperfect competition and the Keynesian cross. *Economics Letters*, 26: 7–13

Rotemberg, J. and Woodford, M. (1992). Oligopolistic pricing and the effects of aggregate demand on economic activity. *Journal of Political Economy*, 100: 1153–1207

Startz, R. (1995). Notes on imperfect competition and New Keynesian Economics, in Dixon, H. D. and Rankin, N. (eds.), *The New Macroeconomics*. Cambridge, Cambridge University Press

Willis, J. (2000). Estimation of adjustment costs in a model of state dependent pricing. PhD dissertation, Boston University

18 Does competition make firms enterprising or defensive?

Jan Boone

18.1 Introduction

The Dixit and Stiglitz (1977) paper provides a tractable way to model competition between firms. This has been used in many areas in economics, such as international trade, industrial organisation and growth theory. This chapter focuses on an application in the intersection of industrial organisation and growth theory: what is the effect of competition on firms' incentives to innovate? In particular, what is the effect of competition on the form of innovation that the firm chooses?

The effect of competition on the amount of innovation by firms has been extensively analysed. Examples are Aghion and Howitt (1992), Aghion, Dewatripont and Rey (1997), Hermalin (1992), Martin (1993) and Schmidt (1997). Instead, this chapter considers the effect of competition on the form of innovation. In particular, I assume that firms can choose between two strategies: a defensive and an enterprising strategy.[1] The 'defensive' strategy keeps a firm's costs low without affecting its competitive position or market share. The 'enterprising' strategy improves a firm's competitive position in the market. The question I want to address is: does a rise in competition make firms more or less enterprising? The two main applications I have in mind here are downsizing and the 'Porter hypothesis', which I discuss in turn.

In the 1980s and 1990s firms invested heavily in downsizing. Examples are National Westminster bank, AT&T, IBM and Scott Paper. In the management literature, downsizing is seen as a defensive strategy. Downsizing mainly cuts labour costs, without making firms more innovative. Moreover, Dougherty and Bowman (1995) and *The Economist* (1995) find

---

[1] The notions of 'defensive' and 'enterprising' investments are also used by economic historians. For instance, Eltis (1996) and Kitson and Michie (1996) argue that Britain's dismal performance in manufacturing since 1960 can be explained by a bias towards defensive investments in the UK. In their terminology 'enterprise' investments increase a firm's output and employment level by increasing the product range or by improving the quality of a firm's products. 'Defensive' investments, on the other hand, cut costs and employment but leave product range and quality unchanged.

that downsizing hinders innovation. A number of people agreed with US Secretary of Labor Robert Reich (1996) that 'downsizing ... has gone way too far'. In other words, these people view downsizing as bad for welfare. Indeed, in the model below where downsizing is formalised as a defensive strategy, it is shown that firms downsize too much. So if a rise in competition makes firms even more defensive, this may be bad for welfare.

It is often CEOs who blame (foreign) competition for their lay-off strategies. The idea being that more competition forces firms to be even more efficient, leaving them no room for more enterprising strategies. On the other hand, Michael Porter scolds US firms for being so defensive and claims that more enterprising investments are more profitable in the long run. In particular, Porter (1990, p. 530) claims that 'American companies, faced with international competitive problems, have chosen bad responses. They have resorted to ... downsizing, cutting overhead ... While this activity has boosted short-term profitability, it has rarely led to competitive advantage. The innovations and upgrading necessary to re-store true competitive advantage have yet to occur.' Interestingly, Porter also makes a connection between international competition and the en-terprising investments needed to create competitive advantage. Porter's idea is that competition should make firms more enterprising.

A similar disagreement appears when considering the effect of com-petition on firms' investments to save the environment. Firms claim that they need to be protected from (foreign) competition in order to be able to invest in environmentally friendly products and production processes. In this claim, they are often joined by environmentalists. The idea is that foreign competition forces firms to lower costs as much as possi-ble. This makes investments in green products and green production technologies all but impossible. In other words, firms need the luxury of (some) monopoly power to invest in such a green way. However, Porter (1998) claims that it is competitive pressure that makes firms enterpris-ing enough to try green solutions to enhance competitive advantage; the so-called 'Porter hypothesis'. This debate about foreign competition and the environment came to a fore in the Seattle protests against the WTO. The claim of the protesters was that globalisation forces firms to be effi-cient and hence leaves no room for investments in the environment. So the question is: who is right? Does competition make firms more enter-prising and green or more defensive?

In a simple formalisation below, I show that firms tend to be too de-fensive from a social point of view. Hence there is reason to worry about the effect of competition on the defensiveness of a firm's strategy.

Related to this is that the economics literature is moving away from Schumpeter's idea that monopoly power is needed to foster innovation. Theoretical papers by, for instance, Aghion, Dewatripont and Rey (1997), Hermalin (1992) and Schmidt (1997) stress the effect that more competition can enhance firms' productivity performance. Empirical studies by Baily and Gersbach (1995), Blundell, Griffith and Van Reenen (1995) and Nickell (1996) seem to confirm these findings. However, these papers do not distinguish between enterprising and defensive strategies. If a rise in competition leads firms to innovate more but in the wrong way, the welfare effects are not unambiguously positive. In the models below, it is the case that the enterprising investments are associated with positive spillover effects, while a defensive strategy like downsizing generates negative externalities. Hence, a social planner would like the firms to become more enterprising. From this it follows that if competition makes firms more defensive, the welfare effects may well be negative.

So what is the effect of competition on a firm's strategy? The main insight of the chapter is that this depends on two things. First, the way in which competition is intensified. Second, on a firm's relative efficiency position in the industry. Both elements are discussed in turn.

There are three ways in which the competition a firm faces can become more intense, and in the Dixit and Stiglitz (1977) framework each of these can be easily parameterised. First, a firm faces a more competitive environment if it faces more opponents. With a CES utility function like $[\int_0^n x_i^\theta \, di]^{1/\theta}$, with $0 < \theta < 1$, where x_i is the output level of firm i, this can be formalised by a rise in n. Second, a firm faces more intense competition if it faces opponents with lower costs. This can be formalised by reducing the marginal cost levels c_j of a firm's opponents. To illustrate, consider the case where domestic firms compete on their own market together with some foreign firms. If the import tariffs that the foreign firms have to pay (per unit of output) are reduced, the domestic firms face more intense competition. Such a reduction in import tariffs can be modelled as a reduction in marginal costs of the foreign firms. Finally, competition becomes more intense if the aggressiveness of interaction between firms increases. This can be modelled as goods becoming closer substitutes, that is θ increases in the utility function above. As goods become closer substitutes, firms have less local monopoly power and become more exposed to each other's actions. Further, as shown below, firms' price cost margins are decreasing in θ. This also suggests that high values of θ can be interpreted as intense competition.

Turning to the effect of competition on a firm's strategy, I show below that a rise in competition through either more firms in the market or more efficient firms in the market always makes a firm more defensive. But if competition becomes more intense through more aggressive interaction between firms, the opposite may happen depending on whether the firm is a leader or laggard in the industry. In particular, a rise in competition makes the most efficient firms in the industry more enterprising, while the same rise in competition makes the least efficient firms more defensive.

This last result reconciles the claims of environmentalists and CEOs blaming globalisation for defensive strategies with the ideas of Porter. It is indeed possible for Porter to give examples of firms which became more enterprising through a rise in competition. These firms were probably leaders in their industry. On the other hand, employees working at firms that are relatively inefficient compared to (foreign) competition are right in fearing lay-offs if competition is further increased. Similarly, relatively inefficient firms in polluting industries will invest less in green products and production processes as competition is increased.

In short, two things are important in assessing whether a rise in (foreign) competition will make (domestic) firms more defensive. First, is the rise in competition a two-way phenomenon? That is, does it make the interaction between firms more aggressive? Or is it one-way in the sense that either more (foreign), competitors can enter the domestic market or that (foreign) competitors get their costs reduced without a similar benefit for the other (domestic) firms? In the one-way case firms become more defensive. In the two-way case, firms become more or less defensive depending on whether they are laggards or leaders in their industry.

The rest of this chapter is organised as follows. Section 18.2 introduces the technology and the three forms of competition. This section formalises defensive and enterprising strategies and derives the effect of competition on the profitability of enterprising strategies. To interpret these results further and to motivate the analysis by introducing welfare considerations, I introduce two simple models. Section 18.3 analyses the effects of competition on strategy in a partial equilibrium model. Section 18.4 extends the analysis to a general equilibrium framework to discuss downsizing. Section 18.5 concludes the paper. The appendix contains the proofs of the results below that are not straightforward to prove.

18.2   The model

In this section, I discuss two building blocks of the model. First, the consumers' utility function and the way firms compete in the product markets are introduced. This determines firms' output levels for given technology. Then, I explain how the technology can be endogenised by introducing enterprising and defensive strategies.

18.2.1 Product markets

Consider an economy with a continuum $[0, 1]$ of identical and infinitely lived agents. An agent derives utility from consuming goods $i \in [0, n]$. Let x_i denote the quantity of good i. Then, the Dixit–Stiglitz utility function of an agent is given by $u(\underline{x}) = [\int_0^n q_i x_i^\theta di]^{1/\theta}$ with $0 < \theta < 1$, where q_i denotes the quality of good i. The quality q_i is endogenously determined by firm i's decisions, discussed below.

Consumers maximise utility subject to a budget constraint. Without loss of generality, I choose total expenditure as numéraire. It is routine to verify that the consumers' maximisation problem with expenditure normalised to 1, that is

$$\max_{\{\underline{x}\}} \left\{ u(\underline{x}) = \left[\int_0^n q_i x_i^\theta di \right]^{1/\theta} \quad \text{subject to} \quad \int_0^n p_i x_i di = 1 \right\}$$

leads to inverse demand functions of the form $p_i(x_i) = q_i A x_i^{-(1-\theta)}$, where

$$A = \left[\int_0^n q_i^{1/(1-\theta)} p_i^{-\theta/(1-\theta)} di \right]^{-(1-\theta)}. \tag{18.1}$$

I assume that each good i is produced by a single firm (also denoted i) and each firm i produces only one good. Firms choose output levels to maximise profits, taking A as given. In other words, there is monopolistic competition in product markets in the sense of Dixit and Stiglitz (1977).

Hence the firm in sector i chooses x_i to solve $\max_{x_i} \{q_i A x_i^{-(1-\theta)} x_i - w x_i\}$, where w denotes the marginal cost of producing output.[2] It follows that

$$x_i = \left(\frac{\theta q_i A}{w} \right)^{1/(1-\theta)} \tag{18.2}$$

$$p_i = \frac{w}{\theta}. \tag{18.3}$$

Notice that each firm's price cost margin equals $(p_i - w)/p_i = 1 - \theta$. Thus a fall in θ leads to a rise in the price cost margin. Therefore, as in Aghion and Howitt (1992), a rise in θ is interpreted as a rise in competition. Substituting the expression for p_i in (18.1) yields

$$A = \left(\frac{w}{\theta} \right)^\theta \left[\int_0^n q_i^{1/(1-\theta)} di \right]^{-(1-\theta)}. \tag{18.4}$$

---

[2] Note that because firms differ in the quality of goods they produce, there is no reason to also introduce heterogeneity in marginal costs. The relevant concept is the margin of value created over marginal costs, that is q_i/w.

For reference below, define s_i as firm i's share in revenue, $s_i \equiv p_i x_i / [\int_0^n p_j x_j dj]$. Because $p_j = w/\theta$ for all firms $j \in [0, n]$, it follows that $s_i = x_i / [\int_0^n x_j dj]$. Then (18.2)–(18.4) imply

$$s_i = \frac{q_i^{1/(1-\theta)}}{\int_0^n q_j^{1/(1-\theta)} dj}. \tag{18.5}$$

With (18.2)–(18.4) utility can be written as

$$u(\underline{x}) = \frac{\theta}{w} \left[\int_0^n q_i^{1/(1-\theta)} di \right]^{(1-\theta)/\theta}. \tag{18.6}$$

Finally, for use below, since total expenditure is equal to 1 and the price of each good equals w/θ, it is the case that

$$\int_0^n x_i di = \frac{\theta}{w}. \tag{18.7}$$

18.2.2   Technology and innovation

In both models below, the firm can choose a combination of fixed costs and quality level of its good. In particular, firm i chooses to which extent its current quality q_i is upgraded to $\gamma_i q_i$. Higher quality, however, is associated with higher fixed costs f_i. In the partial equilibrium model below, the interpretation is that the owner of the firm can exert effort f_i to increase the quality of its product. In the general equilibrium model, the idea is that a firm's strategy either focuses on downsizing, that is cutting fixed labour costs, or on quality improvement. There it is motivated why it is very hard for a firm to pursue both cost-cutting and quality improvements at the same time. In both cases the possible combinations of (γ_i, f_i) for firm i are denoted by the frontier of the innovation possibility set: $\gamma_i = \gamma(f_i)$.

A strategy with low fixed costs f_i and low quality improvements is interpreted as defensive. The firm increases productivity by cutting costs but does not improve its competitive position. An enterprising strategy, however, focuses on enhancing a firm's competitive position by increasing the quality of its product.

In order to find the profit-maximising choice of next period's innovations (γ_i, f_i), use (18.2) and (18.3) to write firm i's profits as

$$\pi(\gamma_i q_i, f_i) = \max_{\{x_i \geq 0\}} \left\{ \gamma_i q_i A x_i^{-(1-\theta)} - w x_i - w_f f_i \right\}$$

$$= \left(\frac{1-\theta}{\theta} \right) w \left(\frac{\theta \gamma_i q_i A}{w} \right)^{1/(1-\theta)} - w_f f_i, \tag{18.8}$$

where w_f is the cost of effort in the partial equilibrium model and w_f equals the wage rate w in the general equilibrium model (see p. 408 below).

Let E_i denote the marginal incentive for firm i to pursue an enterprising strategy, that is $E_i \equiv \partial \pi_i / \partial \gamma_i$. It is routine to verify how firm i's incentive to pursue an enterprising strategy is affected by a change in competition through a rise in the number of i's opponents n, an increase in its opponents' quality level[3] q_j and more aggressive interaction θ between firms. The result can be summarised as follows.

Proposition 1 $\partial E_i / \partial n < 0$; $\partial E_i / \partial q_j < 0$; there exist q^0, q^1 with $\min_i \gamma_i q_i < q^0 < q^1 < \max_i \gamma_i q_i$ such that

$$\frac{\partial E_i}{\partial \theta} \begin{cases} < \\ > \end{cases} 0 \quad \text{if} \quad \gamma_i q_i \begin{cases} < q^0 \\ > q^1 \end{cases}.$$

Before I discuss the interpretation of these results, I note that both the partial equilibrium and the general equilibrium models below show that firms tend to be too defensive from a social point of view. In other words, welfare would be raised if firms became more enterprising. This observation explains why one wants to know the effect of competition on firms' incentives to pursue enterprising strategies.

The interpretation of the first result is that firms become more defensive as the number of their opponents in the market increases. The reason is that upgrading the quality of your good is more profitable the higher your sales are. For a small firm, increasing the quality of its good has almost no effect on profits. For a firm with a high market share increasing quality leads to a big increase in profits. This result is reminiscent of results found by Martin (1993) and Smulders and van de Klundert (1995). They also find that a rise in competition which makes firms smaller tend to reduce their incentive to innovate. This is a way in which economists have formalised Schumpeter's idea that big firms are needed to stimulate R&D and innovation.

The second result shows that if a firm faces more intense competition because its opponents sell higher-quality products, its own incentive to pursue an enterprising strategy is reduced. The intuition is the same as above. As a firm faces opponents with higher quality levels, its own market share is reduced and hence increasing quality becomes less profitable at the margin.

---

[3] Note that the model can also be viewed as one where each firm produces the same quality level, but where marginal costs differ. In particular, in that interpretation firm i's marginal costs equal w/q_i. Hence firm i faces a tougher competitive environment if firm j's quality level is increased, or equivalently if firm j's marginal cost level is reduced.

The last result considers the effect of more aggressive interaction between firms on a firm's incentive to pursue an enterprising strategy. The main result is that this effect is not the same for each firm; it depends on the firm's quality level relative to the quality levels of other firms in the industry. For firms that are lagging behind in quality ($\gamma_i q_i < q^0$) more aggressive interaction between firms makes a defensive strategy more attractive. Meanwhile, the leading firms ($\gamma_i q_i > q^1$) in the industry become more enterprising as the interaction between firms becomes more aggressive. They are spurred on to increase quality by the rise in competition. So increasing competition in this way leads to increasing dominance because the laggards in the industry are pushed back further, while the leaders' advantage increases. The intuition is that the gains from winning are raised for the leaders as competition heats up, while the losers have no chance of winning anyway and hence pursue a defensive strategy which simply reduces costs.

18.3   Partial equilibrium model: appropriability

A simple partial equilibrium model to show that firms under-invest in enterprising strategies is the following. Let $\gamma(f_i)$ denote the maximum quality level that can be achieved for investment f_i in effort by the owner of firm i. I assume that higher effort investments f_i lead to higher quality, but at a decreasing rate, that is $\gamma'(f_i) > 0$ and $\gamma''(f_i) < 0$ for each function $\gamma(f_i)$. Firm i chooses f_i to solve

$$\max_{\{f_i\}} \pi \left[\gamma(f_i)q_i, f_i \right],$$

where the profit function $\pi(\cdot)$ is defined in (18.8) above. The first-order condition for this maximisation problem can be written as

$$E_i \gamma'(f_i) = w_f. \tag{18.9}$$

Clearly, the higher a firm's incentive to pursue enterprising strategies, E_i, the higher its effort and quality levels.

The social planner chooses effort level f_i to maximise utility minus the disutility of effort, that is the socially optimal f_i solves

$$\max_{\{f_i\}} \frac{\theta}{w} \left[\int_0^n \left(\gamma(f_j)q_j \right)^{1/(1-\theta)} dj \right]^{(1-\theta)/\theta} - w_f f_i. \tag{18.10}$$

Let E_i^s denote the social incentive to pursue enterprising investments, that is $E_i^s \equiv \partial u / \partial \gamma_i$ where welfare $u(.)$ is defined in (18.6). Then the first-order condition for the social planner can be written as

$$E_i^s \gamma'(f_i) = w_f. \tag{18.11}$$

It is routine to verify that the social planner wants to be more enterprising than firms are.

Proposition 2 $E_i^s > E_i$.

This explains why one should worry about the effects of competition on the defensiveness of firms' strategies. Firms are too defensive compared to the social optimum. The intuition for this result is the appropriability effect (see for instance Mankiw and Whinston, 1986 and Aghion and Howitt, 1992). By increasing quality firms increase the consumer surplus. But since they appropriate only part of the surplus through profits, their incentive to increase quality is smaller than the social planner's incentive.

This result can be strengthened by assuming that higher-quality products are more friendly for the environment. Porter (1998) gives examples of green technologies and products that have been adopted and created a competitive advantage for firms. One can think of consumers valuing the products of a firm higher because the products are produced in a less polluting way. Alternatively, higher-quality products may be produced using higher-quality inputs which lead to less scrapping and hence are less damaging for the environment. These are the type of enterprising investments that Porter stresses when arguing that green investments can lead to competitive advantage for firms instead of just higher costs.

To model these ideas, one can extend the model above by introducing a negative (environmental) externality of production. Further, the externality created by the production of good i is decreasing in the quality of good i.[4] Firms do not take these externalities into account and hence under-invest in quality.

Turning to Proposition 1, what are the effects of increased competition, for instance through globalisation, on firms' incentives to invest in green products? If the effect of globalisation is the appearance of more foreign firms on the domestic market, one would expect firms to become more defensive and invest less in environmentally friendly products. Similarly, if reductions in import tariffs reduce the marginal costs (or equivalently in the model above increase the quality) of foreign firms, domestic firms become less enterprising. However, more interesting is the effect of globalisation if it causes firms to compete more aggressively on a global market instead of each firm producing on a domestic market protected from foreign competition by trade barriers. In that case, the effect of globalisation depends on a firm's efficiency relative to its foreign competitors. If the domestic firm produces higher quality goods than its competitors,

---

[4] One way to formalise this is to divide the utility in (18.6) by a term which is increasing in total production adjusted for quality, e.g. $\int_0^n (x_j/q_j) dj$.

globalisation will make it even more enterprising. As a result it will invest more in higher-quality green products. If, on the other hand, it produces lower quality goods than its competitors, globalisation will make the firm defensive.

Returning to the discussion in the introduction on whether globalisation makes firms care less about the environment, the model suggests the following arguments. If globalisation is mainly 'one-way' in the sense that it increases the number of foreign firms on the domestic markets or makes these foreign firms more efficient without making domestic firms compete more globally on world markets, then domestic firms become more defensive. However, if the effect of globalisation is that firms become more exposed to each other's actions by competing on a global market, high-quality firms get an additional incentive to upgrade their products. For these firms the fears of environmentalists seem less founded. Yet, for firms with relatively low quality levels it is indeed the case that more (foreign) competition leads to a more defensive strategy.

18.4   General equilibrium model: downsizing

In this section, I analyse a two-period version of the model above. In this case, consumer preferences over these two periods are

$$
\ln\left[\frac{\theta}{w_0}\left[\int_0^n q_{j0}^{1/(1-\theta)}dj\right]^{(1-\theta)/\theta}\right] + \delta\ln\left[\frac{\theta}{w_1}\left[\int_0^n q_{j1}^{1/(1-\theta)}dj\right]^{(1-\theta)/\theta}\right],
$$

(18.12)

where δ is the discount rate, $q_{j0} = q_j$ is the quality of good j in period 0 and $q_{j1} = \gamma_j q_j$ is the quality in period 1. I take firm i's technology (q_{i0}, f_{i0}) in period 0 as given. The firm then decides on its technology (q_{i1}, f_{i1}) for period 1.

Normalising expenditure in each period at 1, we can use the same expressions as above for output, prices, profits, etc.

Each firm produces output using only labour. Firms use both variable and fixed labour. In particular, firm i at time t ($= 0, 1$) uses f_{it} fixed labour and x_{it} variable labour to produce x_{it} units of good i. The fixed-labour component can be interpreted as management. And downsizing is formalised here as reducing this fixed-labour component, $f_{i1} < f_{i0}$. The reason why I interpret lowering fixed costs f_{i1} below the level f_{i0} as downsizing is the following. The downsizing phenomenon involved to a great extent the firing of middle management (see, for instance, Cameron, 1994b; Audretsch, 1995; Sampson, 1995; *Economist*, 1996b). Because the number of middle managers does not vary directly with the amount of output produced, it seems reasonable to model this as a fixed cost.

A firm starting off at time 0 with technology (q_i, f_{i0}) which chooses an innovation (γ_i, f_{i1}) produces at time 1 with technology $(\gamma_i q_i, f_{i1})$. As in the partial equilibrium section on p. 406 above, I assume that the innovation possibility set for firm i can be written as $\gamma(f_{i1})$, with $\gamma' > 0$ and $\gamma'' < 0$. It is possible that the next innovation raises fixed costs compared to the current technology, $f_{i1} > f_{i0}$, to increase quality further. One can think here of hiring additional managers to supervise the quality control process. To capture the idea that some firms have a lot of technological opportunities and are growing while others are in decline, innovation possibility sets differ between firms.

One can think of two ways to interpret the property of the innovation possibility set that $\gamma'(f_i) > 0$. One is that a fixed supply of human capital (which cannot be used in production) is allocated to improve quality or reduce fixed costs. Hence as more human capital is used to raise quality, less human capital is available to reduce fixed costs. To put it another way, human capital can be employed either as management consultants who work to reduce fixed costs or as engineers who work to increase quality.

The other interpretation of $\gamma'(f_i) > 0$ is in terms of the focus of an organisation. The more a firm is focused to increase the quality of next period's product, the less attention can be paid to reducing overhead costs. As Henkoff (1994, p. 32) puts it, 'the problem reflects content clutter, the clangor of conflicting executive directives to cut costs [and] improve quality'. Dougherty and Bowman (1995, p. 30) find that 'downsizing hinders product innovation' because it 'breaks the network of informal relationships used by innovators'. Also, as a survey in the *Wall Street Journal* (6 June 1991) shows, only 9 per cent of firms that downsized in order to improve product quality achieved the desired result.

My chapter does not model why this trade-off exists at the firm level, but looks at the effects of competition on how firms evaluate this trade-off. The social planner takes this trade-off as given in the sense that the innovation possibility sets $\gamma(f_i)$ are the same for the social optimum and the private outcome. It is the choice of the point (γ_i, f_{i1}) that differs.

18.4.1   Labour market

Now I turn to the labour market where the wage and total employment are determined. Using (18.7) total variable labour demand at time $t\ (= 0, 1)$ equals θ/w_t. Then the sum of total variable and fixed labour demand at time t, λ_t^d, equals

$$\lambda_t^d = \int_0^n x_{it}di + \int_0^n f_{it}di = \frac{\theta}{w_t} + f_t, \qquad (18.13)$$

where $f_t \equiv \int_0^n f_{it} di$ equals total fixed-labour demand of all firms i at time t.

The wage w_t is determined in the following way. Assume that agents supply one unit of labour inelastically. In order to introduce unemployment, I assume that the labour market features efficiency wages or labour union bargaining which are modelled here as follows. The wage level depends negatively on the unemployment level $w_t = b(1 - \lambda_t^d)$, with $b'(.) < 0$.

The idea of $b'(.) < 0$ with labour union bargaining is that high unemployment weakens the labour union's bargaining position, thereby leading to lower wage levels. In the Shapiro and Stiglitz (1984) efficiency wage model, a firm offers a high wage to an employee to stop her from shirking. If the employee is found shirking she is fired. When unemployment is high, it will take a fired employee long to find a new job. This is an incentive for the employee not to shirk and hence the firm can offer her a lower wage that still induces the employee to work. Thus both imperfections are captured by the negative relation between wages and unemployment, $w_t = b(1 - \lambda_t^d)$, above.

Lemma 1 shows that a reduction in total fixed-labour cost f_t leads to an increase in unemployment and a reduction in the wage level. Thus, downsizing by firms raises unemployment. Further, an increase in market power, that is a reduction in θ, leads to an increase in unemployment. The intuition is that firms with more monopoly power are inclined to produce less output at a given wage rate. Hence they hire less labour and unemployment is higher. This is the negative static effect of market power on employment as discussed by, for instance Layard, Nickell and Jackman (1991, p. 27). Below, the (dynamic) effect of market power on firms' incentives to downsize and hence on unemployment are analysed.

Lemma 1 $\partial(1 - \lambda_t^d)/\partial f_t < 0$ *and* $\partial w_t/\partial f_t > 0$; $\partial(1 - \lambda_t^d)/\partial\theta < 0$ *and* $\partial w_t/\partial\theta > 0$.

Firms choose (γ_i, f_{i1}) to maximise profits at time 1:

$$f_{i1} = \arg\max_{f_i} \pi[\gamma(f_i)q_i, f_i], \qquad (18.14)$$

where

$$\pi[\gamma(f_i)q_i, f_i] \equiv \left(\frac{1-\theta}{\theta}\right) w_1 \left(\frac{\theta\gamma(f_i)q_i A}{w_1}\right)^{1/(1-\theta)} - w_1 f_i.$$

Because middle managers are paid the same wage as production workers, the parameter w_f in (18.10) equals the wage rate w in this general equilibrium model. Firm i's choice (γ_i, f_{i1}) is described by the following well-known tangency condition.

Lemma 2 *Assuming an interior solution, the private outcome (γ_i, f_{i1}) is determined by*

$$MRS_i^p(\gamma_i, f_{i1}) = \gamma'(f_{i1}) \tag{18.15}$$

where the private marginal rate of substitution is defined as $MRS_i^p(\gamma_i, f_i) \equiv -(\partial\pi/\partial f_i)/(\partial\pi/\partial\gamma_i) = w_1/E_i$.

Note that Lemma 2 gives a necessary condition for (γ_i, f_{i1}) to solve (18.14), but not a sufficient condition. However the results on competition below hold for all solutions to (18.15) so in particular it holds for the optimum.

The social planner chooses f_{i1} to solve

$$\max_{\{f_i\}} \ln\left\{\frac{\theta}{w_1}\left[\int_0^n (\gamma(f_j)q_j)^{1/(1-\theta)}dj\right]^{(1-\theta)/\theta}\right\}, \tag{18.16}$$

where $w_1 = b(1 - [\int_0^n x_{i1}di + \int_0^n f_{i1}di])$.

Lemma 3 *Assuming an interior solution, the social outcome (γ_i, f_{i1}) is determined by*

$$MRS_i^s(\gamma_i, f_{i1}) = \gamma'(f_{i1}) \tag{18.17}$$

where the social marginal rate of substitution is defined as $MRS_i^s(\gamma_i, f_i) \equiv -(\partial u/\partial f_i)/(\partial u/\partial\gamma_i) = (dw_1/df_i)/(w_1 E_i^s)$.

The next result formalises why it is interesting to consider the effect of competition on firms' incentive to downsize.

Proposition 3 $MRS_i^s(\gamma_i, f_i) < MRS_i^p(\gamma_i, f_i)$.

So here, as in section 18.3, we see that firms are less enterprising than the social planner would wish. Firms over-invest in downsizing and under-invest in increasing quality. The intuition for this result follows from two observations. First, as noted above (see Proposition 2), firms under-value a rise in quality because of the appropriability effect. The social planner values a rise in quality to the extent that such a rise increases consumer surplus. Since firms appropriate only part of the consumer surplus as profits, they under-invest in quality. Second, a firm's gain from reducing fixed costs is the wage w_1 that it pays its employees. For the social planner, however, the gain of reducing f_{i1} is the shadow price of labour. Because of the labour market imperfection, due to efficiency wages or labour union bargaining, there is unemployment in equilibrium. In other words, the market wage is above the shadow price of labour. Hence, the social planner has a lower incentive to reduce fixed costs than firms have themselves.

It is straightforward to show that if $MRS_i^p(\gamma_i, f_i)$ is increased for all (γ_i, f_i), then γ_i and f_{i1}, in the solution to (18.14), fall. Similarly, if $MRS_i^s(\gamma_i, f_i)$ is reduced for all (γ_i, f_i), then γ_i and f_{i1} rise.

Before moving back to Proposition 1, I note that it is routine to verify that higher wage levels, either due to higher union bargaining power or due to lower shirking detection probabilities, cause firms to invest more in reducing fixed costs than in quality improvements. The intuition is that higher wages lead to higher cost savings as fixed labour is fired. This result is in line with the finding by Baily, Bartelsman and Haltiwanger (1996, p. 269) that 'downsizing plants had the highest initial real wages'.

Next, in industries where the number of firms increases, the incentive to downsize increases. This happens for two reasons. The first reason is, as shown in Proposition 1, that the incentive to pursue an enterprising strategy E_i is reduced as n rises. The second reason is that as the number of firms n rises, the fixed management costs f_i have to be incurred more often. This raises labour demand and the wage rate. As noted above, a rise in the wage rate causes firms to focus more on downsizing.

If firm i faces a more competitive environment because its opponents' quality levels q_j go up, then firm i downsizes more. This prediction of the model is line with Kang and Shivdasani (1997, p. 61) who find for the USA that 'the likelihood that a firm downsizes is inversely related to firm performance'. The intuition is that as a firm falls behind its opponents in terms of quality, its market share goes down. This reduces the incentive to raise quality, as shown in Proposition 1.

Finally, consider the effect of more aggressive interaction on a firm's incentive to downsize. As competition is increased, firms with below-average quality performance tend to become more defensive and focus more on downsizing. This is due to two reasons. First, as competition is increased firms produce more output and hence (variable) labour demand rises. This rise in labour demand causes a rise in the wage level as shown in Lemma 1. And, as noted earlier, a higher wage level makes reducing fixed-labour costs more profitable. This wage effect holds for all firms. For relatively low-quality firms the wage effect is strengthened by a second effect. As competition rises, high-quality firms increase their market share at the expense of low-quality firms. As low-quality firms' sales fall, they become more defensive. This is the effect described in Proposition 1 for firms with relatively low quality levels.

For high-quality firms the effect of competition on their incentives to invest is ambiguous. On the one hand, the wage effect gives firms a higher incentive to downsize. On the other hand, a rise in competition raises high-quality firms' sales and therefore they become more enterprising and tend to increase quality. Hence a rise in competition has ambiguous effects on high-quality firms' incentives but it unambiguously raises the low-quality firms' incentives to downsize.

This result can be used to interpret the following casual observation. Many CEOs claim that they downsize in response to a rise in competition and that it is downsizing or die (Sloan, 1996). CEOs' claim that the rise in competition brought their firms close to bankruptcy suggests these firms were not market leaders and had a relatively low-quality product. Similarly, as mentioned in the introduction, Porter (1990, p. 530) notes that companies with competitive problems resort to downsizing. The model indeed predicts that a rise in competition increases low-quality firms' incentives to downsize.

18.5   Concluding remarks

In this chapter, I have given a formalisation of the distinction between enterprising and defensive strategies of firms. An example of an enterprising strategy is that a firm creates additional value for its product by producing it in a way that is more friendly to the environment. An example of a defensive strategy is downsizing. Downsizing does increase profits by reducing costs, but it does not create a competitive advantage. Both examples have the feature that firms are too defensive from a social point of view.

The question addressed in this framework is: does a rise in competition make firms more defensive or more enterprising? For instance, many people blame the increased competition caused by globalisation for firms' increased bias towards defensive strategies, that is more downsizing and less investments in green technologies. On the other hand, Michael Porter is the most eloquent defender of the idea that it is precisely competition that forces firms to become more enterprising.

The analysis suggests the following effects of a rise in competition through globalisation. If globalisation is mainly one-way, that is it allows more foreign firms to enter the domestic market or it reduces the marginal costs of these firms without giving comparable advantages for domestic firms on their export markets, then it makes domestic firms more defensive. Such a form of globalisation may be welfare-reducing. However, if globalisation is a two-way process, increasing the aggressiveness of interaction between firms on a global market, then the effect on a firm's strategy depends on the firm's competitive position in the industry. If the firm lags behind other firms in the industry, such a rise in competition makes it more defensive. But if the firm is one of the leaders in its industry, more aggressive interaction with its opponents will make it more enterprising. Hence such a firm will invest less in downsizing and more in the quality of its product due to two-way globalisation.

APPENDIX

Proof of Lemma 1

The first inequality follows from $\partial w_t / \partial f_t = [-b'(.)]/(1 + [-b'(.)]\theta/w_t^2) > 0$, since $b'(1 - \theta/w_t - f_t) < 0$. So an increase in f_t increases the wage rate by reducing unemployment. The second inequality follows from $\partial w_t / \partial \theta = ([-b'(.)]/w_t)/(1 + [-b'(.)]\theta/w_t^2) > 0$.

Proof of Proposition 2

The private incentive to pursue an enterprising strategy is

$$E_i = \frac{\partial \pi_i}{\partial \gamma_i} = \frac{1}{\gamma_i} \frac{(\gamma_i q_i)^{1/(1-\theta)}}{\int_0^n (\gamma_j q_j)^{1/(1-\theta)} dj}.$$

Using a logarithmic transformation of the utility function, the social incentive to pursue an enterprising strategy can be written as

$$E_i^s = \frac{\partial}{\partial \gamma_i} \left(\ln \left[\int_0^n (\gamma_j q_j)^{1/(1-\theta)} dj \right]^{(1-\theta)/\theta} \right)$$

$$= \frac{1}{\theta} \frac{1}{\gamma_i} \frac{(\gamma_i q_i)^{1/(1-\theta)}}{\int_0^n (\gamma_j q_j)^{1/(1-\theta)} dj} = \frac{1}{\theta} E_i.$$

Since θ lies between 0 and 1, we find that $E_i^s > E_i$.

Proof of Proposition 3

Substituting the expressions for E_i^s and E_i derived in the proof of Proposition 2 into the expressions for MRS_i^p and MRS_i^s, the inequality $MRS_i^s < MRS_i^p$ can be written as

$$\frac{\frac{1}{w_1} \frac{dw_1}{df_i}}{\frac{1}{\theta} E_i} < \frac{w_1}{E_i}$$

or equivalently

$$\frac{[-b'(.)] \frac{\theta}{w_1^2}}{1 + [-b'(.)] \frac{\theta}{w_1^2}} < 1$$

which holds because $b'(1 - \theta/w_1 - f_1) < 0$.

REFERENCES

Aghion, Ph., Dewatripont, M. and Rey, P. (1997). Corporate governance, competition policy and industrial policy. *European Economic Review*, 41: 797–805

Aghion, Ph. and Howitt, P. (1992). A model of growth through creative destruction. *Econometrica*, 60: 323–352

Audretsch, D. B. (1995). The innovation, unemployment and competitiveness challenge in Germany. CEPR Discussion Paper, 1152

Baily, M. N., Bartelsman, E. J. and Haltiwanger, J. (1996). Downsizing and productivity growth: myth or reality? *Small Business Economics*, 8: 259–278

Baily, M. N. and Gersbach, H. (1995). Efficiency in manufacturing and the need for global competition. *Brookings Papers: Microeconomics*, 307–358

Cameron, K. S. (1994b). Strategies for successful organizational downsizing. *Human Resource Management*, 33: 189–211

Dixit, A. K. and Stiglitz, J. E. (1977). Monopolistic competition and optimum product diversity. *American Economic Review*, 67: 297–308

Dougherty, D. and Bowman, E. H. (1995). The effects of organizational downsizing on product innovation. *California Management Review*, 37: 28–44

Economist, The (1995). Unthinking shrinking. 9 September, 76

Eltis, W. (1996). How low profitability and weak innovativeness undermines UK industrial growth. *Economic Journal*, 106: 184–195

Henkoff, R. (1994). Getting beyond downsizing. *Fortune*, 10 January, 30–34

Hermalin, B. (1992). The effects of competition on executive behavior. *RAND Journal of Economics*, 23: 350–365

Kang, J. and Shivdasani, A. (1997). Corporate restructuring during performance declines in Japan. *Journal of Financial Economics*, 46: 29–65

Kitson, M. and Michie, J. (1996). Britain's industrial performance since 1960: underinvestment and relative decline. *Economic Journal*, 106: 196–212

Layard, R., Nickell, S. and Jackman, R. (1991). *Unemployment: Macroeconomic Performance and the Labour Market*. Oxford, Oxford University Press

Mankiw, N. G. and Whinston, M. D. (1986). Free entry and social inefficiency. *RAND Journal of Economics*, 17(1): 48–58

Martin, S. (1993). Endogenous firm efficiency in a Cournot principal–agent model. *Journal of Economic Theory*, 59: 445–450

Nickell, S. (1996). Competition and corporate performance. *Journal of Political Economy*, 104: 724–746

Porter, M. E. (1990). *The Competitive Advantage of Nations*. London, Macmillan (1998). *On Competition*. Cambridge, MA, HBS Press

Reich, R. (1996). Has downsizing gone too far? *Challenge*, July–August, 4–10

Sampson, A. (1995). *Company Man: The Rise and Fall of Corporate Life*. London, HarperCollins.

Schmidt, K. M. (1997). Managerial incentives and product market competition. *Review of Economic Studies*, 64: 191–213

Shapiro, C. and Stiglitz, J. E. (1984). Equilibrium unemployment as a worker-discipline device. *American Economic Review*, 74: 433–444

Sloan, A. (1996). The hit men. *Newsweek*, 26 February, 22–26

Smulders, J. and van de Klundert, Th. (1995). Imperfect competition, concentration and growth with firm-specific R&D. *European Economic Review*, 39: 139–160

19   Rationalisation and specialisation
in start-up investment

Christian Keuschnigg

19.1   Introduction

The accumulation of machinery and equipment is one of the prime determinants of productivity growth. As economic historians often argue, the
richest countries were the first in inventing and adopting capital-intensive
production techniques to exploit the productivity gains from rationalisation and mass production. At the same time, equipment investment is
seen as the main vehicle to introduce innovations and to advance the
specialisation and division of labour in industrial production. Unsurpris-
ingly, investment promotion has always been high on the priority list of
policy makers. This interest in encouraging fixed-capital formation implicitly rests on the presumption that private returns fall short of the full
social returns to investment due to some unappropriated spillovers to
the business community. De Long and Summers (1991), for example,
argue along these lines. They found a strong and robust statistical relationship between national rates of machinery and equipment investment
and productivity growth. They claim that the social returns to equipment
investment by far exceed the private returns. Some form of investment
promotion would help. To keep up in high-tech fields, governments are
particularly interested in start-up investment that establishes new firms
and production lines. They are seen as a source of innovative products
and specialised services. Therefore, governments often prefer start-up
subsidies to accelerate the rate of business formation.

We outline an intertemporal equilibrium model with monopolistic
competition among diversified producers and start-up investment in
equipment and machinery. On each machine, a single, differentiated
commodity in the sense of Dixit and Stiglitz (1977) and Ethier (1982) is

I am obliged to seminar participants at the Universities of Cologne, Saarbrücken and
Vienna. I am particularly indebted to G. Grossman, T. Harjes, K. Matsuyama, H.
Schaller, A. Schmutzler and A. Yakita for helpful comments on earlier versions of this
chapter and, in particular, to the seminar participants and discussants at the SOM conference on the Dixit–Stiglitz model. All remaining errors are my own.

assembled. Start-up investment in new workshops introduces new goods and yields productive spillovers to the rest of the economy since the availability of a larger range of tailor-made inputs raises the productivity of final goods production. The novel feature of this model is an endogenously determined trade-off between a more innovative form of investment that addresses specific market niches as opposed to large-scale investment in capital-intensive production techniques that exploits the cost advantages of mass production. Machines may be installed with variable capacity that remains fixed for the rest of their life. They are finitely lived and eventually must be replaced with new equipment which is the next possible date to revise the capacity decision. Aggregate investment reflects the number as well as the size of newly installed machines. Correspondingly, the pre-existing capital stock at each date is composed of different vintages with possibly different capacities. Taking a cross-section of firms, high- and low-cost producers are seen to coexist but heterogeneity in the business sector eventually disappears as old vintages are replaced by new ones of equal capacity in a steady state.[1]

Within this vintage capital framework, the endogenously determined capacity choice is part of the start-up investment decision and determines the direction of aggregate investment. *Intensive* investment adds only a few machines with huge capacities to exploit the cost advantages of mass production. By way of contrast, *extensive* investment opts for a large number of smaller workshops and, thus, contributes to productivity gains from increasing specialisation and division of labour. In view of the productive spillovers of new firms to the rest of the business community, governments often apply start-up subsidies to shift investment towards a more extensive and, thus, more innovative form. Unlike an investment tax credit (ITC) which is proportional to the total value of a project, a subsidy of this type is a fixed amount of cash per project. In order to capture the subsidy more often, investors tend to establish smaller production units. In addition to promoting the level of aggregate investment, it also shifts investment towards a more extensive form. Is the start-up subsidy preferable over a proportional ITC?

The chapter builds on Romer's (1987) model of increasing returns due to specialisation. In this context, Barro and Sala-i-Martin (1992) and Judd (1995) study some public finance aspects of capital income taxation and subsidising capital goods, respectively. Our notion of start-up

---

[1] Recent vintage capital theory is concerned with embodied technological progress where the productive efficiency of new machines increases over time (see Campbell, 1998, Jovanovic, 1998 or Gilchrist and Williams, 1998, for example). In this chapter, all machines are equally productive but the size of the machine determines plant-level productivity by a rationalisation effect.

investment is formally similar to the free entry condition in the R&D-based endogenous growth literature with horizontal product innovation (see Grossman and Helpman, 1991). The dynamic models of monopolistic competition and capital accumulation by Kiyotaki (1988), Hornstein (1993) and Judd (1995) keep the number of firms fixed and, therefore, cannot shed any light on the rate of business formation. Finally, Heijdra (1998) and Broer and Heijdra (1996) study a model of capital accumulation with perfect capital mobility across firms and free entry such that monopoly profits are zero. None of these papers takes account of potential productivity gains from rationalisation of production that may result from setting up new workshops with larger capacities. A start-up subsidy in the context of an endogenous capacity choice has not yet been considered. The novel aspect is that it shifts the direction of investment towards a more extensive and innovative form by accelerating the rate of business formation at the expense of smaller capacity. The gains from increasing specialisation and division of labour must then be weighed against the losses from derationalisation of industrial production.

Much empirical research focused on the interaction between market power, business formation, product diversification and general macroeconomic activity. The main building blocks of the proposed model are well grounded on these findings. Hall (1988) and Domowitz, Hubbard and Petersen (1988), for example, estimate large markups of price over marginal costs in many US industries and find market power to be a pervasive phenomenon. Basu (1995) and Basu and Fernald (1997) report smaller although still significant markups, and report moderate productive spillovers across firms. Davis and Haltiwanger (1990) provide evidence that a large part of macroeconomic fluctuations is associated with business failures and start-ups. Chatterjee and Cooper (1993) report a contemporaneous correlation of 0.54 between detrended real GNP and net business formation. According to Jovanovic (1993), product diversification moves pro-cyclically and increases along with capital accumulation. De Long and Summers (1991) find a strong and robust statistical relationship between national rates of machinery and equipment investment and productivity growth. They conclude that the social returns to equipment investment by far exceed the private returns. This chapter formalises the kind of external economies possibly envisaged by them.

The chapter is divided in five sections. Section 19.2 presents the framework with vintage capital and a detailed account of capacity choice and start-up investment. Section 19.3 discusses the effects of investment promotion in general equilibrium. Section 19.4 identifies market failures and optimal policies by comparing to the social optimum. Section 19.5 briefly summarises the essential results of the chapter.

19.2   The model

This chapter merges models of vintage capital and monopolistic competition and aims to address possible market distortions regarding the direction of investment which could be of a more intensive or extensive nature. To present the framework, this section first introduces preferences, endowments and technology, and then proceeds with the key part of the chapter, i.e. how start-up investment of new workshops determines specialisation and rationalisation of subsequent production.

19.2.1   Consumption

Consumption follows from the intertemporal choices of representative agents. Given an initial stock of assets A_0 and a flow of wage income, households save in order to achieve a preferred flow of future consumption[2] C_s

$$\max \int_0^\infty u(C_s)e^{-\rho s}\,ds \quad s.t. \quad \dot{A} = rA + (w_L - T)/P - C, \qquad A_0 > 0. \tag{19.1}$$

Intertemporal preferences are time-separable with a subjective discount rate equal to ρ. For simplicity, we set the intertemporal elasticity of substitution in consumption equal to unity and specialise to a logarithmic form of instantaneous utility, $u(C) = \ln(C)$. The real interest rate is r, assets A are expressed in terms of the final good. Each agent is endowed with one unit of labour which earns a wage w_L. Government collects a lump-sum tax T. Given a final goods price P, real disposable wage income is $(w_L - T)/P$. In maximising lifetime utility, agents equate the marginal rate of substitution of consumption at any two points in time with the marginal rate of transformation, $\frac{-u'(C_0)}{u'(C_t)}e^{\rho t} = -e^{\int_0^t r_s ds}$, where $u'(C) = \lambda$ denotes marginal utility of income. Differentiating with respect to time yields the usual Euler equation for optimal consumption growth,

$$\dot{C}/C = r - \rho. \tag{19.2}$$

19.2.2   Final goods

The final consumption investment good is composed of N differentiated varieties,

$$D = N^\theta \left[\frac{1}{N} \int_0^N x_j^{1/\beta}\,dj \right]^\beta, \qquad \theta \geq 1, \qquad \beta \equiv \frac{\sigma}{\sigma - 1} \geq 1. \tag{19.3}$$

---

[2] A sub-index refers to time but is suppressed except where it is necessary for clarity.

None of the varieties is essential, each one may easily be substituted by any other with an elasticity of substitution equal to σ. Following Bénassy (1996) and Heijdra (1998), we use the parameter θ to allow for alternative assumptions regarding the strength of the variety effect from introducing new goods. The interpretation of the variety effect as productivity gains from increasing specialisation and division of labour in the sense of Ethier (1982) has recently been given a formal treatment by Weitzman (1994). Setting $\theta = 1$ shuts off any variety effect while a value of $\theta = \beta$ corresponds to the well-known benchmark case introduced by Dixit and Stiglitz (1977) (see Rotemberg and Woodford, 1995, pp. 246–8, for a general discussion of aggregator functions).

Demand D for the final good is for consumption and investment purposes and creates derived demand for specialised intermediate inputs x_j at a total cost $E = \int_0^N p_j x_j dj$ where p_j is the price of brand j. For a given number of inputs, the aggregator function in (19.3) is linear homogeneous. Unit cost is thus given by an exact price index P which, in turn, is equal to the competitive price of the final good,

$$P = N^{\beta-\theta} \left[\int_0^N p_j^{1/(1-\beta)} dj \right]^{1-\beta}. \qquad (19.4)$$

Overall expenditure on intermediates is, thus, $E = PD$. Setting a price p_j for a specialised input results in demand $x_j = N^{(\theta-\beta)/(\beta-1)}(P/p_j)^\sigma D$. Note in particular that the *perceived* own price elasticity of demand is $\sigma = -p_j x'(p_j)/x_j$.

19.2.3   Intermediate goods

Each variety is monopolistically supplied by a specialised producer who operates a single machine. A quantity κ_j of the final good must be acquired to start up a workshop. Production is therefore specialised relative to demand since each new workshop produces a single variety but requires *all* existing varieties embodied in the final good to establish its production facility. In contrast to the strong symmetry assumption in standard monopolistic competition models, we allow for heterogeneity in the business sector that is reflected in different production scale, unit costs and prices. The scale of new production units is determined by the size of investments κ_j in the current period which is explained endogenously as part of the investment decision. The size of older vintages is historically given by previous investments. Once installed, the machine yields a fixed amount of capital services $h_j = h(\kappa_j)$ over its entire lifetime. Henceforth, h_j is called the capacity of the machine. Capacity, or

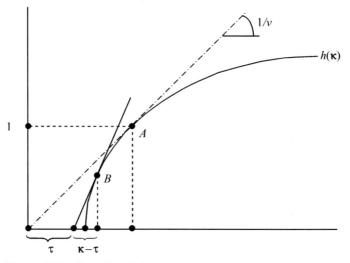

Figure 19.1 Capacity choice

the amount of available capital services, is assumed to increase less than proportionately with the scale of investment, $h'(\kappa) > 0$ and $h''(\kappa) < 0$. A convenient normalisation is $h(1) = 1$ and $h'(1) = 1$. Concavity of the capacity function implies that starting up a workshop requires a fixed installation cost $0 < \kappa_0 < 1$ such that $h(\kappa_0) = 0$ (see figure 19.1). Positive capital services are attained only by an investment scale larger than κ_0. To capture potential savings from mass production, we additionally assume that total factor productivity $A(\kappa_j)$ of the assembly line is increasing and concave in size: $A'(\kappa) > 0$ and $A''(\kappa) < 0$. Thus, we have economies of scale at the plant level which tend to be exhausted with increasing plant size. The subsequent analysis is greatly simplified by parameterising scale economies in a particular way:[3]

$$A(\kappa_j) \equiv h(\kappa_j)^{\beta-1}, \qquad \beta < 2. \tag{19.5}$$

Restricting β to values less than two keeps A concave. Our normalisation of h implies $A(1) = 1$ and $A'(1) = \beta - 1 > 0$. Later on we will emphasise the competitive case of $\sigma = \infty$ and $\beta = \theta = 1$ where all varieties are perfect substitutes, market power is absent and gains from diversification are nil. In that case (19.5) implies that scale economies within the plant are absent as well.

---

[3] Except for scale, assumption (19.5) retains symmetry in production and allows for closed form solutions.

Given capacity and plant productivity, the producer hires labour l_j and assembles a specialised good subject to the technology

$$x_j = A_j y_j, \qquad y_j = F(h_j, l_j) = h_j^{\alpha} l_j^{1-\alpha}. \tag{19.6}$$

The function F is linearly homogeneous in capital and labour services h and l. The overall technology therefore satisfies the replication principle. Doubling factor inputs by adding a second plant of the same size $h(\kappa)$ doubles output. Replication leaves total factor productivity (TFP) unchanged. However, installing a larger machine κ and raising labour input in proportion to capital services boosts TFP and, therefore, raises output more than proportionally. This captures the productivity gains from rationalisation and mass production. Put differently, rationalisation squeezes costs by reducing value added $y = x/A(\kappa)$ per unit of output x.

Each producer specialises in a unique brand and is a monopolist in her market niche. Given capacity, she hires labour in a competitive labour market at a wage rate w_L and maximises current profits subject to (19.6) and a demand curve with a *perceived* own price elasticity equal to σ:

$$\max_{l} \quad p_j x_j - w_L l_j. \tag{19.7}$$

Exploiting market power, she finds it optimal to restrict labour input such that the marginal value product exceeds the wage rate by a markup β: $p_j A_j F_L(h_j, l_j) = \beta w_L$. Denoting the capital/labour ratio by $k_j = h_j/l_j$, we have $x_j = A_j h_j F(k_j, 1)/k_j$ and $F_L = F_L(k_j, 1)$ due to linear homogeneity. Substituting the demand function $p_j = \bar{X}/x_j^{1/\sigma}$ of sub-section 19.2.2 into the optimality condition where $\bar{X}$ is a common shift parameter yields

$$\bar{X}\left[A_j^{1-\sigma} h_j F(k_j, 1)/k_j\right]^{-1/\sigma} F_L(k_j, 1) = \beta w_L.$$

Paying the same wage, producers choose an identical capital/labour ratio $k = h_j/l_j$, since the restriction in (19.5) implies $A_j^{1-\sigma} h_j = 1$. With marginal products being equalised, $p_j A_j$ is uniform across workshops. Consequently, the *imputed* rental rate of capital, $p_j A_j F_K(k, 1) = \beta w_K$, is uniform as well. Except for scale, production is completely symmetric. Labour demand and value added y expand proportionally with installed capacity. Since $F(\cdot)$ is linear homogeneous, it is fully described by unit isoquants. We define unit value-added costs by $\min\{w_K \tilde{h} + w_L \tilde{l} \ s.t. \ F(\tilde{h}, \tilde{l}) \geq 1\}$. Scaling unit inputs $\tilde{h}, \tilde{l}$ by the amount of value-added production gives factor demands consistent with full capacity utilisation,

$$h_j = \tilde{h} y_j, \qquad l_j = \tilde{l} y_j, \qquad y_j = x_j/A_j. \tag{19.8}$$

Multiply the two factor pricing relationships with input quantities. Adding up, applying Euler's theorem on F and using (19.8), we have $p_j A_j F(h_j, l_j) = \beta(w_K \tilde{h} + w_L \tilde{l}) y_j$. It will prove most convenient to choose value-added as the numéraire and normalise prices such that[4] $w_K \tilde{h} + w_L \tilde{l} = 1$. Thus, production decisions result in a constant markup of price over marginal cost $1/A_j$,

$$p_j = \beta / A(\kappa_j). \qquad (19.9)$$

Producers charge identical markups. With $p_j A_j = \beta$, factor prices are $F_L(k, 1) = w_L$ and $F_K(k, 1) = w_K$. Producers may differ with respect to unit costs and output prices since they possibly operate with different capacities. Production is symmetric otherwise. Expanding (19.7) by $w_K h_j$ and using the price normalisation together with (19.8) to write overall factor cost as $w_L l_j + w_K h_j = y_j = x_j / A_j$, we obtain $p_j x_j - w_L l_j = (p_j - A_j^{-1}) x_j + w_K h_j$. Therefore, the overall profit of a workshop is split between pure profits and imputed rental income. Finally, profits depend linearly on installed capacity h_j which is evident from $x_j / A_j = F(h_j, l_j) = h_j f(k)/k$ where $f(k) = F(k, 1)$ is the value-added function in intensive form. It will prove convenient to write pure profits as πh_j where π denotes profits *per unit of capacity*. We obtain

$$p_j x_j - w_L l_j = (\pi + w_K) h_j, \qquad \pi = (\beta - 1) \frac{f(k)}{k}. \qquad (19.10)$$

We summarise. Labour employment depends on a common wage rate and, therefore, results in a uniform capital/labour ratio k irrespective of the size of the workshop. The rental rate w_K as well as the rate of pure profit π *per unit of capacity* are identical as well. Overall cash flow increases linearly with installed capacity. Larger capacity, along with a proportional increase in employment, results in a more than proportional output expansion because a larger scale is associated with higher plant productivity reflecting gains from rationalisation. With lower unit costs, producers are able to cut prices and expand their sales accordingly.

19.2.4   Start-up investment

The start-up investment decision finally determines the size and number of new machines to be added to the pre-existing capital stock and, thereby, resolves an important trade-off between specialisation and rationalisation of subsequent production. Consider a community of identical investors with each one operating a collection of machines. Taking wages as given,

---

[4] While unit value-added costs are equal to one for all workshops, unit costs in terms of output x decline with installed capacity as a result of rationalisation.

the individual agent expects future cash flow from operating a workshop to increase linearly with installed capacity according to (19.10). Capacity remains fixed as long as the machine is used. In real terms, a machine of vintage t with capacity $h_{j,t}$ thus yields income $h_{j,t}(\pi_s + w_{K,s})/P_s$ at some future date $s \geq t$, including imputed rental income plus pure monopoly profits. Equipment deteriorates with age, however, and becomes more accident-prone. Once it breaks down, the plant is closed, production of the product line is discontinued and the cash flow terminates. Machine failure is assumed to occur stochastically with an instantaneous probability equal to δ that is independent across workshops. The expected lifetime of a machine is $1/\delta$ and coincides with the duration of a product cycle. It is further assumed that investors hold a sufficiently large collection of machines, allowing for complete diversification of risk. Investors are thus concerned only with expected values. Given a real interest rate equal to r, the value v *per unit* of capital services reflects the expected present value of marginal future cash flow,

$$v_t = \int_t^\infty \frac{\pi_s + w_{Ks}}{P_s} e^{-\int_t^s (r_u + \delta)du} ds. \tag{19.11}$$

When establishing a new assembly line at date t, the investor decides about how much capacity $h(\kappa_t)$ to install and accordingly invests an amount $\kappa_t > \kappa_0$ of the final good. The government may choose to reduce the private cost of start-up investment by offering an investment tax credit z (ITC). The ITC subsidises *proportionally* the total amount of investment. Alternatively, the government may pay a fixed amount τ irrespective of total investment cost, or it may tax start-up investment if τ is chosen negative. This subsidy, or tax, is in specific rather than ad valorem form. The investor collects it or pays the tax whenever she establishes a new workshop irrespective of the amount of capital actually invested. We call it a start-up or entry subsidy, or a business formation subsidy. Given tax credits, the investor effectively spends $(1 - z)(\kappa - \tau)$ in real terms to start up a new workshop. The overall investment decision must satisfy

$$h'(\kappa_t)v_t = (1 - z), \tag{19.12a}$$
$$h(\kappa_t)v_t \leq (1 - z)(\kappa_t - \tau), \qquad I_t \geq 0. \tag{19.12b}$$

The investor's capacity choice in (19.12a) compares the marginal increase in future returns with the marginal cost of expanding the size of the assembly line. Furthermore, condition (19.12b) implies that investors are willing to establish new workshops as long as the expected present value of marginal future cash flow does not fall short of subsidised start-up costs. In equilibrium, the gross rate of business formation I_t must be positive and the free-entry condition must hold with equality if there is to be some aggregate investment at all. Even if net investment is zero, old assembly lines need to be replaced to prevent a rapid erosion of the economywide capital stock. Combining (19.12a, 19.12b) determines the capacity of a newly established workshop,

$$h(\kappa)/h'(\kappa) = \kappa - \tau. \tag{19.13}$$

Since $h(\kappa)$ is concave, the start-up subsidy τ leads investors to choose a smaller capacity, $\kappa'(\tau) < 0$. Figure 19.1 illustrates this. Our normalisation implies $h(1) = 1 = h'(1)$ at point A. Concavity determines an intersection with the horizontal axis at some κ_0 which is interpreted as a fixed installation or start-up cost. Point A is the optimal solution in the absence of any subsidies where the tangent $h'(\kappa) = 1/v$ according to condition (19.12a) is equal to the line through the origin with slope $h(\kappa)/\kappa = 1/v$ reflecting the free-entry/zero-profit condition (19.12b). Upon inverting it, we have that the present value of marginal cash flow v must not fall short of average cost per unit of capacity, $\kappa/h(\kappa) = v$ if investment is to break even. If a start-up subsidy τ is given, the slope of the tangent at point A would fall short of the slope of the line starting at τ and running through A, $h'(\kappa) = 1/v < h(\kappa)/(\kappa - \tau)$. This inequality reflects profits from further start-up investment since the investor's average cost per unit of capacity is lower than its value, $v > (\kappa - \tau)/h(\kappa)$. With ever more workshops created, the equilibrium value of a machine must fall until profit opportunities vanish at point B where the two lines coincide again.

19.3   General equilibrium

19.3.1   *Aggregation*

Aggregation yields closed form solutions for the final goods price index and real income which greatly simplifies the analysis of intertemporal equilibrium in sub-section 19.3.2. In contrast to the strong symmetry assumption in standard models of monopolistic competition, heterogeneity in the business sector complicates aggregation. Since each level of capacity is associated with a particular scale of production, unit costs and prices may vary across workshops of different vintages if one takes a cross-section of firms at a particular point in time. However, aggregation is simplified by the fact that all producers face the same factor prices and thus state identical unit factor demands. Labour is in fixed supply, $L = 1$. The aggregate capital stock is simply the sum of individual capacities for capital services that have been installed in different workshops. Aggregating (19.8) over all workshops yields economywide resource constraints for labour and capital services,

$$K = \int_0^N h_j\,dj = \tilde{h}Y, \qquad L = \int_0^N l_j\,dj = \tilde{l}Y = 1, \qquad Y = \int_0^N y_j\,dj.$$
$$(19.14)$$

Factor prices are equal to their marginal value added products, $w_L = F_L(h_j, l_j)$. By linear homogeneity, marginal products remain unchanged when inputs are scaled by a common factor Y/y_j. Using (19.8) and (19.14), we have $w_L = F_L(K, L)$, and similarly for w_K. Multiplying (19.14) with factor prices and using the price normalisation $w_L\tilde{l} + w_K\tilde{h} = 1$, one obtains aggregate income at factor cost, $w_L + w_K K = Y$. Invoking Euler's theorem, we may now reconcile the monopolistic production model with the usual notation in neoclassical models of capital accumulation,

$$Y = f(K), \qquad w_K = f'(K), \qquad w_L = f(K) - Kf'(K),$$
$$(19.15)$$

where $f(K)$ is the value-added production function in intensive form. Given labour endowment $L = 1$, the capital/labour ratio is $h_j/l_j = \tilde{h}/\tilde{l} = K$. Having determined income at factor cost, we integrate (19.10) and use (19.14) and (19.15) to compute aggregate profits and the income expenditure identity,

$$E = Y + \pi K = \beta f(K), \qquad \pi = (\beta - 1)\frac{f(K)}{K}, \qquad E = \int_0^N p_j x_j\,dj.$$
$$(19.16)$$

The profit rate π per unit of capital is uniform in the business sector while total profits of a workshop increase linearly with installed capacity.

Next, we investigate the price index to determine real income. In relating plant productivity to capacity as in (19.5), one obtains a simple closed form solution for the price index. Substitute (19.9) into (19.4), use (19.5) and note (19.14) to obtain[5]

$$P = \beta K^{1-\beta} N^{\beta-\theta}. \qquad (19.17)$$

Each machine is used to assemble a unique, specialised product that is a close substitute for other varieties already available. Hence, the number of products is identical to the number of active machines. Investment will affect the price index depending on whether it is intensive or extensive. If investment were only to replace old machines with larger new ones

---

[5] If we didn't restrict the rationalisation effect in (19.5), we could not obtain a closed form solution in K.

without introducing any additional product lines, the rationalisation effect indicated in (19.5) and (19.9) would squeeze the price index which is captured by the exponent of the capital stock. By way of contrast, start-up investment for new workshops contributes to the specialisation and division of labour in industrial production. The average productivity of intermediate inputs in forming the composite final good rises with larger product variety. Reflecting these gains from diversification, the price index falls when the aggregate capital stock expands together with the number of goods. The power of these productivity gains from increased product variety is captured by both stock variables[6] K and N.

The value of final goods production is $E = PD$. Use the income expenditure identity in (19.16) and divide aggregate spending by the price index given in (19.17) to obtain real income or the quantity of the final composite good,

$$D = \frac{\pi K + f(K)}{P} = N^{\theta - \beta} K^{\beta - 1} f(K). \tag{19.18}$$

Demand $x_j = N^{(\theta - \beta)/(\beta - 1)} (P/p_j)^\sigma D$ is the product of real income and unit demand. Substituting (19.5), (19.9) and (19.17), unit demand is $N^{(\theta - \beta)/(\beta - 1)} (P/p_j)^\sigma = N^{\beta - \theta} (h_j/K)^\beta$. It shows how relative prices determine demand structure. A workshop operating with a small scale features high unit costs and prices and, thus, captures only a small share of the market. Consumers tend to substitute away to cheaper mass-produced goods. New suppliers may cut their unit costs by installing larger capacities to rationalise production. With aggregate demand for the composite good given in (19.18), sales of an individual workshop depend on installed capacity according to $x_j = h(\kappa_j)^\beta f(K)/K$. The profit rate $\pi = (p_j - A_j^{-1}) x_j / h_j$ is defined *per unit of capital* and was claimed to be the same for each workshop. To check again, substitute sales and use (19.5) and (19.9) to obtain (19.16).

Capital accumulation reflects turnover in the business sector. Start-up investment expands the aggregate capital stock which otherwise erodes as old equipment wears out. Machine failure is assumed to occur stochastically with an instantaneous probability equal to δ that is independent across workshops. Assume that at date $s < t$, I_s assembly lines have been set up to produce I_s varieties. Due to the law of large numbers, a fraction

---

[6] The influence of the stocks on the price index is most easily understood in case of complete symmetry, $K = hN$, which holds indeed in a stationary equilibrium. (19.17) reduces to $P = \beta h^{1-\beta} N^{-\theta} = p N^{1-\theta}$ where the second equality recognises $p = \beta h^{1-\beta}$ according to (19.5) and (19.9). Intensive investment simply replaces a given number of workshops by larger ones, resulting in lower component prices on account of rationalisation: $\hat{P} = \hat{p} = (1 - \beta)\hat{h}$. Extensive investment adds more workshops of the same size whence the price index declines by $\hat{P} = (1 - \theta)\hat{N}$ on account of gains from specialisation.

δ of all machines in place at any date actually breaks down. Thus, of all the machines installed at date s, only $I_{s,t} = I_s e^{-\delta(t-s)}$ are still working. Goods may similarly be rearranged in order of their date of introduction. Consequently, the interval $[0, N_t]$ is completely divided into sub-intervals $I_{s,t}$ with $N_t = \int_{-\infty}^t I_{s,t} ds$. The number of goods on offer increases or decreases in line with the net rate of business formation $\dot{N}_t = I_t - \delta N_t$ which is the excess of start-ups over plant closures. While I_t new varieties are introduced at date t, the production of a fraction δ of old goods is discontinued because of machine breakdown. Complete symmetry holds within each sub-interval, i.e. machines and products of the same age are identical. Identifying capital goods by their vintages and adding up capacities as in (19.8) gives an alternative expression for the aggregate capital stock,[7]

$$K_t = \int_{-\infty}^t \int_0^{I_{s,t}} h(\kappa_s(j)) dj \, ds = \int_{-\infty}^t h(\kappa_s) I_{s,t} ds,$$

$$\dot{K}_t = h(\kappa_t) I_t - \delta K_t. \tag{19.19}$$

19.3.2   Intertemporal equilibrium

This section analyses the general equilibrium response to tax incentives for investment by deriving and analysing a differential equations system in consumption, capital stock and number of goods. In dynamic equilibrium, accumulated assets must equal the aggregate value of capital, $A = vK$. Differentiating (19.11) with respect to time yields $(r + \delta)v = (\pi + w_K)/P + \dot{v}$. Using this together with (19.19) and (19.12b), $\dot{A} = \dot{v}K + v\dot{K}$ gives a basic no-arbitrage condition $rA = \chi + \dot{A}$ where real dividends $\chi = K(\pi + w_K)/P - (1 - z)(\kappa - \tau)I$ are cash flow less investment outlays. Substituting into (19.1) consolidates the household and investment sectors. With the government budget constraint $T/P = [z(\kappa - \tau) + \tau]I$ and the definition of factor income in (19.15), the aggregate income expenditure identity is $C + \kappa I = (\pi K + Y)/P \equiv D$ where D is *real income* as noted in (19.18). In equilibrium, aggregate monopoly profits, factor income and the price index all depend on the capital stock and the range of currently produced goods. Using the income identity to replace the gross rate of business formation I in the stock flow relationships of subsection 19.3.1, one obtains the aggregate law of motion for the capital

---

[7] Since technology $h(\cdot)$ is uniform and taxes do not discriminate among newly established businesses, (19.12) and (19.13) imply uniform capacity and, therefore, complete symmetry among all *new* workshops. Previously installed machines, however, may be different in size.

stock and the number of goods,

$$\dot{C} = C(r - \rho), \tag{19.20a}$$
$$\dot{K} = (D - C)h(\kappa)/\kappa - \delta K, \tag{19.20b}$$
$$\dot{N} = (D - C)/\kappa - \delta N. \tag{19.20c}$$

Per unit of postponed consumption a number of $1/\kappa$ workshops is started and, thereby, a productive capacity of $h(\kappa)/\kappa$ is added to the capital stock. The first equilibrium condition is the Euler equation in (19.2) where the real interest rate remains to be determined. Investors insist on earning a return on their equipment that at least matches the economywide real interest rate. When government keeps the subsidy rates constant, the value of machines must remain constant as well for investment to be optimal according to (19.12) and (19.13). Consequently, the no-arbitrage condition deriving from (19.11), $(r + \delta)v = (\pi + w_K)/P + \dot{v}$, implies together with (19.12b) an equilibrium real interest rate of [8]

$$r_t = m_t - \delta, \qquad m_t = \frac{h(\kappa)}{(1 - z)(\kappa - \tau)} \frac{\pi_t + w_{Kt}}{P_t}. \tag{19.21}$$

In the appendix, we log linearise the system (19.20) at a stationary state in order to describe the local dynamics. The hat notation indicates percentage changes relative to the initial steady-state position, $\hat{D} \equiv dD/D$, for example. Regarding subsidy rates, we define relative changes $\hat{z} = \frac{dz}{1-z}$ and $\hat{\tau} \equiv \frac{d\tau}{\kappa-\tau}$. The long-run policy effects are easily derived by noting how the real interest rate responds to accumulation of stocks. Referring to (19.15) and (19.16), monopoly profits as a fraction of overall capital income of a workshop amount to $\xi = \frac{\pi}{\pi + w_K} = \frac{\beta - 1}{\beta - 1 + \alpha}$ where $\alpha = Kf'(K)/F(K)$ denotes capital's cost share. According to (19.21), the gross return depends on the profit rate, the imputed rental rate of capital and the price index whence $\hat{m} = \xi\hat{\pi} + (1 - \xi)\hat{w}_K - \hat{P} + \hat{h} + \hat{z} - (\widehat{\kappa - \tau})$. The profit rate in (19.16) is defined per unit of capital and is proportional to average capital productivity. The Cobb–Douglas technology links marginal and average product of capital according to $f'(K) = \alpha f(K)/K$. Thus, both decline with aggregate investment according to $\hat{\pi} = \hat{w}_K = -(1 - \alpha)\hat{K}$. Increasing product diversity and rationalisation squeezes the price index in (19.17) by $\hat{P} = -(\beta - 1)\hat{K} - (\theta - \beta)\hat{N}$. In the benchmark case of $\theta = \beta$, the capital stock is a complete indicator of product diversity. Only if $\theta \neq \beta$, the range of goods enters as a separate stock variable and reflects a diversity effect beyond what is already embodied in the capital stock, and may therefore weaken or strengthen the impact of capital. Finally, the subsidy's effect on capacity choice is

---

[8] In section 19.4 we will find that the optimal τ may be time-dependent. In this case, the interest rate is $r = m - \delta + \dot{v}/v$ where (19.12b) and (19.13) give $\dot{v}/v = -\dot{\tau}/(\kappa - \tau)$.

determined by (19.13), $\hat{\kappa} = -\mu \hat{\tau}$. The elasticity $\mu = -\frac{h'(\kappa)}{\kappa h''(\kappa)}$ reflects the curvature of the installation function $h(\kappa)$. Furthermore, $\hat{h} = \frac{-\kappa\mu}{\kappa-\tau}\hat{\tau}$ and $\widehat{\kappa - \tau} = \hat{h} - \hat{\tau}$. Making the appropriate substitutions, one obtains

$$\hat{m} = -(2 - \beta - \alpha)\hat{K} - (\beta - \theta)\hat{N} + \hat{z} + \hat{\tau}, \qquad 2 - \theta - \alpha > 0. \tag{19.22}$$

In the long run, capacity of new workshops remains constant which fixes the ratio of the two stocks at $K/N = h$, giving $\hat{N} = \hat{K} - \hat{h}$. The parameter restriction ensures that the rate of interest is falling when K and N expand proportionally, and guarantees saddle point stability of the system.[9] Noting that $\hat{m}$ must remain zero for consumption to be stationary in (19.20), the long-run solution for the stocks are obtained as

$$\hat{K}_\infty = \frac{1}{2 - \theta - \alpha}\left[\hat{z} + \hat{\tau} + (\theta - \beta)\frac{\kappa\mu}{\kappa - \tau}\hat{\tau}\right],$$

$$\hat{N}_\infty = \frac{1}{2 - \theta - \alpha}\left[\hat{z} + \hat{\tau} + (\theta - \beta + 2 - \theta - \alpha)\frac{\kappa\mu}{\kappa - \tau}\hat{\tau}\right]. \tag{19.23}$$

Besides incorporating a trade-off between intensive and extensive investment, this framework nests several important models as special cases. With perfect competition, varieties are perfect substitutes in demand ($\beta = \theta = 1$) which leaves room neither for monopoly profits nor for productivity effects from increasing specialisation (see (19.16) and (19.17)). Furthermore, setting β to unity in (19.5) fixes plant productivity to unity as well and excludes productivity gains from rationalisation. Scale economies at the plant level cannot be reconciled with homogeneous goods supplied under perfect competition. In the absence of any markup and any external productivity gains, the price index reduces to unity whence real income is $D = f(K)$ in (19.18). With a zero-profit rate, the gross return in (19.21) is simply proportional to the rental rate $w_K = f'(K)$. Substituting into (19.20) reproduces the standard Ramsey model with perfect competition modified by a capacity decision with (19.20c) being redundant.[10] The terms relating to the scale of investment may

---

[9] Substituting $N = K/h$ into (19.18) with $f(K) = K^\alpha$ gives $D = h^{\beta-\theta}K^{\alpha+\theta-1}$. The condition in (19.22) thus ensures concavity of real income across steady states.

[10] The system becomes

$$\dot{C} = C\left[\frac{\kappa}{(1 - z)(\kappa - \tau)}\frac{h(\kappa)}{\kappa}f'(K) - \delta - \rho\right]$$

and

$$\dot{K} = \frac{h(\kappa)}{\kappa}[f(K) - C] - \delta K,$$

where κ is fixed by (19.13). The dynamics are conveniently analysed with a standard phase diagram.

be interpreted as adjustment costs within the firm. The private capacity decision in (19.13) is determined by concavity of the installation function $h(\kappa)$. If it is not distorted by a start-up subsidy, it maximises the amount of capital services $h(\kappa)/\kappa$ that may be added to the capital stock per unit of postponed consumption. In the absence of any market distortions, investment promotion of any kind would be counterproductive.

As soon as producers are able to differentiate, they obtain market power and contribute to aggregate productivity by either rationalisation or diversification of production. Such external productivity gains translate into increasing returns to scale on the macro level as is evident from (19.18). Both aspects are controlled by the same parameter when intermediate components are aggregated as in Dixit and Stiglitz (1977), $\theta = \beta$. In this case, the capital stock is a sufficient statistic for product diversity whence N does not enter as a separate stock variable. With a CD technology, $f(K) = K^{\alpha}$, the real income function in (19.18) is $D = K^{\alpha+\theta-1}$ and the private return in (19.21) is[11]

$$m = \frac{h(\kappa)}{(\kappa - \tau)(1 - z)} \frac{\alpha + \beta - 1}{\beta} K^{\alpha+\theta-2}.$$

The same condition in (19.22) ensures that the real return to capital keeps falling and $D(K)$ remains concave.[12] With a capital share of a quarter, for example, the critical value of the variety parameter to violate the condition for concavity would be as high as $\theta = 2 - \alpha = 1.75$. This is an unrealistically high value, especially in case of macroeconomic averages. In principle, however, the external economies may be strong enough to give rise to sustained 'growth based on increasing returns due to specialization' (Romer, 1987). In a sense, the model provides a microfoundation for AK-type endogenous growth models where production is linear in the accumulating factor. In the limiting case where $\beta = \theta$ exactly equals its upper bound $2 - \alpha$, aggregate real income is indeed linear in capital, $D = K$ while the gross return is fixed at

$$m = \frac{h(\kappa)}{(\kappa - \tau)(1 - z)\beta}.$$

---

[11] Again, the dynamics reduce to a system in K and C given by (19.20) where (19.20c) becomes redundant. It may easily be analysed with the help of a phase diagram.

[12] The stability condition is on θ rather than β. In the long run, $N = K/h$, and the price index may be written as $P = (\beta h^{1-\beta})(K/h)^{1-\theta}$. With $p = \beta h^{1-\beta}$ according to (19.5) and (19.9), this corresponds with the stationary version of (19.4). The convexification of real income arises because the capital stock reduces the price index via the variety effect while the rationalisation effect on the price index associated with β is imposed exogenously by policy and does not vary with K.

Growth is sustained when $m - \delta$ exceeds the rate of discount ρ. We argue, however, that this limiting case seems rather implausible. Empirical research such as Basu and Fernald (1997) implies that productive spillovers across firms would surely not be so large as to violate our condition.

In general, when the productivity gains from diversification and rationalisation are parameterised differently ($\theta \neq \beta$), the system is three-dimensional where two of the state variables are predetermined and one is forward-looking. The appendix (p. 439) shows that the condition noted in (19.22) guarantees saddle-point stability. Given that the two stable roots are of different magnitude, the transitional solution has some potential for non-monotonicity that may result in U-shaped or hump-shaped trajectories. The long-run solution in (19.23) shows that an ITC raises both stocks proportionally while a start-up subsidy boosts the number of workshops more than proportionally since $\hat{N} = \hat{K} - \hat{h}$. An ITC leaves the scale of investment κ and the size of workshops $h(\kappa)$ unaffected while the start-up subsidy reduces scale by $\hat{\kappa} = -\mu\hat{\tau}$ and capacity per workshop by

$$\hat{h} = -\frac{\kappa\mu}{\kappa - \tau}\hat{\tau}.$$

The number of goods then expands relatively more than aggregate capacity.

19.4   Social optimum

If at all, how must taxes or subsidies be tailored to restore appropriate incentives such that private agents arrive at socially optimal choices? To identify the nature of possible distortions, this section compares the market equilibrium with the socially optimal allocation. In equating the marginal value products of labour in all places, the planner allocates workers across machines in the same way as the private economy. Consequently, maximum real income is given by (19.18). The intertemporal part determines how real income should be spent on consumption and investment. The pre-existing capital stock is installed in N different machines with each one yielding capital services of $h_j = h(\kappa_j)$. To find the optimal rate of business formation and optimal capacity, the planner maximises (19.1) subject to the aggregate resource constraint $C = D - \kappa I$ and the laws of motion for K and N noted in (19.19). From the Hamiltonian $u[D(K, N) - \kappa I] + \lambda_K[h(\kappa)I - \delta K] + \lambda_N[I - \delta N]$, we deduce necessary conditions

$$\kappa u'(C) = h(\kappa)\lambda_K + \lambda_N, \tag{19.24a}$$

$$u'(C) = \lambda_K h'(\kappa), \tag{19.24b}$$

$$\dot{\lambda}_K = (\rho + \delta)\lambda_K - u'(C)D_K, \tag{19.24c}$$

$$\dot{\lambda}_N = (\rho + \delta)\lambda_N - u'(C)D_N. \tag{19.24d}$$

Solving the costate equations yields shadow prices $\lambda_{K,t} = \int_t^\infty u'(C_s)D_{K,s}e^{-(\rho+\delta)(s-t)}ds$ and similarly $\lambda_{N,t}$. Dividing by $u'(C_t)$, we express shadow prices in units of income. Replacing the marginal rate of intertemporal substitution by

$$\frac{u'(C_s)}{u'(C_t)}e^{-\rho(s-t)} = e^{-\int_t^s r_u du},$$

we obtain

$$\frac{\lambda_{K,t}}{u'(C_t)} = \int_t^\infty D_{K,s}e^{-\int_t^s (r_u+\delta)du}ds,$$

$$\frac{\lambda_{N,t}}{u'(C_t)} = \int_t^\infty D_{N,s}e^{-\int_t^s (r_u+\delta)du}ds. \tag{19.25}$$

Before we derive optimal policies, we need to clarify how the returns of capacity and variety are determined by the derivatives of real income D_K and D_N. Aggregate investment, or net business formation, reflects the size and number of newly established workshops, $dK = hdI + Ih'(\kappa)d\kappa$ and $dN = dI$. Investment contributes to real income via three channels: it augments factor income (wages and imputed rental income) and monopoly profits but may also boost aggregate productivity, depending on whether it is of a more extensive or intensive nature. *Extensive* investment establishes a larger number I of workshops with given capacity, $dN = dI$ and $dK = hdI$. In addition to the income effects from larger capital services, it generates income due to productivity gains from increasing specialisation and division of labour in industrial production. By way of contrast, *intensive* investment aims at exploiting scale economies by replacing old vintages with larger capacities rather than setting up a larger number of new workshops,[13] $dN = 0$ and $dK = Ih'(\kappa)d\kappa$. The capital stock expands but the degree of diversification remains constant. In addition to larger factor income and monopoly profits, real income is boosted by the productivity gains from rationalisation due to mass production. Depending on the nature of investment, the productivity effects

---

[13] In this case, $I = \delta N$. The capacity decision relates to new replacement investment since the capacity of previously installed machines cannot be revised any more.

in the final goods sector are reflected in a lower price index (19.17) according to

$$\frac{1}{P}dP = (\beta - \theta)\frac{1}{N}dI + (1 - \beta)\frac{1}{K}[hdI + Ih'(\kappa)d\kappa]. \qquad (19.26)$$

19.4.1 Investment at the intensive margin

Private investors take the price index and the profit rate as given because they perceive themselves as too small to have any impact. The social planner, however, acts on behalf of the total community and coordinates individual investment projects. She recognises the dependence of the price index and profit rate on the level of aggregate investment. Consider first intensive investment, $dK = Ih'(\kappa)d\kappa$. To see how the social return deviates from the private one, we compute the derivative of real income in (19.18) subject to the profit rate in (19.16) and the appropriate version of the productivity effect in (19.26),

$$D_K = \frac{w_K + \pi}{P} + \frac{1}{P}\left[K\frac{\partial \pi}{\partial K} - (f + \pi K)\frac{1}{P}\frac{\partial P}{\partial K}\right] = \beta\frac{w_K + \pi}{P}.$$

$$(19.27)$$

From a social perspective, one may distinguish four distinct effects of intensive investment. First, it marginally increases value-added income by $f'(K) = w_K$. This *value-added* effect corresponds to the competitive remuneration of capital. A second benefit is the *profit creation* effect π per unit of capacity that is added to the capital stock. It results from the profits of newly established businesses. The first part of (19.27) is the privately perceived return to capacity that would obtain in the laissez-faire equilibrium as noted in (19.11). While the private investor fully takes account of the value-added and profit creation effects, she takes the profit rate and the price index as given. Consequently, she fails to recognise that she contributes to a higher aggregate capital stock as well, affecting the other investors' returns. All other investors act the same way which feeds back on her own incentives. The second term in (19.27) reflects the spillovers from investments which are ignored by the individual agent but are internalised by the social planner. A third consequence external to the private investor is that a higher capital stock erodes the sales and the profit rate of existing producers, see (19.16). This *profit destruction* effect is equal to $K\frac{\partial \pi}{\partial K} = (\beta - 1)w_K - \pi$. Finally, in replacing old vintages with larger capacity, intensive investment enables producers to rationalise production and, thereby, cut unit costs and prices. This *rationalisation* effect raises productivity of the final goods sector and is reflected in a lower price index. For this reason, real income rises by $-(f + \pi K)\frac{1}{P}\frac{\partial P}{\partial K} = (\beta - 1)\pi + \pi$ where the increase in the capital stock affects the price index only through the term $dK = Ih'(\kappa)d\kappa$ in (19.26). The rationalisation and profit destruction effects are consolidated to give a total external benefit equal to $(\beta - 1)(w_K + \pi)$. Consequently, the external returns to intensive investment are $(\beta - 1)$ times the perceived private returns. The social return thus exceeds the private one by a factor β precisely as in (19.27).[14]

External benefits could be internalised by a sufficiently generous investment incentive such that private decisions indeed replicate the social optimum. Socially optimal investment at the intensive margin satisfies (19.24b) combined with (19.25),

$$1 = h'(\kappa_t) \int_t^\infty D_{K,s} e^{-\int_t^s (r_u + \delta)du} ds = h'(\kappa_t)v_t\beta. \qquad (19.28)$$

The last equality uses (19.27) together with (19.11) which indicates the private evaluation of a unit of capacity. Comparing with (19.12a), socially optimal investment at the intensive margin is supported in decentralised market equilibrium if the investment tax credit is set to appropriately reward for the external benefits,

$$(1 - z^*)\beta = 1 \qquad \Leftrightarrow \qquad z^* = 1/\sigma. \qquad (19.29)$$

19.4.2   *Investment at the extensive margin*

Investment at the extensive margin augments both aggregate capacity, $dK = hdI$, and the range of intermediate inputs, $dN = dI$. A higher rate of business formation boosts real income by adding capacity in the extensive direction exactly as in (19.27) except that the productivity gains are due to a *variety* rather than a rationalisation effect. Evaluating the term relating to $dK = hdI$ in (19.26) and substituting this term into (19.27) shows that this variety effect raises real income by $-[f + \pi K]\frac{1}{P}\frac{\partial P}{\partial K} = (\beta - 1)\pi + \pi$ which corresponds to the gains from rationalisation noted previously. Adding a unit of capacity therefore boosts real income by exactly the same amount irrespective of whether it is invested at the extensive or intensive margin. The external benefits from extensive investment, however, are due to productivity gains from increasing specialisation and division of labour rather than rationalisation of production. Consolidating with an identical profit destruction effect, the external effects are of the same size as noted in (19.27). Consequently,

---

[14] The wedge between social and private returns would vanish if aggregate demand and productivity spillovers were absent, $\frac{\partial \pi}{\partial K} = \frac{\partial P}{\partial K} = 0$.

the ITC noted in (19.29) fully rewards for the unappropriated gains from business formation in so far as they arise from an expansion in K. The physical capital stock, however, is not a complete indicator of the gains from specialisation. Extensive investment creates a further differential variety effect which may either augment or reduce the productivity gains associated with K. The full gains from specialisation and division of labour noted in (19.26) include a term $dI = dN$ which boosts real income according to

$$D_N = -\frac{f + \pi K}{P} \frac{1}{P} \frac{\partial P}{\partial N} = (\theta - \beta)\frac{D}{N}. \tag{19.30}$$

The social benefits of extensive investment arise from both higher capacity and deeper diversification and specialisation in production. Establishing an additional workshop adds another product line and augments the capital stock by h units, creating value equal to $h\lambda_K$ plus λ_N according to (19.24a). The shadow prices reflect the future gains in real income indicated by (19.27) and (19.30). The optimal rate of business formation weighs these gains against the cost of postponed consumption today. Rearranging, we have

$$\frac{\lambda_N}{u'(C)} = \kappa - h(\kappa)\frac{\lambda_K}{u'(C)}. \tag{19.31}$$

According to (19.25), (19.28) and (19.29), the optimal ITC equates

$$\frac{\lambda_K}{u'(C)} = \frac{v}{1 - z^*}.$$

Consequently, condition (19.31) is replicated by private investors in (19.12b) if extensive investment receives a differential tax or subsidy on top of z^* equal to

$$\tau_t^* = \frac{\lambda_N}{u'(C)} = \int_t^\infty D_{N,s} e^{-\int_t^s (r_u + \delta)du} ds. \tag{19.32}$$

Dixit and Stiglitz (1977) restricted the gains from specialisation by $\theta = \beta$. In this benchmark case, the planner puts no value on variety beyond what is already attained by K, $D_N = \lambda_N = 0$. Private capacity choice is optimal, $\tau^* = 0$. The rate of business formation is sufficiently promoted by the ITC. In case of $\theta < \beta$, the gains from specialisation are comparatively weak whence a tax $\tau^* < 0$ on start-up investment is advised. The tax induces investors to choose larger capacity at the expense of variety and thereby shifts investment towards a more intensive nature to fully exploit the gains from rationalisation due to mass-production. On the other hand, if $\theta > \beta$, the derivative D_N is positive indicating rather strong gains from specialisation and division of labour that are external to individual investors. A special subsidy $\tau^* > 0$ on start-up investment is advised to shift investment towards a more extensive nature at the expense of scale. The subsidy rewards for unappropriated benefits of business formation that are not yet compensated by z^*.

In general, the optimal subsidy or tax on start-up investment varies with time.[15] While the system describing the transitional solution of the social optimum and the associated policy in (19.32) is rather intractable, one may easily characterise the optimal policy in the long run. Multiplying (19.24b) by κ and equating with (19.24a) gives $\kappa^* h'(\kappa^*) - h(\kappa^*) = \lambda_N/\lambda_K$ where the stationary versions of (19.24c, d) are used to replace the ratio

$$\frac{\lambda_N}{\lambda_K} = \frac{D_N}{D_K} = \frac{\theta - \beta}{\alpha + \beta - 1} \frac{K}{N}.$$

The laws of motion dictate $K/N = h$ in the long run. In a stationary state, the socially optimal scale of investment is therefore independent of stocks and is implemented by a tax or subsidy satisfying (19.13), $\tau^* h'(\kappa^*) = \kappa^* h'(\kappa^*) - h(\kappa^*) = \frac{\theta - \beta}{\alpha + \beta - 1} h(\kappa^*)$. We have

$$\theta \gtrless \beta \quad \Leftrightarrow \quad \kappa^* \lessgtr 1 \quad \Leftrightarrow \quad \tau^* \gtrless 0. \tag{19.33}$$

19.5   Conclusions

In a monopolistically competitive economy, start-up investment in new production units yields productivity gains resulting from either rationalisation or increasing diversification of production. Since production is specialised relative to demand, such gains are external to the individual investor. Each producer specialises in a single component good but requires the entire range of specialised inputs to start up a workshop. Being one among many, the private investor takes the profit rate as well as the number and prices of existing specialised capital goods as given. She fails to recognise that the spillovers of her own projects encourage the investment of others. *Extensive* investment adds new workshops and thereby contributes to gains from increasing specialisation and division of labour in industrial production. Notwithstanding a profit-destruction effect, the resulting savings in investment costs would enhance the profitability of the other investors' projects. By way of contrast, *intensive* investment aims to exploit scale economies due to mass production by installing larger capacities once existing workshops terminate and need to be replaced by new ones. Such gains from rationalisation result in lower component prices and benefit other investors as well. In ignoring the external benefits to the

---

[15] The conditions in (19.24a–d) together with the laws of motion give rise to a simultaneous system in κ, C, K, and N which is supported in decentralised equilibrium by appropriate subsidies or taxes.

community, no individual investor is willing to undertake the marginal project. Even though unprofitable unilaterally, a coordinated increase in investment would well be worthwhile from a social perspective. Private investment activities are inefficiently low.

Some form of investment promotion is called for. At the same time, it must appropriately set incentives for the direction of investment. A proportional investment tax credit addresses the problem of under-accumulation but is otherwise neutral with respect to the scale of invest-ment. If the evidence points to comparatively strong gains from specialisa-tion, the ITC should be complemented by a start-up subsidy to encourage investment at the extensive margin by speeding up the rate of business for-mation. If rationalisation effects dominate over gains from variety, how-ever, a specific tax on start-up investment is preferable to strengthen the incentives for more capital-intensive production techniques. The policy problem is, thus, to promote investment and business formation of the right size. The productivity gains from increasing diversification must be weighed against the savings from mass-production.

APPENDIX

The log linearised version of (19.20) will show how the system is displaced from its initial steady-state (ISS) position. In the ISS, the gross return is $m = \delta + \rho$ whence (19.20a) gives $\hat{C} \equiv d\dot{C}/C = m\hat{m}$. Substituting (19.22) results in the first line of (19A.1). Next, (19.20b) yields $d\dot{K} = [D_K dK + D_N dN - dC]h/\kappa - \delta dK + (D - C)d(h/\kappa)$. Define $m_K \equiv D_K h/\kappa$ as well as $m_N \equiv D_N/\kappa$ and divide by K. Using of steady state properties, $K/N = h$, $(D - C)h/\kappa = \delta K$ and $\bar{c} = (h/\kappa)C/K$, we obtain $\dot{\hat{K}} = (m_K - \delta)\hat{K} + m_N\hat{N} - \bar{c}\hat{C} + \delta(\hat{h} - \hat{\kappa})$. Inserting the solutions for $\hat{h}$ and $\hat{\kappa}$ as noted in deriving (19.22) yields the second line of (19A.1). The differential of (19.20c) is $d\dot{N} = (D_K dK + D_N dN - dC)/\kappa - \delta dN - (D - C)/\kappa\hat{\kappa}$. Di-viding by N, using the SS restrictions and inserting the solution for $\hat{\kappa}$ gives the last line of

$$
\begin{bmatrix} \dot{\hat{C}} \\ \dot{\hat{K}} \\ \dot{\hat{N}} \end{bmatrix} = \begin{bmatrix} 0 & -(2 - \beta - \alpha)m & (\theta - \beta)m \\ -\bar{c} & m_K - \delta & m_N \\ -\bar{c} & m_K & m_N - \delta \end{bmatrix} \begin{bmatrix} \hat{C} \\ \hat{K} \\ \hat{N} \end{bmatrix} + \begin{bmatrix} m(\hat{z} + \hat{\tau}) \\ -\frac{\tau\mu\delta}{\kappa - \tau}\hat{\tau} \\ \delta\mu\hat{\tau} \end{bmatrix}.
$$

(19A.1)

The long-run, stationary solution for the stocks is given in (19.23). To check stability, denote the coefficients matrix by A and find the roots of the characteristic polynomial

$$\psi(\omega) = |A - \omega I|$$
$$= (\omega + \delta)[-\omega^2 + \omega(m_K + m_N - \delta) + \bar{c}m(2 - \theta - \alpha)].$$

(19A.2)

The determinant of A is positive if the condition stated in (19.22) is imposed,

$$|A| = \psi(0) = \bar{c}m\delta(2 - \theta - \alpha) > 0 \quad \Leftrightarrow \quad 2 - \theta - \alpha > 0.$$

(19A.3)

The eigenvalues, thus, split into two negative and a positive one,

$$\omega_1 = -\delta,$$
$$\omega_{2,3} = \frac{1}{2}\{m_K + m_N - \delta \mp \sqrt{(m_K + m_N - \delta)^2 + 4\bar{c}m(2 - \theta - \alpha)}\}.$$

(19A.4)

The system is saddle point stable. The two stable roots ω_1 and ω_2 correspond with the two stock variables while the positive root ω_3 goes with forward-looking consumption.

REFERENCES

Barro, R. J. and Sala-i-Martin, X. (1992). Public finance in models of economic growth. *Review of Economic Studies*, 59: 645–661

Basu, S. (1995). Intermediate goods and business cycles: implications for productivity and welfare. *American Economic Review*, 85: 512–531

Basu, S. and Fernald, J. G. (1997). Returns to scale in US production: estimates and implications. *Journal of Political Economy*, 105: 249–283

Bénassy, J.-P. (1996). Monopolistic competition, increasing returns to specialization and output persistence. *Economics Letters*, 52: 187–191.

Broer, D. P. and Heijdra, B. J. (1996). The intergenerational distribution effects of the investment tax credit under monopolistic competition. Erasmus University Rotterdam, OCFEB Research Memorandum, 9603

Campbell, J. R. (1998). Entry, exit, embodied technology, and business cycles. *Review of Economic Dynamics*, 1: 371–408

Chatterjee, S. and Cooper, R. W. (1993). Entry and exit, product variety and the business cycle. NBER Discussion Paper, 4562

Davis, S. and Haltiwanger, J. (1990). Gross job creation and destruction: microeconomic evidence and macroeconomic implications. *NBER Macroeconomics Annual*, 5: 126–168

De Long, J. B. and Summers, L. H. (1991). Equipment investment and economic growth. *Quarterly Journal of Economics*, 106: 445–502

Dixit, A. K. and Stiglitz, J. E. (1977). Monopolistic competition and optimum product diversity. *American Economic Review*, 67: 297–308

Domowitz, I., Hubbard, R. G. and Petersen, B. C. (1988). Market structure and cyclical fluctuations in US manufacturing. *Review of Economics and Statistics*, 70: 55–66.

Ethier, W. J. (1982). National and international returns to scale in the modern theory of international trade. *American Economic Review*, 72: 389–405

Gilchrist, S. and Williams, J. C. (1998). Putty-clay and investment: a business cycle analysis. NBER Discussion Paper, 6812

Grossman, G. M. and Helpman, E. (1991). *Innovation and Growth in the Global Economy*. Cambridge, MA, MIT Press

Hall, R. E. (1988). The relation between price and marginal cost in US industry. *Journal of Political Economy*, 96: 921–947

Heijdra, B. J. (1998). Fiscal policy multipliers: the role of monopolistic competition, scale economies, and intertemporal substitution in labour supply. *International Economic Review*, 39: 659–696

Hornstein, A. (1993). Monopolistic competition, increasing returns to scale, and the importance of productivity shocks. *Journal of Monetary Economics*, 31: 299–316

Jovanovic, B. (1993). The diversification of production. *Brookings Papers: Microeconomics*, 197–247

(1998). Vintage capital and inequality. *Review of Economic Dynamics*, 1: 497–530

Judd, K. L. (1995). *The optimal tax rate for capital income is negative*. Hoover Institution, Stanford, mimeo

Kiyotaki, N. (1988). Multiple expectational equilibria under monopolistic competition. *Quarterly Journal of Economics*, 103: 695–713

Romer, P. M. (1987). Growth based on increasing returns due to specialization. *American Economic Review*, 77: 56–62

Rotemberg, J. J. and Woodford, M. (1995). Dynamic general equilibrium models with imperfectly competitive product markets, in Cooley, Th. F. (ed.), *Frontiers of Business Cycle Research*. Princeton, Princeton University Press

Weitzman, M. L. (1994). Monopolistic competition with endogenous specialization. *Review of Economic Studies*, 61: 45–56

20   Industrial policy in a small open economy

Leon J. H. Bettendorf and Ben J. Heijdra

20.1   Introduction

The pros and cons of industrial policy in an economy with increasing returns to scale industries have been debated time and again by both academic economists and policy practitioners. With the advent of the so-called New Trade Theory (Krugman, 1990), this debate has been given a new lease of life. At least two approaches can be distinguished in the recent literature. The first approach, which is mentioned but not pursued in this chapter, is better known under the name of 'strategic trade policy'. In this branch of literature, the issue of industrial policy is studied in a setting of large duopolistic or oligopolistic firms battling for market share in the international economy (see Dixit, 1987 and Brander, 1995 for an overview and references).

The second approach studies the issue of industrial policy in a world characterised by monopolistic competition.[1] In such a setting there is no strategic interaction between firms, and trade in varieties of a differentiated product takes place between countries. Flam and Helpman (1987), for example, construct a static model of a small open economy with a monopolistically competitive production sector. They use the model to study the effects on allocation and welfare of tariffs, export subsidies, R&D subsidies and output subsidies. Flam and Helpman (1987, pp. 90–1) identify three mechanisms by which welfare of domestic agents is increased in a monopolistically competitive setting. First, an increase in the number of domestic product varieties expands the range of choice by domestic consumers, who are better off as a result provided they exhibit a preference for diversity. Second, a policy that increases the home price of domestically produced varieties has a positive terms of trade effect which

An earlier version of this chapter was presented at the SOM conference on the Dixit–Stiglitz model. We thank our discussant, Peter Neary, as well as Avinash Dixit, Russell Cooper, Steven Brakman, and other conference participants for useful comments.

[1] Early contributions to this branch of the literature are Venables (1985) and Flam and Helpman (1987).

increases welfare of domestic residents. Third, an increase in the output level per domestic firm constitutes a 'pro-competitive' effect and thus increases welfare.

Our chapter is a contribution to the second approach to industrial policy. We study both the product subsidy and the import tariff. While we retain some of the modelling devices of Flam and Helpman (1987), we modify the analysis in several directions. First, we study a dynamic model in which savings dynamics is allowed to play a non-trivial role. Second, we study both temporary and permanent policy shocks and compute the theoretical impulse-response functions. Third, we allow for intergenerational effects by modelling a dynamic overlapping-generations economy. We use the perpetual youth approach of Yaari (1965) and Blanchard (1985), but extend it to an open economy and endogenise the labour supply decision of households. Domestic households purchase domestic and foreign products and use the current account in order to smooth their consumption profiles. The country is *semi-small*, i.e. it is small in world financial markets (and thus faces perfect capital mobility) but it can affect its terms of trade (see Buiter, 1987). There are many small domestic firms producing varieties that are sold at home and abroad. Free exit/entry eliminates excess profits and determines the equilibrium number of firms in the domestic economy. Increasing returns to scale exist because an increase in the number of product varieties boosts the productivity of the variable labour input.

The analysis yields a number of conclusions. First, a permanent increase in the product subsidy boosts labour demand and leads to an expansion of output, employment and the number of product varieties, both at impact and in the long run.[2]

Second, like Sen and Turnovsky (1989) but unlike Flam and Helpman (1987), we find that a permanent increase in the tariff reduces output and employment, in both the short run and in the long run. In our model the tariff shock prompts a negative labour supply response which leads to a reduction in the number of firms. Like Flam and Helpman (1987), we find that the real exchange rate appreciates both at impact and in the long run.

Third, we demonstrate that the impulse-response functions for temporary policy shocks depend critically on demography (as parameterised by the birth–death rate) and on the households' attitude to saving (as determined by the gap between the interest rate and the rate of pure time

---

[2] In the closed economy with fixed labour supply, output and the number of product varieties rise because households accumulate more capital in the long run. See Broer and Heijdra (2001).

preference). The representative-agent version of the model, for example, displays hysteresis, i.e. temporary shocks have permanent effects. Interestingly, in this knife-edge version of the model, a temporary increase in the product subsidy leads to a long-run output reduction while a temporary tariff increase leads to a permanent improvement in the terms of trade!

Fourth, we are able to analytically characterise the pure efficiency effects of the policy shocks.[3] Not surprisingly, in the first-best social optimum, the product subsidy is used to correct for the domestic distortion due to monopolistic competition while the optimal tariff exploits 'national market power' (as in Gros, 1987). More interestingly, in the second-best scenario the two policy instruments are complementary. For example, the second-best optimal tariff not only depends on national market power but also on the pre-existing domestic distortion of monopolistic competition. To the extent that the policy maker has no instrument to combat the domestic monopoly distortion (such as a product subsidy), the second-best optimum tariff is reduced *vis-à-vis* its first-best value. Intuitively, output is already too low due to the domestic monopoly distortion and increasing the tariff only exacerbates this problem. In a similar vein, the second-best optimal product subsidy depends positively on the pre-existing tariff. Our model thus yields precise and intuitively understandable prescriptions about the interaction between the optimum tariff and pre-existing domestic distortions. We thus extend the seminal work by Johnson (1965) and Bhagwati (1967, 1971) on instrument targeting to a dynamic setting of overlapping generations and monopolistic competition.

The remainder of the chapter proceeds as follows. In section 20.2 the model of a semi-small open economy is developed. In section 20.3 the macroeconomic effects of (permanent or temporary) product subsidies and import tariffs are studied, at impact, during transition and in the long run. We distinguish various cases of the model. Section 20.4 is dedicated to the welfare analysis. Finally, section 20.5 contains some concluding remarks and a brief appendix presents the key derivations.

20.2   The model

20.2.1   Households

The basic model of household behaviour builds on the work of Blanchard (1985) and its extension to the open economy by Giovannini (1988). Beside the endogeneity of labour supply, the main difference between these

---

[3] In this chapter we de-emphasise the intergenerational welfare effects of the policy shocks. We refer the interested reader to our earlier papers for a detailed analysis (see Bettendorf and Heijdra, 2001a, 2001b).

two models and ours is the introduction of a diversified consumption good into the utility function of the agents. This in turn opens the scope for imperfectly competitive behaviour on the part of producers.

In this model there is a fixed population of agents each facing a given constant probability of death. During their entire life agents have a time endowment of unity which they allocate over labour and leisure. The utility functional at time t of the representative agent born at time v is denoted by $\Lambda(v, t)$ and has the following form:

$$\Lambda(v, t) \equiv \int_t^\infty \log U(v, \tau) e^{(\alpha+\beta)(t-\tau)} d\tau, \tag{20.1}$$

where α is the pure rate of time preference ($\alpha > 0$), β is the probability of death ($\beta \geq 0$) and $U(v, \tau)$ is the sub-utility which depends on leisure $(1 - L(v, \tau))$ and consumption of domestic and foreign goods ($C(v, \tau)$ and $Z(v, \tau)$, respectively):

$$U(v, \tau) \equiv [C(v, \tau)^\delta Z(v, \tau)^{1-\delta}]^\gamma [1 - L(v, \tau)]^{1-\gamma}, \tag{20.2}$$

with $0 < \gamma \leq 1$ and $0 < \delta < 1$.[4]

The domestic economy consists of imperfectly competitive firms that each produce a single variety of a diversified good. These goods are close but imperfect substitutes in consumption. Following Spence (1976) and Dixit and Stiglitz (1977) the diversified goods can be aggregated over existing varieties $(1, 2, \ldots, N(\tau))$ in order to obtain $C(v, \tau)$:

$$C(v, \tau) \equiv \left[\sum_{i=1}^{N(\tau)} C_i(v, \tau)^{1/\eta} \right]^\eta, \quad \eta \geq 1, \tag{20.3}$$

where $C_i(v, \tau)$ is the consumption of domestically produced variety i in period τ by an agent born in period v ($\leq \tau$). The parameter η captures both the *preference for diversity* (PFD) effect and the extent of monopoly power for producers of individual varieties (Bénassy, 1996, 1998). The true price deflator corresponding to (20.3) is:

$$P(\tau) \equiv \left[\sum_{i=1}^{N(\tau)} P_i(\tau)^{1/(1-\eta)} \right]^{1-\eta}, \tag{20.4}$$

where $P_i(\tau)$ is the price of variety i. The homogeneous imported consumption good is used as the numéraire and features a given world price

---

[4] Hence, it is assumed that the Armington substitution elasticity between domestic and foreign consumption goods equals unity. This assumption is made for simplicity. A non-unitary Armington elasticity does not substantially affect the arguments in this chapter.

$(P_Z(\tau) = 1)$.[5] Hence, $P(\tau)$ represents the *terms of trade*, i.e. the relative price of exports in terms of imports.

The agent's budget identity, expressed in terms of the foreign good, is equal to:

$$\dot{A}(v, \tau) = (r + \beta)A(v, \tau) + W(\tau)L(v, \tau) - T(\tau) - P(\tau)C(v, \tau)$$
$$- [1 + t_M(\tau)]Z(v, \tau), \qquad (20.5)$$

where $\dot{A}(v, \tau) \equiv dA(v, \tau)/d\tau$, r is the fixed world real rate of interest,[6] $W(\tau)$ is the real wage rate (assumed age-independent for convenience), $T(\tau)$ are net lump-sum taxes, $t_M(\tau)$ is an ad valorem import tariff, and $A(v, \tau)$ is real financial wealth. All financial assets are perfect substitutes:

$$A(v, \tau) \equiv B(v, \tau) + F(v, \tau), \qquad (20.6)$$

where $B(v, \tau)$ and $F(v, \tau)$ are, respectively, government bonds and net foreign assets, both measured in terms of the foreign good. We define *full expenditure* $X(v, \tau)$ as the sum of spending on domestic and foreign consumption goods and on leisure, i.e.:

$$X(v, \tau) \equiv P(\tau)C(v, \tau) + [1 + t_M(\tau)]Z(v, \tau)$$
$$+ W(\tau)[1 - L(v, \tau)]. \qquad (20.7)$$

Due to the separable structure of preferences, the choice problem for the representative agent can be solved in two steps. First, the dynamic problem is solved. This leads to an optimal time profile for full expenditure which is described by the agent's Euler equation:

$$\frac{\dot{X}(v, \tau)}{X(v, \tau)} = r - \alpha. \qquad (20.8)$$

In the second step full expenditure is optimally allocated over its component parts:

$$P(\tau)C(v, \tau) = \gamma\delta X(v, \tau), \qquad (20.9)$$

$$[1 + t_M(\tau)]Z(v, \tau) = \gamma(1 - \delta)X(v, \tau), \qquad (20.10)$$

$$W(\tau)[1 - L(v, \tau)] = (1 - \gamma)X(v, \tau), \qquad (20.11)$$

[5] Bettendorf and Heijdra (2001a) model the foreign good as a differentiated commodity. Since we assume that the domestic economy has no influence on the number of foreign varieties or on their price, our approach entails no loss of generality. Z will always be the import good under this interpretation. If, on the other hand, we interpret Z strictly as an internationally traded homogeneous good one could augment the model by allowing for domestic production of Z (an import-competing industry). Obviously, a tariff then benefits domestic Z-producers and causes a shift of labour from the differentiated to the homogeneous sector. We owe this observation to Steven Brakman.

[6] We assume that the domestic economy is small in world capital markets so that it faces a given world real rate of interest r.

where δ thus represents the (constant) share of total goods consumption that is spent on domestic goods and $1 - \gamma$ is the spending share of leisure in full expenditure.[7] Demand for the different varieties of the domestically produced goods is given by:

$$\frac{C_i(v, \tau)}{C(v, \tau)} = \left(\frac{P_i(\tau)}{P(\tau)}\right)^{-\eta/(\eta-1)}. \tag{20.12}$$

A crucial feature of the Blanchard (1985) model (and all models deriving from it) is its simple demographic structure, which enables the aggregation over all currently alive households. Assuming that at each instance a large cohort of size βS is born and that βS agents die, and normalising S to unity, the size of the population is constant and equal to unity and the aggregated variables can be calculated as the weighted sum of the values for the different generations. For example, aggregate financial wealth is calculated as $A(\tau) \equiv \int_{-\infty}^{\tau} \beta A(v, \tau) e^{\beta(v-\tau)} dv$. The aggregated values for the other variables can be obtained in the same fashion. The main equations describing the behaviour of the aggregated household sector are given (for period t) by (T20.1.1) and (T20.1.5)–(T20.1.7) in table 20.1. Equation (T20.1.1) is the aggregate Euler equation modified for the existence of overlapping generations of finitely-lived agents. It has the same form as the Euler equation for individual households (20.8) except for the correction term due to the distributional effects caused by the turnover of generations. Optimal full expenditure *growth* is the same for all generations but older generations have a different full expenditure *level* than younger generations. The correction term appearing in (T20.1.1) thus represents the difference in average full expenditure and full expenditure by newborns:[8]

$$\frac{\dot{X}(\tau)}{X(\tau)} = r - \alpha - \beta(\alpha + \beta)\left(\frac{A(\tau)}{X(\tau)}\right) = \frac{\dot{X}(v, \tau)}{X(v, \tau)}$$
$$- \beta\left(\frac{X(\tau) - X(\tau, \tau)}{X(\tau)}\right), \tag{20.13}$$

where $A(\tau) \equiv F(\tau) + B(\tau)$ is aggregate financial wealth. Throughout the chapter we analyse the case in which there is no government debt in the initial steady state $(B = 0)$. Equation (T20.1.1) shows that steady-state net foreign assets are positive (zero, negative) if the world interest

---

[7] If $\gamma = 1$, labour supply is exogenous and each agent inelastically supplies one unit of labour.

[8] We use the fact that $X(\tau) = (\alpha + \beta)[A(\tau) + H(\tau)]$, $X(\tau, \tau) = (\alpha + \beta)[A(v, \tau) + H(\tau)]$, and $A(\tau, \tau) = 0$ in the second step, where $H(t)$ is human wealth, i.e. the after-tax present value of the household's time endowment: $H(t) \equiv \int_t^{\infty} [W(\tau) - T(\tau)] \exp[(r + \beta)(t - \tau)] d\tau$.

Table 20.1   *Short-run version of the model[a,b]*

$$\dot{X}(t) = (r - \alpha)X(t) - \beta(\alpha + \beta)[F(t) + B(t)] \qquad \text{(T20.1.1)}$$

$$\dot{F}(t) = rF(t) + TB(t) \qquad \text{(T20.1.2)}$$

$$W(t)L(t) = [1 + s_P(t)]Y(t) \qquad \text{(T20.1.3)}$$

$$Y(t) = P(t)[C(t) + E_0 P(t)^{-\sigma_T}] \qquad \text{(T20.1.4)}$$

$$P(t)C(t) = \gamma\delta X(t) \qquad \text{(T20.1.5)}$$

$$[1 + t_M(t)]Z(t) = \gamma(1 - \delta)X(t) \qquad \text{(T20.1.6)}$$

$$W(t)[1 - L(t)] = (1 - \gamma)X(t) \qquad \text{(T20.1.7)}$$

$$Y(t)/P(t) = \Omega_0 L(t)^{\eta} \qquad \text{(T20.1.8)}$$

$$TB(t) = E_0 P(t)^{1 - \sigma_T} - Z(t). \qquad \text{(T20.1.9)}$$

Note: [a] The homogeneous foreign good is the numéraire. $P(t)$ is the terms of trade.
[b] $\Omega_0 \equiv k^{-1}\eta^{-\eta}((\eta - 1)/f)^{\eta-1} > 0$.

rate exceeds (equals, falls short of) the rate of time preference, i.e. $F \gtreqless 0$ for $r \gtreqless \alpha$. Intuitively, net foreign assets are strictly positive (negative) for a patient (impatient) country. The rising (falling) full expenditure profile that this implies ensures that financial wealth is transferred – via the life insurance companies – from old to young (young to old) generations in the steady-state (see Blanchard, 1985). In the knife-edge case, for which $r = \alpha$, households neither save nor dissave, full expenditure is the same for all generations and steady-state net foreign assets are zero.

20.2.2   Foreign sector

The domestic economy has links with the rest of the world through the goods market (via imports of the foreign good and exports of differentiated products) and through the assets market (domestic households can hold foreign assets in their portfolios). Since it is assumed that the domestic economy is small relative to the rest of the world, domestic variables have no impact on foreign macroeconomic variables. Hence, the export equation contains mainly exogenous variables. For simplicity, the following specification is adopted for the export demand equation:

$$[P(\tau)]^{\sigma_T}\left(\frac{E_i(\tau)}{E_0}\right) = \left(\frac{P_i(\tau)}{P(\tau)}\right)^{-\eta/(\eta-1)}, \qquad \sigma_T \geq 1, \qquad (20.14)$$

where E_0 is the exogenous component of export demand. In (20.14), the term $\eta/(\eta - 1)$ summarises how well domestically produced varieties can be substituted by the buyers in the rest of the world. There is also a separate effect of the terms of trade on aggregate exports which is parameterised by σ_T.[9]

The change in net foreign assets is equal to the current account. Since net foreign assets, $F(\tau)$, are measured in terms of foreign goods, the balance of payments equation can be expressed (for period t) as in (T20.1.2) in table 20.1. The first term on the right-hand side is foreign capital income and the second term is the trade balance.

20.2.3   Firms

The domestic economy consists of a single sector characterised by monopolistic competition. Each firm in this sector faces a demand for its product from two sources, i.e. consumption demand from the households sector (represented by $C_i(\tau)$ which is obtained by aggregating (20.12) over individuals), and the demand from the rest of the world (given by $E_i(\tau)$ in (20.14)). There are $N(\tau)$ identical domestic firms that each produce one variety of the differentiated product. Labour is the only productive input[10] and technology features increasing returns to scale at the firm level:

$$L_i(\tau) = kY_i(\tau) + f, \tag{20.15}$$

where $L_i(\tau)$ is labour input, $Y_i(\tau)$ is marketable output, f is fixed cost modelled in the form of 'overhead labour' ($f > 0$), and $1/k$ is the marginal product of labour. Representative firm i's profit is defined by:

$$\Pi_i(\tau) \equiv [1 + s_P(\tau)] P_i(\tau) Y_i(\tau) - W(\tau) L_i(\tau), \tag{20.16}$$

where $s_P(\tau)$ is an ad valorem subsidy on production. The firm chooses its output and price in order to maximise (20.16) subject to the demand restriction $Y_i(\tau) = C_i(\tau) + E_i(\tau)$ and technology (20.15). Assuming that individual firms perceive $P(\tau)$ as given independently of their own price $P_i(\tau)$, the static decision problem yields the familiar pricing rule:

$$P_i(\tau) = \frac{\eta k W(\tau)}{1 + s_P(\tau)}, \tag{20.17}$$

where $\eta > 1$ is the markup. In this chapter the assumption of *Chamberlinian* monopolistic competition is made: competitors' reactions are deemed to be absent and entry/exit is assumed to occur until each active firm makes zero excess profit; the well-known tangency solution (there

---

[9] Flam and Helpman (1987, p. 82) postulate an export demand equation similar to ours.
[10] In Bettendorf and Heijdra (2001a) immobile land is a second production factor. Broer and Heijdra (2001) study a closed economy in which physical capital is the only variable production factor.

are no set-up costs). By using (20.15) and (20.17) in (20.16) we deduce that $\Pi_i(\tau) = W(\tau) [(\eta - 1)kY_i(\tau) - f]$ so that the zero-profit condition pins down a constant firm size:

$$Y_i(\tau) = \bar{Y} \equiv \frac{f}{(\eta - 1)k}. \tag{20.18}$$

Note that if $\eta \to 1$ and $f \to 0$ the model converges to a perfectly competitive economy where varieties are perfect substitutes (no product differentiation) and monopoly profits disappear (no markups).

20.2.4   Government

The government sector is modelled in a very simple fashion. We abstract from macro features of government behaviour such as government spending on goods and services and distortionary taxes on labour income. The periodic budget identity of the government is:

$$\dot{B}(\tau) = r B(\tau) + s_P(\tau) Y(\tau) - t_M(\tau) Z(\tau) - T(\tau), \tag{20.19}$$

where $Y(\tau)$ is national income in terms of the foreign good:

$$Y(\tau) \equiv \sum_{i=1}^{N(\tau)} P_i(\tau) Y_i(\tau). \tag{20.20}$$

Since the government is expected to remain solvent, the following NPG condition is relevant: $\lim_{\tau \to \infty} B(\tau) \exp[r(t - \tau)] = 0$. The government's budget restriction is obtained by integrating (20.19) forward subject to this NPG condition:

$$B(t) = \int_t^\infty [T(\tau) + t_M(\tau) Z(\tau) - s_P(\tau) Y(\tau)] e^{r(t-\tau)} d\tau.$$

20.2.5   Equilibrium and stability

The model is symmetric and can thus be expressed in aggregate terms. All active domestic firms produce the same (constant) amount of output ($Y_i = \bar{Y}$ – see (20.18)), have the same markup, face the same input prices and thus charge the same price ($P_i = \bar{P}$) and hire the same amounts of labour ($L_i = \bar{L}$). As a consequence we have $C_i = \bar{C}$ and $E_i = \bar{E}$ (for $i = 1, 2, \ldots, N$).

The complete dynamic model is given in aggregated form in table 20.1. The dynamic part of the model is given by (T20.1.1)–(T20.1.2) which have been discussed above. The static part of the model is given by

(T20.1.3)–(T20.1.9). Equation (T20.1.3) is the aggregate demand for labour, and (T20.1.4) is the equilibrium condition for the domestic market for differentiated goods, written in aggregate form. Equations (T20.1.5)–(T20.1.6) are, respectively, consumption of the domestic composite good and the foreign good, and (T20.1.7) is labour supply. The aggregate production function for the differentiated goods sector is given in (T20.1.8). It is the aggregated version of (20.15), where use has been made of the zero-pure profit condition.[11] Finally, (T20.1.9) is the trade balance, i.e. the difference between export earnings and imports.

The model nests a number of important cases, depending on the birth–death rate (β) and on the gap between the world interest rate and the rate of time preference ($r - \alpha$). For convenience we state the various sub-cases here.

• Overlapping-generations model ($\beta > 0$)
  – Creditor nation ($r > \alpha$): unique steady state associated with positive net foreign assets
  – Debtor nation ($r < \alpha$): unique steady state associated with negative net foreign assets
  – Non-saving nation ($r = \alpha$): unique steady state associated with zero net foreign assets
• Representative-agent model ($\beta = 0$ and $r = \alpha$[12]): hysteretic steady state.

The dynamical properties of the model are illustrated with the aid of figures 20.1–20.2 (for the overlapping-generations model) and figure 20.3 (for the representative-agent model). Consider the overlapping-generations model first. As in Blanchard (1985, pp. 230–1) the slope of the $\dot{X} = 0$ line depends on the rate of time preference relative to the world interest rate. Since we assume that government debt is zero initially, it follows from (T20.1.1) that the $\dot{X} = 0$ line goes through the origin and is upward (downward) sloping for a creditor (debtor) nation (see figure 20.1). In the knife-edge case, for which $r = \alpha$ the $\dot{X} = 0$ line coincides with the vertical axis (see figure 20.2). For points to the left (right) of

---

[11] Equation (T20.1.8) is obtained as follows. In the symmetric equilibrium, $Y_i = \bar{Y}$ and $P_i = \bar{P}$ so that $Y = N\bar{P}\bar{Y}$. Equation (20.4) implies $P = N^{1-\eta}\bar{P}$ so that $Y/P = N^{\eta}\bar{Y}$. Furthermore, (20.15) and the zero-profit condition imply that $k\bar{Y} + f = \bar{L} = \eta k\bar{Y}$. Aggregation over all active firms yields $N\bar{Y} = L/(\eta k)$, where $L = N\bar{L}$ is aggregate labour supply. By combining these results we obtain $Y/P = \Omega_0 L^{\eta}$ and $N = L/(\eta k\bar{Y})$. Preference for diversity thus causes aggregate output and the equilibrium number of firms to exhibit, respectively, increasing and constant returns to factor supplies. (See Heijdra and van der Ploeg, 1996, and Heijdra, 1998, for further details.)

[12] As is well known in the macroeconomic literature, the representative-agent model for the small open economy has a meaningful steady-state solution only if the interest rate equals the rate of pure time preference, i.e. if $r = \alpha$ (Turnovsky, 1997).

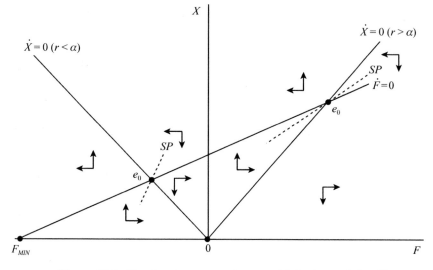

Figure 20.1   Overlapping-generations model ($r \neq \alpha$ and $\beta > 0$)

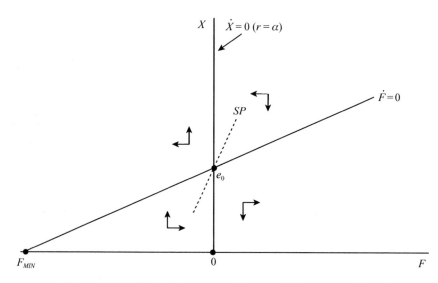

Figure 20.2   Overlapping-generations model ($r = \alpha$ and $\beta > 0$)

the $\dot{X} = 0$ line full expenditure rises (falls), as is indicated with vertical arrows in figures 20.1–20.2.

The derivation of the $\dot{F} = 0$ line is slightly more complicated as it depends on the trade balance which in turn depends on domestic supply and

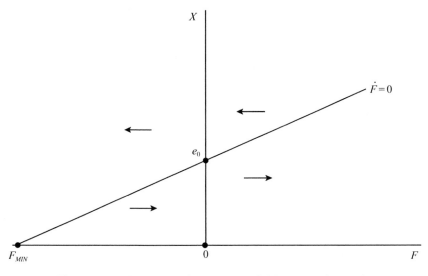

Figure 20.3 Representative-agent model ($r = \alpha$ and $\beta = 0$)

demand conditions and on exports. Below we show, by using (T20.1.3)–(T20.1.9) in table 20.1, that the trade balance depends negatively on the level of full expenditure, i.e. $\partial TB/\partial X < 0$. Intuitively, an increase in full expenditure reduces labour supply and real domestic output, increases the terms of trade, reduces export earnings and increases imports. As a result, the trade balance deteriorates. Since $\partial TB/\partial X < 0$, it follows from (T20.1.2) that the $\dot{F} = 0$ line is upward sloping.[13] Points above (below) the $\dot{F} = 0$ line are associated with a current account deficit (surplus) as has been indicated with horizontal arrows in figures 20.1–20.3.

It follows from the arrow configuration in figures 20.1–20.2 (and from the derivations presented below) that the overlapping-generations model is saddle–point stable for all cases considered (see the equilibria labelled e_0 in (the two panels of) figure 20.1 and figure 20.2). For the creditor (debtor, non-saving) nation steady-state net foreign assets are positive (negative, zero). In all cases the saddle path is upward sloping (see the dashed curves labelled SP in figures 20.1–20.2).

For the representative-agent model, $\beta = 0$ and $r = \alpha$, and it follows from (T20.1.1) that full expenditure dynamics is degenerate, i.e. $\dot{X} = 0$. In terms of figure 20.3, we only have non-degenerate dynamics in net foreign assets (see the horizontal arrows) and the steady state is hysteretic,

[13] It follows from (T20.1.2), (T20.1.6) and (T20.1.9) that $r F_{MIN} \equiv -E_0 P^{1-\sigma T} < 0$.

i.e. determined by past shocks affecting the economy. In figure 20.3 we *assume* that the economy is initially at point e_0.

20.3   Macroeconomic effects of industrial policy

In this section we study the macroeconomic effects of the product subsidy and the import tariff. In order to prepare for the welfare analysis of section 20.4, we compute the comparative dynamic properties of the model by log linearising it around the initial steady state. The resulting expressions are found in table 20.2. We use the following notational conventions. A tilde ($\tilde{\ }$) above a variable denotes its rate of change around the initial steady state, e.g., $\tilde{X}(t) \equiv dX(t)/X$. A variable with a tilde and a dot is the time derivative expressed in terms of the initial steady state, for example, $\dot{\tilde{X}}(t) \equiv \dot{X}(t)/X$. The only exceptions to that convention refer to the policy instruments, the various financial assets, and the trade balance: $\tilde{t}_M(t) \equiv dt_M(t)/(1 + t_M)$, $\tilde{s}_P(t) \equiv ds_P(t)/(1 + s_P)$, $\tilde{B}(t) \equiv rdB(t)/Y$, $\dot{\tilde{B}}(t) \equiv r\dot{B}(t)/Y$, $\tilde{F}(t) \equiv rdF(t)/Y$, $\dot{\tilde{F}}(t) \equiv r\dot{F}(t)/Y$, and $\widetilde{TB}(t) \equiv dTB(t)/Y$.

Table 20.2   *Log linearised version of the model*[a,b,c]

$$\dot{\tilde{X}}(t) = (r - \alpha)\tilde{X}(t) - \beta\omega_Y[\tilde{F}(t) + \tilde{B}(t)] \tag{T20.2.1}$$

$$\dot{\tilde{F}}(t) = r[\tilde{F}(t) + \widetilde{TB}(t)] \tag{T20.2.2}$$

$$\tilde{L}(t) = \tilde{Y}(t) - \tilde{W}(t) + \tilde{s}_P(t) \tag{T20.2.3}$$

$$\tilde{Y}(t) - \tilde{P}(t) = (1 - \omega_X)\tilde{C}(t) - \sigma_T\omega_X\tilde{P}(t) \tag{T20.2.4}$$

$$\tilde{C}(t) + \tilde{P}(t) = \tilde{X}(t) \tag{T20.2.5}$$

$$\tilde{Z}(t) = \tilde{X}(t) - \tilde{t}_M(t) \tag{T20.2.6}$$

$$\tilde{L}(t) = \omega_{LL}[\tilde{W}(t) - \tilde{X}(t)] \tag{T20.2.7}$$

$$\tilde{Y}(t) - \tilde{P}(t) = \eta\tilde{L}(t) \tag{T20.2.8}$$

$$\widetilde{TB}(t) = -(\sigma_T - 1)\omega_X\tilde{P}(t) - (\omega_X + \omega_F)\tilde{Z}(t). \tag{T20.2.9}$$

Shares:

$\omega_{LL} \equiv (1 - L)/L$, leisure/work ratio ($\omega_{LL} > 0$)

$\omega_F \equiv rF/Y$, share of asset income in national income ($\omega_F \gtrless 0$)

$\omega_X \equiv E_0 P^{1-\sigma_T}/Y$, share of exports in national income ($0 < \omega_X < 1$)

$\omega_Y \equiv (\alpha + \beta) Y/(rX) > 0$.

Notes:
[a] We assume that $B = 0$ initially.
[b] Relationship between shares: $\omega_F + \omega_X = Z/Y > 0$.
[c] If $\beta > 0$ and $r \neq \alpha$ then $\beta\omega_Y = (r - \alpha)/\omega_F$.

20.3.1 Model solution

We solve the log linearised model in three steps. In *step 1*, we condense the static part of the model as much as possible. By using (T20.2.3)–(T20.2.9) in table 20.2, the change in real national income $(\tilde{Y}(t) - \tilde{P}(t))$, employment $(\tilde{L}(t))$, the terms of trade $(\tilde{P}(t))$ and the trade balance $(\widetilde{TB}(t))$ can be written in terms of the state variable $(\tilde{X}(t))$ and the policy variables $(\tilde{t}_M(t)$ and $\tilde{s}_P(t))$:

$$\tilde{Y}(t) - \tilde{P}(t) = \eta \tilde{L}(t) = -(\phi - 1)[(\tilde{X}(t) - \tilde{P}(t)) - \tilde{s}_P(t)],$$
$$(20.21)$$

$$\tilde{X}(t) - \tilde{P}(t) = \zeta \left[\tilde{X}(t) + \left(\frac{\phi - 1}{\sigma_T \omega_X} \right) \tilde{s}_P(t) \right],$$
$$(20.22)$$

$$\tilde{W}(t) - \tilde{P}(t) = \left(\frac{\eta - 1}{\eta} \right) [\tilde{Y}(t) - \tilde{P}(t)] + \tilde{s}_P(t),$$
$$(20.23)$$

$$\widetilde{TB}(t) = -[\zeta \phi + \omega_F] \tilde{X}(t) + \zeta (\phi - 1) \left(\frac{\sigma_T - 1}{\sigma_T} \right) \tilde{s}_P(t)$$
$$+ (\omega_F + \omega_X) \tilde{t}_M(t),$$
$$(20.24)$$

where ϕ and ζ are defined as:[14]

$$\phi \equiv \frac{1 + \omega_{LL}}{1 + \omega_{LL}(1 - \eta)} \geq 1, \qquad 0 < \zeta \equiv \frac{\sigma_T \omega_X}{\phi + \omega_X(\sigma_T - 1)} < 1.$$
$$(20.25)$$

It is shown in the appendix (p. 474) that $\zeta \phi + \omega_F > 0$ so that the trade balance depends negatively on full expenditure, as was asserted above.

In *step 2*, we use (T20.2.1), (T20.2.2) and (20.24) to derive the dynamical system for net foreign assets and full expenditure:

$$\begin{bmatrix} \dot{\tilde{F}}(t) \\ \dot{\tilde{X}}(t) \end{bmatrix} = \Delta \begin{bmatrix} \tilde{F}(t) \\ \tilde{X}(t) \end{bmatrix} + \begin{bmatrix} \gamma_F(t) \\ \gamma_X(t) \end{bmatrix},$$
$$(20.26)$$

where the Jacobian matrix of coefficients on the right-hand side (denoted by Δ with typical element δ_{ij}), is defined as:

$$\Delta \equiv \begin{bmatrix} r & -r(\zeta \phi + \omega_F) \\ -\beta \omega_Y & r - \alpha \end{bmatrix},$$
$$(20.27)$$

---

[14] Bettendorf and Heijdra (2001b, p. 339) discuss the condition $0 \leq (\eta - 1)\omega_{LL} < 1$ which ensures that ϕ is positive (and greater than unity for endogenous labour supply).

and where the vector of forcing terms is given by:

$$
\begin{bmatrix} \gamma_F(t) \\ \gamma_X(t) \end{bmatrix} = \begin{bmatrix} r\left(\omega_X + \omega_F\right) \tilde{t}_M(t) + r\zeta\left(\phi - 1\right)\left(\frac{\sigma_T - 1}{\sigma_T}\right) \tilde{s}_P(t) \\ -\left(\beta\omega_Y\right) \tilde{B}(t) \end{bmatrix}.
$$

$$(20.28)$$

The following proposition summarises the dynamical properties of the log linearised system.

Proposition 1 *Consider the model in table 20.2. (a) The overlapping-generations model (for which $\beta > 0$) is saddle point stable and possesses one stable characteristic root ($-\lambda_1 < 0$) and one unstable characteristic root ($\lambda_2 > r$); (b) The representative-agent model (for which $r = \alpha$ and $\beta = 0$) displays hysteresis. Its characteristic roots are $\lambda_1 = 0$ and $\lambda_2 = \alpha$.*

Proof: See appendix. ■

In *step 3* we solve for the impact, transitional, and long-run effects on the state variables of the various policy shocks. The details of the computations are presented in the appendix. The time at which the shock occurs is normalised at $t = 0$. In the remainder of this section we abstract from debt policy ($\tilde{B}(t) = 0$) altogether, i.e. $\gamma_X(t) = 0$ for all t.[15] We focus on the key macroeconomic effects that result from (temporary or permanent) increases in the product subsidy (sub-section 20.3.2) and the import tariff (sub-section 20.3.3). We discuss the intuition behind our results by means of simple graphs.

20.3.2   *Product subsidy*

The effects of an unanticipated (permanent or temporary) increase in the product subsidy can be illustrated with the aid of figures 20.4 and 20.6–20.7. It follows from (20.26) and (20.28) that the shock leads to a leftward shift in the $\dot{F} = 0$ line. Intuitively, for a given level of full expenditure, an increase in the product subsidy boosts labour demand and employment (as labour supply is elastic), increases real domestic output, decreases the terms of trade, increases export earnings and thus improves the trade balance. For convenience we summarise the qualitative results for the permanent shock in table 20.3.

---

[15] The government budget constraint is thus satisfied by changes in the lump-sum tax, T. In doing so we are able to study the two policy instruments independently.

Table 20.3 *Permanent increase in the product subsidy*

	X	F	TB	P	W/P	Y/P	L	C	Z
(a) Creditor nation (r > α)									
$t = 0$	+	0	+	?	++	++	++	+	+
$t \to \infty$	++	+	−	−	+	+	+	++	++
(b) Debtor nation (r < α)									
$t = 0$	++	0	−	+	+	+	+	++	++
$t \to \infty$	+	−	+	−	++	++	++	+	+
(c) Non-saving nation or representative-agent model (r = α)									
$\forall t \geq 0$	+	0	0	−	+	+	+	+	+

Note:
(+)+: (strong) positive effect; (−)−: (strong) negative effect; 0: no effect; ?:
theoretically ambiguous effect. The results in this table assume that labour
supply is endogenous $(0 < \gamma < 1)$ and the diversity effect is operative $(\eta > 1)$.

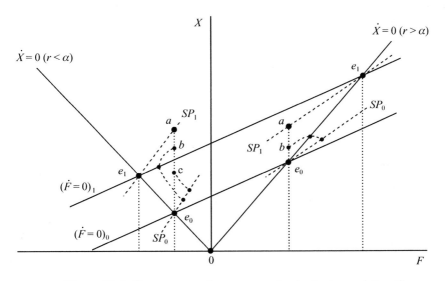

Figure 20.4 Permanent and temporary shocks $(r \neq \alpha$ and $\beta > 0)$

Overlapping-generations model (r ≠ α)
In figure 20.4 we study the overlapping-generations model for the debtor
country (left-hand panel) and the creditor country (right-hand panel).
We discuss the results for a permanent and a temporary shock in turn.

Permanent shock   Consider the creditor country first. As a result of the permanent shock, the economy makes a discrete jump at impact from the initial equilibrium e_0 to point a (on the new saddle path SP_1). Over time, the economy gradually moves along the saddle path from point a to the ultimate equilibrium at e_1. Adjustment in both full expenditure and net foreign assets is monotonic. The impact effect is due to the fact that the policy measure increases the real wage rate and thus the value of human wealth for all agents alive at the time of the shock. At impact, output, employment, imports, and the trade balance all increase, but the effect on the terms of trade is theoretically ambiguous – see panel (a) of table 20.3. Since full expenditure gradually increases over time, it follows that output, employment and the real wage rate all overshoot their respective long-run equilibrium values, and that the terms of trade undershoots its long-run equilibrium.

For the debtor country (left-hand panel of figure 20.4 and panel (b) of table 20.3), the adjustment consists of an upward jump from e_0 to point a at impact, followed by a gradual *decline* of full expenditure and net foreign assets as the economy proceeds along the saddle path SP_1 towards the new steady state at e_1. While the adjustment in net foreign assets is monotonic, full expenditure, domestic consumption and imports overshoot their respective long-run equilibrium during transition.

Temporary shock   Next we consider the case of a temporary increase in the product subsidy. In particular, we assume that the product subsidy shock is positive for $t \in [0, t_E]$ and zero thereafter.[16] The dynamic adjustment of the economy can be deduced by making use of the following intuitive solution principle (Heijdra and van der Ploeg, 2002, p. 91):
- net foreign assets are predetermined at impact
- discrete adjustment in full expenditure is possible only at impact
- for $0 < t < t_E$ the dynamics of the then relevant equilibrium dictates the adjustment
- at time $t = t_E$ the economy must be on the saddle path leading to the long-run equilibrium.

For the creditor country, the intuitive solution principle can be used to deduce that the adjustment path will consist of a discrete jump at impact from e_0 to point b followed by a gradual move towards the saddle path SP_0 for $0 < t < t_E$. At $t = t_E$, the economy has arrived on SP_0 after which it moves gradually to point e_0. The adjustment in both full expenditure and net foreign assets is non-monotonic. As a result of the

---

[16] Obviously, as t_E increases the shock becomes more like a permanent shock. In the limit, as $t_E \rightarrow \infty$, the shock is permanent.

shock, human wealth increases at impact and gradually declines there-after. Households practise consumption smoothing so they save during the early phases of transition. In order to visualise the effects on the re-maining macroeconomic variables, we present the key impulse-response functions for a plausibly calibrated version of the model in figure 20.5.[17] At time $t_E = 50$, the product subsidy shock ends and labour supply and real output fall. The trade balance shifts from surplus to deficit, the terms of trade improve, and net foreign assets are run down. The upward jump in P explains why households cut back domestic consumption at time t_E.

For the debtor country the adjustment path for full expenditure is monotonically declining (following the impact jump) but the path for net foreign assets is non-monotonic (see the left-hand panel in figure 20.4). If the shock is rather long-lasting (and t_E is large), then the economy will jump to point b at impact and follow the trajectory towards SP_0 thereafter. In contrast, if the shock is rather temporary (and t_E is small), then the adjustment path for net foreign assets will consist of the trajectory from point c. The impulse response functions for the remaining variables are very similar to those presented in figure 20.5.[18]

Overlapping-generations model ($r = \alpha$)
In figure 20.6 we study the knife-edge case of the non-saving nation. If the shock is permanent then the economy will jump from the initial equi-librium at e_0 to the new equilibrium at e_1. There will be no transitional adjustment at all. The shock increases human wealth by the same amount for all households. Since $r = \alpha$ households neither save nor dissave (so $F(v, 0) = 0$ for all v) and all households have the same level of full expen-diture, i.e. $X(v, 0) = (\alpha + \beta) H(0)$ for all v. Despite the fact that there are overlapping generations of finitely lived agents, all households are essen-tially identical. Apart from their date of birth (and thus their age) there is no difference between generations.

For a temporary increase in the product subsidy, the adjustment path will be the trajectory emanating from point a. Now there is transitional dynamics because future generations are affected differently by the shock. At impact all existing generations experience an increase in their human

---

[17] We use the following parameters and initial shares: $\eta = 1.3, \sigma_T = 11, s_P = 0.3, t_M = 0.1$, $\alpha = 0.03, \beta = 0.06, \omega_X = 0.2, \omega_{LL} = 2$ and $\omega_F = 0.1$. Using these values the remaining parameters and shares can be computed. The time at which the shock ends is set at $t_E = 50$ (years). Note that the expected remaining lifetime of all households is $1/\beta \approx 17$ (years). Finally, the impulse-response functions for employment and the real wage rate are not shown because they are qualitatively the same as the one for real output.

[18] We use the parameters mentioned in n. 17 except for ω_F which we set at $\omega_F = -0.1$. This choice ensures that $r < \alpha$. For the non-saving nation we set $\omega_F = 0$ so that $r = \alpha$.

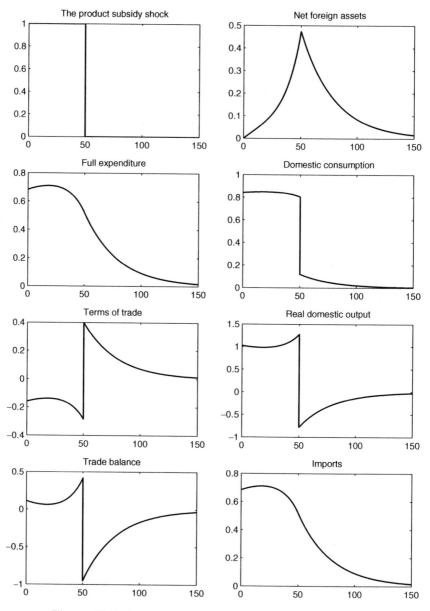

Figure 20.5 A temporary increase in s_P (overlapping-generations model)

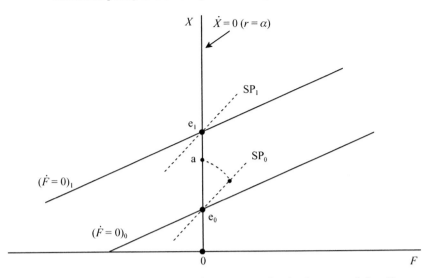

Figure 20.6 Permanent and temporary shocks ($r = \alpha$ and $\beta > 0$)

wealth. Because households want to smooth full expenditure, they start to accumulate net foreign assets. During transition, human wealth declines again as the time at which the policy is ended comes nearer and nearer. From t_E onward, net foreign assets fall and the economy returns to its initial position. Again, the impulse response functions are very similar to the ones presented in figure 20.5.

Representative-agent model
In figure 20.7 we study the representative-agent model. As was demonstrated above, this model features degenerate dynamics in full expenditure. We can nevertheless use figure 20.7 and the intuitive solution principle to deduce the adjustment path following a permanent or temporary shock.

For a permanent increase in the product subsidy the adjustment consists of a discrete jump from e_0 to e_1 at impact. There is no transitional dynamics in this case. Intuitively, there is a once-off increase in human wealth which prompts the representative households to increase full expenditure. There is no need to use the current account for full expenditure smoothing.

If the shock is temporary, then the intuitive solution principle suggests that the economy will jump from e_0 to point a at impact. For $0 < t < t_E$ the economy will gradually move towards point e_2, where it arrives at

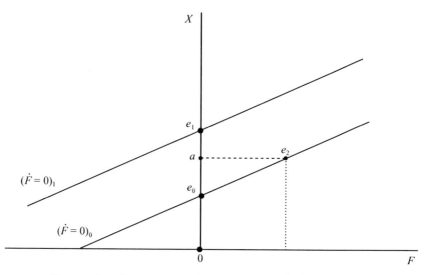

Figure 20.7 Permanent and temporary shocks ($r = \alpha$ and $\beta = 0$)

time $t = t_E$.[19] The key thing to note is that e_2 is the new steady-state equilibrium associated with the temporary shock. The household accumulates net foreign assets in order to be able to sustain its (higher) full expenditure level even after the shock has ended. It follows that the temporary product subsidy has a permanent effect on all variables. Interestingly, in the long run real output, employment and the real wage rate all fall and the terms of trade increases. We visualise the impulse-response functions in figure 20.8.

20.3.3   Import tariff

The effects of an unanticipated (permanent or temporary) increase in the import tariff can also be illustrated with the phase diagrams presented in figures 20.4 and 20.6–20.7. It follows from (20.26) and (20.28) that the shock leads to an leftward shift in the $\dot{F} = 0$ line. Intuitively, for a given level of full expenditure, an increase in the import tariff directly reduces imports and improves the trade balance. For convenience we summarise the qualitative results for the permanent shock in table 20.4 and we show the impulse-response functions for temporary shocks in figures 20.9–20.10. In the interest of brevity we focus on some of the key results.

---

[19] The fourth requirement of the intuitive solution principle is that the economy must arrive on the equilibrium locus $\dot{F} = 0$ exactly at time t_E.

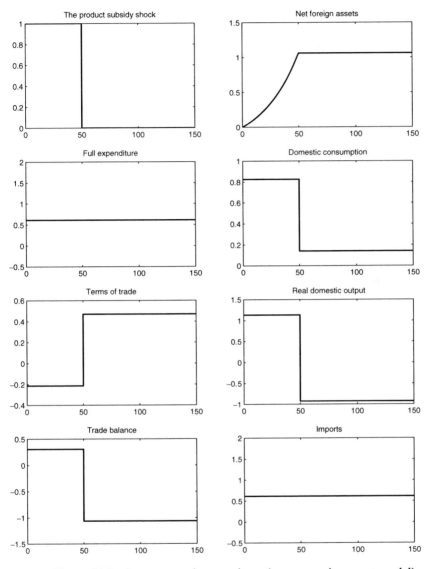

Figure 20.8   A temporary increase in s_P (representative-agent model)

Permanent shock   A permanent increase in the import tariff leads to an increase in full expenditure in the long run – see the move from e_0 to e_1 in Figures 20.4 and 20.6–20.7. Intuitively, the increase in full expenditure is made possible because the country uses the tariff to exploit its national

Table 20.4 *Permanent increase in the import tariff*

	X	F	TB	P	W/P	Y/P	L	C	Z
(a) Creditor nation (r > α)									
$t = 0$	+	0	+	+	−	−	−	+	−−
$t \to \infty$	++	+	−	++	−−	−−	−−	++	?
(b) Debtor nation (r < α)									
$t = 0$	++	0	−	++	−−	−−	−−	++	?
$t \to \infty$	+	−	+	+	−	−	−	+	−−
(c) Non-saving nation or representative-agent model (r = α)									
$\forall t \geq 0$	+	0	0	+	−	−	−	+	−

Note:
(+)+: (strong) positive effect; (−)−: (strong) negative effect; 0: no effect; ?:
theoretically ambiguous effect. The results in this table assume that labour
supply is endogenous ($0 < \gamma < 1$) and the diversity effect is operative ($\eta > 1$).

market power. Net foreign assets rise (fall, stay the same) for the creditor
(debtor, non-saving) nation. For all cases, the increase in full expenditure
gives rise to a fall in labour supply, real output and wages and an increase
in the terms of trade and domestic consumption. The effect on imports
is negative for the debtor nation but ambiguous for the creditor nation.[20]

As was the case for the product subsidy shock, there is no transitional
dynamics if $r = \alpha$, i.e. in the overlapping-generations model for a non-
saving nation (see figure 20.6) and in the representative-agent model (see
figure 20.7). Figure 20.4 covers the remaining cases. At *impact*, net foreign
assets are predetermined and full expenditure jumps to the saddle path
(see the move from e_0 to a in the two panels of figure 20.4). In both cases
full expenditure rises so that employment, real output and wages fall and
domestic consumption rises. The impact response of the trade balance,
however, differs between the two cases. For the creditor nation the jump
in full expenditure is relatively small so that the positive effect of the tariff
shock dominates and the trade balance improves on impact – i.e. point
a in the right-hand panel of figure 20.4 is associated with a rising profile
of net foreign assets ($\dot{F}(0) > 0$). Over time, the economy moves along
the saddle path from a to e_1. The long-run effect on full expenditure
exceeds the short-run effect because the patient residents of the creditor

[20] Tariff-inclusive spending on imports rises in both cases (see (T20.1.6)). The ambiguity
arises in the case of the creditor nation because the rise in full expenditure is large and
may well dominate the effect of the tariff.

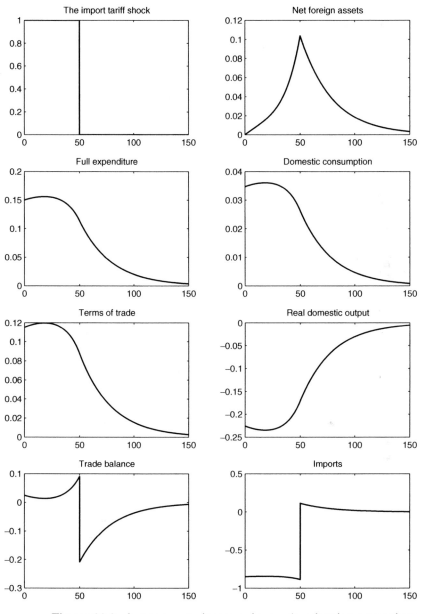

Figure 20.9 A temporary increase in t_M (overlapping-generations model)

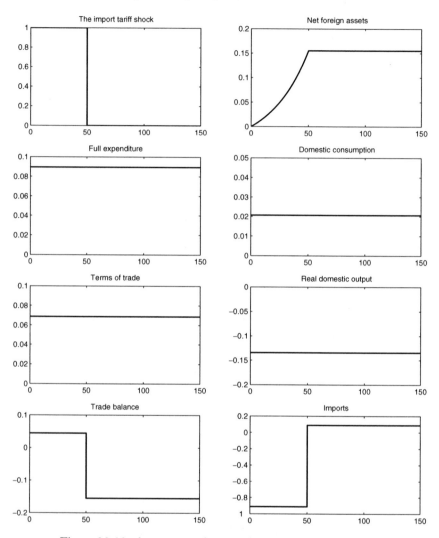

Figure 20.10   A temporary increase in t_M (representative-agent model)

nation accumulate additional net foreign assets during transition so that, over time, the trade balance can deteriorate and full expenditure can rise beyond its impact increase.

The adjustment path for the debtor nation is quite different. The increase in full expenditure at impact is large and dominates the tariff effect so that the trade balance deteriorates at impact and net foreign assets start to fall – i.e. $\dot{F}(0) < 0$ in point a in the left-hand panel of figure 20.4. During transition, the economy moves from a to e_1 along the saddle path. Full expenditure overshoots its long-run equilibrium level at impact. Intuitively, the debtor country is populated by impatient agents who react to the tariff shock by borrowing more from abroad. Over time, interest payments abroad rise and the trade balance must improve, i.e. full expenditure must fall.

Temporary shock   The effects of a temporary shock are illustrated for the overlapping-generations model in figure 20.9 and for the representative-agent model in figure 20.10. In the overlapping-generations model, the shock causes a temporary increase in full expenditure, net foreign assets, domestic consumption and the terms of trade, and a temporary decrease in output, employment and the real wage rate. At the time the shock is ended, the trade balance switches from surplus to deficit (as imports are adjusted upwards) and net foreign assets are decumulated.[21]

In the representative-agent model, a temporary tariff shock has a permanent effect on all variables (see figure 20.10). In the long run, the stock of net foreign assets is permanently higher and the trade balance shows a permanent deficit. Output, employment, and the real wage rate are permanently lower as a result of the wealth effect in labour supply.

20.4   Welfare effects of industrial policy

This section explores the welfare properties of the model. In the most general version of our model (with $r \neq \alpha$ and $\beta > 0$), a change in the product subsidy and/or tariff has both efficiency and intergenerational redistributional effects. The intergenerational effects associated with the two policy instruments have been studied in detail in Bettendorf and Heijdra (2001a, 2001b). It is shown there that an appropriately designed bond policy can eliminate all intergenerational redistributional effects.[22] In the remainder of this chapter we obviate the need for bond policy by limiting attention to (a) permanent shocks and (b) a knife-edge version of the model for which $r = \alpha$. Regardless of the value of β, only the efficiency

---

[21] Figure 20.9 deals with the creditor nation (with $r > \alpha$). Just as for the product subsidy, foreign assets may decline initially in the case of a debtor nation ($r < \alpha$) and a rather permanent shock (t_E large).

[22] Intuitively, this bond policy stops households from using the current account and eliminates all transitional dynamics. This is achieved by making a once-off adjustment in public debt:

$$\tilde{B}(t) = \tilde{B}^* \equiv \left(\frac{\omega_F}{\phi\zeta + \omega_F} \right) \left[(\omega_X + \omega_F)\tilde{t}_M + \zeta(\phi - 1) \left(\frac{\sigma_T - 1}{\sigma_T} \right) \tilde{s}_P \right].$$

effects are operative in that case.[23] In our discussion we assume that the birth rate is positive.

In the knife-edge case the model is essentially static as households neither save nor dissave. Households do not use the current account to smooth consumption ($F(t) = 0$, $\forall t$), and all generations have the same level of (human) wealth, full expenditure and lifetime utility ($X(v, t) = X(t) = (\alpha + \beta)H(t)$ and $\Lambda(v, t) = \Lambda$, $\forall t$). Despite the fact that there are overlapping generations of finitely lived agents, all households are essentially identical. Apart from their date of birth (and thus their age) there is no difference between generations. This property of the knife-edge case is attractive because it allows us to conduct a standard welfare analysis in which a fictional social planner maximises the lifetime utility of the representative household.

The social planner treats all generations the same and thus – like the households – has no reason to use the current account. Suppressing the (now superfluous) time index, the planner chooses C, Z, L, and P in order to maximise lifetime utility of the representative generation:

$$(\alpha + \beta)\Lambda \equiv \gamma\delta \log C + \gamma(1 - \delta)\log Z + (1 - \gamma)\log[1 - L], \tag{20.29}$$

subject to, respectively, the resource constraint[24] and the zero-trade-balance constraint:

$$\Omega_0 L^\eta = C + E_0 P^{-\sigma_T}, \tag{20.30}$$

$$Z = E_0 P^{1-\sigma_T}. \tag{20.31}$$

Straightforward manipulations yield the first-order conditions for the social optimum:

$$\frac{(1 - \gamma)/(1 - L)}{\gamma\delta/C} = \eta\Omega_0 L^{\eta-1}, \tag{20.32}$$

$$\frac{(1 - \delta)/Z}{\delta/C} = \frac{1}{P}\left(\frac{\sigma_T}{\sigma_T - 1}\right). \tag{20.33}$$

[23] Indeed, for the overlapping-generations model (with $\beta > 0$) there are no intergenerational redistributional effects because there are no transitional dynamics (see figure 20.6). For the representative-agent model (with $\beta = 0$) there is no generational redistribution because there is, in effect, only one generation.

[24] Equation (20.30) is the resource constraint in the so-called *constrained social optimum* (CSO) when the planner cannot influence the size of individual firms because lump-sum taxes/transfers at the firm level are deemed to be absent (see Dixit and Stiglitz, 1977). Since we assume, however, that η parameterises both the diversity effect and the monopoly markup the CSO coincides with the unconstrained social optimum (see Broer and Heijdra, 2001, for a related result in a closed economy).

According to (20.32) the marginal rate of substitution between leisure and consumption should be equated to the marginal product of labour. Equation (20.33) says that the marginal rate of substitution between imports and domestic goods should be equated to the relative price of import goods $(1/P)$ corrected for the international markup $(\sigma_T/(\sigma_T - 1))$.

For the decentralised market solution, the corresponding first-order conditions are:

$$\frac{(1-\gamma)/(1-L)}{\gamma\delta/C} = \left(\frac{1+s_P}{\eta}\right)\eta\Omega_0 L^{\eta-1}\left[\equiv \frac{W}{P}\right], \qquad (20.34)$$

$$\frac{(1-\delta)/Z}{\delta/C} = \frac{1+t_M}{P}. \qquad (20.35)$$

By matching, respectively, (20.32) with (20.34) and (20.33) with (20.35) we derive that the decentralised market equilibrium replicates the social optimum for the following values of the tariff and product subsidy:

$$1+s_P^F = \eta, \qquad 1+t_M^F = \left(\frac{\sigma_T}{\sigma_T - 1}\right), \qquad (20.36)$$

where the superscript 'F' stands for first-best. The first-best is an application – in the setting of monopolistic competition – of the so-called 'Bhagwati-Johnson principle of targeting' (Dixit, 1985, p. 335). This principle says that a distortion is best countered by the instrument acting directly on the relevant margin. In the present model, the product subsidy restores productive efficiency and the tariff exploits national trade power.

The model thus incorporates both a domestic distortion, in the form of a monopolistically competitive production structure and an international distortion, in the form of national market power. If the product subsidy is fixed and differs from its first-best value, then the tariff will act on both distortions so that the welfare effect of a tariff increase is complicated by second-best considerations. Vice versa, if the tariff is fixed at a sub-optimal level then the product subsidy will act on the two distortions. In Bettendorf and Heijdra (2001b) we show that the welfare effect of marginal changes in the product subsidy and the import tariff can be written as follows:

$$(\alpha + \beta)d\Lambda = \Phi_P(t_M, s_P)\tilde{s}_P + \Phi_M(t_M, s_P)\tilde{t}_M, \qquad (20.37)$$

where $\Phi_P(t_M, s_P)$ and $\Phi_M(t_M, s_P)$ are complicated functions of the structural parameters and the pre-existing tariff and product subsidy:

$$\Phi_P(t_M, s_P) \equiv \left(\frac{\gamma\eta(1-\gamma)(1+\delta t_M)}{(1-\gamma)(1+t_M)+\gamma(1+s_P)(1+\delta t_M)} \right)$$

$$\times \left[\left(\frac{1-\delta}{1+\delta t_M} \right) \left(\frac{t_M - t_M^F}{1+t_M^F} \right) - \left(\frac{s_P - s_P^F}{1+s_P^F} \right) \right], \qquad (20.38)$$

$$\Phi_M(t_M, s_P) \equiv - \left(\frac{\gamma(1-\delta)}{1+\delta t_M} \right) \left[\delta + \frac{(1-\gamma)(1-\delta)\eta}{(1-\gamma)(1+t_M)+\gamma(1+s_P)(1+\delta t_M)} \right]$$

$$\times \left(\frac{t_M - t_M^F}{1+t_M^F} \right) + \left(\frac{\gamma(1-\delta)}{1+\delta t_M} \right)$$

$$\times \left[\frac{(1-\gamma)(1+\delta t_M)}{(1-\gamma)(1+t_M)+\gamma(1+s_P)(1+\delta t_M)} \right] (s_P - s_P^F).$$

$$(20.39)$$

The interpretation of these results is as follows. First, and rather obviously, if labour supply is exogenous ($\gamma = 1$) then output is fixed and independent of the product subsidy. As a result, $\Phi_P \equiv 0$ and s_P drops out of Φ_M altogether and it follows from (20.37) and (20.39) that the marginal lifetime utility of a tariff is positive (negative) if the initial tariff falls short of (exceeds) the first-best optimal tariff t_M^F. Similarly, for a closed economy ($\delta = 1$) $\Phi_M \equiv 0$ and t_M drops out of Φ_P altogether. It follows from (20.37) and (20.38) that the marginal lifetime utility of a product subsidy is positive (negative) if the initial subsidy falls short of (exceeds) the first-best optimal subsidy s_P^F.

Second, and more interestingly, if labour supply is endogenous ($0 < \gamma < 1$) and the economy is open ($0 < \delta < 1$) then both s_P and t_M feature in the expressions for Φ_P and Φ_M. Implicit expressions for, respectively, the second-best optimal product subsidy, s_P^S, and tariff, t_M^S, are obtained by, respectively, setting $\Phi_P = 0$ in (20.38) and solving for s_P and by setting $\Phi_M = 0$ in (20.39) and solving for t_M:

$$\left(\frac{s_P^S - s_P^F}{1+s_P^F} \right) = \left(\frac{1-\delta}{1+\delta t_M} \right) \left(\frac{t_M - t_M^F}{1+t_M^F} \right), \qquad (20.40)$$

$$\frac{t_M^S - t_M^F}{1+t_M^F} = \left[\frac{1-\gamma}{1-\gamma+\gamma\delta(1+s_P)+(1-\gamma)(\eta-1)\left(\frac{1-\delta}{1+\delta t_M^S}\right)} \right]$$

$$\times (s_P - s_P^F). \qquad (20.41)$$

It follows from (20.40)–(20.41) that the two policy instruments are complementary in a second-best situation (see appendix, p. 481). The intuition behind (20.40) is as follows. If the pre-existing tariff is too high – in the sense that $t_M > t_M^F$ – then domestic production is too low and the terms of trade is too high. The second-best product subsidy is higher than its first-best value because it is aimed at correcting the twin distortions of excessive use of national market power and deficient domestic production.

Similarly, if the pre-existing subsidy policy is too ambitious – in the sense that $s_P > s_P^F$ – then domestic production is stimulated too much

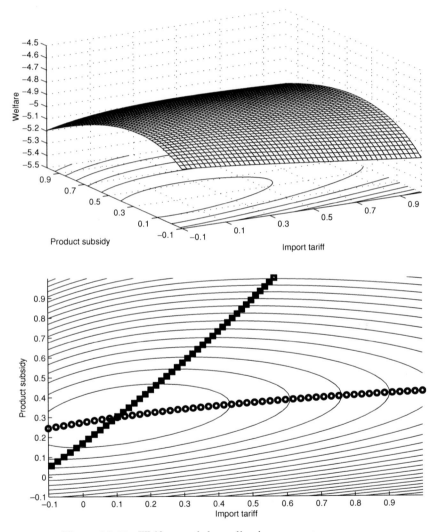

Figure 20.11 Welfare and the policy instruments

and the terms of trade is too low. It follows from (20.41) that the second-best tariff is higher than its first-best value because it is aimed at correcting the twin distortions of deficient national market power and excessive domestic production. At the other extreme, if a country in which diversity effects are present (so that $\eta > 1$ and $s_P^F > 0$) does not subsidise production at all ($s_P = 0$), then the second-best tariff is lower than its first-best value because it must in this case act as a (sub-optimal) substitute for the absent industrial policy.

A rather nice way to visualise the results of this section was suggested by Neary (1995). In the top panel of figure 20.11 we plot the welfare surface for a range of values for the pre-existing product subsidy and import tariff.[25] In the bottom panel we illustrate the contours of the welfare surface. Since the graphs are based on the parameter values $\eta = 1.3$ and $\sigma_T = 11$, the first-best equilibrium is at $s_P^F = 0.3$ and $t_M^F = 0.1$. In the bottom panel of figure 20.11, there are a number of egg-shaped iso-welfare loci around the first-best values – the further away from the first-best equilibrium, the lower is the welfare level on the particular contour.

The second-best optimal product subsidy, s_P^S, can now be visualised by connecting all points for which the iso-welfare loci have a vertical tangent. The resulting schedule is the flat upward sloping line in the lower panel of figure 20.11. Similarly, the second-best optimal import tariff can be found by connecting all points for which the iso-welfare loci are horizontal – see the steep upward sloping line in the bottom panel of figure 20.11. Obviously, the two lines cross in the first-best equilibrium.

20.5   Conclusions

A quarter of a century ago, Avinash Dixit and Joseph Stiglitz formulated a model of monopolistic competition which has become the workhorse model in many diverse fields of economics. In this chapter we use a variant of their model to revisit an old debate in the field of international trade policy, namely the desirability of industrial policy in an economy with increasing returns to scale industries. This debate even predates the first monopolistic competition revolution of the 1930s, but the insights from the second monopolistic competition revolution substantially clarify the key elements.

Using the Dixit–Stiglitz framework and focusing on the semi-small open economy, we show that there are two distortions that must be

---

[25] We use the parameter values that were mentioned in n. 17 except for ω_F which we set equal to zero. This implies that $r = \alpha$.

addressed by the policy maker, namely that due to increasing returns to scale (resulting from monopolistic competition) and that due to national market power (resulting from a downward sloping export demand function). It is natural in this setting to consider two policy instruments, namely the product subsidy and the import tariff. While in the first-best situation the instrument targeting principle is relevant, it turns out that in the second-best case the two policy instruments are complementary. The analytical crispness of the Dixit–Stiglitz framework thus enables us to derive precise and intuitively understandable prescriptions about the interaction between the optimum tariff and pre-existing uncorrected domestic distortions and vice versa. In doing so, we extend the seminal work by Johnson (1965) and Bhagwati (1967, 1971) to the setting of Chamberlinian monopolistic competition.

APPENDIX

In this appendix we derive the key results that are used in the text.

Proof of Proposition 1

Part (a). The determinant of Δ in (20.27) is:

$$|\Delta| = r\left[(r - \alpha) - \beta\omega_Y(\zeta\phi + \omega_F)\right]. \tag{20A.1}$$

If $r \neq \alpha$ then the steady state satisfies $(r - \alpha)/\omega_F = \beta\omega_Y$. If $r = \alpha$ then the steady state is such that $\omega_F = 0$. Hence, equation (20A.1) can be simplified to:

$$|\Delta| = -r\beta\omega_Y\zeta\phi < 0. \tag{20A.2}$$

Since $|\Delta|$ equals the product of the characteristic roots we have one positive root ($\lambda_2 > 0$) and one negative root ($-\lambda_1 < 0$), and we can write $|\Delta| = -\lambda_1\lambda_2$. The characteristic equation of Δ, $g(\lambda) \equiv |\lambda I - \Delta|$, can be written as follows:

$$g(\lambda) = (\lambda + \lambda_1)(\lambda - \lambda_2) = \lambda^2 - (2r - \alpha)\lambda + |\Delta|. \tag{20A.3}$$

The roots, $-\lambda_1$ and λ_2, are the solutions to $g(\lambda) = 0$ in (20A.3). It is straightforward to verify that $-\lambda_1 < 0$ and $\lambda_2 > 0$. Indeed, by using

(20A.3) the following expressions and inequalities for $-\lambda_1$ and λ_2 can be derived:

$$-\lambda_1 = \frac{1}{2}(2r - \alpha)\left[1 - \left(1 - \frac{4|\Delta|}{(2r - \alpha)^2}\right)^{1/2}\right] < 0, \qquad (20A.4)$$

$$\lambda_2 = \frac{1}{2}(2r - \alpha)\left[1 + \left(1 - \frac{4|\Delta|}{(2r - \alpha)^2}\right)^{1/2}\right] > 2r - \alpha > 0.$$
$$(20A.5)$$

Obviously, since the sum of the roots equals $\mathrm{tr}\Delta$ we have that $\lambda_2 - \lambda_1 = 2r - \alpha$.[26]

The proof of $\lambda_2 > r$ proceeds as follows. The characteristic equation $g(\lambda)$ has two roots $(g(-\lambda_1) = g(\lambda_2) = 0)$ and satisfies $g(0) = |\Delta| < 0$ (by saddle path stability), $g(\lambda) < 0$ for $\lambda \in (0, \lambda_2)$, and $g(\lambda) > 0$ for $\lambda \in [\lambda_2, \infty)$. Hence, to show that $\lambda_2 > r$ we must show that $g(r) < 0$. By using (20A.2)–(20A.3) we get:

$$g(r) = r^2 - (2r - \alpha)r - (r\beta\omega_Y\zeta\phi) = -r\beta\omega_Y(\omega_F + \zeta\phi) < 0, \qquad (20A.6)$$

where we have used $(r - \alpha)/\omega_F = \beta\omega_Y$ in the second step. The result $\omega_F + \zeta\phi > 0$ follows from:

$$\omega_F + \zeta\phi = \frac{\omega_X(\sigma_T - 1)(\phi - \omega_X)}{\phi + \omega_X(\sigma_T - 1)} + (\omega_F + \omega_X) > 0, \qquad (20A.7)$$

as $\phi > \omega_X$ and $\omega_F + \omega_X > 0$.

Part b. By setting $r - \alpha = \beta = 0$ in (20A.1) we find that $|\Delta| = 0$ for the representative-agent model. Since $\mathrm{tr}\Delta = \alpha$ in that case it follows that $\lambda_1 = 0$ and $\lambda_2 = \alpha$. ∎

Model solution

In this section we solve the model with the aid of Laplace transforms.[27] The advantage of this method is that we can easily incorporate the hysteretic case and specify quite general shock processes.

[26] We consider only the case of a moderately impatient country, i.e. $\alpha < 2r$. If $\alpha > 2r$ then λ_1 and λ_2 both switch signs but the model remains saddle point stable.

[27] See Judd (1998) for an advanced treatment of the Laplace transform method. Heijdra and van der Ploeg (2002, pp. 678–94) present a simple exposition of the method and discuss the application to hysteretic models.

General solution

By taking the Laplace transform of (20.26) we obtain the following expression:

$$\Lambda(s)\begin{bmatrix} \mathcal{L}\{\tilde{F}, s\} \\ \mathcal{L}\{\tilde{X}, s\} \end{bmatrix} = \begin{bmatrix} \mathcal{L}\{\gamma_F, s\} \\ \tilde{X}(0) + \mathcal{L}\{\gamma_X, s\} \end{bmatrix}, \qquad (20A.8)$$

where we have used the fact that the stock of net foreign assets is predetermined (i.e. $\tilde{F}(0) = 0$), and where $\Lambda(s) \equiv sI - \Delta$, so that $|\Lambda(s)| \equiv (s + \lambda_1)(s - \lambda_2)$. By setting $s = \lambda_2$ and pre-multiplying (20A.8) by $\text{adj}(\Lambda(\lambda_2))$ we obtain the initial condition for the jump in full expenditure:

$$\text{adj}(\Lambda(\lambda_2))\,\Lambda(\lambda_2)\begin{bmatrix} \mathcal{L}\{\tilde{F}, \lambda_2\} \\ \mathcal{L}\{\tilde{X}, \lambda_2\} \end{bmatrix} \equiv \begin{bmatrix} \lambda_2 - (r - \alpha) & -r(\zeta\phi + \omega_F) \\ -\beta\omega_Y & (\lambda_2 - r) \end{bmatrix}$$

$$\times \begin{bmatrix} \mathcal{L}\{\gamma_F, \lambda_2\} \\ \tilde{X}(0) + \mathcal{L}\{\gamma_X, \lambda_2\} \end{bmatrix} = \begin{bmatrix} 0 \\ 0 \end{bmatrix}. \qquad (20A.9)$$

Since the characteristic roots of Δ are distinct, $\text{rank}(\text{adj}(\Lambda(\lambda_i))) = 1$ and there is exactly one independent equation determining $\tilde{X}(0)$. Using the first row[28] of (20A.9) we find:

$$\tilde{X}(0) = -\mathcal{L}\{\gamma_X, \lambda_2\} + \left(\frac{\lambda_2 - (r - \alpha)}{r(\zeta\phi + \omega_F)}\right)\mathcal{L}\{\gamma_F, \lambda_2\}. \qquad (20A.10)$$

Heijdra and van der Ploeg (2002, p. 689) show that the general solution of (20A.8) in terms of Laplace transforms is equal to:

$$(s + \lambda_1)\begin{bmatrix} \mathcal{L}\{\tilde{F}, s\} \\ \mathcal{L}\{\tilde{X}, s\} \end{bmatrix} = \begin{bmatrix} \mathcal{L}\{\gamma_F, s\} \\ \tilde{X}(0) + \mathcal{L}\{\gamma_X, s\} \end{bmatrix} + \text{adj}(\Lambda(\lambda_2))\begin{bmatrix} \dfrac{\mathcal{L}\{\gamma_F, s\} - \mathcal{L}\{\gamma_F, \lambda_2\}}{s - \lambda_2} \\ \dfrac{\mathcal{L}\{\gamma_X, s\} - \mathcal{L}\{\gamma_X, \lambda_2\}}{s - \lambda_2} \end{bmatrix}.$$

$$(20A.11)$$

Specific shocks

The shocks considered in this chapter have the following Laplace transforms (see Spiegel, 1965, p. 254):

$$\mathcal{L}\{\tilde{s}_P, s\} = \psi(t_E, s)\,\tilde{s}_P, \quad \mathcal{L}\{\tilde{t}_M, s\} = \psi(t_E, s)\,\tilde{t}_M, \quad \mathcal{L}\{\tilde{B}, s\} = \frac{\tilde{B}}{s},$$

$$(20A.12)$$

$$\psi(t_E, s) \equiv \frac{1 - e^{-st_E}}{s}, \qquad (20A.13)$$

---

[28] This row is non-trivial even for the representative-agent version of the model (for which $\beta = 0$ and $r = \alpha$).

where $\psi(t_E, s) \equiv \mathcal{L}\{\Psi(t_E, t), s\}$, $\Psi(t_E, t) = 1$ for $t \in [0, t_E]$, and $\Psi(t_E, t) = 0$ for $t \in (t_E, \infty)$. The shocks in s_P and t_M are permanent if $t_E \to +\infty$ and temporary if $0 < t_E \ll +\infty$. We only need to consider permanent shocks in the level of debt (see n. 22).

Impact effects

By using (20.28) and (20A.12) in (20A.10) the jump in full expenditure can be computed:

$$\tilde{X}(0) = \beta\omega_Y \frac{\tilde{B}}{\lambda_2} + \left(\frac{\lambda_2 - (r - \alpha)}{\zeta\phi + \omega_F}\right)\psi(t_E, \lambda_2)\tilde{G}, \qquad (20A.14)$$

$$\tilde{G} \equiv (\omega_F + \omega_X)\tilde{t}_M + \zeta(\phi - 1)\left(\frac{\sigma_T - 1}{\sigma_T}\right)\tilde{s}_P, \qquad (20A.15)$$

where from here on we refer to $\tilde{G}$ as *the* policy shock. Several points are worth noticing about (20A.14). First, the results in section 20.3 of the chapter are obtained by setting $\tilde{B} = 0$ in (20A.14) and distinguishing the various cases. Second, we can derive from (20A.14) that:

$$\frac{\partial \tilde{X}(0)}{\partial t_E} = \left(\frac{\lambda_2 - (r - \alpha)}{\zeta\phi + \omega_F}\right)e^{-\lambda_2 t_E}\tilde{G}. \qquad (20A.16)$$

Since $\lambda_2 \geq r$ (see Proposition 1) we conclude that the jump in full expenditure is larger, the larger is t_E, i.e. the more permanent is the policy shock. Thus, in the left-hand panel of figure 20.4, the trajectory from point b is associated with a more permanent shock than that from point c. Third, by using the second line of (20.26) and imposing $\tilde{F}(0) = \tilde{B} = 0$ we find that the impact effect on full expenditure growth is given by $\dot{\tilde{X}}(0) = (r - \alpha)\tilde{X}(0)$. Similarly, by using the first line of (20.26) and imposing $\tilde{F}(0) = \tilde{B} = 0$ we find that the impact effect on saving can be written as:

$$\frac{1}{r}\dot{\tilde{F}}(0) = -(\zeta\phi + \omega_F)\tilde{X}(0) + \tilde{G}$$

$$= \left[e^{-\lambda_2 t_E} + \left(\frac{r - \alpha}{\lambda_2}\right)(1 - e^{-\lambda_2 t_E})\right]\tilde{G}. \qquad (20A.17)$$

In combination with our earlier results concerning $\dot{\tilde{X}}(0)$ this result explains the slopes of the various trajectories in figures 20.4–20.6. Fourth, for the representative-agent case (with $r = \alpha$ and $\beta = 0$) we find that (20A.14) reduces to:

$$\tilde{X}(0) = \left(\frac{1 - e^{-\lambda_2 t_E}}{\zeta\phi + \omega_F}\right)\tilde{G}. \qquad (20A.18)$$

Government debt is neutral in this case because Ricardian equivalence obtains.

Long-run effects

For the overlapping-generations model only permanent shocks have long-run effects. They can be computed by imposing the steady state in (20.26), i.e. by setting $\dot{\tilde{X}}(\infty) = \dot{\tilde{F}}(\infty) = 0$. After some manipulation we find:

$$\begin{bmatrix} \tilde{F}(\infty) \\ \tilde{X}(\infty) \end{bmatrix} \equiv \begin{bmatrix} \omega_F \\ 1 \end{bmatrix} \frac{\tilde{G}}{\zeta\phi} - \begin{bmatrix} \zeta\phi + \omega_F \\ 1 \end{bmatrix} \frac{\tilde{B}}{\zeta\phi}. \tag{20A.19}$$

The representative-agent model features hysteresis so the long-run effect on full expenditure is given by (20A.18). By using the first row of (20.26) and imposing $\dot{\tilde{F}}(\infty) = 0$ we find the long-run effect on net foreign assets:

$$\tilde{F}(\infty) = (\zeta\phi + \omega_F)\,\tilde{X}(0) - \frac{\gamma_F(\infty)}{r} = \delta(t_E)\,\hat{G}, \tag{20A.20}$$

where $\delta(t_E)$ is a dummy variable:

$$\delta(t_E) = \begin{cases} 0 & \text{for } t_E \to \infty \text{ (permanent shock)} \\ 1 - e^{-\lambda_2 t_E} & \text{for } 0 < t_E \ll \infty \text{ (temporary shock)}. \end{cases} \tag{20A.21}$$

Transitional dynamics

In order to derive the transition path we first note that (20A.12), (20A.15) and (20.28) imply the following Laplace transforms for the shock terms:

$$\mathcal{L}\{\gamma_F, s\} = r\tilde{G}\psi(t_E, s), \qquad \mathcal{L}\{\gamma_X, s\} = -\beta\omega_Y\tilde{B}\left(\frac{1}{s}\right), \tag{20A.22}$$

where $\psi(t_E, s)$ is defined in (20A.13). By using (20A.22) we derive after some manipulations:

$$\frac{\mathcal{L}\{\gamma_F, s\} - \mathcal{L}\{\gamma_F, \lambda_2\}}{s - \lambda_2} = -\frac{r\tilde{G}}{\lambda_2}[\psi(t_E, s) - e^{-\lambda_2 t_E}\psi(t_E, s - \lambda_2)], \tag{20A.23}$$

$$\frac{\mathcal{L}\{\gamma_X, s\} - \mathcal{L}\{\gamma_X, \lambda_2\}}{s - \lambda_2} = \frac{\beta\omega_Y\tilde{B}}{\lambda_2}\left(\frac{1}{s}\right), \tag{20A.24}$$

where we have used the first translation property of the Laplace transform in (20A.23) (Spiegel, 1965, p. 3).

By using (20A.23)–(20A.24) in the first row of (20A.11) we find after some manipulation:

$$\frac{1}{r}\mathcal{L}\{\tilde{F}, s\} = \left(\frac{(r-\alpha)\,\tilde{G} - \beta\omega_Y\,(\zeta\phi + \omega_F)\,\tilde{B}}{\lambda_1\lambda_2}\right)\frac{\lambda_1}{s\,(s+\lambda_1)} - \frac{(r-\alpha)\,\tilde{G}}{\lambda_2}$$

$$\times \frac{e^{-st_E}}{s\,(s+\lambda_1)} + \frac{[\lambda_2 - (r-\alpha)]\,\tilde{G}}{\lambda_2}e^{-\lambda_2 t_E}\frac{1 - e^{-(s-\lambda_2)t_E}}{(s-\lambda_2)\,(s+\lambda_1)}. \qquad (20A.25)$$

For permanent shocks and provided $\beta > 0$ (so that $\lambda_1 > 0$),[29] all except the first term on the right-hand side vanish and $\mathcal{L}\{\tilde{F}, s\}$ can be inverted to obtain:

$$\tilde{F}(t) = \left(\frac{\omega_F \tilde{G} - (\zeta\phi + \omega_F)\,\tilde{B}}{\zeta\phi}\right)[1 - e^{-\lambda_1 t}], \qquad (20A.26)$$

where we have used the fact that $\lambda_1\lambda_2 = r\beta\omega_Y\zeta\phi$ (see (20A.2)) and noted that $r - \alpha = \beta\omega_Y\omega_F$. The term in square brackets is an adjustment function with the following properties.

Lemma 1 *Consider the following adjustment function:*

$$A_1(\lambda_1, t) \equiv 1 - e^{-\lambda_1 t},$$

with $\lambda_1 > 0$. Then $A_1(\lambda_1, t)$ has the following properties: (i) $\mathcal{L}\{A_1(\lambda_1, t), s\} \equiv \lambda_1/[s\,(s+\lambda_1)]$, (ii) (positive) $A_1(\lambda_1, t) > 0$ $t \in (0, \infty)$, (iii) $A_1(\lambda_1, t) = 0$ for $t = 0$ and $A_1(\lambda_1, t) \to 1$ in the limit as $t \to \infty$, (iv) (increasing) $dA_1(\lambda_1, t)/dt \geq 0$, (v) (step function as limit) As $\lambda_1 \to \infty$, $A_1(\lambda_1, t) \to u(t)$, where $u(t)$ is a unit step function.

Proof: For property (i) see Spiegel (1965). Properties (ii) and (iii) follow by simple substitution. Property (iv) follows from the fact that $dA_1(\lambda_1, 0)/dt = \lambda_1[1 - A_1(\lambda_1, t)]$ plus properties (ii)–(iii). Property (v) follows by comparing the Laplace transforms of $A_1(\lambda_1, t)$ and $u(t)$ and showing that they converge as $\lambda_1 \to \infty$. Since $\mathcal{L}\{u, s\} = 1/s$ and $\mathcal{L}\{A_1(\lambda_1, t), s\} = 1/s - 1/(s+\lambda_1)$ this result follows. ■

For temporary shocks, (20A.25) contains two more Laplace transforms on the right-hand side, namely an *adjustment* function and a (temporary) *transition* term. These functions have the following properties.

---

[29] For the representative-agent case, $r = \alpha$ and $\beta = 0$ so that $\lambda_1 = 0$. It follows from (20A.25) that permanent shocks have no effect on $\tilde{F}(t)$ at all.

Lemma 2 *Consider the following adjustment function:*

$$A_2(\lambda_1, t_E, t) \equiv [1 - \Psi(t_E, t)] \left[\frac{1 - e^{-\lambda_1(t - t_E)}}{\lambda_1} \right] \qquad (a)$$

with $\lambda_1 > 0$ and $0 < t_E \ll \infty$. Then $A_2(\lambda_1, t_E, t)$ has the following properties:
(i)

$$\mathcal{L}\{A_2(\lambda_1, t_E, t), s\} \equiv \frac{e^{-s t_E}}{s(s + \lambda_1)},$$

(ii) (positive) $A_2(\lambda_1, t_E, t) > 0$ for $t \in (t_E, \infty)$, (iii) $A_2(\lambda_1, t_E, t) = 0$ for $t \in [0, t_E]$ and $A_2(\lambda_1, t_E, t) \to 1/\lambda_1$ in the limit as $t \to \infty$, (iv) (increasing) $dA_2(\lambda_1, t_E, t)/dt \geq 0$ for $t \in (t_E, \infty)$.

Proof: For property (i) we note that $\mathcal{L}\{e^{-\lambda_1 t}, s\} \equiv 1/(s + \lambda_1)$ and $\mathcal{L}\{1 - \Psi(t_E, t), s\} \equiv e^{-s t_E}/s$ and apply the convolution theorem of the Laplace transform (Spiegel, 1965, p. 45):

$$A_2(\lambda_1, t_E, t) \equiv \int_0^t [1 - \Psi(t_E, \tau)] e^{-\lambda_1(t - \tau)} d\tau$$

$$= \begin{cases} 0 & \text{for } 0 < t \leq t_E \\ \int_{t_E}^t e^{-\lambda_1(t - \tau)} d\tau & \text{for } t > t_E \end{cases}$$

Properties (ii)–(iv) follow directly from (a). ∎

Lemma 3 *Consider the (following) temporary transition function:*

$$T(\lambda_1, \lambda_2, t_E, t) \equiv e^{\lambda_2 t} \Psi(t_E, t) \left(\frac{1 - e^{-(\lambda_1 + \lambda_2)t}}{\lambda_1 + \lambda_2} \right)$$

$$+ e^{\lambda_2 t} [1 - \Psi(t_E, t)] \left(\frac{e^{-(\lambda_1 + \lambda_2)(t - t_E)} - e^{-(\lambda_1 + \lambda_2)t}}{\lambda_1 + \lambda_2} \right) \qquad (a)$$

with $\lambda_1 > 0$, $\lambda_2 > 0$, and $0 < t_E \ll \infty$. Then $T(\lambda_1, \lambda_2, t_E, t)$ has the following properties: (i) $\mathcal{L}\{T(\lambda_1, \lambda_2, t_E, t)\} \equiv \psi(t_E, s - \lambda_2)/(s + \lambda_1)$, (ii) (positive) $T(\lambda_1, \lambda_2, t_E, t) > 0$ for $t \in (0, \infty)$, (iii) $T(\lambda_1, \lambda_2, t_E, t) = 0$ for $t = 0$ and in the limit as $t \to \infty$, (iv) (single peak at $t = t_E$) $dT(\lambda_1, \lambda_2, t_E, t)/dt > 0$ for $t \in (0, t_E]$, $dT(\lambda_1, \lambda_2, t_E, t)/dt < 0$ for $t \in (t_E, \infty)$.

Proof: For property (i) we note that $\mathcal{L}\{e^{-\lambda_1 t}, s\} \equiv 1/(s + \lambda_1)$ and $\mathcal{L}\{e^{\lambda_2 t} \Psi(t_E, t), s\} \equiv \psi(t_E, s - \lambda_2)$ (by the first translation property of the Laplace transform). Next we apply the convolution theorem of the

Laplace transform (Spiegel, 1965, p. 45):

$$T(\lambda_1, \lambda_2, t_E, t) \equiv \int_0^t e^{\lambda_2 \tau} \Psi(t_E, \tau) e^{-\lambda_1(t-\tau)} d\tau$$

$$= \begin{cases} e^{\lambda_2 t} \left(\dfrac{1 - e^{-(\lambda_1 + \lambda_2)t}}{\lambda_1 + \lambda_2} \right) & \text{for } 0 < t \leq t_E \\[3mm] e^{\lambda_2 t} \left(\dfrac{e^{-(\lambda_1 + \lambda_2)(t - t_E)} - e^{-(\lambda_1 + \lambda_2)t}}{\lambda_1 + \lambda_2} \right) & \text{for } t > t_E \end{cases}$$

Property (ii) is obvious as both terms in round brackets in (a) are positive for $t \in (0, \infty)$. Property (iii) follows by simple substitution. Property (iv) is proved as follows. First, for $t \in [0, t_E]$ we have $\Psi(t_E, t) = 1$ so that it follows from (a) that:

$$T(\cdot) = \frac{e^{\lambda_2 t} - e^{-\lambda_1 t}}{\lambda_1 + \lambda_2}, \qquad T'(\cdot) = \frac{\lambda_2 e^{\lambda_2 t} + \lambda_1 e^{-\lambda_1 t}}{\lambda_1 + \lambda_2} > 0.$$

Similarly, for $t \in (t_E, \infty)$ we have $\Psi(t_E, t) = 0$ so that it follows from (a) that:

$$T(\cdot) = e^{-\lambda_1 t} \left(\frac{e^{(\lambda_1 + \lambda_2)t_E} - 1}{\lambda_1 + \lambda_2} \right), \qquad T'(\cdot) = -\lambda_1 \left(\frac{e^{(\lambda_1 + \lambda_2)t_E} - 1}{\lambda_1 + \lambda_2} \right) < 0.$$

It is straightforward to verify that the two branches of $T(\cdot)$ coincide for $t = t_E$ so the function is continuous and has a maximum at $t = t_E$. ∎

By using (20A.23)–(20A.24) in the second row of (20A.11) we find after some manipulation:

$$\mathcal{L}\{\tilde{X}, s\} = \frac{\tilde{X}(0)}{s + \lambda_1} + \frac{r\beta\omega_Y(\tilde{G} - \tilde{B})}{\lambda_1 \lambda_2} \frac{\lambda_1}{s(s + \lambda_1)}$$
$$- \frac{r\beta\omega_Y\tilde{G}}{\lambda_2} \left[\frac{e^{-st_E}}{s(s + \lambda_1)} + e^{-\lambda_2 t_E} \left(\frac{1 - e^{-(s - \lambda_2)t_E}}{(s - \lambda_2)(s + \lambda_1)} \right) \right]. \tag{20A.27}$$

For permanent shocks and provided $\beta > 0$ (so that $\lambda_1 > 0$),[30] all except the first two terms on the right-hand side vanish and $\mathcal{L}\{\tilde{X}, s\}$ can be inverted to obtain:

$$\tilde{X}(t) = \tilde{X}(0)[1 - A_1(\lambda_1, t)] + \left(\frac{\tilde{G} - \tilde{B}}{\zeta\phi} \right) A_1(\lambda_1, t), \tag{20A.28}$$

[30] For the representative-agent case, $r = \alpha$ and $\beta = 0$ so that $\lambda_1 = 0$. It follows from (20A.27) that $\tilde{X}(t) = \tilde{X}(0)$ for both temporary and permanent shocks.

where we have once again used the fact that $\lambda_1 \lambda_2 = r\beta\omega_Y\zeta\phi$ (see (20A.2)) and noted that $r - \alpha = \beta\omega_Y\omega_F$.

Instrument complementarity[31]

In order to prove instrument complementarity we must prove $\partial s_P^S / \partial t_M > 0$ and $\partial t_M^S / \partial s_P > 0$. By using (20.40) we find in a straightforward manner that:

$$\left(\frac{1}{1 + s_P^F}\right)\frac{\partial s_P^S}{\partial t_M} = \left(\frac{1 - \delta}{1 + t_M^F}\right)\left(\frac{1 + \delta t_M^F}{1 + \delta t_M}\right) > 0, \tag{20A.29}$$

provided $t_M > -1/\delta$. By differentiating (20.41) we find:

$$\left[\frac{1}{1 + t_M^F} - \left(s_P - s_P^F\right)\frac{\partial H}{\partial t_M^S}\right]\frac{\partial t_M^S}{\partial s_P} = H + \left(s_P - s_P^F\right)\frac{\partial H}{\partial s_P}, \tag{20A.30}$$

where $H \equiv (1 - \gamma)/G$ and G is defined as:

$$G \equiv 1 - \gamma + \gamma\delta(1 + s_P) + \frac{(1 - \gamma)(\eta - 1)(1 - \delta)}{1 + \delta t_M^S} > 0. \tag{20A.31}$$

It follows from (20A.31) that:

$$\frac{\partial H}{\partial s_P} = -\gamma\delta\frac{H}{G} > 0, \tag{20A.32}$$

$$\frac{\partial H}{\partial t_M^S} = \frac{(1 - \gamma)(\eta - 1)(1 - \delta)\delta}{\left(1 + \delta t_M^S\right)^2}\frac{H}{G} > 0. \tag{20A.33}$$

It follows from (20A.32) that the term on the right-hand side of (20A.30) is positive:

$$H + \left(s_P - s_P^F\right)\frac{\partial H}{\partial s_P} = \frac{H}{G}\left[1 - \gamma + \gamma\delta\left(1 + s_P^F\right)\right.$$
$$\left. + \frac{(1 - \gamma)(\eta - 1)(1 - \delta)}{1 + \delta t_M^S}\right] > 0. \tag{20A.34}$$

---

[31] We thank our discussant, Peter Neary, for detailed notes on how to prove the sign of $\partial t_M^S / \partial s_P$.

Similarly, it follows from (20A.33) that the term in square brackets on the left-hand side of (20A.30) is positive:

$$
\begin{aligned}
[\cdot] &= \frac{1}{1 + t_M^F} - \left(s_P - s_P^F\right) \frac{H}{G} \frac{(1 - \gamma)(\eta - 1)(1 - \delta)\delta}{\left(1 + \delta t_M^S\right)^2} \\
&= \frac{1}{1 + t_M^F} \left[1 - \left(t_M^S - t_M^F\right) \frac{1}{G} \frac{(1 - \gamma)(\eta - 1)(1 - \delta)\delta}{\left(1 + \delta t_M^S\right)^2}\right] \\
&= \frac{1}{1 + t_M^F} \frac{1}{G} \Bigg[1 - \gamma + \gamma\delta(1 + s_P) \\
&\quad + \frac{(1 - \gamma)(\eta - 1)(1 - \delta)}{1 + \delta t_M^S} \frac{1 + \delta t_M^F}{1 + \delta t_M^S}\Bigg] > 0,
\end{aligned}
\tag{20A.35}
$$

where we have used the fact that $H(s_P - s_P^F) = (t_M^S - t_M^F)/(1 + t_M^F)$ in going from the first to the second line. It follows that $\partial t_M^S / \partial s_P > 0$.

REFERENCES

Bénassy, J.-P. (1996). Taste for variety and optimum production patterns in monopolistic competition. *Economics Letters*, 52: 41–47

   (1998). Is there always too little research in endogenous growth with expanding product variety? *European Economic Review*, 42: 61–69

Bettendorf, L. J. H. and Heijdra, B. J. (2001a). Intergenerational and international welfare leakages of a product subsidy in a small open economy. *International Tax and Public Finance*, 8: 705–729

   (2001b). Intergenerational welfare effects of a tariff under monopolistic competition. *Journal of Economics*, 73: 313–346

Bhagwati, J. N. (1967). Non-economic objectives and the efficiency properties of trade. *Journal of Political Economy*, 75: 738–742

   (1971). The generalized theory of distortions and welfare, in Bhagwati, J. *et al.* (eds.), *Trade, Balance of Payments and Growth: Essays in Honor of Charles P. Kindleberger*. Amsterdam, North-Holland

Blanchard, O.-J. (1985). Debt, deficits, and finite horizons. *Journal of Political Economy*, 93: 223–247

Brander, J. (1995). Strategic trade policy, in Grossman, G. and Rogoff, K. (eds.), *Handbook of International Economics, III*. Amsterdam, Elsevier

Broer, D. P. and Heijdra, B. J. (2001). The investment tax credit under monopolistic competition. *Oxford Economic Papers*, 53: 318–351

Buiter, W. H. (1987). Fiscal policy in open, interdependent economies, in Razin, A. and Sadka, E. (eds.), *Economic Policy in Theory and Practice*. London, Macmillan

Dixit, A. K. (1985). Tax policy in open economies, in Auerbach, A. and Feldstein, M. (eds.), *Handbook of Public Economics, I*. Amsterdam, North-Holland

   (1987). Strategic aspects of trade policy, in Bewley, T. F. (ed.), *Advances in Economic Theory*. Cambridge, Cambridge University Press

Dixit, A. K. and Stiglitz, J. E. (1977). Monopolistic competition and optimum product diversity. *American Economic Review*, 67: 297–308

Flam, H. and Helpman, E. (1987). Industrial policy under monopolistic competition. *Journal of International Economics*, 22: 79–102

Giovannini, A. (1988). The real exchange rate, the capital stock, and fiscal policy. *European Economic Review*, 32: 1747–1767

Gros, D. (1987). A note on the optimal tariff, retaliation and the welfare loss from tariff wars in a framework with intra-industry trade. *Journal of International Economics*, 23: 357–367

Heijdra, B. J. (1998). Fiscal policy multipliers: the role of monopolistic competition, scale economies, and intertemporal substitution in labour supply. *International Economic Review*, 39: 659–696

Heijdra, B. J. and van der Ploeg, F. (1996). Keynesian multipliers and the cost of public funds under monopolistic competition. *Economic Journal*, 106: 1284–1296

(2002). *Foundations of Modern Macroeconomics*. Oxford, Oxford University Press

Johnson, H. G. (1965). Optimal trade intervention in the presence of domestic distortions, in Baldwin, R. *et al.* (eds.), *Trade, Growth, and the Balance of Payments: Essays in Honor of Gottfried Haberler*. Amsterdam, North-Holland

Judd, K. L. (1998). *Numerical Methods in Economics*. Cambridge, MA, MIT Press

Krugman, P. R. (1990). *Rethinking International Trade Theory*. Cambridge, MA, MIT Press

Neary, J. P. (1995). Trade liberalisation and shadow prices in the presence of tariffs and quotas. *International Economic Review*, 36: 531–554

Sen, P. and Turnovsky, S. J. (1989). Tariffs, capital accumulation, and the current account in a small open economy. *International Economic Review*, 30: 811–831

Spence, M. (1976). Product selection, fixed costs, and monopolistic competition. *Review of Economic Studies*, 43: 217–235

Spiegel, M. (1965). *Laplace Transforms*. New York, McGraw-Hill

Turnovsky, S. J. (1997). *International Macroeconomic Dynamics*. Cambridge, MA, MIT Press

Venables, A. J. (1987). Trade and trade policy with differentiated products: a Chamberlin–Ricardian model. *Economic Journal*, 97: 700–717

Yaari, M. E. (1965). Uncertain lifetime, life insurance, and the theory of the consumer. *Review of Economic Studies*, 32: 137–150

Index